The Routledge Handbook of Teaching English to Young Learners

The Routledge Handbook of Teaching English to Young Learners celebrates the 'coming of age' for the field of research in primary-level English Language Teaching. With 32 chapters written by international scholars from a wide geographical area including East Africa, Mexico, the South Pacific, Japan, France, the USA and the UK, this volume draws on areas such as second language acquisition, discourse analysis, pedagogy and technology to provide:

- An overview of the current state of the field, identifying key areas of TEYL.
- Chapters on a broad range of subjects from methodology to teaching in difficult circumstances and from Content and Language Integrated Learning (CLIL) to gaming.
- Suggestions of ways forward, with the aim of shaping the future research agenda of TEYL in multiple international contexts.
- Background research and practical advice for students, teachers and researchers.

With extensive guidance on further reading throughout, *The Routledge Handbook of Teaching English to Young Learners* is essential reading for those studying and researching in this area.

Sue Garton is a Reader in TESOL and Associate Dean of External Relations within the School of Languages and Social Sciences at Aston University, UK.

Fiona Copland is a Professor of TESOL and Associate Dean of Research within the Faculty of Social Sciences at the University of Stirling, UK.

Routledge Handbooks in Applied Linguistics

Routledge Handbooks in Applied Linguistics provide comprehensive overviews of the key topics in applied linguistics. All entries for the handbooks are specially commissioned and written by leading scholars in the field. Clear, accessible and carefully edited *Routledge Handbooks in Applied Linguistics* are the ideal resource for both advanced undergraduates and postgraduate students.

The Routledge Handbook of Pragmatics
Edited by Anne Barron, Yueguo Gu and Gerard Steen

The Routledge Handbook of Migration and Language
Edited by Suresh Canagarajah

The Routledge Handbook of Instructed Second Language Acquisition
Edited by Shawn Loewen and Masatoshi Sato

The Routledge Handbook of Critical Discourse Studies
Edited by John Flowerdew and John E. Richardson

The Routledge Handbook of Language in the Workplace
Edited by Bernadette Vine

The Routledge Handbook of English as a Lingua Franca
Edited by Jennifer Jenkins, Will Baker and Martin Dewey

The Routledge Handbook of Language and Superdiversity
Edited by Angela Creese and Adrian Blackledge

The Routledge Handbook of Language Revitalization
Edited by Leanne Hinton, Leena Huss and Gerald Roche

The Routledge Handbook of Sociocultural Theory and Second Language Development
Edited by James P. Lantolf and Matthew E. Poehner with Merrill Swain

The Routledge Handbook of Study Abroad Research and Practice
Edited by Cristina Sanz and Alfonso Morales-Front

The Routledge Handbook of Teaching English to Young Learners
Edited by Sue Garton and Fiona Copland

For a full list of titles in this series, please visit www.routledge.com/series/RHAL

The Routledge Handbook of Teaching English to Young Learners

Edited by Sue Garton and Fiona Copland

Routledge
Taylor & Francis Group

LONDON AND NEW YORK

First published 2019
by Routledge
2 Park Square, Milton Park, Abingdon, Oxon OX14 4RN

and by Routledge
711 Third Avenue, New York, NY 10017

Routledge is an imprint of the Taylor & Francis Group, an informa business

British Library Cataloguing-in-Publication Data
A catalogue record for this book is available from the British Library

Library of Congress Cataloging-in-Publication Data
Names: Garton, Sue, 1961– editor. | Copland, Fiona, 1962– editor.
Title: The Routledge handbook of teaching English to young learners / edited by Sue Garton and Fiona Copland.
Description: Milton Park, Abingdon, Oxon ; New York, NY : Routledge, 2018. | Series: Routledge handbooks in applied linguistics | Includes bibliographical references and index.
Identifiers: LCCN 2018008566 | ISBN 9781138643772 (hardback) | ISBN 9781315623672 (e-book)
Subjects: LCSH: English language—Study and teaching (Primary)—Foreign speakers. | English language—Study and teaching (Elementary)—Foreign speakers.
Classification: LCC PE1128.A2 R69 2018 | DDC 372.652/1—dc23
LC record available at https://lccn.loc.gov/2018008566

ISBN: 978-1-138-64377-2 (hbk)
ISBN: 978-1-315-62367-2 (ebk)

Typeset in Times New Roman
by Apex CoVantage, LLC

Printed and bound by CPI Group (UK) Ltd, Croydon, CR0 4YY

Contents

Contents

Figures

Tables

Contributors

Wendy Arnold, MA in TEYL (University of York, UK), is Co-Founder of ELT-Consultants (www.elt-consultants.com). She taught primary TEYL for 15 years in Hong Kong and has over 25 years TEYL experience in writing TEYL coursebooks and designing/delivering trainer/teacher training programmes and consultancies for ministries of education. Her special interest is early literacy and TEYL in developing countries. E-mail: wendy@elt-consultants.com.

Ruth Ban is a Professor of Education/TESOL in Curriculum and Instruction in the Department of Curriculum, Research and Pedagogy at Barry University in Miami Shores, FL. Previously, she was a teacher educator and curriculum developer for English language teaching programmes in Mexico. Her research interests include foreign language learning for young learners, EFL teacher and professional identity and technology-enhanced language learning.

Isabel Cristina R. Moraes Bezerra is a lecturer at the State University of Rio de Janeiro (UERJ) where she coordinates the Linguistic Studies (PPLIN/UERJ) programme. Currently her research focuses on TEYL, EFL, teacher education, EFL material production, narrative and identity studies. Inspired by Exploratory Practice, she has worked in the development of practitioner research.

Janice Bland is Professor of English Education, Nord University, Norway. Her interests include teacher education in ELT, creative writing, children's literature, critical literacy and global issues, intercultural learning and drama. Her publications include *Teaching English to Young Learners* (2015) and *Using Literature in English Language Education: Challenging Reading for 8–18 Year Olds* (2018).

Coralyn Bradshaw, MA in TEYL (University of York, UK), is Co-Founder of ELT-Consultants. She's a YL coursebook and resource materials author; designer and facilitator of teacher/trainer courses; designer and supervisor of monitoring and evaluation/impact assessment programmes and mentor for teachers and trainers. Her special interest is working within under-resourced contexts. E-mail: coraline@elt-consultants.com.

Walewska G. Braga, Municipal School São Tomás de Aquino, Rio de Janeiro, is a core member of the Rio Exploratory Practice Group. She works to understand life in the classroom and is very enthusiastic about her students' protagonism. Currently, she supervises future teachers within the government-sponsored Teaching Initiation Scholarship Program (PIBID/PUC-Rio).

Yuko Goto Butler is an Associate Professor of Educational Linguistics in the Graduate School of Education at the University of Pennsylvania, USA. She is also Director of the Teaching English to Speakers of Other Languages (TESOL) Program at Penn. Her research interests include language assessment and second and bilingual language learning among children.

Farrah Ching is a doctoral candidate in the Faculty of Education at the University of Hong Kong. She has taught English Language courses in higher education and currently works on K–12 multilingual curriculum development. Her research focuses on language policy and practice in postcolonial contexts and elite multilingualism.

Fiona Copland is Professor of TESOL at the University of Stirling, Scotland, where she is also the Associate Dean of Research in the Faculty of Social Sciences. Fiona has taught English to young learners in Nigeria, Hong Kong and Japan. As well as publishing widely in the field of young learners, her research interests include teacher training and feedback and linguistic ethnography.

Martin Cortazzi is a Visiting Professor at the University of Nottingham Ningbo, China, with extensive experience in teacher training, including teaching early years teachers, supervising research students and researching learners in different countries.

JoAnn (Jodi) Crandall, PhD, is Professor Emerita of Education and the former Co-Director of the MA TESOL Program and Director of the Language, Literacy and Culture PhD Program at the University of Maryland, Baltimore County, USA. Her current research focuses on teacher education and curriculum in English as a global language.

Maria Isabel A. Cunha, CAp/UFRJ, PUC-Rio, teaches Portuguese and English and has been a language teaching consultant to schools and NGOs. She coordinates the Curso de Especialização em Língua Inglesa at PUC-Rio and has been working with the Rio de Janeiro Exploratory Practice Group in the development of practitioner research.

Maria Ellison is an Assistant Professor in the Faculty of Arts and Humanities, University of Porto, Portugal. Her research interests are early foreign language learning, dimensions of teacher reflection, and CLIL. She has researched CLIL as a catalyst for developing reflective practice in primary foreign language teacher education. She also has experience coordinating CLIL projects in primary, secondary and tertiary education in Portugal.

Clarissa X. Ewald works with YLLs at Escola Alemã Corcovado, Rio de Janeiro. She also teaches EFL to adults at IPEL Línguas/PUC-Rio and teaches Issues in Research Methodology at PUC-Rio's Curso de Especialização em Língua Inglesa. Her research focuses on the development of teachers and learners engaged in Exploratory Practice.

Xuesong Gao is an Associate Professor in the School of Education, the University of New South Wales, Australia. His current research interests are in the areas of learner autonomy, language learning narratives, language policy and language teacher education. He is co-editor of *System: An International Journal of Educational Technology and Applied Linguistics*.

Sue Garton is Reader in TESOL, School of Languages and Social Sciences, Aston University, UK. Her research interests are in language teacher education, teaching English to Young learners and classroom discourse. She is Series Editor of the 15-volume Palgrave series *International Perspectives on English Language Teaching* (with Co-Editor Fiona Copland).

Irma-Kaarina Ghosn is Associate Professor of English and ESL at the Lebanese American University, Beirut. She has developed ELT materials for the Lebanese Ministry of Education as well as the UNRWA Education Program in Lebanon. She has conducted over 900 hours of teacher development workshops for primary school teachers.

Kate Gregson, MA in TEYL (University of York, UK), is a freelance trainer, teacher and writer with over 20 years of teaching and training experience, including supervising MA in TEYL and other master's students. She writes training sessions, ELT materials and courses, many in TEYL. Her special interests are bilingualism and progressive education.

Ye Han has a PhD in English language education from the University of Hong Kong and is an assistant professor in the School of Humanities and Social Sciences at Harbin Institute of Technology, Shenzhen. Her research interests include feedback issues in second language writing, individual variations in second language writing and the affective dimension of second language acquisition.

Torill Irene Hestetræet is a university lecturer in English language and didactics at the University of Stavanger, Norway. Her research interests include second language learning in general and vocabulary acquisition and teacher cognition in particular.

Lixian Jin is Chair Professor of Applied Linguistics and Head of the School of English at the University of Nottingham Ningbo, China. For over 30 years she has been training English teachers, supervising research students and conducting externally funded research projects on English learners internationally.

Richard Johnstone is Emeritus Professor at the University of Stirling, Scotland, where he was Head of the Institute of Education and Director of the Scottish Centre for Information on Language Teaching and Research. He has directed research projects on the early learning of additional languages in Scotland, Spain, Italy, Portugal and East Asia.

Yasemin Kırkgöz is a Professor of Applied Linguistics in the ELT Department of Çukurova University, Turkey. Her current research focuses on school-university collaborative action research teacher development, teaching English to young learners, foreign language policy and practice, language teacher education and educational research. She has published widely and presented at numerous conferences.

Kuchah Kuchah is a Lecturer in TESOL at the University of Leeds, UK. Previously he worked in EYL as a teacher, teacher trainer and policy maker in Cameroon. Kuchah's research interests include teaching English to young learners, English-medium instruction, context-appropriate methodology and teacher education. He is Co-Editor of *International Perspectives on Teaching English in Difficult Circumstances* (2018).

Yingying Li is a lecturer in the School of Foreign Languages at He Nan University of Economics and Law. She recently obtained a PhD in English language education from the University of Hong Kong. Her research focuses on written corrective feedback in second language writing and the impacts of individual difference factors on learner use of feedback.

Angel M. Y. Lin is Professor and Canada Research Chair in Plurilingual and Intercultural Education at Simon Fraser University. She is well respected for her interdisciplinary research in classroom discourse analysis, critical literacies, Content and Language Integrated Learning (CLIL) and language policy and practice in postcolonial contexts.

Mario E. López-Gopar is Professor in the Faculty of Languages of Universidad Autónoma Benito Juárez de Oaxaca, Mexico. Mario's main research interest is intercultural and multilingual education of Indigenous peoples in Mexico. He has received over 15 academic awards. His latest book *Decolonizing Primary English Language Teaching* was published in 2016.

Florià Belinchón Majoral graduated from Universitat de Lleida, Catalonia. He works as Head Teacher of a primary school, where he also teaches English, and is a part-time Lecturer at the University of Lleida, where he trains primary teachers in the use of technology in education. He is also Language and Culture Advisor for the Department of Education of Catalonia.

Inés K. Miller Associate Professor at the Pontifical Catholic University of Rio de Janeiro (PUC-Rio), has been researching the reflective discourse generated by learners, teachers and teacher educators. She mentors the Rio Exploratory Practice Group and has been actively engaged in the development and dissemination of Exploratory Practice.

Sandie Mourão, PhD, is a teacher educator, materials writer and educational consultant who works part time at the Nova University Lisbon on the MA for teachers of young learners. Her research interest is in early years language education for small children.

Victoria Murphy is Professor of Applied Linguistics in the Department of Education, University of Oxford. Her research focuses on understanding the interrelationships between child L2/FL learning, vocabulary and literacy development. She has published in a wide range of applied linguistics journals and is the author of *Second Language Learning in the Early School Years* (2014).

Jacob Marriote Ngwaru holds a PhD from the University of Reading, UK. He is Associate Professor at the Aga Khan University, Institute for Educational Development, East Africa. He has published journal papers and book chapters on home school literacy practices, the place of local culture and mother tongue in the classroom and the effect of language policy on learning in Sub-Saharan Africa.

Ming Ni is currently a second-year PhD student in Education at the University of Stirling, Scotland. Her research project focuses on Chinese master's students in the UK and their use of classroom language(s), mainly Mandarin Chinese and English, as well as their translanguaging. She is also interested in linguistic ethnography, especially its practice and ethical concerns.

Adriana N. Nóbrega is a professor at PUC-Rio in the area of Language Studies. Her research focuses on pedagogical contexts, considering the theoretical interface between systemic-functional linguistics and critical discourse analysis, sociocultural theory and narrative and identity studies. She is a member of the Rio de Janeiro Exploratory Practice Group.

Szilvia Papp is a consultant in educational assessment. She was Senior Research and Validation Manager at Cambridge English Language Assessment, working on the Cambridge English Young Learners tests and school examinations between 2007 and 2015. Her current research focuses on language assessment among children and adolescents in pre-school, primary and lower secondary contexts.

Virginia Parker has been involved in ELT internationally for nearly 20 years, as a teacher, teacher mentor and teacher trainer. She has consulted on and written both teaching and assessment materials, as well as delivered numerous conference workshops and CPD to teachers throughout the world.

Simone E. Pfenninger is Associate Professor of Psycholinguistics and Second Language Acquisition at the University of Salzburg, Austria, and Co-Editor of the Second Language Acquisition book series for Multilingual Matters. Her principal research areas are multilingualism, psycholinguistics and individual differences in SLA, especially in regard to quantitative approaches and statistical methods and techniques for language application in education.

Annamaria Pinter is an Associate Professor at the Centre for Applied Linguistics, University of Warwick, UK. She is the author of *Teaching Young Language Learners Oxford Handbooks for Language Teachers* (2nd edition, 2017) and has published extensively in ELT/applied linguistics journals and written numerous book chapters in the broad area of teaching young language learners.

Herbert Puchta holds a PhD in English with an emphasis on ELT pedagogy. He was previously Professor of English at the University College of Teacher Education in Graz, Austria. He has also been President of the International Association of Teachers of English as a Foreign Language (IATEFL). He now works as an independent materials writer and educational consultant and has co-authored numerous coursebooks on the teaching of young learners.

Sarah Rich holds an honorary Senior Lecturership in TESOL at the University of Exeter where she worked for a number of years. She is also a freelance consultant.

Shelagh Rixon has worked extensively in Europe in a young learners connection, in particular in Italy where she was English Language Officer for the British Council. She coordinated the MA in Teaching English to Young Learners at the University of Warwick from 1991 until her retirement in 2009. She now is an Associate Tutor for the University of Leicester, UK.

Peter Sayer is an Associate Professor of Language Education Studies in the Department of Teaching and Learning at the Ohio State University, USA. He is the author of *Tensions and Ambiguities in English Language Teaching* (2012). His current work focuses on the pedagogical, curriculum and sociolinguistic aspects of public school English and bilingual programmes for young language learners.

Euline Cutrim Schmid is full Professor of Applied Linguistics and TEFL at the University of Education Schwäbisch Gmünd, Germany. She has a PhD in linguistics and an MA in language teaching from Lancaster University, UK. Her current research interests are teacher education in computer assisted language learning and plurilingual approaches to language education.

David Singleton is a Fellow Emeritus at Trinity College Dublin and holds professorships at the University of Pannonia, Hungary, and the State University of Applied Sciences, Konin, Poland. He also co-edits the Second Language Acquisition book series for Multilingual Matters. His research publications focus on cross-linguistic influence, lexicon, age factor and multilingualism.

Joan Kang Shin, PhD, is an Associate Professor of Education at George Mason University. She co-authored *Teaching Young Learners English* with Jodi Crandall and is Co-Series Editor of several young learner programmes for National Geographic Learning: *Welcome to Our World*, *Our World*, and *Explore Our World*.

Medadi E. Ssentanda holds a PhD from the Stellenbosch University, South Africa. He teaches in the Department of African Languages at Makerere University and is a Research Associate in the of Faculty of Arts and Social Sciences at Stellenbosch University. His interests lie in early literacy development, language policy and how it is manifested in the classroom, and multilingual education.

Amanda L. Sullivan, PhD, is an Associate Professor of Educational Psychology at the University of Minnesota, USA. She holds a PhD in Educational Psychology from Arizona State University and is a certified school psychologist and licenced psychologist. Her research focuses on special needs among children from culturally and linguistically diverse backgrounds and disparities in the educational and health services they receive.

David Valente is Coordinator of the IATEFL Young Learners and Teenagers SIG and has 20 years' experience as a teacher, academic manager, educational consultant, teacher trainer and materials developer. His specialist interests are primary and secondary ELT and YL ELT management. David has authored teachers' handbooks and primary and secondary programmes and advised Ministries of Education on curriculum development.

Mollie R. Weeks, BA, is a doctoral student in the School Psychology Program at the University of Minnesota, USA. She holds a BA in Psychology from St. Olaf College. Her research centres on mental health disparities in schools and communities, with a special focus on the needs of culturally and linguistically diverse children.

Shona Whyte, PhD Linguistics (Indiana University Bloomington, USA), is Associate Professor of English at the Université Côte d'Azur in Nice, France. Her research interests include computer-assisted language learning (CALL), particularly classroom interaction and teacher integration of technologies, and the didactics of English for specific purposes.

Fiona Willans is a Lecturer in Linguistics at the University of the South Pacific, based at the Laucala Campus in Fiji. Her current research focuses on multilingual classrooms in Melanesia, examining the complexity of Grade 1 teacher talk in a range of schools.

Subhan Zein started his career as a primary EFL teacher in Indonesia. He has taught ESL in Australia since 2009 and has trained teachers in Indonesia and Australia. He currently teaches in the School of Education at the University of Queensland, Australia. He has published in international peer-reviewed journals including the *Applied Linguistics Review* and *Journal of Education for Teaching*.

Acknowledgements

Figure 13.1 is taken from *Teaching Grammar Creatively* by Gerngross, G., H. Puchta and S. Thornbury. © 2006 Helbling Languages. Reprinted with kind permission of the publisher.

Figure 16.2 is reprinted with kind permission of Cláudia Regina Leonardo Abreu.

Figure 17.2 is taken from Thunder Boy, Jr. by Sherman Alexie, illustrated by Yuyi Morales. Text copyright © 2016 by Sherman Alexie. Illustrations copyright © 2016 by Yuyi Morales. Used by permission of Little Brown Books for Young Readers.

Introduction

Sue Garton and Fiona Copland

At the 2014 International Association of Teachers of English as a Foreign Language (IATEFL) conference the *ELT Journal* sponsored a debate on the position 'Teaching English to children in primary schools does more harm than good'. Fiona proposed the topic, which might surprise readers given the focus of this volume. Like many contributors to this book, however, Fiona and Sue (who helped Fiona prepare for the debate) have often felt that the implementation of early English language learning can be flawed and that the evidence base for the early introduction to English is weak.

Opposing this position was Janet Enever, a well-known researcher in the field of young learners. After Fiona's opening arguments, Janet stood up, but rather than voicing opposition to the statement, she took a different approach. She suggested that the point was moot as, in her words, 'the horse had bolted'. Early English language learning, she said, had become so widespread that whatever strong arguments were made, they would have no effect on whether English was taught or not. Given this reality, she argued, we should concentrate instead on investigating the contexts of early language learning with a view to improving approaches so that children and their teachers have good language experiences, inside and outside the classroom.

While we both believe that ideologies of young learner teaching should be challenged when there are grounds, we recognise that Janet's point was both well made and accurate. This volume responds to Janet's challenge.

Until relatively recently the young learner field has been characterised as the Cinderella of applied linguistics research in general and of second language acquisition in particular. However, this no longer holds true. One reason for the increase in interest is the well-documented rise in the number of children who are learning English globally at younger ages (e.g., Johnstone 2009; Garton et al. 2011). Another is the realisation that research with older learners and adults is not necessarily relevant to young learners who are still developing cognitively and emotionally. There is also the recognition that globalisation and consequent movement of peoples around the world creates new contexts of learning, particularly for children. And finally, as researchers begin to debunk a number of myths around young language learners—for example, that it is best to start learning a language early or that children cannot learn two languages at the same time—the focus is shifting increasingly to how

1

children learn languages. Taken together, these circumstances have created a golden age, in which there is a clear and sustained attention on the young learner and the young learner classroom.

Indicative of this growing interest in young language learners in the last twenty years is an abundance of research contributions, especially in the last ten years. A number of books and articles focus on macro perspectives. Enever et al. (2009), for example, examine global policies in teaching English to young learners. Lopez-Gopar (2016) turns his attention to the developing field of critical pedagogy and investigates how it contributes positively to the young learner classroom. Copland et al. (2014) focus on the challenges that young learner teachers face and how they are overcome. Other publications examine micro perspectives and open up new lines of enquiry with regard to young learners. The same year as the IATEFL debate also saw the first ever *ELT Journal* special issue dedicated to young learners (Copland and Garton 2014), which included contributions on learning outside the classroom (Sayer and Ban 2014), appropriate pedagogies for very young learners (Mourão 2014), and gaming (Butler et al. 2014).

A field that was once considered essentially practical now boasts a number of volumes that present research-informed practice. Rich (2014) and Bland (2015), for example, published edited collections that include chapters covering a range of topics of interest to the field but all linking practice with relevant theoretical underpinnings, while Nikolov's (2017) edited collection examines assessing young learners from a variety of perspectives.

Research methods are also of growing interest to the field. Pinter and Zandian's (2014) work involving children in the research process is particularly innovative, while Enever and Lindgren's (2017) volume brings together studies using mixed methods. There is also a keen interest in child second language acquisition: Pinter (2011) and Murphy (2014) both offer far-reaching overviews on studies of children and language learning, and authors in Mihaljević Djigunović and Medved Krajnović's edited collecion (2015) use a Dynamics Systems Theory approach to examine complexities in the young language learner classroom.

It is also noticeable that the young learner field takes a truly international perspective. Edited collections from Rich (2014), Enever et al. (2009) and Copland and Garton (2018) all feature chapters from eminent colleagues around the world, demonstrating the global reach of the field. Indeed, colleagues in TESEP countries (countries where English is taught in tertiary, secondary and primary education, Holliday 1994) have long been interested in young learners (e.g., Nikolov 2009; Butler 2015); colleagues in the West have taken longer to become engaged.

Today the young learner landscape is rich and varied, bringing together theory and practice, large-scale and small-scale projects, which can be both qualitative and quantitative in scope.

These characteristics are reflected in the current volume, which brings the field right up to date, covering a wide range of traditional and new areas of teaching English to young learners and with chapter authors exploring a broad array of recent research in their respective areas.

The scope of the volume

Before giving an overview of the chapters, it is relevant to address two key issues in the discussions of young learners. One is terminology. In the field, a number of labels are used to refer to children learning English. They include: 'young learners' (YLs), 'early language learners' (ELL), 'early English language learners' (EELL) and English young learners (EYL). In this volume, each author has chosen the term they feel is most appropriate for their context. The other issue focuses on age: who exactly is a young learner? Ellis (2014) notes that the term is vague and can lead to confusion, particularly as English has until recently been taught more generally in the secondary sector. In this volume, unless stated differently by the chapter author, young learners are primary school children, with an age range of 5–12.

The volume is organised into six sections. We begin by considering the broader context, examining areas such as policy and motivation. The second section examines the young learner classroom at a more micro level, with chapters on classroom management and teaching through English, amongst others. In the third section, we explore a mainstay of YL research: pedagogy. This large section examines common areas such as teaching grammar and listening and speaking, as well as newer approaches becoming popular with young learners such as CLIL. The fourth section brings together work on curriculum and technology, and section five focuses on researching young learners, including a chapter on involving young learners as researchers. Finally, in section six, chapters provide overviews of EELL in regions where it is growing in popularity: Africa, Asia, Europe, South America and South Pacific.

Part 1 Macro issues

The five chapters in Part 1 of the volume all situate some aspect of TEYL in the broader context in which it takes place. In the first chapter, Johnstone traces the history of early language learning education before discussing the global spread of English for young learners in the twenty-first century. He explores a number of critical issues in primary school contexts that relate to current policy, such as the starting age, the place of English in the curriculum and the effects on language diversity.

The age debate, raised by Johnstone, continues to rage despite studies and discussions which have provided helpful guidance in this area (e.g., Pinter 2011). Singleton and Pfenniger provide a comprehensive overview of research in a number of different contexts and are unequivocal in their conclusions that earlier does not, in most circumstances, mean better. This chapter provides ministries of education globally with important food for thought regarding early English language learning policies and the question of whether the implementation is supporting language learning or is potentially detrimental to it.

Key to the implementation of YL policies is teachers, and research has shown that teacher education is fundamental in successfully bridging the policy-practice gap (see, for example, Garton et al. 2011). In Chapter 3 Rich provides a critical and in-depth account of the current state of early language learning teacher education. She addresses initial and in-service teacher education, identifying core principles and practices and presenting useful recommendations for YL teacher education practice.

Shifting attention to learners, in Chapter 4, Li et al. examine the motivation of young learners, most of whom have few choices about learning English. They show that parental involvement is closely linked to whether children are motivated to learn, as is the social economic status of the family. They also suggest that assessment can have a positive effect on children's language learning, particularly in contexts where children are used to being tested. Li, Han Ye and Gao suggest that children's motivation for language learning is complex, shifting and dynamic, and these features must be taken into consideration in research on young language learners' motivation.

The final chapter in this section looks at a relatively new area of language learning, that of teaching and learning in difficult circumstances. Kuchah Kuchah explores the main factors that contribute to creating difficult environments for young learners, especially in developing contexts. These include the language of instruction, which means many children are educated in a language different from their home languages, large under-resourced classrooms, limited exposure to English language outside the classroom and contexts of conflict. Kuchah also provides examples of bottom-up initiatives and shows the benefits that can be gained in difficult circumstances from collaborative inquiry-based projects involving both teachers and learners.

Part 2 In the YL classroom

The second part of the volume, also consisting of five chapters, shifts from the macro context to the micro context, examining what happens in the YL classroom from a variety of perspectives.

In the first chapter of this section, Ching and Lin focus on contexts where English is not the dominant language but where it is used as the medium of instruction. In this way, children develop academic English skills. They suggest that models of bilingual learning, such as immersion, that were often imposed on teachers and learners alike are no longer as powerful as they once were and that there has been a turn towards more fluid approaches such as translanguaging. Rooting their discussion firmly in issues of power and hierarchy, Chung and Lin put the child at the centre of their recommendations for practice.

Murphy also discusses bi- and multilingualism in Chapter 7 but from the perspective of children who migrate to countries where the dominant language is English. She examines how children from linguistically diverse backgrounds develop reading and writing skills in English and the challenges they face. While highlighting that children benefit cognitively from bilingualism, she also suggests that children from linguistically diverse backgrounds may need specific interventions in order to succeed academically.

The focus of Sullivan and Weeks's chapter is that of differentiated instruction (DI). Defined as an instructional orientation which seeks to enhance students' learning opportunities, this is a relatively new area of concern for TEYL research. The authors therefore draw primarily on studies conducted with DI in English-only general and special education settings. They explore DI practices, emphasising those that can be applied with young English learners (ELs), opening up new avenues for TEYL research.

Moving back to language use in the classroom, in Chapter 9 Copland and Ni address the longstanding debates around the use of learners' first language (L1) in the second language (L2) classroom. They explore how the L1 and L2 are used in the YL classroom and the rationales and the effect of such language use. Based on current research, they make a number of suggestions to support teachers in their language choices.

The final chapter in this section takes a broader view of the YL classroom as Zein looks at research into YL classroom management. In particular, he takes the innovative approach of drawing on research into mainstream classroom management and considering what it has to offer the YL language classroom. He argues for a shift from a classroom-level approach to a whole school-level approach that makes young learner behaviour management a school-wide concern. Zein reviews examples of interventions based on a whole school approach and shows how these may help reduce classroom disruptions and increase learners' self-regulation.

Part 3 Young learner pedagogy

Traditionally in English language teaching, content has been divided into language systems (grammar, vocabulary, pronunciation and discourse) and systems (listening, speaking, reading and writing). Many coursebooks are organised according to these principles and teachers may have to follow that guidance even when they prefer a more holistic classroom approach.

The first part of this section follows this division as authors examine listening and speaking (Kırkgöz), reading and writing (Shin and Crandall), teaching grammar (Putcha) and vocabulary (Hestetræet).

It is common for teachers of young learners to focus exclusively on listening and speaking in the classroom: indeed, some national curricula explicitly urge teachers to take this approach (e.g., Gaynor 2014). In Chapter 11, Kirkgöz examines the research in listening and speaking with young learners with a particular focus on six- to 11-year-olds. She concludes that issues in teaching these skills can be classified as either teacher-related or curriculum-related. She calls for an integrated approach to teaching listening and speaking and provides a series of activities that teachers can try out based on the principles she presents.

Shin and Crandall examine reading and writing with young learners. They explore the links between literacy and learning to read and write in a second language and highlight the benefits that can be gained as children develop literacy in two languages. They uncover the skills learners must develop to read successfully and suggest five stages learners go through when learning to write. The cultural aspects of reading and writing are both emphasised before they suggest a comprehensive set of recommendations for practice.

Putcha begins his chapter by examining the role of grammar in teaching English to children, specifically those in the 5–9 age bracket where cognitive function is not yet fully developed. He points to the interconnectedness of grammar and vocabulary and calls for both to be integrated into other activities such as storytelling. Through responding to a series of questions, such as 'Does explicit grammar work facilitate language use?', Putcha examines effective approaches to grammar teaching to young learners, approaches which he puts into practice in the activities he introduces for use in the classroom.

In Chapter 14 Hestetræet discusses the need for YLs to develop a large vocabulary through focusing on the form, meaning and use of words. She considers research around word frequency and vocabulary size, which have been developed with adult learners in mind, and addresses the need for age-appropriate vocabulary. Going on to explore approaches to vocabulary teaching and learning, she recommends that teachers should aim for a balanced approach that includes both explicit and implicit approaches. As well as suggesting resources such as the use of word cards, graded readers, picture books, oral storytelling and Readers Theatre, she also dicusses the links between vocabulary learning and task-based learning and the use of technology.

While many coursebooks and curricula remain organised around the traditional areas of systems and skills, teachers have begun to work with alternative approaches, recognising that a more holistic approach might be more beneficial for young learners. These are the focus of the second part of this section.

López-Gopar's starting point is that, far from being neutral and apolitical, the spread of English is based on discriminatory practices, social inequality and hegemonic power. In his chapter, he discusses critical pedagogy as a way in which these issues can be addressed in the YL classroom. Whilst critical pedagogy is not new, its application in YL classrooms is far more recent. López-Gopar's chapter therefore provides an overview of critical pedagogies in education in general and how these might be relevant to the EYL classroom, as well as presenting recommendations for critical ELT practice.

In Chapter 16, Ellison provides a comprehensive overview of an approach which is becoming increasingly popular: CLIL (content and language integrated learning). In CLIL, English is learned through focusing on different content areas, for example, history or mathematics. Teachers provide explicit linguistic support to learners to scaffold them in developing content knowledge and academic language skills. Ellison explains how CLIL teachers frame their lessons around the four Cs – content, communication, culture and cognition – and provides helpful examples of lesson plans and class materials.

Storytelling has become an increasingly popular approach to teaching young learners, with some practitioners building a whole syllabus around it (e.g., Yanase 2018). Bland's chapter explores literature-based approaches, which can include stories, poems and more factual pieces. After exploring the historical reach of literature in language learning, Bland sets out a long list of texts that are suitable for young learners, including picture books, graphic novels, story apps and plays, suggesting how these might be used by teachers. Like a number of contributors to this volume, Bland also focuses on the unequal distribution of resources in young learner learning and teaching contexts, and suggests this issue is particularly acute when it comes to the availability of printed resources.

Projects have long been a mainstay in western classrooms as teachers have recognised the potential they have for skills integration and development. In their chapter, Arnold et al. call project work to develop English skills 'language learning through projects' (lltp) and distinguish it from other approaches such as task-based learning. They suggest that there are three phases to project work (choosing a topic, conducting research and representing the findings and presenting the project and receiving feedback) underpinned by three structures: content, processes and products. Although Arnold et al. are convinced of the benefits of lltp for some learners in some contexts, they sound a cautious note about its wholesale exportation to countries which may not have the resources for the approach or where it may not fit easily into current educational norms.

Part 4 Technology and curriculum

Technology is, of course, pervasive in education, and ELT is no exception (see, for example, Dudeney and Hockly 2012). In the first part of this section, three chapters focus on three different aspects of ICT in TEYL: the use of technology outside the classroom in the form of gaming (Butler), the affordances of mobile-learning for use both inside and outside the classroom (Belinchón Majoral) and classroom based ICT (Whyte and Cutrim Schmid).

Butler opens this section with her chapter on digital games. Discussing research into their use with young language learners (age 5–15) as well as in other settings, she shows teachers how digital games can be used as educational tools with the potential to motivate young leaners and enhance their autonomy and learning. However, she notes that the role of the teacher is fundamental in identifying best practices when using digital games and concludes that we need more information about effective design and implementation.

Like Butler, Belinchón Majoral also emphasises the importance of the teacher in mediating between technology and language learners. He discusses the affordances of mobile devices such as tablets, netbooks, laptops and digital readers from a social constructivist and collaborative learning perspective. He concludes with a comprehensive overview of the different ways in which mobile learning can be exploited, with comprehensive suggestions for resources that teachers can draw on.

In the final chapter on technology, Whyte and Cutrim Schmid also discuss how technology can be a key motivating factor for young learners and develop their autonomy. They review previous research on computer-assisted language learning (CALL) focusing on a variety of new technologies for use in the language classroom, such as interactive whiteboards, tablets and telecollaboration. They offer a number of recommendations for the effective integration of new technologies in the primary English curriculum.

The last three chapters in this section focus on the primary English curriculum and specifically on three key aspects: syllabus, materials and assessment. All three of these facets of the curriculum have been identified as key challenges in the successful implementation of primary English (see, for example, Garton et al. 2011).

In their chapter on syllabus design, Parker and Valente look in detail at the challenges in designing the primary English curriculum as a result of of three key factors: the increase in the number of children taking English language; the ever earlier start in learning English and the lack of appropriate pedagogy because of a shortage of qualified teachers. They explore how the spread of the Common European Framework of Reference (CEFR) has led to a washback effect on syllabuses with its influence on coursebook content and on ELL syllabuses. Parker and Valente question whether it is even relevant to talk about the 'syllabus', proposing instead the concept of 'curriculum' with its related schemes better suited to the organization of language learning at the primary level.

As Parker and Valente note, the coursebook is very often the *de facto* syllabus and this is reflected in Ghosn's chapter on YL materials. She presents a wide-ranging review of materials for young language learners and asks what 'good' instructional materials and practices for TEYL are. Unusually, she also offers a glimpse into what materials use in the classroom actually looks like.

In Chapter 24, the final chapter in the section, Papp addresses the sometimes controversial topic of YL assessment, which is often accused of having a negative impact on classroom teaching through washback, especially when high-stakes international examinations are involved. Papp reviews large-scale national and international tests of English language developed for young learners. She explores the factors involved in making informed and appropriate decisions regarding which type of assessment is most effective and beneficial for young learners. Considerations such as age, context of instruction, exposure to English and the reasons for assessment are explored. Papp also goes beyond current tests and addresses new developments in the field such as the assessment of twenty-first century life skills alongside English language competence.

Part 5 Researching young learners

There have long been issues with conducting research 'on' young learners, particularly very young ones, because of ethical and organisational concerns. Nonetheless, there has been a good deal of movement in this area more recently. While much of the research focuses on the teachers of young learners (see Copland and Garton 2018), other studies look outside the classroom and at research 'with' young learners.

Pinter's chapter concerns research with young learners. Drawing on a number of recent projects, she suggests that there can be different levels of children's involvement in research. In most cases, research is performed on children, with the researchers designing the research questions and data collection methods and collecting the data. However, Pinter shows how children can also be involved in decision making around research design as well as active participants in data collection. Pinter argues that children have different questions about learning that directly affect them and therefore should be considered legitimate contributors to research on young learners.

In Chapter 26 Mourão turns her attention to the relatively new phenomena of very young children learning English in nursery and other day care settings. Popular in some Asian, European and South American countries, Mourão highlights key challenges in teaching very young children, from the relative paucity of teaching staff with appropriate skills to understanding appropriate pedagogies for very young children, such as play and storytelling, Mourão suggests that researching these learners can be difficult. She also highlights the issue of equal (or unequal) access to English language learning in very young learner settings, which remains generally an activity in which primarily wealthy families engage.

Sayer and Ban take research outside the classroom and examine how children learn English in other contexts. Distinguishing between incidental learning (learning English while trying to accomplish something else) and intentional learning (focusing on language learning explicitly) they examine how children can learn English in online spaces, for example, when taking part in fan discussion groups. Sayer and Ban draw attention to the difficulty of researching children's learning 'in the wild'; data collection is a particular issue.

Part 6 Teaching English to young learners: regional perspectives

The final five chapters of the volume mark a shift away from the focus of the previous 27 chapters, all of which have focused on a key aspect of TEYL. Instead, this final section takes a different perspective and looks at how TEYL is being implemented in different regions of the world, specifically Africa, East Asia, Europe, Latin America and the South Pacific. Of course, countries within regions vary greatly, as do districts within countries and even schools within districts. What each author in this section has done is focus on a small number of countries in order to illustrate the main challenges and opportunities that can be found in very different areas of the world, and the recommendations for practice in each chapter have clear implications beyond the specific region.

In the first chapter Ssentanda and Ngwaru focus on East Africa to discuss issues of multilingualism in early English language learning in Africa. Far from being the problem that it is often portrayed as, Ssentanda and Ngwaru argue that it can be an opportunity to improve the learning of English, adding value to the linguistic repertoires of children rather than subtracting from them.

In their chapter on East Asia, Lixian Jin and Martin Cortazzi take a broader view of the trends and policies for TEYL in this region. Discussing Singapore, Malaysia, Hong Kong, Japan, Taiwan and especially China, they explore a range of principles and practices situated against the educational and social development contexts of the region. They then focus on China as a case study to highlight some of the research into the impact of learning English. They argue there is a strong need for more empirical research to identify relevant theories and practices for the East Asian context, a call that is undoubtedly relevant to other regions too.

Rixon also takes a policy perspective in her chapter on Europe. She examines European policy making both in terms of what the policies say and the reasons for them, especially in the context of the European Union and its language policies. She also discusses YL teacher education in the region and explores widely used methodologies such as storytelling and CLIL, which are becoming increasingly influential, even outside Europe. Like Papp and

Parker and Valente, Rixon also considers the influence of the CEFR on both syllabus and assessment, specifically in Europe.

A more critical view of the introduction of English into primary schools is taken by Miller et al. in their chapter on Latin America. Focusing on Argentina, Brazil, Chile, Colombia and Uruguay, they look at how the imposition of TEYL has been problematised in the region from a sociolinguist perspective. They call for further research which takes a sociocultural and historical theoretical background.

In Chapter 32, Wilians explores TEYL in an often neglected context, that of the Pacific region. She identifies the policy-practice gaps in a region where English serves as an official language and medium of instruction, but where both teaching and educational use of English varies widely. She focuses on three key issues: the varying status of English, the need to reconcile literacy development and preparation for the use of English as a medium of instruction in the curriculum and teacher training.

Concluding comments

A number of key themes have emerged from the chapters presented in this volume, which in turn raise questions in relation to teaching English to young learners. One is equity—which young learners have access to English and in what contexts? Which young learners are disadvantaged by the global rush to English and which ones are advantaged? Another is appropriate pedagogy—as the age at which children begin to learn English continues to fall, how can we ensure that teaching approaches are fit for purpose across a range of contexts, levels and maturities? A third theme is teacher education—a number of chapters suggest that more support is needed for teachers who are often expected to teach English (or young learners) with very little training. What can be done to support these teachers, particularly in contexts where training is hard to access because of availability or geography? A fourth is resources—as technology develops, how can we ensure that teachers and learners are able to access digital resources for effective language learning?

Of course, the 32 chapters which follow also raise other themes and issues which together with these broader areas represent a strong response to Enever's IATEFL call to better understand young learners and their educational contexts. Indeed, we believe they not only give a timely and comprehensive overview of key issues in the field of teaching English to young learners in the twenty-first century, but also present a plausible research agenda going forward.

References

Bland, J. (Ed.). (2015). *Teaching English to Young Learners: Critical issues in language teaching with 3–12 year olds*. London: Bloomsbury.

Butler, Y. G. (2015). English language education among young learners in East Asia: A review of current research (2004–2014). *Language Teaching*, 48(3), 303–342.

Copland, F., and Garton, S. (2014). Key themes and future directions in teaching English to young learners: Introduction to the Special Issue. *ELT Journal*, 68(3), 223–230.

Copland, F., and Garton, S. (Eds.). (2018). *TESOL Voices: Young learner education*. Alexandria, VA: TESOL Press.

Copland, F., Garton, S., and Burns, A. (2014). Challenges in teaching English to young learners: Global perspectives and local realities. *TESOL Quarterly*, 48(4), 738–762.

Djigunović, J. M., and Krajnović, M. M. (Eds.). (2015). *Early Learning and Teaching of English: New dynamics of primary English*. Bristol: Multilingual Matters.

Dudeney, G., and Hockly, N. (2012). ICT in ELT: How did we get here and where are we going? *ELT Journal*, 66(4), 533–542.

Ellis, G. (2014). "Young learners": Clarifying our terms. *ELT Journal*, 68(1), 75–78.

Enever, J., and Lindgren, E. (Eds.). (2017). *Early Language Learning: Complexity and mixed methods*. Bristol: Multilingual Matters.

Enever, J., Moon, J., and Rahman, U. (2009). *Young Learner English Language Policy and Implementation: International Perspectives*. Reading: Garnet.

Garton, S., Copland, F., and Burns, A. (2011). *Investigating Global Practices in Teaching English to Young Learners*. ELT Research Papers 11–01. London: The British Council.

Gaynor, B. (2014). From language policy to pedagogic practice: Elementary school English in Japan. In Rich, S. (ed.) *International Perspectives on Teaching English to Young Learners*. London: Palgrave Macmillan, 66–84.

Holliday, A. (1994). *Appropriate Methodology and Social Context*. Cambridge: Cambridge University Press.

Johnstone, R. (2009). An early start: What are the key conditions for generalized success? In Enever, J., Moon, J., and Rahman, U. (eds.) *Young Learner English Language Policy and Implementation: International perspectives*. Reading: Garnet, 31–41.

López-Gopar, M. E. (2016). *Decolonizing Primary English Language Teaching (Linguistic Diversity and Language Rights)*. Bristol: Multilingual Matters.

Murphy, V. A. (2014). *Second Language Learning in the Early School Years: Trends and Contexts*. Oxford: Oxford University Press.

Nikolov, M. (2009). *Early Learning of Modern Foreign Languages: Processes and outcomes*. Bristol: Multilingual Matters.

Nikolov, M. (2017). *Assessing Young Learners of English: Global and local perspectives*. New York: Springer.

Pinter, A. (2011). *Children Learning Second Languages*. Basingstoke: Palgrave Macmillan.

Pinter, A., and Zandian, S. (2014). 'I don't ever want to leave this room': Benefits of researching 'with' children. *ELT Journal*, 68(1), 64–74.

Rich, S. (Ed.) (2014). *International Perspectives on Teaching English to Young Learners*. Basingstoke: Palgrave Macmillan.

Yanase, C. (2018). Getting children to be active agents of their own learning. In Copland, F., and Garton, S. (eds.) *TESOL Voices: Young Learner Education*. Alexandria, VA: TESOL Press, 66–74.

PART 1
Macro Issues

Languages policy and English for young learners in early education

Richard Johnstone

Introduction

English for young learners in 'early education'

In this chapter EYL refers to children's learning of English in pre-primary or primary (elementary) school education, for whom English is not their first language. It includes children whose first language is the national language of their country, when learning English there as a additional language. However, there is much more to EYL than that. The globalised world brings many challenges – e.g., movement of people; disparities between small communities in remote rural areas and those in increasingly diverse big cities; and attitudes towards minorities (both indigenous and recently arrived), their cultures and languages – some of which have consequences for EYL. Thus, a child from an EU country in Central Europe learning English in Ireland; a child from Syria being educated in Germany and learning both German and English; children from South America, Africa or Asia learning English in Australia; or in their own country speaking a local language or dialect through which they possibly receive some of their education for a while but at the same time being educated through the country's national language and also learning English – these examples and many more are included in the present chapter.

'Early education' is not only the place where EYL occurs. It is the active process of educating children at school. It has a reciprocal relationship with EYL. Accordingly, one can ask 'What can early education do for EYL?' but also ask 'What can EYL do for early education?' This latter function of EYL in serving the early general education of children at school is of great importance. If EYL were to exist in a linguistic bubble and be solely about developing proficiency in English language, then its rationale for occupying a place in primary school curricula would be weakened.

Languages policy

In the title of this section, the term 'Languages policy' is used because it allows English to be embedded along with other languages in a country's overall approach. While it is true that

Languages Policy has importance at many levels of society – e.g., individual, family, educational institution, peer-group, small community, business, city, region, interest group –in the present chapter it refers mainly to the national/international level.

My reasons for focusing on the national/international dimension of Languages Policy are that it highlights the extent to which a policy caters to all children in a country, rather than an elite minority; it allows for comparison and communication across countries; English as an international language may at times evoke feelings of media propaganda, linguistic imperialism, minority culture suppression or pro-native speaker bias, so it is important to consider what a policy makes of English in the 'early education' of impressionable children; and many governments have allocated substantial funds for EYL in early education, so it is reasonable to ask what arises from this investment.

Languages policy makers

Much has been written about Languages Policy but less about those who make it – e.g., their attitudes, agendas (public or hidden) and political imperatives. Many of the policy makers I have met internationally have been civil servants, national inspectors, national policy advisers, politicians, senior staff co-opted from educational institutions or representatives of civic society (including parents). Their government may possibly assign some of them to languages policy for a while and then move them on. This rotation may provide regular fresh thinking and prevent policy individuals from 'going native' within the languages community, but it may in some cases need to be balanced against possible lack of knowledge of the historical, intellectual and research traditions of the languages field.

Sometimes tensions can arise from key financial decisions being made at a higher level than that of Languages Policy by those exercising responsibility across competing areas of public policy. Given the global financial crisis of 2007 and 2008 and the austerity policies that ensued, languages funding might not be the priority it was at the turn of the century. This reduction in funding can put pressure on the sustainability of some of the EYL initiatives and have an unsettling effect on teachers, students, managers and parents.

Key agencies

Among the key agencies complementing national governments and playing a role in influencing languages-policy development are major transnational entities such as the European Commission (EC) and the Council of Europe (CoE), plus organisations with remits for languages (or a particular language) internationally such as the British Council, the ECML (European Centre for Modern Languages), the Alliance Française and the Confucius Institute. I believe the role of such bodies has largely been positive, though all policies always need to be scrutinized for false claims, for bias and for 'hidden agendas'.

Equally important are international professional associations that among other things support EYL in early education, such as Asia TEFL, IATEFL and AILA. They create a forum for disseminating independent, peer-reviewed research findings, for presenting new ideas and developments, critiquing national and international policies, creating special interest networks and supporting teachers, teacher educators, researchers and policy makers.

Thinking about policies for EYL

It is not always the case that policy makers have a blank sheet of paper. Often, there is an explicit or implicit EYL policy already in existence. If so, then policy makers need to ask questions such as: *'What's wrong with the present policy?', 'Do we simply need to improve it?',* or *'Do we need more radical change?'* As such, they have much to think about, but four considerations seem particularly important:

Aims and values

• *What aims should the policy have and what values should it seek to promote?*

  • Examples of aims: 'proficiency in English'; 'children's general social, cognitive, intercultural, literacy, numerical, aesthetic development'.
  • Examples of values: 'citizenship', 'national identity', 'international outlook', 'humanitarian', 'environmental', 'entrepreneurial'.

Societal factors

• *What factors operating in a nation's society are likely to influence (positively or otherwise) the EYL policy when implemented, and in what ways should the policy address these factors?*

  • Examples of factors: 'public and media attitudes to English and EYL'; 'degree of exposure to English in everyday society'; 'disparities of socioeconomic status and also of geographical location'; 'issues of minority culture, gender, migration, ethnicity, religion, fundamentalism'.

Provision factors

• *What provisions are needed in order to ensure that the policy is adequately financed, resourced and informed?*

  Examples of provisions: 'supply, training and continuing development of teachers'; 'supply of appropriate resources and technology'; 'amount of time allocation per week for EYL'; 'surveys of research on areas relevant to developing the policy'.

Process factors

• *What policy-related processes will need to be put in place?*

  • Examples of processes: 'planning, monitoring, research, evaluation, piloting, decision making, accountability, management, stakeholder consultation and involvement, partnership, international co-operation, fund-raising, long-term sustainability'.

Further examples of these four key considerations are embedded in the remainder of the chapter. They are vital not only in planning and implementing an EYL policy but also in making informed judgements about its outcomes.

Historical perspectives: 1950s to present day

Phase 1: 1950s to late 1960s

Stern (1969) reports on a major UNESCO conference in Hamburg (1962) at which it was claimed that, following World War II, the education of children ought not to be unilingual and unicultural. Many key issues were discussed: e.g., the best age for beginning another language; the effects of an early start in learning an additional language on the further learning of other languages; similarly, on a child's more general development and sense of self; the needs of bi- and multilingual communities; the needs of children from families of immigrants or minority groups; the use of a child's first language in learning an additional language; the use of the additional language for teaching other aspects of the curriculum; the importance of continuity into secondary education; and the supply of trained teachers. These issues from more than half a century ago remain pertinent today.

Phase 2: mid-1980s to roughly turn of the century

The European Commission (EC) and the Council of Europe (CoE) lent strong support to Languages for Young Learners (henceforth LYL), including EYL. Their influence has extended beyond Europe and across much of the world, including website publications, international working groups, networks, research surveys and international conferences for teachers, teacher educators, inspectors, researchers and policy makers. The European Centre for Modern Languages (ECML), within the ambit of the Council of Europe, lends strong support to languages for all ages (including pre-primary – see 'References' for their excellent 'Pepelino' website).

An EC-commissioned research survey (Blondin et al. 1998) drew on published research studies from across the EU and beyond. The research team's analysis concluded that LYL, including EYL, in pre-primary and primary school education could generally promote positive attitudes among children and to some degree language awareness. Many pupils were able to talk fluently and with a good accent but seemed to speak mainly in prefabricated chunks rather than spontaneously through the use of an internalised set of rules.

Phase 3: turn of century to present day

By the end of the twentieth century LYL, including EYL, was truly entering its global phase, thereby astronomically increasing the number of children involved, particularly but by no means exclusively in Asia and South America.

Some societal and cultural issues

Writing on research in China, Taiwan, South Korea and Japan (2004–2014), Butler (2015) claims that despite clear differences, they have certain features in common. Although the number of speakers of English in these countries is rising, most people do not use much English in their everyday lives. So, children do not receive substantial societal exposure to English, and learning English usually takes place at school. Another common feature has been teaching methodologies that have tended to be teacher centred and traditional, with emphasis on vocabulary and grammar. High cultural importance is attached to examinations, and good results are considered to reflect good character, diligence and effort.

With its population of over 1.385 billion, major disparities between cities and rural areas and with substantial variations in primary school class size (Wang 2009), China has faced a mighty challenge. Wang's authoritative account indicates that in 2001 the Chinese government decided to promote English in primary schools, starting from Grade 3, and in some cities from Grade 1 (children begin primary education at age 6). A rapid expansion has taken place across China. The National English Curriculum Standards (NECS) were piloted from 2001 and went nationwide in 2006. Primary English is compulsory within the nine-year compulsory education that connects to the English curriculum of senior high schools. According to Wang (2009) previous English syllabuses in China had prioritised basic knowledge and language skills as primary goals, but NECS broke new ground by highlighting whole-person development and encouraging learners' interest and motivation in learning the language. Wang (2009, p. 280) described this as *'a paradigm-shift from a teacher-centred to a pupil-centred approach'*. To me, the China curriculum for EYL seems a remarkable instance of intention, planning, ambition, boldness, courage and risk-taking in moving forward so quickly across a vastly populated, diverse territory, while also encouraging teachers to find ways to integrate aspects of a more learner-centred approach.

Native speakers

In many countries, by no means limited to Asia, there are feelings of dependence on native-speaker teachers of English – creating a demand that cannot be met. A key policy consideration therefore consists of helping teachers with first languages other than English to develop the competence and the self-confidence to view themselves positively and to be just as good teachers of EYL as some but not all native speakers of English can be. This issue already has an impressive literature, e.g., Copland et al. (2016).

Top-down and/or bottom-up

Butler (2015) has pointed to a tension in East Asia between top-down and bottom-up approaches to policy development and implementation that in fact are characteristic of many countries around the world: she argues that 'top-down' may yield equality of access but create problems at the local level, whereas 'bottom-up', while offering greater local autonomy and diversity, may lead to inequalities – so what is the best way to provide both diversity and equality of access?

Teachers as agents of 'policy distortion' and/or of 'policy enhancement'

Butler's insightful view reflects a related issue already identified by Hamilton over 25 years ago (1990, p. 90). He argues that a curriculum designed by experts may look quite different from the same curriculum implemented in school. This can lead to two differing interpretations: one that the distortion of a curriculum is a retrograde process (implying that teachers need training in how not to distort the new policy); the other that the distortion can add strength (by drawing on teachers' situated craft skills), enabling the curriculum to become what Hamilton (1990, p. 90) calls *'a tried and tested artifact'*. An implication might be that for a curriculum to be truly successful, then 'top-down' and 'bottom-up' approaches must interact with and challenge each other, suggesting an important creative role for teachers' classroom pedagogy.

Teachers' situated craft skills

An example of the tension that can exist between top-down and bottom-up approaches, and of the value of *teachers' situated craft skills* (Hamilton, ibid.), is offered by Lee (2010), who states that South Korea has a national curriculum, with a top-down educational policy. The government decided that traditional teaching of English was inefficient for the modern day and a policy of Teaching English Through English (TETE) was recommended, with extensive use of English in the EYL primary school classroom. Lee reports that Kang's (2007) study of TETE in a Korean primary school acknowledges the benefits of TETE but found that the teacher, who was proficient in English, drew consciously and selectively on the Korean language to sustain students' participation, understanding and interest. This by itself does not necessarily demonstrate that TETE was without merit, but it may imply that the policy had been introduced without sufficient consideration of a possible role for children's first language.

Critical issues

This section discusses three critical issues. These are:

- Early start
- Time allocation
- EYL and other languages.

and the section concludes with a discussion of some implications for EYL policies.

Critical issue 1: early start

The EC's (2003) *Action Plan 2004–2006* recommends the teaching of an additional language to children from an early age across the EU, with a second additional language introduced by the end of primary school education. The Action Plan claims this 1+2 formula will help children acquire a sense of belonging, citizenship and community and develop an understanding of their opportunities, rights and responsibilities as mobile citizens of a multilingual Europe.

Children possess a capacity for implicitly developing more than one first language in their early years, subject to sufficient exposure and interaction in the natural everyday conditions of home, family and community. But what does this mean for the early learning of second, third, fourth languages at primary school? Will this same capacity simply click into action in this very different context?

A recent article by Myles (2017) claims that in primary school conditions young children learn languages more slowly than adolescent learners. This echoes the conclusion of Muñoz (2006) comparing early and late starters who found that late starters consistently learned more quickly. Muñoz (2008, p. 586) states that there is no convincing evidence of 'early start' learners being more advanced than 'later start' learners after the same amount of instructional time. She claims (p. 591) that, to maximise the advantages of the 'early start' in school conditions, children need a substantial amount of exposure to the language, as in immersion classes.

The natural conditions in which young children develop their first language(s) are very different from the non-immersion conditions that normally apply in primary schools for learning a second or other language, where there may be 20–30 or more children in the class, none of whom speak the second language, learning it from one teacher who may not be very proficient in it and for roughly one hour per week during the school year.

Critical issue 2: time allocation

The Eurydice Report (2017) covering all countries in the European Union describes the amount of time allocated to EYL in early education as 'modest', a term I shall borrow for use in relation to one of the three time allocations in this chapter:

> In 2016, the share of instruction time dedicated to foreign languages, compared to total instruction time for the entire primary curriculum, while increasing, is still modest: in the majority of countries, this percentage ranges between 5 and 10%.
>
> *(Eurydice 2017, pp. 14–18)*

Across the world, there can be variation from one country to another, but the verdict would generally be that there too the time allocation is often quite modest.

There are, however, two other contexts in which EYL at primary school receives a time allocation that is less 'modest'. This means that overall there are perhaps three different approaches to time allocation, so I shall call them *'Modest Time'*, *'Significant Time'* and *'Substantial Time'*. These three different time allocations are not about 'time' alone. In each case, 'time allocated' is only one of several factors that form a context in which things happen (or don't happen) within the time that is allocated. They are briefly set out and discussed below:

Modest time

- Roughly 1–1.25 hours per week of EYL.
- Therefore time for exposure to English is limited.
- The exposure is also limited by there being usually one teacher per class, so the children may be mainly exposed to only one (adult) voice.
- In some cases, teachers may lack confidence and proficiency in English, so the children may possibly not be exposed to fluent, confident wide-ranging English that can exploit opportunistic situations.
- Instead, the focus may be on teaching a defined syllabus based on a coursebook.
- In many classes there may be no children who have acquired some fluency in English outside the school, so the children in class may have no models of authentic localised 'children's English' within the 'modest' time allocation.

Despite the limitations of the 'Modest Time' approach, there is much that teachers can still do that is worthwhile. They can show enthusiasm for EYL. They can introduce EYL songs, poems, stories, dramas, games and physical activities. They can make little links between EYL and other aspects of the curriculum that they may teach (such as science, maths, history and geography). They can develop children's 'language awareness' (e.g., by discussing similarities and differences between English and the children's first or other language). They can develop children's cultural and intercultural awareness through English-language songs, poems, stories (featuring English as international language in a wide range of settings, and not as the exclusive cultural 'property' of native speakers of English). They can develop video-conferencing and other technological links (e.g., smartphones) with children in other countries who are also engaged in EYL (these links embracing schools, teachers and parents as well as the children themselves), thereby increasing children's exposure to the language through a wider range of 'real-life' contacts than at school alone and creating a real-life context in which to develop intercultural awareness.

Significant time

- Roughly 20%-30% of total curricular time is made available for EYL combined with learning some other aspect(s) of the curriculum through English.
- Children may spend some of this time learning English and some of it learning other curricular subjects (e.g. maths, history, geography, science) in whole or in part through English.

Sometimes this form of education is called Content and Language Integrated Learning (CLIL) or Content Based Instruction (CBI). It is particularly prominent in the 'Significant Time' allocation, though some writers use the term CLIL in all three time allocations, so long as EYL is combined with learning some other aspect(s) of the curriculum at least in part through English. In some countries there is enormous parental and policy-making interest in CLIL. However, it is not an approach to be embarked upon lightly. It requires teachers who are proficient in English. Eurydice (2017) gives the levels of proficiency for such teachers as: '*usually B2 ("Vantage") or C1 ("effective operational proficiency") levels of the Common European framework of Reference for Languages*' (p. 18). The approach also presupposes approval and strong support from the school management and full consultation with parents.

This model is attracting considerable interest and uptake in several countries, particularly (in my experience) in Spain. Lorenzo (2010) reports, for example, that the Strategic Plan for Languages in Andalusia, for a four-year period beginning in 2005, specified the creation of a network of over 400 bilingual primary and secondary schools; 50 permanent centres to be established for monitoring and supporting teachers; and 50,000 teachers to take appropriate in-service training in bilingual education.

Substantial time

- Roughly 50%–90+% of total curricular time is made available for EYL and learning through English (not as first language) and the remaining time (usually) through a country's national language.
- At least half and often more than half of total curricular subject-content, -skills and -discourse is taught through the medium of English.
- Teachers must be proficient in English, well qualified in the additional curricular areas and able to develop pupils' critical, intellectual and literacy skills in English.
- If it is roughly 50% in English, it may be called Early Partial Immersion, or Early Bilingual Education, and if it is 90+ % in English, it may be called Early Total Immersion Education.

It is worth noting that Early Total Immersion has prominently featured languages other than English: e.g., children from Canada's English-speaking population receiving much or almost all of their education through the medium of French; and children from English-speaking families in Scotland, Wales and Ireland receiving much of their education through the medium of Scottish Gaelic, Welsh or Irish Gaelic. In both of these cases immersion seems to work when it reflects strongly perceived societal needs. In Canada, for example, many English-speaking and other parents put their children into French-immersion schools in order to show solidarity with Canada's French-speaking population; while in the case of Scottish Gaelic, Welsh and Irish Gaelic an overriding reason for early immersion is to help maintain and revitalise these three languages and their associated cultures, and prevent complete takeover by English.

Concluding this section on 'Time Allocation', it may be claimed that there is a big task for policy-related research to inform not only policy makers but also other key stakeholders such as parents, school management and school staff. Researchers will no doubt seek to develop a rigorous understanding of what may reasonably be expected to be the differing outcomes of the different time allocations but also of the most appropriate processes leading to these outcomes and of the factors existing in each specific national, regional or local context that underlie these processes and outcomes. If these factors can be identified, whether singly or in clusters, then a discussion can be had about what can be done about them in order to help children approach their potential.

But what is the situation in contexts where the immersion language is English, and with children having a range of different first languages? This question is addressed in Critical Issue 3.

Critical issue 3: EYL and other languages

Beginning with Europe, Eurydice's (2017) most recent report states that:

- In 2014, at the EU level, virtually all students (97.3 %) studied English during the entire period of lower secondary education.
- The proportion was lower in primary education (79.4 %), as in some countries foreign language learning is not part of the curriculum during the first years of compulsory schooling.
- Many more primary education students learn English compared with students 10 years ago. At the EU level, in 2014, 18.7% more students were learning English in primary education compared with students in 2005. This increase is mainly due to the lowering of the starting age for compulsory learning of the first foreign language. (Eurydice 2017, pp. 14–18)

These statistics show: (a) the dominance of English as additional language overall (primary + lower secondary school stages); (b) the dominance of EYL at primary school; and (c) the steady increase in uptake of EYL at primary school, owing to the lowered starting age.

The British Council Juba Report (McIllwraith 2013) contains a statement of principles for languages education in Africa, endorsed by a group of experts – e.g., importance of linguistic equity; use of African languages in partnership with international languages; learners being taught in basic formal and non-formal education (up to lower secondary level) through the language they know best; need to inform parents, the state and civil society of the educational, social, economic and political benefits of using African languages alongside European languages; and importance of teaching reading and writing, not just in English.

Van Ginkel (2017) reports that in a number of African countries, a local language is in fact used in the initial years of a child's education, but usually only for an initial period of time, after which it 'exits' from the school curriculum. She mentions two 'exit models' whereby the child's local language is replaced by education involving the national language and/or English. 'Early exit' would be after 3–4 years, and 'late exit' after 6–8 years. She also mentions 'submersion', whereby the child's first language, usually a low status minority language, is not used at all. She claims on the basis of research in a number of African countries that 'early exit' and 'submersion' models are not associated with success, that for most children in these programmes *'it is sink or swim'* (p. 19) and that: *'a late exit model provides better learning results'* (p. 16). She also suggests that in the case of children in early exit or submersion programmes:

> because the language and culture of the children is hardly given any space, it harms their self-esteem, relationships, roots and sometimes race.
>
> *(p. 19)*

The Juba conference included a presentation by Kirkpatrick (2013) on English in ASEAN countries. He detected a shift from multilingualism (in Asian languages) to bilingualism (national language plus English). He argues that English as *lingua franca* need not necessarily be taught in the early years of primary school but rather later, when children are able to understand how English as *lingua franca* is used in today's world. This could create space in the earlier years of education for children to develop fluency and literacy in appropriate local or regional languages, nurturing their identity and self-worth.

Some implications of these critical issues for languages policy-planning

First, with regard to 'Early Start', Stern (1976) claims that each age may have its own advantages and disadvantages for language-learning; in the 1960s it was mistaken to expect miracles merely by starting young, but starting late was not the best answer either. An implication for policy makers is that, rather than assuming that 'younger always = better', they should choose the starting-age that best suits their aims and context, and seek to maximise its advantages and minimise its disadvantages.

Second, with regard to 'Time Allocation', if the objective is to generalise EYL across an entire country, then the most feasible option is 'Modest Time'. Even there experience indicates it can take a substantial investment of funds to provide and maintain an adequate supply of good teachers. It therefore becomes most important to have clear and achievable aims for the 'Modest Time' approach, which certainly should include some progression in English language but also the general development of the child (e.g., social, intercultural, cognitive).

With regard to 'EYL and other Languages', in countries where there are a number of first languages, it makes sense for English to be viewed as being in partnership with these and with the country's national language, rather than in competition with them, since children's education may suffer if the first language and the national language are not developed through a child's education.

If it makes sense to help children cope with a version of English intended for all children across the world, it makes equal sense to allow English to adapt to suit national and local circumstances. Building on the insights of Kachru (1992, p. 11), 'pluralism' can be projected as integral to the concept of EYL, helping children to express themselves in part through one or other regional or local varieties of English (or 'Englishes') as first, second or additional languages that occur across the world. Moreover, one category of English that would appeal to all children across continents and cultures may well be imaginative English as found in films, cartoons, songs and great stories for children, with words such as *'snozzcumber'*, *'rummytot'*, *'frobscottle'*, and *'human beans'*, as a *Big Friendly Giant* once said.

Finally, in a world in which the news all too regularly features stories of war, terrorism, trafficking, exploitation, famine, environmental threat and indoctrination, EYL should be linked to generic themes that are central to the development of all children and that are consistent with the UN Convention on the Rights of the Child – Article 13, which states that every child has the right to express their thoughts and opinions and to access all kinds of information, so long as it is within the law. Children's 'right to express their thoughts and opinions' has sociological implications as to when, where and whether they choose to express their thoughts and opinions – e.g., on personal matters – and through which language. It also has pedagogical implications for EYL, in that EYL teachers might well feel that they have much to learn about their own teaching and their pupils' learning from the thoughts and opinions that they have encouraged their pupils to develop the confidence to express.

Current contributions and languages policy-related research

This section is designed to illustrate four themes that are often significant in EYL policy-related research. In some cases it is macro-research on a large scale that has been commissioned by a major body with an investment in policy and that tends to be concerned with the 'big picture'; in other cases it is small-scale micro-research possibly focusing on one theme that is 'closer to the ground', reflecting local circumstances. Both types of research are essential for informing policy.

In illustrating these four themes, I refer to a small number of research studies, but there is no intention here of providing a rounded picture of each research study. In each case, my focus is solely on a theme relevant to EYL policy research that the particular study happens to illustrate.

Theme 1: provision planning beyond the short term

For policies to succeed, planning has to extend beyond the short term, though in my experience 'short-termism' has unfortunately been a feature of several policies (I remember well that in one particular country there were three substantially different policies for LYL succeeding each other within the span of ten years). It was therefore encouraging to find that, in reporting on a large-scale evaluation of the pilot phase of an EYL programme in public elementary schools in Mexico, Sayer et al. (2017) were helped by the long-term thinking and clear parameters of the programme set by the Ministry of Education. It had estimated the number of teachers who would be needed by the time the programme was fully operational (98,300), and the number of students who would be involved from kindergarten through Grade 6 (14.7 million). Moreover, the Ministry had estimated the number of hours that would be made available from kindergarten through Grade 9 (1,060 hours) and how these would be distributed across four phases within that period.

Theme 2: continuity planning

'Continuity' is concerned with smoothness of transfer from primary to secondary education. Lack of 'continuity' has for long posed problems – e.g., Burstall 1965; Blondin et al. 1998) – that prevent children in the early years of secondary education from building on the knowledge and skills they may have developed in elementary school. It is pleasing therefore to read of an impressive initiative on continuity in New South Wales, Australia (Chesterton et al. 2004, p. 262). This set up systems of collaboration across the primary and secondary schools and implemented approved action plans devised by schools in partnership. The evaluation identified a number of key factors for supporting the effectiveness and the sustainability of the pathways that had been created – e.g., initial and continuing cooperation across schools; collaborative establishment and acceptance of a coherent five-year curriculum (which straddles the transition period). An example of **'continuity' in Practice'** is reported in a small-scale study by Uematsu (2012) that focused on the effects of English as a Foreign Language in Elementary Schools (EFLES) in Japan on students after moving on to junior high school. Particularly positive effects were found on Grade 7 students who had received 90 hours of EFLES since Grade 4. Uematsu states: *'EFLES can exert a powerful effect on fostering the foundation of communication skills in English when an English class focusing on communication is continued in junior high school'* (p. 129) – note the 'continuity' of 'focusing on communication skills'.

Theme 3: generalisation

This is understood here as enabling a national policy to extend to all parts of the country, regardless of geographical, socioeconomic, political or other barriers. Vu and Pham (2014) discuss the 2020 Project in Vietnam that aims to introduce English at Grade 3. This implies significant re-training for the country's large number of primary school EYL teachers, hence an issue of generalisation. Their report focuses on a 'cascade' model based on training-of-trainers (ToT), whereby a small number of participants receive training from key trainers and become qualified trainers themselves, *returning to their own areas* (my emphasis) to train future primary English teachers. Despite significant efforts, the author's small-scale qualitative formative evaluation highlights the issue of 'generalisation' by suggesting that *the programmes should better reflect the diverse realities of primary school English teaching across the country* (my emphasis). Writing on a different topic, but one that also puts the spotlight on 'generalisation', Shrestha (2013) claims that how primary school English language learners perceive their experiences of ELT is rarely reported, especially in developing countries such as Bangladesh. Shretha's report focuses on the perceptions of 600 Grade 3 primary school students with regard to technology-enhanced communicative language teaching within the 'English in Action' project in Bangladesh, with funding support from the UK government. The report contains a range of promising findings, but also implies the 'generalisation' theme when it argues that any major languages development project, particularly in developing countries, *needs to take account of local contexts and also learners' views* (my emphasis). 'Generalisation' can also mean ensuring that a policy endowed with prestigious international currency is adapted and 'localised' so as to be successful *within the specific context of a particular country* (my emphasis). Writing about Thailand, Tongpoon-Patanasorn (2011) discusses a new approach aiming to promote learner-centredness in schools, in the case of 25 Thailand primary school teachers of English. Despite laudable intentions and considerable efforts, some problems were identified: e.g., partial knowledge and misconceptions, low self-reported proficiency in English and insufficient prior training for learner-centred education. Needs arising from this included more rigorous training, changes in curricula and *further research on EYL pedagogy in the Thailand context* (my emphasis).

Theme 4: international collaboration

First, *'International Collaboration in Research':* The ELLiE (Early Language Learning in Europe) research study was commissioned by the EC with further support from the British Council. *The project collected data from seven countries from a team of researchers drawn from each of these seven countries* (my emphasis). It included a three-year longitudinal study featuring 6–8 typical state-funded primary schools and 170–200 children per country, aged 7–8 in the first year of the main study. The Ellie Report (Enver 2012) showed that over the three years the children's proficiency in their target language (EYL in six of the seven countries) grew in both oral production and comprehension (p. 67). There was a significant increase in children's vocabulary and an increase in syntactic complexity (p. 129). However, children's main output was formulaic expressions, recalling the earlier finding of Blondin et al. (1998), and there was substantial variation both within and between the seven countries.

Further important findings included a perceived benefit to children's proficiency when their school enjoyed successful ICT links with a partner school in a target language country and had developed an international outlook (p. 148). Not all children had positive attitudes towards learning their additional language, but most continued to show enthusiasm. It was 'good practice' for teachers to be supportive and encouraging, creating a positive environment, ensuring their pupils had successful experiences, showing good classroom management and keeping pupils 'on-task' throughout the lesson (p. 148). These findings suggest that good EYL teaching across an impressive range of countries, even within a small time allocation, can draw substantially on well-established generic primary school teaching skills.

Second, *'International Collaboration Involving Young Learners':* Porto et al. (2016) describe an environmental project in which young learners aged 10–12 in Denmark and Argentina collaborated via the internet on the issue of waste and how to dispose of it. This entailed reflection and action in their local school and community and then collaborating in Denmark-Argentina mixed groups in order to highlight environmental issues. The potential for multilingual development, intercultural learning and international citizenship is clearly considerable. EYL policies of the future will surely lend strong support to initiatives of this sort.

Recommendations for practise

Since this chapter is concerned with policies for EYL, the following recommendations for practice are intended for EYL policy makers, particularly at the national (or regional) or international level:

- **Long-term thinking and development are essential**, rather than one short-term change after another. It is important to **plan for 'generalisation' and 'sustainability' across the country,** if initial pump-priming pilot funding gradually reduces.
- Under appropriate conditions, an early start can bring many advantages, but **all is not lost if a very early start cannot be made**. Each age may have its own advantages and disadvantages for language-learning. Older beginners at primary school, because of their more advanced cognitive development, can make good progress.
- Policy makers should **quantify the basic parameters of the initiative** – e.g., number of teaching staff required for each year; number of pupils projected in each year-group each year; number of hours of EYL per week, per year and for primary school period

overall; and the amount of national and other funding needed each year to meet these provisions. With the support of associated research, this allows an eventual discussion to take place, based on the following question: 'With these given quantified inputs, what does research suggest to us as being a reasonable expectation of outcomes?' If the policy has incorporated an explicit analysis of **'values and aims'** plus **'societal, provision and process factors'**, then the discussion may be further enriched.

- Policies should not be viewed solely as transmissions from experts to practitioners. They should be **appropriated and 'strengthened' by teachers**, drawing on their professional experiences and craft skills, and also by parents and school management. Policies should mainly be judged not by what policy makers or teachers think or do, but by clear evidence of their benefits or otherwise for children.
- Policies should encourage **children's universal right to a 'voice'**, as they learn gradually to express their perceptions of their EYL experiences, thereby providing invaluable feedback for themselves, their teachers and others.
- The **'Modest Time' approach is likely to remain dominant**. As such, it seems essential that careful thought informed by research should seek to identify the key conditions that need to be put in place in order to make EYL in 'early education' work as well as possible to suit the highly diverse contexts in which it is implemented. This approach can help children to make **some basic progress in learning English** but there is much that can also be done in order to **complement it with progress in children's general cognitive, social, intercultural and other development** and their **awareness of important values in life**, e.g., humanitarian, citizenship, entrepreneurial, international outlook.
- At the same time, **other approaches merit careful consideration**, based on different allocations of time and intensity – e.g., CLIL, Bilingual Education, Immersion. These might enhance EYL at given points in children's education.
- The future should include **provision of appropriate technology** that will enable **all children and their schools to interact regularly with partners in other countries**, to help children engage in joint intercultural, multilingual projects.
- It is important **to avoid assuming that English must in all cases be the first additional language**. Often it will, and rightly so, but careful consideration should be given as to how and when EYL will best fit into an overall policy for supporting a child's educational, linguistic, developmental and identity needs. **In particular the needs of the large numbers of children who have a minority first language should be taken into account**, in order to find in their education a productive relationship embracing their first language plus the national language of their country plus possibly EYL as a child's third or other language.
- While it is desirable that EYL should enable children across the world to communicate with and learn from each other, **this does not imply that only one putative universal elite form of English should be taught**. The richness of English as international language lies in part at least in its diversity, its adaptability and its imaginative, inventive uptake by vast numbers of speakers (whether native- or non-native), between countries, within countries, within small communities, and this protean conception of English should be part of the EYL education of all children.

Future directions

There has been a pleasing rise in the numbers of EYL researchers across the world – e.g., in Asia, South America, Africa and Central Europe – who achieve publication in international research journals. Thus, the 'ownership' of EYL research becomes more broadly based as befits a language of massive international, transcultural reach. This can only be good for EYL and for the international multilingual EYL research community.

Given the major societal issues with which EYL is inevitably intertwined, it makes sense for EYL researchers to participate in collaborative, cross-disciplinary, cross-border research on big themes that affect all our lives, such as 'social mobility', 'the environment' and 'international citizenship'. Possibly a Research Council might support research on a cross-disciplinary theme that might be attractive to EYL researchers, but possibly also there might be opportunities for such research in one's faculty or university network involving collaboration with primary school teachers. In principle, this can give EYL researchers an opportunity to play a part in researching something that is bigger than EYL itself and to experience research approaches from other disciplines. Engaging in research that seeks to connect EYL to important aspects of life outside it can find an echo in the elementary school teacher who even in her 'Modest Time' approach seeks to relate EYL to other aspects of the school's curriculum.

An ebbing tide?

In Europe Krzyzanowski and Wodak (2011) argue that EU thinking about the value of languages education may have begun to change. Following the Lisbon Treaty (2009) they claim that EU policies on languages and multilingualism became more focused on skills and competitiveness relevant to the EU economy – and values such as democracy, citizenship and social cohesion began to play a reduced role.

In East Asia and elsewhere in the world I have encountered voices questioning the 'precipitate rush' towards 'EYL in early education', in some cases preferring that children gain a good grasp of their national language, plus their first language (if different from the national language), and their sense of self. This is not surprising, in view of (in some cases) the rapidity of the EYL expansion, a lack of thought as to how it might find a harmonious role within a country's overall languages policy, the linguistic and pedagogical unpreparedness of many teachers and policy makers in some cases relying too much on vague assumptions about the benefits of an early start.

Nonetheless, there is also informal evidence to suggest that EYL remains very strong and that indeed in certain countries in Europe, Asia, South America and possibly elsewhere, too, it is gaining strength through greatly increased interest in going beyond the 'modest time' approach in order to implement some form of CLIL in response not only to the wishes of policy makers but also because of parental demand.

Further reading

1 Butler, Y. G. (2015). English language education among young learners in East Asia: A review of current research (2004–2014). *Language Teaching* 48(03), 303–342.
    A comprehensive and well-informed overview of research in China, Japan, South Korea and Taiwan.

2 Nikolov, M., and Djigunovich, J. M. (2011). All shades of every color: An overview of early teaching and learning of foreign languages. *Annual Review of Applied Linguistics*, 31, 95–119.
    Also a comprehensive and well-informed overview of key theories and developments in the field.

3 Enver, J., and Lindgren, E. (Eds.). (2017). *Early language learning. Complexity and mixed methods*. Bristol: Multilingual Matters, 269–288.

Well-informed, forward-looking overview with interesting findings from a range of different countries. Contains the articles by van Ginkel and by Sayers et al. referred to in my present text and included in the References (below).

4 Pfenniger, S. E., and Singleton, D. (2017). *Beyond age effects in instructional L2 learning: Revisiting the age factor*. Bristol: Multilingual Matters.

An authoritative account of issues relating to age and the learning of additional languages, disposing of some myths in the process.

Related topics

CLIL, assessment, contexts of learning, multilingualism

References

Blondin, C., Candelier, M., Edelenbos, P., Johnstone, R., Kubanek-German, A., and Taeschner, T. (1998). *Foreign Languages in Primary and Pre-School Education: A review of recent research within the European Union*. London: CILT.

Chesterton, P., Steigler-Peters, S., Moran, W., and Piccioli, M. T. (2004). Developing sustainable language learning pathways: an Australian initiative. *Language, Culture & Curriculum*, 17(1), 48–57.

Enver, J. (Ed.). (2012). *ELLiE: Early language learning in Europe*. London: British Council.

ECML. (2012). *PEPELINO – European portfolio for pre-primary educators – The plurilingual and intercultural dimension*. European Centre for Modern Languages of the Council of Europe (ECML/CELV). Graz: 2012-2015. https://www.ecml.at/pepelino. Accessed December 2016.

European Commission (2003). *Promoting Language Learning and Linguistic Diversity: An action plan 2004–2006*. Brussels: European Commission.European Commission/EACEA/Eurydice (2017). *Key Data on Teaching Languages at School in Europe*. Luxembourg: Publications Office of the European Union.

Hamilton, D. (1990). *Learning About Education: The unfinished curriculum*. Philadelphia: The Open University Press.

Kachru, B. B. (1992). World Englishes: Approaches, issues and resources. *Language Teaching*, 25, 1–14.

Kang, D-M. (2007). The classroom language use of a Korean elementary school EFL teacher: Another look at TETE. *System*, 36, 214–226.

Kirkpatrick, A. (2013). *The Lingua Franca Approach to the Teaching of English: A possible pathway to genuine multilingualism in local languages and English*. McIlwraith (ed.). London: British Council. 11–16.

Krzyzanowski, M., and Wodak, R. (2011). Political strategies and language policies: The European Union Lisbon strategy and its implications for the EU's language and multilingualism policy. *Language Policy*, 10(2), 115–136.

Lee, W. (2010). Insights from South Korea. In R. Johnstone (ed.). *Learning through English: Policies, challenges, and prospects: Insights from East Asia*. Printed in Malaysia. London: British Council, 47–68.

Lorenzo, F. (2010). CLIL in Andalusia. In Lasabagaster, D., and de Zarobe, Y. R. (eds.) *CLIL in Spain: Implementation, results and teacher training*. Newcastle-on-Tyne: Cambridge Scholars Publishing.

McIlwraith, H. (Ed.). (2013). *Multilingual Education in Africa: Lessons from the Juba language-in-education conference*. London: British Council.

Muñoz, C. (2008). Symmetries and asymmetries of age effects in naturalistic and instructed L2 learning. *Applied Linguistics*, 29(4), 578–596.

Myles, F. (2017). Learning foreign languages in primary schools: Is younger better? www.meits.org/policy-papers/paper/learning-foreign-languages-in-primary-schools-is-younger-better Multilingualism: Empowering Individuals, Transforming Societies (MEITS) [Accessed 9 August 2017].

Porto, M., Daryai-Hansen, P., Arcuri, E. M., and Schifffer, K. (2016). Green kidz: Young learners engage in intercultural environmental citizenship in English language classroom in Argentina and Denmark. In Byram, M., Golubeva, I., Han, H., and Wagner, M. (eds.) *Education for Intercultural Citizenship – Principles in practice*. Clevedon: Multilingual Matters.

Sayer, P., Ban, R., and de Anda, M. L. (2017). Evaluating the educational outcomes of an early foreign language programme: The design of and impact study for the primary English programme in Mexico. In Enver, J., and Lindgren, E. (eds.) *Early Language Learning: Complexity and mixed methods*. Bristol: Multilingual Matters, 269–288.

Shrestha, P. (2013). English language classroom practices: Bangladeshi primary school children's perceptions. *RELC Journal*, 44(2), 147–162.

Stern, H. H. (1969). *Languages and the Young School Child*. Oxford: Oxford University Press.

Stern, H. H. (1976). Optimum age: myth or reality? Canadian Review of Modern Languages 32, 3, 283–294.

Tongpoon-Patanasorn, A. (2011). Impact of learner-centredness on primary school teachers: A case study in Northeast Thailand. *The Journal of Asia TEFL*, 8(3), 1–28.

Uematsu, S. (2012). The effect of English learning in elementary school on students' English language development in junior high school. *The Journal of Asia TEFL*, 9(4), 113–133.

United Nations (1990). *The United Nations Convention on the Rights of the Child*. London: UNICEF UK.

Van Ginkel, A. J. (2017). Early language learning in complex linguistic settings: Insights from Africa. In Enver, J., and Lindgren, E. (eds.) *Early Language Learning: Complexity and mixed methods*. Bristol: Multilingual Matters, 09–23.

Vu, M. T., and Pham, T. T. T. (2014). Training of trainers for primary English teachers in Viet Nam: Stakeholder evaluation. *The Journal of Asia TEFL*, 11(4), 89–108.

Wang, Q. (2009). Primary English in China: Policy, curriculum and implementation. In Nikolov, M. (ed.) *The Age Factor and Early Language Learning*. Berlin: Mouton de Gruyter, 277–310.

2

The age debate

A critical overview

David Singleton and Simone E. Pfenninger

Introduction

It may seem that childhood must be the best time to start learning a second language (L2). After all, first language (L1) development happens in childhood, so it appears natural to assume that children are better equipped to acquire languages than their seniors and therefore acquire an L2 more effortlessly, more successfully and faster. Observation of children and adults getting to grips with a new language appears to confirm the notion that in the learning of additional languages, younger equals better. For example, we see young immigrant children with a perfectly functional command of the language of the host country acting as interpreters for their parents. It is important to note, nonetheless, that some adult L2 learners also attain very high proficiency levels in the relevant language. One hotly debated issue, then, is whether beginning to be exposed to an L2 as a child is qualitatively different from beginning to be exposed to the language in adulthood. Even more hotly debated, perhaps, is the value of introducing second languages into primary education (see Lambelet and Berthele 2015). Early L2 instruction (especially in English) is a growing trend all over the world despite substantial research findings that early instruction does not yield the advantages one might expect. Studies of the results of primary school L2 instruction go back decades, and there is no solid empirical evidence demonstrating that early L2 beginners outperform adolescent beginners when the number of instructional hours is held constant (see e.g., García-Mayo and García-Lecumberri 2003; Muñoz 2006), Indeed, many studies (e.g., Cenoz 2003; Muñoz 2008a, 2008b; Pfenninger and Singleton 2017) show secondary school beginners by the end of the schooling period completely catching up with primary school beginners with considerably more classroom experience of the L2 in question. There is no real dispute about the scientific facts, which are that primary school instruction in an L2 fails to equip learners with a level of L2 proficiency which by the end of secondary schooling is superior to that of those whose instruction begins later; but because early L2 learning has now been established as the norm (see, e.g., Rixon 2013) and because educational structures have been created to accommodate it, politicians and those with a stake in the educational status quo often direct a particularly envenomed ire at those who point out these facts (see Singleton and Pfenninger 2017).

The question of the ideal age at which to be exposed to an L2 has been puzzled over in various ways throughout history. Researchers now recognise, however, that there is much more to age than maturation, and that age-*related* social, psychological and contextual factors may play as significant role as strictly maturational factors (see, e.g., Moyer 2013, 2014). Indeed, we can point to methodological approaches, both quantitative and qualitative, which now allow us to assess the part played by such social, psychological and contextual factors and their contribution to effects previously ascribed solely to maturation (see discussion in Pfenninger and Singleton 2016, 2017). There is also recognition of the importance of L1 knowledge in relation to the learning of an L2 at a young age (see, e.g., Bourgon 2014; Pfenninger 2014)

Historical perspectives

Some interesting recommendations regarding L2 learning in childhood present themselves in the work of the first-century rhetorician Quintilian. Owing to the ethnic diversity of the Roman population, Rome's admiration of things Greek and the interaction between the Latin-speaking and the Greek-speaking world, many Romans felt obliged to engage with Greek as an L2. Well-to-do families often ensured that their sons received a grounding in the language by having a Greek slave as a live-in teacher (Law 2003). Thus, exposure to Greek as an L2 frequently took place via an immersion experience closer to growing up in a bilingual family than to formal instruction (Law 2003). Quintilian's *Institutio Oratoria* ('Training of an Orator') is a twelve-volume textbook (published around 95 AD; see Murphy 2012) on the education of rhetoricians from childhood to adulthood. The first volume addresses bilingual education, and shows that in regard to the age factor in the teaching/learning of an L2, Roman educators used argumentation comparable to that in modern educational policy documents:

1 Some hold that boys should not be taught to read till they are seven years old, that being the earliest age at which they can derive profit from instruction and endure the strain of learning . . . . Those however who hold that a child's mind should not be allowed to lie fallow for a moment are wiser . . . . Let us not therefore waste the earliest years: there is all the less excuse for this, since the elements of language training are solely a question of memory, which not only exists even in small children, but is especially retentive at that age. (*Institutio Oratoria* I, I, 13–17)

2 Why should we despise the profit to be derived before the age of seven, small though it be? For though the knowledge absorbed in the previous years may be but little, yet the boy will be learning something more advanced during that year, in which he would otherwise have been occupied with something more elementary. Such progress each successive year increases the total, and the time gained during childhood is clear profit to the period of youth. (*Institutio Oratoria* I, I, 17)

In their formative years – according to Quintilian before the age of seven – children, he said, learn from their family, nurses, 'paedagogi' (slaves responsible for 'early training' [*Institutio Oratoria* I, 69]) and peers. There is, he suggests, a clear cut-off point after these formative years. Quintilian also sings the praises of a longer learning period, which, he claims, compensates for the slow learning rate of young children.

The quote in (3) advises *how* young children should be taught:

3   I am not however so blind to differences of age as to think that the very young should be forced on prematurely or given real work to do. Above all things we must take care that the child, who is not yet old enough to love his studies, does not come to hate them and dread the bitterness which he has once tasted, even when the years of infancy are left behind. His studies must be made an amusement: he must be questioned and praised and taught to rejoice when he has done well . . . . And at the tender age of which we are now speaking . . . memory is almost the only faculty which can be developed by the teacher. (*Institutio Oratoria* I, I, 20–21)

Memory work is especially fruitful for the very young, according to Quintilian, as they do not yet have the capacity for intellectual analysis. He insists on the virtue of the young filling their memory with good models rather than their own products, as this will prevent them from perpetuating their faults (Murphy 2012).

It is evident that Quintilian discussed many issues that are still current. The following propositions stand out as particularly pertinent:

- That language instruction should begin before it is 'too late', that children's minds are 'especially retentive'.
- That there is a kind of sensitive period – 'formative years', as he expressed it – between birth and age 7 which should not be 'wasted'.
- That a longer learning period brings about better learning results.
- That early instruction should be pleasurable for the child, focusing on memory-based learning.

The *Institutio* had enormous influence (Murphy 1965), which was still strong in sixteenth-century England. For example, Elyot, in his *Boke Named the Gouernour* (1531), written for future 'gouernours of the publike weale' (quoted in Pollnitz 2015, p. 89), recommended that English boys begin their schooling in Latin and Greek before the age of seven years, because in England these were not 'maternall tongues' (vol. I, pp. 31–32). In line with Quintilian, Elyot also advocated a pleasant learning atmosphere for children.

4   A noble man shulde be trayned in before he come to the age of seuen yeres. Some olde autours holde oppinion that, before the age of seuen yeres, a chylde shulde nat be instructed in letters; but those writers were either grekes or latines, amonge whom all doctrine and sciences were in their maternall tonges . . . I wolde nat haue them inforced by violence to lerne, but accordynge to the counsaile of Quintilian, to be swetely allured therto with praises and suche praty gyftes as children delite in. (*Boke Named the Gouernour* vol. I, pp. 31–32)

Further examples of Renaissance writers favouring an early start to learning are Locke and Montaigne. In his book *Some Thoughts Concerning Education*, Locke described a young child's mind as a *tabula rasa* (blank slate) upon which the child's experiences are written. Because, for Locke, children are born without a natural knowledge of virtue, early education greatly shapes their development, where even 'little and almost insensible impressions on [their] tender infancies have very important and lasting consequences' (*TCE* ed. Grant and Tarcov 1996, § 1). Writing of the learning of classical languages, Montaigne describes 'a method by which they may be acquired more cheaply than they usually are and which was tried on myself' (*Essays* 1.26, quoted in Singleton and Ryan 2004, p. 1): being exposed during his early life to no language other than Latin, he 'learnt to speak as pure Latin as my master without art, book, grammar . . . whipping or a single tear' (quoted in Stern 1983, p. 388). Attempts to teach him Greek formally later, on the other hand, are depicted as less successful. Thinking about language acquisition and the age factor goes back a good deal further. For example, at the end of the fourth century, in his *Confessions*, St Augustine portrays language development as virtually a defining criterion of maturation:

> Passing hence from infancy I came to boyhood, or rather it came to me, displacing infancy. For I was no longer a speechless infant but a speaking boy.
>
> *(Confessions, 1.3)*

Critical issues

One highly influential view is that there is a critical age beyond which it is *impossible* to acquire certain capacities in the new language. This idea that maturation puts constraints on what is attainable by language acquirers is the approach taken by those who favour the *Critical Period Hypothesis* (CPH). Some researchers replace the term *critical period* with the milder-sounding *sensitive period* – although the distinction between the two concepts is variable and ill defined. The CPH was initially applied principally to L1 acquisition (Lenneberg 1967), but it has dominated discussion of differences of attainment between L2 acquirers for many decades. Researchers are increasingly, though, regarding age as a highly complex factor, a 'macrovariable' (Flege et al. 1999), calling for dimensions other than maturation to be taken into account.

Some L1 findings cited in favour of a critical period relate to individuals deprived of the experience of language in childhood. When such children (see, e.g., Jones 1995) are integrated into a language-rich environment in adolescence, they typically exhibit progress in language development – but of a limited kind. Lenneberg was not persuaded, however, of the value of such evidence in regard to the CPH, since it is interpretable in terms of the general damage done to an individual by isolation and deprivation of interaction (Lenneberg 1967, p. 142; cf. Muñoz and Singleton 2011, p. 407). Other L1 evidence comes from profoundly deaf subjects who had no access to sign language in their early years and who then acquired a sign language as their L1 at a later age (e.g., Mayberry and Lock 2003). Research into such cases has not found an abrupt cut-off point to language acquisition or that language completely fails to develop, but they have revealed deficits in the language of later signers. Deprivation of language-mediated social relationships during the period when cognitive development is most intense could have general psychological/cognitive effects (see above); it may well be that such effects are reflected in their later language development.

It is worth bearing in mind that the CPH is actually a cluster of hypotheses with very different predictions (see Singleton 2005). As Aram et al. point out, 'the end of the critical period for language in humans has proven . . . difficult to find, with estimates ranging from 1 year of age to adolescence' (1997, p. 85). Also, there is much discussion about what kinds of linguistic capacities are supposed to be affected, by the critical period at different stages and ages (e.g. Granena and Long 2013; Huang 2014).

The evidence from L2 research favouring the critical period notion is generally derived from immigrant studies. There has been a longstanding plethora of work (e.g., Hyltenstam 1992;

Patkowski 1980; Seliger et al. 1975) showing that younger immigrants arriving in a location where the dominant language is not their home language are more likely than older arrivals to end up passing for native speakers of the new language. It is noteworthy, however, that the younger equals better tendency is *only* a tendency. It is not the case that *all* immigrants who arrive in their new country in childhood end up with a perfect command of the language of the host country; nor that those who arrive later always fail to attain the levels reached by younger arrivals. One can cite in this latter connection Kinsella and Singleton's (2014) study of 20 native English speakers whose average age of significant exposure to French was 28.6 years. Three of the participants scored within French native-speaker ranges on all the tasks they were given.

The relevance of the native speaker concept in this connection goes back to Lenneberg, the 'father of the CPH' who in his 1967 book claimed that individuals who began to learn a second language beyond puberty were incapable of attaining to the proficiency level of native speakers of the language in question. In fact, the native-speaker construct in this context has in more recent times come under a cloud (see Singleton and Muñoz 2011). Cook, for example, argues that the focus should be on L2 users in their own right rather than in comparison with native speakers. He remarks that, while 'ultimate attainment is a monolingual standard rather than an L2 standard' (2002, p. 6), there is no intrinsic reason why the L2 user's attainment *should* be the same as that of a monolingual native speaker. Davies discusses the difficulty of defining what a native speaker actually is. He expresses the view that 'the distinction native speaker – non-native speaker . . . is at bottom one of confidence and identity' (2003, p. 213).

'Hardline' critical period advocates (e.g., Abrahamsson and Hyltenstam 2008; Long 2013), nevertheless, still cling to the 'native-speaker' criterion as enunciated by Lenneberg. For them cases like Kinsella and Singleton's are of no account; *their* criterion for falsification of the CPH is 'scrutinized native-likeness' (Abrahamsson and Hyltenstam 2008) with regard to every detail of the later learner's L2 proficiency. Birdsong, a CPH sceptic, accepts (2014, p. 47) that, because of the interaction of a multilingual's knowledge of his/her languages, 'nonnativelikeness will eventually be found' – so that if 'across-the-board nativelikeness is what is required to disconfirm the CPH, the CPH is invulnerable to falsification'.

The growing consensus is that the relationship between users of additional languages and the relevant languages cannot relate to maturation alone but must also depend on socio-affective factors. We can refer in this context to a study which shows that socio-affective factors rather than maturational considerations may relate to L2 success. The study in question (Walsh and Singleton 2013) focused on the lexical acquisition of nine same-aged Polish children of immigrants to Ireland. The differences among the Polish children were in part explored via the profiles of the two highest-scoring children. Both used Polish at home with their families but also regularly enjoyed activities with friends, in which English was used. Both children's parents had learned English, and so the availability of parental support for their English was also similar. In other words, we see elements which appear partly to account for differences in their performance from that of their age-peers which relate to the enjoyable nature of the experience of English and the degree to which it was supported.

Moyer (2013, p. 19) has suggested that ultimate attainment in additional languages is a function of the quantity and quality of language experience rather than simply a matter of maturation. She comments that 'insights from the empirical research highlight these relationships between age, affect and linguistic experience' (Moyer 2013, p. 19)

Current contributions and research

It is thus widely recognised (Montrul 2008; Muñoz and Singleton 2011) that the age factor is a macrovariable that is systematically and inextricably intertwined with other, co-occurring variables such as contextual, affective and personal factors. For example, in a naturalistic setting, there are factors that seem to operate more favourably in respect to younger learners (e.g., positive attitudes, open-mindedness, greater commitment of time and/or energy, general support system, educational and leisure environment) and so their effects have often been taken to be maturationally rooted. Along these lines Moyer (2013, p. 1) cautions:

> a host of interrelated variables is at play, having to do with learner orientation and experience . . . One valuable contribution of sociolinguistic work in SLA has been to call attention to social, cultural, and psychological circumstances relevant to individual L2 users – a reminder to take a more nuanced look at what underlies age effects in SLA.

In an educational context, age of onset (AO) has been found to interact with school effects or treatment variables (e.g., type of instruction) as well as micro-contextual variables such as classroom and clustering effects (Pfenninger in press). Thus, not only does AO not work similarly across settings (naturalistic vs. school contexts), but also school/class context and climate interact with student-level variables such as AO. Thus, students under conditions of different school context and school climate demonstrate different educational attainment irrespective of AO, which has direct policy implications for policy makers, administrators, teachers, and parents (Pfenninger in press). Finally, not only do different structures like morpho-syntax and lexico-semantics show different sensitivity to age of acquisition (see, e.g., DeKeyser 2012) but also different tasks/skills such as listening skills.

Precisely because it cannot be disentangled from other variables, the significance of starting age and biological age is difficult to determine. The age question therefore demands both a very comprehensive and a very delicate perspective. Pfenninger and Singleton (2016, 2017) claim that it necessitates both qualitative and quantitative methodologies, and that the quantitative approach used needs to go well beyond the kinds of general linear models employed in this area in the past – that family of statistical models which assumes a normal distribution among other features, e.g., t-tests, ANOVA, or multiple regression models (e.g., Plonsky 2013). They suggest that multilevel modelling (MLM) approaches are ideal for a potentially generalizable study of age effects, as these analyses encourage a shift from a myopic focus on a single factor such as the age factor to examining multiple relationships among variables, including contextual variables. Since allowing for the simultaneous generalization of the results on new items and new participants as well as the assessment of the impact of context-varying factors on age, the use of such models enables us to integrate individual-level and contextual-level data in order to assess the impact of context-varying factors in relation to age effects. Although it would be statistically possible to separate the learner from context, it is untenable to do so because this would carry the implication that the two are independent. As Larsen-Freeman (2015, p. 16) puts it, '[w]ith the coupling of the learner and the learning environment, neither the learner not the environment is seen as independent, and the environment is not seen as background to the main developmental drama'.

Furthermore, since it is increasingly felt that age research needs to take account of the social and psychological factors that shape the learner's overall approach to, and experience of, the L2, such research needs to base itself on qualitative as well as quantitative findings, ideally in a methodology in which the two kinds of findings interact. In such a 'mixed methods' approach, qualitative and quantitative research are strategically mixed or combined at the data collection level and/or at the analysis level in such a way that they illuminate each other (see Johnson and Christensen 2004; Tashakkori and Creswell 2007). Mixed methods rest on five rationales: triangulation (corroboration of results from different methods and designs); complementarity (illustration, and clarification between the results of two methods); development (using findings from one method to help inform another method); initiation (discovering elements that lead to the reframing of research questions); and expansion (of the breadth and range of research by using different methods) (see, e.g., Johnson and Onwuegbuzie 2004). However, though most scholars agree that the suitability of combining qualitative and quantitative approaches depends on the research questions and the practical issues in play (Johnson and Christensen 2004), there is no consensus as to the exact mixture considered appropriate. Bachmann (2006) laments that the combination oftentimes appears to be opportunistic and unplanned, but other researchers (e.g., Dörnyei and Ushioda 2011, p. 241) see nothing wrong in 'adding [qualitative] flesh to the bones' if quantitative results cannot be readily interpreted.

There are several advantages of such a mixed methods approach for age factor research. On the one hand, it allows us to answer a broader range of research questions and provides fuller, deeper, more meaningful answers to these questions (see, e.g., Kinsella and Singleton 2014; Winitz, Gillespie, and Starcev 1995). Many insights may be missed if we use only a single method – e.g., understanding which contextual elements may be relevant to motivation in a given classroom, the interaction of AO and other (often hidden) variables such as motivation, attitudes and beliefs, the participants' reflections on their experience of L2 learning, as well as on the early introduction of several additional languages in elementary school, rather than just measuring their learning growth and end state. Furthermore, such an approach results in well-validated and substantiated findings. Multiple approaches in a single study enable us to obtain converging evidence to yield richer and better supported interpretations and insights into the age factor in SLA. This is important inasmuch as age research has important implications for L2 education in relation to decision making about (1) language policies in multilingual countries, (2) early instruction in different languages at primary level, and (3) later instruction in and through different languages at secondary school.

Another major point to be mentioned in the context of current contributions to the age factor debate is the concern about promoting the L1 of L2 learners. In Murphy and Evangelou's (2016, pp. 11–12) words,

> [a]s countries lower the age at which English language education is introduced, . . . we have a situation where a foreign language is introduced at a time when the L1 has not yet fully developed . . . [I]n the zeal to learn English, some educators, parents and policy makers seem to have lost sight of the importance of supporting the L1.

It is well known that L2 learners are able to transfer knowledge from their L1 to the L2 in the domain of academic linguistic, literacy and cognitive skills, which means they do not have to learn everything twice (Geva and Wang 2001). It has also been documented (e.g., Flege 1995) that phonological learning ability is strongly influenced by the learner's L1. Older students therefore have the benefit of a well-developed L1 and, in particular, fully or well-developed L1 literacy skills that can facilitate acquisition of L2 literacy skills (Swain et al. 1990; Sparks et al. 2009). It is generally thought that the level and kind of L1 ability that children acquire prior to coming to school are important predictors of success in school. As early as 1988, Collier suggested that it may be the case that when young children are asked to learn a L2 for use at school before their L1 has sufficiently matured to serve as a source of transferable skills, the learning task is very burdensome and requires more time than older children need – children whose L1 skills are available for transfer. Indeed, in a recent study, Pfenninger (2014) and Pfenninger and Singleton (2017) found that the well-documented fast progress in the first stages of language acquisition that was found for Swiss learners of EFL with a later starting grade could be attributed in part to the late starters' superior literacy skills compared with those of earlier starters, which had a tremendous impact on the learning outcome.

On the other hand, numerous studies have documented that there is no loss of L1 due to early exposure to a new language (e.g., Goorhuis-Brouwer and de Bot 2010). Bilingualism research over the past 50 years and very recently has suggested that (1) learning two languages can have positive cognitive consequences for children (e.g., enhanced metalinguistic awareness), and (2) maintaining continued development of the L1 of young L2 learners is advantageous for their cognitive, academic and social-emotional development (e.g., Bialystok 2001; Paradis 2016).

Recommendations for practice

We have three sets of recommendations for practice. The first relates to the disappointing results concerning early L2 instruction. At the very least, teachers, parents and students should be made aware by those responsible for educational arrangements of the fact that two or three hours a week of L2 instruction at primary school or kindergarten will *not* give them a long-term advantage over those whose instruction in the language in question commences in secondary school. We also recommend in this connection that consideration be given to changing the way in which early L2 instruction is delivered – moving in the direction of more intensive FL programmes. However, time is one of the most valuable pedagogical resources and the most hotly contested; accordingly, it is difficult to increase the student allocation of hours for FLs. One possibility to intensify the input without adding to the timetable is the teaching of the target language in blocks, i.e., alternating more intense periods (e.g., three times per week small groups sessions combined with two times per week individual sessions) with intervals (for examples, see Murphy and Evangelou 2016). Another prominent example is immersion or 'content and language-integrated learning' (CLIL), that is, a dual-focused educational approach in which an additional language is used for the learning and teaching of both content and language, thereby extending the experience of being exposed to a FL and providing a motivational basis for purposeful communication to take place (Coyle et al. 2010). CLIL always allows for a wide range of educational practices, provided that these practices are conducted through the medium of an additional language and that they integrate both language and the subject (see Cenoz et al. 2014) – from a couple of hours a week to 50:50 two-way bilingual programmes – i.e. programmes with 50% German instruction and 50% English – and full CLIL instruction. In contrast to immersion, which is a form of 'additive bilingualism' (Garçia 2009) and is carried out in languages present in the learners' environment, CLIL teachers are normally non-native speakers of the target language and are typically content rather than FL specialists. CLIL lessons are usually timetabled as content-lessons (biology, music, geography, mechanical engineering, etc.), while the target language normally continues as a subject in its own right in the shape of FL lessons. In addition to the general CLIL goal of improving institutional language learning, CLIL education experts have formulated an array of additional goals that CLIL is said to support, such as cultural awareness, FL sensitization, cognitive advantages, deeper content learning, internationalization, self-confidence, motivation, pluriliteracy, learner autonomy and several others (see Coyle et al. 2010).

Since the 1990s, a considerable amount of CLIL research has been carried out in intensive school classes, and various benefits of CLIL have been indicated (despite several methodological pitfalls, see Aguilar and Muñoz 2014, and Bruton 2011), such as advantages in relation to receptive skills and comprehension (listening and reading), oral fluency, syntactic complexity, lexical range and confidence/risk-taking in the target language; improvement of verbal and non-verbal communication skills, cognitive skills and divergent thinking; and minimizing individual differences (e.g., Collins and White 2012; Dalton-Puffer and Smit 2013; Lasagabaster 2011; Serrano and Muñoz 2007). The evidence shows that degree of intensity of input will not, however, change the basic pattern: taking a comparable but in ways dissimilar context, late immersion students (for example, in Canada) seem to catch up with early immersion students in most respects (see, e.g., Genesee 2016). What early immersion delivers in the best circumstances, however, is an early ease with the L2, a genuine capacity to communicate in it at an early age, which early drip-feed instruction does not (for a discussion of this, see Muñoz 2015). This will need to be verified specifically for the somewhat different pattern of CLIL programmes in Europe; in Juan-Garau and Salazar-Noguera's (2015) words, 'the debate continues as to the best age and timing for CLIL' (6), and the issue of an optimum initial proficiency level for CLIL at primary level has not been addressed as an object of research yet (Muñoz 2015). The eventual findings of such research will offer educators and parents choices with respect to when children may begin FL instruction using bilingual education without necessarily compromising outcomes.

Our second set of recommendations concerns researchers working on age and its implications for L2 pedagogy. We have seen that findings in this area have largely been ignored in regard to the trend towards the introduction of additional languages into primary-level curricula, which appears to have been underlain by the widespread belief on the part of parents – whose views feed into the decisions of governments (cf, Spolsky 1989) – that an early start in L2 instruction is a panacea overriding and neutralizing all other factors. It is also true to say that there is in many educational quarters an atmosphere of denial of the basic fact of the non-advantaging nature of early L2 instruction. While more or less everything important has been clarified about the 'catch them young' notion and what it means (and does not mean) in L2 contexts, the main question now is how to induce parents and decision makers to hear such messages. To try to counter the denial of the facts, we need (1) to endeavour to convince people of the need for closer integration between L2 research and pedagogy and (2) to educate them about recent trends in age-related L2 research. Intensive collaboration between practitioners, politicians and researchers is essential in order for mutual interests and concerns to be understood and addressed through shared discussions, data collection, analysis and interpretation. This points to the need for researchers to operate an 'open door' policy – to present their results to lay audiences; to offer workshops for practitioners; to respond positively to invitations for newspaper interviews and radio and television appearances; and to underline the fact that there are numerous factors accounting for the consistent advantages and greater progress of older learners in school contexts. Bachman (2006, p. 182) reminds us that our audiences are not restricted to members of our own research community but also include an audience from a more public, more politically potent sphere, including people that have the power to make real research-inspired decisions in the world. The message should be that the goal is simply to help teachers, politicians and policy makers set realistic expectations for themselves and the students involved.

Our third set of recommendations relates to the importance of the L1 in the context of early L2 instruction. Since the L1 represents a strong foundation for subsequent language learning, as it can both support and enhance L2 development, educators concerned with additional languages should consider the role that initial literacy plays in learning such languages, and should bear in mind that mastery of literacy skills in the primary school years is important for students in this connection. Ordóñez (2016), for instance, laments that even though learning a foreign language from a very young age is not desirable in Colombia since educational provision is not even adequately developing L1, early bilingualism in English is still imposed 'both by policy and common belief' (233). She propounds the implementation of 'a genuinely bilingual curriculum', in which reading and writing in English are not to be introduced before third grade, when reading and writing in Spanish (the L1) are already advanced.

Future directions

a   Perhaps the most pressing desideratum with regard to the future is to move away from the errors which have beset age research in the past: (a) that of placing too much emphasis on unsuccessful adult L2 learners while ignoring older learners who – even in the naturalistic sphere – achieve extremely high levels of L2 proficiency; (b) the overgeneralization of findings from the naturalistic setting to other learning contexts; (c) the misattribution of conclusions about language proficiency to facts about the brain; and (d) exclusively recruiting participants who are highly educated (such as university students).

b   Age-related research has demonstrated increased sensitivity to the contexts of research, the characteristics and diversity of research participants (inter- and intra-learner variability), and the need to consider carefully constraints on the generalizability of results. There are voices – particularly from those who favour the Complex Dynamic Systems Theory (CDST) approach – which opine that the findings of any linguistic investigation must always be partial and provisional and that the potential of classroom research to generalise observations is limited. The theory argues that since language is a complex dynamic system, using traditional approaches to examine language learning will not provide reliable results. By avoiding 'linear causality' and 'generalizable predictions', CDST pursues 'tendencies, patterns and contingencies' (De Bot and Larsen-Freeman 2011, p. 23) instead. That is not to say that forgoing the usual statistical procedures used to generalise means that generalizability is impossible from a CDS perspective. Case studies may not reveal much about a population of language learners, but do have a direct bearing on theory (see, e.g., Verspoor, de Bot and Lowie 2011). According to Duff (2014, p. 242) generalization in relation to a case provides the researcher with 'the opportunity to shed empirical light about some theoretical concepts or principles . . . that go beyond the setting for the specific case'. The downside of such an approach, in our view, is that it neglects to make claims that contain widely generalizable insights, and contribute more broadly to L2 pedagogy. It is important that age researchers try to attach meaning to age-related outcomes by generalizing to other individuals or groups of individuals, or other contexts.

c   One contextual divergence that certainly needs to be taken into consideration, besides that between naturalistic and formal settings, is the difference between early L2 learning in a normal, 'drip-feed' input school situation (two or three hours of L2 input per week) and schooling involving various kinds and degrees of 'immersion' in the L2. As one would expect, significantly more input leads to significantly better results. Young learners seem to achieve quite a high level of proficiency under immersion conditions. The question remains, however, whether this advantage is maintained when compared to the attainments of school students who benefit from full immersion (e.g., bilingual education), or whether the late immersion students simply catch up with the early immersion students. The answer to this question seems to be that catch-up is what indeed occurs, but it would be useful to obtain a detailed, nuanced picture of the speed with which the catch-up happens under different degrees of immersion.

Further reading

1 Lambelet, A., and Berthele, R. (2015). *Age and foreign language learning in school*. Houndmills: Palgrave Macmillan.

   This is a relatively brief but succinct recent review of the age factor research literature as it concerns instructed second language learning. It is a brave attempt to make sense of a complex and controversial domain, and offers a useful source of information both to researchers and to those involved in teaching and educational policy making.

2 Murphy, V. A., and Evangelou, M. (Eds.). (2016). *Early childhood education in English for speakers of other languages*. London: British Council.

   This volume brings together the work of scholars who were invited by the British Council to further develop our understanding of English language learning through 'Early Childhood Education and Care' (i.e., pre-primary L2 learning) and its consequences for appropriate policy, curricula, provision and teacher education.

3 Muñoz, C. (Ed.) (2012). *Intensive exposure experiences in second language learning*. Clevedon: Multilingual Matters.

   Assembled in this volume are a variety of studies dealing with second language learning experiences across a range of contexts which provide intensive exposure to the target language. It sheds light on the role of intensive exposure as a critical distinctive factor in the comparison of learning processes and outcomes.

4 Pfenninger, S. E., and Singleton, D. (2017). *Beyond age effects in instructional L2 learning: Revisiting the age factor*. Bristol: Multilingual Matters.

   In this longitudinal study the authors empirically explore issues regarding the unique profiles of early vs. late learners of EFL, as well as the significance of factors that are stronger than starting age in determining the rate of acquisition and the learning outcomes at the end of mandatory school time, such as effects of school contexts, amount and type of input, L1 literacy skills, and socio-affective variables.

Related topics

Mulitlingualism, contexts of learning, researching very young learners, motivation

References

Abrahamsson, N., and Hyltenstam, K. (2008). The robustness of aptitude effects in near-native second language acquisition. *Studies in Second Language Acquisition*, 30(4), 481–509.

Aguilar, A., and Muñoz, C. (2014). The effect of proficiency on CLIL benefits in engineering students in Spain. *International Journal of Applied Linguistics*, 24(1), 1–18.

Aram, D., Bates, E., Eisele, J., Fenson, J., Nass, R., Thal, D., and Trauner, D. (1997). From first words to grammar in children with focal brain injury. *Developmental Neuropsychology*, 13(3), 275–343.

Bachmann, L. F. (2006). Generalizability. A journey into the nature of empirical research in applied linguistics. In Chalhoub-Deville, M., Chapelle, C., and Duff, P. (eds.) *Inference and Generalizability in Applied Linguistics: Multiple perspectives*. Amsterdam: John Benjamins, 165–207.

Bialystok, E. (2001). *Bilingualism in Development: Language, literacy and cognition*. Cambridge: Cambridge University Press.

Birdsong, D. (2014). The critical period hypothesis for second language acquisition: Tailoring the coat of many colors. In Pawlak, M., and Aronin, L. (eds.) *Essential Topics in Applied Linguistics and Multilingualism*. Heidelberg: Springer, 43–50.

Bourgon, R. (2014). The predictive effects of L1 and L2 early literacy indicators on reading in French immersion. *The Canadian Modern Language Review/La revue canadienne des langues vivantes*, 70(3), 355–380.

Bruton, A. (2011). Is CLIL so beneficial, or just selective? Re-evaluating some of the research. *System*, 39, 523–532.

Cenoz, J. (2003). Facteurs determinant l'acquisition d'une L3: Age, développement cognitif et milieu. *Acquisition et Interaction en langue étrangère*, 18, 37–51.

Cenoz, J., Genesee, F., and Gorter, D. (2014). Critical analysis of CLIL: Taking stock and looking forward. *Applied Linguistics*, 35(3), 243–262. doi:10.1093/applin/amt011.

Collins, L., and White, J. (2012). Closing the gap: Intensity and proficiency. In Muñoz, C. (ed.) *Intensive Exposure Experiences in Second Language Learning*. Bristol: Multilingual Matters, 45–65.

Cook, V. (2002). Background to the L2 user. In Cook, V. (ed) *Portraits of the L2 User*. Clevedon: Multilingual Matters, 1–28.

Coyle, D., Hood, P., and Marsh, D. (2010). *CLIL. Content and Language Integrated Learning*. Cambridge: Cambridge University Press.

Dalton-Puffer, C., and Smit, U. (2013). Content-and-language-integrated learning: A research agenda. *Language Teaching*, 46(4), 545–559.

Davies, A. (2003). *The Native Speaker: Myth and reality*. Clevedon: Multilingual Matters.

De Bot, K., and Larsen-Freeman, D. (2011). Researching SLD from a DST perspective. In Verspoor, M. H., de Bot, K., and Lowie, W. (eds.) *A Dynamic Approach to Second Language Development: Methods and techniques*. Amsterdam and Philadelphia: John Benjamins, 5–24.

DeKeyser, R. (2012). Interactions between individual differences, treatments, and structures in SLA. *Language Learning*, 62(Suppl. 2), 189–200.

Dörnyei, Z., and Ushioda, E. (2011). *Teaching and Researching Motivation*, 2nd ed. Harlow: Longman.

Duff, P. A. (2014). Case study research on language learning and use. *Annual Review of Applied Linguistics*, 34, 233–255.

Flege, J. E. (1995). Second language speech learning: Theory, findings, and problems. In Strange, W. (ed.) *Speech Perception and Linguistic Experience: Issues in cross-language research*. Timonium, MD: York Press, 229–273.

Flege, J. E., Yeni-Komshian, G. H., and Liu, S. (1999). Age constraints on second language acquisition. *Journal of Memory and Language*, 41(1), 78–104.

Garçía, O. (2009). *Bilingual Education in the 21st Century: A global perspective*. Chichester: Wiley-Blackwell.

García Mayo, M. P., and García Lecumberri, M. L. (Eds.). (2003). *Age and the Acquisition of English as a Foreign Language: Theoretical issues and field work*. Clevedon: Multilingual Matters.

Genesee, F. (2016). North America: Rethinking early childhood education for English language learners: The role of language. In Murphy, V. A., and Evangelou, M. (eds.) *Early Childhood Education in English for Speakers of Other Languages*. London: British Council, 21–42.

Geva, E., and Wang, M. (2001). The development of basic reading skills in children: A cross-language perspective. *Annual Review of Applied Linguistics*, 21, 182–204.

Goorhuis-Brouwer, S., and de Bot, K. (2010). Impact of Early English language teaching on L1 and L2 development in children in Dutch schools. *International Journal of Bilingualism*, 14, 289–302.

Granena, G., and Long, M. H. (2013). Age of onset, length of residence, language aptitude, and ultimate L2 attainment in three linguistic domains. *Second Language Research*, 29(3), 311–343.

Huang, B. H. (2014). The effects of age on second language grammar and speech production. *Journal of Psycholinguistic Research*, 43(4), 397–420.

Hyltenstam, K. (1992). Non-native features of near-native speakers: On the ultimate attainment of childhood L2 learners. *Advances in Psychology*, 83, 351–368.

Johnson, R. B., and Christensen, L. B. (2004). *Educational Research: Quantitative, qualitative and mixed approaches*. Boston, MA: Allyn and Bacon.

Johnson, R. B., and Onwuegbuzie, A. J. (2004). Mixed methods research: A research paradigm whose time has come. *Educational Researcher*, 33(7), 14–26.

Jones, P. E. (1995). Contradictions and unanswered questions in the Genie case: A fresh look at the linguistic evidence. *Language and Communication*, 15(3), 261–280.

Juan-Garau, M., and Salazar-Noguera, J. (Eds.). (2015). *Content-based Language Learning in Multilingual Educational Environments*. Cham, Heidelberg, New York, Dordrecht, London: Springer.

Kinsella, C., and Singleton, D. (2014). Much more than age. *Applied Linguistics*, 35(4), 441–462.

Lambelet, A., and Berthele, R. (2015). *Age and Foreign Language Learning in School*. Houndmills: Palgrave Macmillan.

Larsen-Freeman, D. (2015). Foreword. In King, J. (ed.) *The Dynamic Interplay Between Context and the Language Learner*. New York: Palgrave Macmillan, xi–xiii.

Lasagabaster, D. (2011). English achievement and student motivation in CLIL and EFL settings. *Innovation in Language Learning and Teaching*, 5(1), 3–18.

Lenneberg, E. H. (1967). *Biological Foundations of Language*. New York: Wiley.

Locke, J. (1996) [1693]. *Some Thoughts Concerning Education and of the Conduct of Understanding*. Edited by Ruth Grant and Nathan Tarcov. Indianapolis, IN: Hackett.

Long, M. (2013). Maturational constraints on child and adult SLA. In Granena, G., and Long, M. (eds.) *Sensitive Periods, Language Aptitude and Ultimate Attainment*. Amsterdam: John Benjamins, 3–41.

Mayberry, R. I., and Lock, E. (2003). Age constraints on first versus second language acquisition: Evidence for linguistic plasticity and epigenesis. *Brain and Language*, 87(3), 369–384.

Montrul, S. (2008). *Incomplete Acquisition in Bilingualism: Re-examining the age factor*. Amsterdam: John Benjamins.

Moyer, A. (2013). *Foreign Accent: The phenomenon of non-native speech*. Cambridge: Cambridge University Press.

Moyer, A. (2014). Exceptional outcomes in L2 phonology: The critical factors of learner engagement and self-regulation. *Applied Linguistics*, 35(4), 418–440.

Muñoz, C. (2006). *Age and the Rate of Foreign Language Learning*. Clevedon: Multilingual Matters.

Muñoz, C. (2008a). Symmetries and asymmetries of age effects in naturalistic and instructed L2 learning. *Applied Linguistics*, 29, 578–596.

Muñoz, C. (2008b). Age-related differences in foreign language learning: Revisiting the empirical evidence. *International Review of Applied Linguistics (IRAL)*, 46, 197–220.

Muñoz, C. (Ed.). (2012). *Intensive Exposure Experiences in Second Language Learning*. Clevedon: Multilingual Matters.

Muñoz, C. (2015). Time and timing in CLIL: A comparative approach to language gains. In Juan-Garau, M., and Salazar-Noguera, J. (eds.) *Content-based Language Learning in Multilingual Educational Environments*. Cham, Heidelberg, New York, Dordrecht, London: Springer, 87–104.

Muñoz, C., and Singleton, D, (2007). Foreign accent in advanced learners: Two successful profiles. *The EUROSLA Yearbook*, 7, 171–190.

Muñoz, C., and Singleton, D. (2011). A critical review of age-related research on L2 ultimate attainment. *Language Teaching*, 44(1), 1–35.

Murphy, J. J. (1965). Introduction. In James Murphy (ed.) James Watson (trans) *Quintilian: On the early education of the citizen-orator*. Indianapolis, IN: Bobbs-Merrill, vii–xxx.

Murphy, J. J. (Ed.). (2012). *A Short History of Writing Instruction from Ancient Greece to Contemporary America*. New York: Routledge.

Murphy, V., and Evangelou, M. (2016). Introduction. In Murphy, V. A., and Evangelou, M. (eds.) *Early Childhood Education in English for Speakers of Other Languages*. London: British Council, 4–18.

Ordóñez, C. L. (2016). Just singing, role playing and reading: A case study in education for bilingualism. In Murphy, V. A., and Evangelou, M. (eds.) *Early Childhood Education in English for Speakers of Other Languages*. London: British Council, 233–240.

Paradis, J. (2016). Supporting the home languge of English as an additional language (EAL) children with developmental disorders. In Murphy, V. A., and Evangelou, M. (eds.) *Early Childhood Education in English for Speakers of Other Languages*. London: British Council, 159–160.

Patkowski, M. S. (1980). The sensitive period for the acquisition of syntax in a second language. *Language Learning*, 30(2), 449–468.

Pfenninger, S. E. (2014). The literacy factor in the optimal age debate: A 5-year longitudinal study. *International Journal of Bilingual Education and Bilingualism*, 19(3), 217–234.

Pfenninger, S. E. (in press). Not so individual after all: An ecological approach to age as an individual difference variable in a classroom. *Studies in Second Language Learning and Teaching*.

Pfenninger, S. E., and Singleton, D. (2016). Affect trumps age: A person-in-context relational view of age and motivation in SLA. *Second Language Research*, 32(3), 311–345.

Pfenninger, S. E., and Singleton, D. (2017). *Beyond Age Effects in Instructional L2 Learning: Revisiting the age factor*. Bristol: Multilingual Matters.

Plonsky, L. (2013). Study quality in SLA: An assessment of designs, analyses, and reporting practices in quantitative L2 research. *Studies in Second Language Acquisition*, 35, 655–687.

Pollnitz, A. (2015). *Princely Education in Early Modern Britain*. Cambridge: Cambridge University Press.

Quintilian. (1933). Institutio oratoria.In Butler, H. E. (trans.), *Qulintilian*, *I* (LCL; 4 vols.). London: Heinemann.

Rixon, S. (2013). *British Council Survey of Policy and Practice in Primary English Language Teaching Worldwide*. London: British Council.

Seliger, H., Krashen, S., and Ladeforged, P. (1975). Maturational constraints in the acquisition of a native-like accent in second language learning. *Language Sciences*, 36, 20–22.

Serrano, R., and Muñoz, C. (2007). Same hours, different time distribution: Any difference in EFL? *System*, 35(3), 305–321. doi:10.1016/j.system.2007.02.001.

Singleton, D. (2005). The critical period hypothesis: A coat of many colours. *International Review of Applied Linguistics* (*IRAL*), 43(4), 269–285.

Singleton, D., and Pfenninger, S. E. (2017). Reporting on politically sensitive issues: The case of telling the truth about early L2 instruction. In Rose, H., and McKinley, J. (eds.) *Doing Real Research in Applied Linguistics*. London: Routledge, 214–224.

Singleton, D., and Ryan, L. (2004). *Language Acquisition: The age factor*, 2nd ed. Clevedon: Multilingual Matters.

Sparks, R., Patton, J., Ganschow, L., and Humbach, N. (2009). Long-term crosslinguistic transfer of skills from L1 to L2. *Language Learning*, 59(1), 203–243.

Spolsky, B. (1989). *Conditions for Second Language Learning: Introduction to a general theory*. Oxford: Oxford University Press.

Stern, H. (1983). *Fundamental Concepts of Language Teaching*. Oxford: Oxford University Press.

Swain, M., Lapkin, S., Rowen, N., and Hart, D. (1990). The role of mother tongue literacy in third language learning. *Language, Culture and Curriculum*, 3, 65–81.

Verspoor, M. H., de Bot, K., and Lowie, W. (Eds.) (2011). *A Dynamic Approach to Second Language Development: Methods and techniques*. Amsterdam and Philadelphia: John Benjamins, 5–24.

Walsh, P., and Singleton, D. (2013). Variation in English lexical acquisition among Polish migrant children in Ireland. In Singleton, D., Regan, V., and Debaene, E. (eds.) *Linguistic and Cultural Acquisition in a Migrant Community*. Bristol: Multilingual Matters, 156–182.

3

Early language learning teacher education

Sarah Rich

Introduction

The focus of this chapter is on teacher education for teachers of English to young learners (TEYL). Following Freeman (2009), in this chapter teacher education (TED) is understood to serve as an umbrella term, referring to the training and professional development opportunities that teachers undertake in preparation for the job of teaching (hereafter referred to as pre-service teacher education) as well as those that they undertake throughout their career (hereafter referred to as in-service teacher education). Teacher education therefore refers to both planned and unplanned learning opportunities which may take place both in and outside of the workplace.

TED has grown into an important area of inquiry within the field of teaching English language teaching, and the articulation of an English language teacher education (ELTED) strategy is increasingly commonplace in both government and institutional documentation. In part attention to and interest in ELTED reflects a growing awareness of the central role this plays in improving teacher quality, acknowledged to be a critical variable in helping students achieve learning outcomes (Hattie 2003, cited in Enever 2014). It also reflects the rapid expansion and reform of English language instruction worldwide, which is fuelling demand for competent teachers and effective approaches for their preparation and development (Richards 2008), particularly as teachers' access to professional development opportunities is widely seen as pivotal to the success of educational innovations (Wedell 2009).

One of the most significant worldwide reforms of ELT in recent years has been the lowering of the start age of English instruction. Today English instruction is an established component of the primary school curriculum in most countries and is being offered to younger and younger learners, with recent estimates suggesting that more than 7 million teachers are engaged in the TEYL field (Knagg and Ellis 2012). Given this situation, it is not surprising that the development of a teacher workforce with the knowledge and skills to work with young learners (particularly in primary schools) is increasingly reported as a priority by policymakers and researchers alike (Enever 2014), and as a result that the need for teacher education provision targeted at these teachers is quickly becoming an important agenda.

The aim of this chapter is to provide a detailed examination of the current situation regarding TED for TEYL (or TEYLTED). While TEYLTED is an important focus of a growing body of literature and research for teachers of children with English as an additional language in English-speaking countries, for reasons of space, primarily the focus in this chapter will be on a consideration of TEYLTED for teachers in non-English speaking contexts.

Historical perspectives

The emergence of ELTED can be seen to be closely aligned with the development of the field of foreign and additional English language teaching as a distinct professional activity. Richards (2008) argues that the earliest forms of ELTED that emerged in Europe in the 1960s were short training courses designed to equip teachers with the sorts of knowledge deemed necessary to prepare them for work in the field. Since then ELTED activity has expanded considerably worldwide, and an understanding of the scope of ELTED and what a pedagogy for TED should comprise has continued to evolve. In what follows, I will first briefly chart the shifting landscape of ELTED over the last 50 years. This can be seen to provide a useful contextual background to subsequent discussion of the comparatively recent evolution of TEYLTED in the last two decades, which is itself a response to the emergence of TEYL as a new branch of language education.

The expansion of ELTED provision

A growing emphasis on ELTED with its role in maintaining professional standards to ensure a well-qualified and well-prepared teaching workforce is one of the key indicators of the growing professionalization of the field of TESOL (Burns and Richards 2009), and this is reflected in the expectation in most countries that prospective English language teachers complete a formal accredited pre-service training programme typically comprising a number of content modules and a practicum component (Wright 2010). It is also reflected in the steady and growing appreciation of the importance of in-service education to practising teachers in recognition that this is crucial to maintaining the interest, motivation and creativity needed to sustain and improve the quality of professional work (Richards and Farrell 2005). In-service education may take many forms ranging from short training workshops to encouraging teachers to form informal networks, and promoting teachers' self-initiated professional development by making funding and time available for teachers to attend conferences, undertake further accredited learning and other self-directed professional development activities.

The evolution of principles and practices underpinning an effective ELTED strategy

Alongside this expansion of TED as an activity, there has been a gradual evolution in our understanding of the knowledge base of ELTED (Johnson 2009b). This knowledge base, or what Freeman (2009, p. 11) calls the 'scope' of ELTED, comprises attention to three interrelated components:

1   The content that needs to be addressed underpinned by a conception of what good teaching is and what the essential knowledge and skills of teachers are.
2   Teacher engagement or a view of how teachers learn to teach.
3   The influence of teacher education on teachers' practice.

An examination of the historical trajectory of ELTED shows a shift away from a view of the knowledge base of ELTED as merely subject or theoretical knowledge towards an appreciation of the importance of the practical know-how that teachers accrue from their day to day experiences in the workplace. As Freeman and Johnson (1998) point out, the traditional knowledge base of ELTED has been generated from theoretical and research perspectives in the parent disciplines of applied linguistics and second language acquisition, and this has left its mark on the design of pre-service programmes in particular, which often place a heavy emphasis on theory (Wright 2010). However, a move to incorporate insights from professional learning theory in Europe and North America in the 1990s gradually led to a growing appreciation of the importance of promoting an understanding of another form of knowledge – pedagogical knowledge, or knowledge of how to teach within ELTED (Johnson 2009b) – and subsequently to appreciate the ways in which teachers transform and synthesise theoretical and pedagogic knowledge through their teaching into what Shulman (1986) calls pedagogical content knowledge (PCK). While the first two forms of knowledge represent a body of pre-existing external knowledge, PCK is seen as personal knowledge and profoundly interactional, resulting from teachers' efforts to address practical problems in their classrooms (Kumaravadivelu 2012). The growing recognition of the centrality of PCK to effective teaching means that helping teachers develop and refine this is viewed as an important goal of ELTED (Johnson 2015).

This appreciation of the importance of PCK and the emphasis on teachers as 'knowing professionals' (Johnson and Golombek 2002, p. 1) resonates with and has been accompanied by a move to embrace constructivist models of teacher learning over the past two decades. These are ones that view teachers as *actively* engaged in a process of knowledge generation rather than merely passive consumers of knowledge produced by others and view teachers' knowledge and skills as *socially* constructed as they are situated in their engagements with others in their working contexts (Johnson 2015). These perspectives have had a number of important influences on the field of ELTED as discussed below.

Firstly, they have been the stimuli for a large and growing body of research which seeks to better conceptualise teacher knowledge and understand its development and transformation. Research into teacher cognition and more recently teacher identity (e.g., Borg 2009; Miller 2009) has helped shed light on the role of beliefs, emotions, relationships with others, biography and the social worlds teachers occupy (both within and outside school) on teachers' ways of knowing. This has added to a view of teacher knowledge as wide-ranging and has helped shape a view of teacher learning as 'a long-term complex developmental process' (Freeman and Johnson 1998, p. 402).

Secondly, these perspectives have been influential in shaping much of the current thinking on the purpose of teacher education and what is seen to constitute effective ELTED pedagogy. Specifically, they have focused attention on the process of teacher learning and how this can best be supported. There has been a gradual shift of emphasis away from a view of teacher education as primarily focused on *equipping* teachers with new ideas to be employed at a later date through the provision of top-down, expert-driven training programmes towards a view of teacher education as *enabling*; that is contributing to the gradual development and ongoing transformation of teachers' own knowledge and skills (Richards 2008; Prabhu 1987). In line with the growing recognition of teachers as legitimate producers of knowledge, an enabling approach to teacher education is one that sees the role of teacher education as supporting teachers' development and is centred on helping teachers improve what they do over time through the adoption of a reflective model of teacher education (Johnson 2009b). That is a pedagogical model which seeks to uncover teachers' tacit beliefs about teaching, helps them identify agendas for change and provides them with a set of research skills and strategies to investigate and improve their classroom practice (Wright 2010; Malderez and Wedell 2007).

Thirdly, the emphasis on the role of social activities and community relationships in teacher learning highlighted by these perspectives has also contributed to a growing appreciation of the importance of school-based ELTED (e.g., Richards 2008) and the value of activities such as classroom research, peer observation and working with a mentor or coach, allowing teachers to process and try out new ideas encountered in a more formal training session. Finally, given the importance of interaction to teacher learning highlighted by these perspectives, activities which require teachers to collaborate are also increasingly advocated as effective ways to support teacher learning (Johnson 2009a). Moreover, creating informal networks and professional learning communities is seen as an important priority in many contexts. While these may take place within a school, increasingly, the creation of online teacher communities is advocated as an important component of an effective ELTED strategy (Richards and Farrell 2005).

The emergence of interest in the influence of TED on teachers' practice

Underpinning all ELTED initiatives is an assumption that teacher education will help teachers with their work, and, as such, establishing the extent to which it does is seen as an important dimension of an effective ELTED strategy, as Freeman (2009) has highlighted. Until recently, however, little explicit attention has been given to this aspect of ELTED. The acknowledgement of its importance going forward is evident in recent literature and has been heightened by the growing pressure for accountability within the current standards-driven and evidence-based culture in education (e.g., Freeman 2009; Richards 2008).

The development and evolution of TEYLTED

While the introduction of English into primary school curricula in a number of countries in western Europe started more than 25 years ago, it is arguably the dramatic increase in the numbers of teachers engaged in teaching ever younger learners, both in Europe and elsewhere, in the past 15 years that has been the main driver for an emphasis on the importance of TEYLTED initiatives in recent literature. An appreciation of the need and importance of TEYLTED is evident in part in the emergence of publications which provide training resources designed to be used by trainers and others with a vested interest in supporting TEYL teachers (e.g., Slattery and Willis 2001), as well as in setting up special interest groups within professional associations and the availability of specialist web-based resources for TEYL teachers provided by publishers and others.

Pre- and in-service TEYLTED initiatives targeted at prospective or practicing TEYL teachers are also increasingly commonplace. This is evidenced, for example, in the inclusion of specialised TEYL modules in internationally recognised entry-level certified programmes primarily targeted at first language English speaking teachers, such as those offered by Trinity House and International House. Similarly the internationally recognised Cambridge Teacher Knowledge Test (TKT) has a specialised component on TEYL, and the British Council offers a dedicated online certified programme for primary English language teachers (CiPELT). At a national level, TEYLTED provision can be seen to follow a trajectory that Kaplan and Baldauf (1997) observe is commonplace in providing support with educational reforms; namely, to initially prioritise in-service support and to move to establish pre-service support at a later date. Thus in most countries the development of add-on short training programmes to help in-service teachers acquire basic competence in TEYL instruction is seen as a priority area. However, an observable trend in countries where TEYL has now been established for some time, such as in much of western Europe, Turkey and parts of East Asia, is the growth of pre-service TED to ensure that teachers are better prepared and trained for work with young learners from the outset, although this provision is not necessarily always targeted at TEYL teachers in particular (Enever 2014).

Critical issues and topics

As is evident from the historical overview above, while TEYLTED is now firmly established as a priority in many countries worldwide it is still very much a work in progress. The purpose of this section of the chapter is to describe a number of critical issues and topics that need to be addressed to ensure adequate and effective TEYLTED provision.

Access to TEYLTED

There is a widespread consensus that currently there is a shortage of qualified teachers to address the needs of the huge numbers of children engaged in EFL worldwide, not only in countries with relatively short histories of TEYL, such as a number of Asian countries, but also in countries where English has been part of the primary curriculum for some time (Garton,2014; Baldauf et al. 2011). Given this situation, there is clearly an urgent need to both increase TED provision at the pre-service level for teachers entering the field as well as in-service provision for teachers already engaged in TEYL. Yet in many parts of the world pre-service provision remains inadequate. In addition, while some form of inset provision is commonplace in most countries around the world, this is often limited or patchy at best, with teachers in rural areas particularly poorly served (Garton et al. 2011).Thus an urgent priority is to identify ways of increasing the availability of TED opportunities for TEYL teachers in a given setting which acknowledges and works to identify solutions to existing challenges to ensure provision is adequate and appropriate for all.

Meeting the needs of a complex TEYL teacher demographic

Another challenge is the huge diversity in the sorts of teachers currently involved in TEYL, particularly at the primary level, as large-scale transnational studies undertaken by Emery (2012) and Rixon (2013) have shown. In some contexts responsibility for delivering English teaching in primary schools is assigned to generalist or homeroom teachers. While generalist teachers may be trained primary teachers, they may need (and not have received) training in English language instruction and may also have limited English language proficiency. In many contexts specialised English teachers who have transferred from secondary schools are responsible for TEYL. While these teachers will typically have received training in additional language instruction and have a good command of English, they may not be aware of important differences between teaching older learners and children and may be unfamiliar and need support with the use of more child-friendly teaching methods. In addition, in many parts of the world a shortage of teachers means it is still not uncommon to recruit full- or part-time English speakers (both local and first language speakers) who are not qualified teachers, even in countries where TEYL is well established, such as in Europe (Enever 2014). These teachers (sometimes referred to as semi-specialists) present yet another set of training needs.

The need for specialised initial TED for TEYL teachers

Cameron argues that one widespread misconception about TEYL is that it is 'a straight-forward process that can be undertaken by anyone with a basic training in ELT' since 'the language taught to children only needs to be simple' (Cameron 2001, p. xii). Undoubtedly this view contributes to the continued use of unqualified teachers in many TEYL settings and fuels the common practice of reserving specialist and semi-specialist teachers for work with older young learners. Yet the picture emerging from the growing number of accounts of child language learning (see Rich 2014, pp. 26–27, for a summary of these) highlights how TEYL is a demanding and skilled process, particularly with children in the early grades of primary school. Insights from literature and research have highlighted how TEYL teachers need to develop a distinct repertoire of teaching skills and occupational knowledge to work effectively with young learners which include, for example, careful pacing to address children's limited concentration span and planning of short engaging activities (Cameron 2001).

These factors, alongside the fact that TEYL teachers are a critical variable in children's English language learning and are often the key, and in some settings the only resource and source of English input (Copland et al. 2014), presents a strong case for ensuring that specialised pre-service TED is offered to TEYL teachers. Yet in many contexts (even those with a long-standing tradition of TEYL) pre-service provision for English teachers is generically targeted at all prospective teachers, whether of adults or children (Enever 2014). With respect to the preparation of general primary school teachers, while in a few contexts add-on modules are offered to TEYL teachers as part of pre-service TED initiatives, these initiatives are rare, meaning that many general primary teachers do not receive support with special and discreet teaching skills required for additional language teaching.

Better mechanisms and procedures to establish the effectiveness of TEYLTED

While an appreciation of the importance of TED for TEYL teachers means that TED initiatives of some form or another are now in place in almost, if not, all of the different contexts where TEYL is offered worldwide, little is known about the effectiveness of existing provision. More systematic attempts to understand the extent to which teachers are benefiting from and making use of knowledge and skills gained in existing TEYLTED initiatives in their classrooms are important. These can build a picture of what constitutes quality TEYLTED provision and what are the stumbling blocks to realising this, such as poorly trained teacher educators, unsupportive school cultures and teachers' own attitudes and motivations which may impact their uptake of TEYLTED opportunities (Freeman 2009; Richards 2008).

Current contributions and research

In this part of the chapter, literature and the results of published research studies which are contributing to our current understanding of TEYLTED are considered. These include insights from recent transnational studies which reference TEYLTED as part of a broader survey of a number of aspects of current TEYL provision (e.g., Garton et al 2011; Emery 2012; Rixon 2013; Enever 2011) as well as a number of country-specific studies particularly focused on pre- and in-service TEYLTED provision, primarily undertaken in Europe and in Asia. The number of published research studies is still limited, and the fact that the vast majority of these have been published within the last 5 years is one indicator of the ways in which consideration of support for TEYL teachers is a recent and still emerging priority. Below I present a number of cross-cutting key themes identified from my analysis of these studies.

Existing TEYLTED provision

One of the contributions of the large transnational studies in particular has been the development of a solid empirical base regarding the current TED provision for TEYL teachers. With respect to pre-service provision, Rixon's (2013) survey of primary English policy and practice in 64 countries around the world highlights the general lack of attention to English language teaching in pre-service teacher education for generalist primary teachers, with only 26 of the 64 countries currently having provision for this. Several studies also provide insights into the still limited or non-existent provision of suitable pre-service education for specialist TEYL teachers in many contexts (e.g., Baldauf et al's 2011 discussion of the situation in Asia).

In contrast, the picture regarding in-service teacher education provision appears more promising, with the results of a large-scale survey undertaken by Emery (2012) of 2,500 TEYL teachers world-wide, revealing that 85% of TEYL teachers reported that they had received some form of in-service training. However, other studies have highlighted how access to in-service provision remains a problem, with governments struggling to keep up with demand and ensuring equitable access (e.g., Zein 2016; Gimenez 2009). In addition, with regard to in-service specialised training for generalist primary teachers in particular, Rixon's (2013) study identified that this was only in place in 27 of the 63 countries surveyed. Moreover, as Coburn (2016) has highlighted with reference to the situation in Norway, for example, what is provided often fails to meet demand.

The importance of TED to TEYL teachers

A number of studies highlight how the need for TEYL teacher education provision is not only a pressing concern among policy makers but is something that many TEYL teachers and students themselves identify as important. For example, 79% of the teachers surveyed by Emery (2012) indicated that they felt they would like more support, a view that was echoed by teachers in a number of country-specific studies as well (e.g., Kourieos 2011; Zein 2016; ChInh 2017).

Insights into priority content areas for TEYLTED

A major focus of many of the research studies identified was to uncover teacher perspectives on what sorts of knowledge and skills are needed for TEYL teachers to do their jobs effectively and what the implications of this are for TEYLTED provision. Some studies approached this explicitly (e.g., Brining 2015), while others sought to infer needs by asking teachers to stipulate what aspects of their work they found challenging (e.g., Garton et al 2011). Support needs were also identified from teacher accounts of the perceived inadequacy of pre- or in-service initiatives they had attended (e.g., Kourieos 2011). Analysis revealed widespread consensus on priority content areas for TEYL provision from these different lines of inquiry.

1 Support with practical challenges faced in the classroom

A priority area for teachers is support with practical challenges they face (e.g., such as dealing with differentiation and identifying suitable resources). Given that, as Kourieos

(2011, p. 170) noted in her study, many teachers operate with a 'solutions-orientated' perspective with regard to the purpose of TEYLTED, an emphasis on this is perhaps not surprising.

2 Support with the theoretical underpinnings of TEYL

The importance of providing teachers with a grounding in key principles of child learning is also implicit in many of the research studies I reviewed which focus on the difficulties teachers face. For example, Brining's (2015) study highlighted the concerns of the mainly first language speaking teachers in his study whose entry-level certified programme had placed emphasis on the development of skills and techniques for TEYL and very limited attention to important principles of child development and language learning. Other studies highlighted that teachers found much of the theoretical content they received irrelevant and did not target their needs as TEYL teachers (Kourieos 2011; Zein 2016). Taken together, these findings suggest that inclusion of relevant theoretical content in TEYLTED provision is important in the preparation and ongoing support of TEYL teachers.

3 Support with language proficiency and language awareness

There is widespread recognition in the literature on the importance of ensuring that TEYL teachers receive adequate support with English proficiency and knowledge about the English language which can be drawn upon in their teaching (e.g., Butler 2004; Garton et al. 2011; Nunan 2003). Given that these things are the bedrock of teachers professional competence it was not surprising that this was also seen as a priority by teachers in research studies as well (e.g., Kourieos 2011; Coburn 2016).

As Wright (2010) observes, since the vast majority of English teachers worldwide are not first language speakers, attention to improving teachers' language proficiency is an established component of much specialist ELTED pre-service provision, including that targeted at TEYL teachers. Yet in studies which sought out teacher perspectives on their experience with pre-service TEYLTED provision, programmed support with English language proficiency and language awareness was typically seen as either inadequate or, because this often focuses on general language improvement, as inappropriate to their teaching needs (e.g., Kourieos 2011; Dagarin and Andraka 2007).

Effective TEYLTED pedagogic practices

Collectively, insights into the value and effectiveness of TEYLTED pedagogic practices provided by studies highlight that TEYL teachers advocate for the more teacher-centred, interactive and collaborative reflective approaches currently advocated in mainstream ELTED, as reported earlier in the chapter. Thus, for example, a concern raised by teachers in several studies was the disproportionate time devoted to the transmission of theory compared to the teaching practice in pre-service programmes which was seen as crucial to the development of confidence in teaching. (e.g., Mattheoudakis 2007; Dagarin and Andraka 2007; Kourieos 2011).

A related concern identified in research studies, one that is linked to the theory-practice imbalance mentioned above, is teachers' dissatisfaction with teacher education programmes that adopt a non-participatory transmission-driven model of TEYLTED, rather than an emphasis on, reflection, experiential learning and practice opportunities which teachers see as important to help them make connections between TED provision and their teaching realities (e.g., Kourieos 2011; Mattheoudakis 2007). The importance and benefit of the opportunity to engage in dialogue was also highlighted by a number of studies. For example, this was seen as important to both pre-service and in-service teachers in Kourieos's (2011) study, both within formal teacher training programmes, with mentors in schools and through the provision of informal networking opportunities.

Central to those studies which documented innovations in TEYLTED and teachers' reactions to them, the introduction of an online element to enhance access to in-service TEYLTED provision was a recurring theme (e.g., Rich et al 2014, Coburn 2016; Karavas 2014). In all of these studies, the opportunity this provided for teachers to engage in online discussions with other teachers and teacher educators was reported to be a valuable learning opportunity. In those studies where this was used to compliment face-to-face training sessions (e.g., Karavas 2014; Coburn 2016) it was also seen as an important way to extend and increase continuity between training sessions and teaching realities.

Challenges to the success of TEYLTED provision

While research studies have tended to address the issue of quality TEYLTED provision through the lens of content and teacher education pedagogy as described above, a small number of studies have also identified other challenges which can affect the success of teacher education initiatives. Zein (2016) highlights, for example, how in Indonesia selection procedures identifying who can attend training programmes is a problem which can impact a teacher's chance of gaining access to training. Another challenge impacting the delivery of effective TEYLTED is the knowledge base and experience of the teacher trainers themselves (e.g., Kourieos 2011; Zein 2016). In these studies, teachers also commented on the challenges posed by poorly prepared support personnel in schools, such as mentors and advisors, which together with poor channels of communication between external training providers and schools, were perceived to have a detrimental effect on the ongoing support of teachers.

Recommendations for practice

As noted earlier in the chapter, in many parts of the world teachers do not have adequate access to pre-service and/or in-service TEYLTED provision. Moreover, even when they do, as Garton (2014) observes, this often seems to have little tangible effect on teachers continuing to lack the confidence, skills and language proficiency to teach TEYL effectively, pointing, at least in part, to weaknesses in existing provision. In light of this, this discussion of best practice considers both effective ways to improve access to TEYLTED provision as well as quality in terms of the design and delivery of TEYLTED initiatives.

Effective ways to maximise access to TEYLTED

It goes without saying that it is important for policy makers and others with responsibility for TEYLTED to make sure that steps are taken to ensure access to quality pre- and in-service TEYLTED initiatives that meet teacher needs. With regard to pre-service provision, clearly policy makers need to make sure that sufficient places are made available on pre-service programmes to ensure that there is a ready pool of teachers who have both the know-how and English skills needed to teach children effectively. With respect to in-service provision, as was discussed earlier in the chapter, practising teachers' support needs can take many forms, including targeted training, help in locating resources, and opportunities to learn from and dialogue with other teachers. An effective in-service TEYLTED strategy needs to ensure equitable access to all of these different forms of support for practising TEYL teachers who are typically dispersed across a wide geographical area.

The use of cascade models

A popular strategy for ensuring teachers' access to training workshops in particular is to employ a cascade model of delivery. This entails delivery of a workshop to a group of trainers, teachers or lead teachers who then disseminate the workshop to other teachers in their region or school. Cascade models are attractive because they are cost-effective and use existing staff as co-trainers. However, cascading can, as Hayes (2000, p. 137) observes, result in 'the dilution of training' meaning that 'less and less is understood the further down the cascade one goes'. Hayes (2014) proposes two strategies to maximise the efficacy of cascade models of training delivery: firstly to consult a range of stakeholders when designing the materials so that the presentation of new ideas is carefully aligned with and accommodates teaching realities; secondly, to ensure that reflective opportunities for trainers are incorporated in training material at each stage of the cascade, allowing for a degree of reinterpretation and increased sense of ownership of the material by all those involved in delivery.

Technology-enhanced solutions to issues of access

Technology offers considerable potential to maximise access to both formal and more informal forms of in-service education and is gaining in popularity around the world. With respect to the delivery of training workshops in particular, it can be deployed to provide teachers with clear models of good practice which can be shared online or through DVDs. It also offers the potential for training sessions to be delivered via video links or for online teacher training modules to be taken by large numbers of teachers long-distance. However, there are a number of potential challenges associated with the use of technology to enhance formal TEYLTED provision. Apart from technological issues, such as teacher access to a fast and reliable internet connection, without sufficient attention to two-way interactive opportunities and activities which encourage teachers to reflect on and process new ideas, there is a danger that online training programmes may serve as more of a briefing function than a genuine opportunity for teacher learning. In addition, these require moderators to help ensure teachers stay on track and maintain their motivation, particularly as drop rates are often very high (Rich et al 2014). Bearing these points in mind, technological forms of training often work best as a compliment to face-to-face delivery of teacher education.

While the use of technology for training purposes needs to be approached with some caution, it offers considerable potential as a way to provide informal support for TEYL teachers. In a number of countries, online portals (created via platforms like Moodle) are proving to be an effective way of sharing resources (including for those teachers who are developing themselves) and creating networking opportunities for teachers via discussion forums (e.g., Karavas 2014)

The characteristics of quality TEYLTED provision

Echoing Freeman's (2009) conceptualization of the scope of teacher education mentioned earlier in the chapter, the issue of quality in TEYLTED needs to be considered with reference to three important and interrelated dimensions of provision:

1   What needs to be addressed (or CONTENT).
2   How this can be effectively delivered (or PEDAGOGICAL APPROACH).
3   How the success of an intervention can be established (or EVALUATION AND IMPACT).

In what follows, an account of good practice with regard to each of these dimensions will be considered.

Identifying content for TEYLTED programmes

Establishing teachers' needs is a first step in developing an effective teacher education strategy for both pre- and in-service teachers. This will not only ensure that content is relevant and beneficial to teachers but will also help ensure their engagement with TEYLTED initiatives and increase the impact of this on teachers' classroom practice. Consultation with teachers and other stakeholders in schools and observation of TEYL classrooms are therefore important steps to be taken.

More broadly, as the results of studies discussed earlier in the chapter have highlighted, effective TEYLTED provision needs to include attention to targeted support in all of the following:

*   Knowledge of and fluency in English.
*   Knowledge of children's foreign language learning and appropriate teaching strategies.
*   Knowledge of the different cognitive, affective and psychomotor stages children journey through.

Good practice in the delivery of effective TEYLTED

Drawing upon the review of teacher learning presented earlier in the chapter as well as the perspectives of teachers identified in research studies above, a number of operating principles should underpin the development of effective pedagogical approaches to deliver the content areas outlined above.

1   TEYL teachers benefit from pedagogic approaches which help them make connections between new input received and their pre-existing understanding and experience of classroom teaching and learning. As Hayes (2014) argues, this means that support initiatives should be school focused at least, if not also school based. Moreover, they should be grounded in and responsive to a thorough understanding of wider contextual realities which impact possibilities and constraints in teachers' current or future school worlds.
2   Given the ongoing and lifelong nature of teacher learning, it is important to employ pedagogical approaches which help teachers to continue to develop over and beyond any formal input sessions that they receive. This means that it is important to ensure

that support initiatives are designed not only to focus on *equipping* teachers with new knowledge and skills but also to serve an *enabling* function, providing them with resources and strategies to ensure they have the capacity to continue their learning journey over and beyond any formal input they receive.

3   It is important to include pedagogical activities which help teachers interrogate their existing beliefs borne out of their previous experience as learners and/or their existing experience of teaching to date. Beliefs are powerful filters which impact how far and in what ways teachers engage with new ideas, but these are often tacit. By creating activities which require teachers to make these more explicit, teachers are 'readied' to receive new ideas, to see how well these align with existing beliefs or provide powerful alternative ways of working.

4   Dialogue and collaboration with other teachers is a powerful way to support teacher learning, and finding ways to create and increase opportunities for peer learning are therefore important.

These core principles are ones that underline the importance of placing the teacher and their teaching worlds at the centre of TEYLTED endeavours. They also highlight that reflection, experimentation and dialogue should be core components of TEYLTED pedagogy.

In terms of formal provision, whether in the form of pre-service programmes or in-service workshops and reflection, experimentation and dialogue should be combined in ways that:

1   Demonstrate the interconnection between theory and practice.
2   Reveal teachers' prior experience and knowledge.
3   Help teachers develop action plans for future practice.

In pre-service programmes in particular, attention to practice implications should be seen as an essential component of content modules, such as those which focus on theoretical knowledge, language proficiency and awareness and teaching methodology, rather than confined to the teaching practice component of the programme, as is often the case. Not only will this enable student teachers to better see the relevance of these modules to their future teaching, but it can also help ready teachers for the final practicum component of their studies and ensure this is a more beneficial and enriching experience.

Table 3.1 describes an illustrative procedure of how the interconnection between theory and practice can be created in formal teacher education sessions, drawing upon the principles of reflection, experimentation and dialogue.

This procedure is centred on transforming teachers' existing knowledge base and understanding rather than merely the transmission of new ideas. As such this approach entails the use of active-learning and guided discovery techniques and tasks which seek to 'disturb' teachers' established ways of thinking and guide them towards new understandings and action points that can be refined by experimentation.

One of the limitations of formal training programmes, however, is that these do not typically provide teachers with the additional in-school support needed to help put change into practice, and this is often reported as a reason for their limited impact on teachers' practice. Teachers need sustained support over time if they are to transform their practice, and it is important for attention to be given to issues of continuity when planning TEYLTED initiatives. In pre-service programmes, the training of school-based personnel who can act as effective mentors and coaches during the practicum stage is therefore crucial. With regard to in-service provision, where possible, adopting a day-release approach to training

Table 3.1 Steps to the interconnection between theory and practice

Step 1	Introduce the focus of the session (e.g., using games) and invite participants to reflect on a past or recent experience related to the focus that they have had (as a learner or teacher).
Step 2	Ask them to interpret or explain the experience (e.g., their feelings/challenges/successes).
Step 3	Listen to other participants' experiences and look for points of similarity and difference (local knowledge).
Step 4	Read or listen to input from theory or research on the session focus and/or watch a model demonstration of effective practice (external knowledge).
Step 5	Process the various opinions and viewpoints to derive new or revised perceptions and knowledge.
Step 6	Invite participants to reflect on new ideas to try out in future practice.
Step 7	Time permitting, participants can plan how they will implement new ideas and undertake micro-teaching.

(Based on Malderez and Wedell 2007).

is helpful as this allows teachers to try out ideas in school and share their successes and challenges in a follow-on training session. However, where this is not practicable, online forums can play an important support role as discussed above. More broadly, promoting classroom research with teachers is helpful as it provides teachers with a useful set of techniques and strategies to promote self-initiated cycles of reflection and experimentation (Wright 2010).

Good practice in monitoring the quality of TEYLTED

Developing a strategy to evaluate TEYLTED initiatives is an important dimension of effective TEYLTED provision at every level. This should be focused on generating data which not only reveals teachers' views of TEYLTED initiatives themselves, but should also include surveys, interviews and classroom observations which examine the ways in which TEYLTED initiatives are facilitating learning and change in teachers' practice. The results of these evaluations can then be fed back into improving course design for future cohorts of teachers.

Future directions

Although still small, the growing body of research and literature reported in this chapter has provided some important insights into quality TEYLTED provision for a rapidly growing and complex TEYL workforce. It has also signalled some of the contextual constraints that can diminish the quality and likely impact of these initiatives, such as issues around access and the quality of teacher educators. More research into these complicating factors alongside work on the impact of school cultures is important in identifying appropriate forms of effective TEYLTED at a local level and understanding teacher investment in these.

At a practical level, to improve the quality of TEYLTED going forward it is important that more attention be paid to improving the expertise of TEYL teacher educators who play a crucial role in determining the quality of the support that teachers receive. In addition, as discussed above, more attention also needs to be paid to the development and application of a systematic strategy for the evaluation of TEYLTED provision to establish its efficacy and quality.

Further reading

1 Burns, A., and Richards, J. C. (Eds.). (2009). *The Cambridge guide to second language teacher education*. New York: Cambridge University Press.
    This book provides an excellent and comprehensive overview of theory and practice in ELTED today.

2 Enever, J. (2014). Primary English teacher education in Europe. *ELT Journal*, 68(3), 231–242.
    This article provides a valuable account of issues facing the development of TEYLTED in Europe, many of which are also of wider relevance to the development of TEYLTED in other contexts.

3 Karavas., E. (2014). Implementing innovation in primary EFL: A case study in Greece. *ELT Journal*, 68(3), 243–253.
    This article illustrates how an effective teacher education strategy can be developed to help ensure the success of a TEYL reform. In particular, it highlights the value of technology-enhanced solutions to successful TEYLTED initiatives.

4 Malderez, A., and Wedell, M. (2007). *Teaching teachers: Processes and practices*. London: Bloomsbury.
    This book provides a clear and accessible account of how to design and implement effective teacher education programmes.

Related topics

Policies, difficult circumstances, the age debate

References

Baldauf, R. B., Kaplan, R. B., Kamwangamalu, N., and Bryant, P. (2011). Success or failure of primary second/foreign language programmes in Asia: What do the data tell us? *Current Issues in Language Planning*, 12(2), 309–323.

Borg, S. (2009). Language teacher cognition. In Burns, A., and Richards, J. C. (eds.) *The Cambridge Guide to Second Language Teacher Education*. New York: Cambridge University Press, 163–172.

Brining, D. J. (2015). The challenges faced by teachers of English as a foreign language to young learners in international contexts and their training and development needs and opportunities. Unpublished PhD thesis.

Burns, A., and Richards, J. C. (2009). Introduction: Second language teacher education. In Burns, A., and Richards, J. C. (eds.) *The Cambridge Guide to Second Language Teacher Education*. New York: Cambridge University Press, 9–11.

Butler, Y. G. (2004). What level of English proficiency do elementary school teachers need to attain to teach EFL? Case studies from Korea, Taiwan, and Japan. *TESOL Quarterly 38* (2) 245-278.

Cameron, L. (2001). *Teaching Languages to Young Learners*. Cambridge: Cambridge University Press.

Cameron, L. (2003). Challenges for ELT from the expansion in teaching children. *ELT Journal*, 57(2), 105–112.

Chinh, D. N. (2017). Creating spaces for constructing practice and identity: Innovations of teachers of English language to young learners in Vietnam. *Research Papers in Education*, 1(15), 56–70.

Coburn, J. (2016). The professional development of English language teachers: Investigating the design and impact of a national in-service teacher education course. Unpublished PhD thesis.

Copland, F., Garton, S., and Burns, A. (2014). Challenges in teaching English to young learners: Global perspectives and local realties. *TESOL Quarterly*, 48(4), 738–762.

Dagarin, M., and Andraka, M. (2007). Evaluation of teacher training programmes for primary teachers of English – A comparative study. In Nikolov, M., Mihaljević Djigunović, J., Mattheoudakis, M., Lundberg, G., and Flanagan, T. (eds.) *Teaching Modern Languages to Young Learners: Teachers, curricula and materials*. Strasbourg/Graz: Council of Europe/European Centre for Modern Languages, 9–21.

Emery, H. (2012). *A Global Study of Primary English Teachers' Qualifications, Training and Career Development*. London: British Council.

Enever, J. (Ed). (2011). *ELLiE: Early language learning in Europe*. London: British Council.

Enever, J. (2014). Primary English teacher education in Europe. *ELT Journal*, 6(3), 231–242.

Freeman, D. (2009). The scope of second language teacher education. In Burns, A., and Richards, J. C. (eds.), *The Cambridge Guide to Second Language Teacher Education*. New York: Cambridge University Press, 11–20.

Freeman, D., and Johnson, K. E. (1998). Re-conceptualizing the knowledge-base of language teacher education. *TESOL Quarterly*, 397–417.

Garton, S., Copland, F., and Burns, A. (2011). *Investigating Global Practices in Teaching English to Young Learners*. London: British Council.

Gimenez, T. (2009). English at primary school level in Brazil: Challenges and perspectives. In Enever, J., Moon, J., and Raman, U. (eds.) *Young Learner English Language Policy and Implementation: International perspectives*. Reading: Garnet Education, 53–59.

Hattie, J. A. C. (2003). Teachers make a difference: What is the research evidence? Paper presented at the Australian Council for Educational Research Annual Conference on: Building Teacher Quality, October 2003, Melbourne, Australia.

Hayes, D. (2000). Cascade training and teachers professional development. *ELT Journal*, 54(2), 135–145.

Hayes, D. (2014). *Factors Influencing Success in Teaching English in State Primary Schools*. London: British Council.

Johnson, K. E. (2006). The sociocultural turn and its challenges for second language teacher education. *TESOL Quarterly*, 235–257.

Johnson, K. E. (2009a). *Second Language Teacher Education: A sociocultural perspective*. New York: Routledge.

Johnson, K. E. (2009b). Trends in second language teacher education. In Burns, A., and Richards, J. C. (eds.) *The Cambridge Guide to Second Language Teacher Education*. New York: Cambridge University Press, 20–30.

Johnson, K. E. (2015). Reclaiming the relevance of L2 teacher education. *Modern Language Journal*, 99, 515–528.

Johnson, K. E., and Golombek, P. R. (Eds.). (2002). *Teachers' Narrative Inquiry as Professional Development*. Cambridge: Cambridge University Press.

Kaplan, R. B., and Baldauf, R. B. (1997). *Language Planning: From practice to theory*. Clevedon: Multilingual Matters.

Karavas, E. (2014). Implementing innovation in primary EFL: A case study in Greece. *ELT Journal*, 68(3), 243–253.

Knagg, J., and Ellis, G. (2012). *Global Issues in Primary ELT*. http://iatefl.britishcouncil.org/2012/sessions/2012-03-20/british-council-signature-event-global-primary-elt-issues. [Accessed 28 Spetember 2016].

Kourieos, S. (2011). An investigation into the preparation of language teachers at primary level: Implications for an initial language teacher education programme. Unpublished PhD thesis.

Kumaravadivelu, B. (2012). *Language Teacher Education For a Global Society: A modular model for knowing, analyzing, recognizing, doing, and seeing*. New York: Routledge.

Malderez, A., and Wedell, M. (2007). *Teaching Teachers: Processes and practices*. London: Bloomsbury.

Mattheoudakis, M. (2007). Tracking changes in EFL teachers beliefs: A longitudinal study. *Teachers and Teacher Education*, 23, 1273–1288.

Miller, J. (2009). Teacher Identity. In Burns, A., and Richards, J. C. (eds.) *The Cambridge Guide to Second Language Teacher Education*. New York: Cambridge University Press, 172–182.

Prabhu, N. S. (1987). Language education: Equipping or enabling? In Das, B. K. (ed.) *Language Education in Human Resource Development*. Singapore: RELC.

Rich, S. (2014). Taking stock: Where are we now with TEYL? In Rich, S. (ed.) *Global Issues in the Teaching of English to Young Learners*. London: Palgrave Macmillan.

Rich, S., Monteith, S., Al Sinani, S., Al Gardani, M., and Al Amri, H. (2014). Charting new territory: The introduction of on-line CPD opportunities for primary and secondary English teachers in Oman. In Hayes, D (ed.) *Innovations in the Continuing Professional Development (CPD) of English Language Teachers*. London: British Council Publications.

Richards, J. C. (2008). Second language teacher education today. *RELC Journal*, 39(2), 158–177

Richards, J. C., and Farrell, T. S. C. (2005). *Professional Development for Language Teachers.* Cambridge: Cambridge University Press.

Rixon, S. (2013). *British Council Survey of Policy and Practice in Primary English Language Teaching Worldwide*. London: British Council.

Shulman, L. S. (1986). Those who understand: Knowledge growth in teaching. *Educational Researcher*, 15, 4–14.

Slattery, M., and Willis, J. (2001). *English for Primary Teachers*. Oxford: Oxford University Press.

Wedell, M. (2009). *Planning for Educational Change: Putting people and their contexts first*. London: Blackledge.

Wright, T. (2010). Second language teacher education: Review of recent research on practice. *Language Teaching*, 43(3), 259–296.

Zein, M. S. (2016). Government-based training agencies and the professional development of Indonesian teachers of English for Young Learners: Perspectives from complexity theory. *Journal of Education for Teaching*, 42(2), 205–223.

4

Young learners' motivation for learning English

Yingying Li, Ye Han and Xuesong Gao

Introduction

In view of the perceived importance of English competence for individuals' personal and professional pursuits, a rapidly growing number of children are starting to learn English at an early age globally and in diverse contexts, including countries such as China and Spain (e.g., Butler 2015a ; Copland et al. 2014). In these contexts, English has been promoted as an important academic subject in elementary schools, which constitutes 'possibly the world's biggest policy development in education' (Johnstone 2009, p. 33). In addition to formal English education, children of well-off families learn English out of class by attending private tutorials, using learning materials and participating in tailored study-abroad programmes (e.g., Butler 2015a).

The growing global popularity of English among young learners has been followed by an increasing scholarly attention to the learning processes and achievements of young language learners. However, current knowledge about young learners is still limited with regard to (a) what motivates them to learn English; and (b) the motivational process as they progress through schooling. Despite an explosion of studies on adult language learners' language learning motivation, findings generated from studies on adult learners may not be applicable or generalizable to young ones since adults and the young learn English in different situations with different cognitive, psychological and affective levels of maturity (Boo et al. 2015). In this chapter, we present a critical review of research on young learners' motivation to learn English as a second language ('L2') or a foreign language ('FL'). To clarify the scope of this review, young learners are defined as children up to and including the elementary school level (typically up to 12–13 years old) (see Butler 2015a, 2015b).

Historical perspectives

Since language, as 'an integral part of an individual's identity involved in almost all mental activities' (Dörnyei 1996, p. 72), serves as an interpersonal communication system and a tool for social organisation, research on language learning motivation has been influenced by both social and cognitive theories. Among a variety of theories of motivation in the field

(Boo et al. 2015; Dörnyei 2005; Dörnyei and Ryan 2015; Dörnyei and Ushioda 2011), three major theories have dominated the scene: Gardner's (1985) socio-educational model, self-determination theory (Deci and Ryan 1985; Ryan and Deci 2000) and Dörnyei's (2009) L2 Motivational Self System ('L2 MSS'). In the following sections, we introduce theoretical constructs commonly used in contemporary motivational research so that these constructs can be used to discuss research related to young learners' language learning motivation.

Integrative versus instrumental motivation

Drawing on social psychology research, Gardner's (1985) conceptualisation of motivation emphasises individual learners' attitudes towards L2 and the L2 community and differentiates integrative motivation from instrumental motivation. Integrative motivation refers to learners' 'willingness to be like the valued members of the language community' (Gardner and Lambert 1972, p. 271), which can involve L2 learners' positive feelings toward the L2 group and the desire to interact with and even become similar to members of the target language community. In contrast, as the utilitarian counterpart of integrative motivation, instrumental motivation speaks of pragmatic gains from L2 proficiency, such as getting a better job or a higher salary.

Although Gardner's (1985) motivation model dominated the field for many years, we found that most of the related studies covered secondary or post-secondary adult L2 learners. Gardner's (1985) study has not been used to explore young learners' L2 motivation, with only a few exceptions including Donitsa-Schmidt et al. (2004) and Lamb (2004). This lack of research may be due in part to the fact that during the period when this model (integrative versus instrumental motivation) dominated academic research, i.e., from 1950s to 1990s, young learners' L2 learning was scarcely examined, in general. When young learners started to attract more research attention, limitations of Gardner's model of L2 motivation were recognised and criticised. Gardner's (1985) L2 motivation model has also become less applicable to the contemporary world as English is becoming the lingua franca, more widely used between non-native speakers (e.g., Butler 2015a, 2015b; Dörnyei and Ushioda 2011; Kim 2012a, 2012b; Zhang and Kim 2013). Not all learners, therefore, interact and establish connections with the target language community (Butler 2015a). In fact, young learners, especially those in EFL countries with low socioeconomic status ('SES'), usually have little direct contact with English when out of class and have few opportunities to interact with members of a target language community. This probably explains why some of the Indonesian students (11–12 years old) in Lamb (2004, 2013) were found less likely to identify themselves with the target language community and culture even though they were highly motivated to learn the language.

Intrinsic versus extrinsic motivation

Researchers have also conceptualised individual learners' language learning motivation in light of the self-determination theory (SDT) (Deci and Ryan 1985; Ryan and Deci 2000). Unlike the Gardner's motivation model, SDT focuses on individual language learners' selves to explain what motivates them to learn in terms of intrinsic and extrinsic motivations. Intrinsic motivation refers to 'behavior performed for its own sake in order to experience pleasure and satisfaction, such as the joys of doing a particular activity or satisfying one's curiosity' (Dörnyei and Ushioda 2011, p. 23), while extrinsic motivation involves 'performing a behavior as a means to some separable end, such as receiving an extrinsic reward (e.g., good grades) or avoiding punishment' (ibid.).

Previous research has consistently shown that intrinsically driven motivation is more beneficial than the extrinsically controlled motivation as it can enhance learners' self-efficacy, positive emotions and engagement with learning (Corpus et al. 2009; Noels et al. 2000). Therefore, a central question in SDT is how a person originally driven by external factors can become more self-regulated in the presence of social support that meets psychological needs, including autonomy, competence and relatedness.

With regard to young learners, SDT has been more frequently used than other L2 motivation frameworks (e.g., Butler 2015b; Carreira 2006, 2011, 2012; Kissau et al. 2015; Mady 2010; Noels et al. 1999; Wu 2003). Carreira's (2006, 2011, 2012) studies on young learners in Japan have revealed that the participants' motivation may become more internally controlled when psychological needs (such as autonomy, competence and relatedness) are satisfied. In China, Wu (2003) found that teachers can enhance young learners' (four- to six-year-olds) intrinsic motivation by fostering their sense of ownership of the learning process and self-perceived competence. Furthermore, research informed by SDT has shown that development of children's intrinsic motivation and extrinsic motivation may differ across age groups and contexts, demonstrating the complex nature of motivation constructs. However, researchers (e.g., Butler 2015a, p. 319) have cautioned against employing linear statistical models as implied in the SDT framework to explore young learners' motivation and have suggested 'more contextualised approaches to [understanding] motivation' in specific settings.

While previous findings have shown a strong consensus on the decline of intrinsic motivation as children grow older, the developmental path of extrinsic motivation is less clear. Some studies have reported a decline in both intrinsic motivation and extrinsic motivation as students move from the third to the sixth grade (Carreira 2006; see also Enever 2009 for pupils' decreasing positive attitudes towards foreign language learning activities), whereas others have reported an increase in extrinsic motivation in the same period (Anderman et al. 1999). Research has also revealed that extrinsic motivation emerges at age 11 or 12 and is more frequently perceived as the driving force underlying L2 learning by elder learners (11–14 years old) than by younger learners (6–10 years old) (Nikolov 1999).

L2 motivational self system

Echoing the SDT's focus on self, Dörnyei and colleagues (e.g., Csizér and Dörnyei 2005; Dörnyei and Ushioda 2009) proposed a new theoretical model to investigate L2 motivation, i.e., the L2 Motivational Self System (Dörnyei 2009). This model consists of three main components: (1) the Ideal-L2 Self, referring to the idealised images learners have of themselves as future L2 users; (2) the Ought-to L2 Self, composed of idealised images generally intended to please others or avoid negative repercussions; and (3) the L2 Learning Experience, involving 'situated, executive motives which are associated with the immediate learning environment and experience (e.g., the impact of the teacher, the curriculum, the peer group, the experience of success)' (Dörnyei 2009, p. 29). Although the L2 Motivational Self System has gained popularity as a major theoretical framework of L2 motivation (e.g., Haggerty and Fox 2015; Iwaniec 2014; You and Dörnyei 2016), it has not yet been widely used in young learners' motivation research. Lack of research with orientation to the L2 Motivational Self System on young learners is not entirely unexpected since young learners, especially those before or in elementary school, tend to be less self-conscious (suggested in Kissau et al. 2015) and have a vaguer self-system than adults (Iwaniec 2014). Their self-system is still emerging and developing, and the process is most likely to be shaped by the immediate learning environment – parents, peers, teachers and instruction in and out of class. However, this does not mean that the L2 Motivational Self System cannot be applied to young learners of L2; given the paucity of research from this theoretical orientation and the changing nature of self-system of young learners, researchers should consider using the L2 Motivational Self System when exploring participants' L2 motivation.

Although we present the three theoretical frameworks of L2 motivation separately, it is worth noting that empirical research on L2 motivation of young learners does not necessarily follow only one theoretical perspective. It has been quite common for researchers to draw concepts and constructs from more than one framework. For instance, Lamb (2004) investigated instrumental versus integrative motivational orientation but criticised this distinction and suggested the importance of future self as a motivating factor. Cheung and Pomerantz (2012) categorised the motivational orientations emerging in their data into identified motivation, introjected motivation, extrinsic motivation and intrinsic motivation. Thus, the theoretical constructs reviewed earlier may be employed in a variety of combinations in specific empirical studies based on the researchers' operational conceptualisation of L2 motivation.

Critical issues and topics

When appreciating young language learners' motivation, it is important to remember that young learners are less likely to be motivated for integrative reasons, as they usually have limited direct contact with native speakers in many contexts. Unlike adults, they do not face the urgency of getting a good job or entering higher education (motivated for instrumental reasons) (Huang 2011). In addition, their consciousness of selves may be vaguer than that of adults, and still developing. Given these characteristics of young learners, researchers have increasingly recognised that L2 learners' motivation can be mediated by a wide range of factors and specific learning situations that they experience (Dörnyei 1998; Pinter 2017). Specifically, motivation can be shaped by people involved in or related to their learning of English (e.g., parents, teachers and peers) and teaching and learning in the classroom environment (e.g., learning activities and way of instructions), or other related factors. These become the critical issues and topics that need to be explored.

Parental involvement

Research in educational psychology has recognised the important role parents play in their children's educational attainments (e.g., Bakker et al. 2007; Gonzalez-DeHass et al. 2005). Much evidence presented by researchers has shown that parents' involvement in children's learning, such as discussing children's school work with them and offering immediate help for learning whenever needed, can help children foster positive attitudes towards education and strengthen self-efficacy beliefs, which in turn enhance learning achievements (Butler 2015b; Cheung and Pomerantz 2012; Grolnick et al. 2009; Pomerantz and Moorman 2010).

L2 learning research has also acknowledged the critical role of parents (e.g., Sung and Padilla 1998; Gardner et al. 1999; Gao 2012). Empirical research has showed that parental involvement can help predict students' attitudes towards and motivation of learning an L2 (e.g., Mady 2010). Gardner et al. (1999) showed that parents' encouragement motivates children to invest efforts in language learning (also see Mady 2010). Such findings are highly significant since research into challenges and issues of teaching English to young learners (e.g., Copland et al. 2014; Garton 2014) has reported that young learners to some extent lack motivation and interest in learning English, as they may not fully understand the value of learning the language.

It must be noted that many studies on language learning motivation in East Asian countries have projected parental involvement as a common phenomenon since parents tend to impose high standards of academic excellence on their children (Bong et al. 2014). A comparison of Asian parents with European American and Latino parents (Okagaki and Frensch 1998) showed that the former had significantly higher expectations, as well as the 'ideal' image, of their children's educational attainments. Asian parents, especially those with higher socioeconomic status, heavily invest time, energy and money in their children's education. For instance, Gao (2012) examined the parental involvement in adolescents' vocabulary learning in the Chinese context and found parents regulate and control children's learning processes through mediating motivational discourses, beliefs and knowledge. In response, children in East Asian cultures have a strong sense of gratitude and indebtedness to their parents, especially in early school years, so children think it is their obligation to study harder to repay their parents and meet expectations so as to gain their approval (Park and Kim 2006). Although the parent-oriented motivation is controlled rather than autonomous (Cheung and Pomerantz 2012), it may still be beneficial to help enhance children's engagement and ultimate academic achievement as a type of extrinsic motivation.

Parents' socioeconomic status (SES)

Researchers have noted that language learning involves both individual cognitive activities and the efforts to obtain access to resources provided in social activities (e.g., Norton and Toohey 2001; Zuengler and Miller 2006), such as opportunities to communicate with competent speakers of the language and to use materials that can assist learning of the language (Palfreyman 2006). However, considerable differences exist across learners in terms of access to resources for learning English both within and outside the formal school system, which can largely be attributed to differences between SES of parents (e.g., Butler 2015b; Carhill et al. 2008; Gao 2012; Zou and Zhang 2011).

In EFL contexts, English is not used as the major language for communication, and frequent use of English is limited to people in certain communities, such as business and media (Feng 2012). Learners in such contexts often have few opportunities to 'receive sufficient input to acquire practical communicative competency in English' (Butler 2015a, p. 305). To learn and use English thus tends to require learners to pay extra money and to obtain more resources, which may not be affordable for people of low SES backgrounds (Hu 2009). The reality that learning English is costly in these contexts helps to explain the widening 'gaps in accessibility and achievement in English by SES and region' (Butler 2015a, p. 305). The unequal access to English-learning resources and the growing gaps in achievements resulting from SES of parents have prompted empirical research on the association between SES and children's English learning motivation and achievements (e.g., Butler 2015b; Fernald et al. 2013; Gao 2012). Butler's (2015b) mixed-method study on Chinese children found that parents with higher SES adjust their behaviours to their children's changing needs and are able to provide greater opportunities for English communication outside of school, which is conducive to developing self-determined motivation. Gao's (2012) study involving elite young Chinese adolescents also suggests that students whose parents have higher SES may obtain easy access to English-learning resources and are more likely to start learning English at an early age. These advantages may help to establish their confidence and enhance English competence, as well as strengthen motivation for learning it. Therefore, Butler (2015b, p. 411) contends that it is necessary for researchers to integrate the socioeconomic dimension into SLA theories which can help to 'make a more meaningful contribution to improving language education, particularly given its implications of social equity'.

Teacher and teaching-related factors mediating young learners' English learning motivation

Apart from parental involvement and parents' SES, teachers and teaching programmes also mediate children's motivation (Hamada 2011; Kikuchi 2009; Sakai and Kikuchi 2009). In their research on students' (fourth to sixth grade) motivation for learning Arabic as an L2, Donitsa-Schmidt et al. (2004) discovered that students' satisfaction with their Arabic language programme could best predict their motivation. This finding adds support to previous research arguing for the important role of quality language programmes in mediating enthusiasm and satisfaction with the learning environment (e.g., Ushioda 1998), which in turn influences motivation for learning the language. The quality of language programmes is largely dependent on teachers' roles. However, the teacher's role in shaping student motivation is a complex mechanism (e.g., Donitsa-Schmidt et al. 2004; Dörnyei 2001) since it involves various factors, such as teachers' personality, classroom management skills and knowledge of the content. Dörnyei (1998), in his investigation of the relationship between students' attitudes towards L2 and demotivation, found that the teacher is a main factor that demotivates students' learning. Teachers' personality, commitment, competence and teaching method were found to have influenced students' motivation to learn languages. In particular, researchers have examined the impact of teacher instruction on young learners' motivation to learn English (e.g., Huang 2011; Sundqvist and Sylven 2014;). In Taiwan, Huang (2011) found that six-year-old first graders in the Content-Based Language Instruction (CBLI) class displayed more motivated behaviours, such as volunteering more eagerly in class, although he argued that the finding could also be attributed to other factors, such as class/lesson atmosphere, reward, difficulty of questions or tasks, and activity settings. Sundqvist and Sylven (2014) identified that computer-assisted language learning (CALL), in the form of digital games used in learners' English language-related activities outside school, positively influenced fourth-grade English learners' (aged 10–11) motivation to learn in Sweden.

Another influencing factor is assessment, such as standardised high-stakes language tests, which 'possess power to exert an expected influence on teaching and learning because of the consequences they bring about' (Qi 2007, p. 52). Researchers have been much concerned about the considerable influence that high-stakes examinations have on teaching and learning (e.g., Black and William 1998; Haggerty and Fox 2015; Ross 2008; Stobart and Eggen 2012). They have explored the relationship between assessment (such as high-stakes language tests) and students' motivation for learning (e.g., Black and William 1998; Haggerty and Fox 2015; Harlen and Deakin Crick 2003). Choi (2008, p. 53) argued that such tests may create 'unwarranted pressure', 'lead to invalid consequences', and even raise 'ethical issues regarding children's right to learn in an appropriate manner'. Findings have revealed that under-achieving adolescent test takers are more likely to become 'overwhelmed by assessments and demotivated by constant evidence of their low achievement thus further increasing the gap' (Harlen and Deakin Crick 2003, p. 196).

With regard to young learners, Haggerty and Fox (2015) drew on the theoretical model of the L2 Motivational Self System (Dörnyei and Ushioda 2009) to explore the complex relationship between assessment practices and the motivation to learn English as a FL among young adolescents (12–15 years old) in South Korea, where there is a strong tradition of an exam-oriented learning. They found that the participants' L2 motivation is significantly associated with the amount of time spent in L2 test preparation. Less motivated students were found to have spent less time, confirming the role of language assessment in mediating young learners' L2 motivation. The issue deserves further investigation, particularly in test-intensive educational contexts, to further our understanding of influences of assessment on young learners' L2 motivation.

In sum, multiple external factors can impact young learners' dynamic motivation to learn English as an L2 or FL. More research is needed to explore how exactly each factor mediates motivation, how these factors interact with one another and whether the mediation of these factors changes as young learners grow older in specific contexts.

Current contributions and research

Recent research has highlighted the dynamic nature of L2 motivation, especially temporal variations (e.g., Dörnyei 2001; Dörnyei and Ushioda 2009, 2011; Kim 2012a). Dörnyei and Ushioda (2011, p. 6) stated that 'motivation does not remain constant during the course of months, years or even during a single lesson. It ebbs and flows in complex ways in response to various internal and external influences'. In other words, the temporal dimension also constitutes an important aspect of L2 motivation of young learners (Dörnyei 2000). Empirical research has shown the complex and non-static nature of young learners' motivation.

One important pattern of shifts in L2 motivation is that student motivation has been found to be decreasing over school grades (e.g., Carreira 2006, 2011, 2012; Enever 2009, 2014; Kim 2011, 2012a, 2012b). Carreira (2006) looked at young learners' (eight- to 11-year-olds) motivation for English language learning and found students' motivation decreased with age and intrinsic motivation of third graders was significantly higher than their sixth-grade counterparts (also see Carreira 2011 on young learners in Japan). When reviewing literature of developmental trajectories of children's motivation, she argued that the 'developmental decline for motivation for language learning [and learning in general] may be a common phenomenon among school students, despite the contextual differences' (Carreira 2011, p. 92). Some other studies (e.g., Kim 2012a), however, have suggested that the change of motivation can be more complex and nonlinear. Kim (2012a) found that Korean students' L2 learning motivation changed following a curvilinear pattern, with a continuous decrease from the third through the ninth grade and an increase from the 10th to 12th grade.

A follow-up question that interests researchers is the underlying reasons for the high and low points of motivation during their school years. From the perspective of SDT, the decrease of intrinsic motivation can be attributed to the 'inappropriate and/or cognitively undemanding instructional practices' (Carreira 2011, p. 97). Children begin to strive for increased autonomy and personal growth as they grow up, but schools focus on discipline and usually provide few opportunities for decision making (Lepper and Henderlong 2000). In addition, if children have limited access to English (in Carreira 2011, children only attend one English class per week), they may not develop the feeling of competence in English language learning, which can be translated into lack of motivation. As mentioned earlier, parental influences seem to be another main factor mediating children's L2 motivation (e.g., Kim 2012b). Kim's (2012b) qualitative interviews have revealed that parents might exert negative impacts on their children's L2 selves if they fail to provide timely advice and support. In addition, teachers can also play an important role in mediating young learners' L2 motivation. Some research on adolescents has indicated that teacher-related factors might be the most detrimental factor that demotivates students' L2 learning, especially for high school students (Hamada 2011; Kikuchi 2009). Further research on the reasons and processes underlying young learners' L2 motivation can enrich the current understanding of the dynamic nature of motivation.

Recommendations for practice

So far, we have reviewed three popular theoretical perspectives on motivation research and the relevant constructs, factors mediating motivation as well as the dynamic developmental trajectories of young learners' L2 motivation. Relevant research has provided rich insights for researchers, practitioners and parents, especially in terms of the decline of intrinsic motivation as children grow older, and the roles parents, teachers and the teaching and learning environment play in shaping young learners' motivation.

Given parents' involvement, particularly positive beliefs about L2 learning and their actions to regulate children's L2 learning, it is necessary for L2 teachers to closely work together with parents so that they can synergise efforts to foster positive attitudes towards L2 learning among children and enhance their motivation (e.g., Bakker et al. 2007; Gao 2012). Since differences in SES of children result in creating considerable gaps between young learners from different socioeconomic groups, education policy makers should take this phenomenon into consideration and take steps to improve the unequal access to L2 learning resources of high SES- and low SES-young learners (e.g., Butler 2015b). It is likely that low SES children can become more aware of the communicative value of English when provided with more opportunities to interact with English-speaking communities. Encouraging the use of online resources that are free or low-cost in formal English teaching and learning programmes for young learners can have great potential to serve this purpose.

Furthermore, teachers and curriculum developers should be aware that fine-tuning and adjustment of instruction and assessments can help to maintain or improve children's L2 motivation. Classroom activities catering to young learners should be able to develop a sense of competence and relatedness with significant others, and would probably work best if implemented in a form that attracts elementary school students, such as using technology and multimodality. In addition, since young learners' L2 motivation is changing and is subject to multiple external factors, teacher training programmes should explicitly inform teachers about the particularity of young learners and the possible strategies that can help enhance or maintain motivation. In-service teachers facing young L2 learners should also be encouraged to reflect on their students' motivation, beliefs and performance, in order to help them adapt teaching practices accordingly.

Future research directions

This chapter has reviewed the current research on young learners' motivation to learn English as an L2 or FL. We have highlighted theoretical perspectives and constructs widely used in this area of inquiry, the dynamic developmental trajectories of young language learners' motivation, and factors mediating motivation.

Reflecting on the landscape of research on young learners' L2 motivation, we would like to suggest some directions for future research. There might not be any single framework (e.g., SDT) that can account for the complexity of young learners' L2 motivation; therefore, more research taking different theoretical perspectives should be conducted to develop theories of L2 motivation to specifically address young L2 learners. Moreover, while drawing constructs from different perspectives can benefit our understanding of the phenomenon, researchers should make efforts to enhance the conceptual clarity of constructs and terminologies used in their own studies, so as to allow for synthesis or meta-analysis across studies in the future.

Another direction is to continue exploring the dynamic nature of young learners' L2 motivation to understand the developmental trend of intrinsic and extrinsic motivation and how they interact, as well as what factors (in addition to what have been reviewed here) mediate children's L2 motivation and how. Among the factors that were found to mediate young learners' motivation, parental involvement is the most frequently examined. Since most research into parents' influences on L2 motivation has been conducted in East Asia, where parents tend to impose controls over their children's learning, there is far more to explore in other parts of the world with different cultural heritages, especially where parents usually give their children more autonomy (see Okagaki and Frensch 1998). It would also be enlightening to explore L2 motivation of children in East Asia who have received greater autonomy from their parents, i.e., those who were raised less traditionally with the parents as facilitators and friends as opposed to authoritative standard-makers. Our current knowledge about young language learners' language learning motivation would be enriched if more investigations were conducted in diverse sociocultural and socioeconomical contexts. The socioeconomic status (SES) of young learners' parents needs to be further examined in young language learners' motivation research (e.g., Butler 2015b; Gao 2012; Zou and Zhang 2011). It would also be particularly interesting to expand the research on how assessment practices, as well as the innovation of assessments, impact young learners' L2 motivation. In terms of research methods, given that a number of cross-segmental studies have employed questionnaires as a major instrument to look into young learners' L2 motivation, more contextual, qualitative data are needed to complement the quantitative results and to provide in-depth insights into young learners' motivation. For instance, young language learners may be encouraged to use drawings to express their feelings and represent their language learning experiences if they are not able to articulate them through words (İnözü 2018). Their motivations also can be examined through Elicited Metaphor Analysis (EMA), in which 'commonplace metaphorical expressions' such as 'driving' and 'running' were analyzed to identify young language learners' 'conceptual representations of deeper thoughts' with regard to learning English (Jin et al. 2014, p. 289). The EMA approach can be effectively implemented to gather data on young learners' perceptions 'using cards, picture stories, games, drawings, which would be otherwise difficult to obtain" (ibid.). Besser and Chik (2014) have also used a photo-elicitation method, through which young learners took pictures of English learning opportunities and then described them in narratives, to understand young language learners' identity construction in the learning process. Longitudinal research needs to be undertaken to capture the shifting language learning motivations of young language learners over the years. Replication studies can also be conducted to check the generalisability or transferability of previous results to young learners in other sociocultural contexts.

Further readings

1 Boo, Z., Dörnyei, Z., and Ryan, S. (2015). L2 motivation research 2005–2014: Understanding a publication surge and a changing landscape. *System*, 55, 145–157.
    This article surveys the origins and surge of interest in language learning motivation research. It presents an overview of theoretical and methodological trends in relevant research over a decade.

2 Butler, Y. G. (2015). English language education among young learners in East Asia: A review of current research (2004–2014). *Language Teaching*, 48, 303–342.

   This article reviews studies on teaching English to young learners in East Asian contexts including the Chinese mainland, Japan, South Korea and Taiwan with foci on major policy-related discussions and relevant empirical studies of English learning and teaching.

3 Copland, F., Garton, S., and Burns, A. (2014). Challenges in teaching English to young learners: Global perspectives and local realities. *TESOL Quarterly*, 48, 738–762.

   This article reports on the challenges that those teaching English to young learners have to cope with in five different countries. Motivation emerged as one of the most significant challenges faced by these teachers in different contexts.

4 Pinter, A. (2017). *Teaching young language learners*, 2nd ed. Oxford: Oxford University Press.

   This is a comprehensive guide for those teaching language to young learners, covering topics such as assessment, child development, Content language integrated learning (CLIL), intercultural awareness and material development. It has a nice balance of updated research and innovative pedagogical practice.

5 Dörnyei, Z., and Ushioda, E. (2011). *Teaching and researching motivation*, 2nd ed. Harlow: Pearson Education.

   This fully revised edition provides a highly accessible and comprehensive account of motivation research. It offers suggestions on how theoretical insights could be integrated into classroom practices.

Related topics

Assessment, gaming, the age debate, difficult circumstances

References

Anderman, E. M., Maehr, M. L., and Midgley, C. (1999). Declining motivation after the transition to middle school: Schools can make a difference. *Journal of Research and Development in Education*, 32, 131–147.

Bakker, J., Denessen, E., and Brus-Laeven, M. (2007). Socio-economic background, parental involvement and teacher perceptions of these in relation to pupil achievement. *Educational Studies*, 33, 177–192.

Besser, S., and Chik, A. (2014). Narratives of second language identity amongst young English learners in Hong Kong. *ELT Journal*, 68, 299–309.

Black, P., and William, D. (1998). Assessment and classroom learning. *Assessment in Education*, 5, 7–74.

Bong, M., Hwang, A., Noh, A., and Kim, S.-I. (2014). Perfectionism and motivation of adolescents in academic contexts. *Journal of Educational Psychology*, 106, 711–729.

Boo, Z., Dörnyei, Z., and Ryan, S. (2015). L2 motivation research 2005–2014: Understanding a publication surge and a changing landscape. *System*, 55, 145–157.

Butler, Y. G. (2015a). English language education among young learners in East Asia: A review of current research (2004–2014). *Language Teaching*, 48, 303–342.

Butler, Y. G. (2015b). Parental factors in children's motivation for learning English: A case in China. *Research Papers in Education*, 30, 164–191.

Carhill, A., Suarez-Orozco, C., and Paez, M. (2008). Explaining English language proficiency among adolescent immigrant students. *American Educational Research Journal*, 45, 1155–1179.

Carreira, J. M. (2006). Motivation for learning English as a foreign language in Japanese elementary schools. *JALT Journal*, 28, 135–158.

Carreira, J. M. (2011). Relationship between motivation for learning EFL and intrinsic motivation for learning in general among Japanese elementary school students. *System*, 39, 90–102.

Carreira, J. M. (2012). Motivational orientations and psychological needs in EFL learning among elementary school students in Japan. *System*, 40, 191–202.

Cheung, C. S., and Pomerantz, E. M. (2012). Why does parents involvement enhance children's achievement? The role of parent-oriented motivation. *Journal of Educational Psychology*, 104, 820–832.

Choi, I. (2008). The impact of EFL testing on EFL education in Korea. *Language Testing*, 25, 39–62.

Copland, F., Garton, S., and Burns, A. (2014). Challenges in teaching English to young learners: Global perspectives and local realities. *TESOL Quarterly*, 48, 738–762.

Corpus, J. H., McClintic-Gilbert, M. S., and Hayenga, A. O. (2009). Within-year changes in children's intrinsic and extrinsic motivational orientations: Contextual predictors and academic outcomes. *Contemporary Educational Psychology*, 34, 154–166.

Csizér, K., and Dörnyei, Z. (2005). The internal structure of learning motivation and its relationship with language choice and learning effort. *The Modern Language Journal*, 89, 19–36.

Deci, E. L., and Ryan, R. M. (1985). *Intrinsic Motivation and Self-determination in Human Behavior*. New York: Plenum.

Donitsa-Schmidt, S., Inbar, O., and Shohamy, E. (2004). The effects of teaching spoken Arabic on students' attitudes and motivation in Israel. *The Modern Language Journal*, 88, 217–228.

Dörnyei, Z. (1996). Moving language learning motivation to a larger platform for theory and practice. In Oxford, R. L. (ed.) *Language Learning Motivation: Pathways to the new century* (Vol. Tech. Rep. No 11). Honolulu, HI: University of Hawaii Press, 71–80.

Dörnyei, Z. (1998). Demotivation in foreign language learning. Paper presented at the TESOL '98 Congress, Seattle, WA.

Dörnyei, Z. (2000). Motivation in action: Towards a process-oriented conceptualization of student motivation. *British Journal of Educational Psychology*, 70, 519–538.

Dörnyei, Z. (2001). *Teaching and Researching Motivation*. New York: Longman.

Dörnyei, Z. (2005). *The Psychology of the Language Learner: Individual differences in Second Language Acquisition*. Mahwah, NJ: Lawrence Erlbaum.

Dörnyei, Z. (2009). The L2 motivational self system. In Dörnyei, Z., and Ushioda, E. (eds.) *Motivation, Language, Identity and the L2 Self*. Bristol: Multilingual Matters, 9–42.

Dörnyei, Z., and Ryan, S. (2015). *The Psychology of the Language Learner Revisited*. New York: Routledge.

Dörnyei, Z., and Ushioda, E. (2009). *Motivation, Language, Identity and the L2 Self*. Bristol: Multilingual Matters.

Dörnyei, Z., and Ushioda, E. (2011). *Teaching and Researching Motivation*, 2nd ed. Harlow: Pearson Education.

Enever, J. (2009). The status of the target language: Contemporary criteria influencing language choices for early learners in England. In Nikolov, M. (ed.) *Contextualizing the Age Factor: Issues in Early Foreign Language Learning*. Berlin: Mouton de Gruyter, 377–402.

Enever, J. (2014). What can we expect of an early start to foreign language learning in Europe today? Conference proceedings, A Korai Idegennyelvi Feijlesztés Elmélete és Gyakorlata (Early language development theory and practice). In Márkus, E., and Trentinné Benkö, E. (eds.). www.researchgate.net/profile/Janet_Enever/publications.

Feng, A. (2012). Spread of English across greater China. *Journal of Multilingual and Multicultural Development*, 33, 363–377.

Fernald, A., Marchman, V. A., and Weisleder, A. (2013). SES differences in language processing skill and vocabulary are evident at 18 months. *Developmental Science*, 16, 234–248.

Gao, X. (2012). Parental strategies in supporting Chinese children's learning of English vocabulary. *Research Papers in Education*, 27, 581–595.

Gardner, R. C. (1985). *Social Psychology and Second Language Learning: The role of attitudes and motivation*. London: Edward Arnold.

Gardner, R. C., and Lambert, W. (1972). *Attitudes and Motivation in Second Language Learning*. Rowley, MA: Newbury House.

Gardner, R. C., Masgoret, A. M., and Tremblay, P. F. (1999). Home background characteristics and second language learning. *Journal of Language and Social Psychology*, 18, 419–437.

Garton, S. (2014). Unresolved issues and new challenges in teaching English to young learners: The case of South Korea. *Current Issues in Language Planning*, 15, 201–219.

Gonzalez-DeHass, A. R., Willems, P. P., and Holbein, M. F. D. (2005). Examining the relationship between parental involvement and student motivation. *Educational Psychological Review*, 17, 99–123.

Grolnick, W. S., Friendly, R. W., and Bellas, V. M. (2009). Parenting and children's motivation at school. In Wenzel, K. R., and Wigfield, A. (eds.) *Handbook of Motivation at School*. New York: Routledge/ Taylor & Francis, 279–300.

Haggerty, J. F., and Fox, J. (2015). Raising the bar: Language testing experience and second language motivation among South Korean young adolescents. *Language Testing in Asia*, 5, 1–16.

Hamada, Y. (2011). Different demotivators for Japanese junior high and high school learners. *Pan-Pacific Association of Applied Linguistics*, 15, 15–38.

Harlen, W., and Deakin Crick, R. (2003). Testing and motivation for learning. *Assessment in Education*, 10, 169–207.

Hu, G. (2009). The craze for English-medium education in China: Driving forces and looming consequences. *English Today*, 25, 47–54.

Huang, K.-M. (2011). Motivating lessons: A classroom-oriented investigation of the effects of content-based instruction on EFL young learners' motivational behaviours and classroom verbal interaction. *System*, 39, 186–201.

İnözü, J. (2018). Drawings are talking: Exploring language learners' beliefs through visual narratives. *Applied Linguistics Review*, 9, 177-200

Iwaniec, J. (2014). Motivation of pupils from southern Poland to learn English. *System*, 45, 67–78.

Jin, L., Liang, X., Jiang, C., Zhang, J., Yuan, Y., and Xie, Q. (2014). Studying the motivations of Chinese young EFL learners through metaphor analysis. *ELT Journal*, 68, 286–298.

Johnstone, R. (2009). An early start: What are the key conditions for generalized success? In Enever, J., Moon, J., and Raman, U. (eds.) *Young Learner English Language Policy and Implementation: International perspectives*. Reading: Garnet Education, 31–41.

Kikuchi, K. (2009). Listening to our learners' voice: What demotivates Japanese high school students? *Language Teaching Research*, 13, 453–471.

Kim, T.-Y. (2011). 'Korean elementary school students' English learning demotivation: A comparative survey study. *Asia Pacific Education Review*, 12, 1–11.

Kim, T.-Y. (2012a). An analysis of Korean elementary and secondary school students' English learning motivation and their L2 selves: Qualitative interview approach. *Korean Journal of English Language and Linguistics*, 12, 67–99.

Kim, T.-Y. (2012b). The L2 motivational self system of Korean EFL students: Cross-grade survey analysis. *English Teaching*, 67, 29–56.

Kim, T.-Y., and Seo, H.-S. (2012). Elementary school students' foreign language learning demotivation: A mixed method study of Korean EFL context. *The Asia-Pacific Education Researcher*, 21, 160–171.

Kissau, S., Adams, M. J., and Algozzine, B. (2015). Middle school foreign language instruction: A missed opportunity. *Foreign Language Annals*, 48, 284–303.

Lamb, M. (2004). Integrative motivation in a globalizing world. *System*, 32, 3–19.

Lamb, M. (2013). "Your mum and dad can't teach you!": Constraints on agency among rural learners of English in Indonesia. *Journal of Multilingual and Multicultural Development*, 34, 14–29.

Lepper, M. R., Corpus, J. H., and Iyengar, S. S. (2005). Intrinsic and extrinsic motivational orientations in the classroom: Age differences and academic correlates. *Journal of Educational Psychology*, 97, 184–196.

Lepper, M. R., and Henderlong, J. (2000). Turning "play" into "work" and "work" into "play": 25 years of research on intrinsic versus extrinsic motivation. In Sansone, C., and Harackiewicz, J. M. (eds.) *Intrinsic and Extrinsic Motivation: The Search for Optimal Motivation and Performance*. San Diego, CA: Academic Press, 257–307.

Mady, C. J. (2010). Motivation to study core French: Comparing recent immigrants and Canadian-born secondary school students. *Canadian Journal of Education*, 33, 564–587.

Nikolov, M. (1999). "Why do you learn English?" "Because the teacher is short." A study of Hungarian children's foreign language learning motivation. *Language Teaching Research*, 3, 33–56.

Noels, K. A., Clément, R., and Pelletier, L. G. (1999). Perceptions of teacher communicative style and students' intrinsic and extrinsic motivation. *The Modern Language Journal*, 83, 23–34.

Noels, K. A., Pelletier, L. G., Clément, R., and Vallerand, R. J. (2000). Why are you learning a second language? Motivational orientations and self-determination theory. *Language Learning*, 50, 57–85.

Norton, B., and Toohey, K. (2001). Changing perspectives on good language learners. *TESOL Quarterly*, 35, 307–321.

Okagaki, L., and Frensch, P. A. (1998). Parenting and children's school achievement: A multiethnic perspective. *American Educational Research Journal*, 35, 123–144.

Otis, N., Grouzet, F., and Pelletier, L. G. (2005). Latent motivational change in an academic setting: A 3-year longitudinal study. *Journal of Educational Psychology*, 97, 170–183.

Palfreyman, D. (2006). Social context and resources for language learning. *System*, 34, 352–370.

Park, Y. S., and Kim, U. (2006). Family, parent-child relationship, and academic achievement in Korea: Indigenous, cultural, and psychological analysis. In Kim, U., Yang, K., and Hwang, K. (eds.) *Indigenous and Cultural Psychology: Understanding people in context*. New York, NY: Springer Science + Business Media, 421–443.

Pinter, A. (2017). *Teaching Young Language Learners*, 2nd ed. Oxford: Oxford University Press.

Pomerantz, E. M., and Moorman, E. A. (2010). Parents' involvement in children's schooling: A context for children's development. In Meece, J. L., and Eccles, J. (eds.) *Handbook of Research on Schools, Schooling, and Human Development*. Hillsdale, NJ: Erlbaum, 398–416.

Qi, L. (2007). Is testing an efficient agent for pedagogical change? Examining the intended washback of the writing task in a high-stakes English test in China. *Assessment in Education*, 14, 51–74.

Ross, S. (2008). Language testing in Asia: Evolution, innovation and policy challenges. *Language Testing*, 25, 5–13.

Ryan, R. M., and Deci, E. L. (2000). Intrinsic and extrinsic motivations: Classic definitions and new directions. *Contemporary Educational Psychology*, 25, 54–67.

Sakai, H., and Kikuchi, K. (2009). An analysis of demotivators in the EFL classroom. *System*, 37, 57–69.

Stobart, G., and Eggen, T. (2012). High-stakes testing – Value, fairness and consequences. *Assessment in Education*, 19, 1–6.

Sundqvist, P., and Sylvén, L. K. (2014). Language-related computer use: Focus on young L2 English learners in Sweden. *European Association for Computer Assisted Language Learning*, 26, 3–20.

Sung, H., and Padilla, A. M. (1998). Student motivation, parental attitudes, and involvement in the learning of Asian languages in elementary and secondary schools. *The Modern Language Journal*, 82, 205–216.

Ushioda, E. (1998). Effective motivational thinking: A cognitive theoretical approach to the study of language learning motivation. In Soler, E. A., and Espurz, V. C. (eds.) *Current Issues in English Language Methodology*. Spain: Universitat Jaume I, Castello de la Plana, 77–89.

Wu, X. (2003). Intrinsic motivation and young language learners: The impact of the classroom environment. *System*, 31, 501–517.

You, C. J., and Dörnyei, Z. (2016). Language learning motivation in China: Results of a large-scale stratified survey. *Applied Linguistics*, 37, 495–519.

Zhang, Q.-M., and Kim, T.-Y. (2013). Cross-grade analysis of Chinese students' English learning motivation: A mixed-methods study. *Asia Pacific Education Review*, 14, 615–627.

Zou, W. C., and Zhang, S. L. (2011). Family background and English learning at compulsory stage in Shanghai. In Feng, A. (ed.) *English Language Education Across Greater China*. Bristol: Multilingual Matters, 189–211.

Zuengler, J., and Miller, L. (2006). Cognitive and sociocultural perspectives: Two parallel SLA worlds. *TESOL Quarterly*, 40, 35–58.

5

Teaching English to young learners in difficult circumstances

Kuchah Kuchah

Introduction

There is a vast amount of EYL literature which promotes creative, interactive and fun ways of teaching English to young learners (e.g., Moon 2005; Read 2007; Superfine and James 2017) and which discusses the psychological, educational, sociocultural, methodological and ethical as well as pedagogical intricacies of EYL more broadly (e.g., Cameron 2001; Bland 2015; Pinter 2011), but very little, if any, specifically examines the conditions under which the growing numbers of young learners, especially in the developing world, are made to learn English. A number of studies from different contexts around the world (e.g., Butler 2007; Carless 2003; 2004; Kirkgoz 2008; Kuchah 2018a; Nguyen 2011; Nguyen et al. 2016) have specifically examined the disconnections between EYL policy and practice; others (e.g., Kumaravadivelu 2001; 2011; Rubdy 2008; Smith 2011) have called for contextually appropriate forms of ELT pedagogy to be developed, particularly in mainstream formal education institutions in developing countries. Both groups of studies argue that the dominant discourse of ELT methodology, as promoted by local MoE policy makers around the world, has been largely generated in ideal (North) contexts, so it does not reflect the challenging realities of the majority of language teaching and learning contexts in which they are being imposed. What is more, they suggest that the paucity of research *from* Southern contexts means that the predominantly Northern-derived discourse around English language learning and teaching continues to see developing world contexts as inherently problematic, deficient and incapable of generating innovative and effective language teaching principles. In this chapter, I examine the key factors that have contributed to creating difficult environments and conditions for young learner English language education, particularly in developing world contexts where policy decisions such as the lowering age for exposure to English language education (Cameron 2003) and, in some cases, English-medium instruction (Dearden 2014) has meant that more and more children are experiencing formal education in a language different from their home languages and in learning environments that do not meet the minimum conditions for effective language learning (Kuchah 2016a). Then I critically examine the literature on the different contextual challenges faced by EYL practitioners, particularly in contexts with limited exposure to English language outside the classroom, contexts of conflict and forced migration, and in large, multigrade and under-resourced classes amongst others. The chapter also examines different pedagogic approaches as well as teacher education and research possibilities that are embedded in these realities and argues that EYL in these circumstances could benefit from a more sustained dialogue between all key stakeholders including, more importantly, from the development of student and teacher agency.

Historical perspectives

Language teachers around the world work under a variety of conditions and deal with a range of challenges in their day-to-day practices which make a definition of *difficult circumstances* elusive or at best, relative; for example, the circumstances which one teacher might consider challenging may actually constitute a favourable condition for another teacher within the same, or in another, context (Kuchah 2016a). The first known reference to *difficult circumstances* was made by Michael West (1960) in his book *Teaching English in Difficult Circumstances* in which he drew attention to challenges encountered by teachers teaching English language in classrooms:

> 'consisting of over 30 pupils (more usually 40 or even 50), congested on benches . . . accommodated in an unsuitably shaped room, ill-graded, with a teacher who perhaps does not speak English very well or very fluently, working in a hot climate'.
>
> *(West 1960, p. 1)*

15 years later, Nation (1975) echoed West's concerns about the challenging circumstances under which English language was being taught in many parts of the world, explaining that in many countries 'there are economic restrictions that do not allow each student to have a textbook. Classes are large (50 or more learners), absenteeism is high, and there is a wide range of proficiency and ability in one class'. (p. 21). Following these two authors – and with the exception of research initiatives such as the Lancaster-Leeds Language Learning in Large Classes Research Project coordinated by Allwright and Coleman in the 1980s – it was not until the dawn of this twenty-first century that interest in English language teaching in difficult circumstances started to gain grounds in the mainstream literature, notably, it may be suggested, because of the focus on the importance of context in language education (Bax 2003; Holliday 1994; Kumaravadivelu 2001). Maley (2001) suggested that there were equally out-of-school factors affecting language education in developing world countries. He extended the concept of difficult circumstances by describing classrooms of 60 students who had to walk a distance of at least five miles after doing their morning chores and who were crammed in a dirty classroom meant for 30 students in temperatures of 40 degrees Celsius. These students were taught by a poorly paid teacher with rudimentary competence in English language. The textbook represents characters from an unfamiliar luxurious culture; the classroom blackboard is pitted and grey and sometimes there is no chalk.

More recent studies have also highlighted the challenges of teaching children living in dysfunctional societies (e.g., Lovitt 2010) and in contexts of conflict and crisis (Alyasin 2018; Okpe 2016; Phyak 2015). In Brazil, for example, Ball (2018) reports the specific challenges of teaching children who have 'difficult home lives with fragmented family relationships and responsibilities beyond what is normally expected of children of their age'. A significant number of researchers and professionals (e.g., Alyasin 2018; Bertoncino, Murph, and Wang 2002; Copland et al. 2014; Kuchah and Smith 2011; Kuchah 2016a; Kuchah and Shamim 2018; Phyak 2015; UIS 2016; Verspoor 2008) have highlighted the range of challenges affecting both the quality of education more broadly and English language education in particular. The work of these authors point to the fact that the notion of difficult circumstances in language education has become more complex; in fact the concept now seems to include not only micro (i.e., within the language classroom and school) and meso (i.e., within local communities) level constraints affecting teaching and learning, but equally encompasses macro level factors which have a direct or indirect impact on what happens at the micro and meso levels. These include broader policy issues that might affect English language teaching and learning in mainstream as well as non-mainstream educational settings in low-to-mid-income countries (Kuchah 2018a).

Despite the recognition of the existence of contextual challenges which negatively impact language education in developing world countries, there are emerging voices (e.g., Ekembe 2016; Smith 2015) against the conceptualisation of certain contexts as difficult. These scholars argue that the early conceptualisations of *difficult circumstances* were mainly Western/British scholars' perceptions of developing world country contexts (see, e.g., Lamb 2002; Maley 2001; Rogers 1982; West 1960) rather than the perceptions of practitioners from within these contexts. They hold the view that labelling learning contexts as 'difficult' is not only patronizing, but also limits ELT professionals to pathologizing these contexts when indeed ELT could benefit more from acknowledging the diverse range of learning conditions and the pedagogical expertise of teachers in such contexts (Smith 2015). Ekembe (2016) suggests that the conceptualisation of some ELT contexts as 'difficult' is often guided by western conceptions of what is believed to be 'standard' rather than what may be considered adequate and sufficient by stakeholders within the specific context. This notwithstanding, there is growing evidence from practitioners in such contexts that even insiders (see, e.g., Khadka 2015; Kuchah and Smith 2011; Kuchah 2016a; Shamim et al. 2007; UNESCO 1997) perceive their circumstances as difficult although the nature and extent of these difficulties might be different from those which an outsider to the context perceives. The following two excerpts from teachers in Rwanda and Brazil, respectively, illustrate some of the challenges that teachers encounter in their daily work:

> Picking up the pieces is no easy job and when it comes to teaching it is next to impossible [. . .] How can you expect children who have lost their relations to share a classroom peacefully with pupils whose parents took part in the genocide and in some cases actually killed their families? . . . School buildings are in a deplorable state . . . The pupils sit on wooden planks and find it hard to pay attention all day, having walked miles to school. There are no school canteens so most teachers and pupils go without lunch . . . . Another difficulty is shortage of teaching materials; handbooks and textbooks are virtually inexistent. In Grade 6, I have one reader for eight pupils and a French and maths textbook.
>
> *(Thea Uwimbabazi, cited in UNESCO 1997, pp. 4–5)*

> Hunger is a terrible problem here. . . . In a classroom I once found a small boy banging his head repeatedly against the wooden partition. He had also been kicking his classmates. Later, I found out that he hadn't eaten for two days. Aggression is quite common, but it always has a reason. In some extreme cases, mothers give their hungry children drugs to help them sleep at night.
>
> *(Vera Lazzarotto, cited in UNESCO 1997, p. 21)*

Such accounts from practitioners in the field suggest that there are indeed circumstances outside the control of teachers and learners which affect their daily experiences of teaching and learning in significant ways (Kuchah 2016a). These circumstances exist in a large number of contexts in which ELT takes place and as such require greater attention.

Maley (2001) and Smith (2011) argue that the field of ELT has long been dominated by ideas from otherwise privileged Northern contexts, and it is these ideas that were being promoted around the world, sometimes with little or no consideration of the sociopolitical, economic and cultural realities of the contexts in which they were being applied. Drawing attention to such realities is by no means conveying a deficiency in them per se; rather it helps language professionals to reflect more on the issues that affect language education in developing world contexts and to better appreciate and disseminate the resilience and creativity of practitioners in such contexts.

Critical issues

Various factors account for the less-than-ideal circumstances within which young learners experience English language education, particularly in developing world contexts. These can broadly be categorised under three main areas: the promotion and implementation of the *Education for All policy* with its impact on enrolments, resources and the quality of learning, especially at primary school levels in under-privileged and conflict-affected contexts; the phenomenal spread of English language around the globe and its increasing inclusion in primary curricula; and the promotion of communicative and interactive approaches to language teaching (cf. Shamim and Kuchah 2016). In what follows, I examine these factors and show the extent to which they have made teaching and learning circumstances difficult.

The Education for All (EFA) and related challenges

The world conference on Education in Jomtien, Thailand (UNESCO 1990) and the World Education Forum in Dakar, Senegal (UNESCO 2000) led to significant policy decisions that would shape the landscape and quality of education in developing world countries at the dawn of the new millennium. The Jomtien conference came more than 40 years after the declaration of human rights, including the right to basic education. Yet, it was noted that more than 100 million children still did not have access to primary schooling. The Dakar framework for action therefore set 6 key goals for achieving free and quality basic education for all by 2015. One of these goals required countries to ensure

> that by 2015 all children, particularly girls, children in difficult circumstances and those belonging to ethnic minorities, have access to and complete free and compulsory primary education of good quality [emphasising that] all states must fulfil their obligation to offer free and compulsory primary education in accordance with the United Nations Convention on the Rights of the Child and other international commitments.
>
> *(UNESCO 2000, p. 15)*

The implementation of free and compulsory basic education in many developing world countries has led to an exponential growth in the number of children attending primary school without a concomitant increase in human, material and financial resources. A large number of studies in sub-Saharan Africa (e.g., Ampiah 2008; Muthwii 2001; Nakabugo 2008; O'Sullivan 2006; Sawamura and Sifuna 2008; Tembe 2006) have revealed that the implementation of the EFA policy has exacerbated existing challenges such as overcrowded classrooms, lack of textbooks, lack of libraries, low teacher proficiency, qualifications and motivation, and students' limited exposure to English language usage. Underlying these challenges is the lack of financial resources; in fact governments in developing countries are increasingly finding it difficult to cope with the growing numbers of children in state schools. UIS (2016) figures reveal that the total expenditure per student of 10 sub-Saharan African countries in 2014 amounted to only about 25% of what the UK alone spent per student in the same year.

Class size has continued to constitute a major topic in the literature on difficult circumstances, particularly in sub-Saharan Africa. UIS (2016) data from 15 African countries, 10 of which include multigrade classes, showed that the average class size exceeds 70 pupils per class in Malawi, the Central African Republic and Tanzania. What is more, these official numbers are based on official figures which often give a seriously distorted under-representation of the reality of class size. For example, although the pupil-teacher ratio for primary schools in Cameroon was 46:1 in 2012 (UIS 2016), Kuchah (2013) found that class sizes actually ranged from 87 pupils to 124 in the four schools in which his study was conducted. More recently, Coleman (2018) compares official figures on classroom enrolments in Malaysia, eastern Indonesia and countries in Francophone West Africa with actual figures from classroom observations and reveals significant discrepancies between official figures and classroom realities which tend to conceal the true extent of teaching challenges. Coleman concludes that these additional difficult circumstances (undeclared numbers of students in classrooms) need to be systematically and consistently brought to the attention of stakeholders and education authorities so that they can be more explicitly addressed.

Over the last two decades, escalating conflicts and natural disasters have forced millions of people to flee their homes into refugee camps within or even out of their countries (IDMC 2015; Phyak 2015; Okpe 2016). Reports (e.g., by Nicolai et al. 2016; Save the Children 2015; Ekereke 2013) reveal that up to 300 million children are out of school or learning in displacement camps in circumstances that are far removed from traditional conceptualisations of schooling. These circumstances have been described as 'super-difficult circumstances' (Phyak 2015) and 'expanding circles of difficulty' (Kuchah 2018a). Okpe (2016), Alyasin (2018) and Phyak (2015) explain that such circumstances impose on teachers psycho-affective challenges leading to the development of pedagogical practices that are not often discussed in the mainstream EYL literature (e.g., Cameron 2001; Bland 2015; Pinter 2011). At the World Education Forum in Dakar conflict was also acknowledged as a challenge to the achievement of Education for All (UNESCO 2000), leading to the Dakar Framework for Action in which governments and agencies agreed to enable education in such contexts of conflict.

The global spread of English language and the primary school curriculum

The global spread of English language (Graddol 2006) has had a significant impact on language education policies and practices (Nunan 2003). One such policy is the lowering age at which children are taught English language in school (Cameron 2003). Johnstone (2009) describes the introduction of English as a foreign/second language in the primary school system as one of the most significant policy developments in recent years. In this regard, a number of studies (e.g., Copland et al. 2014; Nguyen 2011; Nunan 2003) have examined the policy rhetoric and actual classroom practices and have pointed to disconnections between them. Other studies (e.g., Kouega 2003; Escudero, Reyes Cruz, and Loyo 2012; Nguyen et al. 2016) have examined a variety of challenges faced by teachers and learners in developing world contexts and have raised concerns for language policy, planning and practice. A second policy has been the growing inclusion of English as a medium of instruction in primary schools. Dearden (2014) provides evidence that 52.7% of public primary schools from a survey of 55 countries are increasingly adapting EMI without proper assessment and understanding of the difficulties involved in teaching and learning in a language that both teachers and students do not master (Williams 2011). A major driving force behind these policies, it has been suggested, is the assumed relationship between proficiency in English and socioeconomic development of a country (Dearden 2014; Pinon and Haydon 2010). There is a worldwide perception that an early exposure to English language education, even in state schools, leads to an increase in the human capital on which future national economic development and political power depends (Wedell 2011). In fact, in many countries in sub-Saharan Africa, Asia and South America, English language education is a political imperative regardless of the inadequacy in provision (Baldauf et al. 2011; Forero Rocha 2005; Inostroza Araos 2015; Valenzuela et al. 2013; Williams 2011). Policy decisions have not sufficiently been informed by research with the consequence that there has been a lack of appropriate planning to implement them, causing confusion in the minds of teachers who are called upon to implement the policies (Baldauf et al. 2011). In Nepal, for example, Phyak (2018) suggests that the current English language teaching policy which promotes both the monolingual and the earlier-the-better assumptions itself has created difficult circumstances for both teachers and students towards achieving the national curricular goals for teaching English.

In addition to the top-down policy orientation discussed above, there are also bottom-up pressures from parents for English language education. Tembe and Norton (2011) report from Uganda that although parents in both rural and urban settings recognise the value of local languages, they are not necessarily in favour of teaching or using these in schools; instead, they would prefer that their children be exposed to an international language, English, in order to keep pace with the fast-moving world. Studies in Ghana (e.g., Mfum-Mensah 2005) and Nigeria (e.g., Iyamu and Ogiegbaen 2007) show that attitudes towards mother tongue instruction are divided and that parents, rural communities and even teachers see English and EMI as a means to attaining the benefits of the elite and urban communities (see also Kouega 1999; Kuchah 2016b for examples from Cameroon). In India, Pandey (2011) reports on the erection of a temple to the 'Goddess of English' by the socioeconomically marginalised Banka villagers in the northern Indian state of Uttar Pradesh and cites the local Dalit Leader, claiming that

> English [is] the milk of a lioness . . . only those who drink it will roar. . . . With the blessings of Goddess English, Dalit children will not grow to serve landlords or skin dead animals or clean drains or raise pigs and buffaloes. They will grow into adjudicators and become employers and benefactors. Then the roar of the Dalits . . . will be heard by one and all.
>
> *(n.p.)*

The deification of English language in this way shows the extent to which English language has had a pervasive role in shaping the thinking and aspirations of individuals, communities and countries, particularly in the developing world where education provision is already constrained by other practical difficulties which I will discuss below. Suffice it to say that the attribution of such a high status to English language both as subject and as medium of instruction in the early years of formal education raises questions of justice and human rights (Fraser 2013; Dearden 2014; Skutnabb-Kangas 2009; UNESCO 2003), especially when it comes to providing quality and equitable education (Tomasevski 2003; Kuchah 2016b) to children from poorer backgrounds, particularly in multilingual contexts where the language of instruction presents a barrier to parental involvement in education for children whose parents are not educated in the language of their schooling (Gfeller and Robinson 1998; Bamgbose 2014; Williams and Cooke 2002). There is also abundant evidence that in many developing world countries, school dropout is more likely to affect children for whom English is not spoken out of school (Ampiah 2008; Kuchah 2016b; 2018b; Opoku-Amankwa 2009; Pinnock 2009; Sawamura and Sifuna 2008)

The promotion of communicative and interactive approaches and practical challenges

The spread of the English language around the world and its subsequent inclusion in school curricula have been accompanied by policy decisions promoting communicative forms of teaching (Thornbury 2016). Various English language initiatives have taken aim at making English language teaching effective in mainstream educational contexts around the world. These have included the development of new curriculum, new materials, new teacher education curricula and the introduction of English at younger years (Wedell 2011; Cameron 2003). The goal of these initiatives is to shift away from academic approaches that have dominated traditional school teaching, and as a result the teaching approaches being promoted are thought to be those which would help learners develop communication skills. However, as researchers (e.g., Nunan 2003; Padwad and Dixit 2014; Vavrus 2009; Waters and Vilches 2008; Wedell 2011) affirm, these approaches 'tend to be expressed in terms imported from the "western" literature of Communicative Language Teaching (CLT), Task-Based Language Teaching (TBLT), learner- or child-centredness and constructivist approaches to teaching and learning' (Wedell 2011, p. 276). The extent to which teachers in mainstream educational contexts around the world understand or misunderstand such policy recommendations and how these are translated in their classrooms has been a major preoccupation in ELT. Nunan's (2003) study of seven Asian countries (China, Hongkong, Japan, Korea, Malaysia, Taiwan and Vietnam) indicates that although the emergence of English as a global language is having considerable impact on policies and practices in these countries, there are significant problems, amongst other things, in the disjunction between curriculum rhetoric and pedagogical reality. Despite considerable country-by-country variations, data reveal that teacher education and English language skills of teachers in public-sector institutions in these countries are inadequate for the successful implementation of Communicative Language Teaching (CLT) and Task Based Language Teaching (TBLT) to which policy rhetoric subscribes. Nunan's findings are consistent with those of other young learner related studies in Chile (e.g., Inostroza Araos 2015), Mexico (e.g., Izquierdo et al. 2016), Vietnam (e.g., Nguyen and Nguyen 2007; Nguyen 2011), Hong Kong (Carless 2003; 2004), Ghana (e.g., Ampiah 2008), Uganda (e.g., Tembe 2006; Muthwii 2001), Kenya (e.g., Sawamura and Sifuna 2008), Tazania (e.g., Komba and Nkumbi 2008; Vavrus 2009), India (e.g., Padwad and Dixit 2014) and Cameroon (CONAP 2008; Kuchah 2013) which examine teachers' practical responses to policy, recommending communicative and learner-centred approaches to language teaching. The reasons for the discrepancies between official discourse and classroom reality discussed in the studies cited above are varied and range from the failure of policy makers to take into account factors like the existence of structural-based assessment demands, teachers' language proficiency, training levels especially for elementary level teaching and limited understanding of certain policy decisions as well as the existing teacher-dependent classroom cultures amongst others.

Current contributions and research in EYL in difficult circumstances

Following on from the perspectives of researchers who argue against the conceptualisation of certain contexts as 'difficult' or 'under-resourced' (e.g., Ekembe 2016; Smith 2015; Smith et al. 2017) it could be implied that the disconnections between policy and practice as well as the challenges faced by practitioners in developing world countries to implement imported innovative practices might be a result of the slavish adoption of pedagogic recommendations which are not rooted in the specific realities of the contexts within which they are being applied. Ekembe (2016) suggests, for example, that the perceived lack of resources in so-called under-resourced contexts might be a result of the difficulty in applying North-driven or North-derived methodologies in such contexts that are only different and not actually under-resourced per se. Understanding the specific differences within these contexts, therefore, requires locally focused efforts of a more broadly educational than narrowly linguistic nature, rather than the continuous importation of western innovatory methodological ideas which, as we have seen, have little to offer by way of solutions to the challenges of local EYL practitioners (Maley 2001). Capitalising on the experiences of state school teachers and teacher trainers who already have local knowledge about students and the realities of the classroom and local communities (Kumaravadivelu 2001, 2006) might give us insights into the possibilities which these contexts offer for understanding appropriate language pedagogy in context.

In line with these suggestions, current research into ELT in difficult circumstances has moved away significantly from the early 'problems and solutions' approach (Anmpalagan et al. 2012; Sarwar 2001; Shamim et al. 2007; Shamim 2012), which mainly identified isolated challenges (e.g., managing a large classes, marking assignments in a large class, developing resources in under-resourced classrooms, dealing with mixed ability learners, etc.) and suggested solutions in the form of tips and practical ideas. A major criticism of the problem-solution approach is that most of the solutions represent BANA (Britain, Australasia and North America) type 'best practices' in ELT more generally, which are desirable for teaching English effectively, irrespective of the specific challenges of the classroom (Shamim and Kuchah 2016). Besides, focusing on isolated classroom challenges fails to recognise the complex organic and dynamic nature of classrooms. On the contrary, recent studies are focusing more and more on the holistic nature of classroom encounters and their impact on teaching and learning. Such studies employ different qualitative data collection procedures to explore both teachers' and learners' classroom behaviours in order to identify patterns which promote learning. Also, inquiry-based approaches which encourage the voices of teachers and young learners to emerge (e.g., Kuchah and Shamim 2018; Nguyen et al. 2016; Smith et al. 2017; Smith and Kuchah 2016; Pinter et al. 2016) are beginning to show that the challenges faced by practitioners in developing world contexts actually offer opportunities for enriching our understanding of the complex terrain of English language education as well as for the development of alternative practices which can potentially enrich current theories in ELT (Kuchah 2018a). These classroom-based studies are mostly conducted by outsiders working with teachers and provide evidence of the value of teacher and learner agency in the development and dissemination of good practice in difficult circumstances (e.g., Alyasin 2018; Ekembe and Fonjong 2018; Okpe 2016; Hillyard 2018).

Teaching strategies in difficult circumstances

Several studies (e.g., Alyasin 2018; Kuchah 2013; Nakabugo 2008; O'Sullivan 2006; Phyak 2018) have attempted to investigate good practice in difficult circumstances through observation and interviews with teachers. O'Sullivan's (2006) study in large primary classrooms in Uganda made use of classroom observation and videoed lessons and found that children's answers to questions during lessons, their ability to complete written activities, their engagement in group tasks and their ability to read new words introduced and offer examples all showed evidence of children's learning. She concludes that the effectiveness of these lessons is a result of four basic techniques exploited by the teachers. These include strategies for classroom organisation and management; effective use of basic teaching skills such as effective questioning and use of group work; the use of resources in the environment as well as whole class teaching and the frequency with which the teacher solicits students' opinions and reactions to others' opinions. In Tanzania, Garton et al. (2011) identify the use of realia as an effective strategy for engaging young learners in the language classroom. Underlying these strategies is the energy, animation and enthusiasm of the teachers which contribute to the positive hardworking atmosphere in the classes observed. In Nakabugo's (2008) study, data from interviews and classroom observations of one hundred lessons by 35 early primary school teachers reveal that different teachers in different contexts (rural and urban) have developed strategies to cope with their difficult circumstances and promote learning. Strategies such as group work, the employment of the teacher's enthusiasm and strategies for attracting children's attention through storytelling, singing and questions and answers echo O'Sullivan's (2006) argument that the effective use of generic teaching skills can be a very good way to enhance learning. Kuchah's (2013) study involves young learners and their teachers in identifying good practice, and the findings reveal that teachers and learners possess convergent, and in some cases, divergent notions of good EYL practice; it is these notions, rather than what the MoE promotes, which have the most influence on what happens in the classroom (see also Kuchah and Pinter 2012). Using a variety of participatory data collection and analysis procedures, the study shows how encouraging practitioners to reflect on their own practices and challenging them with insights from students' perspectives enables them to generate new insights about contextually appropriate EYL practices in difficult circumstances.

Studies exploring EYL in conflict-affected contexts (Alyasin 2018; Okpe 2016) have focused on teachers' pragmatic responses to the psycho-affective challenges they and their learners face. In northern Nigeria where terrorist attacks have affected education more broadly, Okpe (2016) found through a survey of the practices of 50 language teachers that they make use of 'restoration strategies' which combine English lessons with counselling and other psychological activities to help restore children to their former psychological state. Alyasin's (2018) study investigates the challenges and coping strategies of an English teacher in a Syrian refugee camp school in Southern Turkey and shows how the teacher develops pedagogic practices, based on her own previous experiences, her understanding of her learners and the specific contextual constraints in which they operate. Vignettes from the teacher's classroom provide an 'exemplary model for challenging difficult circumstances with the capacities available rather than surrendering to the chaotic realities of war' (Alyasin 2018, p. 168).

Bilingual/multilingual practices

Studies have shown that bilingual practices such as translation (Cummins 2007; Hall and Cook 2012) and codeswitching (Clegg and Afitska 2011; Milligan et al. 2016; Madonsela

2015) can be potentially beneficial to English language learning and classroom management more generally. These studies suggest that the use of students' mother tongue or a familiar language as resources in the second or foreign language class can facilitate L2 learning. Milligan et al. (2016), for example, provide findings from an intervention demonstrating the role of language supportive materials and pedagogy – reflected in textbook design, textual characteristics, a range of activity types, the use of vocabulary, the use of visuals and the inclusion of bilingual practices – in improving learning outcomes in English as a foreign language and English-medium education in Rwanda. Teachers in this context have been obliged to transition from French medium instruction to EMI with very minimal support for such a major transition, and the introduction of language supportive materials seems a welcome support mechanism for their own challenges. Writing from South Africa, Makalela (2014) reports on the results of a literacy intervention devised to maintain and support the development of children's L1 literacy while also promoting their literacy development in English language. Factors such as the creation of a print-rich environment in both the local language and English in class, the use of contrastive literacy teaching and the active involvement of parents in reading to their children all contributed to the enhancement of children's English reading development. The use of students' L1 in the English language classroom is particularly relevant in contexts where English-only policy recommendations pose significant barriers to the quality of learning for children who do not have access to the English outside the classroom (Ampiah 2008; Esch 2010; Milligan et al. 2016). However, translation and codeswitching pedagogies are based on the perception of the languages of bilinguals as separate codes (García 2011) which may be compared or contrasted (Cummins 2007; Swain 1985) to foster target language learning. Where they are used, the goal is often subtractive, that is, to transition into target language-only use (Mandalios 2012).

More recent theories of language acquisition, based on a dynamic model of bilingualism/ multilingualism (Cummins 2015; Garcia and Wei 2014), see languages as interrelated and fluid in the human brain and recommend translanguaging as an effective pedagogical strategy to maximise the use of students' and teachers' linguistic, social and cognitive resources. Translanguaging refers to language practices which go beyond the boundaries of named languages and make use of the entire linguistic repertoire of the multilingual individual, rather than of one language at a time (Garcia and Wei 2014; Lewis et al. 2012; Copland and Ni, this volume). It involves meaning making through multiple discursive practices (Garcia 2009) based on functionally grounded hybrid and fluid language practice. Classroom-based studies (e.g., Makalela 2014; 2015; Phyak 2018) show that translanguaging can be an effective strategy for English language teaching and learning in under-resourced multilingual contexts. In Nepal, Phyak (2018) presents classroom vignettes of how teachers mediate classroom learning through the medium of English by employing translingual practices. Translanguaging, in this context, helps break students' silence and increases their participation both in the English language and academic subjects, and as a result enhances both language and subject learning. In South Africa, Makalela's (2015) investigation into the effectiveness of the introduction of teaching African languages – as additional languages – to speakers of other African languages reveals that using translanguaging techniques have both cognitive and social advantages, not typically associated with one-language medium classroom interactions. Through quantitative (test scores) and qualitative (storied reflections) data, the study shows that translanguaging strategies are effective in increasing the vocabulary pool of multilingual speakers as well as in affording them a positive schooling experience which affirms their multilingual identities. These are two significant benefits which might be hampered by one-language-only policies that make L2 teaching challenging for teachers in contexts where resources in the target language might be scarce.

Recommendations for practice

Based on the discussion presented, the following recommendations may be made for the practice of young learner teacher education and TEYL in difficult circumstances:

- Policy makers and teacher educators need to acknowledge the expertise of teachers as a basis for implementing any form of innovation. This requires a major paradigm shift from a deficit perspective of teachers as incapable of implementing imposed innovative practices to an enhancement approach (Kuchah 2013; 2016a) which empowers and motivates teachers to be creative and critically reflective on their classroom practices.
- Classroom practices, such as those promoting interaction and fun, need to be rooted in the sociocultural realities of learners and, at best, elicited from them.
- Teachers need to be encouraged to make use of multilingual practices such as code-switching and translanguaging in order to benefit from the wealth of linguistic and cultural knowledge that children bring to the classroom. In addition, TEYL materials need to be language supportive in nature (see Milligan et al. 2016).
- Learners in contexts of conflict and disaster need more than just English language education; EYL for them has to be embedded in a pedagogy which addresses their socio-affective realities (see Ball (2018) and López-Gopar, this volume, for a discussion of how critical pedagogy can support this approach).

Future directions

There is now a growing body of evidence that teacher research – i.e., 'systematic self-study by teachers (individually or collaboratively) which seeks to achieve real-world impact of some kind' (Borg and Sanchez 2015, p. 1) – can help foster not only the professional development of teachers involved in it, but also the quality of teaching and learning. In fact, social constructivist models of teacher education (Johnson 2006; Borg 2015) have led to the mapping of different forms of teacher/practitioner research such as reflective practice (Griffiths 2000; Lockhart and Richards 1994), action research (Edge 2001) and exploratory practice (Allwright and Hanks 2009). These forms of research legitimise teachers' knowledge and highlight the importance of reflective inquiry into the experiences of teachers as mechanisms for change in classroom practice (Johnson 2006) and present the teacher as a decision maker, an autonomous professional and a reflective practitioner (Stuart and Tatto 2000; Kumaravadivelu 2001). In the area of young learner English language education, research of this kind is scarce, and this is understandably so especially in sub-Saharan Africa where entry qualifications to teacher training institutions are often low and not dependent on English language proficiency and where the low socioeconomic status of primary level teachers means that many enter the profession only as a temporary passage to better opportunities (Mtika and Gates 2011; Akeampong and Stephens 2002). This notwithstanding, modest but significant attempts are being made to support primary level teachers interested in critically exploring their classroom practices and seeking solutions to their day-to-day conundrums.

One such example, which is the first of its kind in the field of EYL, involved 25 young learner teachers exploring their own classrooms in action research cycles with a focus on involving young learners as co-researchers (for details, see Pinter et al. 2016). The different projects undertaken by these teachers are dependent on their contextual circumstances and available support:

> There were two types of project undertaken in classrooms depending on the circumstances and the local levels of support available to each teacher. Some teachers simply elicited children's voices and opinions and this led to more engagement with learning, more meaningful choices and children taking on more responsibility for their own learning. At the other end of the continuum some learners were enabled to undertake an actual inquiry into a matter of interest to them, through using questionnaires or interviews, for example.
>
> *(Pinter et al. 2016, p. 7)*

The results of this project, drawn from a variety of data sources – including teacher diaries and presentations, teacher and learner interviews, as well as secondary data sources including posters, puppets, or books written by the children, activities produced by learners in class and audio or video recordings of classroom episodes – reveal that teacher-research activities which draw upon the opinions and reflections of children can be valuable in developing their cognitive and metacognitive ability as well as their autonomy and agency. This is even more valuable in developing world contexts where resources are limited and where teachers and students might be the only other resources or resource providers (e.g., see Kuchah and Smith 2011).

The ongoing collaborative work of teachers from Bangladesh, India, Nepal and Pakistan (see Smith et al. 2017) is another example which is based not only on sharing best practice through narratives of successful lessons but also on collaborative classroom teacher inquiry. Of the seven stories of teacher-inquiry reported in this collection, three specifically refer to in-country and between-country collaborations between young learner (elementary-level) classroom teacher inquiries and address issues such as correcting written work in large classes, managing multiple classes in one room without partitions (a form of multigrade classrooms) and increasing student participation as well as managing group work – challenges often identified in the literature on teaching in difficult circumstances. What is more, these inquiries are reported in language that is accessible to classroom practitioners (as opposed to the often obscure academic language of academic research journals) and follows a simple pattern including the identification of the (shared) problem faced by these teachers, what they do to set up their inquiries (e.g., formulating research questions, discussing their problems and consulting other colleagues), what they learn from colleagues, what they try in their classes, what they learned from these trials and their shared reflections on the benefits of the process both for student learning and for their own professional development.

Another example of inquiry involving teachers from both secondary and primary levels is the ongoing Teacher Association (TA) research project within the Cameroon English language teacher association (CAMELTA). Smith and Kuchah (2016, p. 215) define TA research as

> systematic inquiry which is derived from members' expressed priorities and officially endorsed by a TA, and which engages members as active participants in what they see as a collective project to improve understanding and practice.

The project, initiated in August 2013, initially involved TA members writing down research questions based on their contextual challenges as a basis for developing a future individual and collaborative research agenda (see Smith and Kuchah 2016, for details of the process and initial outcomes of the project). A recent further development has been the creation of the CAMELTA research group made up of teachers who are specifically interested in pursuing collaborative research on some of the key questions formulated in 2013. As Ekembe and Fonjong (2018) explain, in collaboratively investigating different aspects of classroom practice, the group also aims not only to enrich and share good practice, but also to demonstrate that some of the current practices of its members are good enough to generate pedagogic reflections that are consumable both locally and globally. Activities so far have included identifying relevant research questions from the online database, reading and discussing short articles, developing lesson plans, teaching and observing each other, collecting and analysing feedback from students and reflecting on these to develop principles for good practice in context. Through the use of mobile accessible platforms such as WhatsApp and Facebook, group members are able to engage in ongoing discussions without having to travel to a traditional meeting venue all the time (see Ekembe and Fonjong 2018 for details of what the group has achieved so far).

There are indications that technology might be providing new opportunities for EYL and young learner teacher education. Tyers and Lightfoot (2018) describe and evaluate the outcomes of a British Council m-learning project aimed at enabling young people in India and Bangladesh to develop their English proficiency in order to improve their employability prospects. The authors report large-scale improvements in language proficiency and self confidence in participants who would otherwise not have the opportunity to learn English in formal classroom settings. From Bangladesh, Solly and Woodward (2018) describe and examine a large scale in-service training (INSETT) project which makes use of Mediated Authentic Video with commentary from a local narrator to reach large numbers of teachers through their mobile phones. Through mobile technology, the project aims to reach 50,000 teachers and a cumulative student population of 7 million within a few years in a country where financial, infrastructural and resource challenges make it difficult for the government to provide affordable and effective face-to-face training at scale.

There is an urgent need for research into the exact challenges which young learner teachers face in difficult circumstances as a starting point for reflecting on what might be appropriate for these contexts. Such research should aim at celebrating and refining the positive contributions of teachers in these contexts, rather than at 'pathologising' the contexts. The three examples of bottom-up initiatives presented above indicate that curriculum, materials, and pedagogy can benefit from collaborative inquiry-based projects involving teachers and learners. Future research will need to build on the procedures and findings of these initiatives in order to generate a large bank of accessible ideas for good practice in difficult circumstance. In doing this, it is important to keep in mind that for innovative practices to be considered plausible, they need to involve practitioners, and to some extent, learners in the conception, generation and enactment process.

Further reading

1 Kuchah, K and F. Shamim (Eds.). (2018). *International Perspectives on Teaching English in Difficult Circumstances: contexts, challenges and possibilities*. Basingstoke: Palgrave Macmillan.

   This book offers a holistic practitioner and research-based perspective on English Language Teaching and teacher education in difficult circumstances. The 12 chapters in this collection examine the challenges and problems that emerge from the complex current ELT environment, and present examples of contextualised inquiry-based strategies and interventions to address these challenges.

2   Shamim, F., Negash, N., Chuku, C., and Demewoz, N. (2007). *Maximising learning in large classes: issues and options*. Addis Abbaba: The British Council

This very practical and 'teacher-friendly' publication brings together a range of tasks and reflective activities to help teachers of large classes identify and analyse the difficulties they face as well as develop strategies for overcoming them. It also presents a collection of suggested activities which practitioners can use when teaching language skills in large classes.

3   Smith, R., A. Padwad, and D. Bullock (2017). Teaching in low-resource classrooms: voices of experience. British Council. Available at www.teachingenglish.org.uk/publications

This is an edited collection of stories of success and of teachers-inquiry authored classroom practitioners from Bangladesh, India, Nepal and Pakistan. Each account of successful practice and teacher-inquiry addresses a specific classroom challenge which resonates with those reported in other challenging contexts around the world, and the associated video materials provide a further stimulus for reflection.

Related topics

Critical pedagogy, languages in the classroom, technology, classroom management

References

Akeampong, K., and Stephens, D. (2002). Exploring the backgrounds and shaping of beginning student teachers in ghana: Toward greater contextualisation of teacher education. *International Journal of Educational Development*, 22(3–4), 261–274.

Allwright, D., and Hanks, J. (2009). *The Developing Language Learner: An introduction to exploratory practice*. London: Palgrave Macmillan.

Alyasin, A. (2018). ELT in a war-affected context: One teacher's coping strategies and practical responses in a Syrian camp school. In Kuchah, K., and Shamim, F. (eds.) *International Perspectives on Teaching English in Difficult Circumstances: Contexts, challenges and possibilities*. Basingstoke: Palgrave Macmillan, 155–174.

Ampiah, J. G. (2008). An investigation of provision of quality basic education in Ghana: A case study of selected schools in the central region. *Journal of International Cooperation in Education*, 11(3), 19–37.

Anmpalagan with Smith, R., Ajjan, M., and Kuchah, K. (2012). Large class teaching challenges and responses. www.warwick.ac.uk/telc/strategies/ [Accessed 14 November 2017].

Baldauf Jr, R. B., Kaplan, R. B., Kamwangamalu, N., and Bryant, P. (2011). Success or failure of primary second/foreign Language programmes in Asia: what do the data tell us? *Current Issues in Language Planning*, 12(2), 309–323.

Ball, R. S. (2018). Empowering socially-aware young learners in Brazil through content-based instruction. In Copland, F., and Garton, S. (eds.) *Young Learner Education*. Alexandria, VA: TESOL Press, 123–130.

Bamgbose, A. (2014). The language factor in development goals. *Journal of Multilingual and Multicultural Development*, 35(7), 646–657.

Bax, S. (2003). The end of CLT: A context approach to language teaching. *ELT Journal*, 57(3), 278–287.

Bertoncino, C., Murphy, P., and Wang, L. (2002). *Achieving Universal Primary Education in Uganda: The 'Big Bang' approach. Education notes. World Bank*, Washington, DC: World Bank. https://openknowledge.worldbank.org/handle/10986/10412 [Accessed 10 October 2017].

Bland, J. (2015). *Teaching English to Young Learners*. London: Bloomsbury.

Borg, S. (2015). Researching teacher beliefs. In Paltridge, B., and Phakiti, A. (eds.) *Research Methods in Applied Linguistics: A practical resource*. London: Bloomsbury, 487–504.

Borg, S., and Sanchez, H. S. (2015). Key issues in doing and supporting language teacher research. In Borg, S., and Sanchez, H. S. (eds.) *International Perspectives on Teacher Research*. Basingstoke: Palgrave Macmillan, 1–13.

Butler, Y. G. (2007). Foreign language education at elementary schools in Japan: Searching for solutions amidst growing diversification. *Current Issues in Language Planning*, 8(2), 129–147.

Cameron, L. (2001). *Teaching Languages to Young Learners*. Cambridge: Cambridge University Press.

Cameron, L. (2003). Challenges for ELT from the expansion in teaching children. *ELT Journal*, 57(2), 105–112.

Carless, D. R. (2004). Issues in teachers' reinterpretation of a task-based innovation in primary schools. *TESOL Quarterly*, 38(4), 639–662.

Carless, D. R. (2003). Factors in the implementation of task-based teaching in primary schools. *System*, 31(4), 485–500.

Clegg, J., and Afitska, O. (2011). Teaching and learning in two languages in African classrooms. *Comparative Education*, 47(1), 61–77.

Coleman, H. (2018). An almost invisible 'difficult circumstance': the large class. In Kuchah, K., and Shamim, F. (eds.) *International Perspectives on Teaching English in Difficult Circumstances: Contexts, challenges and possibilities*. Basingstoke: Palgrave Macmillan, 29–48.

CONAP. (2008). *Contribution à la reflexion sur l'arrimage des reformes pedagogiques aux exigencies de la gouvernance educative*. Yaounde: Imprimerie Salvation Print.

Copland, F., Garton, S., and Burns, A. (2014). Challenges in teaching English to young learners: Global perspectives and local realities. *TESOL Quarterly*, 48(4), 738–762.

Cummins, J. (2007). Rethinking monolingual instructional strategies in multilingual classrooms. *Canadian Journal of Applied Linguistics*, 10(2), 221–240.

Cummins, J. (2015). How to reverse a legacy of exclusion? Identifying high impact educational responses. *Language and Education*, 29(3), 272–279.

Dearden, J. (2014). *English as a Medium of Instruction – A Growing Global Phenomenon: Phase 1. Interim report, April 2014*. Oxford: University of Oxford and the British Council.

Edge, J. (Ed.). (2001). *Action Research*. Alexandria, VA: TESOL Press.

Ekembe, E. (2016). Do 'resourceful' methodologies really work in 'under-resourced' contexts? In Murphy, A. (ed.) *New Developments in Foreign Language Learning*. New York: NOVA Science, 121–140.

Ekembe, E. E., and Fonjong, A. S. (2018). Teacher association research for professional development in Cameroon. *ELT Research*, 33, 28-31

Ekereke, S. A. (2013). The effect of Boko Haram insurgency and the school system: A case study of selected states in northern Nigeria. *Science Journal of Sociology and Anthropology*, 10, 1–5.

Esch, E. (2010). Epistemic injustice and the power to define: Interviewing Cameroonian primary school teachers about language education. In Candlin, C. N., and J. Crichton (eds.) *Discourses of Deficit*. New York: Palgrave Macmillan, 235–255.

Escudero, M.D.P, Reyes Cruz, M & Loyo, G.M (2012) The English in public elementary schools program of a Mexican state: a critical, exploratory study. Current Issues in Language Planning 13 (4), 267-283

Forero Rocha, Y. (2005). Promoting oral interaction in large groups through task-based learning. *PROFILE, Universidad Nacional de Colombia*, 6, 73–81.

García, O. (2009). *Bilingual Education in the 21st Century: A global perspective*. Malden and Oxford: John Wiley and Sons.

Fraser, N. (2013) Scales of Justice. Cambridge: Polity.

García, O. (2011). Theorizing translanguaging for educators. In Celic, C., and Seltzer, K. (eds.) *Translanguaging: A CUNY-NYSIEB guide for educators*. New York: The City University of New York, 1–6.

García, O., and Wei, L. (2014). *Translanguaging: Language, bilingualism and education*. New York: Palgrave Macmillan.

Garton, S., Copland, F. and Burns, A. (2011) Investigating global practices in teaching English to young learners. London: British Council.

Gfeller, E., and Robinson, C. (1998). Which language for teaching? The cultural messages transmitted by the languages used in education. *Language and Education* 12(1), 18–32.

Graddol, D. (2006). *English Next*. London: British Council.

Griffiths, V. (2000). The reflective dimension in teacher education. *International Journal of Educational Research*, 33(5), 539–555.

Hall, G., and Cook, G. (2012). Own-language use in language teaching and learning. *Language Teaching*, 45, 271–308.

Hillyard, S. (2018). Resourcing the under resourced English language classroom in state primary special education schools in Buenos Aires, Argentina. In Kuchah, K., and Shamim, F. (eds.) *International Perspectives on Teaching English in Difficult Circumstances: Contexts, challenges and possibilities*. Basingstoke: Palgrave Macmillan, 175–195.

Holliday, A. (1994). The house of TESEP and the communicative approach: The special needs of state English language institutions. *ELT Journal*, 48(1), 3–11.

IDMC (Internal Displacement Monitoring Centre). (2015). Global overview 2015: People internally displaced by conflict and violence. www.internal-displacement.org/assets/library/Media/201505-Global-Overview-2015/201505-Global-Overview-Highlights-document-en.pdf [Accessed 30 December 2017].

Inostroza Araos. M. J. (2015). Examining challenges and complexities in the Chilean young learners classroom: A case of teaching English as a foreign language. Unpublished PhD Thesis, School of English, University of Sheffield.

Iyamu, E., and Ogiegbaen, A. (2007). Parents and teachers' perceptions of mother tongue medium of instruction policy in Nigerian primary schools. *Language, Culture and Curriculum*, 20(2), 97–108.

Izquierdo, J., Martínez, V. G., Garza Pulido, M. G., and Aquino Zúniga, S. P. (2016). First and target language use in public language education for young learners: Longitudinal evidence from Mexican secondary-school classrooms. *System*, 61, 20–30.

Johnson, K. E. (2006). The sociocultural turn and its challenges for second language teacher education. *TESOL Quarterly*, 40(1), 235–257.

Johnstone, R. (2009). An early start: What are the key conditions for generalized success? In Enever, J., Moon, J., and Raman, U. (eds.) *Young Learner English Language Ppolicy and Implementation: International perspectives*. Reading: Garnet Education, 31–41.

Khadka, B. K. (2015). Using learner autonomy approach in large and low resource ELT classroom. *NELTA ELT Forum*. https://neltaeltforum.wordpress.com/2015/07/ [Accessed 10 January 2018].

Kirkgöz, Y. (2008) 'Globalization and English language policy in Turkey.' Educational Policy 23/5: 663 – 684.

Komba, W. L., and Nkumbi, E. (2008). Teacher professional development in Tanzania: Perceptions and practices. *Journal of International Cooperation in Education*, 11(3), 67–83.

Kouega, J. P. (1999). Forty years of official bilingualism in Cameroon. *English Today*, 15(4), 38–43.

Kouega, J. P. (2003). English in francophone elementary grades in Cameroon. *Language and Education*, 17(6), 408–420.

Kuchah, K. (2013). From bilingual Francophones to bilingual Anglophones: The role of teachers in the rising 'equities' of English medium-education in Cameroon. In Ushioda, E. (ed.) *International Perspectives on Motivation*. Basingstoke: Palgrave Macmillan, 60–81.

Kuchah, K. (2016a). ELT in difficult circumstances: Challenges, possibilities and future directions. In Pattison, T. (ed.) *IATEFL 2015 Manchester Conference Selections*. Faversham: IATEFL, 149–160.

Kuchah, K. (2016b). English medium instruction in an English-French bilingual setting: Issues of quality and equity in Cameroon. *Comparative Education*, 52(3), 311–327.

Kuchah, K. (2018a). Teaching English in difficult circumstances: Setting the scene. In Kuchah, K., and Shamim, F. (eds.) *International Perspectives on Teaching English in Difficult Circumstances: Contexts, challenges and possibilities*. Basingstoke: Palgrave Macmillan, 1–25.

Kuchah, K. (2018b). Early English medium instruction in Francophone Cameroon: The injustice of equal opportunity. *System*, 72, 37-47.

Kuchah, K., and Pinter, A. (2012). "Was this an interview?" Breaking the power barrier in adult-child interviews in an African context. *Issues in Educational Research*, 22(3), 283–297.

Kuchah, K., and Shamim, F. (Eds.). (2018). *International Perspectives on Teaching English in Difficult Circumstances: Contexts, challenges and possibilities*. Basingstoke: Palgrave Macmillan.

Kuchah, K., and Smith, R. C. (2011). Pedagogy of autonomy for difficult circumstances: from practice to principles. *Innovation in Language Learning and Teaching*, 5(2), 119–140.

Kumaravadivelu, B. (2001). Towards a postmethod pedagogy. *TESOL Quarterly*, 35(4), 537–560.

Kumaravadivelu, B. (2006). TESOL methods: Changing tracks, challenging trends. *TESOL Quarterly*, 40(1), 59–81.

Kumaravadivelu, B. (2011). *Language Teacher Education for a Global Society: A modular model for knowing, analyzing, doing and seeing*. London: Routledge.

Lamb, M. (2002). Explaining successful language learning in difficult circumstances. *Prospect*, 17(2), 35–52.

Lewis, G., Jones, B., and Baker, C. (2012). Translanguaging: Origins and development from school to street and beyond. *Educational Research and Evaluation*, 18(7), 641–654.

Lin, A. M. Y. (1997). Hong Kong children's rights to a culturally compatible English education. *Hong Kong Journal of Applied Linguistics*, 2(2), 23–48.

Lockhart, C., and Richards, J. C. (1994). *Reflective Teaching in Second Language Classrooms*. New York: Cambridge University Press.

Lovitt, T. C. (2010). What can teachers do for children living in difficult circumstances? *Intervention in School and Clinic*, 45(5), 317–320.

Makalela, L. (2014). Rethinking the role of the native language in learning to read in English as a foreign language: Insights from a reading intervention study in a rural primary school in South Africa. In Rich, S. (ed.) *International Perspectives on Teaching English to Young Learners*. Basingstoke: Palgrave Macmillan, 141–155.

Makalela, L. (2015). Moving out of linguistic boxes: The effects of translanguaging strategies for multilingual classrooms. *Language and Education*, 29(3), 200–217.

Maley, A. (2001). The teaching of English in difficult circumstances: Who needs a health farm when they're starving? *Humanising Language Teaching*, 3(6), November 2001. www.hltmag.co.uk/nov01/martnov014.rtf [Accessed 20 January 2018].

Madonsela, S. (2015). Language anxiety caused by the single mode of instruction in multilingual classrooms: The case of African language learners. *Africa Education Review*, 12(3), 447–459.

Mandalios, J. (2012). Power and pedagogy in ELT: Native-speaker teachers and the case of bilingual dictionaries and L1. *International Journal of Applied Linguistics* 22(2), 1–24.

Mfum-Mensah, O. (2005). The impact of colonial and postcolonial Ghanaian language policies on vernacular use in schools in Two Northern Ghanaian communities. *Comparative Education*, 41(1), 71–85.

Milligan, L. O., Clegg, J., and Tikly, L. (2016). Exploring the potential of language supportive learning in English medium instruction: A Rwandan case study. *Comparative Education*, 2(3), 328–342.

Moon, J. (2005). *Children Learning English*. Oxford: Palgrave Macmillan.

Mtika, P., and Gates, P. (2011). What do secondary trainee teachers say about teaching as a profession of their 'choice' in Malawi? *Teaching and Teacher Education*, 27, 424–433.

Muthwii, M. (2001). *Language Policy and Practices in Kenya and Uganda: Perceptions of parents, pupils and teachers on the use of mother tongue, Kiswahili and English in primary schools*. Nairobi: Phoenix Publishers.

Nakabugo, M. G. (2008). Universal primary education for growth? The paradox of large classes in Uganda. *Journal of International Cooperation in Education*, 11(1), 117–130.

Nation, I. S. P (1975). Teaching vocabulary in difficult circumstances. *ELT Journal*, 30(1), 21–24.

Nguyen, L. C., Hamid, O., and Renshaw, P. (2016). English in the primary classroom in Vietnam: Students' lived experiences and their social and policy implications. *Current Issues in Language Planning*, 17(2), 191–214.

Nguyen, T. M. H. (2011). Primary English language education policy in Vietnam: Insights from implementation. *Current Issues in Language Planning*, 12(2), 225–249.

Nguyen, T. M. H., and Nguyen, Q. T. (2007). Teaching English in primary schools in Vietnam: An overview. *Current Issues in Language Planning*, 8(1), 162–173.

Nicolai, S., Greenhill, R., Jalles d'Orey, M. A., Magee, A., Rogerson, A., Wild, L., and Wales, J. (2016). *Education Cannot Wait: Proposing a fund for education in emergencies*. London: Overseas

Development Institute. www.odi.org/sites/odi.org.uk/files/resource-documents/10497.pdf [Accessed 13 January 2018].

Nunan, D. (2003). The impact of English as a global language on educational policies and practices in the Asia-Pacific region. *TESOL Quarterly*, 37(4), 589–613.

Nunan, D. (2011). *Teaching English to Young Learners*. Anaheim, CA: Anaheim University Press.

Okpe, A. A. (2016). Teaching English in an atmosphere of insurgency: The Nigerian example. In Pattison, T. (ed.) *IATEFL 2015 Manchester Conference Selections*. Faversham: IATEFL, 162–164.

Opoku-Amankwa, K. (2009). English-only language-in-education policy in multilingual classrooms in Ghana. *Language, Culture and Curriculum* 22(2), 121–135.

O'Sullivan, M. C. (2006). Teaching large classes: The international evidence and a discussion of some good practice in Ugandan primary schools. *International Journal of Educational Development*, 26, 24–37.

Padwad, A., and Dixit, K. (2014). Exploring continuing professional development: English teachers' clubs in Central India. In Wright and M. Beaumont (eds.) *Experiences of Second Language Teacher Education*. Basingstoke: Palgrave Macmillan, 153–174.

Pandey, G. (2011). An 'English goddess' for India's down-trodden. *BBC News South Asia*. www.bbc.co.uk/news/world-southasia-12355740 [Accessed 10 January 2018].

Phyak, P. (2015). From 'schooled pedagogy' to 'pedagogy of disaster': The role of EFL teachers in the super-difficult circumstance of post-disaster Nepal. *ELT Choutari*. http://eltchoutari.com/2015/07/from-schooled-pedagogy-to-pedagogy-of-disaster-the-role-of-efl-teachers-in-the-super-difficult-circumstance-of-post-disaster-nepal/ [Accessed 10 January 2018].

Phyak, P. (2018). Translanguaging as a pedagogical resource in English language teaching: A response to unplanned language education policies in Nepal. In Kuchah, K., and Shamim, F. (eds.) *International Perspectives on Teaching English in Difficult Circumstances: Contexts, challenges and possibilities*. Basingstoke: Palgrave Macmillan, 49–70.

Pinnock, H. (2009). *Language and Education: The missing link*. Reading: CfBT Education Trust and Save the Children.

Pinon, R., and Haydon, J. (2010). *The Benefits of the English Language for Individuals and Societies: Quantitative indicators from Cameroon, Nigeria, Rwanda, Bangladesh and Pakistan: A custom report compiled by Eurometer international*. London: British Council.

Pinter, A. (2011). *Children Learning Second Languages*. Basingstoke: Palgrave Macmillan.

Pinter, A., Mathew, R., Smith, R. (2016). *Children and Teachers as Co-researchers in Indian Primary English Classrooms*. London: British Council ELT Research Papers 16.03.

Read, C. (2007). *500 Activities for the Primary Classroom*. Oxford: Palgrave Macmillan.

Rogers, J. (1982). The world for sick proper. *ELT Journal*, 36/3: 144–151.

Rubdy, R. (2008). Diffusion of innovation: A plea for indigenous models. *TESL-EJ*, 12(3), 1–34.

Save the Children. (2015). The cost of war: Calculating the impact of the collapse of Syria's education system on Syria's future. Published March 2015. www.savethechildren.org.uk/sites/default/files/docs/The_Cost_of_War.pdf [Accessed 30 February 2018].

Sarwar, Z. (2001). Adapting individualization techniques for large classes. In Hall, D., and Hewings, A. (eds.) *Innovation in English Language Teaching: A reader*. London: Routledge.

Sawamura, N., and Sifuna, D. N. (2008). Universalizing primary education in Kenya: Is it beneficial and sustainable? *Journal of International Cooperation in Education*, 11(3), 103–118.

Shamim, F. (2012). Teaching English in large classes. In Burns, A., and Richards, J. (eds.) *The Cambridge Guide to Pedagogy and Practice in Second Language Teaching*. Cambridge: Cambridge University Press, 95–102.

Shamim, F., and Kuchah, K. (2016). Teaching large classes in difficult circumstances. In Hall, G. (ed). *The Routledge Handbook of English Language Teaching*. London: Routledge, 527–541.

Shamim, F., Negash, N., Chuku, C., and Demewoz, N. (2007). *Maximising Learning in Large Classes: Issues and options*. Addis Abbeba: The British Council.

Skutnabb-Kangas, T. (2009). What can TESOL do in order not to participate in crimes against humanity? *TESOL Quarterly*, 43(2), 341–344.

Smith, R. (2011). Teaching English in difficult circumstances: A new research agenda. In Pattison, T. (ed.) *IATEFL 2010 Harrogate Conference Selections*. Canterbury: IATEFL, 78–80.

Smith, R. (2015). Teaching English in difficult circumstances: A conversation. *NELTA ELT Forum*. https://neltaeltforum.wordpress.com/2015/07/ [Accessed 10 January 2018].

Smith, R., and Kuchah, K. (2016). Researching teacher associations. *ELT Journal*, 70(2), 212–221.

Smith, R., Padwad, A., and Bullock, D. (2017). Teaching in low-resource classrooms: Voices of experience. British Council. www.teachingenglish.org.uk/publications [Accessed 10 January 2018].

Solly, M., and Woodward, C. (2018). Using mediated authentic video as a potential innovative solution for training at scale: A view from Bangladesh. In Kuchah, K and Shamim, F. (eds.) *International Perspectives on Teaching English in Difficult Circumstances: Contexts, challenges and possibilities*. Basingstoke: Palgrave Macmillan, 221–242.

Stuart, J. S., and Tatto, M. T. (2000). Designs for initial teacher preparation programs: An international view. *International Journal of Educational Research*, 33(5), 493–514.

Superfine, W., and James, M. (2017). *Telling Tales in English*. Peaslake: Delta Publishing.

Swain, M. (1985). Communicative competence: Some roles of comprehensible input and comprehensible output in its development. In Gass, S., and Madden, C. (eds.) *Input in Second Language Acquisition*. Rowley, MA: Newbury House, 235–253.

Tembe, J. (2006). Teacher training and the English language in Uganda. *TESOL Quarterly*, 40(4), 857–860.

Tembe, J., and Norton, B. (2011). English education, local languages and community perspectives in Uganda. In Coleman, H. (ed.), *Dreams and Realities: Developing countries and the English language*. London: British Council, 114–136.

Thornbury, S. (2016). Communicative language teaching in theory and practice. In Hall, G. (ed). *The Routledge Handbook of English Language Teaching*. London: Routledge, 224–237.

Tomasevski, K. (2003). *Education Denied: Costs and remedies*. London: Zed Books.

Tyers, A., and Lightfoot, A. (2018). Using mobile to create low cost, high quality language learning opportunities: Lessons from India and Bangladesh. In Kuchah, K., and Shamim,F. (eds.) *International Perspectives on Teaching English in Difficult Circumstances: Contexts, challenges and possibilities*. Basingstoke: Palgrave Macmillan, 109–130.

UIS (UNESCO Institute for Statistics). (2016). *Education: Pupil-teacher ratio in lower secondary education*. Montreal: UNESCO Institute for Statistics. http://data.uis.unesco.org/ [Accessed 2 January 2018].

UNESCO. (1990). *World Declaration on Education for all and Framework for Action to Meet Basic Learning Needs*. Paris: UNESCO.

UNESCO. (1997). *Portraits in Courage: Teachers in difficult circumstances*. Paris: Global action programme on Education for All. http://toolkit.ineesite.org/resources/ineecms/uploads/1596/Portraits_in_Courage_-_Teachers_in_Difficult.pdf [Accessed February 2018].UNESCO. (2000). *The Dakar Framework for Action: Education for all – Meeting our collective commitments*. Paris: UNESCO.

UNESCO. (2003). *Education in a Multilingual World: UNESCO education position paper*. Paris: UNESCO.

UNESCO. (2005). *Education For All: The quality imperative*. Paris: UNESCO.

UNESCO. (2013). *Toward Universal Learning: Recommendations from the learning metrics task force*. Montreal and Washington, DC: UNESCO.

Valenzuela, J. P., Bellei, C., and de los Ríos, D. (2013). Socioeconomic school segregation in a market-oriented educational system: The case of Chile. *Journal of Education Policy*, 29(2), 217–241.

Vavrus, F. (2009). The cultural politics of constructivist pedagogies: Teacher education reform in the United Republic of Tanzania. *International Journal of Educational Development*, 29, 303–311.

Verspoor, A. M. (2008). *At the Crossroads Choice For Secondary Education in Sub-Saharan Africa: Africa human development series*. Washington, DC: World Bank. https://openknowledge.worldbank.org/handle/10986/6537 [Accessed 28 January 2018].

Waters, A., and Vilches, M. L. C. (2008). Factors affecting reforms: The case of the Philippines basic education curriculum. *RELC Journal*, 39(1), 5–24.

Wedell, M. (2011). More than just 'technology': English language teaching initiatives as complex educational changes. In Coleman, H. (ed.) *Dreams and Realities: Developing countries and the English language*. London: British Council, 269–290.

West, M. (1960). *Teaching English in difficult circumstances*. London: Longmans, Green.

Williams, E. (2011). Language policy, politics and development in Africa. In Coleman, H. (ed.) *Dreams and Realities: Developing countries and the English language*. London: British Council, 41–58.

Williams, E., and Cooke, J. (2002). Pathways and labyrinths: Language and education in development. *TESOL Quarterly*, 36(3), 297–322.

PART 2
In the young learner classroom

6

Contexts of learning in TEYL

Farrah Ching and Angel M. Y. Lin

Introduction

This chapter focuses primarily on TEYL in bi/multilingual contexts, i.e., where English is often used as medium of instruction (MOI) for young learners whose first language is known to be other than English. In these contexts, learning in schools is accessed through English and educational achievement is demonstrated through English. Apart from the BANA countries (Britain, Australasia and North America), many schools in other multilingual societies, such as Hong Kong (Lin 2016), Singapore (Chua 2011), South Africa (Broom 2004) and Zimbabwe (Mufanechiya and Mufanechiya 2011), have also opted for English-medium education to promote the use and learning of English. The latter are often former British colonies, engaged in different processes of postcolonial nation-building in the current globalised world.

In English-dominant BANA countries, the term 'English as an Additional Language' (EAL) is now widely adopted to acknowledge linguistic diversity as an asset for these students. EAL, as a contemporary reconceptualisation of 'English as Second Language' (ESL), reflects an ideological shift in the positioning of bi/multilingual learners and the educational response to them, i.e., mainstreaming (Leung 2016). This categorisation, however, does not denote a homogeneous group but encompasses a range of English learning experience and proficiency (Murphy and Unthiah 2015). In the United States, EAL students are often known as 'English Language Learners' (ELL), a term generally used to refer to students with limited proficiency in English in the American context (Genesee et al 2006).

The teaching of EAL to young learners has seen tremendous growth over the last two decades or so globally and commercially, as evident in the expansion of bilingual and multilingual education (Graddol 2006). English is at the apex of the complex political, economic and cultural hierarchy of languages (Graddol 2007). Its prestige is buttressed by its crucial role in school and higher education, digital communication technology and the entertainment industry. Driven by globalisation and rapid growth in migration, recent years have witnessed a sharp increase in the need for support for EAL children in English-dominant countries. For example, in the UK alone, official statistics (NALDIC 2013) showed that almost one in five primary school pupils do not speak English as a first language; the numbers have doubled in the last decade.

The growing currency of English has prompted policymakers in various parts of the world to introduce the language as integral to primary education (Kirkpatrick 2012, Nikolov 2009). English is a compulsory part of the primary curriculum in all of the ten countries of The Association of Southeast Asian Nations (ASEAN). Among these countries, English is adopted as an MOI in primary schools in Singapore, Brunei and the Philippines (Kirkpatrick 2012). In Hong Kong, where English has been a colonial language, English-medium schooling continues to be more easily accessible to the children of the educated elite due to the streaming policy segregating schools into English-medium and Chinese-medium. In some countries even where the national policy stipulates mother-tongue education, English remains the preferred MOI at the local level, contravening the national policy. For example, it was found that in both urban and rural schools in Kenya, English dominated instruction in all subjects (social studies, mathematics, science, life-skills and religious education) in the first three years of primary education except in Kiswahili and mother-tongue 'language classes' (Trudell and Piper 2014). This is despite the fact that Kenyan children do not speak English at home and their level of English proficiency at that stage presents a serious challenge to their learning through the language.

In pre-school years, there is an increasing trend towards introducing English learning, often as priority language (Gardner 2012, Johnstone 2009). It seems that the TEYL pendulum has swung the other way, some may argue too far, from the earlier myths about bilingualism confusing children (Genesee 1989) to the controversial superiority of 'the younger the better' hypothesis (Pinter 2011). Depending on the specific educational contexts, the definition of 'young learners' could conceivably be extended to a start as early as three years old (Pinter 2006, p. 2). The fashionable discourse of 'winning at the starting line' in Asian societies has also helped to sustain widespread popular beliefs that earlier is better and more is better, despite the lack of empirical evidence supporting this claim in foreign language contexts (Muñoz 2006). Bottom-up forces arising from parent demand for English linguistic capital persist in places such as Hong Kong, Japan and Korea, where affluent parents pay for private English-medium education and tutoring at younger grade levels than the national policy regulates, often in immersion programmes and international schools (de Mejía 2002; Imoto 2011; Song 2012; Yee 2009). Kindergartens in both China and Korea are facing a strong demand for English from parents even though both countries have already ambitiously mandated an early start from Primary 3.

It is important to recognise that the contexts in which young learners are exposed to and engaged in English learning are varied and complex. Children's learning trajectories and outcomes depend on the linguistic and learning conditions provided by their significant others (parents, families, caregivers and schools), and are in turn shaped by wider social processes. The early bird may or may not catch the worm, but for teachers the TEYL boom brings with it many pedagogical challenges (Copland et al 2014).

Historical perspectives

In predominantly English-speaking countries, languages other than English have been historically and primarily regarded as a problem to be remedied by the schools (Ruiz 1984). Improving the English language proficiency of immigrant children from newly decolonised territories was high on the national development agendas of BANA countries in the 1950s. In the case of the UK, it was expected that immigrant children should become 'truly integrated' into the community 'as soon as possible' (Derrick 1977, p. 16). ESL, as it was known until the late 1980s, took the form of separate language provision outside the regular school curriculum. It was usually delivered through full-time or part-time reception ESL classes, and conducted by specialist teachers where resources were available. The assumption was that these young learners would impede the academic progress of local students and should join the mainstream classes when they were adequately prepared. Leung and Franson (2001a) pointed out that ESL provision in the 1950s and 60s in BANA countries was found to be limited and compartmentalised. Using a language-as-structure approach as informed by native-speaker norms, it was a short-term intensive form of initial provision often carried out in isolation from the child's school (Leung 2016).

By the mid-1980s, the pull-out arrangement for new arrivals was being challenged as socially divisive, and national policies began to shift to 'mainstreaming' in response to societal and political demands for equitable access to the mainstream system (Leung and Franson 2001b). The positioning of bilingual learners was changed from being 'outsiders' to 'mainstream participants' in school education. Official documents stated that 'where bilingual pupils need extra help, this should be given in the classroom as part of normal lessons' (DES 1989). In the mainstream classroom, the ESL student and the subject teacher might be supported by an ESL support teacher. This arrangement could be seen as an attempt to provide language-minority children equal access to education (Bourne 1989), but it clearly had to rely on effective collaboration between mainstream and language support teachers.

Another impetus for mainstreaming arose from how language was conceptualised in the development of sociolinguistics (e.g., Hymes 1974) when considerations of communicative competence broadened the notion of correctness beyond grammatical accuracy. The idea that language learning is achieved through the active and meaningful use of language provided the basis for the development of such language pedagogy as communicative language teaching. Cummins (1984, 1993, 2000) makes the distinction between Basic Interpersonal Communication Skills (BICS) and Cognitive Academic Language Proficiency (CALP), while highlighting the need for all teachers to be teachers of language in their subject. The BICS/CALP distinction has contributed to the mainstreaming of EAL students and further discussions on the instruction and assessment of linguistically diverse students (e.g., Coelho 2004, Lin 2016). The shift of emphasis to language as communication and positive findings on bilingual education (Cummins 1984, Lambert 1981) helped to reframe bilingualism as a potential educational advantage.

Between the 1950s and the 1980s researchers and educators in the teaching of English as second or foreign language were preoccupied with 'models' of bilingual education and 'balanced bilingualism' from structural-functional and cognitive perspectives in language majority and postcolonial settings (Martin-Jones 1989, 2007). Most of the formal approaches to language learning took a strong line with regard to classroom language. One of the myths about best practice has been that instruction has to be carried out exclusively in the 'target language': translation between L1 (first language) and L2 (second language) is prohibited in case learners become confused (Conteh et al 2014a). The notion of 'bilingualism without tears' (Swain 1983) was based on the development of bilingualism through parallel monolingualism, separating L1 and L2 by subject, by timetabling and by teacher.

The strategy separating languages by timetabling (as in immersion programmes) found support in studies such as Legarreta (1979). In this study, the children in the only bilingual kindergarten classroom using Spanish and English separately made significantly greater gains in oral comprehension in English than those in the five classrooms that mixed the two languages. Another oft-quoted analysis by Wong-Fillmore (1980) reported children tuning in and out as the teacher translated between Cantonese and English in an American classroom. The students stopped listening attentively when the teacher used the language that they did not understand. The researcher went on to assert the exclusive use of target language in enhancing student motivation (Wong-Fillmore 1985). Dual-language immersion advocates monolingual instruction for adequate language development (Howard et al 2007; Lindholm-Leary 2012), culminating in the negative positioning of L1 and pressure on increasing English time based on the time-on-task rationale. This separation approach also helps to explain why codeswitching has been discouraged in mainstream education contexts as a sign of deficiency (Cheng and Butler 1989). The myth of this approach, which surveils and prohibits students' leveraging of their multilingual resources through restricting their use of L1 and 'mixing' languages, became entrenched in the practices of language teaching up to now (Lin 2015a, Scarino 2014).

Various researchers have discussed the loss or erosion of children's heritage languages among immigrant children in school contexts, i.e., 'subtractive bilingualism'. It was first discussed by Lambert in relation to Canadian immigrant children (Lambert 1977, 1981). The intergenerational language shift within three generations is often the norm (Fishman 1991; Clyne and Kipp 1997). Wong-Fillmore (1991) documented how American native and immigrant children tended to lose their L1, as young children were susceptible to the social pressures against valuing their linguistic or ethnic diversity in the United States. In families whose parents and grandparents spoke little English, such language shift often resulted in native-language loss and intergenerational alienation. Related studies on immigrant and ethnic minority children in Scandinavia and the United States have also given rise to the derogatory label of 'semilingual' (a term first coined by Hansegård 1968, as cited in Martin-Jones and Romaine 1986), characterising the unequal performance of bilingual children in their two languages when compared to monolingual children norms. The lack of equal competence in areas such as vocabulary, linguistic correctness and degree of automaticity was used to highlight a deficit view of bilingual children. However, MacSwan (2000) was careful to point out that the so-called semilingualism was associated more with low socio-economic status rather than language background.

Critical issues and topics

Over the last two decades, multilingualism has been fast becoming an asset to postmodern citizens in the face of globalisation (Canagarajah 2005). In this age of 'superdiversity' (Vertovec 2007), new patterns of transnational migration and their fluid mixing of languages have blurred the traditional boundaries of languages (Blommaert and Backus 2011). On the other hand, researchers have increasingly problematised the static and bounded ideological conceptions of 'language' and monolingual myths in language education as part of the 'multilingual turn' (Conteh and Meier 2014b, May 2014). The growing number of EAL speakers has also prompted examination of issues such as notions of ownership of English (Kramsch and Sullivan 1996, Phillipson 2008) and hierarchical multilingualism (Lin 2015). Critical approaches to language education questioning the power relations and ideology inherent in schooling (Kumaravadivelu 2005) have offered new understandings of how children who come with bi/multilingual repertoires can participate meaningfully in education and negotiate identities through language. In what follows, for critical reflection, we focus on the enduring interrelated issues of monolingual bias and hierarchical multilingualism that have permeated into school practices, as well as their pedagogical implications within the contexts of TEYL. We also discuss how translanguaging can harness children's complete linguistic repertoires to help them learn.

Monolingual bias

The myth of the monolingual nation-state has meant that only the linguistic practices enacted by monolinguals are assumed to be legitimate (May 2014). Although it is now recognised that linguistic plurality has always been a part of life in human history (Canagarajah 2007), young EAL learners are often taught and assessed against monolingual 'standard English' norms unconnected to their local social realities and heritage. 'Bilingualism through monolingualism' stems from uncritical acceptance of received knowledge claims of second language acquisition (SLA) (Lin 2012). By extension, 'balanced bilingualism' has been misguidedly hailed as the idealised benchmark for measuring learners' developmental capabilities in learning additional languages (Martin-Jones 2007). The construction of second language learners as failed monolinguals rather than successful bilinguals runs the risk of condemning them to a permanent 'subaltern' subjectivity (Sridhar 1994).

Critical analyses of language and power in social processes reveal how English-only pedagogical ideologies reproduce social inequality and academic failure (Heller and Martin-Jones 2001; Lin and Martin 2005; Martin-Rojo 2010). It is self-evident that monolingual children tend to perform to the expected mean of standardised tests as they constitute the normative sample for these tests (Oller et al 2007). The monolingual mandate of California's Proposition 227 is a case in point: when children enter the classroom, the teacher speaking only English – 'proper English' – places the burden on her young students to adapt to her delivery (Manyak 2002, p. 434). Chen (2006) found that some kindergarten children in Taiwan have developed a negative attitude to English as a result of being punished for speaking Mandarin in English classes. Such disabling contexts prevent children from fully participating in classroom learning, particularly when in some cases teachers are unable to distinguish between language acquisition and learning disabilities (Orosco and Klingner 2010).

Hierarchical bi/multilingualism

Socially and critically informed understandings of bi/multilingualism in the recent decade (Heller 2007; Pennycook 2010) suggest that language constructs and is constructed by social relationships, characterised by unequal relations of power. In postcolonial contexts, children's more familiar local languages are often relegated to the bottom of the linguistic hierarchy. For instance in Singapore, where English has been installed as the L1 and the chief medium of instruction, 'pragmatic multilingualism' is in practice multilingualism dominated by English (Rubdy 2005). This form of hierarchical multilingualism is also evident in Hong Kong, where higher education has been English-medium since its colonial days and English-medium schooling is favoured by many local parents over mother-tongue (Chinese) education.

In Anglophone countries, the naturalised language practices of the white, educated middle-classes top the language hierarchy (Garcia and Otheguy 2017). Johnson (2016) alerted us to a new generation of minoritised youth borne out of the 'language gap' discourse in the USA today, referring to a so-claimed delay in the vocabulary acquisition in young children of lower socioeconomic status. Language minoritised families are blamed for turning their children into limited language users by not speaking and using English effectively in the family. The 'language gap' is purportedly located at the beginning of the educational process, even before the children enter school. Garcia and Otheguy (2017) cautioned that the 'language gap' is more dangerous than the 'achievement gap' discourse (Mancilla-Martinez and Lesaux 2010; Genesee et al 2006), as it ruptures and devalorises the natural bonding of families through their own home language and cultural practices.

Translanguaging

In response to the dynamic multilingualism ushered in by globalisation, contemporary scholarship has pointed to the 'multilingual turn' (Conteh and Meier 2014b; May 2014). As multilingualism is foregrounded as the new norm in applied linguistics and languages education, children's multilingual repertoire is considered a potential resource rather than impediment to language learning. The idea of drawing on the linguistic repertoire of learners is increasingly known as 'translanguaging' (Hornberger and Link 2012; Lewis et al 2012). To capture the heteroglossic (Bakhtin 1981; Bailey 2007) discursive practices of bilinguals, Garcia and Li (2014) advocate a 'translanguaging' epistemology and pedagogy for developmental bilingual education. Coined in the 1980s by Welsh educator Cen Williams, the term was used originally to refer to the 'planned and systematic use of two languages for teaching and learning inside the same lesson' (Lewis et al. 2012, p. 643). Translanguaging starts from the speaker, and leads us away from a focus on the code or language to a focus on the agency of individuals engaged in communication. In educational settings, it refers to the process by which students and teachers engage bi/multilingually in the many multimodal practices of the classroom, such as reading, note-taking, show-and-tell, discussing and writing (Garcia 2009). It goes way beyond codeswitching and translation to offer educators the possibility of viewing bilingual language practices holistically instead of as two languages competing with each other. In other words, translanguaging seeks to destabilise and remove linguistic hierarchies. For Garcia and Li (2014), translanguaging is a potentially transformative socioeducatonal process that enables students to constantly modify their sociocultural identities as they respond to changing conditions critically and creatively.

Current contributions and research

Current research shows that educators have begun to increasingly leverage their students' multilingual competence in their practices. In the following, we share examples of different translanguaging pedagogies enacted in various TEYL contexts, where emergent bi/multilinguals fall along different points of the bi/multilingual continuum. While not all teachers in the studies can speak their students' heritage languages, they were observed incorporating the young learners' languages in their instruction in productive, creative and sometimes playful ways.

Though traditionally immersion classrooms have been promoting strict separation of languages, it is becoming clear to practitioners that the 'two-solitudes' mode can be counterproductive (Cervantes-Soon et al. 2017; Fitts 2006). In a dual-language school in central Texas, two bilingual teachers were observed modelling translanguaging in their respective pre-kindergarten and Grade 1 classrooms (Palmer et al. 2014). To accommodate their very young emergent bilingual students, these teachers codeswitched purposefully between Spanish and English to validate or mirror their students' language practices. They also raised their students' metalinguistic awareness by drawing attention to the moments when the children noticed similarities between English and Spanish. In the Grade 1 class, the teacher made use of critical bilingual literature, e.g., bilingual poems about naming, to encourage children to think about the power of naming someone and different cultural norms for naming teachers (Garcia-Mateus and Palmer 2017). She went on to ask the students to act out the scenes from the poems, placing them in positions of power by empowering their bilingual identities.

Peer collaboration among students in the forms of helping, practising, sharing and respecting were identified as ways of supporting children's translanguaging and positive identities in an English/Chinese bilingual classroom in Canada (Sun 2016). Two-thirds of the children in this Grade 5 class spoke a variety of Chinese languages and the rest spoke English at home. This study demonstrated how the students actively helped each other by drawing on their varied language and mathematics expertise. They also appropriated strategically their linguistic resources by negotiating, interacting and practising with each other. Both the Chinese-medium and English-medium teachers have encouraged the children to share their Chinese/English writing and assignments so that they could develop biliteracy meaningfully. The students were also observed sharing the method of using the Chinese times table to do multiplication, taking advantage of the monosyllabic characteristic of the Chinese language as a mnemonic aid. Stressing the importance of respect, the teachers were able to cultivate a supportive environment in which young students would ask for help without feeling embarrassed about their lack of language proficiency. The different forms of peer collaboration through translanguaging, promoted by the teachers, legitimated the resources children brought to the classroom and opened up spaces for them to shape their own learning and achievement.

Translanguaging and community literacy activities (Jiménez et al 2009) were used by a third-grade teacher in the USA with her EAL students (Pacheco and Miller 2015), bridging in-school literacy activity with the textual world of multilingual students' lives outside school. The lesson was about making sense of informational texts using text features, such as title, author, caption and chart. The teacher distributed newspapers written in Spanish, Chinese, Arabic and English that she had collected, and asked the children to work in pairs to identify the text features. The young students argued about where to find the author's name written in Arabic, and made attempts to guess the meaning of numbers below a weather map in the Chinese newspaper. Within this 20-minute lesson, the teacher helped students develop conceptual understandings of text features across languages, capitalising on the students' heritage languages. She continued the lesson by reading an English-language article with the assistance of text features.

Another case study, in northern England, also demonstrated how a multilingual teacher in a Primary 4 Geography class tapped into the children's funds of knowledge (Conteh et al 2014b). In this class, over half of the children shared their teacher's first language of Punjabi. During the lesson, the teacher was translanguaging between English and Punjabi fairly extensively. To explain the notion of bartering, she referred to a common practice in the children's communities: buying things 'on tick' from the corner shops. Her approaches to empowering the students' learning highlighted the links between language, social practice, culture and identity.

Findings from a project on composing dual-language e-books revealed how ICT could be incorporated as part of translanguaging to support learning (Pacheco and Miller 2015). In a pre-school class made up of emergent bilinguals with diverse heritage languages, the students had the opportunity to create translanguaging e-books through digital photos, drawings and voice recordings. They were also asked to take photos of their homes and communities, and to label them in English and their heritage language. These images became visual stimuli for the children to learn about each other's lives through translanguaging. Through this activity, the students' heritage languages and lives outside of school were given a visible and valued place in the multilingual classroom.

Emergent bilingual writers have been found to self-regulate during the writing process by translanguaging (Velasco and Garcia 2014). Writing samples from the K–4th grade students in Spanish-English and Korean-English blilingual programmes in New York were collected in a case study. Researchers observed that translanguaging was used by the children in all stages of the writing process: planning, editing and production. It was sometimes used for scaffolding (through vocabulary glosses in the margins or between lines, or using another language for word retrieval), and at other times for rhetorical engagement (to engage the reader through 'another voice'). These practices allowed the learners to resolve problems in creating texts and to develop their own voices.

However, translanguaging process in writing could be contentious when only the author-ised code is permitted. Kiramba (2017) analysed the translanguaging strategies adopted by a fourth-grade class in rural Kenya. The children were proficient in one or more local languages and were acquiring English. (Fourth grade is the transitioning year from mother-tongue instruction to English-only instruction in Kenya.) Although the curriculum dictated the use of only one language in academic writing, the children chose to make their texts clearer by drawing on their diverse communicative repertoires. Words from other languages at their disposal found their way into the texts, indexing the students' multilingual identities and their agency as authors with complex semiotic resources. This study has revealed mul-tilingual children's natural inclination towards translanguaging in their engagement with literacy despite institutional constraints.

Recommendations for practice

Starting with the students' strengths and prior knowledge is the primary principle of all education. While many are impressed with how multilingual children 'pick up' languages, educators are not often wary of how quickly children may 'lose' their heritage languages, particularly when the latter are 'ghettoised' or relegated to a lower status (Cummins 2001). Contemporary studies cited in the previous section exemplify how validating and leverag-ing students' hybrid linguistic and experiential resources can open up spaces for mediating/ enhancing learning and affirm positive multilingual identities. An array of translanguaging pedagogies could be adopted in different TEYL contexts, including:

- Take an *active* stance in welcoming and developing all of a student's linguistic resources. Make it visible by offering a multilingual/multimodal classroom landscape that comprises multilingual word walls/sentence starters, listening and visual centres, etc. (Garcia et al 2017).
- Teachers can model translanguaging and adaptation of language choice when interact-ing with individual students, e.g., through concurrent translation and language broker-ing; or routinely asking children how to say or write words in their heritage languages (Garcia-Mateus and Palmer 2017; Palmer et al. 2014).
- Invite young students to bring along words they choose to share and teach to their teacher and the class, and share stories of cultural heritage, e.g., about festival and cul-tural celebrations. Encourage students to create multilingual and multimodal 'identity texts' to share with multiple audiences for self-affirmation in these interactions (Cum-mins and Early 2011).

- Place multilingual labels on classroom objects; put together a museum of community artefacts with multilingual labels, as well as help children create bilingual picture dictionaries in their home language and English (Linse and Gamboa 2014).
- Use bi/multilingual texts to develop critical metalinguistic awareness across languages and scaffold comprehension, e.g., by comparing language forms and structures (Garcia-Mateus and Palmer 2017; Pacheco and Miller 2015; Palmer et al. 2014; see also Lin 2013 for plurilingual pedagogies that can be adapted).
- Make connections between the children's local community or cultural practices with what they are learning; integrate students' experiences outside of school with the school curriculum (Conteh et al 2014b).
- Bring multilingual community literacy texts into the TEYL classroom (e.g., flyers, posters, signs, advertisements and newspapers) to construct conceptual understandings of literacy across languages and interrogate power relations (Pacheco and Miller 2015; see also Lau 2013 for examples of working with G7/8 emergent English/Chinese bilinguals).
- Promote multilingual students' peer collaboration (Sun 2016) and collaboration between teachers and students by cultivating a supportive learning environment, e.g., asking children to nominate other students who have helped them and awarding students with helper stickers; purposefully asking students for their help in translanguaging; using circle time or centres in classrooms for children to share their learning strategies and help each other solve problems; and making seating arrangements that facilitate peer-sharing and interaction.
- Incorporate ICT with translanguaging: using mobile apps such as Book Creator, Drawing Pad and iBooks for voice recording and literacy work; harnessing audio and visual affordances to encourage dynamic bilingualism (Pacheco and Miller 2015).
- Make meaning or content comprehensible by explaining grammar usage, providing translations for unknown target-language vocabulary, translating and checking comprehension (Luk and Lin 2016).
- Use multimodal resources (e.g., videos, graphic organisers, mind maps, storyboards, comics and bilingual note) for young learners and educators to scaffold and expand children's language and meaning-making repertoire (see Mahboob and Lin 2016 for Lin's Multimodalities/Entextualization Cycle).
- In writing activities, always encourage children to engage with their multilingual semiotic resources during planning, editing and production, such as inserting word glosses in texts for vocabulary acquisition, and employing a 'postponing' strategy by writing down words in a familiar language first for future word retrieval in another language.
- Design content-based units and research tasks that integrate content and language learning, so that students can develop linguistic and discourse competence, as well as strategic translanguaging strategies.

Garcia and Li (2014) advised that while teachers may have varying degrees of bilingual proficiency, they can provide children with opportunities for language use without necessarily setting themselves up as the linguistic authority. Teachers who do not speak the languages of the students may enlist the help of their students in translating and scaffolding, and group linguistically homogeneous children together so they can support each other's learning where appropriate. Teachers may be encouraged to risk saying words in their students' home languages with their help, so they can act as good models for young learners to risk saying more in the target language.

Future directions

As discussed above, current developments in relation to language and language education have led to a growing body of literature on pedagogies that leverage learners' linguistic repertoires. While translanguaging work in schools is still in its infancy and is sometimes even contested in bi/multilingual education programmes, we are beginning to see that all children are capable of competence in additional languages. Through the translanguaging lens, we invite researchers and practitioners to consider the following directions for future investigation:

- Various strategies bridging the in-school and out-of-school lives of children have been documented in the above studies. We need to know more about the experiences of children in their social world and how they can enrich the learning of *all* the students' learning in class.
- How do children use their semiotic resources in peer-learning and collaboration? How do they negotiate and solve problems when working in a multilingual group?
- We need to better understand how children mediate and resist the monolingual bias to achieve their communicative purposes, and how they learn to suppress or activate language features necessary for specific contexts or tasks.
- What strategies can we employ to validate the linguistic practices of young learners in different contexts?
- Translanguaging is potentially transformative and creative (Garcia and Li 2014). How can EAL teachers collaborate with other teachers to engage students in interrogating identity and power relations? (See Bradley et al. 2018 for ideas about a collage workshop to explore communicative repertoires and linguistic landscape.)
- More research is required into content-based or CLIL (Content and Language Integrated Learning) approaches for young EAL learners to access content and academic discourse. (See Lin 2016 and Lin and He 2017 for theory and practice in secondary schools.)

Every learning context is different and students' access to learning opportunities varies. Legitimizing young learners' linguistic repertoires and identities is a necessary step towards translating the multilingual turn into practice, and into policy, for social justice and equal opportunities in learning.

Further reading

1 Conteh, J., and Meier, G. (Eds.). (2014). *The Multilingual Turn in the Languages Education: Opportunities and challenges*. Bristol: Multilingual Matters.
    Exemplifies how schools can value and leverage multilingualism in different contexts.

2 Garcia, O. (2009). *Bilingual Education in the 21st Century: A global perspective*. Oxford: Wiley-Blackwell.
    Provides a comprehensive overview of bilingual education theories, policy and practice with global understandings.

3 Heller, M., and Martin-Jones, M. (Eds.). (2001). *Voices of Authority: Education and linguistic difference*. Westport, CT and London: Ablex.
    Remains a classic volume of ethnographic studies analysing the practices and tensions in relation to the imposition of legitimate language.

4 Lin, A. M. Y., and Martin, P. W. (Eds.). (2005). *Decolonisation, Globalisation: Language-in-education policy and practice*. Clevedon: Multilingual Matters

Provides a collection of studies from Asian and African contexts with critiques of policy and practice.

Related topics

Policies, multilingualism, critical pedagogy, classroom language

References

Bakhtin, M. (1981). *The Dialogic Imagination: Four essays*. Edited by Michael Holquist, translated by Caryl Emerson and Michael Holquist. Austin: University of Texas Press.

Bailey, B. (2007). Heteroglossia and boundary: Processes of linguistic and social distinction. In Heller, M. (ed.) *Bilingualism: A social approach*, Basingstoke: Palgrave Macmillan, 257–274.

Bradley, J., Moore, E., Simpson, J., and Atkinson, L. (2018). Translanguaging space and creative activity: Theorising collaborative arts-based learning. *Language and Intercultural Communication*, 18(1), 54–73.

Broom, Y. (2004). Reading English in multilingual South African primary schools. *International Journal of Bilingual Education and Bilingualism*, 7(6), 506–528.

Canagarajah, S. (Ed.) (2005). Reclaiming the Local in Language Policy and Practice. Mahwah, NJ: Lawrence Erlbaum Publishers, 3-24.

Canagarajah, S. (2007). After disinvention: Possibilities for communication, community and competence. In Makoni, S., and Pennycook, A. (eds.) *Disinventing and Reconstituting Languages*. Clevedon: Multilingual Matters, 233–239.

Cervantes-Soon, C., Dorner, G., Palmer, D., Heiman, D., Schwerdtfeger, R., and Choi, J. (2017). Combating inequalities in two-way language immersion programs: Toward critical consciousness in bilingual education spaces. *Review of Research in Education*, 41(1), 403–427.

Chen, Y. L. (2006). The influence of English immersion programs on kindergarteners' perceptions of languages and cultures. *English Teaching and Learning*, 30(4), 87–109.

Cheng, L. R., and Butler, K. (1989). Code-switching: A natural phenomenon vs language "deficiency". *World Englishes*, 8(3), 293–309.

Chua, S. K. C. (2011). Singapore's E(Si)nglish-knowing bilingualism. *Current Issues in Language Planning*, 12(2), 125–145.

Clyne, M., and Kipp, S. (1997). Trends and changes in home language use and shift in Australia. *Journal of Multilingual and Mulitcultural Development*, 18, 451–473.

Coelho, E. (2004). *Adding English: A guide to teaching in multilingual classrooms*. Toronto: Pippin Publishing.

Conteh, J., Copland, F., and Creese, A. (2014a). Multilingual teachers' resources in three different contexts: Empowering learning. In Conteh, J., and Meier, G. (eds.) *The Multilingual Turn in the Languages Education: Opportunities and challenges*. Bristol: Multilingual Matters, 158–178.

Conteh, J., and Meier, G. (Eds.). (2014b). *The Multilingual Turn in the Languages Education: Opportunities and challenges*. Bristol: Multilingual Matters.

Copland, F., Garton, S., and Burns, A. (2014). Challenges in teaching English to young learners: global challenges and local realities, *TESOL Quarterly*, 48(4), 738–762.

Cummins, J. (1984). *Bilingualism and Special Education: Issues in assessment and pedagogy*. Clevedon: Multilingual Matters.

Cummins, J. (2000). *Language, Power and Pedagogy: Bilingual children in the crossfire*. Clevedon: Multilingual Matters.

Cummins, J. (2001). Bilingual children's mother tongue: Why is it important for education? *Sprogforum*, 19, 15–20.

Cummins, J., and Early, M. (Eds.). (2011). *Identity Texts: The collaborative creation of power in multilingual schools*. Stoke on Trent: Trentham Books.

de Mejía, A.-M. (2002). *Power, Prestige and Bilingualism: International perspectives on elite bilingual education*. Clevedon: Multilingual Matters.

Derrick, J. (1977). *Language Needs of Minority Group Children*. Slough: NFER.

Fishman, J. A. (1991). *Reversing Language Shift*. Clevedon: Multilingual Matters.

Fitts, S. (2006). Reconstructing the status quo: Linguistic interaction in a dual-language school. *Bilingual Research Journal*, 30, 337–365.

Garcia, O. (2009). *Bilingual Education in the 21st Century: A global perspective*. Malden, MA: Wiley-Blackwell.

Garcia, O., and Li, W. (2014). *Translanguaging: Language, bilingualism and education*. Basingstoke: Palgrave Macmillan.

Garcia, O., Ibarra-Johnson, S., and Seltzer, K. (2017). *The Translanguaging Classroom: Leveraging bilingualism for learning*. Philadelphia: Carlson.

Garcia, O., and Otheguy, R. (2017). Interrogating the language gap of young bilingual and bidialectal students. *International Multilingual Research Journal*, 11(1), 52–65.

Garcia-Mateus, S., and Palmer, D. (2017). Translanguaging pedagogies for positive identities in two-way dual language dual education. *Journal of Language, Identity & Education*, 16(4), 245–255.

Gardner, S. (2012). Global English and bilingual education. In Martin-Jones, M., Blackledge, A., and Creese, A. (eds.) *The Routledge Handbook of Multilingualism*. Abingdon: Routledge.

Genesee, F. (1989). Early bilingual development: one language or two? *Journal of Child Language*, 16(1), 161–179.

Genesee, F., Lindholm-Leary,K., Saunders, W. M., and Christian, D. (2006). *Educating English Language Learners: A synthesis of research evidence*. New York: Cambridge University Press.

Graddol, D. (2006). *English Next*. British Council. https://englishagenda.britishcouncil.org/continuing-professional-development/cpd-researchers/english-next. [Accessed 4 August 2017].

Graddol, D. (2007). Global English, global culture? In Goodman, S., Graddol, D., and Lillis, T. (eds.) *Redesigning English*. Abington: Routledge, 243–271.

Hansegård, N. E. (1968). *Tvåspråkighet eller Halvspråkighet?* [Bilingualism or semilingualism?]. Stockholm, Sweden: Aldus Bonnier.

Heller, M. (Ed.). (2007). *Bilingualism: A social approach*. Basingstoke: Palgrave Macmillan.

Heller, M., and Martin-Jones, M. (Eds.). (2001). *Voices of Authority: Education and linguistic difference*. Westport: Ablex.

Howard, E. R., Sugarman, J., Christian, D., Lindholm-Leary, K. J., and Rogers, D. (2007). *Guiding Principles for Dual Language Education*, 2nd ed. Washington, DC: Center for Applied Linguistics.

Hymes, D. (1974). *Foundations in Sociolinguistics: An ethnographic approach*. Pennsylvania: University of Pennsylvania Press.

Imoto, Y. (2011). Producing the 'international' child: Negotiations of language in an international preschool in Japan. *Ethnography and Education*, 6(3), 281–292.

Jiménez, R. T., Smith, P. H., and Teague, B. L. (2009). Transnational and community literacies for teachers. *Journal of Adolescent & Adult Literacy*, 53(1), 16–26.

Johnstone, R. (2009). An early start: What are the key conditions for generalized success?. In Enever, J., Moon, J., and Raman, U. (eds.) *Young Learner English Language Policy and Implementation: International perspectives*. Reading: Garnet Press, 31–41.

Kiramba, L. K. (2017). Translanguaing in the writing of emergent multilinguals. *International Multilingual Research Journal*, 11(2), 115–130.

Kirkpatrick, A. (2012). 'English as an International Language in Asia: Implications for language education', in A. Kirkpatrick and R. Sussex (eds.) *English as an International Language in Asia: Implications for language education*, 29–44, Dordrecht: Springer.

Lambert, W. E. (1977). The effects of bilingualism on the individual: Cognitive and socio-cultural consequences.In Hornby, P. A. (ed.) *Bilingualism: Psychological, social and educational implications*. New York: Academic.

Lambert, W. E. (1981). Bilingualism and language acquisition. In Winitz, H. (ed.) *Native Language and Foreign Language Acquisition*. New York: New York Academy of Science.

Lau, S. M. C. (2013). A study of critical literacy work with beginning English language learners: An integrated approach. *Critical Inquiry in Language Studies*, 10(1), 1–30.

Legarreta, D. (1979). The effects of program models on language acquisition of Spanish speaking children. *TESOL Quarterly*, 13, 521–534.

Leung, C. (2016). English as an additional language – A genealogy of language-in-education policies and reflections on research trajectories. *Language and Education*, 30(2), 158–174.

Leung, C., and Franson, C. (2001a). 'England: ESL in the Early Days. In Mohan, B., Leung, C., and Davison, C. (eds.) *English as a Second Language in the Mainstream: Teaching, learning and identity*. London: Longman, 153–164.

Leung, C., and Franson, C. (2001b). Mainstreaming: ESL as a diffused curriculum concern. In Mohan, B., Leung, C., and Davison, C. (eds.) *English as a Second Language in the Mainstream: Teaching, learning and identity*. London: Longman, 165–176.

Lewis, G., Jones, B., and Baker, C. (2012). Translanguaging: Origins and development from school to street and beyond. *Educational Research and Evaluation*, 18, 641–654.

Lin, A. M. Y. (2012). 'Critical practice in English language education in Hong Kong: Challenges and possibilities'. In Sung, K., and Pederson, R. (eds.) *Critical ELT Practices in Asia*. Rotterdam: Sense Publishers, 71–83.

Lin, A. M. Y. (2015a). Conceptualising the potential role of L1 in CLIL. *Language, Culture and Curriculum*, 28(1), 74–89.

Lin, A. M. Y. (2015b). Egalitarian Bi/multilingualism and Trans-semiotizing in a Global World. In Wright, W. E., Boun, S., and Garcia, O. (eds.) *The Handbook of Bilingual and Multilingual Education*. Chicester, West Sussex: John Wiley & Sons.

Lin, A. M. Y. (2016). *Language Across the Curriculum & CLIL in English as an Additional Language (EAL) Contexts: Theory and practice*. Singapore: Springer.

Lin, A. M. Y., and He, P. (2017). Translanguaging as dynamic activity flows in CLIL classrooms. *Journal of Language, Identity & Education*, 16(4), 228–244.

Lin, A. M. Y., and Martin, P. W. (Eds.). (2005). *Decolonisation, Globalisation: Language-in-education policy and practice*. Clevedon: Multilingual Matters.

Lindholm-Leary, K. (2012). Success and challenges in dual language education. *Theory Into Practice*, 51(4), 256–262.

Linse, C., and Gamboa, A. (2014). Globalization, plurilingualism and young learners in Mexico and beyond. In Rich, S. (ed.) *International Perspectives on Teaching English to Young Learners*. Basingstoke: Palgrave Macmillan.

MacSwan, J. (2000). The architecture of the bilingual language faculty: Evidence from codeswitching. *Bilingualism: Language and Cognition*, 3(1), 37–54.

Mahboob, A., and Lin, A. M. Y. (2016). Using local languages in English language classrooms. In Renandya, Willy A., and Widodo, Handoyo P. (eds.) *English Language Teaching Today: Building a closer link between theory and practice*. New York: Springer.

Makoni, S., and Pennycook, A. (Eds.). (2007). *Disinventing and Reconstituting Languages*. Clevedon: Multilingual Matters.

Mancilla-Martinez, J., and Lesaux, N. K. (2010). Predictors of comprehension for struggling readers: The case of Spanish-speaking language minority learners. *Journal of Educational Psychology* 102(3), 701–711.

Manyak, P. C. (2002). 'Welcome to Salon 110': The consequences of hybrid literacy practices in a primary-grade English immersion class. *Bilingual Research Journal*, 26(2), 421–442.

Martin-Jones, M. (1989). Language, power and linguistic minorities: The need for an alternative approach to bilingualism, language maintenance and shift. In Grillo, R. (ed.) *Social Anthropology and the Politics of Language*. London: Routledge, 106–125.

Martin-Jones, M. (2007). Bilingualism, education and the regulation of access to language resources. in Heller, M. (ed.) *Bilingualism: A social approach*. Basingstoke: Palgrave Macmillan, 161–182.

Martin-Jones, M., and Romaine, S. (1986). Semilingualism: A half-baked theory of communicative competence, *Applied Linguistics*, 7(1), 26–38.

Martin Rojo, L. (2010). *Constructing Equality in Multilingual Classrooms*. Berlin: De Gruyter Mouton.

May, S. (Ed.). (2014). *The Multilingual Turn: Implications for SLA, TESOL and bilingual education*. Abington, Oxon: Routledge.

Moll, L. C., Sáez, R., and Dworin, J. (2001). Exploring biliteracy: Two student case examples of writing as a social practice. *The Elementary School Journal*, 101(4), 435–449.

Muñoz, C. (Ed.). (2006). *Age and the Rate of Foreign Language Learning*. Clevedon: Multilingual Matters.

Murphy, V. A., and Unthiah, A. (2015). A systematic review of intervention research examining English language and literacy development in children with English as an additional language (EAL), The Bell Foundation. www.bell-foundation.org.uk/assets/Documents/EALachievementMurphy. pdf?1422548394 [Accessed 10 June 2017].

Mufanechiya, T., and Mufanechiya, A. (2011). The use of English as medium of instruction in the Zimbawean junior primary schools. *NJLC*, 4(2), 115–127.

NALDIC. (2013). National association for language development in the curriculum, UK. www.naldic. org.uk/research-and-information/eal-statistics/eal-pupils/ [Accessed 15 October 2016].

Nikolov, M. (Ed.). (2009). *Early Learning of Modern Foreign Languages: Processes and outcomes*. Bristol: Multilingual Matters.

Oller, D. K., and Eilers, R. E. (Eds.). (2002). *Language and Literacy in Bilingual Children*. Clevedon: Multilingual Matters.

Oller, D. K., Pearson, B. Z., and Cobo-Lewis, A. B. (2007). Profile effects in early bilingual language and literacy. *Applied Psycholinguistics*, 28(2), 191–230.

Orosco, M. J., and Klingner, J. (2010). One school's implementation of RTI with English Language Learners: "Referring into RTI". *Journal of Learning Disabilities*, 43(3), 269–288.

Pacheco, M. B., and Miller, M. E. (2015). Making meaning through translanguaging in the literacy classroom. *The Reading Teacher*, 69(5), 533–537.

Palmer, D. K., Martinez, R. A., Mateus, S. G., and Henderson, K. (2014). Reframing the debate on language separation; Toward a vision for translanguaging pedagogies in the dual language classroom. *The Modern Language Journal*, 98(3), 757–772.

Pinter, A. (2006). *Teaching Young Language Learners*. Oxford: Oxford University Press.

Pinter, A. (2011). *Children Learning Second Languages*. Basingstoke: Palgrave Macmillan.

Rubdy, R. (2005). Remaking Singapore for the new age: Official ideology and the realities of practice in language-in-education. In Lin, A., and Martin, P. (eds.) *Decolonisation, Globalization: Language-in-education policy and practice*. Clevedon: Multilingual Matters, 56–75.

Ruiz, R. (1984). Orientations in language planning. *NABE Journal*, 8(2), 15–34.

Saunders, G. (1982). *Bilingual Children: Guidance for the family*. Clevedon: Multilingual Matters.

Saunders, G. (1988). *From Birth to Teens*. Clevedon: Multilingual Matters.

Scarino, A. (2014). Situating the challenges in curriculum in current languages education policy in Australia – Unlearning monolingualism. *International Journal of Multilingualism*, 11(3), 289–306.

Song, J. J. (2012). South Korea: language policy and planning in the making. *Current Issues in Language Planning*, 13(1), 1–68.

Sridhar, A. (1994). A reality check for SLA theories. *TESOL Quarterly*, 28(4), 800–805.

Sun, M. (2016). Peer collaboration in an English/Chinese bilingual program in western Canada. *The Canadian Modern Language Review*, 72(4), 423–453.

Swain, M. (1983). Bilingualism without tears. In Clarke, M. A., and Handscombe, J. (Eds.) *On TESOL 82: Pacific Perspectives on Language, Learning and Teaching*, Washington, DC: Teachers of English to Speakers of Other Languages, 35–46.

Trudell, B., and Piper, B. (2014). Whatever the law says: language policy implementation and early-grade literacy achievement in Kenya. *Current Issues in Language Planning*, 15(1), 4–21.

Velasco, P., and Garcia, O. (2014). Translanguaging and the writing of bilingual learners. *Bilingual Research Journal*, 37(1), 6–23.

Vertovec, S. (2007). Super-diversity and its implications. *Ethic and Racial Studies*, 30(6), 1024–1054.

Wong-Fillmore, L. (1980). Learning a second language: Chinese children in the American classroom. In Alatis, J. E. (ed.) *Current Issues in Bilingual Education: Georgetown University round table on languages and linguistics*. Washington, DC: Georgetown University Press.

Wong-Fillmore, L. (1985). When does teacher talk work as input? In Gass, S. M., and Madden, C. G. (eds.) *Input in Second Language Acquisition*, 17–50. Rowley, MA: Newbury.

Wong-Fillmore, L. (1991). When learning a second language means losing the first. *Early Childhood Research Quarterly*, 6, 323–346.

Yee, K. W. (2009). Second language in HK kindergarten: The missing link. In Enever, J., Moon, J., and Raman, U. (eds.) *Young Learner English Language Policy and Implementation: International perspectives*. Reading: Garnet Press.

7

Multilingualism in primary schools

Victoria Murphy

Introduction

More people in the world speak two or more languages than those who speak only one (Grosjean 2010). Bilingualism, therefore, is the norm. Yet surprisingly, when it comes to educating bilingual pupils, many different educational programmes fall short. In this chapter, the focus is on a group of children who are educated through the medium of a majority language at school that is different from their home language. These linguistically diverse children have a home language that is in the minority relative to the language of the wider society, and hence are also often referred to as minority language learners. I will use the term 'linguistically diverse' (LD) in this chapter in an attempt to avoid any potential pejorative implications which might be associated with the term 'minority'. There will be a specific focus on literacy skills in this chapter because a number of studies have demonstrated that some children from LD backgrounds tend to underperform academically relative to their native speaking (or majority language speaking) peers (e.g., Strand et al. 2015). Literacy skills are paramount in academic achievement since children need well-developed reading comprehension skills to access the curriculum, particularly in later primary and secondary school. Additionally, in order to demonstrate their mastery of the curriculum, children need to be able to use their skills in writing effectively. Many children from LD backgrounds tend to have difficulties with reading comprehension and some key aspects of writing. In the UK, for example, a recent analysis of student achievement across the formally assessed levels of education has demonstrated that overall children from linguistically diverse backgrounds consistently underperform relative to monolingual peers on measures of reading (Strand et al. 2015). The good news is that as educators we can do something about it – to try and ameliorate the language, literacy and academic outcomes in this growing population of children around the world.

Historical perspectives

Increased migration and globalization of commerce has meant (among other things) that more people are living in contexts where their native or home languages are not the majority language of the community. A 2016 European Research Council report indicated that in 2014, 3.8 million people had immigrated into one of the 28 European Union (EU) member states, from both in and outside the EU (Eurostat 2016). Additionally, at the time of writing, there is an ongoing international refugee crisis. This means that despite the fact that some countries have expressed a concern about the numbers of immigrants entering their respective countries (e.g., immigration was one of the main concerns behind the UK's vote to leave the EU in June 2016), there are few signs that the rate of immigration is going to slow. The UK has consisted of multiple cultural groups and different identities throughout its recorded history. The first 'Britons' were an ethnically mixed group of individuals retreating from the ice of the Ice Age – and throughout the ages Britain has always 'absorbed' peoples (often from invaders), resulting in a heterogeneous group of diverse peoples (James and Rigby 1997). The case of ancient Britain is but one example. Therefore, the reality of multiple ethnicities and cultural groups living together is an old story and one that has consistently demonstrated how valuable immigration can be to many aspects of society (Dustmann and Frattini 2014).

In 2016, increased immigration has meant that for many countries, a significant proportion of children are being educated in a language that is not their home language. In England, approximately 20% of the primary school population consists of children for whom English is an Additional Language (EAL) (DFE 2016), and in the USA, in the 2012–2013 academic year there were 4.85 million EAL children (Ruiz Soto et al. 2015) – referred to as English Language Learners (ELL) in the US context. These numbers constitute a significant proportion of the school population, and therefore, warrant a close examination of what we can do to ensure that their educational experiences are enabling them to achieve their full potential.

It is important, first, however, to be very clear about who LD learners are and what their linguistic backgrounds are likely to be. The LD population is highly diverse. Just because a child is from a LD background does not mean that they will struggle linguistically or academically. There is plenty of evidence to demonstrate that children from linguistically diverse backgrounds not only do as well as their native-speaking peers but often can exceed their peers' performance. For example, in Strand et al. (2015), EAL pupils were shown to outperform their non-EAL peers at the GCSE examinations on mathematics and modern foreign language. In Scotland, immigrant students also achieve at higher levels on average than their non-immigrant peers in mathematics (OECD 2015). Strand et al. (2015) further demonstrated that ethnicity is a major factor in pupil performance, where some children tagged as EAL in England's National Pupil Database are not only matched to non-EAL peers but consistently outperform them. Additionally, in England, the children who perform the least well in academic achievement are not those with EAL but are boys from white working class backgrounds (Sammons et al. 2015). These findings highlight that being from a linguistically and culturally diverse background does not *a priori* mean that the child will struggle academically. There is an international trend, however, illustrating that EAL pupils often do underperform academically relative to non-EAL pupils as identified in international achievement studies such as PISA (Program for International Student Achievement) and PIRLS (Progress in International Reading Study) (OECD 2012, 2013). There is a real concern, therefore, that many children from ethnic minority backgrounds are not achieving their full academic potential. However, this concern must be tempered by the knowledge that many children from diverse linguistic backgrounds who are emergent bilinguals are at the top of performance scales across a range of subjects around the world.

The other issue that must be noted is that there are many variables that impact whether a child does well at school, not only whether they have another language spoken in the home.

Part of the reason for the heterogeneity in the LD learner population described above will be due to the other factors known to predict academic achievement such as socioeconomic status (SES), level of parents' education, exposure to books (in the home) and so on (e.g., Sammons et al. 2015). Discussing all of these issues in detail is beyond the scope of this chapter, but again, it is worth remembering that linguistic difficulties may not be the (sole) reason for why a child might underachieve at school.

A final point to make relates to the degree of bilingualism of LD pupils in schools. First, bilingualism as a concept is a difficult one to define. Being bilingual can present as a range of different linguistic skills, where individual bilinguals may or may not be bilingual across all four domains of language (speaking, listening, reading and writing). Furthermore, we know from research investigating language dominance that the notion of a completely balanced bilingual with equal skills across all linguistic domains is elusive at best (see Murphy 2014 for discussion). In the context of the discussion in this chapter, the term 'bilingual' refers simply to the notion that a given pupil will have another language in their repertoire. What it does not signify is the nature of that bilingualism (i.e., how proficient the child might be across linguistic skills and within a given language), though this issue is clearly important. Given that LD pupils have another language in the home, usually present from birth, children from linguistically diverse backgrounds have many of the necessary prerequisites in place to become fluently bilingual (i.e., with high levels of proficiency in two languages). The reality, however, for many children from minority language backgrounds is that they don't actually end up becoming bilingual at all. This is because they often undergo a 'language shift' (see Murphy 2014) when they begin to receive formal language arts instruction at school in the majority language. Indeed, many LD pupils do not receive any instruction in or about their home language – unless they participate in a complementary or 'Saturday' school. Even attending such schools, however, LD children typically become dominant in the majority language and, given that many of them fail to develop adequate proficiency in their home language, often do not end up becoming fluently bilingual. Montrul (2008; 2009; 2010 and elsewhere) refers to this phenomenon as a case of 'incomplete acquisition' where due to limitations in the child's linguistic environment, they do not go on to completely acquire their home language. This means then that while children from such backgrounds have the potential to become fluent bilinguals, ultimately many do not.

In summary, children from LD backgrounds have a home language that is not the language of the wider society, and importantly, is not the language in which they are educated. This means that for many such children, when they begin formal schooling, their knowledge of the majority language is likely to be under-developed relative to their monolingual peers. However, many LD children experience a language shift from dominance in the home language to dominance in the majority L2 as they progress through their respective educational experiences provided through the medium of the majority language. Some of the educational consequences of this comparable lack of linguistic skill in the majority language when children commence formal education are discussed below.

Critical issues and topics

There is a wide range of areas of critical interest in children from linguistically diverse backgrounds. Given the focus of this chapter is on literacy, some of the issues which are associated with the development of literacy will be highlighted in this section. It is important to note however, that this discussion does not represent an exhaustive account.

One of the first critical issues was mentioned in the preceding section of this chapter – namely, to what extent are children from LD backgrounds bilingual, and to what extent educational provision supports their bilingual development. As explained above, many children experience the language shift which often means that the children would not really be easily identified as 'bilingual' in the later school years if the development of their home language is not supported. Related to this issue is whether and to what extent supporting the home language has manifest positive consequences on their majority language development and academic achievement. Cummins (2017 and elsewhere) and indeed many other researchers (in the UK, for example, see Conteh and Brock 2011) have for some time noted how important it is to support the home language of LD pupils in order for them to (a) reach their full potential linguistically and take advantage of their emerging bilingualism, (b) to help and support the development of the majority (L2), (c) to take advantage of the *common underlying proficiency* – that is, the underlying linguistic and cognitive system that is shared across all languages an individual will learn (Cummins 1991) and, importantly, (d) to valorise the LD pupils' linguistic identity and culture. These views are more recently associated with the notion of 'translanguaging' in the classroom (García and Li Wei 2014), where it is believed that allowing, and indeed encouraging, children from LD backgrounds to use both their languages as they engage with classroom-based activities is advantageous. However, a recent systematic review examining the empirical evidence which has directly examined use of the child's L1 in the majority language classroom focusing on L2 outcomes has revealed rather mixed results: where some studies revealed no advantage for using the L1, others found advantages, and still others reported lower L2 performance having used the L1 (Chalmers 2017). Future work is necessary, therefore, to examine this issue more critically in the research literature across a range of different educational contexts to further our understanding of the role the L1 can play.

A further related critical issue is the role of the teacher and teacher education. In some contexts where children from linguistically diverse backgrounds all share the same home language (parts of the USA, for example, where many children come from Spanish-speaking homes/communities), teachers can benefit from specific training in how to support their LD pupils. Indeed, there are bilingual education programmes specifically aimed at supporting both languages for bi- or multilingual and monolingual students together (see Murphy 2014 for a discussion). In other contexts, such as the UK, there are so many different languages represented in the LD population that language-specific pedagogy is difficult to develop. Furthermore, it is a reality that the population of pupils in schools is increasingly multilingual, yet in many parts of the world, teacher education speaks to a monolingual norm. The consequence of this approach is then that when a teacher meets pupils from a range of linguistic/cultural backgrounds, they may be (and in many cases are) ill-prepared to meet the needs of all the pupils in their classroom. It is important, therefore, that teacher education programmes around the world, but especially in contexts like the UK with a great deal of linguistic diversity, focus more on developing evidence-based pedagogical approaches which enable teachers to support all their pupils, regardless of their background.

The issue of academic achievement in children from linguistically diverse backgrounds is also directly related to their literacy development. Children from immigrant backgrounds often underperform relative to their non-immigrant peers in international comparative studies of student achievement, and children from minority language backgrounds are typically overrepresented in remedial support programmes (Paradis et al. 2011). For many countries participating in the PISA studies, there is a large gap between first- and second-generation immigrant pupils and non immigrant pupils on reading and mathematics performance

(OECD 2015). International studies such as PISA are, however, somewhat limited as to what they reveal about the language and literacy achievement of young emergent bilingual learners. Fortunately, a considerable amount of research has been carried out in various contexts, most notably the USA and Canada, examining the performance of English Language Learners (ELLs). Specifically, research has been focused on understanding literacy development, as this is such a critical variable underpinning academic achievement. I turn to this research below.

Current contributions and research

Reading skill in minority language learners

In Strand et al. (2015), data on children's reading performance was compared across the major stages of schooling in England for all children tagged as EAL in the National Pupil Database (i.e., regardless of how proficient they are in English and whether they are first, second or later generations of ethnic minorities). They found that at all levels, children with EAL underperformed on reading outcomes relative to non-EAL pupils. The gap was widest at the very earliest stages of education (when children are at the beginning of their formal educational experience) and narrowed considerably by the final stages of secondary school (GCSE), but even then EAL children's reading scores were consistently lower than those of non-EAL pupils.[1] Many studies have identified that LD pupils lag behind majority-speaking peers on measures of reading comprehension (e.g., Hutchinson et al. 2003; Burgoyne et al. 2009; Burgoyne et al. 2011) and that some EAL pupils have similar reading comprehension skills as monolingual children with language weaknesses (Bowyer-Crane et al. 2016). The answer as to why this is the case lies in understanding the skills that underpin reading performance. One of the most widely cited models of reading, particularly with relevance to educational contexts, is Gough and Tunmer's (1986) *Simple View of Reading*. The basic idea behind this model is that there are two fundamental components to reading: word-decoding skills and language comprehension skills. Let's first look at word-decoding skills in pupils with EAL.

Word decoding is the ability to map sounds of language (phonemes) onto the letters (graphemes) and is commonly measured by asking children to read single words out loud or even to provide pseudo-words for children to read. If a child can successfully map phonemes on to graphemes, then their single word (and pseudo-word) reading accuracy will be high because they will be able to sound out words accurately and demonstrate their mastery of the basic phonotactic properties of their language. In order to be good at word decoding, children also need to have well developed phonological and syntactic awareness processes (Jongejan et al. 2007), and research has demonstrated that children who have difficulties in these areas also have difficulties with reading comprehension (Kame'enui and Simmons 2001). Phonological awareness (PA) in particular is the knowledge of the sound structure of a language and the ability to analyse and manipulate those sound units – the metalinguistic knowledge of a language (Burt, Holm, and Dodd 1999; Cheung, Chen, Lai, Wong, and Hills 2001; Jongejan et al. 2007). PA includes the linguistic features associated with grapheme and phoneme correspondence (GPC) knowledge (decoding via matching letters and sounds), extending beyond speech sounds into reading, writing and pronunciation. PA is gradually and implicitly acquired through the oral development of a language and the ability to differentiate between sounds and segment the speech stream into appropriate words and chunks for comprehension. PA is very important in the development of decoding skills at the word level during the emergent stages of literacy (Lindsey, Manis, and Bailey 2003, p. 482). Explicit teaching of PA (e.g., through GPC instruction) is commonly associated with the beginning of formalised schooling; with the introduction of strategic phonics and literacy teaching.

The development of PA and literacy skills has been examined in children who are linguistically diverse, using standardised and experimental measures, comparing LD and non-LD pupils, and surveying home language use and SES. As mentioned above, for many LD students, the point when they begin formalised schooling constitutes their first major and sustained exposure to the majority language, which can then mean they might not have enough knowledge of the majority language to support their emerging literacy skills due to the context of the majority language-only educational system (Paradis, Emmerzael, and Sorenson Duncan 2010). The role of English language proficiency has been repeatedly demonstrated to be one of the most powerful predictors of an EAL child's later academic achievement (Whiteside et al. 2016; Strand and Demie 2005). LD children often have fewer opportunities for the 'auditory discrimination of phonemes' (i.e., they might have less experience with the majority language input), consequently, LD pupils may experience a slower rate of acquisition of GPCs (Verhoeven and Vermeer 2006, p. 726). However, other researchers have suggested that bilingual children have a more advanced phonological sensitivity relative to monolingual children given they have learned (or are learning) two languages. Bilingualism is argued to improve some general cognitive skills during L2 learning due to this dual language processing 'advantage' (Diaz 1985; Diaz and Klinger; Bialystok 2002). This advantage may be responsible for the fact that in many studies LD pupils have not been found to have difficulties in decoding skills relative to monolingual peers (Jean and Geva 2009; Lesaux et al. 2008; Lipka and Siegel 2007; Nakamoto et al. 2007; Verhoeven 1990, 2000). There is strong evidence then that children from LD backgrounds tend not to have any difficulties with the decoding aspect of reading skills. If LD children tend to underperform on reading but do not have difficulties in decoding, what then underpins this weaker reading performance in pupils from linguistically diverse backgrounds?

LD children tend to lag behind their majority-speaking peers in measures of reading comprehension despite comparable skills in single word reading accuracy. For example, in studying the development of phonological awareness and literacy skills, Hutchinson, Whiteley, Smith, and Connors (2003) focused on EAL pupils and non-EAL students in North-West England (i.e., bilinguals vs monolingual pupils). Reading accuracy, comprehension and fluency were tested in years two, three, four, and six. Phonological skills of non-word reading, spoonerisms, alliteration, rhyme, rapid naming of pictures and numbers and fluency were tested with the Phonological Assessment Battery (a standardised test of phonological knowledge and skills developed in the UK). The EAL learners had higher scores than their non-EAL peers on accuracy and fluency; however, the non-EAL students scored higher on measures of reading comprehension. Therefore, despite having mastered phonological processing skills, EAL pupils were nonetheless behind in reading comprehension. One of the main reasons put forward for these lags in reading comprehension in EAL pupils is due to under-developed semantic representations (vocabulary knowledge) – the 'language comprehension' aspect of the Simple View of Reading model (Gough and Tunmer 1986).

Many studies in the L1 domain, and increasingly in studies of young bilingual pupils, have demonstrated the importance of vocabulary knowledge in reading comprehension (Nation et al. 2010; Nation et al. 2004; Nation and Snowling 2004). Studies have also shown that children from LD backgrounds tend to have smaller vocabularies in the majority language than their monolingual peers (Bialystok et al. 2010; Cameron 2002). More recent work has further highlighted the importance of vocabulary knowledge in reading comprehension in LD children. Babayiğit (2012) recruited EAL and non-EAL primary school students in England and administered a range of vocabulary, listening and reading comprehension assessments. Even after 4 years of formal schooling in England the pupils with EAL tended to underperform relative to non-EAL students on measures of listening and reading comprehension and oral language (i.e., vocabulary). Additionally, vocabulary was a significant predictor of performance on reading comprehension tasks, again replicating previous studies. This research underscores the importance of developing vocabulary knowledge in children with EAL and helps us understand the importance of vocabulary knowledge in developing reading comprehension skills.

In summary, the reading research has demonstrated that children from LD backgrounds tend to have no difficulty with the decoding aspects of reading skills, since their ability to map graphemes on to phonemes and single word reading tasks is either the same or even superior to majority-speaking peers. However, for many (but not all) LD pupils, vocabulary knowledge is less well developed than for their peers, which contributes to comparatively weaker performance in reading comprehension tasks.

Writing skill in minority language learners

The other aspect of literacy skill is writing, and there has been far less research on the writing abilities of LD pupils than on reading. Of course writing is absolutely fundamental for all pupils in order to demonstrate their understanding of different aspects of the curriculum (Dockrell et al. 2014). Writing is also a particular challenge for many pupils, regardless of whether they have English as an additional language or not. Teachers often report that finding effective ways of teaching and assessing writing is difficult (Dockrell et al. 2014). Given how important it is, it is somewhat surprising that less attention has been paid to writing, particularly as reading and writing are mutually supportive (Graham and Hebert 2011). Writing, like reading, is generally believed to include knowledge and skill across a range of areas which include working memory, handwriting and spelling and executive functions (Berninger and Amtmann 2003; Berninger and Winn 2006). As with reading, writing takes time to develop and is constrained at the earliest stages by the child's ability to adequately transcribe text onto the page. However, once the child has mastered transcription skills, s/he can then develop higher-level skills such as generating the appropriate content for texts, and organizing and articulating this content in an effective and appropriate manner.

While there is comparatively less research on writing than reading, and less research on the writing development in LD pupils, there have been a few studies which suggest that there are some areas which challenge some LD students. For example, Cameron and Besser (2004) compared the writing performance of EAL pupils in England against that of their non-EAL peers. In particular they focused on two genres: fiction and persuasive writing. Their main findings suggested that EAL pupils were nine percentage points behind their non-EAL peers on the national writing test at Key Stage 2 (end of primary-level education in England). Furthermore, in analyzing their compositions, Cameron and Besser found that the EAL pupils were more likely to make grammatical errors than their non-EAL peers and were less likely to use complex syntax. More recent work examining the writing skills of EAL pupils has also found interesting differences between EAL and non-EAL peers. Babayiğit (2015) examined the writing abilities of EAL pupils in Year 5 (aged 10–11) in England through the administration of a standardised task which required children to write two paragraphs in response to a given prompt (e.g., 'my favourite game is. . . .'). There were no differences between the two groups on spelling accuracy (a finding consistent with previous research), but non-EAL pupils had higher scores on measures of holistic quality, organization, vocabulary and compositional fluency. These findings are also consistent with other work which compared EAL and non-EAL pupils' writing skills. In Murphy et al. (2015), children in Year 5 in England (aged 10–11) were compared on their narrative writing skills. The two groups of children were matched on their English vocabulary and syntactic knowledge. Nevertheless, the EAL pupils still had lower scores than the non-EAL pupils on higher-level writing processes such as organization of ideas – despite the fact that they actually had higher nonverbal IQ scores. These studies together suggest that just as in reading, LD students tend to lag behind native-speaking peers on key aspects of writing – particularly the higher-level features. Unfortunately, it is precisely on these higher-level features of writing that students are required to do well on academic assessments.

One method that seems to have had some success in improving EAL students' writing has been the genre approach. Pioneered in Australia but taken up in other countries, notably in South East Asia (Derewianka 2015), the genre approach, which is derived from systemic functional linguistics (see Martin 2009) explicitly teaches students about text structures and how these are achieved. While some commentators have dismissed the approach as reductionist (Martin 2009), others have noted that the approach provides EAL students with the tools they need to 'successfully write in the second language in the context of school' (Brisk 2011, p. 53).

In summary, children from diverse language backgrounds tend to be as good or better than their native-speaking (monolingual) peers on lower-level aspects of reading (decoding) and writing (transcription), yet they tend to have difficulties on higher-level aspects of reading (comprehension) and writing (organisational structure and content). For both reading and writing, vocabulary has been shown to be an important component underpinning LD students' performance.

Cognitive benefits of bilingualism

The sections above have demonstrated that while LD students constitute a heterogeneous population, international studies of academic achievement, together with specific studies examining reading and writing skills, have demonstrated that many LD pupils lag behind their non-LD peers on academic achievement, reading comprehension and higher-level features of writing. One of the reasons why this pattern is particularly frustrating is that many researchers have argued that bilingual children should benefit cognitively from being bilingual – though this is being hotly debated in the literature at present. The idea that becoming bilingual might be cognitively advantageous is not new. Peal and Lambert (1962) argued that bilingual children (English/French bilinguals in Montréal, Canada) perform better on verbal and nonverbal IQ measures, suggesting that using two languages results in mental 'flexibility' and more diversified mental skills. Peal and Lambert (1962) also showed that the bilingual children in their study had higher scores in academic achievement as well. It should be noted here that the type of bilinguals in this early study examining cognitive advantages of bilingualism were quite different from the LD pupils in focus in this chapter because they were children learning and using both English and French in an English/French bilingual city – in other words, they were not minority language learners, but spoke the two official majority languages of Canada. There are a range of studies arguing that bilingual children do have cognitive advantages on a range of different skills such as concept formation, classification, creativity and analogical reasoning skills (Ben-Zeev

1977; Diaz 1983; Hakuta et al. 1987). Other researchers have argued that bilinguals might be better vocabulary learners as a result of approaching vocabulary learning more flexibly than monolingual children. For example, Marinova-Todd (2012) compared bilingual and monolingual children in Grade 3 (between eight and nine years old) on a word learning task and showed that bilinguals were more successful at deducing novel word meanings than monolinguals – even when the bilinguals had smaller vocabulary sizes. Other researchers have argued bilinguals have advantages over monolinguals in Theory of Mind – the ability to interpret other people's behaviours in terms of their mental states (Geotz 2003; Kovács 2009). Arguably, however, one of the areas that many researchers have more recently been investigating is whether bilingual children have advantages on executive function skills.

Executive function is a general term describing cognitive skills that are at the core of all human cognition, including attention, selection and inhibition processes. Bialystok (1991) claimed that young bilingual children have superior selective attention skills relative to monolinguals and since then, a number of researchers have been attempting to identify the extent to which bilinguals have superior executive control (see, e.g., Bialystok and Barac 2013; Bialystok et al. 2010). However, the findings from these studies is at best mixed, with a number of researchers finding different patterns of results (e.g., Gathercole et al. [2010]) where not all bilingual children show the same cognitive advantages across similar tasks. It is not within the scope of this chapter to delve deeply into this important area of research, but clearly there is more work to be done to resolve the issue of the extent to which there are cognitive advantages for bilingual children on executive function skills.

One area where there does seem to be relatively consistent evidence that bilinguals have advantages over monolinguals relates to metalinguistic awareness – an important predictor of literacy skills. Metalinguistic knowledge refers to the ability to go beyond the meaning of a language and focus on its underlying structure (Bialystok and Barac 2013). Bialystok (1991, 2001) notes, however, that these advantages are not uniformly manifest across all tasks. There is a fair degree of variability in terms of the kinds of bilinguals that different researchers have recruited into their studies (i.e., whether they are bilinguals in a bilingual environment like Montréal, or minority language learners like EAL children in England), the extent to which they are proficient in both their languages and the nature of the tasks used. This variability no doubt has led to some of the variability in the research findings, but the general pattern does seem to suggest bilingual children (in general) have some advantages (see Murphy 2014 for a review). This could be one of the reasons why LD pupils tend to do well on single word reading tasks as described above, because of more well-developed phonological awareness, allowing them to efficiently decode words. A possible advantage in metalinguistic awareness, however, does not seem to help them much with reading comprehension skills, and this is where the importance of vocabulary and supporting vocabulary learning in classrooms comes to the fore.

Recommendations for practise

As demonstrated elsewhere in this chapter, vocabulary knowledge underpins reading comprehension and writing skill, and children from diverse language learning backgrounds often have smaller vocabularies than majority language speaking children. This finding indicates that more focus could be spent on supporting vocabulary development in the classroom. This is particularly relevant given other research which has identified that for some forms of complex (multiword) vocabulary learners may be unaware of the fact that they do not understand the meaning of these items (see Martinez and Murphy 2011; Smith and Murphy 2015). For learners who have sparse vocabulary knowledge and who need to learn lots of words quickly to catch up, explicit teaching of some carefully chosen words can be very productive and efficient (see Murphy and Unthiah 2015 for a review of interventions on vocabulary development for LD pupils). Furthermore, it is a mistake to assume that words can be easily learned from context. Word learning takes time, and multiple exposures are needed to really enable learners to solidify the meaning, to acquire precisely the form, meaning and use of a word and to ensure it is remembered (i.e., learned). Word meanings are often very complex. For example the word 'dog' is a relatively simple word, and easy to learn. However, there are extended meanings of the word 'dog', for example, *His problems continued to dog him* and extended meanings are less likely to be known and understood by some English language learners. Students do not always know when they do not know a word, as has been demonstrated in research studies (Martinez and Murphy 2011; Smith and Murphy 2015), and hence for all of these reasons, some focus on explicit vocabulary teaching and learning in classrooms is warranted. Meaningful exposures, meaningful use, polysemy and structural analysis are all proven approaches to word learning and would benefit children from multilingual backgrounds (as indeed it would benefit all children).

Future directions

In many geopolitical contexts, the issue of how best to educate *all* of their student population has not yet been properly addressed and resolved. There are some educational programmes which have been shown to be particularly helpful for minority language learners, such as the two-way immersion (or dual language) programmes which were spearheaded in the USA (see Murphy 2014 for a review). In these programmes, LD learners are educated alongside their majority language speaking peers in both the minority and the majority language. These additive bilingual programmes aim to support proficiency in both languages, for both groups of children, and have been shown to be more successful than other traditional methods of education where minority language learners either receive no language arts instruction or only remedial support (August and Shanahan 2008). However, in many contexts with high degrees of linguistic diversity, such programmes are not feasible as there are far too many L1 backgrounds. In England, for example, there are over 360 different home languages represented by the EAL population. Which of these would a policy maker choose to implement in a two-way immersion model? For many educators, therefore, focusing efforts on finding the most effective ways to support vocabulary learning in classrooms will prove more fruitful. For researchers, in collaboration with educators, delving more deeply into the relationship between oral language (vocabulary) knowledge and literacy will help inform educational practice.

Roger Bacon is attributed with the quote that 'Knowledge of languages is the doorway to wisdom'. Given the discussion in this chapter we can ask to what extent this is accurate for children from linguistically diverse backgrounds. The selective review of research presented in this chapter demonstrates that many (but not all) learners from multilingual backgrounds are not walking through this door. Educational contexts have a powerful role in shaping children's lives. Hence we need to more carefully consider the best ways to educate our multilingual children to ensure that they can take advantage of all the opportunities that being bilingual presents to them, and shift our thinking so that we no longer adopt a monolingual mindset in a multilingual world.

Further reading

1 Cummins, J. (2000). *Language, Power and Pedagogy: Bilingual children in the crossfire*. Clevedon: Multilingual Matters.

This is a now classic text in which Cummins outlines some of the main political and educational issues relevant for LD pupils. He references some of his main theories (e.g., Common Underlying Proficiency) in arguing that LD students should be afforded the opportunity (where possible) to be educated through the medium of their L1.

2 García, O., and Wei, L. (2014). *Translanguaging*. London: Palgrave MacMillan.

A thorough examination of the construct of 'translanguaging' – using more than one language in the classroom – and why it might be useful.

3 Genesee, F., Lindholm-Leary, K., Saunders, W. M., and Christian, D. (Eds.). (2006). *Educating English Language Learners: A synthesis of research evidence*. Cambridge: Cambridge University Press.

A very detailed and comprehensive summary of key research evidence carried out in the USA evaluating LD children's language and academic achievement.

4 Murphy, V. A., and Unthiah, A. (2015). *A systematic review of intervention research examining English language and literacy development in children with English as an Additional Language (EAL)*. London: Education Endowment Foundation

A systematic review of intervention studies aimed at improving EAL students' language and literacy outcomes. Many of these focus on vocabulary and offer ways of enhancing vocabulary knowledge in classrooms.

Related topics

Classroom languages, contexts of learning, policies, research on learning outside the classroom

Note

1 In England in 2016, for the first time pupils with EAL had an identitcal Attainment 8 (GCSE) score to the national average, they were more likely to achieve the English Baccalaureate than native-speaking peers and were more likely to make greater than average progress. However, this national picture obscures the reality that many sub-groups of pupils with EAL struggle in key ways. For further information see: https://epi.org.uk/publications-and-research/educational-outcomes-children-english-additional-language/

References

August, D., and Shanahan, T. (Eds.). (2008). *Developing Reading and Writing in Second Language Learners: Lessons from the report of the National Literacy Panel on language minority children and youth*. New York: Routledge/CALL.

Babayiğit, S. (2012). The role of oral language skills in reading and listening comprehension of text: A comparison of monolingual (L1) and bilingual (L2) speakers of English language. *Journal of Research in Reading*, 37(1), 22–47.

Babayiğit, S. (2015). The dimensions of written expression: Language group and gender differences. *Learning and Instruction*, 35, 33–41.

Ben-Zeev, S. (1977). Mechanisms by which childhood bilingualism affects understanding of language and cognitive structures. In Hornby, P. A. (ed.) *Bilingualism: Psychological, social and educational implications*. New York: Academic Press.

Berninger, V. W., and Amtmann, D. (2003). Preventing written expression disabilities through early and continuing assessment and intervention for handwriting and/or spelling problems: Research into practice. In Swanson, H. L., Harris, K., and Graham, S. (eds.) *Handbook of Learning Difficulties*. New York: Guildford Press.

Berninger, V. W., and Winn, W. D. (2006). Implications of advancements in brain research and technology for writing development, writing instruction, and educational evolution. In MacArthur, C., Graham, S., and Fitzgerald, J. (eds.) *Handbook of Writing Research*. New York: Guildford.

Bialystok, E. (1991). Metalinguistic dimensions of bilingual language proficiency. In Bialystok, E. (ed). *Language Processing in Bilingual Children*. Cambridge: Cambridge University Press.

Bialystok, E. (2001). *Bilingualism in Development: Language, literacy and cognition*. Cambridge: Cambridge University Press.

Bialystok, E. (2002). Acquisition of literacy in bilingual children: A framework for research. *Language Learning*, 52, 159–199.

Bialystok, E., and Barac, R. (2013). Cognitive effects. In Grosjean, F., and Li, P. (eds.) *The Pscyholinguistics of Bilingualism*. Chichester: Wiley.

Bialystok, E., Barac, R., Blaye, A., and Poulin-Dubois, D. (2010). Word mapping and executive functioning in young monolingual and bilingual children. *Journal of Cognition and Development*, 11(4), 485–508.

Bialystok, E., Luk, G., Peets, K. F., and Yang, S. (2010). Receptive vocabulary differences in monolingual and bilingual children. *Bilingualism: Language and Cognition*, 13(4), 525–531.

Bowyer-Crane, C., Fricke, S., Schaefer, B., Lervåg, A., and Hulme, C. (2016). Early literacy and comprehension skills in children learning English as an additional language and monolingual children with language weaknesses. *Reading and Writing*, 30(4), 771–790. doi:10.1007/s11145-016-9699-8.

Brisk, M. E. (2011). Learning to write in the second language: K-5. In Hinkel, E. (ed.) *The Handbook of Research in Second Language Teaching and Learning Volume II*. New York: Routledge, 40–56.

Burgoyne, K., Kelly, J. M., Whiteley, H. E., and Spooner, A. (2009). The comprehension skills of children learning English as an additional language. *British Journal of Educational Psychology*, 79, 735–747.

Burgoyne, K., Whiteley, H. E., and Hutchinson, J. M. (2011). The development of comprehension and reading-related skills in children learning English as an additional language and their monolingual English-speaking peers. *British Journal of Educational Psychology*, 81, 344–354.

Burt, L., Holm, A., and Dodd, B. (1999). Phonological awareness skills of 4-year-old British children: An assessment and developmental data. *International Journal of Language and Communication Disorders*, 34(3), 311–335.

Cameron, L. (2002). Measuring vocabulary size in English as an Additional Language. *Language Teaching Research*, 6(2), 145–173.

Cameron, L., and Besser, S. (2004). Writing in English as an additional language at Key Stage 2 (rep. No. 586). www.education.gov.uk/ publications/standard/publicationDetail/Page1/RR586.

Chalmers, H. (2017). What does research tell us about using the L1 as a pedagogic tool? *EAL Journal*, Summer.

Cheung, H., Chen, H.-C., Lai, C. Y., Wong, O. C., and Hills, M. (2001). The development of phonological awareness: Effects of spoken language experience and orthography. *Cognition*, 81, 227–241.

Conteh, J., and Brock, A. (2011). 'Safe spaces'? Sites of bilingualism for young learners in home, school and community. *International Journal of Bilingual Education and Bilingualism*, 14(3), 347–360.

Cummins, J. (1991). Interdependence of first and second language proficiency in bilingual children. In Bialystok, E. (ed.) *Language Processing in Bilingual Children*. Cambridge: Cambridge University Press.

Cummins, J. (2017). Teaching for transfer in multilingual school contexts. In García, O., Lin, A., and May, S. (eds.) *Bilingual and Multilingual Education*, 3rd ed. Cham, Switzerland: Springer International.

Department for Education. (2016). *Schools, pupils and their characteristics: January 2016*. www.gov. uk/government/uploads/system/uploads/attachment_data/file/552342/SFR20_2016_Main_Text.pdf.

Derewianka, B. (2015). The contribution of genre theory to literacy education in Australia. In Turbill, J., Barton, G., and Brock, C. (eds.) *Teaching Writing in Today's Classrooms: Looking back to looking forward*. Norwood, Australia: Australian Literary Educators' Association, 69–86.

Diaz, R. M. (1983). Thought and two languages: The impact of bilingualism on cognition. In Gordon, E. W. (ed.) *Review of Research in Education*, X. Washington, DC: AERA.

Diaz, R. M. (1985). The intellectual power of bilingualism. *Quarterly Newsletter of the Laboratory of Comparative Human Cognition*, 7, 16–22.

Diaz, R. M., and Klinger, C. (1991). Towards an explanatory model of the interaction between bilingualism and cognitive development. In Bialystok, E. (ed.) *Language Processing in Bilingual Children*. Cambridge: Cambridge University Press, 167–192.

Dockrell, J. E., Connelly, V., Walter, K., and Critten, S. (2014). Assessing children's writing products: The role of curriculum based measures. *British Educational Research Journal, 41(4)*, 575–595. doi:10.1002/berj.3162.

Dustmann, C., and Frattini, T. (2014). The fiscal effects of immigration to the UK. *The Economic Journal*, 124(580), 593–643.

Eurostat. (2016). *Migration and migrant population statistics*. http://ec.europa.eu/eurostat/statistics-explained/index.php/Migration_and_migrant_population_statistics [Accessed 12 October 2015].

Gathercole, V. M., Thomas, E. M., Jones, L., Guasch, N. V., Young, N., and Hughes, E. K. (2010). Cognitive effects of bilingualism: Digging deeper for the contributions of language dominance, linguistic knowledge, socio-economic status and cognitive abilities. *International Journal of Bilingual Education and Bilingualism*, 13(5), 617–664.

Geotz, P. J. (2003). The effects of bilingualism on theory of mind development. *Bilingualism: Language and Cognition*, 6(1), 1–15.

Gough, P., and Tunmer, W. (1986). Decoding, reading and reading disability. *Remedial and pecial Education*, 7, 6–10.

Graham, S., and Hebert, M. (2011). Writing to read: A meta-analysis of the impact of writing and writing instruction on reading. *Harvard Educational Review*, 81(4), 710–744.

Grosjean, F. (2010). *Bilingual: Life and reality*. Boston, MA: Harvard University Press.

Hakuta, K., Ferdman, B. M., and Diaz, R. M. (1987). Bilingualism and cognitive development: Three perspectives. In Rosenberg, S. (ed.) *Advances in Applied Psycholinguistics: Reading, writing and language learning*. New York: Cambridge University Press.

Hutchinson, J. M., Whiteley, H. E., Smith, C. D., and Connors, L. (2003). The developmental progression of comprehension-related skills in children learning EAL. *Journal of Research in Reading*, 26(1), 19–32.

James, S., and Rigby, V. (1997). *Britain and the Celtic Iron Age*. London: British Museum Press.

Jean, M., and Geva, E. (2009). The development of vocabulary in English as a second language children and its role in predicting word recognition ability. *Applied Psycholinguistics*, 30, 153–185.

Jongejan, W., Verhoeven, L., and Siegel, L. S. (2007). Predictors of reading and spelling abilities in first- and second-language learners. *Journal of Educational Psychology*, 99(4), 835–851.

Kame'enui, E. J., and Simmons, D. C. (2001). Introduction to this special issue: The DNA of reading fluency. *Scientific Studies in Reading*, 5(3), 203–210.

Kovács, A. M. (2009). Early bilingualism enhances mechanisms of false-belief reasoning. *Developmental Science*, 12(1), 48–54.

Lesaux, N. K., Geva, E., Koda, K., Siegel, L. S., and Shanahan, T. (2008). Development of literacy in second-language learners. In August, D., and Shanahan, T. (eds.) *Developing Reading and Writing in Second-Language Learners: Lessons from the report of The National Literacy Panel on language-minority children and youth*. New York: Routledge/CALL.

Lesaux, N. K., Rupp, A. A., and Siegel, L. S. (2007). Growth in reading skills of children from diverse linguistic backgrounds. *Journal of Educational Psychology*, 99(4), 821–834.

Lindsey, K. A., Manis, F. R., and Bailey, C. E. (2003). Prediction of first-grade reading in Spanish-speaking English language learners. *Journal of Educational Psychology*, 95, 482–494.

Lipka, O., and Siegel, L. S. (2007). The development of reading skills in children with English as a second language. *Scientific Studies of Reading*, 11(2), 105–131.

Marinova-Todd, S. (2012). 'Corplum is a core from a plum': The advantage of bilingual children in the analysis of word meaning from verbal context. *Bilingualism: Language and Cognition*, 15(1), 117–127.

Martin, J. R. (2009). Genre and language learning: A social semiotic perspective. *Linguistics and Education*, 20(1), 10–21.

Martinez, R., and Murphy, V. A. (2011). The effect of frequency and idiomaticity on second language reading comprehension. *TESOL Quarterly*, 45, 267–290.

Montrul, S. (2008). *Incomplete Acquisition in Bilingualism: Re-examining the age factor*. Amsterdam: John Benjamins.

Montrul, S. (2009). Knowledge of tense-aspect and mood in Spanish heritage speakers. *International Journal of Bilingualism*, 13(2), 239–269.

Montrul, S. (2010). Current issues in heritage language acquisition. *Annual Review of Applied Linguistics*, 30, 3–23.

Murphy, V. A. (2014). *Second Language Learning in the Early School Years: Trends and contexts*. Oxford: Oxford University Press.

Murphy, V. A., Kyriacou, M., and Menon, P. (2015). Profiling writing challenges in children with English as an Additional language (EAL). Nuffield Foundation Report. www.nuffieldfoundation.org/writing-challenges-children-learning-eal.

Nakamoto, J., Lindsey, K. A., and Manis, F. R. (2007). A longitudinal analysis of English language learners' word decoding and reading comprehension. *Reading and Writing*, 20, 691–719.

Nation, K., Clarke, P., Marshall, C. M., and Durand, M. (2004). Hidden language impairments in children: Parallels between poor reading comprehension and specific language impairment. *Journal of Speech, Hearing & Language Research*, 47, 199–211.

Nation, K., Cocksey, J., Taylor, J. S. H., and Bishop, D. (2010). A longitudinal investigation of early reading and language skills in children with poor reading comprehension. *Journal of Child Psychology & Psychiatry*, 51(9), 1031–1039.

Nation, K., and Snowling, M. (2004). Beyond phonological skills: Broader language skills contribute to the development of reading. *Journal of Research in Reading*, 27, 342–356.

OECD. (2012). Percentage of immigrant children and their outcomes. www.oecd.org/els/soc/49295179.pdf.

OECD. (2013). *PISA 2012 Results: Excellence through equity: Giving every student the chance to succeed. vol. II*. PISA: OECD Publishing. http://doi.org/10.1787/9789264201132-en.

OECD. (2015a). Helping immigrant students to succeed at school and beyond. www.oecd.org/education/Helping-immigrant-students-to-succeed-at-school-and-beyond.pdf.

OECD. (2015b). Improving schools in Scotland: An OECD perspective. www.oecd.org/education/school/Improving-Schools-in-Scotland-An-OECD-Perspective.pdf.

Paradis, J., Emmerzael, K., and Sorenson Duncan, T. (2010). Assessment of English language learners: Using parent report on first language development. *Journal of Communication Disorders*, 43, 474–497.

Paradis, J., Genesee, F., and Crago, M. (2011). *Dual Language Development and Disorders: A handbook on bilingualism and second language learning*, 2nd ed. Baltimore, MD: Brookes Publishing.

Peal, E., and Lambert, W. E. (1962). The relation of bilingualism to intelligence. *Psychological Monographs: General and Applied*, 76(27), 1–23.

Ruiz Soto, Ariel G., Hooker, Sarah, and Batalova, Jeanne. (2015). *States and Districts with the Highest Number and Share of English Language Learners*. Washington, DC: Migration Policy Institute. www.migrationpolicy.org/research/states-and-districts-highest-number-and-share-english-language-learners.

Sammons, P., Toth, K., and Sylva, K. (2015). *Background to Success: Differences in A-level entries by ethnicity, neighbourhood and gender*. Report for the Sutton Trust. London.

Sammons, P., Toth, K., Sylva, K., Melhuish, E., Siraj, I., and Taggart, B. (2015). The long-term role of the home learning environment in shaping students' academic attainment in secondary school. *Journal of Children's Services*, 10(3) 189–201.

Smith, S. S., and Murphy, V. A. (2015). Measuring productive elements of multi-word phrase vocabulary knowledge among children with English as an additional or only language. *Reading and Writing*, 28(3), 347–369.

Strand, S., and Demie, F. (2005). English language acquisition and educational attainment at the end of primary school. *Educational Studies*, 31(3) 275–291.

Strand, S., Malmberg, L., and Hall, J. (2015). *English as an Additional Language (EAL) and Educational Achievement in England: An analysis of the National Pupil Database*. Report for the Educational Endowment Foundation. London, UK.

Verhoeven, L. (1990). Acquisition of reading in a second language. *Reading Research Quarterly*, 25(2), 91–113.

Verhoeven, L. (2000). Components of early second language reading and spelling. *Scientific Studies of Reading*, 4, 313–330.

Verhoeven, L., and Vermeer, A. (2006). Literacy achievement of children with intellectual disabilities and differing linguistic backgrounds. *Journal of Intellectual Disability Research*, 50(10), 725–738.

Whiteside, K. E., Gooch, D., and Norbury, C. F. (2016). English language proficiency and early school attainment among children learning English as an additional language. *Child Development, 88(3)*, 812–817. doi:10.1111/cdev.12615.

8

Differentiated instruction for young English learners

Amanda L. Sullivan and Mollie R. Weeks

Introduction

Diversity is a cornerstone of the modern classroom. Children vary not only in their funds of knowledge and academic skills, but on a range of intersecting cultural dimensions such as ethnicity, nationality, language, socioeconomic status, gender and religion. In many schools and classrooms, increasing diversity is largely attributable to rising enrolments of migrant children, including immigrants, refugees and asylees, who may enter school with a myriad of linguistic and educational experiences that create a range of readiness for planned curriculum and instruction (Sullivan et al. 2016). Yet, to the potential detriment of students, many educators 'still harbor the myth of "homogeneity by virtue of chronological age"' where teachers instruct all students uniformly regardless their diverse needs (Tomlinson et al. 2003, p. 119). This attitude can be especially problematic when the students comprising a classroom come from diverse cultural and linguistic backgrounds.

Educators can implement differentiated instruction (DI) to respond systematically to students' varied learning needs and language skills. DI is an instructional orientation wherein 'teachers proactively modify curricula, teaching methods, resources, learning activities, and student products to address the diverse needs of individual students and small groups of students to maximise the learning opportunity for each student in a classroom' (Tomlinson et al. 2003, p. 121). In short, DI is a framework for tailoring curriculum and instruction to students' readiness and interests so that students acquire desired knowledge and skills and avoid disengagement that often follows instruction misaligned to students' present knowledge and skills (Tomlinson et al. 2003). This chapter provides an overview of DI and its component practices that can be applied in order to achieve instructional tailoring to unique student needs, with an emphasis on its application with young English learners (ELs).

Historical perspectives

As a general concept, DI has been around for many years and discussed in a variety of terms (e.g., differentiated learning, tailoring, individualization, adapting to individual differences, universal design). As a unified approach, however, development of DI has largely taken place in the last twenty years. In this section, we describe the historical origins of DI, including its theoretical roots, as a basis for the practices to be discussed in later sections.

Teachers in one-room schoolhouses and multigrade classrooms had to differentiate instruction to ensure students of varying developmental stages and skill levels progressed (Washburn 1953). As many school systems moved to graded classrooms of like-aged children, attention to differentiation waned. Nonetheless, as student diversity grows and policies encourage or mandate inclusion of students from diverse cultural, linguistic, and ability groups, DI has been refined as an increasingly valuable means of supporting students' learning. Indeed, since few classrooms are characterised by truly homogenous learner needs, all educators should engage in some degree of differentiation to promote learning. As a unified concept, contemporary conceptualization of DI gained traction from Tomlinson's work in the late 1990s and early 2000s and centres around adaptation of the instructional strategies, curriculum, learning environment and student products in response to students' diverse learning needs.

The DI approach described herein is informed by multiple developmental and learning theories and constructs. Of particular relevance is Lev Vygotsky's zone of proximal development (ZPD), 'a point of required mastery where a child cannot successfully function alone, but can succeed with scaffolding or support' (Tomlinson et al. 2003, p. 126). When instruction targets students' ZPDs with appropriate teacher support, students build academic skills and develop greater independence. One child's ZPD is likely unique from another's, so scaffolding allows for tailoring of support to meet children's varied needs. Consistent with Vygotsky's ZPD, research indicates children learn best when given tasks that are slightly beyond their skill level but not so challenging as to cause failure (Case-Smith and Holland 2009). This means teachers should identify the task features wherein a child is able to succeed while building additional language or academic skills and offer necessary supports to facilitate mastery.

In addition, applied behaviour analysis (ABA), an approach to supporting development of meaningful behaviours by altering the environment, provides a foundation for research-based practices within DI. In ABA, the provider considers how the environment influences behaviour to identify how environmental factors can be modified to promote desired outcomes (Ardoin et al. 2016). Thus, from an ABA approach, we do not blame students for educational difficulties but instead consider ways in which the learning environment can impede or facilitate students' progress and adjust instruction, materials or other dimensions of the classroom environment to achieve desired outcomes (Ardoin et al. 2016). When engaging young ELs, examining environmental causes for difficulties helps underscore the many contextual factors influencing language acquisition, especially second language acquisition, and related academic development of ELs (e.g., inadequate vocabulary instruction; Martinez et al. 2014). Adjusting instruction accordingly increases the likelihood of student success by implementing increasingly individualised or intensive practices to reinforce linguistic development.

DI is also informed by motivation theory. While external factors have a significant impact on language acquisition and academic development, it is also prudent to examine student motivation throughout the process of learning. Self-determination theory (SDT) explores the relationship between various types of motivation and how they relate to behaviour. Behaviour that is extrinsically motivated is directed by certain tangible outcomes (i.e., earning a specific grade on a test, developing foundational knowledge for a future career, avoiding punishment/sanctions). Intrinsic motivation, on the other hand, is often related to curiosity or other internal drivers. Appropriately supporting student learning and student competence and autonomy creates educational environments that spark curiosity and capitalise on intrinsic motivation. One way to support autonomy is by allowing choice and self-direction during learning (Ryan and Deci 2000). DI can promote intrinsic motivation by encouraging student interest and self-competence (Tomlinson et al. 2003).

Critical issues and topics

Because DI is an orientation or framework for instruction, there are several necessary elements and related practices to achieve its goals. In this section, we describe the basic elements of DI and core practices in assessment since effective assessment is necessary to plan and evaluate instructional adaptations that occur within DI. DI scholarship specific to TESOL and young ELs is limited, so we have drawn primarily in this chapter on studies conducted with DI in English-only general and special education settings with largely early elementary-aged students. Further, this literature has largely emerged from scholars and research studies based in the United States. We address how DI may be applied with young ELs, recognizing that its application may have to be adapted in non-US contexts.

Basic elements of DI

Proactive instructional design responsive to learner differences is the basis of effective DI. Teachers taking this approach design curricula with learner diversity in mind as opposed to only adapting whole-class instruction as challenges arise. Instruction can be differentiated by focusing on curricula, instructional strategies, classroom environment or materials and student products, or the reciprocal relationships among them. Figure 8.1 presents several guiding questions that can inform DI planning with young ELs.

DI is planned relative to students' readiness for instruction given that not all students will benefit from a one-size-fits-all approach to curriculum and instruction. Among young ELs, readiness may be determined by a variety of factors: language proficiency, educational experience, prior funds of knowledge, academic skills, abilities and special needs, and others. Finding the right starting point for instruction links directly back to the importance of the ZPD since instruction should be targeted just beyond a child's current level of language skills and content mastery, and provide appropriate scaffolding. Educators must gauge students' individual readiness well enough to determine the best entry point for additional instruction. Through screening, progress monitoring and diagnostic assessments (discussed in detail below), school personnel can determine which students need additional assistance to progress and how best to adapt relevant dimensions of the instructional environment by understanding the nature of language and skill deficits, planning changes to core curriculum and matching students to appropriate targeted supports (Hosp and Ardoin 2008).

DI often relies on flexible grouping and pacing. In recognizing the variability in students' language skills and performance, teachers make allowances for variable response times and completion rates. Groupings can be made to provide DI to breakout groups of students with similar needs. Alternatively, heterogeneous groups can be used to capitalise on the social nature of learning via implementation of research-based paired or group learning strategies so that peers provide scaffolding. Another core feature of DI is using students' interests and experience to enhance learning. Teachers should consider students' interests and background knowledge as a means to increase not only students' persistence and motivation, but achievement and productivity as well (Tomlinson et al. 2003).

Instructional Strategies	Learning Environment
How do I structure instructional time within the classroom (lecture, choral responding, popcorn reading)? Can I present material through different means (audio, visual, varying text sizes, etc.)? Do some students respond differently to different types of instruction? Are there ways to shape instruction to meet individual student language needs? Can I utilize peers to assist with language instruction and socialization?	Is my classroom conducive to learning? Could I minimize clutter to help increase student focus? Do certain students require special environments to maximize learning and performance (i.e.,quiet testing areas)? How do I create a welcoming environment for all students? Can I find ways to acknowledge and celebrate the diversity of cultures within my classroom? Are students grouped appropriately for small group instruction?

Guiding Questions for DI

Curriculum	Student Products
Does my classroom's core curriculum support all learners? Are any students at risk for language difficulties? Can I vary instructional materials accordingly? Can I find ways to vary content by student interest? Can I alter the curriculum to focus on areas in need of additional instruction?	How do I assess students' language and content mastery? Do I offer options for students to showcase what they know and can do in a variety of formats? Would a variety of different assessments (exams, papers, projects, etc.) increase depth of learning and engagement with course material? Can I capitalize on the diverse linguistic strengths within my classroom when creating assignments and assessments? Are there opportunities for students to work in groups? Are grading rubrics varied by skill level?

Figure 8.1 Questions to guide DI, derived from Skinner et al. 1996; Martinez et al. 2014; Delbridge and Helman 2016; Grinder 1993; Watts-Taffe et al. 2012; Ernest et al. 2011

Assessment to inform DI

The goal of assessment is to determine what students need to learn and how to best teach it (Hosp and Ardoin 2008). In order to differentiate instruction efficiently and effectively and determine the value of adaptations, teachers should engage in data-based decision making (DBDM). Put simply, DBDM is a set of systematic procedures for collecting data on student performance and modifying instruction based on those data (Carta et al. 2016). Educators act as problem analysts, identifying potential causes for students' problems and strategizing methods for solving the problem (Christ and Arañas 2014). When discrepancies exist between an expected level of performance and an observed level of performance, practitioners work to uncover the variables that both cause and maintain particular problematic behaviours or performance challenges.

The basic principles of DBDM are derived from the scientific method. To change student outcomes and performance (dependent variables) teachers implement instructional strategies or interventions (independent variables), based on hypotheses about students' learning needs, and collect data before and during implementation to determine the effects of changes (Deno 2016). Any change made within DI can be considered a testable hypothesis about the potential effect on student learning. From there, school personnel are able to engage in the ongoing process of assessment, modification and hypothesis testing until student outcomes reflect desired results.

Accordingly, a common first step in DBDM is school- or classwide screening, a process of briefly assessing all students to determine each individual student's performance in comparison to peers or language or performance standards. The data obtained from this process can be used to evaluate instruction and determine students' learning rates, progress, and mastery of instructional objectives (Barrera and Liu 2010; Brown-Chisdey and Steege 2005). In the United States, DBDM is often achieved through use of curriculum-based measurement or evaluation, which are quick, reliable, cost-effective standardised formative assessment procedures drawn directly from classroom instruction and curriculum (Deno 2003; Howell and Hosp 2014; for detailed instructional guides, see Burns and Parker 2014; Hosp et al. 2016).

Depending on the results of screening and progress monitoring, instructional or curricular modifications may occur for the entire class, small groups or individuals. Ongoing assessment is essential to determining the effectiveness of any given strategy since there is no way to determine if specific interventions will work *a priori* for specific students. Research provides insight on what is likely to work under certain conditions; ongoing assessment allows for determination of actual effect on any given individual. Teachers should select instructional strategies and interventions based on the best available evidence, assess student progress to determine effects and change strategies if performance does not improve. For students who demonstrate chronic or severe difficulties despite multiple attempts at differentiation, diagnostic assessment can guide further individualization.

DI for learners with special needs

When young ELs demonstrate inadequate linguistic development or academic performance that appears unresponsive to DI, it can be challenging to determine whether students' performance is attributable to insufficient opportunities to learn or special needs (Linan-Thompson and Ortiz 2009) since test scores alone do not allow for determination of whether difficulties arise from lack of instruction or learning problems (Barrera and Liu 2010). A problem-solving orientation to identify the cause of students' difficulty is especially valuable given the behavioural parallels between language acquisition and learning problems. More specifically, both ELs and students with learning disabilities may struggle to identify unfamiliar words, follow directions or participate in activities. Before considering that a student may have a learning problem, educators should rule out contextual determinants like language proficiency, cultural variability and educational experience (Sandberg and Reschly 2011). The iterative process of assessment and differentiation can assist in ruling out these factors.

To understand what children can and cannot do with proper instruction, practitioners may turn to dynamic assessment wherein the assessor provides explicit instruction in a new skill and monitors progress over a discrete period of time (Barrera and Liu 2010). Similar to their English proficient peers, ELs with learning disabilities generally show limited growth whereas a child whose challenges are due to typical language acquisition will show consistent gains in skill after explicit instruction (Linan-Thompson and Ortiz 2009). A small percentage of students have learning disabilities. ELs with learning disabilities comprise a heterogeneous group of students who experience complex interactions between language, culture, and language-learning ability. These students likely encounter literacy difficulties in both their native language and English, which complicates second language acquisition. This may increase the cognitive demand associated with engaging with classroom materials, necessitating additional scaffolding and differentiation (Garcia and Tyler 2010).

Current contributions and research

In this section, we briefly discuss the current context of research on DI with ELs. Little scholarship has focused on DI for language instruction. Available research evidence, however, suggests that DI supports literacy development, particularly phonological awareness, reading comprehension and narrative storytelling, when the types and extent of instructional supports are varied according to student differences (August et al. 2014; Healy et al. 2005; Reis et al. 2011; Weddle et al. 2016). DI practices utilised in this research included introducing books with discussion, cognitive strategy instruction, listening to students read aloud one-on-one, small group enrichment, buddy reading, phonological awareness interventions, encouraging students to repeat stories they hear then elaborate on their own experiences and creativity exercises.

The research support for assessment tools for young ELs is also limited and characterised by longstanding concerns for their reliability and validity (e.g., Baker et al. 1998). Recently, academic assessment systems have been developed and validated with ELs in mind (e.g., curriculum based measurement; for examples, see Richards-Tutor et al. 2012; McConnell et al. 2015). Given the dearth of research on DI for TESOL specifically, this chapter draws necessarily on scholarship addressing DI generally with students from culturally and linguistically diverse backgrounds, especially research related to literacy development in young ELs.

Recommendations for practice

Thus far, this chapter had addressed the historical and theoretical foundations of DI, basic elements of effective DI implementation and the current research base. In this section, we summarise the practices that may be used to enact the previously described elements and features commonly enumerated in DI scholarship. We focus on how DI can be tailored to young ELs by linking DI scholarship to effective instruction of young ELs in general education and TESOL contexts, and include recommendations for how to address common concerns about engaging students' families to maximise learning and integrating DI with other instructional initiatives.

Putting DI into practice for young ELs

Implementation of the DI framework requires teachers to engage in several foundational approaches to instruction. These are detailed in Table 8.1 along with related classroom practices for young ELs, including instructional practices shown to be effective for supporting language and literacy development for ELs (August et al. 2014; Martinez et al. 2014; Tomlinson et al. 2003). However, teachers cannot effectively implement DI without first acquiring thorough knowledge in the subject area taught and current developments in research-based instruction and assessment in a given subject area (Watts-Taffe et al. 2012). For early childhood educators, firm understanding of typical and atypical child development is also critical.

Table 8.1 Key features and related practice for effective DI

Key Feature	Sample Related Practices
Design curriculum with learner variance in mind.	• Consider students' first language proficiency, English proficiency, academic skills, educational experience, learning rates and interests in design and planning of instructional supports. • Use a variety of modes of presentation. • Engage in ongoing formative assessment to gauge student progress and identify students for differentiation. • Use progress monitoring data to identify appropriate instructional goals for groups and individuals. • Align instructional materials and tasks with students' present level of proficiency.
Ensure students' understanding of key concepts, principles and skills in a given content area.	• Thoroughly understand local curriculum and subject matter to be taught. • Use end goals for knowledge and skills students should have at the end of a sequence, unit or timeframe to plan differentiated lessons and activities. • Provide explicit instruction in phonics, vocabulary, phonological awareness, readings fluency and comprehension, writing mechanics, grammar, etc. • Use pictures or other visual aids to illustrate meanings and contexts. • Reinforce material through repeated exposures to strengthen learning (e.g., postreading vocab activity).
Capitalise on students' interests and prior knowledge.	• Use active learning strategies. • Construct novel and/or challenging tasks. • Link instruction to students' experiences. • Use materials that feature authentic multicultural identities. • Encourage questions or conversations in and out of classroom context. • Allow student choices of materials, tasks or topics when possible. • Discuss linkages between current learning and prior knowledge or experience. • Discuss relevance and utility of new knowledge or skills.
Use students' first language proficiency to support development of new knowledge and skills.	• Preview or review English materials or tasks in student's first language. • Allow for conversation during instruction in first language. • Provide bilingual glossaries.
Allow flexible pacing.	• Allow sufficient wait-time (>10 seconds) when soliciting student responses to allow for cognitive processing. • Allow students to progress through an assignment or activity at different speeds.
Incorporate small-group instruction.	• Use groupings flexibly, based on students' current knowledge and skills. • Match instructional materials to instructional needs of small groups.

(Continued)

Table 8.1 (Continued)

Key Feature	Sample Related Practices
	• Engage in frequent progress monitoring to determine appropriate groupings. • Use both heterogeneous groupings and skill-based groupings to achieve varied learning goals. • Use peer-assisted learning strategies, cooperative learning activities and learning centres.
Provide scaffolding to support development of new knowledge and skills.	• Model the process or task before having the student do it. • Create opportunities to use new vocabulary. • Incorporate opportunities for teacher-student interactions with materials. • Preview materials. • Use graphic organisers. • Teach and model metacognitive and problem-solving strategies.

Engaging families with limited English proficiency

Interactions between families and schools impact children's learning and social-emotional development (Reschly and Christenson 2012). Ideally, schools work to build school-family partnerships in which the worlds of home and school are brought into congruence through shared goals, contributions and accountability (Reschly and Christenson 2012). To do so, teachers should eschew assumptions about 'hard-to-reach' families as being unconcerned about or uninvolved with their children's education since research contradicts this assumption (Mapp and Hong 2010). Instead, teachers should recognise that families may hold a variety of notions about appropriate involvement in schools and adults' roles (e.g., teachers as the unquestioned expert), and that dominant expectations are often implicit and unknown to families from culturally and linguistically diverse backgrounds (Arzubiaga et al. 2009). Schools should accommodate multiple means of family involvement and recognise their capacity to assist with learning (Mapp and Hong 2010).

Systematic strategies to cultivate positive relations and family engagement include treating families as equals in educational processes; encouraging parent-to-staff and parent-to-parent interactions; involving parents in decision making and school leadership; and enlisting outside agencies to act as cultural brokers within local communities (Mapp and Hong 2010). In addition, educators can emphasise instructional methods that place families in the role of educators and demonstrate value for the skills they possess in supporting young children's English development such as authoring dual language texts and family literacy nights (Delbridge and Helman 2016).

Integrating DI with other initiatives

Beyond its theoretical foundations, DI is applicable to – and can be implemented within the context of – other contemporary educational initiatives that emphasise acknowledging and responding to diverse learners' needs through differentiation. Often, the desire to implement any new initiative, including DI, is pitted against schools' and teachers' limited resources. School leaders and teachers can reduce the burden by integrating initiatives wherever feasible. DI should not be considered adjunctive to or separate from educational initiatives like multitier systems of support (e.g., response to intervention [RTI]), culturally responsive teaching [CRT], or universal designs for learning [UDL], but as a means for achieving the goals of these frameworks and vice versa. Such integration can increase general efficiency and a positive climate that benefits both teachers and students.

Many educators are familiar with response to intervention (RTI), a framework for instruction and intervention based on the multitier public health model of increasingly individualised and intensive supports to meet learner needs. The goal of RTI is to support learning by providing a high-quality curriculum for all students and supplementing instruction with differentiated supports when necessary (Gettinger and Stoiber 2012). DI strategies such as small-group instruction and matching instructional materials to individual needs are often employed when students demonstrate needs beyond the universally provided research-based curriculum and instruction (Tomlinson et al. 2003; Al Otaiba et al. 2011; Gettinger and Stoiber 2012). RTI also provides several tools to facilitate identification of learner needs and appropriate differentiation through DBDM.

Integration of DI may also bolster efforts to engage in CRT, which calls for teachers to establish strong relationships with their students, understand their cultural backgrounds and differentiate instruction to be responsive to students' backgrounds and needs (Klingner and Edwards 2006). DI's emphasis on individualization and capitalizing on students' interests and experiences makes it well suited for application within a CRT framework. In turn, CRT places great value on teachers' understanding of students' cultures, community values and home learning practices, and using that knowledge to enhance instruction and provide a classroom environment more conducive to learning by incorporating culturally based practices (e.g., storytelling). In this way, CRT is complementary to DI. In addition, CRT highlights the importance of embracing cultural differences and the cultural nature of learning, such as the following: challenging interpersonal biases, practices or procedures that disadvantage students from culturally diverse backgrounds (e.g., beliefs that all students must be taught the same way and progress at same rates; application of punitive discipline procedures; dismissal of cultural knowledge and preferences); eschewing privilege to support equitable educational access, participation and outcomes; and believing all students are capable of educational success (Klingner et al. 2005). All of these notions are compatible with DI.

Similarities can also be drawn between DI and UDL, an approach to designing learning spaces by emphasizing flexibility and versatility to ensure all students can access the space, curriculum and instruction through multiple means of representation, engagement and expression (Horn and Banerjee 2009; Kaderavek 2009). Universal design of learning was originally conceptualised as a movement to make physical spaces universally accessible, and later expanded to UDL to emphasise educational and informational accessibility (Rao and Skouge 2012). Educators are encouraged to tailor instruction to address a wide variety of abilities, allow students to interact with material in ways they find most interesting or as needed given sensory or learning differences (e.g., visual or hearing impairments, reading disability) and provide a platform for students to respond to class material in a variety of ways that demonstrate what they know (e.g., allowing oral, written, graphic and pictorial responses). At their core, both DI and UDL serve as means for all students to access and participate in the same curriculum (Horn and Banerjee 2009; Watts-Taffe et al. 2012). For educators, application of UDL's principles of flexibility in providing varied means of representation, engagement and expression based on learner needs and preference can be essential to effective DI.

Future directions

Here, we discuss avenues for future research given the current knowledge base for DI. In particular, we consider how future DI research can clarify issues related to appropriate assessment and instruction for young ELs in TESOL contexts.

There is a robust and growing research base for DBDM, and numerous studies to support use of DI, but there is less known about the effectiveness of these practices with young children and ELs. Additional research is necessary to validate assessment tools with young ELs and to establish new ways in which to evaluate the language and literacy abilities of culturally and linguistically diverse students, particularly those who are bilingual or learning English. Most research on ELs has included students with similar language and socioeconomic backgrounds, which may not generalise to heterogeneous contexts, or researchers do not report on the linguistic or cultural diversity of participants, which does not allow for inferences about the generalizability of findings to specific EL subpopulations. Better, more culturally responsive assessments will allow for more accurate identification of learner needs and effective DI.

DI can also be challenging in pre-kindergarten settings that lack formal curriculum, which makes it difficult to determine whether or not students are in need of additional supports (Carta et al. 2016). In addition, extensive variation between pre-kindergarten programmes in academic resources, quality of instruction, training and credentialing of staff, hours of operation and other features can impede implementation of research-based assessment and instructional practices because of the difficulty in identifying and adapting applicable research (Carta et al. 2016). Nonetheless, when operating from an orientation of DBDM, early childhood educators can make instructional decisions based on the best available research and assess effects to identify where additional adaptations or strategies are warranted.

Culturally responsive instruction and assessment are promising methods for preventing inappropriate educational practices that hinder students' development; however, evidence must be gathered in order to validate instructional practices and determine what works with diverse populations of students. The issue of effectiveness becomes more complex when we conceptualise instructional practices within an ecological context because it emphasises the importance of considering for whom and under what conditions a given practice is effective. A proper interpretation of existing literature requires educators to ask probing questions (Klingner et al. 2005): Were the students in the sample similar to the students in my setting? Is the context of research similar to my own? Without consideration of these questions in practice – and without research that allows practitioners to respond affirmatively to these questions – students are vulnerable to ineffective and culturally unsupportive instruction.

DI serves as a powerful tool within the classroom; however, the strength of its impact relies on correct implementation. Evidence suggests that active coaching can help instructors implement evidence-based practices with fidelity. By developing relationships with knowledgeable and experienced coaches, teachers acquire the knowledge and tools for effective DI (Snyder et al. 2015). Yet, many questions remain about the best way to implement coaching: Who needs additional coaching? How should it be delivered? How often? With additional research focused on these questions, practitioners will gain a better understanding of how to support teachers in their efforts to differentiate instruction accurately.

Evidence-based practice (EBP) occurs when practitioners make decisions based on the best available research, student and family characteristics and preferences and site resources. One challenge for implementing research-based practices is identifying the factors which may facilitate or hinder implementation, and how adaptations to research-based practices affect students' outcomes. Yet, DI relies heavily on iterative adaptations, so we need to test empirically common adaptations. This knowledge base can be enhanced through practice-based evidence research (PBER) wherein practitioners collect data on the effects of adaptations or modifications to interventions in order to increase their overall ability to support students' outcomes (Kratochwill et al. 2012). Moreover, thoughtful PBER has the potential to provide evidence about the extent to which certain instructional practices are culturally responsive. While PBER is conceptually appealing, there is no consensus about standard criteria for practice-based evidence. It is thus the responsibility of the scientist-practitioner to adopt methodologies with sound foundations in order to collect accurate information.

Further reading

1   Buysse, V. (2013). *Handbook of response to intervention in early childhood.* Baltimore, MD: Paul H. Brookes.

This book provides information on the application of RTI in early childhood education settings, and includes chapters on RTI for young ELs, and language and literacy development.

2   Jimerson, S. R., Burns, M. K., and Mathany VanDerHeyden, A. (2016). *Handbook of response to intervention: The science and practice of multi-tiered systems of support,* 2nd ed. New York: Springer.

This handbook provides comprehensive coverage of conceptual and practical aspects of RTI to support students' academic development in elementary and middle school.

3   Lapp, D., Fisher, D., and DeVere Wolsey, T. (2009). *Literacy growth for every child: Differentiated small-group instruction K-6.* New York: Guilford Press.

This book describes collaborative learning strategies and small group activities to facilitate differentiated instruction.

4   McGee, L. M., and Richgels, D. J. (2014). *Designing early literacy programs: Differentiated instruction in preschool and kindergarten,* 2nd ed. New York: Guilford Press.

This book provides an overview of DI, including RTI, and describes the application of DI in language and literacy instruction for young children, highlighting learning activities and assessment with examples, vignettes and reproducible materials.

Related topics

Classroom management, assessment, teaching grammar, projects

References

Al Otaiba, S., Connor, C. M., Folsom, J. S., Greulich, L., Meadows, J., and Li, Z. (2011). Assessment data-informed guidance to individualize kindergarten reading instruction. Findings from a cluster-randomized control field trial. *The Elementary School Journal,* 11(4), 535–560.

Ardoin, S. P., Wagner, L., and Bangs, K. E. (2016). Applied behavior analysis: A foundation to response to intervention. In Jimerson, S. R. et al., eds, *Handbook of Response to Intervention.* New York: Springer Science+Business Media, 29–42.

Arzubiaga, A. E., Nogeuron, S. C., and Sullivan, A. L. (2009). The education of children in immigrant families. *Review of Research in Education,* 33, 246–271.

August, D., McCardle, P., and Shanahan, T. (2014). Developing literacy in English language learners: Findings from a review of the experimental research. *School Psychology Review,* 43(4), 490–498.

Baker, S. K., Plasencia-Peinado, J., and Lezcano-Lytle, V. (1998). The use of curriculum-based measurement with language-minority students. In Shinn, M. R. (ed.) *Advanced Applications of Curriculum-based Measurement.* New York: Guildford Press, 175–213.

Barrera, M., and Liu, K. K. (2010). Challenges of general outcomes measurement in the RTI progress monitoring of linguistically diverse exceptional learners. *Theory Into Practice*, 49, 273–280.

Brown-Chidsey, R., and Steege, M. W. (2005). Using RTI procedures with students from diverse backgrounds. In Brown-Chidsey, R., and Steege, M. W. (eds.) *Response to Intervention: Principles and strategies for effective practice*. New York: Guilford, 99–107.

Burns, M. K., and Parker, D. C. (2014). *Curriculum-based Assessment for Instructional Design: Using data to individualize instruction*. New York: Guilford Press.

Carta, J. J., Greenwood, C. R., Atwater, J., McConnell, S. R., Goldstein, H., and Kaminski, R. A. (2015). Identifying preschool children for higher tiers of language and early literacy instruction within a response to intervention framework. *Journal of Early Intervention*, 36(4), 281–291.

Carta, J. J., Greenwood, C. R., Goldstein, H., McConnell, S. R., Kaminski, R., Bradfield, T. A., Wackerle-Hollman, A., Linas, M., Guerrero, G., Kelley, E., and Atwater, J. (2016). Advances in multi-tiered systems of support for prekindergarten children: Lessons learned from 5 years of research and development from the center for response to intervention in early childhood. In Jimerson, S. R. et al. (eds.) *Handbook of Response to Intervention*. New York: Springer Science+Business Media, 587–606.

Case-Smith, J., and Holland, T. (2009). Making decisions about service delivery in early childhood programs. *Language, Speech, and Hearing Services in Schools*, 40, 416–423.

Christ, T. J., and Arañas, Y. A. (2014). Best practices in problem analysis. In Harrison, P. L., and Thomas, A. (eds.) *Best Practices in School Psychology Data-Based and Collaborative Decision Making*. Bethesda, MA: National Association of School Psychologists, 87–98.

Delbridge, A., and Helman, L. A. (2016). Evidence-based strategies for fostering biliteracy in any classroom. *Early Childhood Education Journal*, 44, 307–316.

Deno, S. L. (2003). Developments in curriculum-based measurement. *The Journal of Special Education*, 37(3), 184–192.

Deno, S. L. (2016). Data-based decision-making. In Jimerson, S. R. et al. (eds.) *Handbook of Response to Intervention*. New York: Springer Science+Business Media, 9–28.

Ernest, J. M., Thompson, S. E., Heckman, K. A., Hull, K., and Yates, J. (2011). Effects and social validity of differentiated instruction on student outcomes for special educators. *The Journal of International Association of Special Education*, 12(1), 33–41.

Garcia, S. B., and Tyler, B. (2010). Meeting the needs of English language learners with learning disabilities in the general curriculum. *Theory Into Practice*, 49, 113–120.

Gettinger, M., and Stoiber, K. C. (2012). Curriculum-based early literacy assessment and differentiated instruction with high-risk preschoolers. *Reading Psychology*, 33, 11–46.

Grinder, M. (1993). *ENVoY: Your personal guide to classroom management*. Battle Ground, WA: Michael Grinder & Associates, 280.

Healy, K., Vanderwood, M., and Edelson, D. (2005). Early literacy interventions for English language learners: Support for an RTI model. *Contemporary School Psychology*, 10, 55–63.

Horn, E., and Banerjee, R. (2009). Understanding curriculum modifications and embedded learning opportunities in the context of supporting all children's success. *Language, Speech, and Hearing Services in Schools*, 40, 406–415.

Hosp, J. L., and Ardoin, S. P. (2008). Assessment for instructional planning. *Assessment for Effective Intervention*, 33(2), 69–77.

Kaderavek, J. N. (2009). Perspectives from the field of early childhood special education. *Language, Speech, and Hearing Services in Schools*, 40, 403–405.

Klingner, J. K., Artiles, A. J., Kozleski, E., Harry, B., Zion, S., Tate, W., Zamora Duran, G., and Riley, D. (2005). Addressing the disproportionate representation of culturally and linguistically diverse students in special education through culturally responsive educational systems. *Education Policy Analysis Archives*, 13(38), 1–43.

Klingner, J. K., and Edwards, P. A. (2006). Cultural considerations with response to intervention models. *Reading Research Quarterly*, 41(1), 108–117.

Kratochwill, T. R., Hoagwood, K. E., Kazak, A. E., Weisz, J. R., Hood, K., Vargas, L. A., and Banez, G. A. (2012). Practice-based evidence for children and adolescents: Advancing the research agenda in schools. *School Psychology Review*, 41(2), 215–235.

Linan-Thompson, S., and Ortiz, A. A. (2009). Response to intervention and English-language learners: Instructional and assessment considerations. *Seminars in Speech and Language*, 30(2), 105–120.

Mapp, K. L., and Hong, S. (2010). Debunking the myth of the hard-to-reach parent. In Christenson, S. L., and Reschly, A. L. (eds.) *Handbook of School-family Partnerships*. New York: Routledge, 345–361.

Martinez, R. S., Harris, B., and Brunson McCain, M. (2014). Practices that promote English reading for English learners (ELs). *Journal of Education and Psychological Consultation*, 24, 128–148.

McConnell, S. R., Wackerle-Hollman, A. K., Roloff, T. A., and Rodriguez, M. (2015). Designing a measurement framework for response to intervention in early childhood programs. *Journal of Early Intervention*, 36(4), 263–280.

Rao, K., and Skouge, J. (2012). Using multimedia technologies to support culturally and linguistically diverse learners and young children with disabilities. In Hieder, K. L., and Renck Jalongo, M. (eds.) *Young Children and Families in the Information Age*. Dordrecht: Springer Science+Business Media, 101–115.

Reis, S. M., McCoach, D. B., Little, C. A., Muller, L. M., and Kaniskan, R. B. (2011). The effects of differentiated instruction and enrichment pedagogy on reading achievement in five elementary schools. *American Educational Research Journal*, 48(2), 462–501.

Reschly, A. L., and Christenson, S. L. (2012). Moving from "Context Matters" to engage partnerships with families. *Journal of Educational and Psychological Consultation*, 22(1–2), 62–78.

Richards-Tutor, C., Solari, E. J., Leafstedt, J. M., Gerber, M. M., Filippini, A., and Aceves, T. C. (2012). Response to intervention for English learners: Examining models for determining response and non-response. *Assessment for Effective Intervention*, 38(3), 172–184.

Ryan, R. M., and Deci, E. L. (2000). Intrinsic and extrinsic motivations: Classic definitions and new directions. *Contemporary Educational Psychology*, 25, 54–67.

Sandberg, K. L., and Reschly, A. L. (2011). English learners: Challenges in assessment and the promise of curriculum-based measurement. *Remedial and Special Education*, 32(2), 144–154.

Skinner, C. H., Fletcher, P. A., and Henington, C. (1996). Increasing learning rates by increasing student response rates. *School Psychology Quarterly*, 11(4), 313–325.

Snyder, P. A., Hemmeter, M. L., and Fox, L. (2015). Supporting implementation of evidence-based practices through practice-based coaching. *Topics in Early Childhood Special Education*, 35(3), 133–143.

Sullivan, A. L., Houri, A., and Sadeh, S. (2016). Demography and early academic skills of students from immigrant families: The kindergarten class of 2011. *School Psychology Quarterly*, 31, 149–162.

Tomlinson, C. A., Brighton, C., Hertberg, H., Callahan, C. M., Moon, T. R., Brimijoin, K., . . . Reynolds, T. (2003). Differentiated instruction in response to student readiness, interest, and learning profile in academically diverse classrooms: A review of literature. *Journal for the Education of the Gifted*, 27(2/3), 119–145.

Washburne, C. W. (1953). Adjusting the program to the child. *Educational Leadership*, 138–147.

Watts-Taffe, S., Laster, B. P., Broach, L., Marinak, B., McDonald Connor, C., and Walker-Dalhouse, D. (2012). Differentiated instruction: Making informed teacher decisions. *The Reading Teacher*, 66(4), 303–314.

Weddle, S. A., Spencer, T. D., Kajian, M., and Peterson, D. B. (2016). An examination of multitiered system of language support for culturally and linguistically diverse preschoolers: Implications for early and accurate identification. *School Psychology Review*, 45(1), 109–132.

9

Languages in the young learner classroom

Fiona Copland and Ming Ni

Introduction

This chapter examines languages in the young learner classroom. Specifically, it explores how both the learners' first language (L1) and the second language (L2) have been used as pedagogical tools and the rationales for and effects of doing so. It begins by giving a historical overview of classroom language use before turning to critical issues such as translanguaging. Current contributions particularly in the field of young learner research are then introduced and suggestions made for how teachers might decide how and when to use the L1 or L2. Finally, it will provide a future research agenda for this topic, which includes a focus on classroom data.

Definitions

In this chapter, we use the term L1 for the first language of students or the mother tongue (MT). The language children are learning at school is called the L2, which can also be called the target language (TL). Some children learn two (or more) languages from birth: these children are bilingual (BL). Children and adults can also become bilingual through learning a second language at school or in a social environment. Bilingualism does not therefore mean that control of two languages is flawless (see Conteh and Brock 2006, 2011; Murphy, this volume) or that bilinguals can do the same things in both languages to the same degree (e.g., it is rare to find a bilingual who can write an academic essay in two languages to the same level).

Terminology is generally contested and this is true for the terms introduced here. For example, Hall and Cook (2012) prefer the terms 'own language' for L1 and 'new language' for L2 because the order of learning does not necessarily represent the priority a person gives to each language. Mother tongue has been critiqued because it suggests that it is only the mother who speaks to a child and that other parents or carers do not have input. In terms of bilingualism, García and Kleifgen (2010, cited in Palmer et al. 2014) suggest that the term dynamic bilingualism more accurately describes the repertoire of related language practices available to people using more than one language. While we welcome the nuance that this term provides, for simplicity we use bilingualism in this chapter to describe those who have some capacity in two or more languages. We also prefer L1 and L2 as they are most commonly used in the literature and because in many classroom contexts children are indeed learning a second language.

Historical perspectives

In this section we will provide a brief overview of how L1 and L2 have been used in classrooms over the years in line with classroom methodologies and shifts in emphases. It is a broad stroke description, and it is important to acknowledge that theory and practice did not always coincide; teachers did not always do what the method demanded in terms of classroom language. The discussion takes a broad view before focusing in specifically on young learner classrooms.

Children have always learnt languages, but not always in a classroom context. Indeed, wide-scale, school-based language learning is a fairly recent phenomenon in Europe at least, starting as it did in the eighteenth century (Howatt and Smith 2014) (previously, students had studied the classical languages, Latin and Greek, but not what we would recognise as 'modern foreign languages'; see Singleton and Pfenninger, this volume). Whether and when to use the L1 or L2 to teach the target language has in part been directed by the methodological approach that teachers have followed over the years. In the early days, it was likely that most language teaching used the grammar translation (GT) method as this was used to teach the classical languages, where the focus was on reading to understand texts, and writing to some extent, but not on listening and speaking. Translating texts from one language to another was a regular feature of grammar translation classroom practice, as was a focus on the grammar and vocabulary of a language. Students also memorised chunks of texts, such as poems, and learnt rules, such as how tenses are formed and used (Larsen-Freeman and Anderson 2013). In GT, where it was important to know about the language as well as how to use it, the teacher would use the students' L1 as the medium of instruction (EMI), explaining concepts and syntactical patterning and giving L1 equivalents for new words (Larsen-Freeman and Anderson 2013). Of course, teachers and students would use the L2, but in general it was a controlled use, for example when they read texts out loud, performed translations or asked and gave answers to comprehension questions.

Not all children went to school in the eighteenth century, so learning a foreign language formally remained the privilege of the wealthy until the mid-twentieth century, at least in Europe and the USA. During this time, language learning pedagogies were undergoing significant changes as they were influenced by both advances in understandings of psychology and changes in the social world. In terms of the former, behaviourism (Skinner 1938) had a very strong influence. Focusing on how we learn a first language, Skinner suggested it was a result of positive and negative feedback (Brown 2007). In terms of the latter, the United States was at war in Korea and required soldiers to learn the language of both its allies and its enemies. Drawing on behaviourist theory, the America Army developed the audio-lingual method (AL), which was very different from GT (Brown 2007). The method encouraged speaking and listening, focusing on social, everyday language, such as greetings, asking questions and getting things done. Indeed, in some classrooms, reading and writing were not permitted, at least until after a word or phrase had been introduced, practised orally and memorised (Larsen-Freeman and Anderson 2013). In AL classrooms, teachers were encouraged to use the L2 to communicate with students and to present new language items to them. The students were discouraged from using their L1 and to immerse themselves in the L2.

In the late 50s and into the 60s and 70s, AL was very popular and was adopted in many schools in the UK and the USA (Fiona's first French lessons were delivered through an AL approach). However, by this time Chomsky had debunked many of Skinner's ideas. He posited that rather than stimulus-response being responsible for language learning, it was an inevitable result of being human as we are all born with the capability to learn languages through what Chomsky called our language acquisition device (LAD) (Chomsky 1965): we need only to be put into the right environment in order to do so. Krashen (1987) drew on Chomsky's work to develop his own theories of and pedagogies for language learning. A key feature was the notion of comprehensible input (CI). CI posits that exposure to language ('information' in Krashen's terms) is central to language learning but that any new language must not be too difficult or the student will not be able to draw on what he or she knows in order to make sense of it. Learners can be supported in this sense-making, through, for example, the teacher using gesture, visuals and repetition. Creating comprehensible input requires the teacher to use only the target language with students, although this must be made comprehensible through modification (sometimes called 'grading' language) in order not to overwhelm students and to ensure that they are able to understand most of what the teacher is saying (Krashen demonstrates this approach in a video on YouTube: https://youtube/lxKvMqPl6j4).

Krashen was one of the first scholars to study what has become known as second language acquisition (SLA) and he developed theoretical positions which the next wave of SLA researchers empirically tested (see Ellis (2015) for an overview). A number of his ideas were challenged through this research, and scholars went on to suggest other language learning theories. Interactionism (e.g. Long 1996), for example, drew on Vygotskian ideas of social constructivism (e.g. Burr 2003, 2015) and posited that second languages were learnt through students using the TL in interaction with others. This theory supported the development of Communicative Language Teaching (CLT) and a number of hybrids (e.g. Task based learning [TBL]). Proponents of AL and CLT share a belief that recreating a target language world within the classroom can provide learners with maximum opportunities to hear and use the language. Therefore, the L2 is used as much as possible, for classroom management, for doing 'chit-chat' and for explanations of grammar and vocabulary, even when they are quite complex. Struggling to make and understand meaning is believed to be key to learning, and mistakes are considered to be further evidence of progress, hence the focus is on fluency rather than accuracy. Although CLT was originally developed for adult learners in small classes (see Holliday 1994, for a critique) in recent years, CLT has been introduced into classrooms around the world, including the young learner classroom (see Garton et al. 2011).

More recently, CLIL (content and language integrated learning) has been growing in popularity, particularly in young learner classrooms (e.g., Anderson et al. 2015; Pinter 2017). In CLIL, teachers use the target language to teach a different area of the curriculum, such as history or math (see Coyle et al. 2010 for a detailed explanation; Ellison, this volume). You can see a typical CLIL classroom at this YouTube link: www.youtube.com/watch?v=kR6OnEqq1Fc. The focus is therefore on teaching the topic effectively rather than explicitly on learning language. CLIL offers an interesting contradiction in terms of classroom language. As we have explained, the class is taught through the target language; however, the teacher is often not an expert user of the language but rather an expert in the content area (he/she may be assisted by the language teacher to prepare materials and to deliver the lesson). Therefore, although he/she is using the target language, he/she may not always be accurate. Proponents of CLIL suggest that the subject teacher provides a strong role model to students of what can be achieved if you are prepared to 'have a go'. They also suggest that underachieving students are well served by this approach to subject teaching as the teacher(s) have to work hard to make meaning clear, often introducing a range of visual aids (Hellekjær 2010) and staged tasks (Grandinetti et al. 2013) to support this. Recent iterations of CLIL have described a somewhat more relaxed view of introducing the L2 into classes than was encouraged in the earliest iterations of the methodology (see Ellison, this volume).

As indicated at the beginning of this section, what we have presented so far is a Western-centric view of L1 and L2 use in language classes and also an idealised one in that teaching and learning rarely proceed in line with a given methodological orthodoxy. The history of language use in the English language classroom in other contexts is less documented. However, in countries in southeast Asia, such as China, Japan and South Korea, where English has been part of the school curriculum for some years, there have been various approaches to classroom language use.

Traditionally in Japan, for example, English has been taught using an approach called *yakudoku*, which is similar to grammar translation. As English has been considered an academic subject, rigorously examined through reading, writing, grammar and vocabulary tests, this approach has been considered appropriate. In *yakudoku*, teachers generally use Japanese as the medium of instruction (Nishino and Watanabe 2008). In China, performing well in assessments is also the paramount concern of students, and English is treated as a subject for study instead of a way of communicating (Pan and Block 2011). Therefore, Chinese is mostly used to deliver English classes, which is especially true in Mainland China, even though the Ministry of Education encourages the use of English for English classrooms (Littlewood and Yu 2011).

In recent years, CLT has been adopted in many Asian countries and teachers have been encouraged to use the target language throughout the class. Indeed, in South Korea, 'Teaching English through English' has been mandated by the national government starting from primary school at around the age of six (Choi 2015). In Japan, the Ministry of Education (MEXT) has introduced a new policy that will be enacted in 2020, which will require teachers to use English in junior and senior high school English classes (from the age of 13 to 18) as much as possible (Sekiya 2017). As an alternative to traditional English teaching approaches such as drill-based and audio-lingual methods, which have been long criticised, CLT does have its own advantages in improving students' communication ability, though it also brings with it some challenges (see Butler 2011).

While CLIL has been extensively researched in European countries and regions, it is relatively under-researched in Asia (Yang 2015). Furthermore, within Asia, the development of CLIL practices is rather diverse due to the various sociocultural and education contexts among and within the countries (Lin 2015). Indonesia, Malaysia, the Philippines and Thailand, for instance, differ in the speed and scale at which English language education is implemented in primary schools, and therefore Marsh and Hood (2008) argue that it is 'neither possible, nor appropriate' (p. 45) to generalise the classroom practice of these countries in CLIL research at the primary school level.

Notwithstanding these different methodological approaches to language teaching and the emphases they place (or not) on target language use, it is true to say that the majority of young learner teachers globally are not following a particular methodology but rather following the coursebook provided by the ministry of education or the school (Garton et al. 2011). Partly because of this, recent academic literature has been less concerned with whether the L1 should be used or not, but rather with how much should be used and when. A number of scholars have suggested that teachers should aim for 'judicious' language use. In this perspective, the how, why and when aspects of using L1 are examined and debated, with the view to develop 'guidelines' for L1 use in the classroom (e.g., Macaro 2009; Turnbull and Dailey-O'Cain 2009). Macaro (2009) suggests that teachers' judgement should determine how much of each language is used in class but based on a rationale. This viewpoint lines up with those of scholars such as Prabhu (1990) and Kumaravadivelu (2003; 2012), who believe teachers are in the best position to know how to teach their classes based on their knowledge of the children, the educational and sociopolitical contexts and what is both practical and possible under these constraints. While there are few studies which examine the important link between coursebook, context and classroom language use, Mahboob and Lin's (2018) study shows how English language teachers in Hong Kong manage this nexus in their English classes, and how target language education can benefit from the use of local language.

Critical issues and topics

In this section, we will posit three critical issues that affect how languages are used in the classroom: the demand for communication skills; the value of using the first language to teach the second; and how the decrease in the age children are being taught English affects classroom languages.

The demand for communication skills in English

The first critical issue we wish to examine is the rise in demand in many countries for citizens who can use English to communicate orally and the consequences of this demand. As English has become a global lingua franca (see, e.g., Seidlhofer 2011) and is used extensively in business, academia and cultural exchange, governments around the world have examined the English language curricula in schools and found them to focus too much on knowledge about English (e.g., grammatical rules) and not enough on how to use English (e.g., to exchange meanings). While some might argue that this demand for English has been created by western governments who are keen to remain influential in international spheres (see Phillipson 2017, for an outline of this position), the fact that globally children are learning English at increasingly younger ages is testament to this demand (Copland et al. 2014; Johnstone 2009).

The first consequence of the demand for English oral competence has been a turn to communicative pedagogies which focus on listening and speaking skills. Communicative pedagogies generally require teachers to use the target language as the medium of instruction. This is obviously easier to achieve for an expert user, or at least a confident one. In some contexts, local English teachers are not offered the training required to reach this level and so their competence is limited (Garton et al. 2011). Often oral skills are a particular problem as their education in English has focused on the written word, and teaching through the target language for these teachers is not only difficult but impossible (see Garton et al. 2011).

However, teaching through the target language is considered easy for another group of teachers – native English speaker teachers (NESTs) – and a second consequence of the demand for communication skills in English language therefore has been their employment. Currently, particularly in southeast Asia, many NESTs work on government schemes, such as JET (Japanese English Teachers) and NET (Native English Teachers in Hong Kong) where they spend time in state schools and support local English teachers (LETs) (see Copland et al. (2016) for a full discussion). Many others work autonomously in private language schools, which are numerous, ubiquitous and often unregulated. However, many NESTs are inexperienced and unqualified in English language teaching (see Copland et al. 2016). Others struggle with local educational norms which are often very different from those in the countries in which they were educated (ibid.). In terms of using the target language as the medium of instruction, there are also issues, but as Krashen has suggested, teachers need to be able to moderate their English so that students can understand them. This skill may not come easily to NESTs who may be ignorant of the fact that their language use will often contain complex constructions and be highly idiomatic. Ironically, they therefore struggle with the skill for which they are employed.

Valuing L1 in the language classroom

A second critical issue relates to the usefulness of using the L1 to teach the L2, which has been explored in recent literature (see, e.g., Hall and Cook 2012). This position goes beyond the judicious use approach described above and makes the case for choosing to use L1 to support development of L2. For example, Copland and Yonetsugi (2016) explain how a bilingual teacher drew on L1 explicitly to contrast sounds between the L1 and L2 and to provide children with personalised learning experiences. The learners' L1 can also be used effectively to contribute to positive classroom 'affect', that is, the emotional side of learning (Mitchell et al. 2013). In this regard, Auerbach (1993) claims that using L1 'reduces anxiety, enhances the affective environment for learning, takes into account sociocultural factors, facilitates incorporation of learners' life experiences, and allows for learner centred curriculum development' (p. 20). Copland and Neokleous (2011) and Brooks-Lewis (2009) both suggest that teachers can use the L1 to engage and motivate students, and Littlewood and Yu (2011) explain that using the L1 can reduce learner anxiety; in a study from South Korea, for example, young learners were less comfortable in an L2 only classroom than were adult learners (Macaro and Lee 2013). From these pedagogical perspectives, therefore, rather than L1 use being considered a mistake, it is considered a tool. Nonetheless, there remains an L2 hegemony in English language teaching, summed up by Ellis and Shintani (2013), who argue that teachers should:

> maximise the use of L2 inside the classroom. Ideally this means that the L2 needs to become the medium as well as the object of instruction, especially in a foreign language setting.
>
> *(p. 24)*

The age drop

A third critical issue is the continuing reduction in age at which children are taught English. In many countries, children in the first years of primary school are now learning English (e.g., Mexico, Germany, China) and in many others, children may be enroled in (private) kindergartens which promise an English language environment (e.g., in South Korea and France). This decrease in age has implications for classroom language use. In some cases, schools promise an immersion experience with all interaction carried out in English. In others, English is the language of instruction and children are encouraged to use it as much as possible. However, as researchers note, it is challenging with very young children to insist on using the L2 only particularly when the children (and the teachers) all share another language and where the emphasis is on learning through play rather than on formal learning (see, e.g., Mourão (2014) on Portugal, and McPake et al. (2017) on Gaelic medium kinder-gartens in Scotland).

Mourão (2014) suggests that changing pedagogical practices can support children in using the L2 in a natural and playful way. She describes how an 'English Corner' was introduced into a kindergarten in Portugal. Materials, such as flashcards and picture books, that the teacher used during a circle time storytelling activity were placed into the English Corner at the end of the storytelling section of class. Children were free to visit the Corner or not and to play with the materials. Mourão (2014) found that children spontaneously used the English they had heard in the storytelling activity in their play, helping each other to remember and pronounce the English words as they took on the role of teacher and learner. This contrasts with the somewhat stilted and artificial insistence on Gaelic which McPake et al. (2017) found in their kindergarten study, where there was no reason for children to use the L2 except to respond to teacherly questions on what they were doing in the activities.

Current contributions and research

This section examines current contributions to the field of classroom language and will focus on two areas: first, we will explore recent research into classroom language in young learner classrooms, and, second, we will examine how research in bilingualism can support our understanding of classroom languages in contexts where English is taught as a foreign language.

Research into classroom language use in the young learner classroom

In terms of the young learner classroom, language use is little researched. Carless (2002) found that pupils in Hong Kong used L1 (Cantonese) more frequently in complicated lan-guage tasks (maybe because it is difficult and time-consuming for them to tackle the tasks through communication in English) or when they had lower English proficiency (which makes it hard for them to talk with each other in English). In terms of teachers' perspectives, an English teacher in Inbar-Lourie's (2010) research in Israel held the opinion that her aims were to provide exposure and inspire interest for low-grade students rather than to teach the language, and therefore she used more L1 with younger learners, and decreased the amount as the students improved. Enever (2011), drawing on a large-scale study of early language learning in Europe (ELLiE), suggests that target-language-only classrooms were not com-mon in the seven European countries in the study. This may be because, as Weschler (1997) argues:

> There comes a point beyond which abstract concepts simply cannot be conveyed through obvious gestures, pictures and commands.

Fisher (2005) points out, pre-literate learners have little recourse to means of expressing themselves other than their L1; they cannot look up a word in a dictionary, their narrow range of vocabulary makes it difficult for them to give an example sentence to clarify their meaning and even their ability to use gestures is immature. To expect these young learners, therefore, to function effectively in a learning and teaching context in the L2 is naïve.

Copland and Yonetsugi (2016) investigated how teachers and young learners use Eng-lish and Japanese in a classroom in a private primary school in Japan. They compared the language use in classrooms taught by two different teachers: one bilingual and the other who only spoke the L2, English. In order to ensure a level of comparability, the teachers taught the same lesson which they had planned together to two different classes of six- to seven-year-olds. The classes were observed, recorded and transcribed, and the teachers were interviewed about the classes.

In their data, Copland and Yonetsugi (2016) show how the bilingual teacher modelled pronunciation drawing on the learners' L1 and that she provided more opportunities for learning by translating the learners' meanings into English sentences, practices not available to the monolingual teacher. An example of the latter practice can be seen in the following extract. At the time the data were recorded, students were looking in their picture dictionaries at a page of insects in order to select an example to practise the language point of the lesson, which was responding to the question 'What animal do you like?' with the response 'I like/don't like (animal + s)'. During this activity, over 18 separate interactions with the bilingual teacher were initiated by the students (indented lines indicate the words spoken: left aligned lines are translations into English)

Extract 1

S1: 先生、毛虫嫌い
  Teacher, I don't like hairy caterpillars.
Teacher: 本当!何で?可愛いじゃない?
  Really! Why? They are cute.
S1: いや!年中のとき刺された、痛かった
  No way! I was bitten by a hairy caterpillar when I was inkindergarten. It was sore
Teacher: それはそうだよね,じゃあ
  I can understand that. In that case I don't like caterpillars.
S1: I don't like caterpillars.

Altogether, students produced nine full English sentences providing a personalised response to the question. In contrast, in the monolingual teacher's class, children spoke only to each other, and in total produced only four utterances using 'I like/don't like (animal + s)'. From this and other data, the authors claim that the bilingual teacher in this context is better able to support the children's English language development than the monolingual teacher and suggest that, where possible, bilingual teachers should be recruited to teach languages to young children.

What we can learn from the bilingualism research

In terms of the classroom, bilingualism research has consistently and effectively made the case that separating languages is neither natural nor desirable as it does not mirror what happens either in the brain (see Birdsong 2006) or in the outside world, where most people are bilingual and draw on two or more languages as a matter of course (Canagarajah 2013). García and Wei (2014) highlight 'the complex language practices that enable the education of students with plurilingual abilities' (p. 3), and this has led to a new approach to classroom languages called 'translanguaging' (Creese and Blackledge 2010), a flexible approach to using both the first and target languages. In a translanguaging classroom, learners and teachers draw on all their linguistic resources: all languages are valued and are regarded as making different but equal contributions to language learning and meaning making (see, e.g., Palmer et al. 2014).

Scholars differentiate translanguaging from codeswitching in a number of ways. First, codeswitching implies that speakers have two separate systems which they move between; translanguaging supports the case for speakers having one linguistic system (Birdsong 2006) which is often called the linguistic repertoire (e.g., Busch 2014). A second difference is in how codeswitching and translanguaging are regarded. Codeswitching has often been used to highlight deficiencies in a person's language skills: users 'switch' when they are unable to produce the word or phrase for something in the target language; in the language classroom, teachers codeswitch to the L1 when they cannot explain something in the L2 (see, e.g., Copland and Neokleous 2011). Third, codeswitching implies that monolinguals' language practices are the norm, not those of bilinguals (García and Wei 2014), which makes it fail to fit in the modern world where at least half of the population is bilingual (Conteh 2007; Grosjean 2010).

Translanguaging can be seen in the following extract (taken from Conteh et al. 2014), where the teacher, Meena, is bilingual in English and Punjabi and she is teaching in a state primary school in England where English is the medium of instruction. The children (25 altogether) were aged eight to nine years old. About 15 spoke Punjabi as a first language; one or two spoke Polish as a first language and the remaining six or seven children spoke English. Meena was teaching a lesson from the National Geography Curriculum (2011, p. 2). In this extract, the teacher is drawing on her knowledge (and that of some of her students) of bartering in the Swat Valley of Pakistan. As can be seen, Meena draws on both English and Punjabi to explain the practice (the same transcription conventions are used as in extract 1).

Extract 2

001	Meena:	When you . . . I know that . . . jilaythusa rai amithayabba
002		janaynadukarnay par paysayarvacthdanay.. dukarn
002		janaynadukarnay par paysayarvacthdanay.. dukarn
003		daray.. koi.. jraaykhusa nay kol
		When your mum and dad go to the 'corner shops' and they pay the shop-keepers, do they pay the shopkeeper there and then.. I mean the shops that are near you
	Meena:	When you . . . I know that . . . **jilaythusa rai amithayabba**
		janaynadukarnay par paysayarvacthdanay . . . dukarn
		janaynadukarnay par paysayarvacthdanay . . . dukarn
		aray . . . koi . . . jraaykhusa nay kol
		When your mum and dad go to the 'corner shops' and they pay the shop-keepers, do they pay the shopkeeper there and then . . . I mean the shops that are near you
004	Child 1:	No, they can give . . . .
005	Meena:	Kay karnai?
		What do they give?
006	Child 2:	Paysaydaynayna
		They give money
007	Meena:	Paysaysarai day nay?
		Do they give all the money?
008	Child 3:	No . . . (unintelligible)
009	Meena:	Who said 'no'? What does your mum do when she goes to the
010		shop? Paysaydaynay . . . kai kithabay par liknaysaabkithab
		Do they pay (upfront) or do they write it in a book, i.e. 'all your goods'

011	Child 2:	Paysaydaynay nah
		They pay
012	Child 3:	Liknaythaypaysaydaynay
		They write it and pay
013	Meena:	I know . . . I know . . .

De Oliveira and Ma (2018) provide further evidence of a teacher translanguaging in English and Spanish in a state primary school in the USA to ensure all the children in her class are developing literacy skills, not only the English monolingual children. In South Africa, translanguaging is a common pedagogy in state education (Probyn 2015) although not formally condoned. Makoe and McKinney (2014) argue that in a country where languages are inevitably linked to political ideologies, and where children have a little exposure to English outside school, recognising translanguaging as a legitimate resource in formal education settings is one important step towards creating and providing 'equal learning opportunities and access to all' (p. 372).

While EFL researchers have been slow to recognise the theoretical purchase that translanguaging might offer as a way of explaining how teachers use languages concurrently in class to support language learning, some scholars have started to explore its potential. Phyak (2018) adopts the term in his discussion of a Nepalese teacher's practice, and argues that translanguaging allows the teacher to engage children in a deeper understanding of subject matter and to ensure that children keep on task and can negotiate meanings successfully, while Copland and Yonetsugi (2016) suggest that translanguaging provides the bilingual teacher in their study with the resources to support her pupils' meaning making (see extract 1).

In tandem with a growing interest in general, translanguaging has been of increasing interest in immersion language classrooms. As the name suggests, the prevailing pedagogy in terms of language use in these classrooms is monolingualism, in that the target language is used exclusively to teach all classroom subjects. In some settings, dual-immersion is growing in popularity. In this model, children are taught the curriculum through one language in the morning and another in the afternoon, or on alternate days. In the USA, the languages are usually English and Spanish (see García et al. 2011), but in Canada the languages can also be Mandarin and English (e.g., Sun 2016). Meier (2010) reports on a similar approach in Germany, where children in Hamburg are taught through Portuguese and German, which reflects the languages spoken by the local population.

As current discussions in the literature show, proponents of immersion and dual-immersion can be fiercely opposed to language mixing or to translanguaging in class (McPake et al. 2017) as it can lead to the minority or less prestigious language being undervalued (Gomez et al. 2005). Many immersion teachers believe that children are best served by being surrounded by the language they are learning and that language, therefore, should be separated in the classroom (Stephen et al. 2016). McPake et al. (2017) take issue with this stance, however, and suggest that at least in the young learner Scots Gaelic immersion setting with which they are familiar, translanguaging offers a useful approach to scaffold children to learn the new language, while simultaneously providing a safe space for children to make their own meanings. Furthermore, Palmer et al. (2014) suggest that teachers in dual-immersion programmes in Texas can themselves struggle to separate languages, as doing so conflicts with goal of modelling dynamic bilingualism (see 'definitions' above).

In the ELT world, the notions that languages exist in one system and that bilingualism is the everyday reality for most people globally (Canagarajah 2013) have been less explored than in the bilingualism literature, perhaps because a good deal of the research in teaching English as a foreign language focuses on countries where the dominant language is either considered to be more common or more necessary (Lao 2004), for example, in Japan, China and South Korea. It may also be because the ELT industry is for the most part predicated on a communicative language teaching model, where a target-language-only classroom is believed to be the ideal environment for language learning. Nevertheless, it is also fair to say that throughout language teaching history, teachers have used classroom languages based on context and students' needs, and have not necessarily stuck to the tenets of a particular methodology, even when doing so has resulted in feelings of guilt (see, e.g., Copland and Neokleous 2011). We hope that Hall and Cook (2012) are right that 'entrenched monolingualism' (p. 297) is now a thing of the past, but question if teachers who had the choice of which language to use ever let dogma override appropriate pedagogy (see Butzkamm 2003 for a discussion of this point).

As with most issues in TESOL, there is no one-size-fits-all response to which languages children and teachers should use in class. Indeed, the choice of languages might be dictated at a different level from the classroom. Ministries of education sometimes expound on the issue (e.g., see Heo 2017 on South Korea), and sometimes head teachers will make a ruling (see Yanase 2016). In addition, as we have shown, different language teaching methodologies support different approaches to L1 and L2 use, from the ban on L1 in total immersion to the tolerance of teachers and students drawing on their linguistic repertoires in translanguaging approaches. In CLT, there has generally been a relaxing of the preference for target language use, although researchers continue to advocate its use in order to provide ultimate conditions to learn the language (e.g., Ellis and Shintani 2013). Researchers who advocate appropriate pedagogies (e.g., Holliday 1994; Kumaravadivelu 1994, 2001) would expect the teacher to make decisions about classroom languages based on their local context. These different approaches and ideologies make it difficult to advise on practice, but in this section we will provide some general suggestions.

First, it is important to meet the needs of the student, and this is especially true for younger students. Teachers of English to young learners should recognise their responsibility to educate the whole child and not only to teach him/her English. As research in education shows, a child must be nurtured, made to feel valued and allowed to develop his/her identity in order for him/her to become a confident young person (Cameron 2001; Chi et al. 2016; Johnstone 2009). Language learning can contribute to successful development but only if it is carefully done. Classroom language use is especially important in this regard because children need to feel understood and able to make their own meanings.

A related but slightly different point concerns the purpose of teaching young learners English (or any language). As Singleton and Pfenninger (this volume) explain, an early start does not result in gains over students with a later start in terms of language proficiency. Given this finding, the most compelling reason for an early start is to engender in children an interest in languages through providing enjoyable experiences (Johnstone, this volume). Being flexible in terms of classroom language use is more likely to produce a low-anxiety environment conducive to learning (see Brooks-Lewis 2009; Copland and Neokleous 2011), which we believe should be the primary concern of teachers of English to young learners.

A further recommendation concerns the hiring of NESTs by government agencies and schools to teach young learners. Often recruited because they can teach English using English, inexperienced and unqualified NESTs may not have the knowledge and understanding of children's development to teach young learners successfully. Furthermore, if they are newly arrived in country, they are unlikely to know the children's L1, which can hamper their efforts to engage and motivate young learners (Copland and Yonetsugi 2016). Often left in charge of classes despite their inexperience (see Copland et al. 2016 for a detailed description of the roles of NESTs in primary and secondary schools), NESTs can flounder (see for example, Ng 2014). On the other hand, experienced/qualified, bilingual NESTs can make excellent teachers of the young (see, e.g., Copland and Yonetsugi 2016; Yanase 2016) and can support the local teacher to provide quality education in learning English. We would suggest that those responsible for hiring NESTs should think carefully about the skills they require in a NEST and consider providing training in child development and in the local language to ensure NESTs are prepared for the young learner classroom.

Future directions

A clear route forward for research into young learners is to examine appropriate pedagogy. Currently, the tendency is for pedagogies designed to teach adults, such as CLT and TBL, to be introduced to the young learner classroom, where they may not be suitable. As described above, Mourão (2014) explores how English play corners can provide safe spaces for children to rehearse the English they have learnt through self-directed play. While a play corner might not be suitable for older children, the principle of pedagogies being fit for purpose depending on age and level pertains. We need more research of this kind with different young learner age groups so we can provide learning that is engaging and motivating.

A second direction is to find out more about children's views on classroom language use. As stated above, Macaro and Lee (2013) found that children were less tolerant of a target-language-only classroom than their adult counterparts. In a recent study conducted at the University of Stirling, UK, Imray (2016) found that Thai students preferred to be taught by teachers who could use both English and Thai.

However, students' preferences are only one part of the picture: more research is needed on how different kinds of interactions lead to learning. Copland and Neokleous (2011), Conteh et al. (2014), Copland and Yonetsugi (2016), Mahboob and Lin (2016) and Yanase (2017) are amongst a small number of researchers now exploring this and other L1/L2 issues through analyzing classroom data. More studies of this type could provide useful insights on the link between language use and language learning.

Finally, while translanguaging seems to offer a different ideological and pedagogical approach to language use in the classroom, there are currently too few studies to support a useful discussion of the approach in the young learner classroom in traditional EFL settings.

Concluding comments

Studies show that whether to use L1 in the young learner classroom is not a decision merely about the best way to teach language but 'can underpin learners' sense of who they are and who they want to be in a complex, multilingual world' (Hall and Cook 2012, p. 279). Young learners are especially vulnerable when it comes to developing their sense of worth and identities, and developing confidence in language learning can be positive in these regards.

Recommended reading

1 Hall, G., and Cook, G (2012). Own-language use in language teaching and learning. *Language Teaching*, 45(3), 271–308.

This state-of-the-art article provides a detailed overview of historical perspectives on using L1 and L2 in class and describes arguments used by both sides. It is a little light on young learner perspectives, but this is because there are few research papers on the subject.

2 Copland, F., and Yonetsugi, E. (2016). Teaching English to young learners: Supporting the case for the bilingual native English speaker teacher. *Classroom Discourse*, 7(3), 221–238.

This paper examines the interactions between students and teachers in two classrooms in a primary school in Japan. One teacher is monolingual and the other bilingual. The authors present a number of data extracts from the class and make the case for using L1 and L2 with young learners based on their findings.

3 Palmer, D. K., Mateus, S. G., Martínez, R. A., and Henderson, K. (2014). Reframing the debate on language separation: Towards a vision for translanguaging pedagogies in the dual-immersion classroom. *Modern Language Journal*, 98(3), 757–772.

In this paper, the authors describe how teachers in a dual-immersion programme, where languages are supposed to be strictly separated, draw on a number of translanguaging pedagogies to support their pupils' language development and positive identities as dynamic bilinguals. It is an excellent introduction to translanguaging and provides a strong discussion of bilingualism.

Related topics

Difficult circumstances, critical pedagogy, policies, CLIL

References

Anderson, C. E., McDougald, J. S., and Cuesta Medina, L. (2015). CLIL for young learners. *Children Learning English: From Research to Practice*, 137–151.

Auerbach, E. R. (1993). Reexamining English only in the ESL classroom. *TESOL Quarterly*, 27(1), 9–32.

Birdsong, D. (2006). Age and second language acquisition and processing: A selective overview. *Language Learning*, 56(1), 9–49.

Brooks-Lewis, K. A. (2009). Adult learners' perceptions of the incorporation of their L1 in foreign language teaching and learning. *Applied Linguistics*, 30(2), 216–235.

Brown, H. Douglas. (2007). *Teaching by Principles*, 3rd ed. New York: Pearson.

Burr, V. (2003). *Social Constructionism*, 2nd ed. London; New York: Routledge.

Burr, V. (2015). *Social Constructionism*, 3rd ed. London; New York: Routledge.

Busch, B. (2014). Building on heteroglossia and heterogeneity: The experience of a multilingual classroom. In Blackledge, A., and Creese, A. (eds.) *Heteroglossia as Practice and Pedagogy*. Netherlands: Springer, 21–40.

Butler, Y. G. (2011). The implementation of communicative and task-based language teaching in the Asia-Pacific region. *Annual Review of Applied Linguistics*, 31, 36–57.

Butzkamm, W. (2003). We only learn language once: The role of the mother tongue in FL classrooms: Death of a dogma. *Learning Journal*, 28(1), 29–39.

Cameron, L. (2001). *Teaching Languages to Young Learners*. Cambridge: Cambridge University Press.

Canagarajah, S. (2013). *Literacy as a Translingual Practice: Between communities and classrooms*. London: Routledge.

Carless, D. (2002). Implementing task-based learning with young learners. *ELT Journal*, 56(4), 389–396.

Chi, S., Kim, S. H., and Kim, H. (2016). Problem behaviours of kindergartners: The affects of children's cognitive ability, creativity, and self-esteem. *South African Journal of Education*, 36(1), 1–10.

Choi, T. H. (2015). The impact of the 'Teaching English through English' policy on teachers and teaching in South Korea. *Current Issues in Language Planning*, 16(3), 201–220.

Chomsky, N. (1965). *Aspects of the Theory of Syntax*. Cambridge and London: MIT Press.

Conteh, J. (2007). Opening doors to success in multilingual classrooms: Bilingualism, codeswitching and the professional identities of ethnic minority primary teachers. Education in Pakistan. *Journal of Multilingual and Multicultural Development*, 25(4), 333–353.

Conteh, J., and Brock, A. (2006). Introduction: Principles and practices for teaching bilingual learners. In Conteh, J. (ed.) *Promoting Learning for Bilingual Pupils 3–11: Opening doors to success*. London: Sage, 1–12.

Conteh, J., Copland, F., and Creese, A. (2014). Multilingual teachers' resources in three different contexts: Empowering learning. In Conteh, J., and Meier, G. S. (ed.) *The Multilingual Turn in Languages Education: Opportunities and challenges*. Bristol: Multilingual Matters, 158–178.

Copland, F., Davis, M., Garton, S., and Mann, S. (2016). *Investigating NEST Schemes around the World: Supporting NEST/LET collaborative practices*. Teaching English. London: British Council.

Copland, F., Garton, S., and Burns, A. (2014). Challenges in teaching English to young learners: Global perspectives and local realities. *TESOL Quarterly*, 48(4), 738–762.

Copland, F., and Neokleous, G. (2011). L1 to teach L2: Complexities and contradictions. *ELT Journal*, 65(3), 270–280.

Copland, F., and Yonetsugi, E. (2016). Teaching English to young learners: Supporting the case for the bilingual native English speaker teacher. *Classroom Discourse*, 7(3), 221–238.

Department of Education (DfE). (2011). National curriculum coverage for geography using the rivers project. www.google.co.uk/url?sa=t&rct=j&q=&esrc=s&source=web&cd=1&cad=rja&uact=8&ved=0ahUKEwjllqjnkIXYAhVHJsAKHUo5DtUQFgguMAA&url=http%3A%2F%2Fwww.suffolk learning.co.uk%2Fdo_download.asp%3Fdid%3D2859&usg=AOvVaw2L4Ha-kKDqL2r2MarimJdo [Accessed 12 December 2017].

Ellis, R. (2015). *Understanding Second Language Acquisition*, 2nd ed. London: Oxford University Press

Ellis, R., and Shintani, N. (2013). *Exploring Language Pedagogy through Second Language Acquisition Research*. New York: Routledge.

Enever, J. (Ed.). (2011). *ELLiE: Early language learning in Europe*. London: British Council.

Fisher, R. (2005). *Teaching Children to Think*. Cheltenham: Nelson Thornes.

García, O., Flores, N., and Chu, H. (2011). Extending bilingualism in U.S. secondary education: New variations. *International Multilingual Research Journal*, 5(1), 1–18.

García, O., and Wei, L. (2014). *Translanguaging: Language, bilingualism and education*. Basingstoke: Palgrave Macmillan.

Garton, S., Copland, F., and Burns, A. (2011). *Investigating Global Practices in Teaching English to Young Learners*. London: British Council.

Gomez, L., Freeman, D., and Freeman, Y. (2005). Dual language education: A promising 50–50 model. *Bilingual Research Journal*, 29(1), 145–164.

Grandinetti, M., Langellotti, M., and Ting, Y. L. T. (2013). How CLIL can provide a pragmatic means to renovate science education – Even in a sub-optimally bilingual context. *International Journal of Bilingual Education and Bilingualism*, 16(3), 354–374.

Grosjean, F. (2010). *Bilingual*. Cambridge and London: Harvard University Press.

Hellekjær, G. O. (2010). Language matters: Assessing lecture comprehension in Norwegian English-medium higher education. In Dalton-Puffer, C., Nikula, T., and Smit, U (eds.) *Language Use and Language Learning in CLIL Classrooms*. Amsterdam and Philadelphia: John Benjamins, 233–258.

Heo, N. (2017). "We are not simply 'multicultural'": intersecting ethnic and religious identities of Japanese-Korean young adults in South Korea. *Ethnic and Racial Studies*, 1–20.

Holliday, A. (1994). *Appropriate Methodology and Social Context*. Cambridge: Cambridge University Press.

Howatt, A. P., and Smith, R. (2014). The history of teaching English as a foreign language, from a British and European perspective. *Language & History*, 57(1), 75–95.

Imray, M. (2016). Thai young learners' perceptions of using L1 and L2 in English classes. MSc dissertation, University of Stirling.

Inbar-Lourie, O. (2010). English only? The linguistic choices of teachers of young EFL learners. *International Journal of Bilingualism*, 14(3), 351–367.

Johnstone, R. (2009). An early start: What are the key conditions for generalized success? In Enever, J., Moon, J., and Raman, U. (eds.) *Young Learner English Language Policy and Implementation: International perspectives*. Reading: Garnet Education, 31–41.

Krashen, S. D. (1987). Principles and practice in second language acquisition, 1982–1982, http://scholar. google.co.uk/scholar_url?url=http%3A%2F%2Faces.ir%2Fattachments%2F22d1286622494-

communicative-approach-stephen-crashen.pdf&hl=en&sa=T&oi=ggp&ct=res&cd=0&ei=s2oxWv P1DNSLmAHw-4eQCw&scisig=AAGBfm0tA_l9VzuDcI6YfalNwYOL_C1OOw&nossl= 1&ws=1280x832.

Kumaravadivelu, B. (1994). The postmethod condition: (E) merging strategies for second/foreign language teaching. *TESOL Quarterly*, 28(1), 27–48.

Kumaravadivelu, B. (2001). Toward a postmethod pedagogy. *TESOL Quarterly*, 35(4), 537–560.

Kumaravadivelu, B. (2003). *Beyond Methods: Macrostrategies for language teaching*. New Haven, CT: Yale University Press.

Kumaravadivelu, B. (2012). *Language Teacher Education for a Global Society*. London: Routledge.

Lao, C. (2004). Parents' attitudes toward Chinese – English bilingual education and Chinese-language use. *Bilingual Research Journal*, 28(1), 99–121.

Larsen-Freeman, D., and Anderson, M. (2013). *Techniques and Principles in Language Teaching*, 3rd ed. Oxford: Oxford university Press.

Littlewood, W., and Yu, B. (2011). First language and target language in the foreign language classroom. *Language Teaching*, 44(1), 64–77.

Long, M. H. (1996). The role of the linguistic environment in second language acquisition. In Bhatia, T., and Ritchie, W. (eds.) *Handbook of Second Language Acquisition*. San Diego, CA: Academic Press.

Luciana C. de Oliveira and Amber Ma (2018). Planned and interactional scaffolding in kindergarten. In Copland, F., and Garton, S. (eds.) *Voices From the Classroom*. Alexandria, VA: TESOL Press, 101–110.

Macaro, E. (2009). Teacher use of code-switching in the second language classroom: Exploring 'Optimal' use. In Turnbull, M., and Dailey-O'Cain, J. (eds.) *First Language Use in Second and Foreign Language Learning*, 35–79. Bristol: Multilingual Matters.

Macaro, E., and Lee, J. H. (2013). Teacher language background, codeswitching, and English-only instruction: Does age make a difference to learners' attitudes? *TESOL Quarterly*, 47(4), 717–742.

Mahboob, A., and Lin, A. M. Y. (2016). Using local languages in English language classrooms. In Renandya, W. A., and Widodo, H. P. (eds.) *English Language Teaching Today*. New York: Springer, 25–40.

Mahboob, A., and Lin, A. M. Y. (2018). Local languages as a resource in (language) education. In Selvi, A. F., and Rudolph, N. (eds.) *Conceptual Shifts and Contextualized Practices in Education for Glocal Interaction*. Singapore: Springer, 197–217.

Makoe, P., and McKinney, C. (2014). Linguistic ideologies in multilingual South African suburban schools. *Journal of Multilingual and Multicultural Development*, 35(7), 658–673.

Marsh, D., and Hood, P. (2008). Content and language integrated learning in primary East Asia contexts (CLIL PEAC). In *The Proceedings of Primary Innovations Regional Seminar*, 43–50. www.pefja. kg.ac.rs/preuzimanje/TEYL%202015/TEYL_Conference_2010.pdf.

McPake, J, Macdonald, A., Wilson, M., O'Hanlon, F., and Andrew, M. (2017). *Transformative Pedagogies for Gaelic Revitalisation: Report to Soillse of a study of Gaelic-medium teachers' perspectives on the potential of translanguaging as a classroom pedagogy*. [Report]

Meier, G. S. (2010). Two-way immersion education in Germany: Bridging the linguistic gap. *Journal of Bilingual Education and Bilingualism*, 13(4), 419–437.

Mitchell, R., Myles, F., and Marsden, E. (2013). *Second Language Learning Theories*, 3rd ed. New York: Routledge.

Mourão, S. (2014). Taking play seriously in pre-primary English classes. *ELT Journal*, 63(3), 254–264.

Ng, M. L. (2014). Difficulties with team teaching in Hong Kong kindergartens. *ELT Journal*, 69(2), 188–197.

Nishino, T., and Watanabe, M. (2008). Communication-oriented policies versus classroom realities in Japan. *TESOL Quarterly*, 42(1), 133–138.

Palmer, D. K., Mateus, S. G., Martínez, R. A., and Henderson, K. (2014). Reframing the debate on language separation: Towards a vision for translanguaging pedagogies in the dual-immersion classroom. *Modern Language Journal*, 98(3), 757–772.

Pan, L., and Block, D. (2011). English as a "global language" in China: An investigation into learners' and teachers' language beliefs. *System*, 39(3), 391–402.

Phillipson, R. (2017). Myths and realities of 'global' English. *Language Policy*, 16(3), 313–331.

Phyak, P. (2018). Translanguaging as a pedagogical resource in English language teaching: A response to unplanned language education policies in Nepal. In Kuchah, K., and Shamim, F. (eds.) *International Perspectives in Teaching English in Difficult Circumstances: Contexts, challenges and possibilities*. London: Palgrave Macmillan.

Pinter, A. (2017). *Teaching Young Language Learners*. Oxford: Oxford University Press.

Prabhu, N. S. (1990). There is no best method – Why? *TESOL Quarterly*, 24(2), 161–176.

Probyn, M. (2015). Pedagogical translanguaging: Bridging discourses in South African science classrooms. *Language and Education*, 29(3), 218–234.

Seidlhofer, B. (2011). *Understanding English as a Lingua Franca*. Oxford: Oxford University Press

Sekiya, Y. (2017). The current state of English language teacher education in Japan. Presentation given at the Symposium on English teacher learning and development, Kanda University of International Studies, Chiba, Japan, 12th November, 2017.

Skinner, B. F. (1938). *The Behavior of Organisms: An experimental analysis*. Cambridge, MA: B. F. Skinner Foundation.

Stephen, C., McPake, J., Pollock, I., and McLeod, W. (2016). Early years immersion: Learning from children's playroom experiences. *Journal of Immersion and Content-Based Language Education*, 4(10), 59–85.

Sun, M. (2016). Peer collaboration in an English/Chinese bilingual program in Western Canada. *Canadian Modern Language Review*, 72(4), 423–453.

Turnbull, M., and Dailey-O'Cain, J. (2009). "Concluding reflections: Moving forward." In Turnbull, M., and Dailey-O'Cain, J. (eds.) *First Language Use in Second and Foreign Language Learning*. Bristol: Multilingual Matters, 182–207.

Weschler, R. (1997). Uses of Japanese (L1) in the English classroom: Introducing the functional translation method. *The Internet TESL Journal*, 3(11). Online.

Yanase, C. (2016). From an assistant to a team member: a perspective from a Japanese ALT in primary schools in Japan. In Copland, F., Garton, S., and Mann, S. (eds.) *LETs and NESTs: Voices, views and vignettes*. London: British Council, 195–210.

Yanase, C. (2017). Functional L1 usage in English classrooms. Presentation given at JALT Conference 2017, Tsukuba, Japan, 18th November 2017.

Yang, W. (2015). Content and language integrated learning nextin Asia: Evidence of learners' achievement in CLIL education from a Taiwan tertiary degree programme. *International Journal of Bilingual Education and Bilingualism*, 18(4), 361–382.

10

Classroom management for teaching English to young learners

Subhan Zein

Introduction

Effective classroom management sets the stage for optimal learning. This explains why classroom management positively correlates with higher student participation, greater learning satisfaction, dropout prevention and reduced disruptive behaviour (Evertson 2013; Evertson and Weinstein 2006), and it is even suggested as the single variable with the strongest impact on student achievement (Marzano and Marzano 2003). Defined as the ability of teachers to establish and maintain order in a classroom within an education system that aims to foster learning as well as social and emotional growth, classroom management encompasses all of the teacher's practices related to developing mode of instruction (e.g., lecturing, group work) and dealing with learner behaviour (Elias and Schwab 2006, Emmer and Sabornie 2015). The instructional dimension of classroom management includes teachers' works such as grouping and seating, regulating classroom routines, timing activities, setting up and sequencing tasks, giving instructions, providing feedback and monitoring the learners. The learner behaviour management dimension, on the other hand, includes activities such as preventing, correcting and redirecting inappropriate student behaviour and developing learner self-regulation.

The bulk of research on classroom management has been drawn from Western classrooms where language education is not necessarily the focus. This chapter attempts to address this issue by bringing what the mainstream classroom management research has to offer to the English for Young Learners (EYL) classroom. The chapter first provides an overview of the historical perspectives of classroom management, shifting from its early development in the 1900s to the emergence of the ecological and the behavioural approaches to recent approaches to classroom management. The chapter further discusses five critical issues related to EYL classroom management, namely theoretical approaches, educational cultures, teachers' backgrounds, classroom conditions and technology. Third, the chapter demonstrates how current contributions in EYL pedagogy have been devoted to the fairly mechanical aspects of instructional management with little attention paid to young learners' behavioural management. Next, the chapter provides recommendations for practice to assist teachers with managing young learner behaviour. Finally, the chapter points to future directions for EYL pedagogy at both the theoretical and practical levels and the much-needed reorientation in teacher education for EYL teachers.

Historical perspectives

Early development

One of the early modern Western educators, Bagley (1908), wrote that educators prior to the twentieth century embraced the machine-like and 'military organization' (p. 30) style of classroom management, while at the turn of the twentieth century, 'most of the advanced and progressive educators' were proponents of the self-government theory of classroom management (p. 31). The machine-like style of classroom management placed emphasis on rules and punitive consequences to manage student behaviour, whereas the self-government theory focused on the development of self-discipline within students. This conceptualisation of classroom management is consistent with the dual meanings of the term 'discipline' (Emmer and Sabornie 2014). The first meaning refers to the creation and maintenance of an orderly learning environment conducive to learning in which punitive consequences are used for correcting and prevent problem behaviour. On the other hand, the second meaning of discipline refers to 'self-discipline', also referred to as 'self-regulation', 'responsibility' and 'autonomy' within students. In this chapter, the term *self-regulation* is used, as it is associated with the students' ability to inhibit inappropriate behaviour and exhibit pro-social behaviour under their own volition.

Throughout the first half of the twentieth century, the development of self-regulation was the primary aim of classroom management. Within this perspective, teachers employed a combination of teacher-centred and student-centred techniques, with greater emphasis on the latter (Emmer and Sabornie 2014). However, as a consequence of increasing behaviour problems in the second half of the twentieth century, there was a shift on the focus of classroom management and prevention from developing self-discipline to establishing order and managing student behaviour (McClellan 1999). With the prevalent views in the 1970s and 1980s pointing to school discipline as the greatest problem, classroom management was equated with maintaining classroom order and controlling student behaviour. The use of teacher-centred techniques of prevention and correction was the emphasis of practice and research, as seen in the emergence of the process-product, the ecological and the behavioural approaches.

The process-product approach

Researchers embracing the process-product tradition aimed to identify predictors of teacher effectiveness by drawing from the methodology of systematic classroom observation (Emmer and Sabornie 2014). They explored the relationships between classroom processes (particularly teacher behaviour and teacher-student interaction patterns) and subsequent outcomes (particularly adjusted achievement gain). The focus was on the system-level characteristics of schools that were successful in promoting high achievement and positive classroom behaviour among students (Doyle 2006). This perspective led to the notion of the importance of activity management, including how the teacher engages students and minimises disruptive behaviour by keeping activities on track, preventing intrusions and maintaining the flow of activities. Brophy (2006) stated that various studies within this tradition demonstrate that effective classroom managers: (1) provide sufficient advance preparation to enable most, if not all, of their students to begin seatwork and other independent activities smoothly; and (b) monitor progress and provide individual assistance where necessary, but ensure the brevity and privacy of these interactions.

Much of the first process-product research focused on individual behaviours or routines (e.g., brisk instructional pace, wait time, performance feedback), but more recent work has examined the efficacy of comprehensive models of teaching and classroom management derived from individual studies. Contemporary process-product research now defines effective teaching primarily through synthesis. Individual behaviours and processes related to positive student outcomes are combined into an effective teaching composite such as explicit instruction, authoritative classroom management and positive behaviour support. The idea is that teachers can be taught to employ process-product research findings in their classrooms, and that such strategies have positive correlation with student achievement and behaviour. Components of effective teaching and classroom management drawn from process-product research have been used as the foundation for many teacher education programmes (Gettinger and Kohler 2006).

The ecological approach

Brophy (2006) explained that the ecological research on classroom management resulted from studies of the characteristics of different classroom settings (e.g., whole class, small group, individual) and the unfolding of the activities occurring within them. The basic tenet of 'the ecological approach is *habitat*, the physical niche or context with characteristic purposes, dimensions, features and processes that have consequences for the behavior occupants in that setting' (Doyle 2006, p. 98). Thus, classrooms are environmental settings (ecologies) that can be examined according to the adaptation potential of different individuals. As a consequence, when the notion of person-environment fit is applied to classrooms, the settings' physical characteristics and the affordances or constraints created by teachers, peers, administrators and others need to be taken into account.

The ecological approach research peaked in the 1980s, with a large emphasis on the 'school effectiveness' in relation to classroom management (Doyle 2006). Emmer and Sabornie (2014) stated that researchers within the ecological perspective employed descriptive and correlational methodologies to demonstrate that what best differentiated effective from ineffective classroom managers was not how teachers remedied misbehaviour but how they prevented it from appearing in the first place and from worsening and spreading. In preventing misbehaviour, teachers would be aware of classroom management dimensions, namely: (1) multidimensionality: a multitude of events and tasks in classrooms take place; (2) simultaneity: many things occur in the classroom at the same time; (3) immediacy: there is a fast pace of classroom events; (4) unpredictability: classroom events often take unpredicted turns; (5) publicness: classrooms are public, meaning classroom events are done and seen in public; and (6) history: a class accumulates a common set of experiences, routines and norms (Doyle 2006). By taking into account these dimensions, effective classroom managers would develop characteristics such as: (1) withitness – closely monitoring student behaviour and intervening early when misbehaviour is first observed and before it interferes with instruction; (2) overlapping – dealing with multiple events or demands at the same time; (3) momentum – starting and presenting lessons at a brisk pace, while allowing for only brief and efficient transitions; (4) smoothness – presenting lessons at an even flow, free from interruptions; and (5) group alerting – establishing and maintaining the attention of all students.

The behavioural approach

Another major line of research on classroom management is the behavioural approach. This approach recognises the importance of prevention, using positive reinforcement as its strategy of choice for preventing misbehaviour. Positive reinforcement refers to the effect 'that is observed when a behaviour is made more likely to recur by a contingently applied stimulus that follows that behavior' (Landrum and Kauffman 2006, p. 48). One prominent and effective application of positive reinforcement in classrooms is the use of provisional teacher attention that is aimed to increase students' positive behaviour. The premise is simple: teachers attend positively to students when they are engaged in desired, appropriate task-related activity or behaviour. Compared with the ecological and process-product approaches, the behavioural approach places greater emphasis on correcting behaviour techniques, such as negative reinforcement and extinction. Negative reinforcement refers to the contingent removal of a stimulus in order to create the desired behaviour; for example, a teacher tells the students that they will not be given homework if they complete the task on time. Extinction, on the other hand, is 'the phenomenon of a behaviour decreasing in rate or likelihood of occurrence when the reinforcement that has been maintaining it is removed' (Landrum and Kauffman 2006, p. 50).

Applications of the behavioural approach commenced in the 1960s and 1970s. These applications, widely known as applied behavioural analysis, focused on the management of stimuli and consequences through controlled programming of reinforcement, extinction, response cost and other practices of punishment to promote desirable behaviours and to decrease the undesirable ones. Applied behaviourists emphasised the use of reinforcement to bring behaviour under the control of stimuli. The stimulus is a prompt that directs students to understand that certain forms of behaviour are desired, and performing them will result in reinforcement. Inability to perform the desired behaviour immediately will yield gradual improvement towards target performance level; it is maintained by reinforcing it often enough to guarantee its continuation. On the other hand, the behaviours that are incompatible with the desired pattern are overcome through non-reinforcement, or repressed through punishment. Early studies within this perspective often took place in special education settings and typically focused on the management of individuals' behaviour. However, more recent research has broadened the scope of its application to groups, classrooms and schools, employing measures such as group contingencies, direct social skills training and school-home communication. The research has allowed researchers to examine the impact of interventions (e.g., reinforcement, extinction) on individual students (e.g., staying in the seat, remaining quiet) using single-subject or single-case experimental designs (Emmer and Sabornie 2014, Landrum and Kauffman 2006).

Recent developments

It is apparent that from the 1960s and into the 1990s classroom management had taken on a new meaning that was in contrast to the one that directed educators in the first half of the century (Emmer and Sabornie 2014). It is more common now to understand classroom management as 'actions taken by the teacher to establish order, engage students, or elicit their cooperation' (Emmer and Stough 2001, p. 103). Concurrently, there has been a reemergence of self-regulation development, as scholars have attempted to conceptualise classroom management and school discipline more broadly than that of order and compliance (Emmer and Stough 2001, Evertson and Weinstein 2006).

This shift of paradigm marks the application of the behavioural principle that started in the 1990s and is common nowadays, called the School-Wide Positive Behavioural Interventions and Supports (SWPBIS). Within SWPBIS, behaviour management is a school-wide concern, and classroom management is a central component that needs to be coordinated across administrators, teachers and other staff (Lewis, Mitchell, Trussell, and Newcomer 2014). This notion is embodied by Positive Behaviour Support (PBS), which is a collection of effective practices, interventions and system change strategies with evidence-based support. The scope is on the entire school as the unit of analysis, focusing on the school-wide, classroom and individual levels. There are three components involved: (1) the adoption of evidence-based practices; (2) data to categorise current status and effectiveness of intervention; and (3) systems that allow staff to accurately implement and sustain practices. This is a comprehensive approach that gives primacy to problem solving as well as action planning with a focus on accurate, sustainable and wide implementation across a continuum of settings and levels (Lewis et al. 2014).

A direct behavioural approach to PBS is seen in how students are taught social skills; the skills taught are identified in a behaviour matrix that comprises where students are to perform the specific social skills (Lewis et al. 2014). A recent national survey of social skills taught in SWPBIS schools demonstrates that the most common social skills found in matrices are those that 'emphasize student compliance' and those that are within three general categories of behavioural expectations: responsibility, respect and safety (Lynass et al. 2012, p. 159). In learning responsibility, for example, students are repeatedly directed (and reinforced) to 'keep hands and feet to self' in hallways, to 'raise your hand for assistance' in the cafeteria, and to 'accept consequence of your behavior' in the classroom. Similarly, in learning respect they are directed to 'work quietly' in the classroom, use 'voice Level 2' in the cafeteria and to 'allow others to pass' in hallways (Lynass et al. 2012, p. 155).

Following the emergence of SWPBIS, there was a call 'for an approach to classroom management that fosters the development of self-regulation and emotional competence' (Evertson and Weinstein 2006, p. 12). Scholars under the Social and Emotional Learning (SEL) approach responded to this call. They did not believe in the traditional goal of classroom management that prescribes the teacher to enforce discipline. While this 'control' goal of classroom management is undeniably important for the effective functioning of a classroom, it is teacher- and instruction-centred, and not student-centred. With schools becoming more focused on social, emotional and academic learning, a more holistic and student-centred goal for classroom management is necessary, and this goal is best achieved through internal control (i.e. self-regulation) (Elias and Schwab 2006).

The SEL approach perceives children's ways to communicate, to deal with emotions and to solve problems as part of a school's classroom management programme. Since prevention is viewed in this manner, it includes promotion or development of social, emotional and behavioural skills that underlie self-regulation. Although it branches out from SWPBIS, the SEL approach is more concerned with the promotion of mental health and wellbeing. It includes programmes often referred to as positive youth development, resilience, character education, positive psychology, emotional development and moral education. It also embraces programmes for preventing mental health issues and risk behaviours such as alcoholism, drug abuse, teen pregnancy, bullying, school violence and suicide (Durlak et al. 2011). The SEL approach certainly views the importance of teachers' cognitions and actions, but it considers it to be only one of multiple factors along with individual student, peer, cultural, developmental, home, school and community factors – all these factors operate in a transactional, dynamic fashion in determining student behaviour (Dodge, Coie, and

Lynam 2006). In the SEL approach, lessons are taught both directly and indirectly using a mixture of instructional techniques involving students, such as applying social problem solving to real-life problems in the classrooms, moral reasoning discussions, social perspective taking, as well as training in relaxation, communication and anger management (Emmer and Sabornie 2014).

Critical issues

In this section, I will focus on five critical issues in the EYL classroom management. These issues are associated with educational approaches to classroom management, educational cultures, teachers' backgrounds, classroom conditions and the presence of technology.

First of all, there appears to be no evidence of direct, deliberate application of the theoretical approaches to classroom management discussed in the previous section in the EYL classroom. Teachers resort to using various strategies in order to maintain classroom order and control young learner behaviour (Schneiderová 2013, Stelma and Onat-Stelma 2010, Zein 2013), but they appear to be short-gap measures rather than being underpinned by certain theoretical approaches to classroom management. The absence of a theoretical approach to teachers' practices in classroom management indicates that teachers may not be informed of various educational and psychological approaches to classroom management due to lack of specificity in their pre-service education. This is true because in contexts such as Vietnam (Le and Do 2012), Indonesia (Zein 2015, 2016) and Europe (Enever 2014), the generic teacher preparation at pre-service level places a large emphasis on instructional management but leaves little attention to the management of young learner behaviour.

The second critical issue of EYL classroom management is related to educational cultures. Much of the work on classroom management comes from the general education field in Western contexts such as the USA (e.g., Evertson 2013, Durlak et al. 2011, Emmer and Sabornie 2015), where the ideas of student-centred learning and developing self-regulation are prominent. Little is known, however, as to how teachers manage the EYL classroom in other educational cultures, especially in the Eastern contexts. This is especially relevant because teachers face many challenges when implementing Western-imported methodologies such as communicative language teaching (CLT) and task-based language teaching (TBLT), which are not conducive to local classroom ecologies. For example, Eastern classrooms (and many in Africa and South and Central America, too) are generally large with limited facilities and resources. These factors constrain the implementation of communicative pedagogy (Butler 2011, Enever and Moon 2009). In addition, CLT and TBLT encourage learners to be autonomous; the role of the teacher is to facilitate this process of self-analysis rather than explicitly teach the language (Butler 2011). The autonomous role given to learners is in line with the perspective of self-regulation in classroom management that is widely embraced in the West. However, classrooms in the Asia-Pacific region, for example, place a large emphasis on teacher authority. Learners are expected to obey teachers – the focus of classroom management is on the development of classroom discipline rather than self-regulation. Thus, an issue of great concern is how teachers could manage a locally fitting and culturally responsive classroom to create a learning environment that is comfortable, caring, embracing, affirming, engaging and facilitative (Gay 2006).

Third, various studies have shown that teachers of different backgrounds demonstrate varying degrees of resourcefulness when it comes to managing young learners (Le and Do 2012, Oga-Baldwin and Nakata 2013; Schneiderová 2013, Shohamy and Inbar 2007, Stelma and Onat-Stelma 2010, Zein 2016, 2017). Generalist teachers who teach English along with other general subjects, such as maths and basic literacy, tend to demonstrate anxiety about their English language proficiency, as they overuse their first language (L1) due to their lack of confidence in English (Butler 2004, Copland et al. 2014, Enever 2014, Zein 2016, 2017), while others use students' L1 in order to maintain control and develop discipline because they cannot do it in the TL (Zein 2013). Despite this challenge, generalist teachers tend to be more adaptable in dealing with young learners (Zein 2013, 2017), and they also appear to be more eclectic in integrating English and other subjects (Le and Do 2012, Oga-Baldwin and Nakata 2013, Shohamy and Inbar 2007).

The second group of teachers consists of reassigned teachers, that is, those who formerly taught English to older learners in other sectors before being required to teach EYL, typically find managing young learners over-challenging. As these teachers face a new teaching situation, they struggle to organise learning. For example, the various strategies they employ to control young learner behaviour, such as raising one's voice, moving noisy children to different seats and using non-verbal cues to keep children silent, are often unsuccessful (Stelma and Onat-Stelma 2010). Native-speaking English teachers often have a similar issue. They may be able to provide richer input than local non-native English speaking teachers (Unsworth, Persson, Prins and de Bot 2015), but evidence suggests that native English-speaking teachers exert less influence on young learners' learning behaviour because they have no L1 knowledge to discipline them (Oga-Baldwin and Nakata 2013) and demonstrate poor pedagogical context knowledge (Luo 2007). Specialist local teachers who have relevant qualifications in English language pedagogy and only teach English also have their own classroom management issue. They may be able to provide richer language input than local generalist teachers (Unsworth, et al 2015), yet studies suggest that they struggle to manage young learner behaviour (Shohamy and Inbar 2007, Zein 2013, 2017). This is primarily attributed to their lack of professional preparation; in Zein's (2015, 2016) studies, for example, the pre-service education the teachers had undertaken was not sufficient to prepare them with adequate educational approaches to managing young learners.

Classroom conditions are also a major hindrance to effective management, as it has been found in studies at the global level (Copland et al. 2014) as well as local level studies in Vietnam (Le and Do 2012) and Indonesia (Zein 2017), among others. The large number of students in the classroom may even be more influential than the professional and educational backgrounds of the teachers in determining the way they manage the classroom (Zein 2017). Zein's (2013, 2016, 2017) studies demonstrate that although generalist local teachers exhibited greater versatility in managing the classroom than specialist local teachers, both were often overwhelmed when dealing with simultaneous classroom events and learner demands in a classroom consisting of 40–50 students. This holds true especially when they had to teach in a classroom with the rigid four-row seating arrangement. On the other hand, specialist local teachers who only had to teach 20 children or fewer could manage their classroom without much difficulty. This was supported by the fact that when the classroom had removable chairs and desks, the teachers could easily switch from one pattern of classroom organisation to another. As Copland et al. (2014) suggested, unless language-in-education policies in countries with unfavourable classroom conditions change the situations, the current classroom management issue would remain.

The fifth critical issue is how teachers can effectively manage the EYL classroom with the presence of innovative technologies (e.g., games, smartboards, Power Point). Teachers in various contexts such as China (Li and Ni 2011), South Korea (Suh et al. 2010) and Japan (Butler et al. 2014) generally hold positive attitudes towards the value of technological innovations for teaching young learners. Nevertheless, the extent to which the presence of technology affects EYL classroom management is unclear. Li and Ni (2011), for example, argued that teachers mainly use technology for teacher-centred purposes such as lesson preparation and instructional delivery, and in such a case emphasis on developing children-centred learning is absent. Another issue lies at how teachers manage the balance between children's degrees of enjoyment and learning, because highly enjoyable games do not necessarily warrant learning (Butler et al. 2014).

Current contributions and research

Current contributions in language education have paid very limited attention to classroom management. Wright's (2005) contribution on classroom management in language education provides a thorough overview of classroom management as it relates to language pedagogy and social contexts as well as implications for research; and yet it makes limited reference to teaching young learners. The issue of classroom management is even absent in publications on teaching EYL such as Bland (2015), Pinter (2011) and Rich (2014) and is only covered in one chapter in Moon (2006), Nunan (2011) and Shin and Crandall (2014). This is despite classroom management being reported as one of the most serious challenges in EYL classrooms at the global level (Copland et al. 2014) as well as in specific contexts such as China (Zhang and Adamson 2007), Indonesia (Zein 2013, 2016, 2017) and Japan (Aline and Hosoda 2006).

Moon (2006), Nunan (2011) and Shin and Crandall (2014) primarily emphasised the fairly mechanical aspects of instructional management including grouping and seating, setting up tasks and sequencing activities. Despite showing adjustments on aspects of teaching young learners, the heavy emphasis on the instructional procedures of classroom management shows resemblance to popular publications on language pedagogy (e.g., Harmer 2007, Richards 2015). This indicates that research on classroom management in the EYL pedagogy has not shown significant progress from the mainstream language pedagogy. By the same token, recent studies have underscored how EYL classrooms worldwide are characterised by learners' inattentiveness (Copland et al. 2014), lack of discipline (Garton 2014), recurrent chatting and misbehaviour (Zein 2013, 2017) and unexpected anxiety (Yim 2014), suggesting that the work of EYL teachers is not merely limited to instructional management. The paucity of research into EYL teachers dealing with the complex issues of young learner behaviour management further reflects partiality in understanding classroom management, as it is only understood within the instructional management dimension. The other dimension of EYL classroom management, that is, young learner behaviour management, escapes the attention of researchers.

Current educational practices of classroom management have embraced the SWPBIS and the SEL approaches that combine the development of classroom discipline and self-regulation in association with the school-wide management, but there are no signs that these approaches have been reflected in the mainstream EYL classroom. Publications such as Moon (2006), Nunan (2011) and Shin and Crandall (2014) give little indication as to whether their classroom management techniques are underpinned by a theoretical approach to classroom management. Wright (2005) identified classrooms as multidimensional, highlighting the role of institutional and affective aspects of classroom management. For example, he underscored that classrooms are invariably located in institutions, and this institutional issue is influential in affecting classroom participation. He also stressed that teachers must attend to ways to engage students in classroom activities, something that he argued is a core issue of the affective aspect of classroom management. However, it appears that none of the thematic approaches that Wright (2005) elaborated on are related to any specific approaches to classroom discipline and self-regulation, such as SWPBIS and SEL. This lack of a systematic theoretical approach to classroom management enmeshing EYL pedagogy suggests that much research needs to be done.

Recommendations for practice

Readers wishing to explore the instructional management procedures such as grouping, seating and timing; setting up and sequencing tasks or activities; giving instructions; and monitoring in the EYL classroom may want to consult Moon (2006), Nunan (2011) and Shin and Crandall (2014). This section discusses young learner behaviour management, given the scarcity of sources on it. The section focuses on the underexplored issues of dealing with learners' lack of respect and attention-seeking behaviours.

O'Grady et al. (2011) stated that with the increasing number of students displaying challenging behaviour, the respect that teachers receive today has arguably decreased from two decades ago, and yet its significance within an educative relationship at any level is undeniable. They argued that learners who show lack of respect tend to exhibit rudeness against their teacher, and this could adversely affect teachers' confidence. Teachers who receive various instances of disrespect and rudeness tend to feel undermined by learners who do not acknowledge them as a teacher, or they may feel a lack of acknowledgment as a human being. This certainly would diminish the interpersonal respect that the teachers have towards the learners and negatively affect the classroom atmosphere.

EYL teachers wanting respect do not need to impose themselves upon young learners. Instead, they need to demonstrate integrity and professionalism, which can be done in some contexts by meeting the following characteristics: (1) being punctual; (2) being well prepared; (3) being consistent in their manners and attitudes; (4) treating students fairly; (5) trying not to let personal feelings about individual students influence their professionalism; (6) not ignoring problems and work instead on addressing them; and (7) never losing their temper (Gower et al. 2008). When teachers are able to demonstrate these characteristics, they build a figure of authority; they can serve as a role model for their leaners. When teachers become a role model, learners recognise the teacher's efforts, appreciate them and under their own volition self-regulate themselves to develop a sense of respect for the teacher (Gower et al. 2008). This is the beginning for the development of self-regulation on the part of the learners (O'Grady et al. 2011).

Learners may exhibit lack of respect not only to their teacher but also other learners. EYL teachers could address this problem by implementing applied behavioural approach to establish respect among learners. One common strategy used is classroom rules. Classroom rules may apply both positive and negative reinforcements. The rules are meant to form a predictable atmosphere that maintains classroom discipline, prevents disruptions and encourages young learners to self-control. Things that may need to be included in the class rules are guidelines on arriving late, interrupting other students, forgetting to do homework and not paying attention. Learners would be reminded that adherence to these rules exhibits respect. The rules need to be based on moral, legal, safety and educational considerations, and they also need to be age appropriate, simple and be stated in positive terms. Involving learners to develop the rules is advisable, as learners who participate in creating the rules have higher understanding and are more likely to adopt the rules and obey them (Schneiderová 2013). Teachers may want to allow the learners to produce illustrated classroom rules by themselves; they may create and draw the rules as they see fit. These rules may need to be displayed on the wall in order to help learners learn and follow them more easily. Teachers can point to them when the need arises. Once the rules are set, teachers may want to apply some behavioural procedures that reinforce appropriate behaviours such as 'Good Behaviour Game' where learners are put into teams and compete to receive prizes based on which team receives the lowest scores for negative behaviour (Lemlech 1999; Schneiderová 2013).

The second issue is attention-seeking behaviours. Attention-seeking behaviours are commonplace in the young learner classroom; they can be disruptive to the lesson and may be time consuming to deal with. When it comes to overcoming attention-seeking behaviours, teachers need to be aware of the types. The first type of attention-seeking behaviours is not entirely negative. These include showing off having completed tasks or assignments, desiring to be praised and asking unnecessary questions. Integrating a series of behavioural approaches to this type of attention-seeking behaviour has proven useful. While sometimes teachers should ignore learners exhibiting these kinds of behaviours, at other times they should deliver positive attention to the learners. These can be done by: (1) making eye contact and smiling at the learner(s); (2) (culture permitting) patting the learner(s) on the shoulder; (3) checking in with the learner(s) about how they are progressing with their work; (4) passing the learner(s) a cheerful comment or compliment of their attitudes or work; and (5) calling on the learner(s) in class to share their answer (Lemlech 1999, Schneiderová 2013).

On the other hand, there are negative attention-seeking behaviours such as being loud, opposing or responding negatively to teachers' authority and bullying other students. These behaviours are detrimental to building a positive classroom atmosphere and often interfere with the teachers' abilities to maintain order and proceed with academic tasks. In dealing with these kinds of behaviours, teachers may need to implement preventive strategies such as asking questions to draw students' attention, talking to the learner(s) and rewarding them. Teachers may also do corrective strategies such as warning the learners or setting up a conference meeting with their parents (Gower et al. 2008, Lemlech 1999, Schneiderová 2013).

At the extreme of attention-seeking behaviours are children who are diagnosed with attention-deficit hyperactivity disorder (ADHD). These children are likely to exhibit management problems such as non-compliance and oppositional behaviours. Researchers have suggested the use of straightforward approaches when dealing with ADHD learners (Blotnicky-Gallant, Martin, McGonnell, and Corkum 2015, Kapalka 2006, Reid and Johnson 2012). Reducing repetition has been suggested as a useful classroom-based intervention by Kapalka (2006). Blotnicky-Gallant et al. (2015) proposed interventions such as training learners to self-monitor their behaviour, reducing task duration/workload, allowing for oral rather than written task completion, chunking information into smaller sections, providing choice in activities and breaking homework and assignments into smaller segments. Reid and Johnson (2012) emphasised the sparing use of negative reinforcement such as reprimand and admonishment while maintaining the importance of setting up predictable classroom routines. All these interventions could help generate compliance of ADHD learners and restore order, allowing the teacher to introduce a new activity that provides a change of focus.

Future directions

Classroom management is a large issue that vitally influences the overall quality of learning environments and experiences, and determines whether they are conducive to the maximum performance of all students. A classroom conducive to learning is one that is facilitative and builds a comfortable, caring, embracing, affirming and engaging atmosphere – in such a classroom learners' discipline is less likely to be an issue and instruction can proceed smoothly (Gay 2006). EYL classroom management should be aimed towards the development of such a conducive classroom. Teachers' instruction will not be effective unless the classroom is conducive.

With EYL pedagogy still generally focusing on instructional management, a shift of paradigm among EYL practitioners and researchers is vital: classroom management does not only comprise the instructional dimension but also the behavioural one. This paradigm shift needs to occur at both theoretical and practical levels.

At the theoretical level, addressing specific issues of young learner behavioural management is an important research agenda. Aspects of misbehaviour such as lack of respect and rudeness as well as seeking attention in the EYL classroom have not been explored in the literature. Furthermore, we know little about the way EYL teachers manage their emotions. Little, if not none, research has been done on the emotional strategies that EYL teachers employ in order to manage young learner misbehaviour. This issue of emotional regulation deserves attention in future research.

While conducting research into those areas is important, this direction should not create another partiality of classroom management. Teachers' instruction and learner behaviour are inseparable – each shapes and is shaped by the other. Thus, research into teacher instructional management cannot be done solely on the pedagogical perspective per se without close scrutiny to its impact on young learner behaviour. This means research into corrective feedback in teaching EYL, for example, takes into account behavioural aspects such as learners' responses to feedback. The same thing applies to research on young learner behaviour – considerations on how the behaviour impacts the teacher's instruction need to be taken into account. Doing so will ensure future research tackles both dimensions of classroom management set out earlier in this chapter: instruction and behaviour.

At the practical level, the development of a classroom conducive to learning is central in EYL pedagogy. To achieve this, an integration of approaches to classroom management where teachers play an authoritative, *not* authoritarian, role has been found to characterise the most effective teachers and schools (Bear et al. 2011, Gregory, Cornell, Fan, Sheras, Shih, and Huang 2010). Authoritative teachers are similar to authoritative parents, as they prevent misbehaviour and stimulate compliance in the short run but also develop self-regulation in the long run. This is accomplished through the creation of balanced dimensions between child rearing and classroom management where responsiveness and demandingness are concomitantly applied (Gregory et al. 2010). An authoritative approach may help teachers to create such a balance, as they more effectively and efficiently achieve the dual aims of classroom management: (1) order, engagement and compliance and (2) self-regulation.

Emmer and Sabornie (2014) argued that the implementation of the authoritative approach allows teachers to integrate techniques from the ecological, behavioural and SEL approaches through a school-wide perspective of classroom management that involves teachers, management, administrators and other parties. This has implications for language instruction: it ceases to be seen in isolation and devoid of the school context; rather, it moves towards an holistic framework of EYL classroom management that aims to foster young learners' learning development while being an integral part of the school curriculum and educational agenda. This means classroom management is seen in the context of the development of self-regulation within individual students as well as the maintenance of discipline within the school as the large learning ecology.

An SWPBIS approach to EYL pedagogy seems befitting, making young learner behaviour management a school-wide concern, and not just the concern of an individual EYL teacher. This is especially relevant because in many EYL contexts, English is introduced to children alongside other subjects, and is usually in a multilingual classroom where other languages exist. However, it remains to be seen how the practice of managing the EYL classroom is perceived alongside the management of teaching other subjects or languages. The concern is that given the wide importation of Western methodologies that might not be entirely appropriate to the local contexts, more behavioural issues might manifest in English language classrooms rather than in classes in other subjects or languages. A school-wide approach ensures a balanced focus on self-regulation and classroom discipline. The implementation of a SWPBIS approach to EYL pedagogy could provide solutions to the problem created by the implementation of Western-imported methodologies such as CLT and TBLT that emphasise the development of self-regulation. Holistic classroom-based interventions prescribed by the SWPBIS approach may help reduce classroom disruptions to minimal while, increasing learners' self-regulation emphasised by those imported Western methodologies.

This commands coordination across administrators, teachers and other staff and takes into account the affordances and constraints (Lewis et al. 2014). Further, it requires specialist EYL teachers to work collaboratively with classroom teachers or teachers of other subjects through different levels of schooling to achieve positive classroom management. This is relevant in many EYL contexts worldwide where teaching English to children is a confluence of interests of different stakeholders (Enever and Moon 2009). Promoting order, discipline, engagement, compliance and self-regulation is a joint interest of relevant parties who take into account the broad spheres of language-in-education policy, national ideology, societal values, misbehaviour rates and the school's educational cultures.

Third, it is vital to reorient teacher education. Classroom management should be an integral component of teacher education programmes, with a view to develop methodologically versatile specialist EYL teachers. These are teachers who can teach English properly and can deal with young learners appropriately. There has been a call to move from generic preparation of EYL teachers to training in specific areas to produce such versatile teachers (Enever 2014; Zein 2015, 2016), and yet major concerns seem to remain on teachers' language proficiency and instruction (Butler 2015). If teacher education programmes wish to tackle those focal concerns, a cross-fertilising approach may be implemented. Such an approach allows prospective EYL teachers to study cross-departmentally or institutionally. They could undertake relevant courses that provide them with adequate preparation on the management of young learner behaviour in, for instance, child psychology or classroom-based interventions. Another approach is an integrative one; EYL teacher education programmes can retain their focus on teachers' language proficiency while developing learning-teaching options that integrate instructional and behavioural management dimensions. Courses on teaching methodologies and second language acquisition within the programmes are therefore designed to ensure this integration. The suggestion for cross-fertilising and integrative approaches is, nevertheless, still within the realm of theoretical speculation. Further research is warranted.

Further reading

1 Emmer, E. T., and Sabornie, E. J. (Eds.). (2015). *Handbook of classroom management*, 2nd ed. New York: Routledge.

This handbook is the most current and comprehensive account of classroom management that includes classroom management approaches, models and programmes.

2 Evertson, C. M. (2013). *Classroom management for elementary teachers,* 9th ed. Boston, MA: Pearson.

This book provides teachers with the skills, approaches and strategies necessary to establish effective management in the primary school classroom.

3 Evertson, C. M., and Weinstein, C. S. (Eds.). (2006). *Handbook of classroom management: Research, practice and contemporary issues.* Mahwah, NJ: Lawrence Erlbaum.

This handbook provides a rich account of classroom management that includes classroom management approaches, models and programmes.

4 Reid, R., and Johnson, J. (2012). *Teacher's guide to ADHD.* New York: The Guilford Press.

This book provides a comprehensive overview of ADHD including introduction, assessments of ADHD learners, medication, classroom-behaviour interventions and self-regulation strategies.

Related topics

Motivation, differentiation, difficult circumstances, classroom language

References

Aline, D., and Hosoda, Y. (2006). Team teaching participation patterns of homeroom teachers in English Activities classes in Japanese public elementary schools. *JALT Journal,* 28, 5–21.

Bagley, W. (1908). *Classroom Management.* New York: Palgrave Macmillan.

Bear, G. G., Gaskins, C., Blank, J., and Chen, F. F. (2011). Delaware school climate survey-student: Its factor structure, concurrent validity, and reliability. *Journal of School Psychology,* 49, 157–174. doi:0.1016/ j.jsp.2011.01.001.

Bland, J. (Ed.). (2015). *Teaching English to Young Learners: Critical issues in language teaching with 3–12 year olds.* London: Bloomsbury.

Blotnicky-Gallant, P., Martin, C., McGonnell, M., and Corkum, P. (2015). Nova Scotia teachers' ADHD knowledge, beliefs, and classroom management practices. *Canadian Journal of School Psychology,* 30(1), 3–21. doi:10.1177/0829573514542225.

Brophy, J. (2006). History of research on classroom management. In Evertson, C., and Weinstein, C. (eds.) *Handbook of Classroom Management: Research, practice, and contemporary issues.* Mahwah, NJ: Erlbaum, 17–43.

Butler, Y. G. (2004). What level of English proficiency do elementary school teachers need to attain to teach EFL? Case studies from Korea, Taiwan, and Japan. *TESOL Quarterly,* 38(2), 245–278. doi:10.2307/3588380.

Butler, Y. G. (2011). The implementation of communicative and task-based language teaching in the Asia-Pacific region. *Annual Review of Applied Linguistics,* 31, 36–57. doi:10.1017/S0267190511000122.

Butler, Y. G. (2015). English language education among young learners in East Asia: A review of current research (2004–2014). *Language Teaching,* 48, 303–342. doi:10.1017/S0261444815000105.

Butler, Y. G., Someya, Y., and Fukuhara, E. (2014). Online games for young learners' foreign language learning. *ELT Journal,* 68(3), 265–275. doi:10.1093/elt/ccu008.

Copland, F., Garton, S., and Burns. A. (2014). Challenges in teaching English to Young Learners: Global perspectives and local realities. *TESOL Quarterly,* 48(4), 738–762. doi:10.1002/tesq.148.

Dodge, K. A., Coie, J. D., and Lynam, D. (2006). Aggression and antisocial behavior in youth. In Damon, W., and Learner, R. M. (Series eds.) and Eisenberg, N. (Vol. ed.), *Handbook of Child Psychology: Vol. 3. Social, emotional, and personality development,* 6th ed. New York: Wiley, 719–788.

Doyle, W. (2006). Ecological approaches to classroom management. In Evertson, C. M., and Weinstein, C. S. (eds.) *Handbook of Classroom Management: Research, practice, and contemporary issues.* Mahwah, NJ: Erlbaum, 97–125.

Durlak, J. A., Weissberg, R. P., Dymnicki, A. B., Taylor, R. D., and Schellinger, K. B. (2011). The impact of enhancing students' social and emotional learning: A meta-analysis of school-based universal interventions. *Child Development,* 82, 405–432. doi:10.1111/j.1467–8624.2010.01564.x.

Elias, M. J., and Schwab, Y. (2006). From compliance to responsibility: Social and emotional learning and classroom management. In Evertson, C., and Weinstein, C. (eds.) *Handbook of Classroom Management: Research, practice, and contemporary issues*. Mahwah, NJ: Erlbaum, 309–341.

Emmer, E. T., and Sabornie, E. J. (2014). Introduction to the second edition. In Emmer, E. T., and Sabornie, E. J. (eds.) *Handbook of Classroom Management*, 2nd ed. New York: Routledge, 3–12.

Emmer, E. T., and Stough, L. M. (2001). Classroom management: A critical part of educational psychology, with implications for teacher education. *Educational Psychologist*, 36, 103–112. doi:10.1207/S15326985EP3602_5.

Enever, J. (2014). Primary English teacher education in Europe. *ELT Journal*, 68(3), 231–242. doi:10.1093/elt/cct079.

Enever, J., and Moon, J. (2009). New global contexts for teaching primary ELT: Change and challenge. In Enever, J., Moon, J., and Raman, U. (eds.) *Young Learner English Language Policy and Implementation: International perspectives*. Reading: Garnet Education, 5–21.

Evertson, C. M., and Weinstein, C. S. (Eds.). (2006). *Handbook of Classroom Management: Research, practice and contemporary issues*. Mahwah, NJ: Lawrence Erlbaum.

Garton, S. (2014). Unresolved issues and new challenges in teaching English to young learners: The case of South Korea. *Current Issues in Language Planning*, 15(2), 201–219. doi:10.1080/14664208.2014.858657.

Gay, G. (2006). Connections between classroom management and culturally responsive teaching. In Evertson, C., and Weinstein, C. (eds.) *Handbook of Classroom Management: Research, practice, and contemporary issues*. Mahwah, NJ: Erlbaum, 343–370.

Gettinger, M., and Kohler, K. M. (2006). Process-outcome approaches to classroom management and effective teaching. In Evertson, C. M., and Weinstein, C. S. (eds.) *Handbook of Classroom Management: Research, practice, and contemporary issues*. Mahwah, NJ: Erlbaum, 73–95.

Gower, R., Phillips, D., and Walters, S. (2008). *Teaching Practice: A handbook for teachers in training*. Oxford: Palgrave Macmillan.

Gregory, A., Cornell, D., Fan, X., Sheras, P., Shih, T., and Huang, F. (2010). High school practices associated with lower student bullying and victimization. *Journal of Educational Psychology*, 102, 483–496. doi:10.1037/a0018562.

Harmer, J. (2007). *The Practice of English Language Teaching*, 4th ed. Harlow: Longman.

Kapalka, G. M. (2006). Avoiding repetitions reduces ADHD children's management problems in the classroom. *Emotional and Behavioural Difficulties*, 10(4), 269–279. doi:10.1177/1363275205058999.

Landrum, T. J., and Kauffman, J. M. (2006). Behavioral approaches to classroom management. In Evertson, C., and Weinstein, C. (eds.) *Handbook of Classroom Management: Research, practice, and contemporary issues*. Mahwah, NJ: Erlbaum, 47–71.

Le, V. C., and Do, T. M. C. (2012). Teacher preparation for primary school English education: A case of Vietnam. In Spolsky, B., and Moon, Y-I. (eds.) *Primary School English-language Education in Asia: From policy to practice*. New York: Routledge, 106–121.

Lemlech, J. K. (1999). *Classroom Management: Methods and techniques for elementary and secondary teachers*, 3rd ed. Prospect Heights, IL: Waveland Press.

Lewis, T. J., Mitchell, B. S., Trussell, R., and Newcomer, L. L. (2014). School-wide positive behavior support: Building systems to prevent problem behavior and develop and maintain appropriate social behavior. In Emmer, E. T., and Sabornie, E. J. (eds.) *Handbook of Classroom Management*, 2nd ed. New York: Routledge, 40–59.

Li, G., and Ni, X. (2011). Primary EFL teachers' technology use in China. *RELC Journal*, 42(1), 69–85. doi:10.1177/0033688210390783.

Lynass, L. L., Tsai, S-F., Richman, T. D., and Cheney, D. (2012). Social expectations and behavioral indicators in school-wide positive behavior supports: A national study of behavior matrices. *Journal of Positive Behavior Interventions*, 14, 153–161. doi: 10.1177/1098300711412076.

Luo, W.-H. (2007). A study of native English-speaking teacher programs in elementary schools in Taiwan. *Asia Pacific Education Review*, 8(2), 311–320.

Marzano, R. J., and Marzano, J. S. (2003). The key to classroom management. *Educational Leadership*, 61(1) (September), 6–13.

McClellan, B. E. (1999). *Moral Education in America: Schools and the shaping of character from colonial times to the present*. New York: Teachers College Press.

Moon, J. (2006). *Children Learning English: A guidebook for English language teachers*. Oxford: Palgrave Macmillan.

Nunan, D. (2011). *Teaching English to Young Learners*. California: Annaheim University Press.

O'Grady, E., Hinchion, C., and McNamara, P. M. (2011). The importance of respect in teaching and learning: Perspectives of final year pre-service teachers in a regional university in Ireland. *European Journal of Teacher Education*, 34(4), 501–518. doi: 10.1080/02619768.2011.592978.

Pinter, A. (2011). *Children Learning Second Languages*. Basingstoke: Palgrave Macmillan.

Rich, S. (Ed.). (2014). *International Perspectives on Teaching English to Young Learners*. London: Palgrave MacMillan.

Richards, J. C. (2015). *Key Issues in Language Teaching*. Cambridge: Cambridge University Press.

Schneiderová, P. (2013). The effective classroom management in young learners' language classes. Unpublished Bachelor thesis. Faculty of Education, Masaryk University, Brno.

Shin, J. K., and Crandall, J. A. (2014). *Teaching Young Learners English*. New York: National Geographic Learning.

Shohamy, E., and Inbar, O. (2007). Effective teaching of EFL to young learners: Homeroom or FL teachers? Paper presented at TeMoLaYoLe conference, University of Pécs, Hungary.

Stelma, J., and Onat-Stelma, Z. (2010). Foreign language teachers organising learning during their first year of teaching young learners. *The Language Learning Journal*, 38(2), 193–207. doi:10.1080/09571731003790490.

Sugai, G., and Horner, R. H. (2009). Defining and describing schoolwide positive behavior support. In Sailor, W., Dunlap, G., Sugai, G., and Horner, R. (eds.) *Handbook of Positive Behavior Support*. New York: Springer, 307–326.

Suh, S., Kim, S. W., and Kim, N. J. (2010). Effectiveness of MMORPG-based instruction in elementary English education in Korea. *Journal of Computer Assisted Learning*, 26, 370–378.

Unsworth, S., Persson, L., Prins, T., and de Bot, K. (2015). An investigation of factors affecting early foreign language learning in the Netherlands. *Applied Linguistics*, 36(5), 527–548. doi:10.1093/applin/amt052.

Wright, T. (2005). *Classroom Management in Language Education*. London: Palgrave Macmillan.

Yim, S. Y. (2014). An anxiety model for EFL young learners: A path analysis. *System*, 42, 344–354. doi:http://dx.doi.org/10.1016/j.system.2013.12.022.

Zein, M. S. (2013). Language teacher education for primary school English teachers in Indonesia: Policy recommendations. Unpublished PhD thesis. Canberra: The Australian National University.

Zein, M. S. (2015). Preparing elementary English teachers: Innovations at pre-service level. *Australian Journal of Teacher Education*, 40(6), 104–120. doi:10.14221/ajte.2015v40n6.6.

Zein, M. S. (2016). Pre-service education for primary school English teachers in Indonesia: Policy implications. *Asia Pacific Journal of Education*, 36(S1), 119–134. doi:10.1080/02188791.2014.961899.

Zein, M. S. (2017). Professional development needs of primary EFL teachers: Perspectives of teachers and teacher educators. *Professional Development in Education*, 43(2), 293–313. doi:10.1080/19415257.2016.1156013.

Zhang, E. Y., and Adamson, B. (2007). Implementing language policy: Lessons from primary school English. In Feng, A. (ed.), *Bilingual Education in China: Practices, policies and concepts*. Clevedon: Multilingual Matters, 166–181.

PART 3
Young learner pedagogy

11

Fostering young learners' listening and speaking skills

Yasemin Kırkgöz

Introduction

In an increasingly globalised world proficiency in English, the world's *lingua franca*, is perceived by many non-English-speaking countries as vital to professional communication, delivering long-term economic development and improving quality of opportunities for young people (Enever 2011). The response to the ever-increasing demand for English has led to pressure on governments 'to ensure there is an English speaking workforce' (Garton et al. 2011, p. 4). Along with this, there has been a growing tendency among many Asian countries to reform language education systems and introduce English at earlier ages in elementary schools (Murphy 2014). Likewise, as noted by Enever (2014), 'substantial attention has been given to the introduction of English from the very start of schooling in many European countries' (p. 231). In other countries, too, such as Turkey, following the introduction of English as a compulsory subject for young learners in primary grades four through eight (age nine) in 1997, the most recent curriculum change, starting with the 2013–2014 teaching year, is that English is now being taught at a much younger age in primary grade two (age six).

As a result of such developments, the field of teaching English to young learners (TEYLs) has expanded. The school curriculum for foreign language learning in primary schools in many countries has now privileged the development of communicative competence with an emphasis on the oral skills of listening and speaking (Enever 2011). Hence, teachers of English as a second/foreign language (ESL/EFL) are expected to make the improvement of children's listening and speaking skills as the main aim of teaching.

This chapter illustrates how young learners' listening and speaking skills can be effectively promoted. After providing definitions of key words, and a theoretical perspective on listening and speaking in general, the characteristics of young learners (YLs) will be related to the nature of listening and speaking. This is followed by a discussion of the critical issues in listening and speaking skills in young learner classrooms. A survey of the research relevant to this area is given, followed by a presentation of the listening and speaking activities that can promote listening and speaking in young learner classrooms. The chapter concludes with suggestions for future directions in this area of research.

The following three sections provide definitions of the three key terms used in this chapter.

Listening

Listening is the receptive use of language. It is the process of interpreting messages by using context and one's knowledge of language and the world. The development of listening skills has an impact on the development of other skills (Rost 2002; Linse 2005) because listening provides input for other language skills including speaking and writing. Listening is not an easy skill to acquire as it requires listeners to make sense of the meaning from the oral input, produce information in their long term memory and make their own interpretations of the spoken passages (Richards 2008). That is, listeners need to be active processors of information. This is also the case for young learners who must select and interpret information that comes from auditory and visual clues in order to define what the speakers are trying to express with a focus on meaning (Cameron 2001).

Speaking

As a productive language skill, speaking is the active use of language to express meaning. Speaking involves expressing ideas, opinions or a need to do something and establishing and maintaining social relationships and friendships (McDonough and Shaw 2003). For YLs, the spoken language is usually the medium through which a new language is encountered, understood, practised and learnt. While listening is the initial stage in first and second language acquisition, and the skill that children acquire first (Scott and Ytreberg 1990), speaking will often quickly follow and provide evidence to the teacher of learning, whether this is superficial or deep. It goes without saying that listening and speaking, therefore, are closely interrelated, particularly in the young learner classroom.

Young learners

The term young learners covers a range of learners who share commonly accepted characteristics such as having short attention spans and learning holistically, but differs in terms of their physical, psychological, social, emotional, conceptual and cognitive development. Although the age range the term young learners covers may vary according to the educational system of a country, Ellis (2014) suggests labels for the different age groups according to the terms commonly used in the educational systems to which children belong. Accordingly, pre-schooler or pre-primary children cover two to five years and they are commonly known as very young learners or early starters; primary school pupils are within the age range of six to 10/11 years old and they are commonly known as young learners; secondary school pupils are within the age range of 11–14 years, and are also known as young learners or early teens; and those within the age range of 15–17 years are known as young adults. In this chapter, I will focus on the 6–11 age group.

Historical perspectives

This section provides a theoretical overview of listening and speaking in general and the nature of listening and speaking for YLs in particular, taking their developmental characteristics into consideration.

As I suggested in the introduction, English language teaching (ELT) in primary schools is a recent phenomenon. However, English has been a core part of school curricula in many countries for some time. For example, Japanese children have been learning English in junior high schools for over 30 years, while in Turkey children in state primary schools have been learning English for the last 20 years (Kırkgöz 2008b). By this age, children have developed cognitively and academically and these factors have contributed to the approach taken to ELT, in the state system at least, which has focused for the most part on following a coursebook which teaches grammar and vocabulary through reading and writing exercises (Kırkgöz 2011). The fact that these features of English are relatively easy to assess has also played a part in their being prominent in post-primary contexts. However, introducing English in the early years has meant a change in approach. Not only are primary school children less cognitively aware than their secondary school peers, but they are still developing literacy in their first language. This has meant that emphasis has been placed in many countries on listening and speaking rather than reading and writing. Indeed, in Japan, reading and writing are actively discouraged in the guidance prepared on introducing foreign language activities in the primary sector by the Ministry of Education (MEXT) (Gaynor 2014).

In addition to development factors, it is also fair to say that there has been a communicative turn in school-based ELT more generally. Many governments, exasperated by the fact that children leave schools after years of English language tuition barely being able to speak a few words in English, never mind communicate with other English users, have introduced new curricula which highlight communication, often drawing on Communicative Language Teaching (CLT). In China, for example, the curriculum reform labelled 'quality-oriented education' (Wang 2013) was introduced in 2001, which resulted in the introduction of English to primary schools. A further reform in 2011 introduced some communicative approaches (Wang ibid.). The result is that listening and speaking are emphasised in many primary classrooms, with coursebooks focusing on enhancing these skills.

Luckily, our understanding of listening and speaking skills has increased significantly over the last twenty years. We now know, for example, that to comprehend a listening text, learners employ two types of processing: top-down and bottom-up. Top-down processing requires the listener to activate his or her schema (Brown 2001), that is, knowledge of the world, to understanding the general meaning of a listening text. For a young learner, this might mean knowing that a listening activity that begins with 'once upon a time' is going to be a fairy tale (see, too, Bland, this volume). Bottom-up listening, in contrast, requires a listener to make sense of individual sounds, words or phrases. For example, a young learner needs to distinguish between the sounds /i/ and /i:/ to know that ship is a sailing vessel and sheep is an animal. In real-life listening, both processes are usually combined, giving more emphasis to one or the other depending on the reason for listening (Oh and Lee 2014).

In terms of speaking, understanding has also moved on, as summarised in Butler (2005). Drawing on research conducted in three Asian countries, Butler identified three factors that need to be considered in developing the oral activities in English. First, it is important to provide a theoretically consistent and operationalised definition of communicative competence for YLs, namely, what constitutes 'teaching for communicative purposes' needs to be clear. In addition, socially and cognitively meaningful motives and goals for the activities need to be specified so that the introduction of communicative activities into classrooms will lead to children learning. Based on children's developmental stages, effective mediational support also needs to be identified and given to YLs. These principles suggest that teachers need to consider carefully the focus and purpose of speaking activities so that they meet both the English language and developmental needs of learners.

The nature of listening and speaking for YLs

Listening and speaking for YLs needs to be considered relative to the characteristics that differentiate this group of learners from more mature ones. The first differentiating trait is that YLs learn indirectly and holistically rather than directly (Cameron 2001). Pinter (2017, p. 167) clarifies:

> learners are not yet able to analyse and manipulate language in an abstract way. They are learning by understanding meaningful messages. For example, in a song children will not understand every word but they will have an idea about what they are singing.

Accordingly, YLs need to be provided with extensive and continuous exposure to language contextualised in meaningful and enjoyable ways (Cameron 2001; Pinter 2011). They also need to be encouraged to communicate through purposeful, real here-and-now experiences. Arnold (2016) has suggested in this regard that listening can be made more comprehensible by using exaggerated intonation to hold the child's attention, emphasising key words, presenting the topics that are familiar to the child, repeating and paraphrasing frequently, and keeping sentences short and grammatically simple.

Secondly, YLs have short attention spans (Cameron 2001; Brewster et al. 2002; Slattery and Willis 2001), and they are not capable of focusing on one task for long periods of time. Therefore, they need variety in listening and speaking tasks. It is essential that such tasks be short, varied, motivating and interesting, and that, in line with Butler (2005), teachers mediate and offer concrete support.

In addition, YLs are active and they need physical movement in the classroom due to their high levels of energy (Brewster et al. 2002). As they enjoy learning through playing, acting, making and doing (Slattery and Willis 2001), these characteristics of YLs can be exploited through Asher's TPR method (Asher 2009). TPR is based on the theory that people learn best when they are actively involved and understand the language they hear, which is especially true of children whose physical and cognitive development can be supported by relating meaning to movement. TPR involves students listening and actively carrying out movements related to what they hear. Incorporating TPR and miming are considered to be effective ways to reinforce meaning while young learners listen. For example, the teacher shows picture cards of key words such as 'plane', 'car' and 'teddy', and introduces the words one at a time to the whole class. Then, the teacher contextualises each word within a sentence and does the action such as 'fly your plane', 'drive your car' and 'hug your teddy' with the children imitating the actions. Later, the teacher asks children to do the action according to the command given. A useful link to a class where children are doing this TPR activity is: www.youtube.com/watch?v=1Mk6RRf4kKs. Overall, this approach involves multisensory processing and it appeals to auditory, visual and kinesthetic learners. It also allows active children to expend some energy and enjoy the fun of uninhibited movement and mimicry.

Another characteristic of YLs is their ability to learn through repetition and to imitate the sounds of the target language (Slattery and Willis 2001). Listening to stories, songs and rhymes is specifically recommended for children to become aware of the rhythm, intonation and pronunciation of language (Brewster et al. 2002). Teachers can use such listening materials as a source of input to develop a speaking activity. For example, children can take the roles of characters in the songs and stories or they can recreate the activity in an activity corner (see Mourão 2014).

A final characteristic that YLs display is that they learn through the here-and-now prin-ciple (Nunan 2011), which implies that they need to be supported to communicate through purposeful, real, here-and-now experiences. Accordingly, YLs need to be provided with a language environment where 'they have the opportunity to listen to and respond to a great variety of meaningful target language input' (Pinter 2014, p168), with each listening and speaking task having purpose and intention (as recommended, too, by Butler 2005).

Critical issues and topics

With the recent introduction of English into the young learner primary ELT curricula in many countries around the world, development of children's oral-aural skills has been high-lighted, and the learning and teaching of listening and speaking has started to receive more attention. However, teaching listening and speaking skills to YLs is found to be highly challenging by teachers. Consequently, a number of critical issues and topics have arisen. The first critical issue concerns teachers' low proficiency level in English (or their lack of confidence in their English ability), which is almost universally identified as a problem (Baker 2008; Kuchah 2009; Littlewood 2007; Nunan 2003). It is generally accepted that to teach using the communicative approach, teachers need to have good levels of English or at least confidence in their ability to use English. This is partly because communicative approaches have traditionally encouraged a target-language-only classroom, which means teachers must use English as much as possible. In this regard, Kuchah (2009) found that teaching in the target language caused anxiety for teachers in Cameroon and caused them to question their own speaking and listening skills.

Furthermore, communicative approaches focus on learners' communicating their own meanings, rather than answering questions based on written texts or completing grammar or vocabulary exercises; the language skills required for the first exceed those required for the second. A primary way of helping children participate as listeners and speakers in conversa-tions is for teachers to model good listening and speaking techniques themselves, for which they need an advanced level of fluency (Enever 2019).

A further critical issue is that teachers find teaching speaking skills particularly difficult. In a global study of the experiences of young learner teachers of English reported in Cop-land et al. (2014), teachers overwhelmingly and across countries and contexts stated that teaching speaking was the greatest challenge they faced. Problems included getting children to speak it, teaching pronunciation and setting up and managing speaking activities. Studies have also revealed that children are not prepared for spontaneous communication (Butler 2005; Enever 2019). In the same global survey, Copland et al. (2014) found that not only are children reluctant, but they also lack adequate language to produce the meanings they want. These findings have been confirmed by several other studies conducted in Turkey (Kırkgöz 2008b) and elsewhere (Baker 2008; c.f. Kuchah 2009; Littlewood 2007).

Another critical issue concerns how L2 listening input is delivered to children (and the role of the teacher during this process). Studies have found that listening to CDs is one of the most frequent activities in the young learner classroom (Butler 2005; Copland et al. 2014). Although video and digital recordings are becoming more accessible (see Bland, this volume, on digital books) CDs remain the dominant medium through which listening activities are delivered. By their nature, these recordings lack visual input and so can be challenging for learners, particularly when texts are relatively long and require learners to listen intensively. Copland et al. (2014) suggest that teachers' reliance on the CD player as the main source of listening input may be due to concerns about their own levels of English or their lack of confidence in their spoken English. Teachers may also worry that they do not provide a good model for students as they do not sound like 'native speakers'. Recent discussions of World Englishes (e.g., Galloway and Rose 2015) have tried to dispel the myth that the native speaker is a model to aspire to (see, too, Copland 2011). Nonetheless, it is not uncommon for teachers to hold these beliefs which contribute to their lacking confidence in their own spoken English.

An important characteristic of YLs with regard to listening and speaking is their ability to imitate the new sounds of the target language (Brewster et al. 2002; Slattery and Willis 2001). It is also acknowledged that successful listening and speaking skills are acquired over time and with ample practice. It is therefore important that children are exposed to ample opportunities to listen to English from a variety of sources where the speakers use English in a variety of contexts. Unfortunately, it has been found in some contexts that students receive little dedicated listening and speaking practice in their classes, and in some cases they get almost none (for example, see Kırkgöz 2008a).

Another concern relates to how many hours of input children receive in schools and what happens in the lessons. Nunan (2003) suggests that at least 200 hours per year of instruction are needed for measurable progress to be seen in L2. However, Ho (2003) found that in many countries in East Asia, the hours in primary schools varied, from between one and two hours in South Korea to between four and six hours in Malaysia or Singapore. Currently, in Turkish state primary education, students in primary Grades 2 and 3 receive an average of 76 hours of instruction per year, which is far below the minimum number of hours needed for significant progress in English.

Differentiation has also been found challenging in terms of listening and speaking. Differentiation is the reality that children in class have different needs, levels, ways of learning and motivations. Nunan (2003) argues that by the very nature of their job as a teacher of young learner, teachers must be aware of children's basic physical and psychological needs. So that they can provide the best instruction possible, they need to adjust educational experiences to meet the developmental stages of the individual child. A particular issue in terms of differentiation for state school teachers of English to young learners is that some young learners go to after-school English classes while others do not. As many of these classes focus on developing communication skills, the teacher has to deal with supporting children with different listening and speaking levels. Other learners may be exposed to English in other ways, through family members or friends or from other out-of-school activities (see Sayer and Ban 2014 for a description of how children in Mexico access English out of class). As noted by Djigunovic and Krajnovic (2015), as a result of different exposure to English, learners bring into the classroom various linguistic skills, learning strategies and sensibilities that the teachers and teaching materials should aim to accommodate.

Another potential problem relates to the curriculum materials for listening and speaking in state education in particular, which may not always be appropriate. In the global survey reported by Copland et al. (2014), it was found that in some countries such as South Korea and Malaysia, one prescribed textbook for each grade is used. In other countries, a range of government-approved textbooks for teachers are available to choose from. In yet other countries, such as Italy, schools can choose their own textbooks from those available on the market. Perhaps most bizarrely, in Mexico, children in the same classroom can be issued coursebooks produced by different publishers (Copland, personal communication). With a view to examining the listening input children receive in Turkey, Kırkgöz (2011) evaluated four locally published English textbooks used in state primary schools. Her findings show that some textbooks lacked a listening component, which suggests that the centrality of listening to developing young learner English is not well understood in Turkey at least. Where textbooks are inadequate, teachers could be trained to create their own materials. They could also have a number of useful items such as CDs with songs and stories, flashcards, puppets and a collection of realia to allow them to improvise listening activities. In such circumstances the teacher can use his or her voice as the audio source. However, several studies have shown that teachers often lack the time and expertise to develop appropriate materials (Ghatage 2009; Ho 2003).

To conclude, the picture that emerges concerning the current issues in listening and speaking to YLs can be summarised under two headings: teacher-related issues and curriculum-related issues. Teacher-related issues focus on teachers' low proficiency level in English or their lack of confidence in their English ability; the challenges they face around teaching speaking and differentiating for learning. Curriculum-related issues focus on insufficient time allocated to listening and speaking in school curricula and problems related to teaching materials for listening and speaking, particularly in state education.

Current contributions and research

Research in listening and speaking with YLs focuses on two areas: pedagogy and second language acquisition (SLA). In terms of pedagogy, there is a good deal of interest in how songs, chants and stories can enhance listening and speaking skills. For example, YL researchers (e.g. Coyle and Gracia 2014; Graham 2006; Lechel 2010) have found that teaching song-based activities provides memorable and enjoyable language practice, especially in fostering listening skills, understanding of basic nouns, aiding pronunciation, and learning and retention of vocabulary and structures over a shorter time period.

In relation to teaching speaking, researchers have investigated the effect of games, puppets, stories, drama and role play on enhancing YL speaking. For games and plays Linse (2005) posits that they are a 'vital and important aspect of a child's development and language is a part of that play' (p. 47). English-speaking puppets, animated by the teacher, have an effect on influencing children to use more English during speaking activities and make children more relaxed and motivated. During storytelling, using visuals, non-linguistic support and limited use of the mother tongue was found to facilitate comprehension of a story (Haven 2000). Investigating the use of narratives in the young learner classroom, Bland (2015a) focused on oral storytelling and sharing of a picture book whereby particularly the pictures 'can focus the children's attention through their continuous and repeated presence' (p. 186). She highlights the educational value of stories for empathy and intercultural understanding. In another study, Bland (2015b) highlights using drama for oracy development in the young learner classroom. She stresses the cognitive, sociological, affective and psychological dimensions of holistic learning offered by using the potential of drama noting that 'children are extremely involved in learning through imitation and playful experimentation' (p. 221). Integrating technology in the young-learner classroom is another area of pedagogic research. Schmid and Whyte (2015) used technology-enhanced tasks through video conferencing to allow learners to negotiate meaning and repair communication breakdown. Computer-mediated communication has been found to offer considerable opportunities as well as challenges. Verdugo and Belmonte (2007) used animated stories in language instruction. The study demonstrated that YLs' listening comprehension was improved with the infusion of digital stories. The visual, interactive and reiterative character of digital stories had a crucial effect on this result. Using a multimedia storytelling website, Tsou, Wang, Tzeng (2006) found that the retention of words, phrases and sentences from the storyline and the general story recall of the participants had increased. The researchers indicated that the extra visual and audio stimuli received through the multimedia storytelling website may have facilitated story recalls and the children's' creativity in recreating stories.

In the field of second language acquisition (SLA), research undertaken with children remains limited. However, as reviewed by Oliver and Azkarai (2017), recently there has been a growing body of research on child second language (L2) learners with a pedagogical focus. One aspect of SLA research is situated on child interaction. Guilfoylea and Mistryb (2013) investigated how role play supports the development of speaking and listening skills. Observations of case study children over a period of one month demonstrated effectiveness of role play in language development for children and improvement in a range of language learning strategies (LLS), including experimenting with language, repeating key language items and memorising and internalising new vocabulary. Also, the use of metacognitive strategies increased, suggesting that the pupils were able to organise and evaluate their own language development through self-speech.

Another line of research investigated the provision and use of feedback. Mackey et al. (2003) provided empirical support for the use of pairwork in classrooms by demonstrating that child learners are able to provide the type of feedback that leads to improved language production. A similar study by Pinter (2006) found that children used various strategies to complete different tasks and suggested that the children's interactions facilitated L2 acquisition as they contained opportunities for comprehensible input and feedback. Other SLA research is concerned with the role of L1 in L2 development. Azkarai and García Mayo (2017) explored the use and functions of L1 in Spanish EFL learners' (9–10 years old) repetition in a spot-the-differences task. They found that the children used their L1 in their interactions for various purposes (clarification requests, confirmation checks), to indicate lack of knowledge and to appeal for help.

Recommendations for practice

This section offers recommendations based on issues previously discussed in the chapter and provides suggestions for useful techniques and activities for enhancing listening and speaking skills for YLs.

Although listening is a receptive skill, children should be actively engaged while listening. In any listening activity, it is important to orient students towards what they are going to listen to before beginning the activity. Language acquisition takes place most effectively when the input is meaningful and interesting to the learner. Teachers should, therefore, ensure that the materials used for listening and speaking are comprehensible to YLs and appropriate developmentally and culturally for them to maximise the potential for language acquisition. Teachers should also relate the topics to what children already know by establishing a meaningful context to promote effective language acquisition (Slattery and Willis 2001).

Illustration of listening tasks

A variety of listening comprehension tasks illustrated below can be conducted in class to promote YLs' listening skills. The same activity can easily be adjusted to various topics and levels by varying content and language.

Listen and do

TPR focusing on the use of physical activity is a useful approach for YLs, who listen to their teacher's instructions generally in the form of commands and then follow those instructions by moving their bodies, drawing, writing or gap-filling. As noted by Ur (1984) a good listening task is one with 'active responses occurring during, or between parts of, the listening passage, rather than at the end' (p. 4). The following YouTube clip gives an example of a 'listen and do' activity in which the teacher performs a TPR activity by engaging the children through commands on the topic 'shapes': www.youtube.com/watch?v=3ZNLBonSXpA

Listen and repeat

Listen-and-repeat activities give the learners a chance to practise parts of the language – the sounds, stress, rhyme and the intonation – to promote effective pronunciation. When performed in combination with movements, objects or pictures, chants, songs and story refrains, they help learners to establish a link between words and meaning (Scott and Ytreberg 1990). An example of a story refrain 'Were-Going-On-A-Bear-Hunt' can be accessed from the following YouTube clip: www.youtube.com/watch?v=kL36gMrHJaI

Listen and Draw

This task can be done in any age group to help learners practise listening and language in context, e.g., prepositions. For example, the teacher describes three objects (e.g., a present, a clock and a box) without saying any of these words in his or her description. The descriptions should be about size, shape and details, not naming the object or saying what it does. Learners listen carefully and draw their own version of the picture. To illustrate, the teacher gives a description of a monster, and children draw it after the instructions, as in the given example:

> Let's draw a monster!
> The monster has one eye.
> The monster has three arms.
> The monster has four legs.

Listen and arrange

Learners are given scrambled pictures of a story or a text, and they can be asked to put the pictures in the correct order while listening. The following sample activity is designed for six- to eight-year-old children. In this activity, the teacher reads the text and, meanwhile, children listen and sequence the pictures:

> I am ready to go to school. First, I put on my green shirt and blue trousers. Then I grab my backpack which is red. Next, I put my books in my backpack. And then, I put my lunch in my backpack. Finally, I go outside and wait for the bus. At school, I meet my friend <Sally>.
> Figure 11.1. shows scrambled pictures of the story.

Figure 11.1 A sample listening activity

Sources: Image a: 'Pictures Of Lunch Ladies #2062389'. *Images For Lunch Lady Clip Art – Clip Art Library*, clipart-library.com/clipart/pc78g8aoi.htm.; Image b: *Free Clipart For Kids #14950*, mzayat.com/single/ 14950.html.; Image c: 'T-Shirt Shirt Clipart Clipartfest'. *ClipartBarn*, clipartbarn.com/t-shirt-clipart_17884/.; Image d: '66 Awesome Library Book Clip Art Images'. *Weclipart*, weclipart.com/library+book+clip+art.; Image e: 'Mens Pants Cliparts #2489978'. *Pic Of Jeans – Clip Art Library*, clipart-library.com/clipart/ 1739340.htm.; Image f: 'Daily Routine Work – Lessons – Tes Teach'. *Tes Teach with Blendspace*, www.tes. com/lessons/NsAaJUsLnhhyKg/daily-routine-work

Listen and colour

Since children love colouring, in such tasks, instead of letting children simply colour the picture, teachers can make it into a language activity, as illustrated in the following sample story, which can be used with eight- to 10-year-old learners. The teacher passes out colouring sheets, on which there is a picture of what she or he will describe to YLs, and tells the purpose of the activity. The teacher reads the instructions below one at a time. When the activity is finished, she or he checks the pages together with the students. Figure 11.2 below shows the picture of the shopping trip.

The shopping trip

It was getting close to Christmas. Mrs Wilson went Christmas shopping. Colour Mrs Wilson's jacket green and her skirt red. Colour Mrs Wilson's shoes black. Colour Mrs. Wilson's hair purple and her purse yellow. She left the house and the dog decided to go shopping too.

Figure 11.2 The shopping trip

The dog's name is Blue. Colour the dog blue. Colour the dog collar orange. A cat followed them. The cat's name is Grey. Colour the cat grey. Mrs Wilson has four packages. Colour the package that the cat is standing on: one side orange, and the other side red. Colour the package that is above the striped package yellow. Colour the other two boxes with your favourite colour. Mrs Wilson has tubes of paper for her daughters. Colour the tubes of paper: one red, one blue and one green.

Speaking task

Speaking tasks with children should provide plenty of support in terms of structure to enable them to use language confidently and effectively. In the following game, children describe cartoon characters in short oral texts that are scaffolded through stem sentences. First, the teacher prepares cards with cartoon characters and their features, and calls on a student to pick up one card and describe it to the class.

> Using the gapped text below, learners describe the cartoon for classmates to guess.
> My name is . . . .
> I am a (white duck).
> I have (yellow-orange feet and legs).
> I wear (a sailor shirt and cap).

Techniques to promote listening and speaking skills

Becker and Roos (2016) state that 'in order to become truly communicatively competent, learners should be provided with manifold opportunities through activities that support their natural desire to interact with peers and allow them to make use of their rich resources of imagination, creativity, curiosity, and playfulness' (p. 23).

There are many techniques that can be used to enhance children's oral language. Bland (this volume) covers a key area – children's literature and storytelling. Here I present three other approaches that are popular in young learner classrooms.

Songs

Songs can make an important contribution to YLs' listening skills, pronunciation, vocabulary, sentence structures and repetition that might otherwise be tedious (Cameron 2001). Songs help children gradually to internalise the structures and patterns of the foreign language and to learn specific vocabulary items. The length of a phrase in a typical children's song is short and often uses simple conversational language, which can allow learners to process the language easily (Murphy 2014). The 'hide and seek' song from super simple song teaches not only how to count from 1 to 10, but also the children can learn to play hide and seek in English. It is also fun because they can do an actual hide and seek game while singing (see www.youtube.com/watch?v=Tt_S9qoupAk)

Animation

The art of animation involves giving life and soul to lifeless materials. Presenting language to YLs through a puppet, having conversations with it and presenting dialogues are some of the most effective ways to teach English. For example, a puppet 'bear' can be created as a personality to support childrens' listening and speaking, helping them to communicate much more spontaneously. Bear can be included in songs, chants, rhymes, games, dialogues and stories by the teacher. Similarly, children can use puppets for retelling what they have learned (Slattery 2008). The following YouTube link illustrates how a YL teacher can use puppets to get children talking in English: www.youtube.com/watch?v=f-P7CFSps0U.

Dialogues and role play

Dialogues and role play based on real-life conversations are oral activities that can be used to bridge the gap between guided and free tasks. Learners can find them entertaining and motivating as they take on the role of an imaginary character. The use of puppets, physical movements and realia can make a dialogue come alive for YLs, giving them a communicative purpose (Brezigar 2010). Several examples of role play activities can be found in the following YouTube link: www.youtube.com/watch?v=AA5hOCxlRaI&list=PLii5rkhsE0L d3xCgxG6j5fw7RlG2S5czO

Future directions

I would like to suggest some areas for future investigation, specifically relating to listening and speaking emerging from the discussion thus far.

Educational research continually reminds us that the teacher is the most important factor in any child's education (Hu 2007; Kırkgöz 2008a; Garton et al. 2011). Research findings bring to attention the need to support the provision of quality language teacher preparation at the level of pre-service and in-service teacher education programmes to address the listening and speaking problems identified. As noted by Enever (2014), attention should turn to ensuring that teachers of English to young learners are trained effectively and have opportunities for continuing professional development.

In pre-service primary courses, prospective teachers need to have the appropriate skills for teaching listening and speaking and expertise relevant to the age group. Effective teacher education programmes for YLs therefore need to educate prospective teachers to have:

- Age-appropriate pedagogies for teaching listening and speaking skills.
- Fluency and confidence particularly in their English speaking to provide both a good language model and a plausible model for children to aspire to.
- Basic classroom management skills in establishing, monitoring and giving feedback on communicative listening and speaking tasks.
- The ability to differentiate teaching to meet the learning needs of young learners who may have different levels, learning styles and motivations.

In-service teacher development programmes could champion collaborative action research teacher development projects (e.g., Kırkgöz 2016), in which university teacher educators collaborate with English language teachers to support teachers' ongoing professional development in areas identified by the teachers as challenging. As highlighted by Curtain and Dahlberg (2010), 'it should be the goal of the language teachers to support the learning of every student, appealing to a variety of learning styles, and to nurture all the forms of intelligence represented in each of our classes' (p. 10).

Given the similarities in the concerns of young learner teachers globally, there is a need for greater opportunities for sharing ideas and experiences amongst primary school teachers of English both nationally and internationally. This could be achieved in a number of ways, including: teacher development groups; trainer training opportunities for young learner teachers who can then support other teachers in their local schools; websites for teachers where teachers can exchange ideas, experiences and activities; and online conferences and seminars for young learner teachers, with contributions mainly from young learner teachers themselves (Copland et al. 2014).

There is no doubt that many teachers are already effectively teaching listening and speaking skills in English to young learners. Nonetheless, there are few studies which effectively investigate appropriate approaches by level and age and which provide useful support for teachers. Moving forward, we must work to better understand how children can learn languages effectively and efficiently in school contexts so that language learning can be celebrated as a successful addition to the primary curriculum.

Further reading

1   Bland, J. (2015a). Oral storytelling in the primary English classroom. In Bland, J. (ed.) *Teaching English to young learners critical issues in language teaching with 3–12 year olds*. London: Bloomsbury, 183–198.

     This chapter illustrates the centrality of storytelling in the young learner classroom followed by the use of a picture book whereby pictures focus the children's attention through their repeated presence.

2   Cameron, Y. (2004). *Teaching languages to young learners*. Cambridge: Cambridge University Press, 37–70.

     The chapter focuses on the development of children's spoken language built around the principles that meaning comes first and children need to participate in discourse and build up knowledge and skills to develop oral proficiency illustrated with an analysis of a task in action.

3   Hugo, A. J., and Horn, J. A. (2013). Using music activities to enhance the listening skills and language skills of grade 1. *English First Additional Language Learners Per Linguam*, 29(1), 63–74.

     This article describes how music activities can be used to develop and enhance young learners' listening abilities. A six-month experimental research study was applied to test whether or not daily music activities had an effect on young learners' listening abilities. The findings reveal that using daily musical activities improved children's listening skills in English.

4   Pinter, A. (2006). *Teaching young language learners*. Oxford: Oxford University Press, 45–64.

     This chapter focuses on key issues in children's language learning with reference to listening and speaking. It specifically covers activities and discusses what can realistically be achieved in young learner classroom in terms of listening and speaking.

Related topics

Curriculum, teacher education, reading and writing, classroom management

References

Arnold, W. (2016). Listening for young learners. www.teachingenglish.org.uk/article/listening-young-learners [Accessed 12 December 2017].

Asher, J. J. (2009). *Learning Another Language through Actions*, 7th ed. Los Gatos, CA: Sky Oak Productions.

Azkarai, A., and García Mayo, M. P. (2017). Task repetition effects on L1 use in EFL child task-based interaction. *Language Teaching Research*, 21(4), 480–495.

Baker, W. (2008). A critical examination of ELT in Thailand: The role of cultural awareness. *RELC Journal*, 39(1), 131−146.

Becker. C., and Roos, J. (2016). An approach to creative speaking activities in the young learners' classroom. *Education Inquiry*, 7(1), 9–26.

Bland, J. (2015a). Oral story telling in the primary English classroom. In Bland, J. (ed.), *Teaching English to Young Learners Critical Issues in Language Teaching with 3–12 Year Olds*. London, Bloomsbury, 183–198.

Bland, J. (2015b). Drama with young learners. In Bland, J. (ed.) *Teaching English to Young Learners Critical Issues in Language Teaching with 3–12 Year Olds*. London: Bloomsbury, 219–238.

Brezigar, B. (2010). How does the introduction of an English speaking puppet influence the use of English in group speaking activities? Teaching English to young learners third international TEYL research seminar 2005–2006. Papers Edited by Annie Hughes and Nicole Taylor, 6–13.

Brewster, J., Ellis, G., and Girard, D. (2002). *The Primary English Teacher's Guide*, New ed. England: Pearson Education Limited.

Brown, H. D. (2001). *Teaching by Principles: An interactive approach to language pedagogy*. Beijing: Foreign Language Teaching and Research Press.

Butler, Y. G. (2005). Comparative perspectives towards communicative activities among elementary school teachers in South Korea, Japan and Taiwan. *Language Teaching Research*, 9, 423–446.

Cameron, L. (2001). *Teaching Languages to Young Learners*. Cambridge: Cambridge University Press.

Copland, F. (2011). Teaching young learners in a global context. *The Language Teacher*, 35(4).

Copland, F., Garton, S., and Burns, A. (December 2014). Challenges in teaching English to young learners: Global perspectives and local realities. *TESOL Quarterly*, 48(4), 738–762.

Coyle, Y., and Gracia, R. G. (July 2014). Using songs to enhance L2 vocabulary acquisition in preschool children. *ELT Journal*, 68(3), 276–285.

Curtain, H. I., and Dahlberg, C. A. A. (2010). *Languages and Children: Making the match, new languages for young learners*, 4th ed. London: Pearson.

Djigunovic, J. M., and Krajnovic, M. M. (Eds.). (2015). *Early Learning and Teaching of English New Dynamics of Primary English*. Bristol: Multilingual Matters.

Ellis, G. (2014). "Young learners": Clarifying our terms. *ELT Journal*, 68(1), 75–78.

Ellis, G., and Brewster, J. (2002). *Tell it Again! The new storytelling handbook for primary teachers*. England: Pearson Education Limited.

Enever, J. (2011). Policy. In Enever, J. (ed.) *ELLiE – Early language learning in Europe*. London: British Council, 23–43. www.teachingenglish.org.uk/publications/early-language-learning-europe.

Enever, J. (July 2014). Primary English teacher education in Europe. *ELT Journal*, 68(3), 231–242.

Enever, J. (2019). Current policy issues in early foreign language learning. *CEPS Journal*, 2(3), 9–26.

Garton, S., Copland, F., and Burns, A. (2011). *Investigating Global Practices in Teaching English to Young Learners: ELT research papers 11–01*. London: The British Council.

Galloway, N., and Rose, H. (2015). *Introducing Global Englishes*. London: Routledge.

Gaynor, B. (2014). From language policy to pedagogic practice: Elementary school English in Japan. In Rich, S. (ed.) *International Perspectives on Teaching English to Young Learners*. Houndmills: Palgrave Macmillian, 66–86.

Ghatage, M. M. (2009). Introduction of English from Grade 1 in Maharashtra, India. In Enever, J. Moon, J., and Raman, U. (eds.) *Young Learner English Language Policy and Implementation: International perspectives*. Reading: Garnet Education, 45–51.

Graham, C. (2006). *Creating Chants and Songs. Resource books for teachers*. Oxford: Oxford University Press.

Guilfoylea, N., and Mistryb, M. (2013). How effective is role play in supporting speaking and listening for pupils with English as an additional language in the Foundation Stage. *Education 3–13*, 41(1), 63–70

Haven, K. F. (2000). *Super Simple Storytelling: A can-do guide for every classroom, every day*. Englewood, CO: Teacher Ideas Press.

Ho, W. K. (2003). English language teaching in Asia today: An overview. In Ho, W. K., and Wong, R. Y. L. (eds.) *English Language Teaching in East Asia Today: Changing policies and practices*. Singapore: Eastern Universities Press, 1–32.

Hu, Y. (2007). China's foreign language policy on primary English education: What's behind it? *Language Policy*, 6, 359–376.

Kırkgöz, Y. (2008a). A case study of teachers' implementation of curriculum innovation in English language teaching in Turkish primary education. *Teaching and Teacher Education*, 24, 1859–1875.

Kırkgöz, Y. (2008b). Curriculum innovation in Turkish primary education. *Asia-Pacific Journal of Teacher Education*, 36(4), 309–322.

Kırkgöz, Y. (2011). An evaluation of English textbooks in Turkish primary education: Students' and teachers' perceptions. *Egitim Arastirmaları- Eurasian Journal of Educational Research*, 44, 188–206.

Kırkgöz, Y. (2016). Improving teaching practices through a university-school collaboration in young learner classrooms. In Dikilitaş, K., Wyatt, M., Hanks, J., and Bullock, D. (eds.) *Teachers Engaging in Research*. Kent: IATEFL, 89–99.

Krashen, S. D. (1991). The input hypothesis: An update. In Alatis, J. E. (ed.), *Georgetown University Round Table on Languages and Linguistics*. Washington, DC: Georgetown University Press, 409–431.

Kuchah, K. (2009). Early bilingualism in Cameroon: Where politics and education meet. In Enever, J., Moon, J., and Raman, U. (eds.) *Young Learner English Language Policy and Implementation: International perspectives*. Reading, England: Garnet Education, 87–94.

Lechel, F. (2010). What is the effect of using children's songs on young learners' understanding of basic nouns? Third International TEYL Research Seminar 2005–2006 Papers Edited by Annie Hughes and Nicole Taylor, 58–67.

Linse, C. T. (2005). *Practical English Language Teaching: Young learners*. New York: McGraw-Hill.

Littlewood, W. (2007). Communicative and task based language teaching in East Asian classrooms. *Language Teaching*, 40, 243–249.

Mackey, A., Oliver, R., and Leeman, J. (2003). Interactional input and the incorporation of feedback: An exploration of NS-NNS and NNS-NNS adult and child dyads. *Language Learning*, 53, 35–66.

McDonough, J., and Shaw, C. (2003). *Materials and Method in ELT*, 2nd ed. United Kingdom: Blackwell.

Mourão, S. (2014). Taking play seriously in the pre-primary English classroom. *ELT Journal*, 68(3), 254–264.

Murphy, V. (2014). *Second Language Learning in the Early School Years: Trends and contexts*. Oxford: Oxford University Press.

Nunan, D. (2003). The impact of English as a global language on educational policies and practices in the Asia-Pacific region. *TESOL Quarterly*, 37(4), 589–613.

Nunan, D. (2011). *Teaching English to Young Learners*. Anaheim, CA: Anaheim University Press.

Oh, E., and Lee, C. (2014). The role of linguistic knowledge and listening strategies in bottom-up and top-down processing of L2 listening. *English Teaching*, 69, 149–173.

Oliver, R., and Azkarai, A. (2017). Review of child second language acquisition (SLA): Examining theories and research. *Annual Review of Applied Linguistics*, 37, 62–76.

Pinter, A. (2006). Verbal evidence of task related strategies: Child versus adult interactions. *System*, 34, 615–630.

Pinter, A. (2011). Children Learning Second Languages. London: Palgrave Macmillan.

Pinter, A. (2014). Child participant roles in applied linguistics research. Applied Linguistics, 35(2), 168–183.

Pinter, A. (2017). Teaching Young Language Learners, 2nd ed. Oxford, UK: Oxford University Press.

Richards, J. (2008). *Teaching Listening and Speaking*. New York: Cambridge University Press.

Rost, M. (2002). *Teaching and Researching Listening*. London: Longman.

Sayer, P., and Ban, R. (2014). Young EFL students' engagements with English outside the classroom. *ELT Journal*, 68(3), 321–329.

Schmid, E. C., and Whyte, S. (2015). Teaching young learners with technology. In Bland, J. (ed.) *Teaching English to Young Learners Critical Issues in Language Teaching with 3–12 Year Olds*. London: Bloomsbury, 239–260.

Scott, W. A., and Ytreberg, L. H. (1990). *Teaching English to Children*. London: Longman.

Slattery, M. (2008). *Teaching with Bear: Using puppets in the language classroom with young learners*. Oxford: Oxford University Press.

Slattery, M., and Willis, J. (2001). *English for Primary Teachers*. Oxford:Oxford University Press.

Tsou, W., Wang, W., and Tzeng, Y. (2006). Applying a multimedia storytelling website in foreign language learning. *Computers and Education*, 47(1), 17–28.

Ur, P. (1984). *Teaching Listening Comprehension*. Cambridge: Cambridge University Press.

Verdugo, D. R., and Belmonte, I. A. (2007). Using digital stories to improve listening comprehension with Spanish young learners of English. *Language Learning and Technology*, 11(1), 87–101.

Wang, B. (2013). Ten years review of basic education new curriculum implementation in southwest rural area in China: Present situation, experience, problems and strategies. In Hao, W. (ed.) West China education report 2013 [Xibu jiaoyu baogao 2013] (Vol. 3, pp. 161–190). Beijing, China: Educational Science Publishing House. [in Chinese]

12

Teaching reading and writing to young learners

Joan Kang Shin and JoAnn (Jodi) Crandall

Introduction

Reading and writing are dynamic and interactive processes. They require skills and strategies to make meaning from and create printed text. For many, this ability to read and write is known as literacy. Unlike learning to speak, literacy is not acquired naturally. Children usually learn to read and write in their first or native language (L1) in school during early childhood, from kindergarten through third grade. Whether students are learning these skills in English as their first language or an additional language, the process requires instruction that is informed and deliberate. In the field of Teaching English to Young Learners (TEYL), teachers of children at the primary school level (five to 10 years old) must first understand the process of becoming literate in an L1 as well as the challenges of becoming literate in English as an additional language.

Creating meaning from print

Literacy instruction should include the three main cueing systems that students utilise to create meaning from print: graphophonic cues, semantic cues and syntactic cues:

- Graphophonic cues: Students gain meaning by decoding – that is, using their knowledge of sound – symbol relationships of language to make mean from text.
- Semantic cues: Students gain meaning from text using their background knowledge.
- Syntactic cues: Students gain meaning from text using their knowledge of language patterns and grammar.

All three are essential to being able to read and write in a language. Effective literacy programmes provide opportunities for students to integrate these cueing systems. Walter (2004) suggests that 'Good readers tend to be flexible, using and integrating the systems interdependently. Developing readers, however, may rely too heavily on one system, typically graphophonic cues. Each system, used in isolation, presents special challenges for English learners' (48). For some EYL programmes, there is a heavy emphasis on phoneme-grapheme correspondence, particularly through phonics instruction. This is commonly the case when students' L1 does not have the same alphabetic writing system as English. However, the process of decoding and encoding through sound-symbol relationships in isolation is only one part of the dynamic, interactive process of reading and writing.

Reading and writing are interactive processes

It is important to understand the interactive process that occurs between the reader and text, as well as the reader and the writer. Most people think reading is gaining meaning from the text. However, the reader actually brings meaning to the text and interacts with the meaning that is encoded in the text. Our comprehension of text is often based on making connections from the text to our own experience and background knowledge. This background knowledge is often referred to as schema. For instance, when children read a story about *Chicken Little*, they bring their knowledge or schema of animals who live on a farm to the text, which will help them understand the story more easily. Reading can be seen as an interactive process involving the reader, the text and the writer.

Writing is also an interactive process that involves thinking about who will read the text. Writers must make decisions about what to write and how to write it based on the reader. While these decisions involve word choice, vocabulary, grammar and mechanics (such as spelling and punctuation), they also involve more choices related to tone, style (formal or informal), and so forth, related to the type of text (e.g., the ways in which we communicate ideas by email to friends differs substantially from the ways in which we write more formally by memo or report to co-workers). We often read what we write multiple times to make sure we are communicating our intended meaning to the potential reader. For example, if we write an email, we may read it over at least once before sending it to make sure our information and purpose are clearly stated. The interaction between the reader and writer through text is a dynamic process that requires many skills to learn.

Historical perspectives

Towards a balanced literacy approach

Our understanding of teaching reading and writing has historically focused on early literacy approaches based on learning to read and write in L1. Educators have been discussing and debating the effectiveness of phonics versus whole language instruction for years (Adams 1997; Chall 1967; Goodman 2005; National Reading Panel 2000). Although this debate was grounded in first language literacy instruction, it has affected how we understand teaching young learners how to read and write in English as a foreign or additional language. A phonics approach teaches the sound-symbol relationship in order to decode written language. It is considered a bottom-up approach starting with building phonemic awareness, which helps discriminate sounds in English, and then moving on to learning the relationship between the sounds and letters in order to decode words. For example, vowel sounds in English can be represented by a number of different letters; note how the 'a' sound in English can be rendered in print: day, eight, train. A whole-language approach focuses on top-down processing skills, which starts from children's knowledge of the world and experience with language and texts and builds strategies for making meaning from text and creating text.

Modern day researchers and practitioners in the fields of first, second, and foreign language literacy promote taking a balanced literacy approach, which integrates aspects of both whole language and phonics. Researchers recommend using an interactive reading process model, which proposes that readers use both bottom-up and top-down processing skills simultaneously during the reading process in both first and second languages. This process utilises both schematic knowledge as well as decoding skills at the letter or word level to comprehend text (Herrera, Perez, and Escamilla 2015). Just as reading is interactive – between the text and the reader – so is writing. Writing involves interaction with a reader. Writing is more meaningful if children have an audience and a purpose for their writing. Reading can provide a scaffold for children learning to write. Because both processes are interactive, reading and writing are frequently taught together in an integrated way.

EYL teachers need to be sure to take a balanced literacy approach that helps YLs build both bottom-up and top-down processing skills. The time spent on bottom-up focused phonics instruction could vary depending on how similar or different the L1 writing system is from English. In addition, teachers should work on both reading and writing in an integrated way.

Toward a sociocultural perspective of literacy

Traditionally, literacy practices were shaped by cognitive or psycholinguistic perspectives and focused on skills like phoneme-grapheme correspondence or fluency. However, sociocultural perspectives on literacy have become increasingly important not only as a theoretical framework but also in classroom practice. According to Gee (1996), language is always connected to social, cultural and political contexts. Barton and Hamilton (2000) describe literacy in terms of social practice, given that literacy practices are 'what people do with literacy' (7). They note that 'literacy practices are more usefully understood as existing in the relations between people, within groups and communities, rather than as a set of properties residing in individuals' (8). As Perry (2012) notes, 'Conceptualizing literacy as something one does, as opposed to a skill or ability one has, helps us understand the real-world ways in which real people actually engage with real texts, which ultimately could help educators make formal literacy instruction more meaningful and relevant for learners' (62). This perspective broadens our understanding of literacy beyond linguistic skills to decode the printed page and situates literacy within a context that is bound by both cultural and social practices. Certainly for YLs of a foreign language, schematic knowledge essential to comprehend text in English could present challenges. When EYL teachers use authentic texts written for native speakers of English, the readers and writers will not share the same sociocultural background. Therefore, YLs may need more context and culture specific background knowledge in additional to linguistic knowledge in order to make sense of text.

Critical issues and topics

The balance between L1 and English literacy

In the field of Teaching English to Young Learners (TEYL), children are often learning to read and write in English while they are working on first language (L1) literacy. Parents, teachers, school administrators and curriculum developers often discuss how to approach teaching reading and writing to children in EYL contexts while they simultaneously learn their L1. Some worry that learning English at young ages will affect children's language and literacy in their L1 negatively. In fact, some EFL programs delay reading and writing instruction for YLs in the early grades and only focus on listening and speaking skills. For example, in Japan, English instruction in primary school grades focuses on oral language skills creating difficulty in the transition to secondary school where the emphasis is on grammar and reading (Gardner 2017). However, developing reading and writing skills in a foreign language can begin as early as foreign language instruction begins (National Academies of Sciences, Engineering, and Medicine 2017). In fact, as Dlugosz (2000) states, 'including the teaching of reading in language programmes will benefit all young beginners, including pre-schoolers, i.e., children who have not yet been taught to read in their native tongue . . . If reading is emphasized in their curriculum from the very beginning of their language education, these young children will progress faster not only in learning to read, but also in understanding and speaking the language' (p. 285).

Young learners (YLs) of English as a foreign language may already be literate in their native language or L1, which is an asset for building literacy in a new language. It is well-known that skills used in reading and writing in the L1 can transfer to another language, such as English, and serve as a foundation for literacy in a new language (Cummins 1999; Proctor, August, Carlo, and Snow 2006). Young learners can utilise their understanding of the relationship between oral and written language and how to make sense of printed text in their L1 and apply it to English. As we know, 'the better developed the conceptual foundation of children's first language, the more likely children are to develop similarly high levels of conceptual abilities in their second language' (Cummins 1999, p. 51).

For very young learners (VYLs) under seven years old who are still learning to read and write in the L1, studies have shown that they can transfer literacy skills successfully between the two languages (Dlugosz 2000; Verhoeven 1994). This transfer of literacy skills is bidirectional. In fact, the language of initial literacy does not need to be students' L1 (Dlugosz 2000; Lenters 2004/2005; Verhoeven 1994). For administrators or parents who worry about starting reading and writing instruction too early, studies show that integrating reading and writing instruction can actually assist in oral language development (Dlugosz 2000).

Even VYLs who are not literate in their L1 can build reading readiness and phonemic awareness by reading aloud using big books with print or using songs and rhymes to focus on the sounds of English. They can also engage students in writing readiness exercises like tracing, connecting the dots and coloring. These are fun and effective activities for building early literacy with young EFL learners. Building children's motor skills for more control when holding a pencil and putting pencil to paper is essential and another example of skills that can be developed in both languages simultaneously.

The differences between the young learners' L1 and English

YLs can transfer many literacy skills to reading and writing in English. However, differences between L1 and L2 writing systems can create challenges for early learners. Here are some areas of difficulty depending on differences in students' L1:

1 L1 uses a non-alphabetic writing system (Chinese).
2 L1 uses a different alphabet than English (Russian or Greek).
3 L1 uses the Roman alphabet with sound or symbol differences (Spanish).
4 L1 is read from right to left (Arabic) or top to bottom (traditional Chinese).

All students will benefit from explicit instruction for decoding and encoding using English orthography. Naturally, children who share the same alphabet with English will have less difficulty learning to read and write in English than those who do not use an alphabet or use a different alphabet (Cameron 2001; Nunan 2011). In fact, all children, including native speakers, find it challenging to learn the different ways in which English represents sounds. According to Moats (2010), English has 26 letters that represent 44 sounds with more than 500 ways to spell them. English has what is known as a 'deep' orthography. It can be difficult to sound out many words from the way in which they are written or spelled. In contrast, Spanish or German have a 'shallow' orthography, which makes them more predictable in sounding out words based on how they are written (Geva and Wang 2001). As Shin and Crandall (2014) point out, the sound /i/ in English can be represented in many combination of letters, e.g., *be, bee, key, sea, ski, skied, receive* (and more). Alternatively, there are many ways of pronouncing the same set of letters, such as 'ea' in *read, bread,* and *break.* This is why phonics instruction is necessary for all learners of English. Teaching students to decode words by transforming letters into sound can be used effectively with children ages five and older (Dlugosz 2000).

The stages of children's writing development

YLs learn to write their first language through several developmental stages although at different rates and in different sequences (Samway 2006). First, children engage in scribble writing and drawing. The scribbles often reflect the orthography of their L1, and the letters are often approximations that resemble standard letters. Then children use strings of letters to express themselves in writing. In this stage, there is no sound-symbol correspondence and spacing between letters is often absent. After stringing letters together, children begin to learn to use letters to represent whole words and thoughts. There is some sound-symbol correspondence, and children can usually spell high frequency or sight words correctly. Children begin putting spacing between words and show accuracy with beginning consonants, then ending consonants, then medial consonants and finally vowels. It is noticeable that children at this stage may have difficulty reading their own texts.

Next is the stylised writing stage. Children use patterns with lots of repetition, such as 'She is_____. She is _____.' They rely on familiar words, especially ones displayed in the classroom. At this time, children can usually read their own texts. As children start to write longer messages and take more risks with writing, teachers will notice invented spelling. This is unconventional spelling that may reflect how words sound, such as writing 'sed' instead of 'said.' Finally, children will begin to produce standardised writing that is more organised and focused. Children's spelling and punctuation becomes more standardised and word choice is more varied.

It is useful for EYL teachers to understand these stages. For instance, children from any language background may invent spellings to words they do not know. However, not all children will pass through all of the stages, e.g, scribbling is unusual for older YLs. Also, in some cases, YLs may stay longer in a particular stage. For example, children with Arabic L1 will often ignore spacing in English. Understanding the stages may support teachers in giving appropriate feedback; they might, for example, be more lenient when correcting spelling, particularly when children produce a good approximation, with a view to encouraging them to enjoy the writing process. It may also help them to plan effective writing activities, allowing plenty of opportunity and time for students to copy and practise forming letters and write very short texts (such as gap fill).

Helping children to make their own meanings through writing takes a good deal of effort, work and patience and it can be counter-productive when children are very young or when their English levels are low as it can discourage them or make them feel inadequate. Instead, teachers should focus on modelling and providing simple interactive writing activities (see recommendations for practice), so that children can begin to learn the conventions of writing, such as spelling, spacing between words, punctuation, etc. with a view to eventually expressing themselves more fluently and accurately in writing.

The importance of vocabulary in reading comprehension

Because word recognition is essential for reading comprehension, vocabulary instruction is extremely important. Studies have confirmed that learners need to know as many as 95–98% of words in a text for independent or unassisted comprehension (Hu and Nation 2000; Laufer 1989; Laufer and Ravenhorst-Kalovski 2010; Schmitt, Jang, and Grabe 2011). For young EFL learners, this is very challenging, particularly when using authentic texts in the classroom which can have a wide range of vocabulary meant for native speaker children. However, EYL teachers can help learners by focusing instruction on the highest frequency words, which are words that are used most frequently in all written text in English. Eldredge (2005) identified the 300 highest frequency words used in first-grade basal readers (collections of stories written at specific grade levels) and trade books (books written for a broad audience, not specifically leveled). These 300 words account for 72% of the words beginning readers of English read. Analysis of written texts in English show that 50% of all written text is made of up the 100 most frequently used words in English. The following are the 25 most frequently used words; they make up one third of all printed text: *the, of, and, a, to, in, is, you, that, it, he, was, for, on, are, as, with, his, they, I, at, be, this, have, from*. It is believed that automatic recognition of these words helps children comprehend and create text more easily. These words have been compiled in lists, most notably the Dolch and Fry word lists, and are often used by teachers who focus vocabulary instruction on them.

Based on L1 literacy instruction for native speakers of English, EYL teachers often work on automatic recognition of these high frequency or sight words, from kindergarten through second or third grade. In fact, many EFL texts and graded readers are written to use these most frequently used words. Many of these words are used very frequently in children's lives and are easy to remember and then recognise in print, such as *big, little, blue, red, yellow, come, go, look, jump, play, run, see, one, two, three* (Pre-K Dolch sight word list).

Cultural differences and background knowledge in English texts

As we described above, many books used to teach children English come from contexts where English is the language of classroom instruction and often of the home. English language learners may face cultural barriers when they try to interpret these texts. These types of texts are often used for storytelling activities and to promote extensive reading. However, YLs in foreign language contexts may have difficulty understanding the cultural context of the stories and even the picture or visuals used. For example, in the popular storybook *Library Lion* by Michelle Knudsen and illustrated by Kevin Hawkes, which is an engaging story with lovely illustrations, there could be cultural references that are not familiar to students in other countries. Although children may have the concept of 'lion', the things the lion does in the story, such as going to a library with a circulation desk, might not be as familiar. Other cultural norms in the story such as 'story time' at the library and 'story corner' might also be unknown. Teachers might therefore need to build background knowledge before reading the text or may need to find books that have culturally familiar content to help students gain comprehension of text. It is more common now to find multicultural storybooks, which represent diverse cultures and different ways of seeing the world. These stories, published by both local and global publishers, might provide more relevant content for young English language learners.

Current contributions and research

Review of phonological-based instruction

Huo and Wang (2017) conducted a review of 15 experimental and quasi-experimental studies published from 2000 to 2016 on the effectiveness of phonological-based instruction focused specifically on teaching English as a foreign language to young learners in Grades K–6. The implication for practice of this study is that including phonological-based instruction in the current English curriculum may be beneficial for young EFL students so that they can better learn to phonologically decode English words. It is interesting to note that the majority of the studies implemented *a synthetic phonics approach*, which focuses on 'explicit instruction of alphabetic principles and applying the knowledge to sounding out novel words' (Huo and Wang 2017: 9). Few studies used an analytic phonics approach, which focuses on 'phonetically analysing words which are already familiar to students' and utilises activities' such as sight word recognition and word family analysis' (Huo and Wang 2017: 9). Although a synthetic phonics approach may seem more appropriate for young learners in an EFL context because it does not require prior knowledge of English, studies by Wu (2005) and Yang (2009) showed that both synthetic and analytic phonics approaches can be equally effective. There is also evidence of the effectiveness of integrating an instructional method of comparing L1 and English writing systems with a synthetic phonics approach (Nishanimut et al. 2013).

Huo and Wang's (2017) review found inconclusive results in word recognition, which showed that children had difficulty transferring phonological skills to word recognition. Based on the results, they suggest: 'Semantic and syntactic information of words are not the focus on phonological-based instruction and are often gained from large exposure to print and oral language' (10). Their review also highlighted the importance of vocabulary and oral language proficiency and emphasised that none of the studies solely used phonics and phonological awareness in their English programme, but as a supplement to daily English language classes, stating that it was 'most effective when delivered regularly and discretely' (11).

Making sense of different writing systems

Nam (2017) recently conducted a qualitative study to understand how young EFL learners understand and develop more than one writing system simultaneously, particularly with two completely different scripts, e.g., Roman and non-Roman alphabetic scripts. This is one of the first studies of its kind conducted in an EFL setting. The study focused on Korean EFL learners who are five to six years old and examined how children understand two different writing systems: Korean alphabet (Hangul) and English alphabet (Roman) in a peer-teaching setting. In each tutoring pair, a six-year-old tutored a five-year-old learner. The findings showed that children could discover key orthographic principles which characterise each script as well as find similarities and differences between Hangul and English. They could articulate differences in shapes of letters/words (block shaped vs. linear), language units (syllables vs. letters) and sound-letter relationship (shallow vs. deep orthography). As Nam (2017) explains, 'young children are able to look for key concepts in different writing systems by constructing their own ideas about the principles of reading and writing from an early age as active language learners' (1). This provides good support for literacy instruction in two languages simultaneously and the relevance of comparing two writing systems during instruction with VYLs.

Use of technology-enhanced storybooks

Two recent studies show positive effects from technology-enhanced storybooks for improving a variety of reading and writing skills. Walker, Adams, Restrepo, Fialko, and Glenberg (2017) focused their study on Spanish-speaking dual language learners in Grades 2–5 in an American context. Children were given one narrative text and one expository text. They read the texts using an iPad application called EMBRACE (Enhanced Moved by Reading to Accelerate Comprehension in English), which has interactive features that simulate the story events. As students read the text, they can touch the screen and manipulate the images on the screen to match the text. The findings showed that when children read grade-appropriate texts that were written in a familiar narrative style, the simulation of text content using EMBRACE helped their comprehension. However, with advanced expository text, simulation of text content using the iPad application helped good decoders gain comprehension but did not help students with poor decoding skills. In another study, Alsamadani (2017) implemented the use of 'talking story books' – illustrated storybooks with audio from the Lady Bird series – with 11–12-year-old Saudi students. The results showed positive effects on their reading and writing skills, i.e., understanding stories, phonics skills, spelling skills and story retelling skills.

These studies support the use of interactive tablet applications and talking storybooks (audiobooks) to enhance literacy instruction. It also promotes a balance between top-down and bottom-up instruction, perhaps with additional supports for students struggling decoders with unfamiliar texts.

Recommendations for practice

Young learners of English are more successful when they receive meaningful exposure to language and plenty of opportunities to practise. EYL teachers can integrate reading and writing activities with oral language instruction for children at an early age, focusing as well on helping children to understand speech-to-print differences, as well as similarities between their L1 and English. Some helpful ways to ensure your EFL literacy programme is meaning-based and balanced, include the following:

- Immerse students in print and literature
- Give explicit instruction in phonics
- Build vocabulary and automaticity of high frequency words
- Utilise and build students' background knowledge
- Model and teach various reading and writing strategies
- Involve young learners in literacy activities
- Use a 'To/With/By' approach.

Immerse students in print and literature

Young EFL learners need a 'print-rich' environment where they are surrounded by environmental print (for example, maps, daily schedules and birthday calendars) and engage in multiple activities with that print, such as labelling objects in the classroom and adding words to word walls as they learn new vocabulary (Shin and Crandall 2014). They also need to participate in reading experiences with a variety of texts. Those texts should include not only stories, but also poetry and information texts (which can be drawn from their other classes), and a wide array of texts from the Internet. We also need to engage young learners in drawing and labelling pictures, as well as creating their own stories, poems and class books, all of which can be shared with their peers during independent reading time or with parents and the wider school community (Curtain and Dahlberg 2016; Pinter 2006; Collins 2004). 'For young learners to become effective and engaged readers and writers, they must have multiple opportunities to explore, read and write a variety of texts and to talk about what they are going to read or write or what they have read or written' (Shin and Crandall 2014: 164).

Give explicit instruction in phonics

As mentioned previously, effective literacy instruction needs to incorporate both bottom-up and top-down skills. Phonics instruction will help young EFL learners to develop bottom-up skills to decode text in English, and over time, they will be able to develop automaticity in decoding and spelling English texts. Even young native speakers need explicit instruction because of the complexity of English sound-symbol relationships. The amount of time needed and the specific kind of phonics instruction will differ depending on the writing system and literacy practices of the L1.

Build vocabulary and automaticity of high frequency words

Children need explicit vocabulary instruction to make sense of oral and written texts as well as multiple opportunities to see and use that vocabulary in various contexts. In order to develop a balanced literacy programme, young learners need a balance between authentic children's texts (trade books) as well as graded readers. Teachers can equip students with word-learning strategies that include figuring out the meaning of words using context clues. However, young learners can become overwhelmed with too many unknown words or language structures in authentic texts. As a result, teachers often use graded readers, which are purposely written to control the vocabulary and language in a text. Graded readers can help young learners become familiar with the most frequently used words in English, while also systematically introducing new vocabulary in a meaningful context. Graded readers also recycle vocabulary learned in preceding books. They are often based on stories that children have heard or read in their own language, promoting transfer of skills across the two languages.

Use and build students' background knowledge

Young EFL learners may have prior experience with different topics and text types from their L1 and can tap into their background knowledge to help make sense of text in English. For example, many cultures have a 'Cinderella' story with which children can compare and contrast and build their intercultural understanding. After all, English is a global language and connected to cultures around the world. Building cultural knowledge helps prepare learners to be effective readers and writers of English across cultures. Teachers can also use content-area texts on a variety of topics, which help students make cross-curricular connections and promote comprehension of text.

Model and teach various reading and writing strategies

Young EFL learners need a variety of strategies to both understand and create different texts. One way to help young learners build reading and writing skills is to model the skills and strategies the students need to use. In a *read-aloud*, the teacher models how to read fluently and with expression, while also communicating interest and enthusiasm for reading. Some skills the teacher can model are previewing a text by focusing on visuals, headings, etc.; predicting what happens in the text; and highlighting text structures, such as the beginning, middle and end of stories or texts (Shin 2017). Teachers can model writing by providing simple writing activities, such as tracing or copying words and sentences, unscrambling words and sentences or providing gap-filling activities in order to help lower level students learn the basics of writing in English. They can also model more complex writing strategies in *writing think-alouds*, explaining their thinking as they write a text on the board or a flip chart. Some skills a teacher might model are brainstorming ideas to write; identifying a particular audience and purpose for the text; using a graphic organiser (e.g., word web, t-chart, or table) to help structure the text; and even paragraph writing for more advanced young learners.

Involve young learners in literacy activities

Children learn by doing and need to actively participate in literacy activities. Not only does this mean participating in the actual reading and writing activities themselves, but also engaging in discussions about texts, comprehension strategies and the writing process. This can be a gradual process after the teacher models. The following are some useful reading and writing activities that range from less to more independent.

- *Shared Reading*. Teachers can use a big book to do a shared reading with the whole class, modelling reading strategies and skills while encouraging children to join in when they can, especially if there is a repeated line in the story. For example, in *The Gingerbread Man* children can repeat with the teacher, 'Run, run as fast as you can; you can't catch me, I'm the gingerbread man.' The teacher can also encourage students to participate in reading skills and strategies, including using new vocabulary through a repeated structure. For example, in *Brown Bear, Brown Bear, What Do You See?* when the story repeats 'I see a . . . looking at me', children can show they recognise each animal. For example, the teacher can pause, 'I see a . . .' and wait for students to say '. . . red bird looking at me.' (For more activities built around this book, see *Crazy Animals and Other Activities for Teaching Young Learners*.)
- *Choral Reading and Readers Theatre*. In choral reading, children (individually, in pairs or in small groups) take turns reading a text out loud. If the text is a story, children can do a dramatic reading, acting out or reciting character dialogue in an activity known as 'Readers Theatre' or 'Reader's Theater' (Young, Stokes, and Rasinski 2017). They can also dress up as the characters and act out while they are reading their parts out loud.

Many children's books already have a narrator and dialogue. If not, the teacher can prepare a script for the children to read. (See the Reading A–Z webpage: www.readinga-z. com/fluency/readers-theater-scripts/ for Reader's Theater scripts.)

• *Guided Reading.* In guided reading, learners meet in groups with similar reading levels to read the same text together. They each receive a copy of the text selected by the teacher for their level and work together to make sense of it, with the teacher providing assistance when needed. They can also work together to produce a labeled drawing or simple text about the characters or plot in the story they have just read. In guided activities, learners should feel comfortable taking risks and experimenting. They may not always make the right predictions when reading or may end up inventing spelling (e.g., 'wuz' instead of 'was'). Teachers need to provide supportive feedback to help students improve their literacy skills and strategies, while also valuing students' ideas and encouraging them to keep taking risks.

• *Language Experience Approach.* Teachers can use the Language Experience Approach (LEA), which is a shared writing activity. This activity encourages learners and the teacher to create a text together. Texts can include a summary of a story or a video, a letter or email to the author of a story and a thank-you note (Dixon and Nessel 1983; Nessel and Jones 1981; Shin and Crandall 2014; Van Allen and Allen 1976; Ashton-Warner 1963). Shin and Crandall (2014), suggest the following steps:

1 Participate in a common experience (a field trip, a story, a celebration, a visitor, a picture that evokes feelings).
2 Have a discussion (can be in L1, depending on students' level).
3 Decide what to write, using a brainstorming web or other graphic organiser.
4 Dictate the 'story' to the teacher, who writes it so all can see.
5 Read back what the teacher has written (The teacher may read it first, with students following along, and then they read it together.).
6 Decide if they want to edit anything.
7 Copy what is written on the board into their notebooks. (176–177)

• *Interactive Writing.* This activity is similar to shared writing activities like the Language Experience Approach, but the teacher does not do the actual writing (Shin 2017). Instead, the bulk of the responsibility for writing is passed to the students. However, it is still scaffolded thoroughly by the teacher though discussion. Interactive writing focuses on 'constructing texts filled with personal and collective meaning' (Button, Johnson, and Ferguson 1996: 446). Button et al. (1996) provide an example of a kindergarten teacher's use of interactive writing after children have heard 'Goldilocks and the Three Bears' read aloud many times. Here are the steps:

After a reading or telling a story, ask children about various parts of the story, such as *Who are the characters? Where are they? What happened?* As they dictate or share ideas in their L1, the teacher can record the key words and ideas on the board. Then the teacher uses the text as an opportunity to engage students in writing. While doing this, the teacher can draw students' attention to the text and engage in writing as well. If lower level students need more scaffolding, the teacher could point out some of the conventions of English writing, from left to right, from top to bottom, the spaces between the words, initial capital letters and use with names, etc. Children can also come to the board and write some of the words after the teacher has had them repeat the words several times and tells them the letters to write as they write them on the board and/or at their seat. For higher level students, the teacher can give them time to draft the text themselves after discussion or write more independently, such as creating a new ending for a story or adding their own details.

Use a To/With/By approach

We know that young EFL learners need effective scaffolding to become independent readers and writers. After all, they learn language through social interaction with support and scaffolding from the teacher (Shin and Crandall 2014). The recommended practices above provide step-by-step scaffolding from the teacher through modelling as well as guided activities that help move children towards becoming more independent readers and writers. Teachers may find it helpful to conceptualise the process of scaffolding students to become more independent using the *To/With/By approach* (Cappellini 2005; Mooney 1990; Walter 2004).

- Reading and writing *to* students: The teacher provides a model to learners of reading and writing skills and strategies, e.g., read-alouds and think-alouds.
- Reading and writing *with* students: After modelling, the teacher reads and writes with students, gradually giving learners more responsibility for reading and writing, e.g., big book shared reading, the Language Experience Approach, Reader's Theater and small group guided reading.
- Reading and writing *by* students: After guided practice with the teacher, learners can begin to read and write independently, e.g., through literacy centres, literature circles, interactive and collaborative writing and research projects.

The To/With/By approach is a simple but effective step-by-step framework for teachers to help young learners become readers and writers in English.

Future directions

Multiliteracies

In the twenty-first century, additional skills should be addressed in relation to teaching reading and writing in TEYL contexts. The notion of 'literacy' as a sociocultural practice can be further explored in relation to creating meaning from printed text. Furthermore, literacy instruction should also include 'new literacies' or multiliteracies, which Perry (2012) describes as viewing literacy as 'involving multiple modes of visual, gestural, spatial, and other forms of representation' (p. 58–59). This can include new media and digital literacies, which could be seen as an expanded view of printed text. They can also include visual literacies which involve students learning to understand visual media such as advertisements, photographs and film.

Reading and writing English as a global language

The status of English as a global language requires us to take a critical stance on the texts we incorporate into our classrooms, which should not only represent the dominant discourses from the USA or the UK, as is common for authentic texts in English. We will need further exploration of how we produce and select texts we use to teach reading and writing in EYL classrooms. Such texts may include:

- Texts that represent other Englishes (i.e., varieties of English spoken around the world).
- Texts that integrate cultural information from other countries and cultures.
- Texts that are written for a global audience.

These texts will require cross-cultural interpretation skills to understand cultural content that comes from diverse cultures and represents other Englishes. This can include cross-cultural visual literacy since the images accompanying text will be diverse as well.

Conclusion

Teaching young EFL learners to read and write is a challenging yet exciting endeavor. EYL classrooms may focus primarily on oral language skills, but as the chapter has shown, integrating literacy instruction even in the early years is highly encouraged. We can produce effective readers and writers of English through engaging activities described in this chapter and provided in additional texts described and listed below. It is important to take a balanced literacy approach that is meaning focused but also provides explicit instruction in phonics and bottom-up processing skills. Young learners need to be actively involved in reading and writing, and teachers can effectively scaffold young learners to become independent readers and writers by using techniques such as the To/With/By approach. Hopefully teachers can connect young learners to literacy practices in linguistically and culturally appropriate ways and look ahead to new literacies in the future.

Further reading

1 Curtain, H., and Dahlberg, C. A. (2016). *Languages and learners: Making the match*. Boston, MA: Allyn and Bacon.

Curtain and Dahlberg provide an excellent foundation for teaching foreign languages to young learners in Grades K–8. They focus on foreign language instruction in the US context, but the well-researched practices can also be applied in English as a foreign language (EFL) contexts effectively. This book, which serves as a guide for both administrators and teachers, has a robust chapter on building literacy, with many practice examples.

2 Shin, J. K., and Crandall, J. A. (2014). *Teaching young learners English: From theory to practice*. Boston, MA: National Geographic Learning/Cengage Learning.

Shin and Crandall's foundational work on teaching young learners English as a foreign or international language bridges theory to practice. It has a comprehensive chapter on teaching reading and writing to young learners that provides teachers with a theoretical foundation in the process of reading and writing and gives numerous activities and a sample lesson plan with a diverse array of ideas to integrate into their classroom.

2 Tompkins, G. E. (2017). *Literacy for the 21st century: A balanced approach*. Boston, MA: Allyn and Bacon/Pearson.

This textbook brings literacy instruction into the twenty-first century by promoting a balanced approach to diverse student populations. It provides both theory and practice for effective reading and writing instruction for learners of all ages and includes ideas for digital teaching and learning. This is the e-book version of the textbook published in 2013.

Related topics

Listening and speaking, teaching grammar, differentiation, assessment

References

Adams, M. (1997). *Beginning to Read: Thinking and learning about print*. Cambridge, MA: MIT Press.

Alsamadani, H. A. (2017). The effect of talking story books on Saudi young EFL learners' reading comprehension. *English Language Teaching*, 10(5), 204–213.

Ashton-Warner, S. (1963). *Teacher*. New York: Simon and Schuster.

Barton, D., and Hamilton, M. (2000). Literacy practices. In Barton, D., Hamilton, M., and Ivanič, R. (eds.) *Situated Literacies: Reading and writing in context*. London: Routledge, 7–15.

Button, K., Johnson, M. J., and Ferguson, P. (1996). Interactive writing in a primary classroom. *The Reading Teacher*, 49(6), 446–454.

Cameron, L. (2001). *Teaching Languages to Young Learners*. Cambridge: Cambridge University Press.

Cappellini, M. (2005). *Balancing Reading & Language Learning: A resource for teaching English language learners, K–5*. Portland, ME: Stenhouse Publishers.

Chall, J. (1967). *Learn to Read: The great debate*. New York: McGraw Hill.

Collins, K. (2004). *Growing Readers*. Portland, ME: Stenhouse Publishers.

Copland, F., and Garton, S., with Davis, M. (Eds.). (2012). *Crazy Animals and Other Activities for Teaching Young Learners*. London: British Council and BBC. www.teachingenglish.org.uk/article/crazy-animals-other-activities-teaching-young-learners.

Cummins, J. (1999). Alternative paradigms in bilingual education research: Does theory have a place? *Educational Researcher*, 28(7), 26–32.

Curtain, H., and Dahlberg, C. A. (2016). *Languages and Learners: Making the match*, 5th ed. Boston, MA: Allyn and Bacon.

Dixon, C., and Nessel, D. (1983). *Language Experience Approach to Teaching Reading (and Writing): LEA for ESL*. Hayward, CA: Alemany Press.

Dlugosz, D. W. (2000). Rethinking the role of reading in teaching a foreign language to young learners. *ELT Journal*, 54, 284–291.

Eldredge, J. L. (2005). *Teach Decoding: How and why*, 2nd ed. Upper Saddle River, NJ: Merrill/Prentice Hall.

Gardner, W. (2017, April). Modify instruction to improve English skills. *Japan Times*.

Gee, J. (1996). *Social Linguistics and Literacies: Ideology in discourses*. London: RoutledgeFalmer.

Geva, E., and Wang, M. (2001). The development of basic reading skills in children: A cross-linguistic perspective. *Annual Review of Applied Linguistics*, 21, 182–204.

Goodman, K. (2005). *What's Whole in Whole Language?* Berkeley, CA: RDR Books.

Herrera, S. G., Perez, D. R., and Escamilla, K. (2015). *Teaching Reading to English Language Learners: Differentiating literacies*, 2nd ed. New York: Pearson.

Hu, M., and Nation, I. S. P. (2000). Vocabulary density and reading comprehension. *Reading in a Foreign Language*, 13(1), 403–430.

Huo, S., and Wang, S. (2017). The effectiveness of phonological-based instruction in English as a foreign language students at primary school level: A research synthesis. *Frontiers*, 2(15), 1–13.

Laufer, B. (1989). What percentage of text lexis is essential for comprehension? In Lauren, C., and Nordman, M. (eds.) *Social Language: From humans thinking to thinking machines*. Clevedon: Multilingual Matters, 316–323.

Laufer, B., and Ravenhorst-Kalovski, G. C. (2010). Lexical threshold revisited: Lexical coverage, learners' vocabulary size and reading comprehension. *Reading in a Foreign Language*, 22(1), 15–30.

Lenters, K. (2004/2005). No half measures: Reading instruction for young second-language learners. *The Reading Teacher*, 58(4), 328–336.

Moats, L. C. (2010). *Speech to Print: Language essentials for teachers*. Baltimore, MD: Paul H. Brookes.

Mooney, M. (1990). *Reading to, with, and by Children*. Katonah, NY: Richard Owen.

Nam, K. M. (2017). How young children make sense of two different writing systems: Korean written in the Hangul alphabet, and English written in the Roman alphabet. *Journal of Early Childhood Literacy*, 1–28.

National Academies of Sciences, Engineering, and Medicine. (2017). *Promoting the Educational Success of Children and Youth Learning English: Promising futures*. Washington, DC: National Academies Press.

National Institute of Child Health and Human Development. (2000). *Teaching Children to Read: Summary Report of the National Reading Panel*. Washington, DC: U.S. Government Printing Office.

National Reading Panel. (2000). *Teaching Children to Read: An Evidence-based Assessment of the Scientific Research Literature on Reading and its Implications for Reading Instruction*. Washington, DC: U.S. Department of Health and Human Services.

Nessel, D. D., and Jones, M. B. (1981). *Language Experience Approach to Reading*. New York: Teachers College Press.

Nishanimut, S. P., Johnston, R. S., Joshi, R. M., Thomas, P. J., and Padakannaya, P. (2013). Effect of synthetic phonics instruction on literacy skills in an ESL setting. *Learning and Individual Differences*, 27, 47–53.

Nunan, D. (2011), *Teaching English to Young Learners*. Anaheim, CA: Anaheim University Press.

Perry, K. H. (2012), What is literacy? – A critical overview of sociocultural perspectives. *Journal of Language & Literacy Education*, 8(1), 50–71.

Pinter, A. (2006). *Teaching Young Language Learners*. Oxford: Oxford University Press.

Proctor, C. P., August, D., Carlo, M., and Snow, C. (2006). The intriguing role of Spanish language vocabulary knowledge in predicting English reading comprehension. *Journal of Educational Psychology*, 98(1), 159–169.

Samway, K. D. (2006). *When English Language Learners Write: Connecting research to practice, K-8*. Portsmouth, NH: Heinemann.

Schmitt, N., Jang, X., and Grabe, W. (2011). The percentage of words known in a text and reading comprehension. *The Modern Language Journal*, 95(1), 26–43.

Shin, J. K. (2014). Teaching young learners in ESL and EFL settings. In Celce-Murcia, M., Brinton, D. M., and Snow, M. A. (eds.) *Teaching English as a Second or Foreign Language*, 4th ed. Boston, MA: National Geographic Learning/Cengage Learning, 550–567.

Shin, J. K. (2017). *Literacy Instruction for Young EFL Learners: A balanced approach*. Boston, MA: National Geographic Learning.

Shin, J. K., and Crandall, J. A. (2014). *Teaching Young Learners English: From theory to practice*. Boston: National Geographic Learning/Cengage Learning.

Van Allen, R., and Allen, C. (1976). *Language Experience Stories*. Boston, MA: Houghton Mifflin.

Verhoeven, L. T. (1994). Transfer in bilingual development: The linguistic interdependence hypothesis revisited. *Language Learning*, 44, 381–415.

Walter, T. (2004). *Teaching English Language Learners*. White Plains, NY: Pearson.

Wu, C. J. (2005). *A Comparison of the Effects of Explicit Phonics Instruction and the Revised Silent Way on EFL Elementary Students' Pronunciation*. Tainan, Taiwan: National Cheng Kung University.

Yang, H. C. (2009). Improving phonological awareness and reading through rhyme picture books for EFL elementary school students. *ProQuest Dissertations and Theses*. San Diego: Alliant International University.

Young, C., Stokes, F., and Rasinski, T. (2017). Readers theatre plus comprehension and word study. *The Reading Teacher*, 71(3), 351–355.

13

Teaching grammar to young learners

Herbert Puchta

Introduction

When young children start learning English at school, they approach the new language (L2) in significantly different ways from those used by older learners. Younger learners do not perceive language as a system that needs to be learnt, but as communication. They want to understand what you (and later their classmates) are saying to them in the L2. They listen to a story, and as the narrative unfolds in their own imagination they get more and more drawn into the L2.

Grammar is of course an integral part of such language encounters, but for young learners it is not a part they are aware of. What is much more the focus of their attention is the sounds of the L2, its rhythm, the process of interacting with you and their classmates, the fun they have when playing games, the fascination with stories, songs and chants and their growing wish to express themselves meaningfully in the L2.

When we talk about learning grammar in general, we usually refer to the need to develop knowledge of how words in their correct forms (word grammar) are put together to create meaningful sentences (sentence grammar), and how sentences are organised to form coherent texts (text grammar).

However, when it comes to teaching younger children, experience shows that grammar as a formal system that needs to be understood and mastered is *not* an issue. Rather, we need to look at grammar from the perspective of the learner, bearing in mind that children tend to 'grow their grammar' (Nunan 2005, p. 45), not learn it as a formal system. Cameron (2001, p. 100) distinguishes between 'external grammars' (the grammars in grammar books and teaching materials) and 'internal grammars'. (The latter are the ways in which grammar is organised in each student's mind – a process that does not follow the grammar progression as taught by the teacher any more than it is found in the syllabus or the teaching materials.) The outcomes of conveying grammar to younger students can only be measured by how well your students are able to understand a new structure in context – and later, whether or not they can use it meaningfully in their own production.

Following on from what has been said so far, I would like to stress that unless otherwise stated I use the term 'young learners' in this chapter in order to refer to children aged 5 to 9.

Focusing mainly on this age group is a deliberate choice I have made because of the limited space available for this chapter, but also because it is the lower segment of the young learners age bracket, where teaching grammar needs to be dealt with in ways that are very different from children aged ten and upwards – when learners' cognitive capabilities make it increasingly possible for them to think about language in more abstract and explicit ways.

Historical perspectives

The following reflections on the history of teaching grammar are in no way complete, nor are they a detailed overview of the developments. Rather, I intend to give a speeded-up motion picture of how language teaching has developed over time and what role the teaching of grammar has played in that process in general. As Cameron (2001, p. 105) speeded-up, 'Young learner classrooms are inevitably affected by the trends that sweep through foreign language teaching', and a cogent reason for that seems to lie in the fact that teachers of young children often teach other age groups too. It is also important to point out that the various methods and approaches mentioned here do not always have clear-cut boundaries; they have not developed completely separately, several of them having influenced others.

We also need to consider the growing demand for teachers of young learners, necessitated by the 'rapid introduction of Primary ELT' (Enever 2016, p. 361) – according to Johnstone (2009, p. 36) 'possibly the world's biggest policy development in education'. One outcome of this development has been that teachers of older students or even adults have not infrequently ended up in front of young learners' classrooms. Naturally, those colleagues tend to have belief systems about language teaching that are based on their experiences, techniques and knowledge as teachers of those older age groups, which will influence their ways of teaching the younger ones.

As far as state school systems in particular are concerned, another issue often needs to be considered: the lowering of the age when children start learning English has led to a situation where not enough qualified teachers are available. 'This often means that many teachers who are assigned to teach English hold qualifications in other disciplines and have either received no training or insufficient training, such as short, intensive courses' (Burns et al 2013, p. 7). Unsurprisingly, many unqualified teachers do not speak English well enough to teach children successfully. We can infer, too, that they will have a very limited understanding of how grammar might emerge in the young learners' classroom without being properly taught, and their beliefs about this process will be influenced by their own experiences as learners of grammar at school rather than by sound pedagogical knowledge and up-to-date insights into how young children learn language.

Teaching grammar explicitly

It is a fact that 'for 2500 years the teaching of grammar had often been synonymous with foreign language teaching' (Celce-Murcia 1991, p. 459). This explicit approach to teaching language clearly focuses on grammar rules, the exceptions to them and their application – mainly in the form of the translation of (often meaningless) sentences from one language to the other. It was based on how languages such as ancient Greek and Latin were taught for centuries, the main purpose being to translate literature rather than to learn to communicate in the L2. Within the framework of this kind of grammar teaching, mistakes were not tolerated – a sharp contrast to the modern-day view that errors are not only unavoidable, but are natural phenomena that are an integral part of the language learning process.

The audio-lingual method

Around the middle of the twentieth century, the amalgamation of insights from behaviour-ism with those from linguistic structuralism led to the development of audiolingualism. The main claim of this theory of language teaching and learning was that students would learn to speak English by following a stimulus-response routine based on oral drills of gram-matical structures that according to Celce-Murcia (1991, p. 460) were 'carefully sequenced from basic to more complex (based on linguistic description)'. In audio-lingual classrooms, grammar was hardly ever taught explicitly, nor would the teacher attempt to tackle the rules governing it.

In the UK, this led to the so-called structural-situational method being developed for teaching modern foreign languages. Coursebooks for children from that era often presented page spreads with situational dialogues on the left-hand page, followed by exercises aimed at drilling the key structure(s) from the dialogue on the right-hand page. The language in the dialogues used was a clear departure from the often meaningless sentences on which the explicit grammar lessons of the previous era had been based, and a large amount of teaching time was now spent on oral drills in which the students listened to model sentences that they then had to manipulate according to grammatical cues given by the teacher or the audio tape. This was often carried out in language laboratories.

Other teaching techniques used were dialogue memorization and question-and-answer formats based on a substitution table. As Richards (2015, p. 64) comments, 'Great atten-tion to accurate pronunciation and accurate mastery of grammar was stressed from the very beginning stages of language learning, since it was assumed that if students made errors, these would quickly become a permanent part of the learner's speech'. Celce-Murcia (1991, p. 460) explains that this belief was so strong because language learning was seen as habit formation, hence mistakes were 'regarded as bad habits' and 'the result of interference from the first language'.

For many teachers, the fact that a lot of the language practice involved speaking drills created the impression – and indeed the hope – that their students were thus learning lan-guage that would be useful for social interaction. But with the hindsight of several decades, and the insights into authentic spoken language use provided by corpus linguistics, we can now see how bizarre the dialogues were that students had to listen to, repeat and learn by heart: here's an extract from one of the leading coursebooks, *Look, Listen and Learn* (Alex-ander 1968), based on the structural-situational method for children:

Mother:	This egg is for you, Sandy!
Sandy:	Thanks, Mum.
Sue:	Listen, Sandy!
	That's Dad's car.
	Eat your egg quickly!
	Now put the egg in the egg-cup like this.
Father:	Good evening, Betty.
Mother:	Good evening, Jim.
Father:	Good evening, children.
Children:	Good evening, Dad.
Sandy:	Tea's ready, Dad.
	This egg is for you.
Father:	An egg!

	That's nice.
	I'm hungry.
Father:	Oh! It's empty!

Of course, nobody would claim nowadays that the above is an authentic dialogue, and we don't need to consult language corpora to confirm that. After all, even the middle-class children of the 1960s would have been highly unlikely to greet their father on arrival home from work by saying, 'Good evening, Dad'. And Dad would have been highly unlikely to have reacted to the children's invitation to eat an egg by saying: 'An egg! That's nice. I'm hungry!'.

But we can easily understand the enthusiasm many teachers felt for the new approach, because what we're doing here is comparing the quality of this dialogue with the language that had been used in explicit grammar teaching. A look at Richards and Rodgers (2014, p. 5) quoting sentences used for grammar translation listed by the Italian scholar Titone (1968, p. 28) may make this clear:

> The philosopher pulled the lower jaw of the hen.
> My sons have bought the mirrors of the Duke.
> The cat of my aunt is more treacherous than the dog of your uncle.

As a young teacher, I myself was among those of us who put a lot of hope into the structural-situational method. However, together with others, I soon noticed that after the first few weeks of teaching, and as soon as the utterances in the dialogues became a bit longer, kids had problems remembering the sentences and acting them out by heart – and worse, rather frustratingly, the realization dawned on us that children definitely weren't learning grammar through the drills we had used.

Nevertheless, Hall (2018, Location 1625, p. 66) has observed that 'drills are still used by many teachers today, whether or not they explicitly associate such techniques with Audiolingualism and know about the structuralist view of language and behaviourist theory of learning that underpins this method'. Likewise, other techniques associated with lingualism – such as learning short dialogues by heart, and getting students to answer teacher questions with the help of substitution tables and choral drills – have certainly not vanished from young learners' classrooms and we will see later that there are justifiable reasons for using them.

Comprehensible input – the natural approach

Krashen (1982, p. 18) argued that 'mechanical drills can be, and often are, done without understanding on the part of the learner' and that language is far too complex to be consciously learnt. Hence students should ideally 'acquire' (rather than 'learn') a new language in the classroom through plenty of 'comprehensible input' and a focus on meaning, in a process similar to the way children pick up their own language. 'Learning' a language, on the other hand, refers to the process that results from the teacher explaining rules to the students, and getting them to practise language consciously.

Grammar, according to the theory laid out by Krashen and Terrell in their book *The Natural Approach* (1983), is acquired through lots of comprehensible input, provided students are in an emotional state that allows them to pick up language; this is a process that does not work well if students are scared of making mistakes or nervous because they have negative beliefs about their language learning capabilities. The development of the students' internal grammar runs independently from the grammar they have learnt, following a natural order of acquisition influenced by the quality of input and their emotional state. The students' knowledge of grammar and grammar rules edits their language correctness via their internal monitor. This is a kind of editing processor in the students' minds that ideally corrects the students' production without interrupting its flow; so, not too much monitor or too often, as that creates inhibited students (monitor overusers), or students whose language has become fossilised (underusers.) What type of user a student turns out to be depends on their personality. Introverted people are usually overusers, while extroverted people tend to be underusers.

While much of Krashen's early work has come under scrutiny in the last twenty years, his notion that input should be largely comprehensible to children has – thankfully – been generally adopted in teaching young learners. This seems reasonable, particularly as decoding more complex texts requires cognitive skills that young learners have often not yet developed. This is not to say that children have to understand everything in a text, but that their ability to grasp the overall meaning of narratives in particular is paramount as it gives them a sense of security and keeps them engaged.

Communicative language teaching (CLT)

CLT was developed from a multidisciplinary perspective that according to Savignon (2007, p. 209) 'includes, at least, linguistics, psychology, philosophy, sociology, and educational research'. It can be seen as a result of the early days of globalization in the 1960s and 70s which 'was beginning to have an impact on travel, communications, education, commerce and industry. The world was becoming smaller, and proficiency in English was becoming a more urgent priority for countries in many parts of the world. The language-teaching profession was challenged to provide a response' (Richards 2015, p. 68). In Europe, research and classroom practice in a number of countries had shown the limitations of audiolingualism and a merely grammar-oriented approach to language teaching and learning, so researchers from various fields, supported by educational politicians from the Council of Europe, were working together on a theory of language learning that specified the student's *communicative competence* as the goal of learning. This early vision of students achieving communicative competence focused on the analysis of the learners' future needs, in the form of a description of the roles and situations they would find themselves in (e.g., as a customer in a shop), and the language functions they would need to master (e.g., asking for the price of something), and the lexis they would need for that. When Ek (1991) published the so-called Threshold Level that specified what students of various European languages should be able to do with the language at certain levels of their learning process, this was the beginning of great enthusiasm in teachers, methodologists, linguists and authors of ELT materials. Soon afterwards, the first functional-notional coursebooks became available. The description of the linguistic needs for communicative competence was then widened to include the development of the students' strategic competence, with the goal of furnishing them with the language needed to negotiate meaning, take turns in conversation, ask for clarification, paraphrase language that a partner did not understand, and the like.

The prospect of preparing students more efficiently to be able to communicate successfully in the real world had an important impact on the teaching of adult learners. However, teaching language 'not primarily through memorization, but through meaningful tasks involving real communication' (Nunan 20011, Location 741) was soon going to become influential in the teaching of young learners, too.

Critical issues and topics

The role of grammar itself has been the source of a lot of confusion among teachers since the early days of communicative language teaching. The two opinions – grammar needs to be formally taught vs. grammar cannot be taught but will take care of itself as long as the focus of language use is on meaning and its practice is motivating and fun – still represent the two extremes between which the pendulum of language teaching methodology has swung during the last three decades.

What happens in the primary classrooms has been strongly influenced by such swings, by the teachers' knowledge about how children learn, by the teachers' beliefs and theories about learning and their own experiences as language learners, and not least by the materials and the technologies they are using. Hereafter, a number of critical issues in the form of questions is discussed. Hopefully, the discussion will offer a kind of roadmap towards the principled teaching of grammar to young learners.

Can grammar be taught in isolation?

Wilkins (1972, pp. 111–112) states that 'while without grammar very little can be conveyed, without vocabulary nothing can be conveyed'. The point is obvious – in order to communicate and to become more articulate, learners need both.

Van Lommel et al. (2006, p. 255) argue in line with the lexical approach (Lewis 1993; Long 1996) that vocabulary acquisition is a first and necessary step to acquire grammar, as 'language consists of grammaticalized lexis, not lexicalized grammar; that is, learners do not first acquire rules and then vocabulary to apply it to. Rather, they learn collections of complex but initially unanalyzed chunks of language, which they then progressively analyse, and thus extract grammatical regularities'.

Although I agree with the gist of this assertion, we need to be wary of claims that learners learn grammar by 'progressively analysing' language, at least in the young learners' classroom. Such a claim could lead to the misunderstanding that all the teacher needs to do is provide rich lexical input, and the analysis of this input and the subsequent development of grammatical understanding will follow automatically. As Pinter (2017, p. 85) argues, there is sufficient evidence that 'learning grammar is a messy process requiring the teacher to provide lots of meaningful input, recycling and guidance in attending to language form'. The following extract is, I believe, a good example of how grammar and vocabulary develop together as part of such a process. It comes from a research project at an Austrian primary school I was involved in at the time of writing this chapter.

In that beginners' class, the teacher was doing a word revision activity, asking learners to call out words from lexical sets that had been taught, while she counted how many words they remembered. She asked the students to 'name words for things we can eat' (using gestures to support the children's understanding). Several words were mentioned:

S1:   Apple . . .
T: Do you like apples?
S1:   Yes.
T: I love apples. (adding a point to the tally list on the board) And I love apple pie.
S2:   Apple pie. Apple pie. (looking quizzical)
T: Look. (draws a piece of apple pie on the board) Apple pie. Yummy. I love.
S3:   Apple pie yummy.

S4: Yummy strawberry. (nonverbally expressing delight by rubbing her tummy)
S5: Pie pie. Strawberry pie.
T: Wow. That's a new word. You like strawberry pie. It's good, isn't it?
Ss: Is good . . . strawberry pie.
Ss: Banana. (word incomprehensible)
T: Ah. Do you like banana pie?
Ss: Yes, yes. Banana pie.

This short extract shows how grammar and lexis are interconnected. The children had not learned the phrase 'apple pie' until the teacher introduced it. Then, when S4 mentioned the word 'strawberry' (which had been taught before) a classmate created 'strawberry pie' following the 'apple pie' word pattern (first fruit, then 'pie'). Finally, another classmate said 'banana', followed by an indeterminate word, which the teacher interpreted as a possible attempt to form the word 'banana pie'. When the teacher prompted the word, what the students said and their body language suggested to the teacher that her interpretation had been right.

As pointed out by Cameron (2001, p. 104), 'rote-learnt chunks of language will make up a substantial part of early learning, and . . . the learnt chunks also provide a valuable resource for developing grammar, as they are broken down and reconstituted. Ways of teaching that help learners notice words inside chunks and how other words can be used in the same place may help with the development of grammar.'

Does explicit grammar work facilitate language use?

Thornbury (2001, p. 43) maintains that 'grammar is less a *thing* than something that we *do:* it is a process. Learning, producing and understanding language involve engaging in processes of 'grammaring', as above, when the learners created the words 'strawberry pie' and 'banana' and the latter followed by the teacher facilitating, but not teaching it explicitly. Thornbury stresses that 'this contrasts with a product view of grammar, which construes grammar as an "out there" phenomenon: a body of facts about the language that have to be learned and then taken down off the shelf, so to speak, every time an utterance is produced or interpreted'. The metaphor of grammar *growing* or *emerging* over time rather than *being taken in* from outside through the teacher teaching it explicitly – by using rules and labels such as 'demonstrative pronoun' – is becoming more and more accepted these days among ELT specialists (although its application to practical teaching is still far away). One of the reasons for this insight is the commonsense understanding that children tend to learn in a holistic way and therefore 'little explicit grammar instruction is needed', as Celce-Murcia (1991, p. 463) argues.

The very few studies looking at the outcome of explicit grammar teaching in young learners' classrooms do not contradict this claim, as Bouffard and Sarkar (2008, p. 21) conclude in a study analysing the training of 8-year-old French immersion students in metalinguistic analysis: 'it is clear that a pedagogy oriented towards language analysis and metalanguage use will improve language awareness, but less clear that it will improve language use'. However, the analysis by Marsden (2016, p. 282) of various studies shows that drawing learners 'attention' to aspects of the language (promoting intentional and explicit learning)' is far more promising and 'has most convincingly demonstrated that intentionally and explicitly orientating students' attention to features of the language tends to lead to larger learning gains than instruction that hopes to do so incidentally and/or implicitly' (ibid.).

Does imitation facilitate grammatical competence?

It is folk wisdom that children learn skills through imitating significant adults or their older siblings. It would be surprising, however, if grammatical competence was acquired through mere imitation. A search for the effect of imitation on the development of grammatical competence has not come up with any recent studies. However, a surprisingly clear answer comes from a study carried out almost two decades ago: Tager-Flusberg and Calkins (1990, p. 591) argue that the 'results of this study suggest that across a broad range of children, including some with disorders in language acquisition, imitated speech is neither longer nor grammatically more advanced than non-imitated, spontaneous speech. Despite the very small number of exceptions to these overall results, our conclusion is that imitation does not facilitate grammatical development.'

Reflection on those research outcomes helps produce at least three reasons supporting the argument that imitation does not lead to grammatical competence: first, as mentioned above, some kind of 'grammaring' is needed in order for learners to be able to 'grow' grammar, or for grammar to 'emerge' in the students' language repertoire.

Secondly, neurobiology shows that the brain is not a machine that stores sentences that have been imitated and then lets the learner retrieve them later. On the contrary, as Schnelle (2010, p. 133) states: 'the speakers of the language select spontaneously phrasings and structures from the repertoires of possible expressions and "construe" what they consider as appropriate in the communicative situation'. According to this view, the brain is like a growing system where new things get connected with what is already known, and learning is a process that involves going through phases where errors are not only unavoidable, but an inherent ingredient of the learning process. If imitation was all that's at work, children would simply repeat sentences they have previously heard, and although the sentences might be correct, they would not necessarily be meaningful or communicatively useful. However, we know that language learning is about communicating messages.

Thirdly, the short-term or working memory that we use when we imitate sentences is, well, short term; it is not suitable for storing information for a longer time and then enabling us to 'retrieve' it. As Schnelle (2010, p. 50) argues, 'this kind of activation is often misleadingly called retrieval in thought processes, though there is no agent in the brain that retrieves something'.

Is meaning-focused input sufficient to develop grammatical learning?

A growing body of research indicates that it is not enough to expose students in language classrooms to input, however meaningful and engaging it may be, and hope they will then pick up the correct forms. Cameron (2001, p. 101), for example, argues that 'It seems increasingly likely that paying attention to grammatical features of the language is not something that happens automatically in communicating, and that therefore some artificial methods of pushing attention are needed, i.e. teaching! In line with this argumentation, Nassaji (2004, p. 127) sums up the literature on the importance of 'noticing' – a process of 'registration of the occurrence of a stimulus event in conscious awareness and subsequent storage in long term memory', as suggested by Schmidt (1994, p. 179) – and argues that students will 'fail to process and acquire' grammatical forms unless they (1) are given the opportunity to notice them, (2) are frequently exposed to input that focuses on them, and (3) get plenty of opportunities to practise forms and to use them in output-oriented activities.

When it comes to teaching young children, beginners in particular, it seems important to stress that until a structure gets brought into conscious awareness, the process requires time and patience. The teacher can support it by keeping in mind that the third suggestion above does not necessarily need to focus on output, but can (and in the case of beginners must) consist of 'comprehension based input tasks'. Some recent studies focusing on incidental grammar acquisition for young beginner learners were carried out by Shintani (2012 and 2015). Using listen-and-do tasks with Japanese beginners, the author explores whether noticing two grammatical structures – plural -s and copular *be* – leads to learning, and concludes that 'the only way to conduct the task-based teaching needed for FonF (focus on form) is through input-based tasks' (2014, p. 137). The classroom excerpts quoted in the articles show how the process of noticing is closely connected to the learners' private speech used for 'self-regulation' and 'language play', which the author says 'have both been considered facilitative of L2 acquisition'. The children's speech was shown to result in fairly realistic classroom interactions, with turn-taking 'mostly managed by the students' and 'repair' initiated by the students and then completed either by them or their teacher. Shintani reports a high level of motivation in the children to communicate in English in order to complete the task, and concludes that the learners' 'social speech increased considerably over time', referring to other studies (Pinter 2005; Van den Branden (1997) showing that 'task repetition leads to greater participation of children in tasks' and 'task familiarity makes meaning negotiation easier' (Shintani 2012, p. 266).

Another important condition for the incidental (from the learner's point of view) and focus-on-form-oriented (from the teacher's point of view) learning is that it seems to work with those structures in which the teacher can design tasks based on the principle of a 'functional value' rather than a mere 'grammatical need'. Plural -s has functional value: if you have two pictures, one showing one apple and the other six, and you say to your learners 'Point to the apples', then in order to point to the right picture the students need to understand the meaning of the plurality marker -s as against no -s ('Point to the apple'). N.B. This looks like an extremely important principle that could lead to the creation of a range of incidental focus-on-form-based activities, perfect for very young and beginner learners – see also Puchta and Elliott (2017, p. 11).

However, in the third person singular although the -s must be used for grammatical correctness it has no functional value, and seems far more difficult for children to understand and produce. The practical suggestions section in this chapter contains an idea on how you can increase your learners' awareness of such structures.

Can output help with learning grammar?

There seems to be solid evidence that expecting children to produce a target structure that the teacher has chosen to 'teach' too early could be counterproductive. However, once children have received more input and are at ease with the L2, it is 'equally important that learners have the chance to use new language (both vocabulary and grammar) in meaning-focused output in situations where they have control over the choice of language' (Pinter 2006, 85).

Nassaji (2004) has analysed various studies on textual enhancement and its effect on drawing learners' attention to grammar. He argues that while visually manipulating the appearance of structures in a text (through bolding, italicizing, etc.) may have helped learners notice those forms, this 'did not result in gains in accuracy using the target form' (Nassaji 2004, p. 130), and quotes Batstone (1994, p. 59), arguing that in order for learners to learn grammar effectively, they have to 'act on it, building it into their working hypothesis about how grammar is structured'. In terms of what kinds of output tasks are particularly effective, Nassaji quotes various research studies, specifically mentioning 'collaborative output tasks' and 'discourse-based approaches'.

When should teachers start teaching grammar more explicitly?

There is obviously no clear-cut answer to this question as there is a broad range of variables influencing a child's ability and motivation to deal with grammar more explicitly, such as the child's levels of maturity and cognition, the number of teaching hours, the methodology used, the quality of the classroom interaction, and the teacher's level of experience, to name just a few.

Pinter (2011, p. 142) offers a comprehensive analysis of research findings into the 'age factor' in language learning and the differences between younger and older children. She stresses that 'some recent work also shows that adolescents are more similar to adults in their L2 acquisition processes whereas younger children follow a somewhat different order of acquisition, at least in some areas of grammar'. Other differences mentioned refer to younger children's tendency to 'rely more on imitation skills, repetition and implicit learning' (ibid.), while older ones use 'their cognitive and analytical abilities and more explicit learning methods'. Although the majority of the research available pertains to natural learning contexts (and looks for example at immigrant children learning a second language rather than children learning a foreign language), Pinter (ibid.) cautiously concludes that 'even in foreign language contexts . . . research suggests that more challenges should be offered to young learners in addition to fun activities'. These insights further confirm some of the claims that have been made above, namely that – age and maturity of the learners permitting – the teacher needs to challenge children by going beyond simply giving them a good time in the ELT classroom to progressively including activities that challenge their ability to notice and think about language.

Current contributions and research

For many years, the young learners' classroom did not receive the level of attention it deserved from researchers. It has only been in recent years that a noticeable change has got under way, although a lot more research into various aspects of ELT to young learners is still needed, and the teaching of grammar is certainly among them. I agree with Enever (2016, p. 361) who states, 'It can no longer be claimed that there is little research in the field of primary ELT. However, while the wealth of linguistic, sociocultural and education-focused research worldwide is now strongly developing in the field of primary ELT, there remain a number of areas still hardly explored by empirical research'.

There are now a number of studies available that look at the differences and similarities of young language learner contexts in various countries and regions. The so-called 'ELLiE' (Early Language Learning in Europe) research project (Enever 2011), for example, examines – among other aspects of teaching English to young learners – the outcomes of teaching languages in state primary schools in various European countries. One of the chapters in a research report (Szpotowicz and Lindgren 2011) titled 'Language Achievements: A Longitudinal Perspective' convincingly shows 'significant correlations between lexical diversity and syntactic complexity in Year 3 indicating that the more varied children's vocabulary was, the more determiners they used. Thus, the results indicate that children tended to syntactically complexify their language once they had a large enough vocabulary size'

(p. 129). A number of concrete suggestions are made, one of them in the form of a recommendation to policy makers to make available TV programmes and films in the original language versions in order to provide children with more frequent contact with the target language.

Two substantial longitudinal studies carried out in Croatia (Djigunović and Krajnović 2015) have made available key insights into the language developments of children over time. With the study focusing on 'the learner as an individual' (p. 217) the data showed significant differences in the learning gains between individual students. A comprehensive meta-study (Butler 2015) analyses the situation of teaching English in schools in East Asia. The analysis of various studies into the development of children's interlanguage suggests that 'while some features observed seem to be unique to this group, other features are similar to those experienced by adult L2 English learners and/or child L1 English learners' (ibid., p. 317).

An important discussion on 'Cognitive perspectives on classroom language learning' can be found in Hall (2016). The authors, Collins and Marsden, argue that modern SLA research has had to move beyond 'borrowing concepts from cognitive psychology to the elaboration of sophisticated research methodologies and theoretical constructs' (ibid., p. 281). They make the point that 'as more of the research is now conducted in classrooms, in addition to the more controlled laboratory environments, there are clear implications for teaching' (ibid.). Evaluating the research in language learning cognition in recent years, they differentiate between 'five issues relevant to teaching and learning that have been well-researched and about which some level of consensus has been reached': '(1) *Implicit and explicit learning and explicit and implicit knowledge;* (2) *Practice and automatisation of explicit knowledge;* (3) *Roles of working memory and attention*; (4) *Characteristics of the input influencing learning*; and (5) *Making form-meaning connections* (ibid., p. 282). The authors list 'three areas of debate: one related to language knowledge and two to language use' (ibid., 285): (1) Influence of previously learned languages; (2) Benefits of comprehension and production practice; and (3) Contributions of formulaic language and exemplars to learning.

A passionate plea to include formulaic language in young learners' classrooms can be found in Bland (2015). Based on the outcomes of various studies, Kersten 2015 argues that frequently exposing young learners to lexical chunks rather than just isolated words, and guiding learners to notice and play with the parts of the chunks, gives them the opportunity to unpack or analyse 'formulaic language into its components, which then leads to an abstraction of the underlying construction with all its constraints as well the acquisition of its parts' (p. 129). This approach is in line with what children naturally do in their own language, as observed by Cook (2010).

Recommendations for practice

Below are a number of recommendations for practice in the form of suggestions aimed at helping children to notice the relationship between linguistic form and meaning, by practising form through short behavioural activities in tandem with noticing tasks, and bringing form and lexical practice together in creative ways through language play. These activities have been selected particularly with a view to being used in larger classes too, where it is usually more challenging to find tasks that are meaningful and engaging at the same time. This refers to a family of activities that help students notice why the choice of an 'item – as opposed to the choice of another, or zero choice – matters' (Thornbury 2001, p. 38).

Here is an example of such a practice activity (see Gerngross et al 2006). It supports the students' noticing of the differences in the use of the present perfect for completion (rather than the present progressive).

Assuming that students have been introduced to the present progressive and the present perfect already, the teacher can first introduce or revise the verb phrases *have lunch, wash the dishes, write postcards* and *bake a cake*. The teacher then tells the students they will see a column of pictures and hear sentences. After hearing each sentence, they should quickly call out the number of the picture that goes with that sentence. The teacher presents only the left-hand column of the pictures below (Figure 13.1), and, giving the students little time, says the following sentences: *Ben has washed the dishes. Bridget has had lunch. Barney has baked a cake. Betty has written five postcards*. Students will often match sentences and pictures based on the semantic links between them (*have lunch, wash the dishes*, etc.), without noticing that the grammatical structures they are hearing, and the content of the pictures do not match at all.

The teacher then presents all the pictures and says 'Bridget has had lunch'. Inevitably, students will notice that 'have lunch' is somehow connected to both pictures 1 and 2. If the teacher then offers another sentence 'Brenda is having lunch', he or she can scaffold the students' understanding of the structure. Sentence pairs for the remaining horizontal picture pairs are as follows:

N.B.: It is highly recommended that the same activity be used several times (initially with the same pictures, later with other pictures) as there is evidence that 'task-repetition leads to greater participation of children in tasks' and 'task familiarity makes meaning negotiation easier' (Shintani 2012, p. 266).

Mini-grammar lessons

As early as (1991, p. 473) Celce-Murcia stressed the need for professional teachers to be able to get students to focus briefly on a certain grammar problem so that they 'become aware of both the error and the correct form, and practice the correct form briefly'. It is up to the teacher when to carry out such a 'mini-grammar lesson', but an appropriate moment may be when the teacher has noticed the frequent occurrence of a certain error in the students' production.

Let's imagine that the teacher notices that in a role-play where students go shopping for clothes, they have problems with the correct form of be in the phrase 'How much is/ are . . .?' After the role-play the teacher can write on the board two sentences that the students need to complete with one of the two possible endings in brackets:

How much is (the T-shirt/the T-shirts)?
How much are the (jumpers/jumper)?

The teacher tries to elicit the correct answer, and maybe afterwards an explanation from the students as well. This could be followed by an activity where the teacher presents a picture showing one item (e.g., a pullover), and another picture showing two items (e.g., pullovers). The teacher then calls out a stem sentence, e.g., 'How much is . . .?' and the students have to point at the correct picture. The teacher can then react and say, e.g., 'That's right. How much is the pullover?' etc.

In the next lesson, this could be followed by a short drill. The teacher can have pictures (e.g., items of clothing) ready and then hold up one picture after the other and get students to call out questions along the lines of, 'How much are the jeans? How much is the jumper?', etc. Note that error correction in this case works best when not done by the teacher, but by the students themselves (prompted by the teacher's non-verbal reaction indicating that there is something wrong in a sentence).

I should like to stress that there are serious arguments (e.g., Nassaji 2004, p. 128, quoting Skehan 1996, p. 18) that 'the belief that a precise focus on a particular form leads to learning and automatization no longer carries much credibility in linguistics or psychology'.

Figure 13.1 Activity from Gerngross et al (2006, p. 131)

Images from Gerngross et al. (2006, p. 131)

However, I believe that there is enough evidence from practical classroom research that encourages the use of short noticing tasks in tandem with brief form drills. No doubt more research is needed to substantiate this claim.

Restructuring and output-focused activities

Based on careful analysis of various studies, Nassaji (2004) examines the outcomes of textual enhancement on the development of grammar and in particular the question of whether 'frequent exposure to target items enhances their saliency and hence results in noticing their forms', and comes to the conclusion that mere visual enhancements (e.g., highlighting or bolding certain structures in a text) does not produce 'gains in accuracy using the target form' (p. 140). However, output-focused activities seem to have a greater impact on the development of the learners' grammar than enhanced input. Concerning the quality of output-focused activities, there seems to be evidence that process-oriented output tasks (as opposed to just product-oriented output) that involve learners in collectively and accurately reproducing language forms are important (ibid., p. 131). From a similar viewpoint, Bland (2015, p. 161) has observed that exposing children to poems and engaging them in cognitive play with the linguistic patterns presented in them can lead to the acquisition of grammatical categories as templates for future language use.

Here is an example aimed at practising third person singular/*doesn't*.

The teacher engages the learners in a dictogloss activity. She tells her students that she is going to read out a poem. She tells them that when she has finished reading out the poem, students should pick up pen and paper and try to reconstruct the poem as accurately as possible. They then get together with a partner, compare what they have got and improve their texts together. Finally, the teacher asks the students to dictate back to her the whole poem, word for word, while the teacher writes it on the board. Whenever the students 'make a mistake', the teacher does not immediately correct it, but tries to elicit the correct form from the group until the board shows the poem the teacher had initially dictated.

> She likes chocolate
> she likes music
> she likes good movies
> but
> she doesn't like
> two things:
> unfair people and lies.

The teacher now engages the class in a gradual deletion activity, erasing individual words from the poem and frequently getting students to reconstruct the whole text orally, so that eventually only the following prompts can be seen on the board:

```
_____ l_____ _____
_____ l_____ _____
_____ l_____ _____ _____
but
_____ d_____ l_____
_____ _____:
_____ _____ and _____.
```

The teacher now gets students to think of a person they know well. They first need to think of three things the person likes and two things they don't like. They then write their own poem about the person, following the structure set out by the prompts on the board. Later, the teacher 'edits' the learners' texts and gets them to read the texts out, or display them on the walls of the classroom.

Anticipatory form introduction

While the activities above are aimed at practising grammar forms that have already been introduced, the purpose of the ideas presented here is to introduce a grammar form before it is formally introduced. That is, in the lessons before the formal introduction, the teacher occasionally uses a structure she knows she will teach in one of the next few lessons in such a way that students can understand – with guidance from the teacher – the meaning of the structure.

Here is an example of how to pre-introduce pronouns *this*, *that*, *these* and *those* (for deixis):

Before the lesson, the teacher places various pairs of objects in various locations in the classroom, e.g., two boxes on her desk, one closer to where she usually stands and one clearly further away. During the lesson, the teacher incidentally asks one student, e.g., 'Maria, can you give me the box, please?', pointing vaguely at her desk. When Maria reaches for the box closer to the teacher, the teacher can say, 'No, not **this** box. I mean **that** box, there!' It is advisable not to go into explaining the structure or giving any rules at all at this point of time, but classroom experience seems to indicate that if students get pre-exposed to a new structure several times before the teacher formally introduces it, they have in some ways already 'been there' before and so find it much easier to understand and learn.

Future directions

More research is needed to shed light on teachers' beliefs, perceptions and practices of teaching grammar to young learners. We need to find out, for example, how familiar teachers are with concepts such as noticing, and what they actually do to initiate and maintain such processes in their classrooms. We need more narrative accounts of best-practice grammar teaching to young learners, including examples of student utterances and teacher-student or student – student interaction.

Collins and Marsden (2016, p. 289) stress the importance of repetitive practice and the lack of research into this area: 'Fluent, automatic use of language is the result of considerable practice, and repetition clearly plays a role in the process.' Given the time constraints that many teachers of young learners are subjected to (at least in state schools), we can assume that indeed very little time (if any at all) is spent on repetitive practice.

Finally, we need more research to find out how the materials available for teaching grammar to young learners are in line with latest insights into the cognitive processes of how children learn grammar. And finally, as discussed above, further research is needed to find out more about the possible advantages and constraints of using formulaic language with young learners, and the role of output-oriented activities in the process.

Further reading

1　Bland, J. (2015). *Teaching English to young learners: Critical issues in language teaching with 3–12 year olds*. London: Bloomsbury.

An edited collection of research papers and pedagogical themes containing thought-provoking articles on the use of formulaic language and poetry in teaching grammar to young learners.

2 Cameron, L. (2001). *Teaching languages to young learners*. Cambridge: Cambridge University Press.
   This book offers valuable insights into the principles of learning-centred grammar teaching and what happens in classrooms where it is applied.

3 Pinter, A. (2017). *Teaching young language learners*, 2nd ed. Oxford: Oxford University Press.
   This book provides an accessible, comprehensive overview of the issues surrounding the teaching of young learners.

4 Shintani, N. (2015). The incidental grammar acquisition in focus on form and focus on forms instruction for young beginner learners. *Tesol Quarterly*, 49, 115–140.
   This paper reports a study of children's incidental grammar acquisition of two grammatical features in two types of instruction – focus on form and focus on forms.

Related topics

Vocabulary, assessment, languages in the young learner classroom, materials

References

Alexander, L. G. (1968). *Look, Listen and Learn: Student's book 1*. Harlow: Longman.

Bland, J. (2015). *Teaching English to Young Learners: Critical issues in language teaching with 3–12 year olds*. London: Bloomsbury.

Bouffard, L. A., and M. Sarkar (2008). Training 8-year-old French immersion students in metalinguistic analysis: An innovation in form-focused pedagogy. *Journal of Language Awareness*, 17(1).

Burns, A., Morris-Adams, M., Garton, S., and Copland, F. (2013). *Key Factors and Challenges in Transition from Primary to Secondary Schooling in ELT: An international perspective. Practical guidelines for working at transition levels*. London: the British Council. ELT Research Papers 13–08.

Butler, Y. G. (2015). English language education among young learners in East Asia: A review of current research (2004–2013). *Language Teaching*, 48(3), 303–342.

Cameron, L. (2001). *Teaching Languages to Young Learners*. Cambridge: Cambridge University Press.

Celce-Murcia, M. (1991). Grammar pedagogy in second and foreign language teaching. *Tesol Quarterly*, 25(3), 459–480.

Collins, L., and Marsden, E. (2016). Cognitive perspectives on classroom language learning. In Hall, G. (ed.) *The Routledge Handbook of English Language Teaching*. London: Routledge, 281–294.

Cook, G. (2010). *Language Play, Language Learning*. Oxford: Oxford University Press.

Djigunovic, J. M., and Krajnovic, M. M. (2015). *Early Learning and Teaching of English: New Dynamics of Primary English*. Bristol: Multilingual Matters.

Enever, J. (2011). *ELLiE: Early language learning in Europe*. London: The British Council.

Enever, J. (2016). Primary ELT: Issues and trends. In Hall, G. (ed.) *The Routledge Handbook of English Language Teaching*. London: Routledge.

Gerngross, G., Puchta, H., and Thornbury, S. (2006). *Teaching Grammar Creatively*. Helbling Languages. Innsbruck.

Hall, G. (Ed.). (2016). *The Routledge Handbook of English Language Teaching*. London: Routledge.

Hall, G. (2018). *Exploring English Language Teaching: Language in action*, 2nd ed. London: Routledge.

Johnstone, R. (2009). An early start: What are the key conditions for generalized success? In Enever, J., Moon, J., and Raman, U. (eds.) *Young Learner English Language Policy and Implementation: International perspectives*. Reading: Garnet Education, 31–42.Krashen, S. D. (1982). *Principles and Practice in Second Language Acquisition*. Oxford: Pergamon.

Krashen, S. D., and Terrell, T. D. (1983). *The Natural Approach: Language acquisition in the classroom*. London: Prentice Hall Europe.

Lewis, M. (1993). *The Lexical Approach: The state of ELT and a way forward*. Hove: Language Teaching Publications.

Long, M. H. (1996). The role of the linguistic environment in second language acquisition. In Ritchie, W. C., and Batia, T. K. (eds.) *Handbook of Second Language Acquisition*. San Diego CA: Academic Press, 413–468.

Lugo-Neris, M. J., Jackson, C. W., and Goldstein, H. (2010). Facilitating vocabulary acquisition of young English language learners. *Language, Speech and Hearing Services in Schools*, 41, 314–327.

Magdalena Szpotowicz, M., and Lindgren, E. (2011). Language achievements: A longitudinal perspective. In Enever, J. (ed.) *ELLiE: Early language learning in Europe*. London: The British Council, 125–144.

Nassaji, H. (2004). Current developments in research on the teaching of grammar. *Annual Review of Applied Linguistics*, 24, 126–145.

Nunan, D. (2011). *Teaching English to Young Learners*. Anaheim: Anaheim University Press.

Perozzi, J. A., Chavez Sanchez, M. L. (1992). The effect of instruction in L1 on receptive acquisition of L2 for bilingual children with language delay. *Language, Speech and Hearing Services in Schools*, 23, 348–352.

Pinter, A. (2011). *Children Learning Second Languages: Research and practice in applied linguistics*, Kindle ed. London: Palgrave Macmillan.

Pinter, A. (2017). *Teaching Young Language Learners*, 2nd ed. Oxford: Oxford University Press.

Puchta, H., and Elliott, K. (2017). *Activities for Very Young Learners*. Cambridge: Cambridge University Press.

Richards, J. C. (2015). *Key Issues in Language Teaching*. Cambridge: Cambridge University Press.

Richards, J. C., and Rodgers, T. S. (2014). *Approaches and Methods in Language Teaching*. Cambridge: Cambridge University Press.

Ritchie, W. C., and Batia, T. K. (Eds.). (1996). *Handbook of Second Language Acquisition*. San Diego CA: Academic Press, 413–468.

Savignon, S. J. (2007). Beyond communicative language teaching: What's ahead? *Journal of Pragmatics*, 39, 207–220.

Schmidt, R. W. (1994). Implicit learning and the cognitive unconscious: Of artificial grammars and SLA. In Ellis, N. C. (ed.) *Implicit and Explicit Learning of Languages*. San Diego, CA: Academic Press, 165–209.

Schnelle, H. (2010). *Language in the Brain*. Cambridge: Cambridge University Press.

Shintani, N. (2012). Input-based tasks and the acquisition of vocabulary and grammar: A process-product study. *Language Teaching Research*, 16(2), 253–279.

Shintani, N. (2015). The incidental grammar acquisition in focus on form and focus on forms instruction for young beginner learners. *Tesol Quarterly*, 49, 115–140.

Skehan, P. (1996). Second language acquisition research and task-based instruction. In Willis, J., and Willis, D. (eds.) *Challenge and Change in Language Teaching*. Oxford: Heinemann, 17–30.

Tager-Flusberg, H., and Calkins, S. (1990). Does imitation facilitate the acquisition of grammar? Evidence from the study of autistic, Down's syndrome and normal children. *Journal of Child Language*, 17, 591–606.

Thornbury, S. (2001). *Uncovering Grammar*. Oxford: Macmillan Heinemann.

Titone, R. (1968). *Teaching Foreign Languages: An historical sketch*. Washington, DC: Georgetown University Press.

Van Ek, J. K., and Trim, J. L. M. (1991). *Threshold 1990*. Strasbourg/Graz: Council of Europe.

Van Lommel, S., Laenen, A., and d'Ydewalle, G. (2006). Foreign-grammar acquisition while watching subtitled television programmes. *British Journal of Educational Psychology*, 76, 243–258.

Wilkins, D. (1972). *Linguistics in Language Teaching*. London: Edward Arnold.

Willis, J., and Willis, D. (Eds.). (1996). *Challenge and Change in Language Teaching*. Oxford: Heinemann, 17–30.

14

Vocabulary teaching for young learners

Torill Irene Hestetræet

Introduction

Developing a large, functional and age-appropriate L2 vocabulary is as important as ever before in YLL teaching of English. Many young learners receive massive out-of-school media exposure to the English language due to the significant role that it has as a lingua franca in today's globalised world. Children therefore start learning English informally very early, and may have prior knowledge of English vocabulary when they enter primary school (Lefever 2013). In many European countries, for example, the starting age of learning English has been lowered (Rixon 2015). Against this backdrop, the significance of L2 vocabulary for children's ability and need to express themselves becomes evident.

Before going any further, it is necessary to define some of the terms that will be used in this chapter.

Chunks, or *lexical chunks* or *multiword units*, can be defined as 'a group of words that commonly occur together, like "take a chance"', but the concept can also refer to 'word groups that are intuitively seen as being formulaic sequences, that is, items stored as single choices' (Nation 2013, p. 479). They are also referred to as *formulaic language* or *collocations*.

A *corpus* is a large electronic collection of written and spoken text. There are L1 corpora, learner corpora and child language corpora.

Explicit learning refers to learning that occurs through focused, deliberate study (Schmitt 2008), while *implicit learning* of vocabulary happens incidentally through exposure and use (Schmitt 2008).

A *word family* can be defined as a word and its main inflections and derivations, and the words within it all share 'a common meaning', such as the noun *leak* with its inflected forms *leaks* and *leaked* and derivations *leaky*, *leakiness* and *leakage* (Read 2000, pp. 18–19).

The concept *young learners* is defined as 'those at pre-primary and primary level, roughly from the age of 3 up to 11 or 12 years old' (Copland and Garton 2014, p. 224).

Historical perspectives

There is now a large body of research into the learning of L2 vocabulary (Schmitt 2008). This represents both recognition of the role of vocabulary and a shift away from grammar, which for a long time received more focus, both in teaching and research (Zimmerman 1997). Corpus linguistics research since the 1990s has had a huge impact on the way the nature of vocabulary is now understood (Schmitt 2010; Wray 2009), most importantly because of 'the use of corpus evidence to provide an empirical basis for determining vocabulary behavior, instead of relying on appeals to intuition or tradition' (Schmitt 2010, p. 12). Most dictionaries today are based on electronic corpora with authentic examples of written and spoken language use, such as the British National Corpus (BNC), the Corpus of Contemporary American English (COCA) and the Collins Corpus. This means that our knowledge about how vocabulary is used and how words are combined into formulaic language has increased tremendously. There are also corpora of learner language, e.g., the International Corpus of Learner English (ICLE), and L1 child language, e.g., the Child Language Exchange System (CHILDES), which give us information about young learner langue use specifically.

In a similar vein, Communicative Language Teaching (CLT) and sociocultural views on learning have brought about changes in the teaching of vocabulary to children. These perspectives are more learner-centred and allow for socal interaction and learner-selected vocabulary, indicating a teacher role as facilitator for learning (Richards and Rodgers 2014, Mitchell et al. 2013).

Owing to research in the last few decades, we now have considerable knowledge about the way vocabulary is learned, both in L1 and L2 (Schmitt 2008). The L2 research mostly concerns older learners and, even though there are some studies of YLL vocabulary development (Orosz 2009), research on young learners is still scarce. There is broad agreement that a balance of explicit and implicit teaching approaches is to be recommended (Schmitt 2008; Nation 2013), although there has been a debate about how prominent the role of extensive reading should be in L2 vocabulary acquisition, in which Cobb (2008) argued against McQuillan and Krashen's view that reading alone is enough for L2 vocabulary development (Cobb 2008, McQuillan and Krashen 2008). Explicit study of vocabulary is also necessary (Cobb 2007). This balanced view mainly concerns vocabulary teaching in general, and thus tends to assume older learners or adults, rather than young language learners. However, the research literature does take into consideration the beginner stages of vocabulary learning, and this, together with the general nature of the research, may therefore be seen as being generally applicable to YLL vocabulary development as well.

Such a balanced approach to vocabulary teaching in general is reflected in Nation's four strands for the teaching and learning of vocabulary, which may also be relevant when addressing and balancing the vocabulary needs of children. The strands, applied to YLL vocabulary, are the following: *meaning-focused input*, which allows for input and exposure, for example, from children listening to stories, watching films or reading graded readers *meaning-focused output*, which may involve children taking part in spoken interaction or writing creative stories; *language focused learning*, which includes explicit study of the high frequency vocabulary items that the children need the most; and *fluency development*, which focuses on the recycling and consolidation of the vocabulary that is already familiar to the children (Nation 2013, pp. 1–2).

Recent YLL research has made some very interesting contributions to our knowledge about the L2 vocabulary development of very young children. This research suggests that learners pick up vocabulary and manage to engage in short dialogues even before they start school (Lefever 2013) and that pre-primary school children actively use chunks in child-initiated play in English (Mourão 2014).

Critical issues and topics

What vocabulary do young learners need?

Young learners are motivated by and enjoy learning the L2 vocabulary that they need in order to express their intended meaning, and they are eager to use this vocabulary productively, either in interaction or in writing (Hestetræet 2015, Szpotowicz 2009). With this in mind, it is evident that learning L2 vocabulary is of major significance in children's current and future lives. Long and Richards (2007) consider vocabulary as 'the core component of all of the language skills' and explain how it plays 'an important role in the lives of all language users, since it is one of the major predictors of school performance, and successful learning and use of new vocabulary is also key to membership of many social and professional roles' (Long and Richards 2007, p. xii). Its role as a predictor of mastery may be more essential than ever, both in countries where children are massively exposed to English vocabulary in and out of school, but also in parts of the world where this is not the case. Many children are expected to use English in their future private and professional lives. Thus children need to develop their L2 vocabulary both for their existing as well as their future lives, and this seems to be of critical importance.

The first critical issue in YLL vocabulary learning is vocabulary size development. When children start learning vocabulary, high-frequency words are the most important ones. These are the 3,000 most frequently occurring words in English. Knowing these words, learners can understand spoken English with 95% coverage, which means that that is the rate of words known, and 5% of the words will be unknown (Nation 2013, Nation 2006). Mid-frequency words are the 3,000–9,000 most frequent words, and high-frequency words are those above the 9,000 level.

A five-year-old child knows about 5,000 words in her L1, and goes on learning around 1,000 words a year. An educated L1 speaker knows about 20,000 words (Nation and Waring 1997, p. 7). Newer L1 research indicates similar, but slightly lower, results in vocabulary size. According to Biemiller (2005) and Biemiller and Slonim (2001), as explained by Anthony et al. (unpublished article), young L1 speakers of English learn 800–1000 words a year. For five-year-olds the average word family size was 3,000 and for eleven-year-olds it was 9,000. Based on these results, L1 learner vocabulary size can be estimated as 'age minus 2 times 1000' (Anthony et al. unpublished article). Thus the estimated vocabulary size of a nine-year-old would be: $9 - 2 \times 1000 = 7000$. These figures indicate both the possibilities and the challenges the vast number of words in English pose to the L2 speaker. This does not imply, however, that it is necessary for a YLL child to learn all of these words, as there are other considerations to be made.

YLL vocabulary size matters when it comes to what children may be able to understand in an L2. In order to be able to guess meaning from context when listening or reading, which is considered a very important vocabulary learning strategy, the optimal condition is to have 98% coverage and only 2% unknown words (Nation 2013). This constitutes one in every 50 running words. With this coverage, it takes 6,000 words to understand a children's movie, 7,000 to understand spoken English, 8,000 to understand newspapers, and 9,000 to understand novels (Nation 2013, 2006). With 95% coverage, it takes 3,000 words to understand spoken English and 4,000 for the remaining genres (Nation 2013, 2006). Recent research indicates that it is possible for L2 children to explicitly learn at least 300 words or more per year, with a vocabulary uptake of six words per hour of instruction (Orosz 2009). The critical issue in YLL vocabulary learning is therefore to develop vocabulary sizes large enough for the children to reach the goals of understanding spoken and written English, with a focus on high-frequency vocabulary.

One critical factor to consider when choosing what vocabulary to teach children is select-ing age-appropriate vocabulary that relates to the children's cognitive development. Cam-eron (1994, 2001) outlines how within cognitive linguistics it is maintained that children learn basic level concepts, such as *chair* and *dog*, before they learn the more specific lower level concepts, such as *rocking chair* and *spaniel*, and the more general higher level con-cepts, such as *furniture* and *animal* (Cameron 1994; Cameron 2001). According to Cameron (1994), the higher level and lower level concepts 'will be acquired mainly through social interaction within educational institutions, because they are socially determined' (Cameron 1994, p. 32). Further, she maintains that this knowledge has implications for how vocabu-lary is chosen and taught, both when it comes to syllabuses and texts. It then follows that basic level concepts should be introduced first, gradually followed by lower and higher level ones as the children develop cognitively.

A second crucial factor concerns choosing age-appropriate vocabulary in the sense that the children find it meaningful. Meaningfulness is one of the principles within Communica-tive Language Teaching, stating that 'language that is meaningful to the learner supports the learning process' (Richards and Rodgers 2014, p. 90). When children self-select vocabulary that is relevant and meaningful to them, they become more involved and their motivation to learn is likely to increase. In this way, the teacher and the children can develop a dia-logue about the vocabulary needs of the learners. The choices may involve what items to be expressed, to be learned and to be tested. Giving learners a choice promotes motivation, reflection, awareness and autonomy (Dam 2011, p. 43).

Interaction and vocabulary learning

Interaction is another significant issue in vocabulary development, relating to how to teach and learn the vocabulary that YLL learners need. Interaction supports YLL vocabulary learning. This view is grounded in both theory, mainly the interactionist approach, which 'is sucessfully demonstrating many interconnections between L2 interaction and L2 learning' (Mitchell et al. 2013, p. 187), and sociocultural theory, where dialogic communication 'is seen as central to the joint construction of knowledge (including knowledge of language forms)' (Mitchell et al. 2013, p. 248), and in YLL and vocabulary research. Nation explains that when learners interact to solve tasks, their attention to language features may support vocabulary learning (Nation 2013, pp. 172–173). Rixon (2015) asserts that it is not enough with 'mere exposure'; interaction is also 'required for optimum take-up and development' (Rixon 2015, p. 42). However, the transition from learning words explicitly to using vocab-ulary to partake in interaction seems to be a challenging transition for both young learners and their teachers (Hestetræet 2015). Attending to interaction through child-initated play in the early years of learning English vocabulary, as suggested by Mourão (2014), may seem to help. Young children introduced to chunks to support child-inititated play in English learning areas (English corners) in pre-primary school successfully managed to interact in English, recycling the chunks they had learned and helping one another, even when the teacher was not present (Mourão 2014, p. 261). Developing teacher competence and knowledge about the role of interaction in children's language learning is another way it may be strengthened in countries around the world (Rixon 2015, p. 42). From a learner autonomy perspective, Dam suggests that authenic communication in the classroom promotes interaction:

> If we want our learners to be genuine users of the target language, including outside the
> classroom, we must create a learning environment that is real life in its own right. This

means that ongoing communication between teacher and learners must be authentic. This implies that the participants act and speak as *themselves* within their respective roles in the teaching/learning environment.

(Dam 2011, p. 44)

Choice of tasks in the YLL classroom also influences interaction and vocabulary development. According to Pinter (2015), stories used in task-based learning (TBL) 'inherently elicit interaction and feedback' (Pinter 2015, p. 119). Further, she explains, through the interaction the learners motivate 'their partners to produce cognitively and linguistically modified, better-quality output.' (Pinter 2015, p. 119).

The incremental process of knowing a word: form, meaning and use

In order for children to know a word, it is vital to know its form, meaning and use, both productively and receptively (Nation 2013, Schmitt 2008). The noun *dog* may serve as an illustration. To know the form of this word means to know its pronunciation, its spelling and its grammar. To know its meaning is to know that it denotes 'an animal with four legs and a tail, often kept as a pet' (Oxford Learners Dictionary). As the children grow older, they will also learn other senses the noun *dog* has, such as 'a male dog' as opposed to 'a female dog', and the synonyms and associations that it has, along with specific examples of dogs, such as *spaniels*, and that it is an example of the higher level concept *animal*. To know the use of the word *dog* involves knowing the collocations it forms, such as *to have a dog, to feed the dog, to walk the dog, a friendly dog, a family dog*, and *dogs bark*. It also means gradually knowing that it is a frequent word and knowing its register, for example that the word also has disapproving senses that are only used in informal contexts.

Children learn L2 vocabulary incrementally. This means that words are learned little by little, over time. It takes many encounters to develop word knowledge of form, meaning and use, and for this knowledge to be consolidated and enhanced. At the beginning stages of learning a word, Schmitt suggests, explicit study is to be recommended whereas later in the process learning from context, implicitly, can improve word knowledge (2008, p. 334).

Chunks for young learners

Learning chunks is also a critical issue for young language learners when building a functional vocabulary, because they provide children with ready-made phrases they can use to express meaning. They are also referred to as lexical chunks, multiword units, collocations and formulaic language. Learning chunks can help children develop fluency and express themselves more easily. Chunks, or multiword units, can generally be defined as 'a group of words that commonly occur together, like "take a chance" ', but since there are different types of them, it should also be mentioned here that they can also refer to 'word groups that are intuitively seen as being formulaic sequences, that is, items stored as single choices' (Nation 2013, p. 479). Chunks have been described as being very useful for children, both when expressing their needs and when building up an L2 (Wray 2002).

Chunks serve important communicative functions in the language of both native speakers and non-native speakers. Wray (2002) reviewed existing studies of the use of chunks in L2 young learner language, mainly from the late 1970s and 1980s, some of them from an L2 naturalistic setting, others from an L1 environment. She found that children use chunks for socio-interactional purposes. These functions (Wray 2002, pp. 161–169) include to get things done, such as in *Milk, please* and *Can I play with this?*; to demonstrate group membership, e.g., *How are you? Have a nice day! See you tomorrow* and *I'm sorry*; and demonstrate individuality, e.g., *I can do this, I know this*. Another function included using chunks to gain control of their language learning development, such as in *What's that?*; *I don't understand*. Since chunks seem to have these functions, it also seems important to provide young learners with them. Wray suggests that very young L2 learners 'seem naturally adept at employing formulaic sequences' and that in primary school L2 learning is enhanced in social interaction with peers (Wray 2002, p. 148). From this it may be concluded that the teaching of vocabulary may allow for both plentiful numbers of chunks as well as social interaction between the learners.

Very young learners in the pre-primary English classroom have also been shown to use chunks in interaction, during child-initiated play and in a Portuguese study (Mourão 2014). The children used chunks such as 'Let's play . . . ', 'Your turn!', 'Raise your hand!', 'What's missing?', 'They're the same' and 'Help please' (Mourão 2014, p. 261), indicating that functions of the chunks were to initiate and take part in the play, as well as ask for help. The children were strongly motivated and were 'observed correcting each other, reminding each other of English words and expressions, and actively helping each other to play in English' (Mourão 2014, p. 261). Thus these Portuguese children managed to both interact and play through the use of chunks.

Some researchers, such as Wray, claim that chunks are prefabricated and 'stored and retrieved whole from memory' (Wray 2000, p. 465). There is a debate whether children learn chunks as a whole and then later unpack the grammar of them, or whether the chunks are rote-learned and dropped when the process of rule-governed grammar competence takes over (Myles et al. 1998, p. 327, cited in Kersten 2015, p. 134), or if both of these processes are at play.

Current contributions and research

One current research contribution to the vocabulary development of young learners comes from an Icelandic context, where a study of young learner language indicates that the children had picked up English vocabulary from exposure prior to starting school. The children were able to recognise vocabulary and participate in conversations. Media exposure is suggested as one of the most important factors influencing early incidental learning. A teaching implication pointed out in the study is that it is important to build on the prior English vocabulary knowledge young children have when they start school (Lefever 2013).

The second contribution is an investigation of the vocabulary size development of young Hungarian learners of English. Promoting childrens's vocabulary size development is one of the major tasks of the YLL teacher, and research may yield information about the process of vocabulary growth and how much vocabulary children may learn. The Hungarian study suggests a vocabulary uptake of 'about six words per contact hour' in the first years of learning English (Years 3–6, ages 9–12) (Orosz 2009, p. 191). An average of ten words were presented in each class (Orosz 2009, p. 183). There was an average growth of 348 words per year in Years 3 and 4, 481 in Year 5, and 280 in Year 6 (Orosz 2009, p. 188). The mean vocabulary size estimates ranged from 348 in Year 3 to 696 in Year 4, 1177 in Year 5 and 1457 in Year 6 (Orosz 2009, p. 188). The results indicate that the vocabulary growth is consistent and the teaching programme successful (Orosz 2009, p. 191). It could also be mentioned that in 'the first year of English, the most able performers appear to learn 1000 words' and that in Year 6 'the most able learner scored over 3000 words in the vocabulary size test' (Orosz 2009, p. 191).

Another recent contribution concerns the beliefs and practices of YLL vocabulary teachers. Language teacher cognition can be explained as 'what language teachers think, know and believe and the relationships of these mental constructs to what teachers do in the language teaching classroom' (Borg 2003, p. 81). Teacher cognition research has yielded insight into the beliefs and practices YLL teachers have, and contributed understanding that is useful for teachers and teacher educators in further developing professional knowledge (Borg 2009; Gao and Ma 2011). Some studies have been conducted into the vocabulary teaching of YLL English teachers. Lau and Rao (2013) carried out a qualitative study of the vocabulary instruction in early childhood classrooms in Hong Kong. Their main findings indicate that the teachers employed a 'limited variety of instructional practices in teaching vocacbulary' (Lau and Rao 2013, p. 1378), with a focus on word recognition and memorisation, and these practices were in line with the teachers' beliefs. Similar results were found in another qualitative study of vocabulary instruction, in Year 7 in a Norwegian setting (Hestetræet 2015). The teachers did not seem to use the full range of teaching possibilites available, focusing on teacher-selected decontextualised vocabulary, leaving less room for spontaneous interaction. The teachers' prior language learning experiences seemed to influence them to either choose similar or quite dissimilar instruction (Hestetræet 2015, p. 50). Both of these studies suggest a need for balanced vocabulary teaching, which also includes contextualised vocabulary, such as in storytelling and reading and meaning-focused output, such as in spontaneous interaction.

Research on the use of ICT to promote language learning and vocabulary development provides interesting and innovative contributions to the field of YLL research. Schmid and Whyte (2015) investigated the use of interactive whiteboards and videoconferencing to support collaboration between young learners in primary schools in Germany and France. They explain how the use of ICT 'offers opportunities for exchanging meaningful information and ideas in authentic tasks' and how it 'allows interaction with speakers who do not share a native language and can provide scaffolding to support this interaction' (Schmid and Whyte 2015, p. 241). Citing Camilleri, Sollars, Poor, Martinez del Pinal and Leja (2000), they further maintain that 'oral, synchronous interaction is best suited to young learners who do not master the written language and cannot sustain motivation over weeks and months') (Schmid and Whyte 2015, p. 241). The findings of the study included motivational gain and 'enhanced communication skills' (Schmid and Whyte 2015, p. 252). What is more, the teachers and learners expressed that they found the activites authentic and that they preferred them over traditional ones, even though there was also room for more spontaneous interaction among the learners, as well as more learner-centredness.

Recommendations for Practice

The main recommendations for practice include having a varied and balanced approach to teaching YLL vocabulary. This means that it should allow for both explicit and implicit teaching and learning, which are processes that complement one another (Nation 2013, p. 348), and for Nation's (2013) four strands of meaning-focused input, meaning-focused output, language-focused learning and fluency development. Naturally, the use of ICT also belongs in a modern YLL classroom to support vocabulary learning.

Explicit vocabulary teaching: pre-teaching and word cards

The main benefits of explicit, direct vocabulary teaching include that it is fast and efficient and provides opportunities for conscious focus and controlled repetition, as well as development of the word knowledge necessary for productive use (Nation 2013, p. 444). Such explicit teaching is most useful for high-frequency words, as these are the words that children need to learn first. They need these words to be able to understand when listening and reading, and to be able to express themselves through interaction and in writing. Pre-teaching may aid both text comprehension and vocabulary learning, and should involve rich instruction. Rich instruction includes aspects of meaning, form and use, as well as the context in which the words appear and the collocations in which they combine (Nation 2008, pp. 60–62). Rich instruction is time-consuming and should therefore be used only with the high-frequency words that the young learners need the most. Using pictures, objects and actions makes it easier for children to understand the meaning, and it aids memorisation, due to the meaning being 'stored both linguistically and visually' (Nation 2013, p. 121).

Another example of explicit teaching is to use word cards (Nation 2013, pp. 437f). By using cards children may develop their vocabulary size quickly. One of the reasons for this is that having to retrieve the meaning of the word on the card supports learning, and it gives better results than memorising lists where both the words and their meaning are provided. Spaced retrieval has proved to be particulary beneficial, as it allows for improving word knowledge every time. The word form, in spelling, is provided on one side of the card, and the meaning on the other. The meaning can be explained in the L2, translated into the L1 or be a picture that shows the meaning.

Implicit vocabulary teaching: graded readers, picturebooks, oral storytelling and Readers Theatre

Reading extensively is one of the most important ways in which children can learn vocabulary implicitly and further develop their vocabulary knowledge (Stahl and Nagy 2012, p. 49). Both L1 and L2 studies show that there is a strong relationship between children's vocabulary knowledge and reading comprehension (Droop and Verhoeven 2003). Extensive reading can be explained as 'the reading of large numbers of texts largely chosen by the learners where there are 5% or less unknown running words' (Nation 2013, p. 219). With such a low percentage of unknown words, it is possible for young learners to practise the important strategy of guessing the meaning of these words from context. However, as young learners may still be in the process of learning to read in their L1, learning to read in their L2 may require support. Arnold and Rixon (2014) suggest what they they refer to as a 'bridge' between the decoding stage and the 'lift-off' stage of reading for meaning and for pleasure to support YLL reading (2014, p. 30). Graded readers are simplified, complete books 'that have been prepared so that they stay within a strictly limited vocabulary' (Nation 2013. p. 247). These books are divided into different vocabulary levels, so that as the children's vocabulary level develops, they can read books that have slightly more advanced vocabulary. According to Arnold and Rixon (2014), referring to the work of Claridge (2012), there is a lack of graded readers for YLL children, and therefore many teachers use graded readers that are developed for L1 learners, usually younger than the YLL children. As a result, the L2 learners may find the content of the books to be 'of "low interest"' (Arnold and Rixon 2014, p. 38). If the content is more mature, the learners may need support with cultural, cognitive and textual challenges (2014, p. 32). In Arnold and Rixon's (2014) study about the implementation of an extensive reading programme with YLL children aged 6–12 in Hong Kong, L1 reading materials were employed, but adapted to fit the needs of these L2 learners of English. These adaptions included plenary sessions that focused on reading strategies, such as phonemic, grammatical and semantic awareness, but also on how to guess meaning from context by using cues from pictures and the text (2014, p. 36). The use of graded readers may support the consolidation and fluency development when the children encounter and retrieve the meaning of familiar vocabulary, as well as the development of reading skills in general (Nation 2013, pp. 248–249, Beglar et al. 2012).

Picturebooks represent another type of reading material that may support implicit YLL vocabulary learning and literacy development. Picturebooks combine text and pictures, and the pictures provide a context that facilitates the comprehension of unfamiliar vocabulary. According to Bland, 'the visual images in picturebooks are regarded and acknowledged as an effective scaffolding context, supporting comprehension' (Bland 2013, p. 31). The use of picturebooks encourages interaction between the pictures and the words, the teacher and the learners and between the learners themselves, inspiring the children's imagination. Mourão (2015) explains that with 'picturebooks, young learners are given a multitude of opportunities to use language that represents the pictures and the words and the interpretations created from the two modes coming together' (Mourão 2015, p. 214). Using picturebooks that capture the young learners' imagination is also a way of supporting their 'aesthetic, cultural, cognitive and emotional development' (Mourão 2015, p. 214). The authentic language in picturebooks is often rich in chunks (Kersten 2015, p. 138, Bland 2013, pp. 152–153) and includes repetitions of vocabulary items (Birketveit 2013, Kersten 2015). These repeated exposures support YLL vocabulary learning, as it may take at least 8–10 encounters to learn a word, and since word knowledge is consolidated when words are used repeatedly, but in different contexts (Schmitt 2010, p. 31). This illustrates that vocabulary is learned incrementally, little by little, through recycling. Another advantage of using picturebooks is that they 'provide visual support for weak or reluctant readers' and the learners can choose whether to 'rely mostly on the pictures or mostly on the verbal text or go back and forth between the two according to where their cognitive strength lies' (Birketveit 2013, pp. 17–18).

Oral storytelling is another example of how to teach vocabulary implicitly, through listening, in the YLL classroom, particularly for the very young learners. Oral stories 'have traditionally been told by word of mouth, with, these days, many retellings in written form and remediations in digital form or film.' (Bland 2015, p. 185). Oral stories contain short sentences and are rich in repetitive vocabulary and formulaic language and therefore offer plentiful exposures and recycling of vocabulary. What is more, oral stories have a plot with an archetypal story template, which young children easily relate to and which captures their imagination. This template has '*a logically linked series of events, a structure that includes a beginning, a middle and an end, characters that remain the centre of attention throughout, and to whom the story happens, and a resolution that offers some resolution or release*' (Crago 2011, p. 211, cited in Bland 2015a, p. 186, italics in the original). According to Bland, narrative such as storytelling to children who are not fluent in reading yet 'can play an enormous role in their L2 acquisition' (Bland 2015, p. 185).

Readers Theatre 'is essentially an activity in which a group reads a text aloud' (Drew and Pedersen 2012, p. 71). For young children it can be used with stories and literature, such as *Mr. Twit's Revenge* or *Rumpeltstilskin*, but also with simplified factual texts. The chosen text is made into a script with shorter parts that the children first rehearse and read aloud in turn, performing for one another and the rest of the class. This type of activity promotes word recognition and the understanding of vocabulary (Drew and Pedersen 2012, p. 81). It also provides a context and allows for plentiful recycling of words both during the rehearsal and performance, and learners find it motivating to participate in the activity. According to Rinehart, Readers Theatre is 'an integrated language event with an authentic communication purpose' (Rhinehart 1999, p. 87).

The use of ICT in vocabulary teaching

ICT, too, can be used to support both explicit and implicit vocabulary learning. An example of the former is to use electronic flashcard programmes. According to Nakata (2017), such programmes 'have been developed in a way that maximises vocabulary learning' (Nakata 2011, p. 17). As with ordinary flashcards, the learner is 'asked to associate the L2 word form with its meaning, usually in the form of a first language (L1) translation, L2 synonym, or L2 definition' (Nakata 2011, p. 17). The main benefits of using electronic flashcards include the efficiency with which they allow for learning a large number of words in a short period of time, and that the learners go on to use these words for ordinary, meaningful purposes. Nakata outlines how most flashcard programmes are flexible, so that it is possible for children to make their own cards, to choose between L2 definitions/synonyms or L1 translations depending on learner needs and to include both chunks and individual words. It is also possible to use sound files, images or video clips to link the programme to own or external vocabulary database, and to allow for receptive and productive retrieval and recognition and allow for generative use, which means to 'encounter or use previously met words in novel contexts' (Nakata 2011, p. 22, referring to Joe 1995, 1998; Nation 2001, pp. 68–70). Finally, the programmes have adaptive sequencing and expanded rehearsal functions, which means, respectively, that words that are hard to learn can be studied more and that words are studied more frequently right after the first encounter and then less frequently and between longer intervals as they become more familiar to the learners (p. 23).

ICT can also be used to promote meaning-focused output through online interaction between YLL learners from different countries. As shown in the study by Schmid and Whyte (2015) of young learners from Germany and France, video communcation can be used for task-based learning. Using drag-and-drop functions, the children collaborated online to solve tasks such as creating an ID-card for all the learners, designing funny animals, and selecting food items to buy in the supermarket and to serve for breakfast. The tasks promoted production of comprehensible output through learner interaction, as well as improved communication skills and motivation (Schmid and Whyte 2015, p. 252). However, both the teachers and the learners from this study thought that there was more room for spontaneous interaction in which the learners could express themselves. This means that such considerations should be made in creating ICT tasks for the young learners. In both this study as well as in the use of ICT and websites generally, pictures, or the visual mode, have an important function. According to Stone (2007), 'non-linguistic modes, particularly the visual, are gaining dominance' and to 'ignore the role of modes such as images, movement, sound, and layout would be to ignore central systems of meaning' (Stone 2007, p. 52).

Teaching vocabulary through TBL

Choosing meaningful tasks, for example through task-based learning (TBL), may promote learner involvement and vocabulary production in the YLL classroom. Task involvement creates a need for using both familiar and unfamiliar vocabulary in a context. Learner interaction is essential in task-based learning. Pinter addresses this when explaining that the 'underlying principle behind both CLT and task-based learning is that authentic learner interaction, motivated engagement and purposefulness are important in making progress in language learning.' (Pinter 2015, p. 114). For example, when children create TBL stories, it is the puzzle of the story that generates vocabulary production, and 'learning happens by confronting gaps between the young learners' existing linguistic repertoire and what emerges as a need/gap while talking about the puzzle with others' (Pinter 2015, p. 119). Thus, by taking part in the interaction, the learners develop their awareness about the familiar vocabulary they already know and the unfamiliar vocabulary that they need to narrate the story. Pinter distinguishes between linguistic, social, cognitive and metacognitive demands that tasks may present to the young learner, and suggests that teachers contemplate the extent to which the learners have the necessary language, interaction skills and maturity when selecting suitable tasks for them (Pinter 2015, p. 119). Similarly, she recommends the learners to develop their TBL awareness by asking themselves questions such as if they understand the vocabulary communicated by their partner, if there is a need for repetition, if the language is difficult, if the information conveyed is important or not and if they are making task progress (Pinter 2015, p. 119).

The importance of tasks for incidental vocabulary learning is reflected in Laufer and Hulstijn's (2001) *task involvement hypothesis*, in which it is suggested that the cognitive components *search* and *evaluation* and the motivational component *need* (Laufer and Hulstijn 2001, pp. 14–15, Nation 2013, p. 98) influence acquisition. The need component has to do with necessity, the search component with finding meaning of unfamiliar vocabulary and the evaluation component with selection of appropriate meaning, all of them either receptively or productively. For example, there is more task involvement in writing tasks than in reading tasks, because the need for vocabulary is stronger.

Writing tasks, for example through TBL, create a need for vocabulary for the children (Nation 2008, p. 83). However, learners are more likely to use vocabulary that they are familiar with than use words that they have just encountered (Coxhead 2007, p.335, Nation 2013, p. 270). This may suggest that young learners also need support when building up their writing skills.

Future directions

The massive exposure to English that many young learners are subject to is, undoubtedly, beneficial for their vocabulary development. Even though it is natural to embrace this early exposure, it still represents challenges for the teaching and learning of vocabulary. A logical implication is, of course, that vocabulary teaching must build on the learners' existing knowledge when they start school, in order to remain meaningful to the children. Another consequence of the learners' prior L2 vocabulary knowledge is that language teacher education should include methodology on how to teach young learners who already have this knowledge. A challenge from the learner perspective is that exposure to vocabulary does not necessarily involve acquisition, which may take many encounters as well as opportunities for receptive and productive retrieval. To this day, there is a scarcity of studies into young learner vocabulary development. More research is needed on children's L2 vocabulary size and vocabulary knowledge from countries around the world, both where there is major and minor exposure to English. Further research is also needed in the field of teacher cognition about vocabulary teaching to find out what teachers believe and do in relation to current vocabulary theory and recommendations for practice. Finally, the use of ICT offers tremendous opportunities for vocabulary learning in the future, through text, images and sound alike. Still, it seems that interaction between learners in the classroom will not go out of fashion.

Further reading

1 Bland, J. (Ed.). (2015). *Teaching English to young learners: Critical issues in language teaching with 3–12 year olds*. London: Bloomsbury.

   This book has a collection of recent research from YLL scholars about a wide range of aspects relevant to YLL teaching, such as pre-primary English, immersion teaching, task-based learning, chunks, grammar, intercultural understanding, storytelling, picturebooks, drama and ICT.

2 Hasselgreen, A., Drew, I., and Sørheim, B. (2012). *The young language learner. Research-based insights into teaching and learning*. Bergen: Fagbokforlaget.

   This is a collection of chapters on YLL research about a wide range of topics, including use of the the European Language Portfolio, reading stories, approaches to teaching reading, Readers Theatre, incidental pre-primary language learning, phonological competence, vocabulary and assessment.

3 Lefever, S. C. (2013). Incidental foreign language learning in young children. In Hasselgreen, A., Drew, Ion, and Sørheim, Bjørn (eds.) *The young language learner: Research-based insights into teaching and learning*. Bergen: Fagbokforlaget.

   Lefever's study offers interesting insight into Icelandic young learners' knowledge of English prior to starting school.

4 Nation, I. S. P. (2013). *Learning vocabulary in another language*, 2nd ed. Cambridge: Cambridge University Press.

   The second edition of Nation's book is an essential reference work about current research on vocabulary for students, teachers and researchers alike.

5 Nikolov, M. (Ed.). (2009). *Early learning of modern foreign languages: Processes and outcomes*. Bristol: Multilingual Matters.

   This book, edited by Nikolov, presents recent YLL research from many different international scholars and perspectives, such as for example using the Early Years Literacy Programme in a Norwegian context, the age factor and reading, vocabulary size development, factors in YLL vocabulary acquisition and target language use in China.

6 Orosz, A. (2009). The growth of young learners' English vocabulary size. In Nikolov, M. (ed.) *Early learning of modern foreign languages: Processes and outcomes*. Bristol: Multilingual Matters.

   The study by Orosz offers valuable insight into the vocabulary development of young Hungarian learners of English.

Related topics

Grammar, assessment, materials, syllabus, technology in the classroom

References

Anthony, L., van Hees, J., and Nation, P. (unpublished article). *The Vocabulary Sizes of Young Native-Speakers of English*.

Arnold, W., and Rixon, S. (2014). Making the moves from decoding to extensive reading with young learners: Insights from research and practice around the world. In Rich, S. (ed.) *International Perspectives on Teaching English to Young Learners*. Basingstoke: Palgrave Macmillan.

Beglar, D., Hunt, A., and Kite, Y. (2012). The effect of pleasure reading on Japanese University EFL learners' reading rate. *Language Learning*, 62, 665–703.

Birketveit, A. (2013). Picturebooks. In Birketveit, A., and Williams, G. (eds.) *Literature for the English Classroom: Theory into Practice*. Bergen: Fagbokforlaget.

Bland, J. (2013). *Children's Literature and Learner Empowerment: Children and Teenagers in English Language Education*. London: Bloomsbury.

Bland, J. (2015). Oral storytelling in the primary English classroom. In Bland, J. (ed.) *Teaching English to Young Learners: Critical Issues in Language Teaching with 3–12 Year Olds*. London: Bloomsbury.

Borg, S. (2003). Teacher cognition in language teaching: A review of research on what language teachers think, know, believe and do. *Language Teaching*, 36, 81–109.

Borg, S. (2009). Language teacher cognition. In Burns, A., and Richards, J. C. (eds.) *The Cambridge Guide to Second Language Teacher Education*. Cambridge: Cambridge University Press.

Cameron, L. (1994). Organising the world: Children's concepts and categories, and implications for the teaching of English. *ELT Journal*, 48, 28–39.

Cameron, L. (2001). *Teaching Languages to Young Learners*. Cambridge: Cambridge University Press.

Cobb, T. (2007). Computing the vocabulary demands of L2 reading. *Language Learning & Technology*, 11, 38–63.

Cobb, T. (2008). Commentary: Response to McQuillan and Krashen (2008). *Language Learning & Technology*, 12, 109–114.

Copland, F., and Garton, S. (2014). Key themes and future directions in teaching English to young learners: Introduction to the Special Issue. *ELT Journal*, 68, 223–230.

Coxhead, A. (2007). Factors and aspects of knowledge affecting L2 word use in writing. In Davidson, P., Coombe, C., Lloyd, D. and Palfreyman, D. (eds.) Teaching and Learning Vocabulary in Another Language. Dubai: TESOL Arabia, 331–342

Dam, L. (2011). Developing learner autonomy with school kids: Principles, practices, results. In Gardner, D. (ed.) *Fostering Autonomy in Language Learning*. www.researchgate.net/publication/259368185_ Fostering_autonomy_in_language_learning: Faculty of Education at Zirve University, Gaziantep, Turkey.

Drew, I., and Pedersen, R. R. (2012). Readers theatre: A group reading approach to texts in mainstream EFL classes. In Hasselgreen, A., Drew, I., and Sørheim, B. (eds.) *The Young Language Learner: Research-based insights into teaching and learning*. Bergen: Fagbokforlaget.

Droop, M., and Verhoeven, L. (2003). Language proficiency and reading ability in first- and second-language learners *Reading Research Quarterly*, 38, 78–103.

Gao, X., and Ma, Q. (2011). Vocabulary learning and teaching beliefs of pre-service and in-service teachers in Hong Kong and mainland China. *Language Awareness*, 20, 327–342.

Hestetræet, T. I. (2015). Vocabulary instruction in 7th-grade English classes. In Amdal, A., Fjørtoft, H., and Guldal, T. M. (eds.) *Faglig kunnskap i skole og lærerutdanning II*. Bergen: Fagbokforlaget.

Kersten, S. (2015). Language development in young learners: The role of formulaic language. In Bland, J. (ed.) *Teaching English to Young Learners: Critical issues in language teaching with 3–12 year olds*. London: Bloomsbury.

Lau, C., and Rao, N. (2013). English vocabulary instruction in six early childhood classrooms in Hong Kong. *Early Child Development and Care*, 183, 1363–1380.

Laufer, B., and Hulstijn, J. 2001. Incidental vocabulary acquisition in a second language: The construct of task-induced involvement. *Applied Linguistics*, 22, 1–26.

Lefever, S., C. (2013). Incidental foreign language learning in young children. In Hasselgreen, A., Drew, Ion, and Sørheim, Bjørn (eds) *The Young Language Learner: Research-based insights into teaching and learning*. Bergen: Fagbokforlaget.

Long, M. H., and Richards, J. C. (2007). Series editors' preface. In Daller, H., Milton, J., and Treffers-Dallers, J. (eds.) *Modelling and Assessing Vocabulary Knowledge*. Cambridge: Cambridge University Press.

McQuillan, J., and Krashen, S. (2008). Commentary: Can free reading take you all the way? A response to Cobb (2007). *Language Learning & Technology*, 12, 104–108.

Mitchell, R., Myles, F., and Marsden, E. (2013). *Second Language Learning Theories*, 3rd ed. London: Routledge.

Mourão, S. (2014). Taking play seriously in the pre-primary English classroom. *ELT Journal*, 68, 254–264.

Mourão, S. (2015). The potential of picturebooks with young learners. In Bland, J. (ed.) *Teaching English to Young Learners: Critical Issues in Language Teaching with 3–12 Year Olds* London: Bloomsbury.

Nakata, T. (2011). Computer-assisted second language vocabulary learning in a paired-associate paradigm: A critical investigation of flashcard software. *Computer Assisted Language Learning*, 24, 17–38.

Nation, I. S. P. (2006). How large a vocabulary is needed for reading and listening? *The Canadian Modern Language Review*, 63, 59–82.

Nation, I. S. P. (2008). *Teaching Vocabulary: Strategies and Techniques*. Boston, MA: Heinle, Cengage Learning.

Nation, I. S. P. (2013). *Learning Vocabulary in Another Language*. Cambridge: Cambridge University Press.

Nation, I. S. P., and Waring, R. (1997). Vocabulary size, text coverage and word lists. In Schmitt, N., and McCarthy, M. (eds.) *Vocabulary: Description, Acquisition and Pedagogy*. Cambridge: Cambridge University Press.

Orosz, A. (2009). The growth of young learners' English vocabulary size. In Nikolov, M. (ed.) *Early Learning of Modern Foreign Languages*. Bristol: Multilingual Matters.

Pinter, A. (2015). Task-based learning with children. In Bland, J. (ed.) *Teaching English to Young Learners: Critical Issues in Language Teaching with 3–12 Year Olds*. London: Bloomsbury.

Read, J. (2000). *Assessing Vocabulary*. Cambridge: Cambridge University Press.

Rhinehart, S. D. (1999). "Don't think for a minute that I'm getting up there": Opportunities for Readers theater in a tutorial for children with reading problems. *Reading Psychology*, 20, 71–89.

Richards, J. C., and Rodgers, T. S. (2014). *Approaches and Methods in Language Teaching*, 3rd ed. Cambridge: Cambridge University Press.

Rixon, S. (2015). Primary English and critical issues: A worldwide perspective. In Bland, J. (ed.) *Teaching English to Young Learners*. London: Bloomsbury.

Schmid, E. C., and Whyte, S. (2015). Teaching young learners with technology. In Bland, J. (ed.) *Teaching English to Young Learners: Critical Issues in Language Teaching with 3–12 Year Olds*. London: Bloomsbury.

Schmitt, N. (2008). Review article: Instructed second language vocabulary learning. *Language Teaching Research*, 12, 329–363.

Schmitt, N. (2010). *Researching Vocabulary: A vocabulary research manual*. Basingstoke: Palgrave Macmillan.

Stahl, S. A., and Nagy, W. E. (2012). *Teaching Word Meanings*. Abingdon: Routledge.

Stone, J. C. (2007). Popular websites in adolescents' out-of-school lives: Critical lessons on literacy. In Knobel, M., and Lankshear, C. (eds.) *A New Literacies Sampler*. New York: Peter Lang.

Szpotowicz, M. (2009). Factors influencing young learners' vocabulary acquisition. In Nikolov, M. (ed.) *Early Learning of Modern Foreign Languages: Processes and Outcomes*. Bristol: Multilingual Matters.

Wray, A. (2000). Formulaic sequences in second language teaching: Principle and practice. *Applied Linguistics*, 21, 463–489.

Wray, A. (2002). *Formulaic Language and the Lexicon*. Cambridge: Cambridge University Press.

Wray, A. (2009). Future directions in formulaic language research. *Journal of Foreign Languages*, 32, 2–17.

Zimmerman, C. B. (1997). Historical trends in second language vocabulary instruction. In Coady, J., and Huckin, T. (eds.) *Second Language Vocabulary Acquisition*. Cambridge: Cambridge University Press.

15

Critical pedagogy and teaching English to children

Mario E. López-Gopar

Introduction

Children from across the globe have been 'adding' English to their linguistic repertoire. In different parts of the world, English language teaching (ELT) differs tremendously in terms of historical, socioeconomic and political dimensions (Mohanty 2006; López Gopar 2016; Pennycook 2016). This addition of English, whether or not imposed by the educational system, to children's linguistic repertoire (López-Gopar, Núñez Méndez, Montes Medina and Cantera Martínez 2009) is by no means 'neutral', 'apolitical' or 'ahistorical' but rather inherently connected to discriminatory practices, social inequality, hegemonic power and identity negotiation in the aforementioned contexts (Chun 2015; López-Gopar 2014; Motha 2014). In order to address these issues and thereby resist the imperialistic nature of the English language (Canagarajah 1999), especially in the face of English being taught sub-tractively and resulting in social class division (López-Gopar and Sughrua 2014; Mohanty 2006; Ricento 2012), teacher educators, researchers and classroom teachers have found in critical pedagogy a theoretical starting point to critically analyse the effects of ELT around the globe. Grounding their teaching 'praxis' or otherwise 'reflection plus action' (Freire 1970) in the local contexts and physical realities of their students, many teachers resist the effects of the ELT industry and negotiate their and their students' identities within the search for social justice (Canagarajah 1999; Cummins 2001).

Critical pedagogy emerged from the work of several authors in Europe, North America, and South America (Kirylo 2013). Paulo Freire, a Brazilian educator, is widely considered the father of critical pedagogy. 'Freire's legacy is unprecedented for an educator: None other has influenced practice in such a wide array of contexts and cultures, or helped to enable so many of the world's disempowered turn education toward their own dreams' (Glass 2001, 15). Freire believed that every single person could teach us something, including students to teachers. Showing the world how much he had learned from the Brazilian peasants was Freire's greatest teaching.

Defining critical pedagogy remains a challenge and is open to contestation. According to Porfilio and Ford (2015), 'The question, "What is critical pedagogy?" is one that will elicit various and probably irreconcilable answers' (xv, quotations in original). Following from Freire (1970) who held critical pedagogy as a non-prescriptive method, educators have appropriated and reinvented critical pedagogy according to their own contexts as well as the lived experiences of their students. Hence, Porfilio and Ford (2015) from general education studies as well as Norton and Toohey (2004) from language education refer to critical *pedagogies* (in the plural) so as to acknowledge the multiple approaches and practices of educators and their students who are concerned with how to work against discriminatory practices and alleviate human suffering through pedagogy. Critical pedagogies are 'concerned with the ways that schools and the educational process sustain and reproduce systems and relations of oppression, [and how education] can also potentially be a site for the disruption of oppression' (Porfilio and Ford 2015, p. xvi). Critical pedagogies thus become 'an empowering way of thinking and acting, fostering decisive agency that does not take a position of neutrality in its contextual examination of the various forces that impact the human condition' (Kirylo 2013, p. xxi). Focusing on the education of young children, critical pedagogues attempt 'to create an equitable educational system and model where all classes, ethnicities, sexual orientations, nationalities, languages, and voices are included' (Christensen and Aldridge 2013, p. 5).

Although critical pedagogy and its connections to English language teaching have been theorised for the last three decades (Auerbach 1986; Canagarajah 1999; Cummins 2000, 2001; Pennycook 2001; Phillipson 1992; Peirce 1989; Norton and Toohey 2004), its introduction into classrooms with young learners has not been well documented or summarised. Hence, the purpose of this chapter is to provide an overview of different attempts to reinvent critical pedagogies in ELT classrooms with young students (K–6). To this end, in the following sections of this chapter, I provide a historical overview of critical pedagogies in education in general and their connection to ELT; address the critical problematisation of ELT; discuss current studies of critical pedagogies in ELT; present recommendations for critical ELT practice; and contemplate future directions of critical ELT. I begin with critical pedagogy in general.

Historical perspectives

Critical pedagogy as a recognised academic construct is relatively new. It began in the early-1970s, prompted by Freire's seminal work *Pedagogy of the Oppressed* (1970). Nevertheless, as Kirylo (2013) points out, 'the consciousness of it as a way of thinking and acting has been around through the ages' (xix). After Freire, several authors have followed in 'reinventing' critical pedagogy, naming it 'a pedagogy of love' (Darder 2002), 'transformative education' (Ada and Campoy 2004), 'transformative pedagogy' (Cummins 2000) and 'revolutionary pedagogies' (Trifonas 2000). In addition, Porfilio and Ford (2015) have identified three waves of critical pedagogy during the last five decades. These waves are not exclusive but rather overlap in time, while concurring on social justice as their main goal.

The first wave of critical pedagogy emerges from Freire's early work and the introduction of that work in education in North America during the 70s and 80s. In this first wave, according to Porfilio and Ford (2015), critical pedagogy 'inherited most directly the theoretical inclinations of the Frankfurt school and its insistence upon the centrality of class' (xvii, quotation in original). Using Marxism as his starting point, Freire (1970) focused on the notions of oppressor and oppressed from the perspective of social class while working with and for Brazilian peasants. In the area of ELT, also focusing on social class, Auerbach (1986) noticed that although ESL teachers were teaching students how to follow orders in low-paying jobs, they were not questioning the nature of those jobs. During this first wave,

Freire's work, along with that of Giroux (1988) and McLaren (1989), was criticised on the basis of its alleged deterministic view of social class, male-dominant theorization and failure to exemplify itself within an educative context (Crookes and Lehner 1998; Ellsworth 1989; Johnston 1999; Yates 1992). This last criticism, the avoidance of classroom application, resulted in the second wave of critical pedagogies.

The second wave began around the late 80s and early 90s and now included applied linguists questioning the 'neutral' role of the English language and the ELT industry around the world. At this time, as stated by Porfilio and Ford (2015), critical pedagogies embarked on two routes: the feminist/poststructural philosophy as well as the postmodern philosophy, both of which acknowledge class domination. The work of Jim Cummins with minority children in the late 80s falls into the second wave. By analysing why minority groups have failed in schools, Cummins (1986) realised that the work of critical pedagogy should focus on the relationships between educators, children and the children's families and thereby challenge the way these children are viewed from a deficit perspective in terms of their cultural and linguistic background. Valuing the linguistic background of children, Cummins questioned the notion of the 'English-only unproblematized school.' This type of critical stance was adopted by applied linguists as well.

Applied linguists developed their own critical pedagogies during the second wave by following or combining the two routes: the feminist/poststructural and postmodern philosophies. For instance, Graman (1988) criticised adult ESL classes. He argued that the exclusively linguistic-based instruction seemed irrelevant and non-engaging to students as it was not tied to the students' own lives. In more general terms, questioning the role of English as a globalised language, Phillipson (1992) argued that English had been spread for economic and political purposes and posed a major threat to other languages. In the late 90s, critical pedagogy in ELT again gained momentum with a special edition of *The TESOL Quarterly* entitled 'Critical Approaches to TESOL', edited by Pennycook (1999), as well as with the work of Canagarajah (1999) on resisting linguistic imperialism, Morgan (1998) on teaching grammar around community concerns, and Pennycook (2001) on critical applied linguistics. In addition, Norton and Toohey (2004) edited the book *Critical Pedagogies and Language Learning*, arguing that 'advocates of critical approaches to second language teaching are interested in relationships between language learning and social change' (1).

At the beginning of the twenty-first century and into the fourth and fifth decade of critical pedagogy, a third wave has begun to evolve. This wave returns to social class while maintaining the problematisation of 'underlying assumptions about the operations of power and oppression, ultimately leading to the inclusion of various forms of identity and difference' (Porfilio and Ford 2015, p. xviii) that were developed in the second wave. According to Porfilio and Ford (2015), the return to issues of class 'does not represent a retreat . . . [but] comes as a result of a resurgence of Marxist educational theorizing . . . and the economic crisis of 2007–2008' (xviii). This crisis gained the attention of educators in education in general and in ELT as they realised 'the devastating ways that processes of capitalist value production . . . can make and remake our daily lives' (Porfilio and Ford 2015, p. xviii) and the realities faced by young children in schools. Recently, in applied linguistics, different authors have also started to focus on social class (Block 2014; Block et al. 2012; Chun 2017). In addition, the work of López-Gopar and Sughrua (2014) on the connection of modernity/coloniality and social class within ELT emphasises the inherent role of ELT teachers as accomplices of class division if their teaching is not problematised.

To conclude this history of critical pedagogies, it can be said that 'the field of critical pedagogy now represents a constellation of insights from other intellectual fields, including feminist studies, environmental studies, critical race theory, cultural studies, and Indigenous studies' (Porfilio and Ford 2015, p. xviii). Critical pedagogy is now an intellectual bricolage of its three waves of development, without ignoring the issues faced by educators and children and their communities in their current sociopolitical contexts. These issues will be the focus of the next section, in which I expand on the focus of the third wave of critical pedagogies in connection to the introduction of ELT in primary schools worldwide.

Critical issues and topics

In the same way that critical applied linguists have criticised the 'neutral' role of the English language, the rapid spread of ELT in public elementary schools must be problematised, especially because it has become a world trend. Enever (2016) states: 'The unprecedented scale of reform in the rush towards English has been consolidated over the first two decades of the twenty-first century' (354). This rush to learn English raises important issues in terms of inherent ideologies and material consequences for the contexts and children. Such a rapid and seemingly non-reflective manner of ELT making its way into elementary schools seems fuelled by a neoliberal ideology that equates English with economic success (Pennycook 2016). When school administrators and parents decide to bring English into children's education, they base their rationale on the idea that English will open doors to a 'brighter' economic future. Indeed, Sayer (2015) documents how different language policies in different countries base the inclusion of ELT in elementary schools on 'national development and modernization' (China), 'economic development' (Malaysia), 'economic imperative' (Taiwan), '[i]nternationalization of Chilean economy' (Chile), 'developing human capital . . . [and] economic development of the country' (Bangladesh) and 'enhance[ment] of Vietnam's competitive position in the international economic and political arena' (Vietnam) (pp. 49–50). Sayer (2015) concludes these policies are 'couched strongly in a neoliberal discourse of economic development' (p. 50).

The neoliberal ideology behind ELT has been challenged and problematised. Pennycook (2006), for instance, points out the 'many myths about English as a "marvelous tongue"' and its 'exclusionary and delusionary effects' (p. 100–101, quotation marks in original). In terms of exclusion, Pennycook (2006) argues that the 'door opened' by the English language lets in very few people and leaves thousands of people out. In their analysis of social class and ELT in Mexico, López-Gopar and Sughrua (2014) state that in Mexico only 5% of the country can afford some sort of English education, ranging from elite bilingual elementary schools to private English institutes. Concerning the delusionary effect, most jobs in Mexico that require some level of English do not offer salaries much higher that those of other jobs that do not require English (López-Gopar and Sughrua 2014). This is also the case in other countries, such as Colombia, which promote English proficiency from an early age: 'the payoff of knowing English is almost inexistent for accessing the labour market, since only a very small percentage of jobs require bilingual proficiency and most of them are located in Bogotá, Colombia's capital' (Herazo Rivera, Jerez Rodríguez and Lorduy Arellano 2012, p. 209). These authors – as echoed by Block (2014), López-Gopar and Sughrua (2014), Mohanty (2006) and Ricento (2012) – conclude that bilingualism (English and Spanish) contributes to 'deepening the social educational inequity . . . that has traditionally existed in Colombia and Latin America in general' (209). Similarly, Lamb (2011) has found that ELT could widen the social class gap in Indonesia as higher-status children make more progress in English than do more disadvantaged children. Not only does ELT in primary schools impact social and economic inequality, but it also affects the minoritised languages in the local contexts. This is another issue to be problematised.

In the same way that ELT in elementary schools is connected to neoliberalism, ELT also juxtaposes with the local linguistic realities in which it is being implemented. The sole focus on English as a medium of instruction or as a second or foreign language has resulted in 'othered' languages being pushed aside. These languages become 'otherised' since they are perceived as inferior to English and not worthy to be learned or promoted through public and/or private funding (López-Gopar 2016). In other words, English has become the (only) language to learn. For instance, Indigenous languages such as Zapotec in Mexico, Quechua in Perú and many others abound in Latin American countries (Mejía 2009; Sayer 2015) as well as Asian countries (Spolsky and Moon 2012), yet in the elementary schools of these countries the teaching of additional languages remains primarily focused on English rather than on a multilingual approach allowing room for all languages. This phenomenom has had detrimental effects on minoritised and Indigenous languages (Rahman 2010). Indigenous language practices have been confined to private spaces and associated with shame while English is seen as progress and modernity.

The preponderance of English over 'othered' languages is tied to social class as well. Focusing on India in particular, Mohanty (2006) states, 'As the voiceless minorities suffer the sinister exclusion of mother tongues, the silent elites enjoy the pre-eminence of dominant languages, such as English' (5). Mohanty goes on to argue that 'English thrive[s] at the cost of other languages, and in many countries the myth of English medium superiority is propagated to the detriment of the poor and the marginalised' (p. 5). For example, as Mejía (2011) argues, in Colombia 'the development and promotion of one powerful language – English – is privileged at the expense of other languages which form part of the local language ecology' (14). Regarding English, othered languages and social class, Mejía further states that the elite bilingualism (English/Spanish) usually attained by the rich who can afford access to elite bilingual schools 'provides access to a highly "visible", socially-accepted form of bilingualism'; whereas other forms of bilingualism (Spanish/Indigenous languages or creoles) 'leads . . . in most cases to an "invisible" form of bilingualism in which the native language is undervalued and associated with underdevelopment, poverty and backwardness' (7–8, quotations in original). It seems important, though, to move away from this 'either, or' stance; that is, having to choose either an Indigenous or minoritised language or the English language. As Pennycook (2006) argues, the way forward is 'not so much in terms of language policies to support other languages over English but rather in terms of opposing language ideologies that construct English in particular ways' (112).

In opposing these ideologies, one should place ELT materials and textbooks on the table and subject them to critical scrutiny. ELT materials and textbooks, often forming the course programme, become the main or sole encounter with the English language for many children. This includes whatever content, worldviews and ideologies are behind and within the materials and textbooks. For this reason, critical linguists have paid particular attention to the discourses represented in ELT materials, especially because 'European and North American publishers exercise a powerful influence on ELT publishing globally' (Gray 2016, p. 96). In addition, as Gray (2016) further suggests, 'textbooks (when not produced locally) can be methodologically and culturally inappropriate' (97, parenthesis in original). McKay and Bokhorst-Heng (2008) take a more critical stance, arguing that in the same way the ideologies behind English has otherised languages, ELT materials tend to produce othered cultures, rendering these cultures inferior to the ones represented in the materials, which are 'portrayed as having modern and desirable behaviour' (184).

Regarding ELT materials used by children in Mexico, López-Gopar, Núñez Méndez, Montes Medina and Cantera Martínez (2009) conducted a critical analysis of *Inglés Enciclomedia*, one of the first attempts of the Mexican government to bring English into public elementary schools through the use of technology and textbooks that all Mexicans children nationwide were to use in order to learn English. Influenced by the US-style production of ELT materials, the software and textbooks used in this programme were designed and published in the USA. In this study, the authors discuss the example of an 'engineer' represented in a photograph by a white man who is being assisted by a black man, making the point that this seems to reinforce racialised discourses present in the USA (See Chun 2016, for a similar discussion related to didactic materials used in the teaching of English for academic purposes.) López-Gopar, Núñez Méndez, Montes Medina and Cantera Martínez (2009) conclude that these ELT materials used by millions of Mexicans focus on a fake reality far from the one experienced by children in Mexico and thereby allude to a supposed superiority of US ways of being and knowing that render Mexican children's own cultures as inferior.

Even though materials present hegemonic discourses of the English language, ELT materials are mediated by teachers and their interactions with the students. This makes room for resistance (Chun 2015, 2016) and carves out spaces for students' othered languages and cultures. This resistance, then, pushes back against the neoliberal ideology of ELT in elementary schools as well as the colonial legacy of the English language vis-à-vis Indigenous and minoritised languages. This seems achievable, at least as a full first step, by addressing ELT programmes, materials and teacher preparation from a critical perspective. This criticality is ongoing at the present time; and for that reason, in the next section, I describe various critical pedagogues' current studies that attempt to problematise the issues addressed above.

Current contributions and research

Current critical research on teaching English to children falls between the second and third waves of critical pedagogy, utilizing ethnographic and critical action research methodologies while incorporating new theories in education in general and applied linguistic in particular. In this section, I describe critical research projects decidedly not treating students as objects but rather as subjects of their own histories as well as experiencers of complex and emotional lives. These studies, in Lau's (2017) terms, attempt to 'illuminate . . . the complex shifting interstices between power, identities, and agency within the classroom and wider social environment' (77).

Current research projects in elementary schools reinvent critical pedagogy by challenging the monolingual and assimilationist ideologies prevalent in different societies while attempting to negotiate children's affirming identities. In Canada, Cummins and Early (2011) led the Multiliteracies Project. In this project, researchers collaborated with classroom teachers to explore the use of multimodalities in the creation of identity texts, which can be considered 'the products of students' creative work on perfomances carried out within the pedagogical space orchestrated by the classroom teacher' (Cummins and Early 2011, p. 3). The different case studies documented in Cummins and Early's (2011) edited collection (and also showcased online at www.multiliteracies.ca) prove that change can actually happen and that 'actuality implies possibility' (19). Hence, it is possible for minority students, usually viewed as deficient, to perform their 'identity as intelligent, imaginative and linguistically talented' (p. 4). For instance, in one case study included in the edited collection, the classroom teacher had three students collaborate to create a bilingual multimodal text entitled *The New Country*, which reflected the experience of an Urdu-speaking student who migrated to Canada. The girls in the study not only shared their linguistic resources and developed linguistic and literacy skills, but also invested their identities in this text, which made them feel proud that they were capable of authoring stories.

Building on the Multiliteracies Project, Stille (2016) conducted research in a multilingual and multicultural elementary school in a large Canadian city. By analysing the creation of children's migration stories, she concludes that '[l]anguage teaching and learning is not distinct from students' lived experiences . . . [which] tend to be interpreted according to monolingual, monocultural assumptions and educational practices' (p. 494). In another study, where a French teacher and an English teacher collaborated in a multi-age classroom (Grades 4–6) with children from different backgrounds, Lau et al. (2016) transgressed the monolingual hegemony by using both English and French and by adopting a literature-based curriculum and a critical literacy approach in order to address the issue of children's rights. They claim that 'students came to appreciate the importance of dynamic bi- and multilingualism,' acquired 'a nuanced and measured understanding of social prejudice as well as their own embodied fear and assumptions toward those in the social margins' and most importantly 'bec[a]me critical bilingual users to enact social change' (121). These studies, which move away from an English-only policy and which recognise and value students' bi-multilingual repertoires,

> give a larger purpose to language teaching and learning; such initiatives highlight openings and agentive social movements within which students and their teachers can enact change and resistance to dominant and potentially marginalizing monolingual, monocultural approaches to English language teaching.
>
> *(Stille and Prassad 2015, p. 619)*

Researchers in different parts of the world have also worked with children to go beyond the English-only ideology in order to promote multilingualism. Conteh and Meier (2014) brought together researchers from continental Europe, the UK, China, Mauritius, the USA and Australia who reflected on the possibilities and challenges of the multilingual turn in language education. As an example in Europe, Hélot (2016) as well as Hélot and Young (2006) report that mainstream/monolingual children begin to regard othered languages as interesting when they are introduced to the languages through meaningful class activities such as language and culture presentations by the parents or children who speak the othered languages. In language awareness projects, the human aspect is the *sine qua non* of the promotion of languages and interculturalism. Also, language awareness projects must be considered only the first step, and othered languages must become part of the curriculum should they not want to remain tokenistic. In this regard, Hélot (2016) concludes that language awareness could be instrumental 'in redressing the unequal balance of power between dominant and dominated languages, and between their speakers, only if it allows for a debunking of language ideologies and opens the door to a truly multilingual education for all students' (p. 12). In the USA, Woodley and Brown (2016) discuss how a teacher worked with a complex classroom, which they succinctly describe as: 'Eight home languages. Twenty-seven students. Twenty-seven levels of English language development, home language literacy, and content knowledge' (p. 83). By honouring and welcoming all students' languages into classroom, Woodley and Brown argue: 'All students deserve to hear what their classmates have to say about how they use languages. This can help to dispel stereotypes or negative perspectives about multilingualism' (p. 96).

Other critical researchers have been concerned with the role of English vis-à-vis Indigenous or minoritised languages. In Colombia, as mentioned above, the government has implemented the goal of making students bilingual in English and Spanish. Clavijo Olarte and González (2017) are therefore 'concerned with the role of English as a foreign language among Indigenous minority groups that arrive in Bogotá's public school because of forced displacements' (p. 431). By using a community-based pedagogy with a critical perspective, Rincón and Clavijo Olarte (2016) have started to meet the needs of Indigenous children and to teach English by engaging 'students in rich schooling experiences as a way to reconcile the curriculum with the real life of students within their communities' (p. 68). In Brasil, Ball (in press) has also been using English, and Portuguese, to address community issues important in chidren's lives by developing materials for the real world. These studies demonstrate that English can be used to discuss critical issues in children's lives. In China, Adamson and Feng (2014) looked at four different models for trilingual education including Mandarin, English and Indigenous languages. They conclude that English does not have a detrimental effect as long as the Indigenous language is maintained and the ethnic identity fostered. They also make the case against the neoliberal ideology prevalent in ELT, claiming that 'for a minority group the value of trilingual education goes beyond mere financial benefits to include greater confidence in one's culture and identity' (p. 41). In Mexico, for the last ten years, López-Gopar (2014, 2016) with the collaboration of other researchers as well as student teachers (López-Gopar, Jiménez Morales and Delgado Jiménez 2014) has attempted to teach English critically by developing the student-teacher's critical awareness about the myths of the English language and its connection to neoliberalism, social class, modernity and its alleged benefits for all. Using the teaching praxicum as an opportunity to dialogue with children, the student-teachers have used 'English in favor of Indigenous and *othered* children's way of knowing, culturing, languaging, and living' (López-Gopar 2016, p. 15, italics in original). They have developed critical thematic units, which are taught in English, Spanish and different Indigenous languages, to address important community issues such as water shortage, health and eating habits and discriminatory practices.

The studies summarised in this section are only some current examples of critical pedagogies in primary English language teaching. These studies demonstrate that researchers, teachers, student teachers and children have the agency to fight against discriminatory practices in ELT. Based on the studies presented in this chapter, in the following section I provide recommendations for practice that must be critically analysed, adapted and/or rejected according to each and every context.

Recommendations for practise

It is important, first of all, to remember that critical pedagogy is not a method to be prescribed and followed. It is a political stance and a humanistic position. Being critical means to truly believe in each student and her reflective and agentive capacity: 'Different children have different talents. No matter what form of knowledge they pursue, it should be valued and encouraged' (Christensen and Aldridge 2013, p. 86). It is also imperative to remember that critical pedagogy requires a hope that change, transformation and social justice will occur, especially in current times when groups of peoples and cultures are treated as second-class citizens. Furthermore, critical pedagogy is not about changing the world. It is about small things, and the small changes in a classroom that can make a student feel intelligent, creative and truly appreciated at that particular moment. The student, then, can hopefully go on to change the world.

Authoring identity texts should be one of the most important aspects of critical pedaogies. 'Language pedagogy in schools can be invigourated by an approach that emphasizes imagination, curiosity, and the growth of students' critical consciousness. These capacities can be developed as students learn to read and produce culturally relevant, *plurilingual* multimodal texts' (Stille and Prassad 2015, p. 620, my emphasis). In English classes where authorship is valued, English can be learned revolving around a common theme, health issues for instance. The teachers can focus on grammatical patterns and vocabulary needed to produce 'simple', yet powerful sentences, such as 'beans make me stronger and keep me healthy', which can later be part of a larger text such as books, posters or video story lines. In these classes, the children can also author these same texts in the languages they already know. Multimodal identity texts can work as a 'three-dimensional prism [that] refracts light into an infinite rainbow of possibilities' (Prassad 2016, p. 511). In addition, texts created in the classroom are able to challenge the 'othering' discourses present in ELT materials and textbooks. They also challenge the myths of the English language and present a different story to the world in a multimodal form and by way of English used together with othered languages. Finally, creating texts is feasible and economical as it goes against the neoliberal industry of ELT that has facilitated transnational publishing companies to profit from low-SES, middle-class people and outer-circle countries, such as Mexico, which desire English.

If child authors emerge in the classroom, then it is the children's own lives that drive the curriculum. Stille (2016) argues: 'Inviting students to bring the full range of their cultural and linguistic resources and diverse histories into the educational context potentially creates conditions for students to invest themselves into classroom activities and therefore support their language learning' (494). When curricula, locally produced materials and teaching strategies revolve around the child, the complex lives and realities of the children become part of the conversation. Children do not only become experts in the classroom, but they also become agents of change as they start talking about real problems in their communities and in their own lives. Hence, classroom walls move beyond the classroom and encompass the children's geographical and virtual communities. As Rincón and Clavijo Olarte (2016) state,

> students' communities provided alternatives for creating meaningful learning environments in the EFL classroom, transforming mechanical and decontextualized language practices into flexible ways to communicate what matters to students. When students are intellectually and emotionally engaged, better learning is achieved. (p. 80)

Once the children's lives become the curriculum, their languages and cultural practices share the classroom grounds along with an English language and culture, rather than being subjugated to the language and culture. Most children around the world have directly heard that their languages and culture are not welcome in the ELT classroom. Hence '[s]tudents need direct messages and encouragement to develop or regain interest and pride in using their home languages in school' (Stille et al. 2016, p. 499). When children's languages are welcomed into the classroom, both children and family members become the teachers, and the English teacher, the student. In critical pedagogies, teaching and learning must be a two-way avenue. English has been detrimental to othered languages, especially when it has been positioned in educational policy as the only language to learn. The critical ELT classroom, where the policy of English-only is changed to all-languages-and-semiotic-resources-welcome, can speak boldly against the ideology of English as the language of worldwide communication.

Future directions

Critical pedagogies in primary English language teaching owe a great deal to children, student teachers and teachers. Their voices, desires and feelings must be taken seriously should we not want critical pedagogy to be yet another grand narrative and imposition in their lives. In future research, both children and teachers should be co-researchers as well. In this way, as Pinter (2014) points out, childhood can be understood 'from children's own perspectives' (69). Pinter (2014) adds:

> As research is a type of collaborative social practice that is likely to impact on children's lives, it follows that children could be considered as co-researchers. Becoming co-researchers implies that adults need to hand over at least some of the control and responsibility.
>
> *(174)*

Not only must critical pedagogy make room for children's perspectives, but student teachers and teachers' voices must be heard and their daily educational and personal lives' constraints must be seriously addressed. ELT teachers reinvent real critical pedagogies on a daily basis by testing out their own theories and making immediate changes to their teaching practice. Researchers and teacher educators have a role as well. This role, however, is that of collaborator and not authoritarian. We must also understand that ELT teachers around the world are exploited (López-Gopar and Sughrua 2014), undervalued and denied job stability (Ramírez Romero et al. 2014). Once researchers and teacher educators acknowledge the realities currently faced by the ELT teacher, they can start developing respectful and collaborative research projects. Consequently, more studies will be needed to document these types of collaboration, especially now when millions of ELT teachers will soon be needed to supply the rush of ELT into primary and kindergarten school.

Further reading

1   Cummins, J., and Early, M. (Eds.). (2004). *Identity texts: The collaborative creation of power in multilingual schools*. Stoke on Trent: Trentham Books.
      This edited collection offers both a theoretical background and classroom examples regarding the construct of identity texts in different countries and at different educational levels.

2   Copland, F., and Garton, S. (Eds.). (2014). Special issue: Teaching English to young learners. *ELT Journal*, 68(3).
      This journal special issue includes different studies on ELT and children, covering a wide range of current topics and issues from different theoretical perspectives.

3   Pinter, A., and Zandian, S. (2014). 'I don't want to leave this room': Benefits of researching 'with' children. *ELT Journal*, 68(1), 64–74.
      This article focuses on the experience of two researchers who have conducted projects in which children have actively participated in and shaped the research activities in their own way.

Related topics

Difficult circumstances, reflective voices from South America, contexts of learning

References

Ada, A. F., and Campoy, I. (2004). *Authors in the Classroom: A transformative education process*. New York: Pearson.

Adamson, B., and Feng, A. (2014). Models for trilingual education in the People's Republic of China. In Zenotz, V., Gorter, D., and Cenoz, J. (eds.) *Minority Languages and Multilingual Education*. New York: Springer, 29–44.

Auerbach, E. (1986). Competency-based ESL: One step forward or two steps back? *TESOL Quarterly*, 20(3), 411–429.

Ball, S. B. (in press). Empowering socially-aware young learners in Brazil through content-based instruction. In Copland, F., and Garton, S. (eds.) *Voices from the Classroom: Insiders and outsides perspectives of young language learners*. Alexandria, VA: TESOL Publications.

Block, D. (2014). *Social Class and Applied Linguistics*. New York: Routledge.

Block, D., Gray, J., and Holborow, M. (2012). *Neoliberalism and Applied Linguistics*. New York: Routledge.

Canagarajah, S. (1999). *Resisting Linguistic Imperialism in English Teaching*. Oxford: Oxford University Press.

Christensen, L. M., and Aldridge, J. (2013). *Critical Pedagogy for Early Childhood and Elementary Educators*. New York: Springer.

Chun, C. (2015). *Power and Meaning Making in an EAP Classroom: Engaging with the everyday*. Clevedon: Multilingual Matters.

Chun, C. (2016). Addressing racialized multicultural discourses in an EAP textbook: Working toward a critical pedagogies approach. *TESOL Quarterly*, 50(1), 109–131.

Chun, C. (2017). *The Discourses of Capitalism: Everyday economists and the production of common sense*. New York: Routledge.

Clavijo Olarte, A., and González, A. P. (2017). The missing voices in Colombia Bilingüe: The case of Ebera Children's in Bogotá, Colombia. In Hornberger, N. (ed.) *Honoring Richard Ruiz and His Work on Language Planning and Bilingual Education*. Bristol: Multilingual Matters, 431–458.

Conteh, J., and Meier, G. (Eds.). (2014). *The Multilingual Turn in Languages Education: Opportunities and challenges*. Bristol: Multilingual Matters.

Crookes, G., and Lehner, A. (1998). Aspects of process in an ESL critical pedagogy teacher education course. *TESOL Quarterly*, 32(2), 319–328.

Cummins, J. (1986). Empowering minority students: A framework for intervention. *Harvard Educational Review*, 56(1), 18–36.

Cummins, J. (2000). *Language, Power and Pedagogy*. Toronto: Multilingual Matters.

Cummins, J. (2001). *Negotiating Identities: Education for empowerment in a diverse society*, 2nd ed. Los Angeles: California Association for Bilingual Education.

Cummins, J., and Early, M. (Eds.). (2011). *Identity Texts: The collaborative creation of power in multilingual schools*. Stoke on Trent: Trentham Books.

Darder, A. (2002). *Reinventing Paulo Freire: A pedagogy of love*. Boulder: Westview Press.

Ellsworth, E. (1989). Why doesn't this feel empowering? Working through the repressive myths of critical pedagogy. *Harvard Educational Review*, 59(3), 297–324.

Enever, J. (2016). Primary ELT. In Hall, G. (ed.) *The Routledge Handbook of English Language Teaching*. London: Routledge, 353–366.

Freire, P. (1970). *Pedagogy of the Oppressed*. New York: Continuum.

Giroux, H. (1988). *Schooling and the Struggle for Public Life: Critical pedagogy in the modern age*. Minneapolis: University of Minnesota Press.

Glass, R. D. (2001). Paulo Freire's philosophy of praxis and the foundations of liberation education. *American Educational Research Association*, 30(2), 15–25.

Graman, T. (1988). Education for humanization: Applying Paulo Freire's pedagogy to learning a second language. *Harvard Educational Review*, 58(4), 433–448.

Gray, J. (2016). ELT materials. In Hall, G. (ed.) *The Routledge Handbook of English Language Teaching*. London: Routledge, 95–108.

Hélot, C. (2016). Awareness raising and multilingualism in primary education. In Cenoz, J., and Hornberger, N. (eds.) *Encyclopedia of Language and Education*. New York: Springer International Publishing, 1–15.

Hélot, C., and Young, A. (2006). Imagining multilingual education in France: A language and cultural awareness project at primary level. In García, O., Skutnabb-Kangas, T., and Torres-Guzmán, M. E. (eds.) *Imagining Multilingual Schools*. Toronto: Multilingual Matters, 69–90.

Herazo Rivera, J. D., Rodríguez, S. J., and Arellano, D. L. (2012). Opportunity and incentive for becoming bilingual in Colombia: Implications for Programa Nacional de Bilingüismo. *Íkala: Revista de lenguaje y cultura*, 17(2), 199–213.

Johnston, B. (1999). Putting critical pedagogy in its place: A personal account. *TESOL Quarterly*, 33(3), 557–565.

Kachru, B (1992) *The Other Tongue: English across cultures*. Urbana: University of Illinois Press.

Kirylo, J. D. (Ed.). (2013). *A Critical Pedagogy of Resistance: 34 Pedagogues we need to know*. Rotterdam, Netherlands: Sense Publishers.

Lamb, M. (2011). A 'Matthew Effect' in English language education in the developing world. In Coleman, H. (ed.) *Dreams and Realities: Devoloping countries and the English language*. London: British Council, 186–206.

Lau, S. M. C. (2017). Classroom ethnography on critical literacy teaching and learning. In Mirhosseini, S. A. (ed.) *Reflections on Qualitative Research in Language and Literacy Education*. Dordrecht, Netherlands: Springer, 77–90.

Lau, S. M. C., Juby-Smith, B., and Desbiens, I. (2016). Translanguaging for transgressive praxis: Promoting critical literacy in a multi-age bilingual classroom. *Critical Inquiry for Language Studies*, 14(1), 99–127.

López Gopar, M. (2016). *Decolonizing Primary English Language Teaching*. Bristol: Multilingual Matters.

López-Gopar, M. E. (2014). Teaching English critically to Mexican children. *ELT Journal*, 68(3), p. 310–320.

López-Gopar, M. E., Jiménez Morales, N., and Delgado Jiménez, A. (2014). Critical classroom practices: Using 'English' to foster minoritized languages and cultures. In Zenotz, V., Gorter, D., and Cenoz, J. (eds.) *Minority Languages and Multilingual Education*. New York: Springer, 177–200.

López-Gopar, M. E., Núñez Méndez, O., Montes Medina, L., and Cantera Martínez, M. (2009). Inglés enciclomedia: A ground-breaking program for young Mexican children? *Teaching English to Younger Learners [Special Issue]. Mextesol Journal*, 33(1), 67–86.

López-Gopar, M. E., and Sughrua, W. (2014). Social class in English language education in Oaxaca, Mexico. *Journal of Language, Identity and Education*, 13, 104–110.

McKay, S. L., and Bokhorst-Heng. (2008). *International English in its Sociolinguistic Contexts*. New York: Routledge.

McLaren, P. (1989). *Life in Schools*. New York: Longman.

Mejía, A. M. de (2009). Teaching English to young learners in Colombia: Policy, practice and challenges. *Mextesol Journal*, 33(1), 103–114.

Mejía, A. M. de (2011). The national bilingual programme in Colombia: Imposition or opportunity? *Conference Special Issue of Apples-Journal of Applied Language Studies*, 5(3), 7–17.

Mohanty, A. (2006). Multilingualism of the unequals and predicaments of education in India: Mother tongue or other tongue? In García, O., Skutnabb-Kangas, T., and Torres Guzmán, M. E. (eds.) *Imagining Multilingual Schools*. Clevedon: Multilingual Matters, 262–283.

Morgan, B. (1998). *The ESL Classroom: Teaching, critical practice and community development.* Toronto: University of Toronto Press.

Motha, S. (2014). *Race, Empire, and English Language Teaching: Creating responsible and ethical anti-racist practice.* New York: Teachers College Press.

Norton, B., and Toohey, K. (Eds.). (2004). *Critical Pedagogies and Language Learning.* Cambridge: Cambridge University Press.

Peirce, B. N. (1989). Toward a pedagogy of possibility in the teaching of English internationally: People's English in South Africa. *TESOL Quarterly*, 23(3), 401–420.

Pennycook, A. (1999). Introduction: Critical approaches to TESOL. *TESOL Quarterly*, 33(3), 329–348.

Pennycook, A. (2001). *Critical Applied Linguistics.* Mahwah, NJ: Lawrence Erlbaum Associates.

Pennycook, A. (2006). The myth of English as an international language. In Makoni, S., and Pennycook, A. (eds.) *Disinventing and Reconstituting Languages.* Cleveland: Multilingual Matters, 90–115.

Pennycook, A. (2016). Politics, power relations and ELT. In Hall, G. (ed.) *The Routledge Handbook of English Language Teaching.* London: Routledge, 26–37.

Phillipson, R. (1992). *Linguistic Imperialism.* Oxford: Oxford University Press.

Pinter, A. (2014). Child Participant Roles in Applied Linguistics Research. *Applied Linguistics*, 35(2), 168–183.

Porfilio, B. J., and Ford, D. R. (2015). Schools and/as barricades: An introduction. In Porfilio, B. J., and Ford, D. R. (eds.) *Leaders in Critical Pedagogy: Narratives for understanding and solidarity.* Boston, MA: Sense Publishers, xv–xxv.

Prassad, G. (2016). Beyond the mirror towards a plurilingual prism: Exploring the creation of plurilingual 'identity texts' in English and French classrooms in Toronto and Montpellier. *Intercultural Education*, 26(6), 497–514.

Rahman, T. (2010). A multilingual language-in-education policy for indigenous minorities in Bangladesh: Challenges and possibilities. *Current Issues in Language Planning*, 11(4), 341–359.

Ramírez Romero, J. L., Sayer, P., and Pamplón Irigoyen, E. N. (2014). English language teaching in public primary schools in Mexico: The practices and challenges of implementing a national language education program. *International Journal of Qualitative Studies in Education*, 27(8), 1020–1043.

Ricento, T. (2012). Poltical economy and English as a 'global' language. *Critical Multilingualism Studies*, 1(1), 31–56.

Rincón, J., and Clavijo-Olarte, A. (2016). Fostering EFL learners' literacies through local inquiry in a multimodal experience. *Colombian Applied Linguistics Journal*, 18(2), 67–82.

Sayer, P. (2015). 'More & earlier': Neoliberalism and primary English education in Mexican public schools. *L2 Journal*, 7(3), 40–56.

Stille, S (2016). Identity as a site of difference: Toward a complex understanding of identity in multilingual, multicultural classrooms. *Intercultural Education*, 26(6), 483–496.

Stille, S., Bethke, R., Bradley-Brown, J. Giberson, J., and Hall, G. (2016). Broadening educational practice to include translanguaging: An outcome of educator inquiry into multilingual students' learning needs. *Canadian Modern Language Review*, 72(4), 480–503.

Stille, S., and Prassad, G. (2015). 'Imaginings': Reflections on plurilingual students' creative multimodal texts. *TESOL Quarterly*, 49(3), 608–621.

Trifonas, P. (2000). Introduction. In Trifonas, P. (ed.), *Revolutionary Pedagogies.* London: Routledgefalmer, xi–xxi.

Woodley, H. H., and Brown, A. (2016). Balancing windows and mirrors: Translanguaging in a linguistically diverse classroom. In García, O., and Kleyn, T. (eds.) *Translanguaging with Multilingual Students: Learning from classroom moments.* New York: Routledge, 83–99.

Yates, L. (1992). Postmodernism, feminism and cultural politics or, if master narratives have been discredited, what does Giroux think he is doing? *Discourse*, 13, 124–133.

16

CLIL in the primary school context

Maria Ellison

Introductions and definitions

As foreign languages are increasingly being introduced into pre-school education and have become compulsory in more primary school curricula, questions about what is appropriate and effective methodology for teaching them at this educational level naturally arise. This is particularly pertinent given the widely held belief that children best acquire language when they are immersed in contexts where there is natural exposure and opportunities for authentic use of it for other learning, rather than when it is taught as a separate and sometimes 'isolated' subject. This brings into question the role of a foreign language in primary education and is one of the reasons why Content and Language Integrated Learning (CLIL), 'an educational approach in which an additional language is used for the learning and teaching of both content and language' (Coyle et al 2010, p. 1), could be considered suitable, not only for enhancing the development of foreign languages in such contexts, but of fulfiling broader, more far-reaching educational goals. In this chapter, young learners (YLs) are those aged between 6 and 10 years.

Content and Language Integrated Learning (CLIL) is a complex phenomenon. This is in part due to the range of interpretations across contexts which have led to the acronym being considered something of a generic umbrella term under which may be included, somewhat controversially, 'immersion', 'bilingual education' and 'content based instruction' (for discussions on this, see Pérez Cânado 2016;Cenoz et al 2014; Dalton-Puffer et al 2014). CLIL is about teaching school curricular content through the use of an *additional* or *vehicular* language. This language may be a foreign language, other national language or minority or heritage language. Aims for introducing CLIL may relate to improving performance in, developing positive attitudes towards or 'reviving' this language. In this chapter, the additional language referred to is English, which is also taught as a foreign language in many primary school contexts. In CLIL, pupils are learning content *and* language in a dual-focused way. This normally requires methodological shifts in practice which go beyond simply changing the medium of instruction. In the primary school context, CLIL could involve learning about a science topic through English, for example, food chains, habitats or electrical circuits. The same content would not be pre- taught in the mother tongue. The teacher would make the content as explicit and accessible as possible to learners using a range of means and resources to teach key terms, principles and processes. He or she would create opportunities for the learners to apply new knowledge and express their understanding using the additional language, providing them with appropriate support when necessary. In CLIL, the use of the additional language can make teaching and learning more engaging and cognitively challenging for both children and teachers, i.e., both have to think a lot more!

The amount of CLIL will depend on the school context—this could mean entire subject areas taught through English over one or more academic years or modules or topics within curricular areas amounting to short sequences of lessons. Teaching objectives for CLIL may be more content or language oriented. The former is often referred to as 'hard' or 'strong' CLIL, and the latter, 'soft' or 'weak'. Hard/strong CLIL focuses on the development of the knowledge, skills and understanding of the content area (e.g., geography) and as such is 'content-driven'. Soft/weak CLIL is 'language-driven' and is what foreign language teachers do when they bring content or techniques from other curricular areas such as maths and science into their lessons as in cross-curricular and theme/activity-based approaches to language teaching (see Halliwell 1992; Vale and Feunteun 1995; Cameron 2001; Brewster et al 2007). In most CLIL contexts, separate lessons in the additional language are also part of the school curriculum.

CLIL draws on second language acquisition theories relating to exposure to language through comprehensible input and opportunities for interpreting meaning and use in risk-free, naturalistic contexts (Krashen 1982; Coonan 2005), and socioconstructivist and socio-cultural approaches to learning where children are supported by the teacher or their peers whilst they work together to construct knowledge and understanding mediated through the additional language (Vygotsky 1978; Lantolf 2002). The limited number of English language lessons for YLs in some contexts may mean that fewer opportunities are provided for activities involving learning by doing. Lessons may focus on vocabulary learning at the word level with little genuine communicative purpose in activities which are cognitively undemanding. Any teaching of YLs at school, whether using the mother tongue or foreign language, needs contextualised content from the 'real' context of school so that it becomes meaningful and relevant. If this is absent, there may be an abstraction of the language itself (Snow et al 1989, p. 202). CLIL for YLs provides opportunities to learn curricular content whilst capitalising on the inhibition, curiosity and appetite for discovery of many children, which provide the momentum for learning.

CLIL in the primary context can support holistic development and interdisciplinary learning when there is a combined focus on what have come to be known as the 4Cs of CLIL: content, communication, cognition and culture, all of which make it compatible with the default *integrationist* ethos of primary education. For CLIL to be CLIL there is a 'planned pedagogic integration' of the 4Cs (Coyle et al. 2010, p. 6). It is said that this gives CLIL its 'added value'. The 4Cs may be viewed as a set of principles, a curriculum and a framework for lesson planning, as can be seen in Figure 16.1.

Content consists of the main concepts, knowledge and skills of the subject area, so from the science topic *electricity*, this could be understanding how a battery-powered electrical circuit works. Children may be involved in constructing one in small groups and then predicting and testing which materials conduct electricity. The content determines the language which will be used both to transmit and construct knowledge and express understanding i.e., **Communication.** This may be categorised in terms of key subject terminology, *language of learning* or *content obligatory language*, and the language with which this combines within any given curricular area, *language for learning* or *content compatible language*, such

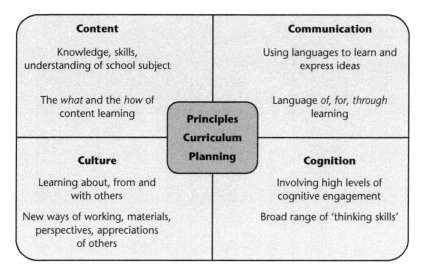

Figure 16.1 CLIL: the 4Cs Principles, curriculum and framework for planning (drawing on Coyle 2002; Coyle et al. 2009; Coyle et al. 2010)

as functional exponents for defining, predicting and explaining, which may be common, though not exclusive to the subject. So for electrical circuits this would be the language for the parts of the circuit, the principles behind how the circuit works and the language for experimenting with materials within it. This is language required of the topic/subject area. It is not 'graded' nor does it follow a pre-set order as in a grammatical hierarchy, which is often the procedure in teaching English as a foreign language. However, language *of* and *for* learning are predictable, and support for them can be planned and provided during lessons. In addition, there is the language learners use when interacting with each other and the teacher to express their learning – language *through* learning. This is less predictable; it is the language that emerges when learners are immersed in tasks in which they apply new understandings which challenge their thinking. **Cognition** plays a key role in CLIL. Learners should be given opportunities to think about content in different ways so that they may exercise both lower and higher order thinking skills in order to achieve a deeper level of understanding. This will be enhanced if their thoughts and ideas are shared with others in the additional language. This implies collaboration and cooperation with their peers in group tasks within and sometimes beyond the classroom. **Culture** embraces the classroom as a *community* for learning and supports *intercultural dynamics*, which nurtures an appreciation of oneself and the potential for understanding and appreciating others. In sum, CLIL may be considered a unique 'multidimensional approach connecting different goals within the same conceptualization' (Ruiz de Zarobe 2013, p. 234). Table 16.1 illustrates a teacher's planning of the 4Cs for a lesson about food chains for a class of eight- and nine-year-olds. It is the third in a sequence of lessons which follows on from ones about animal habitats.

CLIL may be taught by primary generalist teachers who have a high degree of functional competence in English or English language teachers who have a very good knowledge of the curricular content. It requires methodological shifts from both types of teacher in order to accommodate the dual focus so that they become content- and language-sensitive. Ideally, within any given CLIL context, both types of teacher should plan CLIL lessons and design materials together, since each offers a necessary high degree of expertise in their

Table 16.1 A teacher's 4Cs planning based on the framework of Coyle et al (2010, pp. 80–81)

Unit: 'Animal world' – LESSON 3	LEVEL: *Third Grade*	TIMING: *60 minutes*

Teaching Aims

- To recall previous knowledge (revision of what a habitat is)
- To introduce vocabulary related to food and animals
- To make students aware of what they already know about animals' food
- To teach how we classify animals according to their eating habits (carnivores, herbivores . . .)
- To introduce the notion of food chain, producers, consumers and predators
- To develop Ss' listening and speaking skills

Learning Outcomes

By the end of this lesson learners will be able to:

- classify animals according to what they eat (herbivore, carnivore, insectivore, omnivore)
- understand the concept of a food chain
- create their own food chain
- use familiar and new language for learning

Assessment Criteria

Teacher and learner assessment of learning to:

- identify what animals eat
- classify animals according to what they eat
- match definitions with words
- understand what a food chain is by building one on their own
- co-operate with his/her colleague
- participate in all tasks and activities

4Cs Objectives

Content

- The concept of food chain
- Animal eating habits
- What producers, consumers and predators are in a food chain

Cognition

- Classifying animals according to their eating habits
- Comparing animals
- Understanding what a food chain is
- Applying their knowledge to construct a food chain

Culture/Community

- To understand that animals have their own way of life as we do
- To respect animals and the differences between them
- To understand that animals need to eat each other to survive
- To appreciate that we can learn from and with each other in class

Communication

Language of Learning	Language *for* Learning	Language *through* Learning
Key Vocabulary:	*Frogs **eat** insects.*	Making statements
Animals: spider, grasshopper, hawk, frog, rabbit, fox, goat, kangaroo, snake, pig, penguin, parrot, fish, whale, lion, bird, elephant, horse, zebra, polar bear, shark, camel, giraffe	***They are** insectivores.*	Asking questions
	***I think** lions **eat** meat.*	Understanding and applying new language with already known language
Food: meat, fish, grass, plants, insects	**Asking/answering questions**	Using language from their own and other resources
Categories of animal eating habits	*What do lions eat?*	
carnivore, herbivore, insectivore, omnivore, food chain, consumer, producer, predator	*Can a carrot eat a rabbit? No*	

subject area which is essential to integrated learning in CLIL. All primary CLIL teachers need a good understanding of the theories of child development, how children acquire languages and the objectives of curricular areas.

Historical perspectives

The use of additional languages as tools for other learning is not a recent phenomenon. In fact, it can be traced back to ancient civilizations as empires expanded and the privileged sections of society were educated in these languages in order to reap the benefits of newly acquired territories (Mehisto et al. 2008, p. 9; Coyle et al. 2010, p. 2).

In more recent times, learning through additional languages has been propelled by a number of factors related mainly to social and economic change brought about by globalization which have made them decidedly less a luxury and commodity of the elite, and more an entitlement of the mainstream (Coyle et al. 2010, pp. 6–9; Pérez-Cañado 2012, p. 315).

The term 'CLIL' was first used in 1994 to describe what was considered to be a distinctly European phenomenon which responded to the need to support languages education and enhance plurilingualism in the continent where its increasingly mobile populations, hugely diverse in cultures and languages, need to communicate more effectively in more than one language. The drive towards this was manifest in European policy statements including the Commission's white paper of 1995, 'Teaching and Learning: Towards the Learning Society' followed by the announcement at the Barcelona European Council that 'every European citizen should have meaningful communicative competence in at least two other languages in addition to his or her mother tongue' (MT + 2) from an early age which was to become part of the Action Plan 2004–2006, 'Promoting Language Learning and Linguistic Diversity' (for an in-depth account of European policy initiatives relating to CLIL, see Marsh 2013). Realising the MT + 2 ideal in schools was an operational challenge. Some member states increased the number of foreign language lessons at higher levels of schooling and others lowered the onset of learning to primary school. CLIL was seen as a pragmatic solution to this essentially language problem. Teaching subjects through additional languages would provide more exposure and raise motivation in them through immediate application and authentic use, hence the subsequent and oft-cited mantra 'learn now, use now'. This is summed up well by Coyle et al. (2006, p. 26) who state that 'CLIL is not only a pragmatic solution to curriculum delivery but also an essential feature of an entitlement to plurilingual, pluricultural learning, offering cohesion and progression in the language learning apprenticeship.'

Some advocates of CLIL have drawn parallels with French immersion programmes such as those set up during the 1960s in Canada. The positive results of scholarly research into these programmes has often been used to justify implementing CLIL in European contexts. However, comparisons have also been dismissed on the grounds of very distinctive contextual and pedagogic differences (for discussions on this topic, see Zarobe and Cenoz 2015; Cenoz et al 2014; Dalton-Puffer et al 2014).

Many projects implementing and developing CLIL in Europe have been endorsed as have publications disseminating CLIL activity, such as the Eurydice report 'Content and Language Integrated Learning at School in Europe' (2006), which documented the variation in CLIL practices across the continent. In the survey report, 'Key Data on Teaching Languages at School in Europe 2017' (Eurydice 2017), CLIL is described as part of mainstream provision in nearly all European countries across educational levels although it is not widespread.

Even though considered a European construct, CLIL is practised in its many guises around the world. In South America there is reported CLIL activity in Argentina (Bandegas 2011) and also in Colombia (McDougald 2015) from where the *Latin American Journal of Content and Language Integrated Learning* (LACLIL) emerged. As English language education for YLs continues to expand in East Asia (see Marsh and Hood 2008; Butler 2015), interest in CLIL is growing across educational levels as is evident from studies in Japan (Yamano 2013; Pinner 2013), China (Wei and Feng 2015) and the challenges of pilot projects such as that in Thailand (Suwannoppharat and Chinokul 2015; MacKenzie 2008), the Phillipines (Miciano 2008) and Malaysia (Yassin et al. 2009), where it is increasingly becoming part of ministry of education initiatives to develop English language proficiency.

Critical issues and topics

Language development and cognitive maturity

Concerns regarding CLIL with young learners relate to understanding key concepts in the curricular area and the parallel development of these with the mother tongue.

In school contexts, children need to develop language to express their understanding of specific academic content. Their ability to do this may be referred to as Cognitive Academic Language Proficiency (CALP). This runs alongside the development of language for general communication known as Basic Interpersonal Communicative Skills (BICS). These terms were coined by Cummins (1979; see also Cummins 2008), who also stated that CALP is part of a 'common underlying proficiency' of skills which once learned in one language should be transferable to any other. This theory has consequences in relation to 'cognitive maturity' to learn through another language, with older children considered to be more advantaged as CALP would have had more time to develop in their first language (Pinter 2011, p. 75). Since it is thought that CALP takes five or more years to develop in the child's mother tongue, there are concerns as to whether it is appropriate to introduce CLIL at a very young age before such proficiency has had time to develop.

However, there are scholars who believe that such a rigid dichotomy between BICS and CALP is not helpful as 'language relates to the situation, context and purpose of use' and that with age-appropriate support for the understanding of content, learners may 'move from academic to colloquial and vice versa' until content is processed and conceptualised (Meyer et al 2015, pp. 50–51). Ball et al. (2015, p. 62) put it in a similar way stating that '[e]ffective CLIL harnesses CALP, makes it salient, then practices and balances it through the calming influence of BICS'. The simple fact is that 'CLIL involves learning to use language appropriately while using language to learn effectively' (Coyle 2006, p. 9) which is a clear endorsement for CLIL at any age.

As a plurilingual approach, CLIL is accepting of the mother tongue in the classroom. Used strategically, this can be a useful tool and resource. It is quite common for there to be codeswitching within and between utterances and translanguaging with the child's own language and the additional language of CLIL, particularly at the beginning of a CLIL programme. Language-sensitive CLIL teachers will be aware of this, and actively accommodate it in their classes. They need to be aware of how they may employ effective scaffolding to support the development of both whilst not compromising either. Progress in CLIL may be slower than when content is taught in the mother tongue as teachers find that they need to provide for more varied, strategic input and opportunities for practical expressions of understanding. Modular CLIL, in which a part of a subject or topic is taught through English which alternates with other parts taught through the mother tongue allows for content knowledge to be recycled in the mother tongue, thus allaying fears of any detriment to either.

Scaffolding learning

The term 'scaffolding' is frequently used in education to describe the temporary support given to learners in order to help them develop understanding of key concepts and reach learning outcomes. It is part of a

> process that enables a child or novice to solve a problem, carry out a task or achieve a goal which would be beyond his unassisted efforts. This scaffolding consists essentially of the adult 'controlling' those elements of the task that are initially beyond the learner's capacity, thus permitting him to concentrate upon and complete only those elements that are within his range of competence
>
> *(Wood et al. 1976, p. 90).*

Scaffolding is frequently associated with Vygostky's Zone of Proximal Development, the distance between what a child can do alone and what they can do with the help of a capable other (Vygotsky 1978, p. 86). Inherent in this is the concept of learning as part of a socially constructed process in which children learn from and with each other, to understand, develop skills, create new knowledge or 'transform understandings' for themselves (Hammond and Gibbons 2001, pp. 12–13).

In CLIL, scaffolding is a complex process for the teacher given the need to achieve the right balance of cognitive and linguistic demands when creating materials and during lesson delivery without compromising on the content concepts. It requires planned action at 'macro-level' and flexibility in practice or 'micro-level' 'moment-to-moment' support (Walqui 2006, p. 159). A range of strategies should be considered so that support is given to all areas of development. Strategies which come from both content teaching and language teaching can be drawn upon. For young learners these should be concrete, multisensory and multimodal so as to take account of cognitive development, how children experience the world and their natural desire to be active meaning makers. Language teaching strategies include modifying language, use of cognates, repetition, recasts, stressing key words during spoken discourse and providing visual stimuli and graphic organisers to support understanding of written texts (see Massler et al. 2011, for a range of techniques related to verbal, content and learning process scaffolding). Children's thinking can be scaffolded through, for example, strategic use of graded questions which support different types of thinking demanded by school curricula, from checking knowledge through closed questions to gradually using more open-ended questions which engage children in applying, analyzing and evaluating as associated with taxonomies of cognitive processes (see Bloom 1956; Anderson and Krathwohl 2001). Teachers may encourage children to use a range of means to express their knowledge and understanding; these may be verbal and non-verbal and could include the use of mime, gestures and drawings. Table 16.2 presents an accumulative taxonomy of scaffolding strategies compiled from observations of CLIL lessons in primary contexts and studies of the literature. It is intended for use by CLIL teacher educators for observation of CLIL lessons and may be used by teachers as a checklist in the planning stage in order to raise consciousness of the need for scaffolding before and during lesson delivery.

Table 16.2 Taxonomy of scaffolding strategies for CLIL lessons (Ellison 2014, p. 414)

Planning

- aims for 4Cs (content, communication, cognition, culture)
- anticipates language demands: language for/of/through learning
- builds on prior learning
- anticipates learning demands: appropriate sequencing of tasks from lower to higher order thinking skills; linguistic and content demands balanced
- considers a variety of interaction patterns

Materials

- makes appropriate choices for developmental level (content and language)
- uses visuals, realia, technology, film to support learning
- language is supported (e.g., simplified, key words highlighted/underlined)
- cognition is supported (e.g., use of diagrams, pictures which show relationships between key ideas)
- materials are balanced in terms of language and cognitive demands

Delivery of lesson

Teacher's language

- models language accurately and clearly with good pronunciation
- demonstrates knowledge of subject-specific language
- translanguaging and codeswitching – can decide when to use L1 effectively

Teacher talk: modifying language

- modifies delivery
- lengthens sounds
- stresses key words
- uses repetition
- modifies vocabulary (e.g., use of synonyms/antonyms)
- organises input (e.g., signals/use of discourse markers)
- uses variety of questions to guide/develop understanding, support and check learning, promote thinking from lower order to higher order, e.g., guided display/convergent questions; declarative with rising intonation; tag questions; referential

Communicative functions to support learning

- gives clear instructions
- monitors and repairs
- backtracks when problems are encountered
- uses functional exponents appropriately for explaining, describing, emphasizing, exemplifying, comparing, paraphrasing, summarizing, consolidating – demonstrating again, reminding, repeating, reviewing
- uses comprehension checks for students to demonstrate understanding of meaning and form
- uses variety of feedback techniques to check content message and language
- applies corrective strategies which support learning, e.g., facial expression, questions, auto/peer correction
- praises students' efforts

(*Continued*)

Table 16.2 (Continued)

Supporting content and cognition

- establishes 'route' for the lesson, e.g., tells learners about the 'topic' at beginning of the lesson
- establishes patterns of input/systematic routine in presentation and feedback
- exposes students to input at a challenging level
- explains concepts and processes in ways appropriate to the level of the class, using simple language and familiar/concrete examples
- breaks complex information into smaller simpler parts and tasks into clear steps
- pauses to enable thinking time
- uses body language, visuals, diagrams, gestures, realia to support understanding
- provides demonstrations with accompanying language
- elicits/draws on prior knowledge/experience
- supports lower order and higher order thinking skills such as remembering, understanding, applying, analyzing, evaluating, creating
- provides opportunity to negotiate meaning
- provides opportunities for students to learn from and with each other

Supporting language/communication

- provides language *of* and *for* learning
- raises awareness of language form in speech and writing
- hints using initial letter or sound
- models key words in isolation and context
- echoes correct examples
- raises awareness of pronunciation and provides opportunities for practice, e.g., in mini-drills
- encourages students' productive use of language in class, pair and groupwork
- provides written models of language (key words/structures), e.g., in substitution tables
- allows children to use L1 to communicate when their L2 productive language is limited.

Assessment

Assessment of young learners in primary education is multifaceted. This is due to the range of subject areas which primary education includes and the integration of their multiple literacies, as well as the development of positive behaviours and attitudes to learning, all of which are the responsibility, in many contexts, of a single generalist teacher. Such teachers will likely be adept at integration-enhanced assessment, and good practice may well include formative or learning-oriented techniques, which allow for regular monitoring of the various facets within this holistic development.

CLIL brings another layer of complexity to assessment because of the dual focus attributed to the approach where content and language are often envisaged as equally weighted, separately assessable subjects (Ball et al. 2015, p. 214). Another issue is the extent of integration at any one time in CLIL; there may be times where there is more of a focus on language and others which focus more on content, which may also depend on the model of CLIL adopted (whether soft or hard). Commonly voiced questions are: 'What should I assess here – just the content; content *and* language?' As Genesse and Hamayan (2016, p. 100) state when planning content and language objectives for CLIL lessons:

> you can rarely focus on one without the other. Because students are learning new concepts through a language in which they are not fully proficient, it is necessary to make

sure that they are familiar with the language that is needed to learn about academic content topics or themes.

Knowing the technical terms to label an electrical circuit, for example, is important language in primary science which children need to know in order to explain how the circuit works. An added difficulty is how to interpret learner responses. Does an incomplete or inaccurate answer reveal a lack of content knowledge, language or lack of understanding of the rubric itself? Good practice in assessment aligns itself with specific learning outcomes, which in CLIL should reflect the 4Cs: content, communication (language), cognition (thinking skills) and culture (also community/cultures of learning which incorporate attitudes to learning, learning to learn and working with others).

What is important is that there is compatibility between learning objectives and methods with the *what* and *how* of assessment. It would be unfair, for example, to assess children's knowledge of the water cycle in L1 if they had been introduced to it in English. Methods of assessment therefore, should mirror classroom practices, i.e., the typical tasks and activities planned by the teacher in order to reach the desired learning outcomes. To this end, for young learners a blend of diagram completion, gap-fills, matching sentences and opportunities for more extended written or verbal answers may be employed. Assessment should not only be of a product of learning, but the process itself (Massler 2011, p. 120). Therefore, it should include group activities where children can be observed working cooperatively with each other. Learner engagement should be closely monitored as events unfold in acts of learning in the classroom. This may be done through focused observation using grids with specific criteria related to learning outcomes, which may function as checklists where progress is ongoing, recorded and dated. The use of individual or small group 'think alouds' may be considered where children can be observed verbalizing their thoughts or prompted to do so in L1 or L2. This, for instance, would afford the teacher the opportunity to identify instances of codeswitching – where there may be gaps in language knowledge and use.

Managing such assessment is not easy, especially where class sizes are large. A key here would be to focus assessment on smaller groups of children in turn. Where it is possible, other teachers, or language assistants who are familiar to the children, may also be involved in this procedure. Teachers may collaborate to assess children where there are parallel foreign language lessons, for example. Each teacher could assess separate foci. Children's engagement in dialogue with the teacher about their work and progress should be a regular part of primary practice as it enhances metacognitive awareness. This may be done in L1 or L2. A common practice involving all the class is the use of KWL charts (*what I know, what I want to know, what I learned*) or WALT and WILF statements (*We are learning to . . . What I'm looking for . . .*). Another is through written 'can do' statements which take into consideration the 4Cs. These may also be in L1.

The examples below are related to the digestive system and food chains:

For the digestive system:
I can label the organs of the digestive system.
I can identify the route within the digestive tract.
I can explain the function of the large intestine to my partner and my teacher.
For food chains:
I can categorise living things into omnivores, herbivores, carnivores and insectivores.
I can label elements in a food chain.
I can create a food chain on my own and explain how it works to my friends.

Scholars are in agreement that language should not be an obstacle for learners expressing their understanding of content knowledge (Ball et al. 2015, pp. 214–215; Coyle et al. 2010, p. 123). Teachers may attempt to get around the latter by offering a range of scaffolds, which may include rubrics in L1, or teacher reading aloud of rubrics or translating them into L1, visual representations and allowing children to respond through gesture, drawing, or even to choose the language they want to answer in if the focus is on content knowledge in summative tests (Massler 2011, pp. 119–121). As Coyle et al. (2010, p. 131) put it, 'we need to assess what students can do with support before we can assess what they can do without it'. The example in Table 16.3 below taken from a teacher's log illustrates the negotiation between teacher and learners before and during a mini-test (see Figure 16.2) intended to

Table 16.3 Teacher-learner negotiation of test procedure

The instructions given	*Their reactions*
– Write your name and class, and date – Silence, concentrate – If you have questions, raise your hands	They agreed with their heads (nodded) I used gestures

Their questions	*I answered*
They spoke in Portuguese. *(Before the test)*	
– *Teacher, will we write the name of the animals or will we have them in written form and is it only choosing the right option? I haven't memorised all of them.*	Don't worry. You have the names.
(During the test)	
– *Here do we have to draw arrows?*	– Yes.
– *What's 'monéki'?*	– I said the word correctly and she immediately recognised it.
– *In Exercise 5 is it the Food Chain?*	– Yes, it's the food chain.
– *In Exercise 6 is it just drawing or do we have to write the name of the animals*	– Just drawing, but you can write the names of the animals too, if you want . . . (I said this in Portuguese)
– *But I don't know how to write in English . . . .*	– Write in Portuguese
– *How do I write 'couve' in English? Can I write in Portuguese?*	– Yes.
– *In Exercise 6 do we have to draw the animals from Exercise 5?*	– No. You can draw what you want (said in English and Portuguese)
– *In Exercise 6 can I write the animal names in Portuguese, but if I know in English can I also write in English?*	– Yes.
– *In Exercise 6 is this eaten by this one or is it the other way around?*	– Remember the lesson. What do you think? (said in Portuguese)
– *In Exercise 4, what are the animals for?*	– Look, questions here . . .

Their reaction to the test *(They spoke in Portuguese)*	
SPOKEN – Just one sheet of paper – So easy, look! – Oh, we have here the words. – Oh, this exercise I don't understand (Ex. 6)	**NON – SPOKEN** – Looking at the test puzzled by Exercise 6 – Some were saying words silently to remember them

4. Look at these animals.

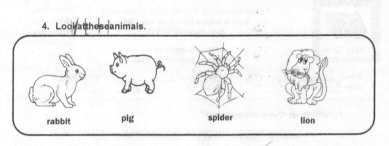

rabbit　　pig　　spider　　lion

4.1. Which animal is a carnivore? _lion_ ✓
4.2. Which animal is a herbivore? _rabbit_ ✓
4.3. Which animal is an insectivore? _spider_ ✓
4.4. Which animal is an omnivore? _pig_ ✓

5. Complete this FOOD CHAIN.

FOOD CHAIN

6. Draw your FOOD CHAIN.

lion　　rabbit　　erva

Figure 16.2 Sample test

check understanding and application of knowledge about food chains administered to eight- and nine-year-olds in a primary school in Portugal. Only part of the test is included. The comments reveal children's doubts about the test, which are mainly procedural and related to which language to use, and the degree and type of support given by the teacher.

Attempts have been made to provide supporting frameworks for assessment in CLIL. The CLILA project (CLIL Learner Assessment) developed a tool for the measurement of content and language ability of primary school pupils in CLIL lessons in German and Swiss primary schools (see Massler et al 2014). It is a 3-D tool based on the Common European Framework of Reference, descriptions of subject area competences, curricula of the subjects and their thematic categories. Xavier's (2015) framework for assessment in primary CLIL contexts is based on a learning-oriented approach which combines objectives for content, language, cognition (based on Bloom's taxonomy), learning to learn and behaviour/attitudes towards learning. The work comprises an in-depth study of assessment types and examples from primary CLIL practice.

In primary CLIL it is important to include a range of assessment types so that an all-round picture of learning emerges which may be used in the evaluation of the CLIL programme as a whole. Ultimately, the focus of assessment in any given context will be determined by the main goals of the programme.

Current contributions and research

Despite the growth of CLIL around the world, its research agenda has largely focused on secondary and tertiary education. There is still little research on CLIL with young learners. What exists in Europe largely consists of stakeholder responses to implementation in national pilot projects or grassroots initiatives (see, for example, the evaluation reports of the British Council Bilingual Projects in Spain (Dobson et al 2010) and more recently in Portugal (Almeida et al 2014), which point to generally positive results for young learners; Infante et al 2009 – Italy; Massler 2014 – Germany; Pladevall-Ballester 2015 – Catalonia). However, the lack of a strong evidence base clearly leaves CLIL vulnerable to criticism, and calls for further rigorous studies (Pérez-Cañado 2012; Bonnet 2012; Coyle 2013; Cenoz et al 2014; Murphy 2014) as well as more classroom-based research are frequent, not only about language development, but also 'subject matter knowledge, attitudinal and motivational approaches, cognitive development and brain research' Van de Craen et al (2007). More recent specialised studies that have emerged include comparative language use of EFL and CLIL learners (García Mayo and Hidalgo 2017; Yamano 2013); assessment (Xavier 2015); dimensions of teacher reflection (Ellison 2014); affect and cognition (Otwinowska and Forys 2015); and vocabulary learning (Tragant et al 2016).

Other contributions to the area of CLIL for young learners have come from European-financed projects involving consortia from various national contexts in the development of teaching and learning tools, sets of guidelines for implementation, teacher education and dissemination of good practices. Examples of these include TIE CLIL Translanguage in Europe – Content and Language Integrated, an early example of a teacher training guide for implementing CLIL in schools; 'EUCLID European CLIL in Development: A Primary Phase Consortium' (2008), which amongst other things focused on developing a profile for the primary CLIL teacher; PROCLIL which led to a set of guidelines for the implementation of CLIL in Primary and Pre-primary education (2011); and more recently 'CLIL for Children', a consortium which is developing an online training programme and materials for primary CLIL. Academic interest in CLIL continues to grow across the world with an increasing number of Special Interest Groups (SIGs), journals (e.g., *International CLIL*

Research Journal, Latin American Journal of CLIL), special editions of established publications, a research network (CLILReN) and conferences.

Recommendations for practice

Implementing CLIL

It goes without saying that any new pedagogic intervention in a school requires a great deal of prior reflection, teacher education and preparation of materials and tasks for lessons. CLIL is no exception. In fact, implementing CLIL needs the support of many stakeholders within and beyond the school community – parents, school directors, teachers (generalist and additional language), lower secondary schools in the area which the primary children will one day attend, faculty or governmental support agencies for external monitoring and teacher education, and other similar communities of practice in schools within the national context and further afield. This is because, as a 'complex whole approach' (Wolff 2002, p. 48), it will lead to change in the entire ethos of the school community.

A realistic set of goals and a coherent model that fits the context are essential. It must therefore be made clear to the entire school community why and how CLIL will be implemented. Modular CLIL is advisable at the start of a programme. This gives both teachers and children time to adapt and gain confidence in new ways of working. Depending on how the primary day is organised, modules may amount to one to three hours of lessons in a sequence over a week or two so as to complete a topic. This could be increased for another topic in another term. If the children also have separate English language lessons in the school then these lessons may provide 'language rehearsals' of key content language of and for learning. Both teachers should be given time to observe each other in order to identify key techniques and strategies used in each area which may come together in the CLIL classroom. Thus, a spirit of collaboration should be nurtured so that CLIL becomes a fusion of best practices from both primary and English language teaching. Both teachers may work together towards developing a literacy rich, plurilingual classroom environment which through bilingual displays and use of language demonstrates the importance of learning and acceptance and appreciation of languages and culture.

Planning CLIL lessons

A major part of ensuring quality in CLIL programmes is in lesson preparation. This requires a great deal of time and effort given the need to focus on the integration of content and the additional language in a way that maintains linguistic and cognitive challenge without diluting the subject content. An additional problem is that many teachers cannot rely on a ready-made supply of CLIL materials which will fit their context and national curriculum objectives. More often than not, teachers will need to either adapt or create their own materials for use with their learners. They should also be wary of materials labelled as CLIL in ELT coursebooks (Bandegas 2014). Whilst these will likely support the use of curricular content in English language lessons, they will not necessarily be developing key concepts and learning skills in the curricular area to the same extent, as the main objective will be to use content to enhance language development. For example, curricular content may be used in an ELT coursebook with the main purpose of practising simple dialogues using basic structures such as *do* in an exchange about what magnets attract. *Does the magnet attract the paper clip? Yes, it does. Does the magnet attract the piece of string? No it doesn't.*

The 4Cs may be used as a conceptual framework for planning lessons. A useful starting point is to identify the national curriculum targets for content in the specific area. Teachers should then formulate aims and learning outcomes based on these. Next, teachers may brainstorm the content area in light of each of the 4Cs. They must then decide on how best to sequence the elements of their schema into lessons which provide for a logical, coherent, cognitive route ensuring planned opportunities for the development of all 4Cs with appropriate scaffolding. This will involve planning for teacher input, and learner involvement. Activities, tasks and materials must be designed carefully so as to ensure that they are balanced in terms of cognitive and linguistic demands in accordance with the children's stage of development.

Throughout the planning process and well into lesson delivery, teachers should be conscious of the strategies they may use to scaffold all 4Cs. The attention to each of the 4Cs may vary within a sequence of lessons depending on how much new content or language is introduced. It may be useful to think of this in terms of a 'content and language familiarity and novelty continuum' (Coyle et al. 2010, p. 95) which will help to ensure balance between known and new, prevent language from becoming an obstacle and content knowledge from being diluted and oversimplified. There should be a steady increase in challenge as the lesson proceeds. The lesson plan below (Table 16.4) intended for eight- to nine-year-olds who have parallel EFL lessons serves to illustrate the above. It is the third in a sequence and was preceded by lessons about animal habitats.

Future directions

All over the world, young children are growing up with increasing amounts of exposure to many languages and as a consequence bring more knowledge and even experience of using them to primary school. With this comes an enhanced awareness of language as a tool for communication in all aspects of life including classroom use. For CLIL to be the 'added value' that it is claimed to be, there must be more investment in research for it in primary education, as well as a serious commitment to providing quality teacher education, particularly within pre-service programmes for future primary teachers and English language teachers, which include both theoretical modules and practica in schools. This is because CLIL:

- makes teachers aware of their responsibility to educate the 'whole' child';
- forces language teachers to look beyond language and address other essential learner needs;
- improves teachers' knowledge about the content of the primary curriculum;
- develops their understanding of the cognitive and linguistic demands of this level of education;
- develops awareness of the important role of language across the curriculum;
- unites language and primary generalist teachers in partnerships where they work together to achieve broad educational goals (adapted from Ellison 2015, p. 59).

Theoretical modules should contain an analysis of the knowledge bases of primary content areas and English language teaching for young learners focusing on the unique features and similarities of each as a basis for considering the fusion of these for CLIL. Applying the 4Cs to an analysis of the primary curriculum would be useful in determining demands in L1 medium instruction so that challenges may be realistic when planning for future CLIL lessons.

Table 16.4 Primary CLIL lesson plan on food chains

TEACHING/LEARNING ACTIVITIES

Time Interaction	Stage – Procedures	Aims	Scaffolding strategies
5 m T-Ss	**Lead-in** T starts by asking where animals live. Ss recall the definition of a habitat. T asks Ss how animals can survive. T waits for answers and then says that FOOD is very important.	To remind Ss of what they have previously learnt	Powerpoint with visuals and language
5 m T-Ss	T asks what animals eat. Some may say things like plants, meat. T tells Ss that it can be plants, meat or insects	To involve Ss in the topic and remind them that they already know some information	Using visuals in the PowerPoint to make the vocabulary clear
10 m Groups	**Thinking Task** T divides class in small groups and tells them they are going to discuss what animals eat and gives them a worksheet of visuals of animals and food to prompt them T asks groups to speak about this in the plenary by prompting them with questions such as, 'Do you think snails eat meat'? T asks: What do lions eat? T gives them a multiple choice task. Ss have to choose between plants, meat and insects.	To engage Ss in discussion with each other To make Ss think about what animals eat To give them time to speak and express their thoughts To consolidate understanding of concept and language	Provide language of/for learning in grid on the board Pause to enable students to think and speak
10 m T-Ss	**Thinking Task** T says that animals can be classified into herbivores, insectivores, carnivores and omnivores	To introduce categories of classifying animals according to food habits	Powerpoint Flashcards Worksheets
Pairs	T asks them to match these words with written definitions on flashcards on the board. T asks some students go to the board to match them. In pairs Ss complete a gap-fill of a diagram of the categories T provides feedback when checking the worksheet with Ss	To apply understanding of the categories and which animals belong to them To interpret the written form of words	

(Continued)

Table 16.4 (Continued)

TEACHING/LEARNING ACTIVITIES

Time Interaction	Stage – Procedures	Aims	Scaffolding strategies
10 m Individual work	**Introducing FOOD CHAIN** T shows visuals of grass, a rabbit and a fox and asks *Who do you think eats who?*	To make Ss think logically and apply what they already know.	Powerpoint Visuals and accompanying words to demonstrate the food chain
T–Ss	T explains that this is a FOOD CHAIN. *The grass is food for the rabbit and the rabbit is food for the fox.* T explains what a food chain is and gives an example	To apply what they have learnt To introduce new terminology	T points to the arrows in the food chain while explaining
Ss	T shows a picture of several food chains and asks Ss to explain who eats who T gives them time to explain T introduces the notion of *producers, consumers and predators* and explains what they are *Producers are food. They don't eat other plants or animals. Consumers eat. And the predator is at the top of the food chain.*		
10m Groups	**Practice** T gives each group some pictures of animals. Ss construct their own food chain using the pictures. Ss stick their food chains on the wall so that everyone can see them. They explain their food chain.	To apply what they have learnt To cooperate with each other while doing the task	The pictures have words (e.g., producer) on them to help A grid on the board with language to help them speak
10m Individual Pairs Plenary	**Further Practice** Ss complete a worksheet, and now they have to draw arrows to make a food chain Ss draw their own food chain and talk about it with each other Ss show their food chains to the class and talk about them	To apply and demonstrate what they have learnt To reflect on their learning during the lesson	

The framework may also be applied to English language lessons for young learners so that teachers may consider in what way these may be enriched in terms of content, cognition and culture. Practica should include observation of both generalist and English language teachers of young learners teaching within their areas, which would help develop an understanding of pedagogic content knowledge in practice.

CLIL can be a positive contribution to teachers' personal and professional development as it makes them question their regular practice as either generalist or language teachers as illustrated in the extract below from a language teacher's reflection on her experience:

> The way I plan my lesson activities and materials has changed, because now I spend more time thinking of my scaffolding strategies and planning tasks that are cognitively more demanding. I keep asking them the 'why' question to make them think. Personally and professionally I think that this CLIL experience, and knowledge of what CLIL is, has helped me to become a better teacher.

CLIL can also be a valuable addition to a teacher's profile as it opens up a realm of possibilities for new roles within schools, as well as employment opportunities within and outside national contexts. It is vital that communities and networks of primary CLIL practitioners are set up so that teachers may exchange ideas and materials as well as their practical theories which will help propel the evidence base for CLIL in new directions. Then primary CLIL will truly 'come of age' and be seen as providing a legitimate contribution to the education of primary-aged children.

Acknowledgement

The author would like to thank Cláudia Abreu for her assessment material and lesson plan.

Further reading

1   Ball, P., Kelly, K., and Clegg, J. (2015). *Putting CLIL into practice*. Oxford: Oxford University Press.
    A refreshing comprehensive handbook which challenges as well as adds new perspectives on some of the established principles and practices of CLIL.

2   Coyle, D., Hood, P., and Marsh, D. (2010). *CLIL: Content and language integrated learning*. Cambridge: Cambridge University Press.
    Essential core reading about CLIL from theory to practice by leading experts in the field which includes a useful 'CLIL toolkit' for practitioners initiating CLIL projects.

3   Ioannou-Georgiou, S., and Pavlou, P. (Eds.). (2011). *Guidelines for CLIL implementation in primary and pre-primary education*. Brussels: European Commission.
    A rare publication specifically related to CLIL for young learners that contains recommendations based on practical experiences of implementation at this level.

4   Mehisto, P., Marsh, D., and Frigols, M. J. (2008). *Uncovering CLIL: Content and language integrated learning in bilingual and multilingual education*. Oxford: Palgrave Macmillan.
    This handbook was the first of its kind about CLIL. It is a very clear first guide into CLIL and includes practical examples from primary practice.

Related topics

Languages in the classroom, policy, projects, syllabus, materials

References

Almeida, M., Costa, E., Pinho, A. Antão, V., and Rocha, P. (2014). *Evaluation Study on the Effectiveness of the Implementation of the Early Bilingual Education Project in Portugal*. Portugal: DGE/MEC.

Anderson, L. W., and Krathwohl, D. R. (Eds.). (2001). *A Taxonomy for Learning, Teaching, and Assessing: A revision of Bloom's taxonomy of educational objectives*. New York: Longman.

Ball, P., Kelly, K., and Clegg, J. (2015). *Putting CLIL into Practice*. Oxford: Oxford University Press.

Bandegas, D. L. (2011). Content and language integrated learning in Argentina 2008–2011. *Latina American Journal of Content and Language Integrated Learning*, 4(2), 33–50. doi:10.5294/laclil.2011.4.2.4 ISSN 2011–6721.

Bandegas, D. L. (2014). An investigation into CLIL-related sections of EFL coursebooks: Issues of CLIL inclusion in the publishing market. *International Journal of Bilingual Education and Bilingualism*, 17(3), 345–359.

Bloom, B. S. (Ed.). (1956). *Taxonomy of Educational Objectives, Handbook I: Cognitive domain*. New York: Longman.

Brewster, J., Ellis. G., and Girard, D. (2007). *The Primary English Teacher's Guide*. Harlow: Pearson Education Limited.

Butler, Y. (2015). English language education among young learners in East Asia: A review of current research (2004–2014). *Language Teaching*, 48(3), 303–342.

Cameron, L. (2001). *Teaching Languages to Young Learners*. Cambridge: Cambridge University Press.

Cenoz, J., Genesse, F., and Gorter, D. (2014). Critical Analysis of CLIL: Taking stock and looking forward. *Applied Linguistics*, 35(3), 243–262.

Coonan, C. M. (2005). The natural learning of a foreign language. CLIL as a possible partial solution for the primary school. *Scuola e Lingue Moderne*, 4–5.

Coyle, D. (2002). Relevance of CLIL to the European Commission's language learning objectives. In Marsh, D. (ed.). *CLIL/EMILE The European Dimension: Action, Trends and Foresight Potential*. Brussels: European Commission, 27–28.

Coyle, D. (2006). Content and language integrated learning: Motivating learners and teachers. *Scottish Languages Review*, 13, 1–18.

Coyle, D. (2013). Listening to learners: an investigation into 'successful learning' across CLIL contexts. *International Journal of Bilingual Education and Bilingualism*, 16, (3), 244-266.

Coyle, D., Holmes, B. and King, L. (2009). *Towards an integrated curriculum – CLIL National Statement and Guidelines*. England: The Languages Company on behalf of the Department for Children, Schools and Families.

Coyle, D., Hood, P., and Marsh, D. (2010). *CLIL: Content and Language Integrated Learning*. Cambridge: Cambridge University Press.

Cummins, J. (1979). Cognitive/academic language proficiency, linguistic interdependence, the optimum age question and some other matters. *Working Papers on Bilingualism*, 19, 121–129.

Cummins, J. (2008). BICS and CALP: Empirical and theoretical status of the distinction. In Street, B., and Hornberger, N. H. (eds.) *Encyclopedia of language and education, 2nd edition, volume 2: literacy*, New York: Springer Science and Business Media LLC, 71–83.

Dalton-Puffer, C., Llinares, A., Lorenzo, F., and Nikula, T. (2014). *"You Can Stand Under My Umbrella"*: Immersion, CLIL and billingual education: A response to Cenoz, Genesse and Gorter (2013). *Applied Linguistics*, 35(2), 212–218.

Dobson, A., Murillo, M. D., and Johnstone. R. (2010). *Bilingual education project Spain: Evaluation report*. Spain: Ministério de Educación de Españha and British Council.

Ellison, M. (2014). CLIL as a catalyst for developing reflective practice in foreign language teacher education. Unpublished doctoral thesis. Porto: Faculty of Arts and Humanities, University of Porto.

Ellison, M. (2015). CLIL: The added value to foreign language teacher education for young learners. *Linguarum Arena*, 6, 59–69.

European Commission. (1995). *White paper on education and training. Teaching and learning: Towards the learning society*. Brussels: European Commission.

Eurydice. (2006). *Content and language integrated learning (CLIL) at school in Europe*. Brussels: Eurydice.

Eurydice. (2017). *Key data on teaching languages at school in Europe*. Brussels: Eurydice.

García Mayo, M. P., and Hidalgo, M. A. ((2017). L1 use among young EFL mainstream and CLIL learners in task-supported interaction. *System*, 67, 132–145.

Genesse, F., and Hamayan, E. (2016). *CLIL in context: Practical guidance for educators*. Cambridge: Cambridge University Press.

Halliwell, S. (1992). *Teaching English in the primary classroom*. Harlow: Longman.

Hammond, J., and Gibbons, P. (2001). What is scaffolding? In Hammond, J. (ed.) *Scaffolding: Teaching and learning in language and literacy education*. Newtown: Primary English Teaching Association, 1–14. http://files.eric.ed.gov/fulltext/ED456447.pdf.

Infante, D., Benvenuto, G., and Lastrucci, E. (2009). The effects of CLIL from the perspective of experienced teachers. In Marsh, D., Mehisto, P., Wolff, D., Aliaga, R., Asikainen, R., Frigols-Martin, M. J., Hughes, S., and Langé, G. (eds.) *CLIL practice: Perspectives from the field*. University of Jyväskylä, 156–163.

Ioannou-Georgiou, S., and Pavlou, P. (Eds.). (2011). *Guidelines for CLIL implementation in primary and pre-primary education*. Brussels: European Commission.

Kiely, R. (2009). CLIL – The question of assessment. www.developingteachers.com/articles_tchtraining/clilpf_richard.htm.

Krashen, S. (1982). *Principles and practice in second language acquisition*. Oxford: Pergamon.

Lantolf, J. P. (2002). Sociocultural theory and second language acquisition. In Kaplan, R. B. (ed.) *The Oxford handbook of applied linguistics*. New York: Oxford University Press, 104–114.

MacKenzie, A. S. (2008). CLILing me softly in Thailand: Collaboration, creativity and conflict. www.onestopenglish.com/clil/clil-teacher-magazine/your-perspectives/cliling-me-softly-in-thailand-collaboration-creativity-and-conflict/500927.article.

Marsh, D. (2008). *CLIL in primary East Asia contexts: Primary innovations in East Asia: Indonesia, Malaysia, Thailand, Philippines*. East Asia: British Council.

Marsh, D. (2013). *The CLIL trajectory: Educational innovation for the 21st century iGeneration*. Córdoba: Servicio de Publicaciones, Universidad de Córdoba.

Marsh, D., and Hood, P. (2008). Content & language integrated learning in primary East Asia contexts (CLIL PEAC). *Proceedings of Primary Innovations Regional Seminar in Bangkok*. British Council, 43–50.

Massler, U. (2011). Assessment in CLIL learning. In Ioannou-Georgiou, S., and Pavlou, P. (eds.) *Guidelines for CLIL implementation in primary and pre-primary education*. Brussels: European Commission, 114–136.

Massler, U., Stotz, D., and Queisser, C. (2014). Assessment instruments for primary CLIL: The conceptualisation and evaluation of test tasks. *The Language Learning Journal*, 42(2), 137–150.

McDougald, J. (2015). Teachers' attitudes, perceptions and experiences in CLIL: A look at content and language. *Columbian Applied Linguistics Journal*, 17(1), 25–41. https://doi.org/10.14483/udistrital.jour.calj.2015.1.a02.

Mehisto, P., Marsh, D., and Frigols, M. J. (2008). *Uncovering CLIL: Content and language integrated learning in bilingual and multilingual education*. Oxford: Palgrave Macmillan.

Meyer, O., Coyle, D., Halbach, A., Schuck, K., and Ting, T. (2015). A pluriliteracies approach to content and language integrated learning – Mapping learner progressions in knowledge construction and meaning-making. *Language. Culture and Curriculum*, 28(1), 45–57.

Miciano, R. V. (2008). CLIL PEAC case study: The division of Quezon city, Philippines. *Proceedings of Primary Innovations Regional Seminar in Bangkok*. British Council, 51–56.

Murphy, V. (2014). *Second Language Learning in the Early School Years: Trends and Contexts*. Oxford: Oxford University Press.

Otwinowska, A., and Forys, M. (2015). They learn the CLIL way, but do they like it? Affectivity and cognition in upper-primary CLIL classes. *International Journal of Bilingual Education and Bilingualism*, doi:10.1080/13670050.2015.1051944.

Pérez-Cañado, M. L. (2012). CLIL research in Europe: Past, present, and future. *International Journal of Bilingual Education and Bilingualism*, 15(3), 315–341.

Pérez Cañado, M. L. (2016). From CLIL craze to the CLIL conundrum: Addressing the current CLIL controversy. *Bellaterra Journal of Teaching and Learning Language and Literature*, 9(1)1, 9-31.

Pinner, R. (2013). Authenticiy of Purpose: CLIL as a way to bring meaning and motivation into EFL: *Asian EFL Journal*, 15(4), 138–159.

Pinter, A. (2011). *Children learning second languages*. Basingstoke: Palgrave Macmillan.

Pladevall-Ballester, E. (2015). Exploring primary school CLIL perceptions in Catalonia: Students', teachers' and parents' opinions and expectations. *International Journal or Bilingual Education and Bilingualism*, 18(1), 45–59.

Ruiz de Zarobe, Y. (2013). CLIL implementation: From policy-makers to individual initiatives. *International Journal of Bilingualism and Bilingual Education*, 16(3), 231–243.

Snow, M. A., Met, M., and Genesse, F. (1989). A conceptual framework for the integration of language and content in second/foreign language instruction. *TESOL Quarterly*, 23(2), 201–217.

Suwannopphrat, K., and Chinokul, S. (2015). Applying CLIL to English language teaching in Thailand: Issues and challenges. *Latina American Journal of Content and Language Integrated Learning*, 8(2), 237–254. doi:10.5294/laclil.2015.8.3.8.

Tragant, E., Marsol, A., Serrano, R., and Llanes, À. (2016). Vocabulary learning at primary school: A comparison of EFL and CLIL. *International Journal of Bilingualism and Bilingual Education*, 19(5), 579–591.

Vale, D., and Feunteun, A. (1995). *Teaching children English: A training course for teachers of English to children*. Cambridge: Cambridge University Press.

Van de Craen, P., Mondt, K., Allain, L., and Gao, Y. (2007). Why and how CLIL works: An outline for a CLIL Theory. *Vienna English Working Papers, Current Research on CLIL 2*, 16(3), 70–79.

Vygotsky, L. S. (1978). *Mind in society: The development of higher psychological processes*. Massachusetts: Harvard University Press.

Walqui, A. (2006). Scaffolding instruction for English language learners: A conceptual framework, *International Journal of Bilingual Education and Bilingualism*, 9(2), 159–180, doi:10.1080/13670050 608668639.

Wei, R., and Feng, J. (2015). Implementing CLIL for young learners in an EFL context beyond Europe. *English Today*, 31(1), 55–60. doi.org/10.1017/S0266078414000558.

Wolff, D. (2002). On the importance of CLIL in the context of the debate on plurilingual education in the European union. In Marsh, D. (ed.) *CLIL/EMILE The European dimension*: *Action, trends and foresight potential*. Brussels: European Commission, 47–48.

Wood, Bruner, J. S., and Ross, G. (1976). The role of tutoring in problem solving. *Journal of Child Psychology and Psychiatry*, 17, 89–100.

Xavier, A. (2015). Assessment for Learning in EBE/CLIL: A learning-oriented approach to assessing English language skills and curriculum content at early primary level. Unpublished Masters dissertation. Lisbon: Faculdade de Ciências Sociais e Humanas, Universidade Nova de Lisboa.

Yamano, Y. (2013). Utilizing the CLIL approach in a Japanese primary school: A comparative study of CLIL and EFL lessons. *Asian EFL Journal*, 15(4), 160–183.

Yassin, S., Marsh, D., Tek, O., and Ying, L. (2009). Learners' perceptions towards the teaching of science through English in Malaysia: A quantative analysis. *International CLIL Research Journal*, 1(2), 54–69.

Zarobe, Y. Ruiz, and Cenoz, J. (2015). Way forward in the twenty first century in content-based instruction: Moving towards integration. *Language, Culture and Curriculum*, 28(1), 90–96. doi:10.1080/07 908318.2014.1000927.

17

Learning through literature

Janice Bland

Introduction

English language *and* literature teaching to young learners has received far too little attention to date from applied linguists and scholars of children's literature. This is surprising, for English language teaching (ELT) as a primary-school subject and as a teaching medium is expanding rapidly on a global scale, and both language and content are involved in all holistic, content-based approaches to language education. This chapter is based on the assumption that waiting until language learners are old enough to include adult literature in the language-learning setting creates a delay in students' development in the literacy spectrum, affective and cognitive development, as well as intercultural learning, that may be difficult to reverse. Additionally, literary texts offer contextualised access to stretches of authentic discourse that sensitise learners to grammatical relations and the semantic associations of words as well as formulaic sequences; and should be included in the input as early as possible (Hoey 2004, Kersten 2015), due to the implicit learning mechanisms and tolerance of ambiguity that characterise young language learners (Bland 2015b, Murphy 2014).

The rationale for teaching with children's literature includes perspectives from applied linguistics, as literary texts can support learners in the development of rich lexical representations and can promote creative reading and writing in English (Maley 2013). However, children's literature offers a valuable study in its own right, as well as an educational benefit – by means of windows into other worlds (Bishop 1990), intercultural understanding (Bland 2016), aesthetic pleasure (Nodelman and Reimer 2003), visual literacy (Arizpe et al. 2014), critical literacy (Bland 2013) and, an important skill in an increasingly rapid world, deep reading (Nikolajeva 2014). This chapter focuses on using English-language literary texts that were not published for ELT or any educational context specifically, and are aimed at children, not teenagers or adults. My examples of using literature in the classroom are taken from ELT settings with young learners, mostly in Europe.

Historical perspectives

Before the development of communicative language teaching (CLT) syllabuses, canonical English literature for adults had a privileged place in language teaching (Hall 2015,

p. 2). CLT signalled a move away from English literature to a more functional focus on oral communication. However, since the cultural turn in the last decades of the twentieth century, the understanding of literature has been re-conceptualised to become broader and pluralistic – the study of a wide variety of texts. Both for adults and children we now refer to world literatures in English, and the inclusion of literature in ELT may embrace postcolonial and migrant literature in an almost overwhelming array of formats. It is now understood that literary texts form a gateway to new perspectives and intercultural awareness – in the case of English through the many literatures in English from nations throughout the world. Further still, attention has shifted from a literary product to the communicative process of reception: 'Analysis has been extended to all texts as cultural products, with the notion of culture seen as increasingly dynamic and co-constructed interactively, as an emergent and specifically linguistic process rather than as a completed product' (Carter 2015, p. 316).

With the coming of the digital age it became clear that literacy in a wide sense is of pivotal educational concern, with the understanding that 'the complexities of literacy are linked to the patterns of social practices and social meanings. From now on there will be multiple literacies' (Meek 1993, p. 96). The need for a wider understanding of literacy is ever more apparent in the twenty-first century, with the hugely influential role of unsubstantiated claims often made through texts on social media, and the dangers of 'a culture where a few claims on Twitter can have the same credibility as a library full of research' (Coughlan 2017). Consequently many educators, particularly among those responsible for teacher education of ELT with young learners and teenagers, refer to multiple literacies – not only learning to read and write (functional literacy), but also learning to use the Web wisely and skilfully for information (information literacy), learning to read the aesthetic nature of a literary text (literary literacy), learning to read all texts critically and understanding their manipulative power (critical literacy) and also reading pictures for information both deeply and critically (visual literacy). The habit of literature is considered to be a social good, as an opening to lifelong learning – teaching multiple literacies in English as well as in the majority language extends opportunities for achieving a citizenry that reads to expand their knowledge of the world. At the same time, there is huge interest now in all teachers (also in countries where English is the majority language) being able to work on literacy development with linguistically diverse children – as plurilingualism in classrooms becomes increasingly common and pluricultural competence increasingly respected. Nonetheless, the move towards including children's literature in language education with young learners follows several huge strides behind the larger development over the last fifty years that Enever (2015, p. 13) calls 'a general trend worldwide towards introducing the teaching of additional languages from the very earliest phases of compulsory schooling'.

Children's literature is notoriously difficult to define, and furthermore is changing rapidly. Whereas the picturebook has been gaining in popularity for primary ELT for several decades: 'a journey that began with the communicative language teaching approach in the 1970s' (Mourão and Bland 2016, p. ii), the story app – sometimes called a digital picturebook – is a newly developed multimodal format. The concept of multimodality 'characterizes any kind of text which draws from language, sound, music, images or other graphic elements in various combinations' (Wales 2011, p. 279). This definition would include most texts on the Web as well as film, so that children's out-of-school reading and listening is increasingly multimodal and very often in English. This is hugely advantageous for second language acquisition – yet suggests all the more the need for some in-depth critical literacy with literary texts in the classroom.

I will distinguish a number of formats of children's literature, with some examples of when and how they are employed in ELT in various European countries. It is useful to distinguish format from genre: 'Genre is a fluid category, of course, but it refers primarily to *the type of story content* the reader will experience – historical fiction, fantasy, romance, and so on – rather than to *how* that story will be delivered. And the *how* is exactly what the format is all about' (Oziewicz 2018, p. 30).

Multimodal formats of children's literature

Picturebooks. This is the format that is currently perhaps best known and most widely used in ELT with young learners. Indeed the picturebook seems to have become the default young-learner narrative format, as studies focusing on story-based pedagogy for young learners (e.g., Ellis and Brewster 2014, Hsiu-Chih 2008 and Yanase 2018) most often refer to picturebooks rather than other forms of narrative, such as chapter books, graded readers or oral storytelling. The picturebook has received in-depth critical attention from literary and education scholars, to the extent that it has been called 'one of the richest and potentially most rewarding of literary forms' (Hunt 2001, p. 291). Usually fiction but including non-fiction, whether a traditional or postmodern narrative (such as when the pictures and words tell somewhat different stories), the picturebook is essentially defined by the interaction between the words and pictures as being vital to the meaning. This leads to complex opportunities for discovery and interpretation of meanings that are created by the combination of pictures, verbal text, creative typography and design, as well as 'the drama of the turning of the page' (Bader 1976, p. 1). Consequently, to emphasise its compound nature, the format is now frequently spelled as a compound noun: *picturebook*. As an artefact rich in meaning and dialogic opportunities, the picturebook can offer ideal matter for ELT with young learners, and increasingly scholars working in this area of ELT encourage teachers 'to select picturebooks at the more complex end of the picture-word dynamic, so that learners are challenged to think and fill the gaps between the pictures and the words' (Mourão 2016, p. 39).

Graphic novels

This format is swiftly gaining attention due to a sudden surge in high quality, seriously themed, award-winning graphic novels in recent years. Whereas the picturebook is mostly, but not exclusively, aimed at children in primary or even pre-primary school, the graphic novel is more likely to be shared with higher grades. However, the format is also popular with young learners due to the similarity of graphic novels and comics. Sarah Garland's graphic novel *Azzi in Between* (2012) can, for example, be shared with children aged eight and nine in an ELT context in Germany (Bergner 2016). Although the graphic novel format is particularly fluid, variously sharing features with comics, the picturebook or with film (Oziewicz 2018), it is generally a novel-length narrative distinguished by the inclusion of panels, gutters, speech balloons and captions. The size and shape of panels and gutters – the space between panels – are significant. It is due to these gaps, 'a silent dance of the seen and the unseen' (McCloud 1993, p. 92), that active participation is required as students mentally construct the relationships between the stopped moments of each panel. They close these gaps in their imagination, in shared booktalk or, for example, in creative writing. Many educators have now discovered the value of the graphic novel: 'Teachers use graphic novels because they *enable* the struggling reader, *motivate* the reluctant one, and *challenge* the high-level learner' (McTaggart 2008, p. 32, emphasis in the original). The potential of the graphic novel in the ELT classroom similarly stretches from a support for reluctant second language (L2) readers to a challenge for high-level L2 readers (Ludwig and Pointner 2013).

Story apps

The story app is a new format that is neither a book nor a film but has some similarities with both. As Al-Yaqout and Nikolajeva (2015), referring to picturebooks, write: 'Tapping, touching and tracing become embodied actions to reading and viewing that enhances the user's affective engagement'. Story apps take these interactive elements in a different direction with reader-activated animation, music and background noises as well as audio narration that can be activated by the reader. Integrated choices and tasks activated by the learner clicking on an action hotspot ensure high involvement, and sometimes feedback is given on the action taken.

In a recent study with 8 to 11 year-old young learners using story apps in pairs in an ELT extensive-reading setting, the researchers identified 'four main elements that helped the students derive meaning from the texts: audio narration, animation and sound, vocabulary support and readers' participation and co-creation' (Brunsmeier and Kolb 2017, pp. 7–8). The young learners had control of the reading process – the opportunity to hear the story narrated aloud, while reading along quietly and deciding on the pace of the storytelling. As such, story apps seem to be highly useful for extensive, autonomous reading – which is particularly difficult in ELT with young learners – as well as extensive listening. However, the action hotspots, offering for example a game or reader-activated vocabulary support, also caused distraction. Such action hotspots frequently 'trigger childrens' curiosity but lead them away from the story without contributing any useful information to the plot' (Brunsmeier and Kolb 2017, p. 14).

Performative formats

Playground and nursery rhymes

Always popular with young learners, there is a wealth of material for rhythmic and participatory pleasure in the ELT classroom to satisfy children's need for rhythm and pleasure in rhyme. Playground rhymes – shared amongst children at play, and consequently often with rather 'naughty' content – may be counting-out chants, skipping and clapping songs, jokes and riddles. Well-known contemporary poets, such as Roger McGough and Michael Rosen (Children's Laureate 2007–2009), have successfully emulated the strong rhythms, fun and naughtiness of playground rhymes, with their vibrant poetry for performance that may also plunge into serious themes – highly meaningful for teachers as well as their students.

Nursery rhymes are usually short, popularly transmitted poems that are familiar worldwide in English-speaking countries in families, pre-school and primary school. With their vivid characterization of comic characters – often helped by lively illustrations – they aid visualization of language. An example of a favourite anonymous nursery rhyme is:

> Hey diddle, diddle!
> The cat and the fiddle,
> The cow jumped over the moon;
> The little dog laughed

To see such sport,
And the dish ran away with the spoon.

The rhyme seems nonsensical, yet in its few brief catchy lines, it creates not only a viva-cious personification of the animals, the musical cat, sportive cow and the laughing dog, but also invites the listener to infer a love story to the personified dish and the spoon. However – in the true spirit of children's literature – the fun is due not only to the pleasure of playing with words, but also to the images that often stay in children's memory long after they have forgotten any particular illustration.

These archived mental images are initiated by the humour of pictures children have seen – 'Hey diddle, diddle' illustrators invariably show the dish and spoon running away hand in hand, the dog laughing merrily, the cow mid-jump over the moon, a moon that is tradition-ally given a smiling face (see Figure 17.1). Clearly visualization of language is strongly supported: mental images that develop while listening or reading may enter an archive of images in memory along with the verbal text (Bland 2015d). The larger-than-life characters may become lifelong friends, and this in itself is a useful introduction to the pleasure of story. The Web provides both rhymes and images that are in the public domain. It may also supply invented interpretations that are not supported by scholarship. Nursery rhymes are more important to children as language play – and for L1 and L2 literacy development – than for any historical meanings (see also Bland 2013, pp. 156–187).

Oral storytelling

Oral storytelling is an important vehicle for ideas generally, and a specific skill for teachers of English with young learners. Stories have been used with all age groups to pass on ideas, organise information and lighten the dark long before most children had the opportunity to attend school and learn to read and write. Young learners in ELT contexts usually learn to read English fluently a number of years after they have acquired functional literacy in the majority language. At school they will hopefully also have the important opportunity to learn functional literacy in their home language, which can differ from the majority lan-guage in many contexts worldwide. English may then be the third or even fourth language – and the time allotted to ELT very brief. This time is well spent in the earliest years of ELT by listening to and interacting with stories well told, before the children are reading in English.

The stories we tell to young learners are intrinsically motivating; they are often con-nected to 'the warmth of early childhood experiences' (Cameron 2001, p. 160). Short oral tales are, for example, fables, legends and folk tales from around the world. One of the defining characteristics of what was once *only* oral literature – tales told by word of mouth – is that there is no one 'correct' or authoritative version (Zipes 2004, p. 118). Nonetheless we know stories from folk literature now mostly through their written expression, for example, the numerous versions of fairy tales by the Brothers Grimm, or reimagined and remediated as film, such as the ubiquitous Disney versions.

Yet, storytelling in the classroom is not the same as sharing a book or film – oral storytelling can and should be moulded to the particular audience – shaped by the needs of the listeners. However, the standard story patterns and formulaic language (such as: Once upon a time, little cottage, wicked wolf, deep dark woods) must remain unchanged. Audience participation is anticipated – young learners join in with the reassuring and comforting repetition: 'Whatever its pedagogical benefits, repetition is also a source of enjoyment. Witness the pleasure of repetitive rhythmic patterns in music and language'

Figure 17.1 Illustration by Edward Cogger of the anonymous nursery rhyme *Hey Diddle Diddle* (circa 1885, public domain)

(Nodelman 2008, p. 233). Repetition is important as a support for the teacher-storyteller and crucial for the listener – especially when the story is in a foreign language. Oral tales cannot sustain the complexity of written literature with regard to language, characterisation, setting and theme. Additive language is used, avoidance of complex sentences, familiar stock characters, iconic settings with few details and recurrent themes and triples (such as three brothers or sisters, three wishes, three attempts). This characteristic helps young learners to predict, and it activates their prior knowledge of the creatures of tales, such as witches, monsters and trolls. It also compels children to listen carefully to confirm or disprove their hypotheses, and it helps them to notice new ideas. The use of scaffolding such as pictures, puppets and realia is very helpful in oral storytelling in ELT settings. However, I suggest creative teacher talk is the most important technique of the teacher-storyteller:

> The teacher-storyteller employs a varied paralanguage involving expressive prosodic features (pitch, tempo, volume, rhythm – including dramatic pauses), exuberant intonation, gasps, and, where suitable, even sighs. Some storytellers employ exaggerated gesture and facial expressions, while others have a quieter style. This will also depend on the story and the age of the young learners; the younger the child, the more the storytelling (and classroom discourse generally) should resemble repetitive child-directed speech.
>
> *(Bland 2015c, p. 190)*

Michael Morpurgo, award-winning author of children's literature, locates the importance of stories in the area of intercultural understanding:

> without stories, and without an understanding of stories, we don't understand ourselves, we don't understand the world about us. And we don't understand the relations between ourselves and those people around us. Because what stories give us is an insight into ourselves, a huge insight into other people, other cultures, other places.
>
> *(Morpurgo 2014, n.p.)*

Plays

Children's drama has long played a role in ELT as offering an opportunity to perform language, using whole-body response to support students in learning to trust and enjoy their linguistic resources and extend their repertoire (Fleming 2013). Unscripted drama conventions such as freeze-frames, speaking objects, questioning-in-role and teacher-in-role provide context-embedded, stimulating language-learning opportunities and are now well established in ELT (Bland 2015a, Farmer 2011). It is rather more difficult to locate play scripts suitable for young learners to act out, as task-based, multisensory, embodied learning. David Wood, an acclaimed playwright for children, considers: 'Plays for very young children to perform need to involve a large group or a whole class (. . .) without giving any one child too much responsibility' (1994, p. 9). This is even more the case when children are playing roles in ELT – many roles with short, rhythmical lines and very short scenes that can be rehearsed separately, as well as, ideally, a well-known story, are called for. The following extract from a Christmas story script gives an idea of these characteristics:

knock, knock, knock

Cat:	Not **another** knock at the door!
Horse 1:	Quiet cat!
Horse 2:	We have space for more.
Pig 1:	Hallo, would you please let us in?
Pig 2:	It's so cold.
Piglet 3:	And we've lost our way!
Cow 1:	Yes, but be quiet!
Cow 2:	Come in.
Calf 3:	See the baby asleep in the hay!
Pig 1:	Wonderful!
Pig 2:	Tiny and sweet!
Piglet:	Do babies like nuts to eat?
Cow 1:	He drinks milk at his mother's breast.
Cow 2:	For babies milk is best.
Piglet:	I'd rather have nuts any day.
Calf:	My Mum gives me milk that way.
	(from: Bland 2009, pp. 27–28)

Serrurier-Zucker and Gobbé-Mévellec (2014) report on a rewarding ELT drama project in France, whereby teachers chose to act out carefully selected picturebooks with young learners. It was shown in the study that acting out provides multisensory clues to meaning, and supports a motivating classroom environment. Reynolds and Chang (2018) describe how they prepared pre-service teachers in Taiwan to use picturebooks with children and their parents in a community service project. The student teachers scripted picturebooks into interactive plays with which to involve pre-school children and their parents in a 'Weekend English Story Time' project at their university library. In Germany, a scripted drama project in ELT, 'Coming Together', involving student teachers and young learners, proved to be a highly effective way to introduce teachers to a 'team-teaching and bridge-building peda-gogy' (Bland 2014, p. 172). This study, located at the primary to secondary school transition, again showed the advantages of working on a play together for a motivating classroom environment. It is to be hoped that the choice of a play for young audiences as a new addition to the *Harry Potter* oeuvre, *Harry Potter and the Cursed Child* (Thorne et al. 2016), which is well-suited to acting out in the secondary school, will reinvigorate the format of play scripts for children just as much as Rowling's novels reinvigorated young adult fiction.

Formats of children's literature for fluent readers

Chapter books and graded readers

The chapter book is a format for those children who are beginning to read independently, and the books consequently have far more text than a picturebook. Chapter books have very short chapters 'for children who have mastered basic reading skills but still require simple, illustrated texts' (Agnew 2001, p. 139). Although typically quite richly illustrated, the pictures are not essential for the meaning of the story, in contrast to the larger-formatted picturebook. Jeff Brown's *Flat Stanley* (1964) is a well-known chapter book, later turned into a series, which has inspired intercultural primary-school project work internationally.

Begun in Canada, this project work has been 'connecting kids from around the world with literacy since 1995' (www.flatstanley.com/about). The protagonist, Flat Stanley, has exciting adventures due to his thinness, for example, he is mailed in an envelope to visit a friend in California. In the global literacy project, a paper Flat Stanley becomes the mutual friend of the project partners, and is mailed from school to school accompanied by reports of what he has experienced in other countries and contexts. Fleta and Forster (2014) have reported on a recent international ELT project, carried out in Portugal, Estonia, Spain, Slovakia, Switzerland, Latvia, the United Arab Emirates and Cameroon, based on this idea.

The many graded readers that are produced for the international ELT market are mostly quite similar to the chapter book format, but are typically less richly illustrated, with a less cohesively patterned text (Bland 2013, p. 8), and the majority are without the child-focused content, as even the beginner titles are often aimed at teenager and adult ELT. In contrast to chapter books, graded readers frequently include comprehension questions and other activities to support the teacher, and are offered for particular language levels with the vocabulary and grammar correspondingly controlled. In many ELT classrooms, this is considered an essential aid, although answering comprehension questions does not in most cases support the joy of playful language, intercultural awareness and deep reading. In ELT curricula with young learners, for example in Europe, acquiring intercultural competence is often considered as important as learning the language.

In an extensive reading programme for young learners aimed at pleasure reading and language enrichment, teachers should ideally offer titles of all possible formats for a wide reader choice. Access and the opportunity to enjoy self-selected material are particularly important with children who are in danger of losing the love of reading, which happens frequently around the age of 12 (Harmgarth 1999, p. 18). For, as Bamford and Day express it: 'Only by discovering the rewards of reading through actually engaging in it will students become people who both *can* and *do* read' (1997, emphasis in the original).

Verse novels, young adult novels and crossover novels

The verse novel is a fairly recent format that is very promising, however mostly for teen readers rather than young learners – an example for younger readers is Sharon Creech's *Love that Dog* (2001). The word scenery of verse novels and the musicality of the language often reflects the strong emotions of adolescence; as in poetry, feelings reverberate in the omissions, lingering in the moment of what can be said and what can only be felt. For the ELT classroom there is ample potential for slower, deep reading of the poetry. The most successful verse novels not only offer the vivid depth of feeling that poetry can deliver, but they are also convincing as stories.

Young adult literature is included in the umbrella term children's literature (Bland et al. 2015, p. ii). It is usually considered to aim at the liminal phase between childhood and adulthood, and so falls outside the field of potential material for young learners. The topics of young adult literature often include concepts that children are normally sheltered from, such as sex and death. Some novels seem to be equally read by teenagers and adults – by all those who love a compelling story – and thus recently the term crossover literature has been introduced. *The Hunger Games* series is a high profile example of crossover literature.

Critical issues and topics

The lag in including children's literature in language education with young learners is due to a number of problematic issues – connected firstly to the lack of access to texts through (school) libraries and consequent equity issues, and secondly to teacher education.

A reading apprenticeship for young learners in ELT for development of (critical) literacies, intercultural awareness and the ability to read deeply will give learners the chance to prepare themselves playfully and pleasurably for the very rewarding but challenging adult canon, which is often an aspect of ELT syllabuses in higher grades. However a major area of concern is access to suitable texts. This is not only a question of social class and equity of opportunity, but also of information about selecting suitable reads:

> In the case of EFL worldwide, it is not only the children of poverty who have no access to compelling reading in English. Apart from *Harry Potter* and perhaps *The Hunger Games*, compelling titles for children and young adults in the lingua franca are not at all well known by parents generally, as well as being very expensive. Most parents will be at a loss to choose compelling books for their children in English. The library with a certified librarian can supply this access immediately, and free of charge.
>
> *(Krashen and Bland 2014, p. 9)*

Unfortunately, nowadays school libraries with a certified librarian scarcely exist anywhere except in private schools, but it may be possible to make an arrangement with the local library. If communities, schools and parents are all unable to finance books, the teacher has a heavier burden – which is usually the case. There are many YouTube renderings of picturebooks that can be shared if they can be projected in the classroom. If at all possible, teachers need to supply at least two print copies of the books for children to read and enjoy. An excellent source of second-hand children's books can be found in the thousands of charity shops in the UK. However, the lack of resources generally and books in particular in many countries is a huge disadvantage for children learning English. Oral storytelling and nursery rhymes require little or no funding, but these performative formats demand well-trained teachers with very good language skills. Another barrier to using children's literature in class can be the educational culture. In many countries, storytelling is not central to the curriculum and teachers tend to rely on traditional coursebooks.

Within teacher education, three major aspects of studying children's literature have been identified as important for future ELT teachers, according to Narančić Kovač (2016). The researcher describes a study programme of primary English at the Faculty of Teacher Education in Zagreb, Croatia, that aims to provide the following:

- Experience of a wide range of children's literary texts.
- The theory of children's literature, for example, the picturebook.
- The ability to evaluate the potential of a book for ELT and design activities for young learners.

Pre-service teacher education in ELT worldwide is often exclusively designed by applied linguists with a focus on language, but no experience either in teaching young learners themselves or in the wide-reaching educational affordances, the breadth and depth, of children's literature.

The ability to evaluate the potential of a book for ELT refers to language and communication affordances, to aesthetic criteria and also to content. English-language children's literature is not for the most part published for any particular market, and some books will be unconventional, even controversial in some contexts. Challenging ideas make for genuine discussion, potentially transformative content, motivated reading and listening, more tolerance of unfamiliar vocabulary and hence language development. For example young adult literature largely avoids the self-censorship that troubles the ELT international graded reader and textbook market (avoiding politics, alcohol, religion, sex, narcotics, isms and pork – the PARSNIP policy). This is a huge advantage for critical literacy approaches and intercultural learning. However, teachers must themselves pre-select with regard to cultural sensitivity in their own context as well as consider the language level for their students.

An understanding and appreciation of out-of-school learning – wide or extensive reading – as well as in-school deep reading and critical literacy, should accompany all pedagogical, administrative and financial decisions on teaching English to young learners. Thus there is still much work to be done in the area of theory building – connecting conceptual and empirical research in ELT with young learners – in order to close the gap regarding children's literature in language education, specifically in the primary and early secondary grades, where most compulsory ELT takes place.

Current contributions and research

Current research into learning through literature with young learners divides roughly into areas of applied linguistics and second language acquisition on the one hand and areas that connect to children's literature scholarship and pedagogy, such as visual and critical literacies and intercultural learning, on the other.

The usage-based approach to language acquisition provides a valuable understanding of the role of context, formulaic language and usage (for example, reading as receptive usage and booktalk as productive usage) in children's language acquisition. This approach highlights the exemplar-based nature of language acquisition and how lexical and grammatical knowledge can emerge through engaging with extended input, 'with language, as with other cognitive realms, our experiences conspire to give us competence' (Ellis, O'Donnell and Römer 2013, p. 45). Frequency and salience (which includes prominence of meaning and whether the feature – from a morpheme to a formulaic sequence – is easy to notice) are crucial. Repeated encounters with oral stories, poems and picturebooks with electrifying characters and exciting storyworlds, which entice children to revisit them again and again with their teachers, are arguably the best if not the only way to supply extensive input for young learners, when they cannot yet read autonomously in English. Usage frequency seems to be the ideal condition for second language acquisition: 'Psycholinguistic research provides the evidence of usage-based acquisition in its demonstrations that language processing is exquisitely sensitive to usage frequency at all levels of language representation' (Ellis et al. 2013, p. 30). The patterned nature of most children's literature connects to concerns such as literacy (reading and writing skills) as well as oracy (listening and speaking skills). This supports discourse skills, while making language pleasurable and salient for young learners: 'The ability to understand, recall, and produce songs, rhymes, chants, and stories [. . .] are all examples of discourse skills' (Cameron 2003, p. 109). Research by Kaminsky (2016), Lugossy (2012) and Mourão (2012; 2016) has shown that if young learners' response is taken seriously in an approach that utilises and values the multimodality of children's literature, then authentic communication emerges from the interaction between the learners, their books and their teacher.

A fertile source of research and contributions on learning through literature with young learners is the peer-reviewed journal *Children's Literature in English Language Education* (*CLELEjournal*), an open access journal that was established in 2013. Many articles published in the *CLELEjournal* connect to international children's literature scholarship, such as exploring visual literacy, critical literacy, diversity in literary texts and intercultural learning, while exploring the different formats and genres in the ELT classroom. This area of research is expanding particularly fast, with children's literature scholars involved in education becoming ever more cognizant of the plurilingual and pluricultural nature of classrooms across the world – where English is the vehicle of teaching, but many children in the classroom have a home language other than English – and the need to prepare in teacher education for emergent bilinguals.

There is consequently an ever-increasing demand for teaching English to young learners, who must learn English over many years. Children need to be motivated in ways that make sense to them; and meaningful stories and patterned language, such as rhythmical poems, can activate their implicit learning mechanisms (Bland 2015b). Learning through literature with young learners sits well alongside the current focus on content-based teaching, the acquisition of intercultural understanding, multiple literacies and an initiation into the pleasures of literature. Unsurprisingly, teaching English with children's literature is now a rapidly expanding research area. However implementation in primary school ELT is patchy and poorly resourced in most countries. The frequent attitude of policy makers that teachers for young learners need less English language competence than teachers for advanced learners is extremely damaging for the necessary progress in this area.

Recommendations for practice

While suggestions on methodology and *how* to teach language and literature to young learners have been available for some decades, for example the three editions of Ellis and Brewster (1991, 2002 and 2014), there has been less analysis to date of *what* to teach and *why*. I will focus in this section on the picturebook as a frequently used literary text with young leaners. Important questions to ask when selecting picturebooks (particularly with a view to reflecting diversity and practising intercultural understanding) would include:

1   Is the language and content accessible for the target group?
2   Do the pictures add layers of meaning to the story?
3   Does the characterisation in words and illustrations encourage empathy?
4   Is diversity mirrored in some of the chosen texts?
5   Is the story compelling, e.g. exciting, humorous, surprising or moving?
6   Can the children relate to the narrative – is the import of the story meaningful for them as individuals so that they will wish to revisit it?
7   Is the representation of the world and of people accurate and respectful?
8   Does the story encourage a questioning stance and genuine communication? (Bland 2016)

An exemplar: Thunder Boy Jr

Teachers may find, depending also on the cultural context of their teaching environment (the humorous use of language in the excerpt below, for example, may not be acceptable in all settings), that Sherman Alexie's picturebook *Thunder Boy Jr* (2016) fulfils the above criteria. The verbal text is very brief: the reader is introduced, through colourful words and powerful pictures (Yuyi Morales), to a vibrant Native American family. Thus the book reflects a minority culture in the USA, but is emphatically upbeat – the struggles of the young hero, Thunder Boy Smith, are presented both in the pictures and in the language with life-affirming humour. The small, empathetic hero is busily working on his agency – it is easy for children to relate to his story as he invents names for himself that should express his vivacious sense of self. He was named after his dad, Thunder Boy Smith Sr,

> People call him **BIG THUNDER.**
> That nickname is a storm filling up the sky.
> People call me
> LITTLE THUNDER.
> That nickname makes me sound like a burp or a fart.
>
> *(Alexie 2016, unpaginated)*

Many picturebooks play with language. Young language learners will enjoy this use of language – scatological humour is particularly popular with children as they understand it to be 'naughty'. This adds to the fun of the book: 'Just as intense emotion is an elementary force setting the tone for many a successful children's book, so is humour' (Tabbert and Wardetzky 1995, p. 3). The little boy's spirited temperament also empowers him – his characterisation is humorous due to the subversion of the pattern that small is powerless – and not only the dynamic illustrations but also the typographic creativity support his demand for agency. His speech bubbles are frequently filled with shouting capitals, such as '**I WANT MY OWN NAME**'. Thunder Boy's emotions are expressed in words, in symbolic pictures (for example, a howling wolf, a hissing snake and a growling bear to express frustration), in colours and even in the shape and outline of his speech bubbles. All of this encourages a questioning stance and genuine communication. While he shares his hatred of his name with the reader, he loves his father and fears to upset him by revealing his dislike of their shared name.

This picturebook is suitable for the youngest language learners, and the respect they may feel for Thunder Boy could be considered the first step towards intercultural understanding. It is important to remember that classroom activities should develop strategies for understanding other texts as well as the particular text children are sharing, and 'simply preteaching all the unknown words [. . .] does not help them to know what to do the next time they come to an unknown word' (Gibbons 2015, p. 145). Once the children have heard the story read aloud, and have become acquainted with the family through the lively illustrations, the teacher can decide to spend more time – and more than one lesson – on selected pages.

Thunder Boy Smith goes on to create new and wonderful names for himself, which are also energetically illustrated, for example

> I love playing in the dirt,
> so maybe my name should be
> MUD IN HIS EARS.

and

> I like to go to garage sales
> with my mom, so maybe
> my name should be
> OLD TOYS ARE AWESOME.

The story is full of communicative potential, as the example shows (Figure 17.2). The children will be keen to name the toys and describe their own toys when they see a similarity or difference. As Ghosn writes: 'In literature-based lessons students can remain in their

Figure 17.2 From *Thunder Boy, Jr.* by Sherman Alexie, illustrated by Yuyi Morales. Text copyright © 2016 by Sherman Alexie. Illustrations copyright © 2016 by Yuyi Morales. Used by permission of Little Brown Books for Young Readers

own persona while exchanging ideas about the story content, which results in meaningful discourse, during which children can draw on their L1 when necessary' (2010, p. 32). The teacher thus has the important role of supplying input that models language and clarifies vocabulary, for instance by recasting children's L1 utterances into English. Teachers might tell an anecdote about their experience with 'garage sales', or the closest equivalent in their culture. A jumble sale of toys might be arranged at school – for example to raise money to buy picturebooks for the classroom.

Young children often talk to their toys, so it is meaningful for them if the teacher elicits dialogue for the toys illustrated (Figure 17.2). For example: 'What does the crocodile say?' The teacher typically needs to make the first suggestion as a model, such as 'Perhaps the crocodile says: I want my dinner', which will prompt the children's inventive suggestions (I want my Mom, I want a friend, I want my river, I want to swim, I want to play, I want to sleep, etc.) All the toys could be given a voice: What does the robot say? What does the dog on wheels say? What does the elephant (or horse/mouse/rabbit/rattle) say? And the children may choose a favourite toy (from their own lives or from the book) to draw with a speech bubble. The children can focus on Thunder Boy and his sister Lillian: They love skipping, they love riding, they love playing, they like old toys, they like noise, they like fun. And the children can also voice their own preferences. Thunder Boy plays with names on this and other pages, and this suggests many creative and fun opportunities for inventing new personality names with young language learners.

Humour is supplied by the gentle, carnivalesque nature of Thunder Boy's wishing to determine his own name, creatively and innovatively, and reject his given name. Although the expressive illustrations and bold typographical creativity suggest conflicting emotions, the humour of the story is the prevailing mood: 'The best antidote to the anxieties and disasters of life is laughter; and this children seem to understand almost as soon as they are born' (Opie 1992, Introduction). Thunder Boy does not want to hurt his father, which causes his dilemma and the tension. But all is happily resolved in the end (and will not be revealed here) – with the ingredients of a strong and loving father-son relationship – providing a happy counterbalance to the many picturebooks that focus on mother-child relationships.

Future directions

A number of institutions must become more actively involved for the future development of learning through literature with young learners. These are universities and colleges responsible for pre-service and in-service teacher education, publishers of children's literature and ELT materials, schools, school libraries and local libraries. A pedagogical study of children's literature in ELT teacher education is essential in order to test and discover its potential for creative reading and writing, as well as performance, intercultural understanding and critical literacy. However, a literary study of children's literature from the outset in teacher education is crucial in order to equip future teachers with the know-how to select the finest possible texts for their individual classes – which involves the ability to analyse the potential of a variety of formats and genres for ELT. The best training in the long run is wide or extensive reading and deep reading, booktalk and reflective classroom practice. For the sake of crucial educational goals, including literacy development, intercultural awareness and the ability to read deeply, the ever-multiplying and diversifying ocean of literary texts for children should be made accessible to a vastly greater extent than they currently are – conceptually through teacher education courses and materially through school or local libraries – for all those involved in ELT with young learners and adolescents. As Barack Obama observed, in the last days of his presidency:

> When so much of our politics is trying to manage this clash of cultures brought about by globalization and technology and migration, the role of stories to unify – as opposed to divide, to engage rather than to marginalize – is more important than ever.
>
> *(Obama 2017)*

Further reading

1 Bland, J. (2013). *Children's literature and learner empowerment. Children and teenagers in English language education*. London: Bloomsbury.

   A book that covers the full breadth of children's literature in ELT in depth, including picturebooks, graphic novels, fairy tales, poetry, creative writing, plays and young adult novels, with an emphasis on creative response, critical literacy and intercultural learning.

2 Ellis, G., and Brewster, J. (2014). *Tell it again! The storytelling handbook for primary English language teachers*, 3rd ed. British Council. www.teachingenglish.org.uk/sites/teacheng/files/D467_Storytelling_handbook_FINAL_web.pdf [Accessed 14 January 2017].

   A seminal publication with a hands-on approach. Systematic criteria for selecting stories are included with reference to psycholinguistic, sociological and intercultural affordances of the picturebook to support the development of the whole child.

3 Ghosn, I.-K. (2010). Five-year outcomes from children's literature-based programmes vs. programmes using a skills-based ESL course – The Matthew and Peter effects at work? In Tomlinson, B., and Masuhara, H. (eds.) *Research for materials development in language learning*. London: Continuum, 21–36.

   The chapter reports on a study which examines 10 to 11-year-old children's English learning outcomes in Lebanon. Two different programmes with 106 children in four schools were researched – one literature-based programme and the other following an international ESL course. The results are illuminating.

4 Mourão, S. (2016). Picturebooks in the primary EFL classroom: Authentic literature for authentic responses. *Children's Literature in English Language Education*, 4(1), 25–43. http://clelejournal.org/authentic-literature-for-an-authentic-response/ [Accessed 8 October 2016].

   This article surveys the manifold promising connections between picturebooks and the central concern of ELT – rich and meaningful communication. Mourão analyses picturebooks as artefacts, and then details and reports on systematic categorizations of children's engaged oral response when a picturebook is offered as a compound literary form.

5 O'Sullivan, E., and Rösler, D. (2013). *Kinder- und Jugendliteratur im Fremdsprachenunterricht*. Tübingen: Stauffenburg.

   The authors combine children's literature scholarship with a rich methodological repertoire to illustrate the benefits of children's literature in the foreign language classroom to promote literary reading and intercultural communicative competence.

Related topics

Teacher education, Materials for early language learning, Young learners' motivation, and CLIL

References

Agnew, K. (2001). Chapter books. In Watson, V. (ed.) *The Cambridge Guide to Children's Books in English*. Cambridge: Cambridge University Press, 139.

Al-Yaqout, G., and Nikolajeva, M. (2015). Re-conceptualising picturebook theory in the digital age. *Nordic Journal of ChildLit Aesthetics*, 6, x–x. www.childlitaesthetics.net/index.php/blft/article/view/26971/pdf_11 [Accessed 6 January 2017].

Alexie, S. (2016). *Thunder Boy Jr.* Y. Morales (illus.). New York: Little, Brown and Company.

Arizpe, E., Colomer, T., and Martínez-Roldán, C. (2014). *Visual Journeys through Wordless Narratives: An international inquiry with immigrant children and the arrival*. London: Bloomsbury.

Bader, B. (1976). *American Picturebooks From Noah's Art to the Beast Within*. New York: Palgrave Macmillan.

Bamford, J., and Day, R. (1997). Extensive reading: What is it? Why bother? *The Language Teacher*, 21(5). www.jalt-publications.org/tlt/articles/2132-extensive-reading-what-it-why-bother [Accessed 8 January 2017].

Bergner, G. (2016). *Azzi in between* – A bilingual experience in the primary EFL classroom. *Children's Literature in English Language Education*, 4(1), 44–58. http://clelejournal.org/a-bilingual-experience-in-the-primary-efl-classroom/ [Accessed 6 January 2017].

Bishop, R. S. (1990). Mirrors, windows, and sliding glass doors. *Perspectives: Choosing and Using Books for the Classroom*, 6(3), ix–xi.

Bland, J. (2009). *Mini-plays, Role-rhymes and Other Stepping Stones to English. Book 3: Favourite festivals*, 2nd ed. California: Players Press.

Bland, J. (2013). *Children's Literature and Learner Empowerment: Children and teenagers in English language education*. London: Bloomsbury.

Bland, J. (2014). Interactive theatre with student teachers and young learners: Enhancing EFL learning across institutional divisions in Germany. In Rich, S. (ed.) *International Perspectives on Teaching English to Young Leaners*. Basingstoke: Palgrave Macmillan, 156–174.

Bland, J. (2015a). Drama with young learners. In Bland, J. (ed.) *Teaching English to Young Learners: Critical issues in language teaching with 3–12 year olds*. London: Bloomsbury, 219–238.

Bland, J. (2015b). Grammar templates for the future with poetry for children. In Bland, J. (ed.) *Teaching English to Young Learners: Critical issues in language teaching with 3–12 year olds*. London: Bloomsbury, 147–166.

Bland, J. (2015c). Oral storytelling in the primary English classroom. In Bland, J. (ed.) *Teaching English to Young Learners: Critical issues in language teaching with 3–12 year olds*. London: Bloomsbury, 183–198.

Bland, J. (2015d). Pictures, images and deep reading. *Children's Literature in English Language Education*, 3(2), 24–36. http://clelejournal.org/pictures-images-and-deep-reading-bland/ [Accessed 10 October 2016].

Bland, J. (2016). English language education and ideological issues: Picturebooks and Diversity. *Children's Literature in English Language Education*, 4(2), 41–64. http://clelejournal.org/article-3-picturebooks-and-diversity/ [Accessed 6 January 2017].

Bland, J., Lütge, C., and Mourão, S. (2015). Editorial. *Children's Literature in English Language Education*, 3(1), ii–iii. http://clelejournal.org/contents-and-editorial-2/ [Accessed 12 August 2017].

Brunsmeier, S., and Kolb, A. (2017). Picturebooks go digital – The potential of story apps for the primary EFL classroom. *Children's Literature in English Language Education*, 5(1), 1–20. http://clelejournal.org/article-1-picturebooks-go-digital/ [Accessed 12 August 2017].

Cameron, L. (2001). *Teaching Languages to Young Learners*. Cambridge: Cambridge University Press.

Cameron, L. (2003). Challenges for ELT from the expansion in teaching children. *ELT Journal*, 57(2), 105–112.

Carter, R. (2015). Epilogue: Literature and language learning in the EFL classroom. In Teranishi, M, Saito, Y., and Wales, K. (eds.) *Literature and Language Learning in the EFL Classroom*. Basingstoke: Palgrave Macmillan, 316–320.

Creech, S. (2001). *Love that Dog*. New York: HarperCollins.

Coughlan, S. (2017). What does post-truth mean for a philosopher? *BBC NEWS*, 12 January. www.bbc.com/news/education-38557838 [Accessed 14 January 2017].

Ellis, G., and Brewster, J. (2014). *Tell it Again! The storytelling handbook for primary English language teachers*, 3rd ed. www.teachingenglish.org.uk/article/tell-it-again-storytelling-handbook-primary-english-language-teachers [Accessed 12 October 2016].

Ellis, N., O'Donnell, M., and Römer, U. (2013). Usage-based language: Investigating the latent structures that underpin acquisition. *Language Learning*, 63(Supp. 1), 25–51.

Enever, J. (2015). The advantages and disadvantages of English as a foreign language with young learners. In Bland, J. (ed.) *Teaching English to Young Learners: Critical issues in language teaching with 3–12 year olds*. London: Bloomsbury, 13–29.

Farmer, D. (2011). *Learning through Drama in the Primary Years*. Norwich: Drama Resource.

Fleming, M. (2013). Drama. In Byram, M., and Hu, A. (eds.) *Routledge Encyclopedia of Language Teaching and Learning*, 2nd ed. London: Routledge, 209–211.

Fleta, T., and Forster, E. (2014). From *Flat Stanley* to *Flat Cat*: An intercultural, interlinguistic project. *Children's Literature in English Language Education*, 2(1), 57–71. http://clelejournal.org/from-flat-stanley-to-flat-cat-an-intercultural-interlinguistic-project/ [Accessed 7 January 2017].

Garland, S. (2012). *Azzi in Between*. London: Francis Lincoln Children's Books.

Ghosn, I.-K. (2010). Five-year outcomes from children's literature-based programmes vs. programmes using a skills-based ESL course – The Matthew and Peter effects at work? In Tomlinson, B., and Masuhara, H. (eds.) *Research for Materials Development in Language Learning*. London: Continuum, 21–36.

Gibbons, P. (2015). *Scaffolding Language, Scaffolding Learning*, 2nd ed. Portsmouth, NH: Heinemann.

Hall, G. (2015). *Literature in Language Education*, 2nd ed. Basingstoke: Palgrave Macmillan.

Harmgarth, F. (1999). *Das Lesebarometer – Lesen und Umgang mit Büchern in Deutschland*. Gütersloh: Bertelsmann Stiftung.

Hoey, M. (2004). *Lexical Priming: A new theory of words and language*. London: Routledge.

Hsiu-Chih, S. (2008). The value of English picture story books. *ELT Journal*, 62(1), 47–55.

Hunt, P. (2001). *Children's Literature*. Oxford: Blackwell.

Kaminsky, A. (2016). *The Use of Singing, Storytelling and Chanting in the Primary EFL Classroom: Aesthetic experience and participation in FL learning*. Unpublished doctoral thesis. Swansea: University of Swansea.

Kersten, S. (2015). Language development in young learners: The role of formulaic language. In Bland, J. (ed.) *Teaching English to Young Learners: Critical issues in language teaching with 3–12 year olds*. London: Bloomsbury, 129–145.

Krashen, S., and Bland, J. (2014). Compelling comprehensible input, academic language and school libraries. *Children's Literature in English Language Education*, 2(2), 1–12. http://clelejournal.org/compelling-comprehensible-input/ [Accessed 14 January 2017].

Ludwig, C., and Pointner, F. (Eds.). (2013). *Teaching Comics in the Foreign Language Classroom*. Trier: Wissenschaftlicher Verlag Trier.

Lugossy, R. (2012). Constructing meaning in interaction through picture books. *C.E.P.S Journal*, 2(3), 97–117.

Maley, A. (2013). Creative writing for L2 students and teachers. In Bland, J., and Lütge, C. (eds.) *Children's Literature in Second Language Education*. London: Bloomsbury, 161–172.

McCloud, S. (1993). *Understanding Comics: The invisible art*. New York: HarperCollins.

McTaggart, J. (2008). Graphic novels. The good, the bad and the ugly. In Frey, N., and Fisher, D. (eds.) *Teaching Visual Literacy using Comic Books, Graphic Novels, Anime, Cartoons, and More to Develop Comprehension and Thinking Skills*. Thousand Oaks, CA: Corwin Press, 27–46.

Meek, M. (1993). What will literacy be like? *Cambridge Journal of Education*, 23(1), 89–99.

Morpurgo, M. (2014). www.storymuseum.org.uk/about-us/testimonials/ [Accessed 10 October 2016].

Mourão, S. (2012). *English Picturebook Illustrations and Language Development in Early Years Education*. Unpublished PhD Thesis. Aveiro: University of Aveiro.

Mourão, S. (2016). Picturebooks in the primary EFL classroom: Authentic literature for authentic responses. *Children's Literature in English Language Education*, 4(1), 25–43. http://clelejournal.org/authentic-literature-for-an-authentic-response/ [Accessed 8 October 2016].

Mourão, S., and Bland, J. (2016). Editorial vol. 4, issue 2: The jurney. *Children's Literature in English Language Education*, 4(2), ii–xi. http://clelejournal.org/contents-and-editorial-4/ [Accessed 6 January 2017].

Murphy, V. (2014). *Second Language Earning in the Early School Years: Trends and contexts*. Oxford: Oxford University Press.

Narančić Kovač, S. (2016). Picturebooks in educating teachers of English to young learners. *Children's Literature in English Language Education*, 4(2), 6–26. http://clelejournal.org/article-1-picturebooks-educating-teachers-english-young-learners/ [Accessed 14 January 2017].

Nikolajeva, M. (2014). *Reading for Learning: Cognitive approaches to children's literature*. Amsterdam: John Benjamins.

Nodelman, P. (2008). *The Hidden Adult: Defining children's literature*. Baltimore, MD: The John Hopkins University Press.

Nodelman, P., and Reimer, M. (2003). *The Pleasures of Children's Literature*, 3rd ed. Boston, MA: Allyn and Bacon.

Obama, B. (2017). President Obama on what books mean to him. *The New York Times*, 16 January. www.nytimes.com/2017/01/16/books/transcript-president-obama-on-what-books-mean-to-him.html?emc=eta1&_r=0 [Accessed 20 January 2017].

Opie, I. (1992). Introduction. In Opie, I., and Opie, P. (eds.) *I Saw Esau*. Sendak, M. (illus.), 2nd ed. London: Walker Books.

Oziewicz, M. (2018). Exploring challenges of the graphic novel format: Brian Selznick's *The Invention of Hugo Cabret, Wonderstruck* and *The Marvels*. In Bland, J. (ed.) *Using Literature in English Language Education: Challenging reading for 8–18 year olds*. London: Bloomsbury, 25–40.

Reynolds, B. L., and Chang, S. (2018). Empowering Taiwanese preservice EFL teachers through a picture book community service project. In Copland, F., and Garton, S. (eds.) *Voices from the Classroom: Teaching English to young learners*. Alexandria, VA: TESOL Press.

Serrurier-Zucker, C., and Gobbé-Mévellec, E. (2014). The page is the stage: From picturebooks to drama with young learners. *Children's Literature in English Language Education*, 2(2), 13–30. http://clele journal.org/from-picturebooks-to-drama-with-young-learners/ [Accessed 8 January 2017].

Tabbert, R., and Wardetzky, K. (1995). On the success of children's books and fairy tales: A comparative view of impact theory and reception research. *The Lion and the Unicorn*, 19(1), 1–19.

Thorne, J. (2016). *Harry Potter and the Cursed Child*, based on a story by J. K. Rowling and J. Tiffany. London: Little, Brown Book Group.

Wales, K. (2011). *A Dictionary of Stylistics*, 3rd ed. London: Longman Linguistics.

Wood, D. (1994). *Meg and Mog. Four Plays for Children.* London: Puffin.

Yanase, C. (2018) Getting children to be active agents of their own learning. In Copland, F., and Garton, S. (eds.) *Voices from the Classroom: Teaching English to young learners*. Alexandria, VA: TESOL Press.

Zipes, J. (2004). *Speaking Out: Storytelling and creative drama for children*. New York: Routledge.

18

Language learning through projects

Wendy Arnold, Coralyn Bradshaw and Kate Gregson

Introduction

This chapter will analyse the characteristics of projects and how they function within different overall approaches to teaching English as a foreign language to Young Learners (YL). Young learners are children between the ages of six and 16 years learning English, at primary (elementary) and secondary (high school) levels. 'Learners' and 'students' will be used synonymously unless indicated otherwise.

What is learning through projects?

The use of projects for learning is based on a constructivist, learner-centred approach to inquiry-based learning, and has been part of mainstream education for decades (Beckett 2002; Thomas 2000) if not centuries (Taylor et al. 1998; Knoll 1997).

According to Phillips et al. (1999, p. 6) projects are 'an integrated unit of work' with distinct parts, 'beginning, middle and end' (ibid.). The essential features are that a project requires independent research into a topic and results in a product. This can be in the form of text alone, but usually involves pictures, diagrams and other visual displays. Projects may be carried out by individuals or by small groups working together. Projects typically take more than a single lesson to complete and require some work to be done outside class; the learner develops holistically without language learning being the only focus – skills including 'intellectual, physical/motor, social and learner independence' (1999, p. 6, 2012) are also developed. Projects help to develop learner autonomy by encouraging making choices and taking responsibility, as well as transferable skills such as research. Projects lend themselves well to mixed-ability classes; they can also be used to supplement or complement an existing language programme, or the syllabus can be designed around them (Phillips et al 1999).

In summary, a project is an extended task; learners work through a number of activities towards an agreed goal; it involves 'planning, gathering of information, discussion, problem solving, oral or written reporting, and display' (Hedge 2004, p. 49).

What is language learning through projects?

The term Language Learning Through Projects (LLTP) will be used to distinguish the use of projects in the ELT context from other project-based approaches. Diane Philips describes that although the teacher controls the planning, it is the learners' ideas and personal interests that drive the project. The challenge for the teacher is to select the specific language and linguistic skills to be used or developed during project work. LLTP also has an outcome or authentic end product for the learners to show to others (2012, pp. 1–2).

In summary, what makes LLTP unique is that whilst learning through projects is a well-known mainstream method for learning, in LLTP language is deliberately integrated into one of the learning objectives alongside subject content. However, within English Language Teaching (ELT), LLTP remains an under-exploited and generally misunderstood type of activity (Alan and Stoller 2005).

Historical perspectives

The first section in this chapter will trace the history of using projects in the mainstream educational classroom and describe the initial transference of the concept of project work to the field of ELT.

With the rise of the philosophical movement Pragmatism in the late nineteenth and early twentieth century in the USA, project work became the focal point of a new progressive educational approach. John Dewey's seminal educational theories were presented in a series of publications between 1897 and 1938. The most influential of these being, arguably, Dewey's *Democracy and Education* (1926, p. 11), where, as in other works, he argues that education and learning are social and interactive processes, where students interact with the curriculum and take part in their own learning. Kilpatrick (1918) was the first American reformer to coin the term 'Project Method', thereby challenging the traditional view of the student as passive recipient of knowledge and the teacher as the transmitter of a static body of facts. Meanwhile in Europe, themes around project work were emerging with the work of, among others, Gaudig (in Fragoulis 2009), responsible principally for the idea of group work in pursuit of problem solving. The important concepts of the constructivist educational psychologists Piaget (1952), Vygotsky (1978) and Bruner (1978) are interwoven into this view of learning as investigative, problem solving, co-operative and reflective, and diametrically opposed to the traditional notions of passive rote learning.

Within the field of educational linguistics the movement towards more proactive learning did not go unnoticed. From the middle of the twentieth century the straitjacket of behaviourist and structural linguistics was discarded. Jacobs and Farrell (2003, p. 16) suggest that a 'Communicative Language Teaching (CLT) paradigm shift' occurred, wherein project work first featured in the field of ESL (English as a Second Language) under 'Project Based Learning' (PBL) in the USA (which is discussed below) and subsequently in what are traditionally called EFL (English as a Foreign Language) contexts. This shift was towards a more sociocognitive, contextualised and meaning-based view of language learning. Project work in ESL and ELT evolves within this CLT framework.

There are several mainstream education initiatives using projects that we will explore below in chronological order. These all share common goals of engaging students in exploring real-world issues and solving practical problems.

The project approach

The Project Approach, evolving from Kilpatrick's Project Method, was coined by Katz and Chard (1993) who underlined that 'including project work in the curriculum promotes children's intellectual development by engaging their minds in observation and investigation of selected aspects of their experience and environment' (Katz and Chard 2000, p. 2). Katz (1994) outlines the approach as involving three phases: Phase 1: students and their teacher select and discuss a topic to be explored; Phase 2: students conduct investigations and then create representations of their findings; Phase 3: students present their project and receive feedback. The underpinning structure of a project is therefore envisaged as (1) content, (2) processes and (3) products.

Project-based learning or project-based instruction

Project-Based Learning (PBL) described by Thomas (2000), sometimes referred to as Project-Based Instruction (PBI) (Hedge 2004; Stoller 1997; Becket 1999), takes the principles of the Project Method and crafts them into a more rigorous form. Thomas (2000) provides a detailed definition of PBL, underscoring the students' need for more in-depth autonomous enquiry, as well as collaborative skills, supported by research using twenty-first century technological tools.

The Buck Institute for Education carefully reviews the work of Larmer, Mergendoller and Boss (2015, pp. 2–4) in order to put together a framework for what is referred to as the Golden Standards for project work. They list seven 'Gold Standard' essential project design elements, which suggest a fundamental requirement of PBL as including higher order thinking skills such as reflection and critical analysis:

- Challenging problem or Question
- Sustained Inquiry
- Authenticity
- Student Voice and Choice
- Reflection
- Critique and Revision
- Public Product.

Furthermore, Bradley-Levine and Mosier (2014, p. 1) identify a major development of PBL/PBI from the Project Method:

> In PBL, projects requiring students to apply the knowledge and the skills they learn are the focus of the curriculum rather than being added as a supplement at the end of traditional instruction.

LLTP in TEYL

Turning to TEYL, literature on and research into the use of projects with young learners of English is scant. Indeed, the most prominent evidence of projects appears in published materials, including coursebooks written for an international market, usually in the private sector (Oxford Discover 2013–2014; Cambridge Global English 2014a, b; Projects Fourth Edition 2014). A number of glocal coursebooks (Arnold and Rixon 2008, p. 40) written for a specific context but with a global perspective, usually used in the public or state education sector, also use an LLTP approach (English for Palestine 2011; New Magic 2008).

A number of education reforms in TEYL have included cross-curricular, thematic-based language learning through projects, for example in Hong Kong (EdB 2004, p. 104), giving the rationale that the inclusion of projects for learning is intended to involve learners in integrating language within a thematic-based investigation in order to 'develop independence and a sense of responsibility', as well as making choices, linking school and the outside world, real-life investigations, planning and organizing.

There is also anecdotal evidence that teachers use an LLTP approach as discussed in Part 4 below from the online survey.

Summary

There is no clear pathway that has led to the evolution of the use of projects into LLTP; indeed it seems to have come from an eclectic combination of mainstream project-based approaches, topic/thematic-based learning, activities, features of learning how to learn and sometimes uses PBL with a learner-centred and CLT approach.

Critical Issues

A general critical issue that has an impact on TEYL is the fast-growing number of countries introducing English at ever-younger ages. References supporting an early start to learn English are prolific, widely offering the advantage that learners have longer to learn the language. However, caveats exist, such as the need for teacher education that acknowledges different areas of child development including second/foreign language, culturally appropriate curriculum, assessment and provision of learning materials, and support from parents and school management. Without this, the success of implementation will be limited and unsustainable (Rixon 2013 and 2015; Rich 2014; Enever and Moon 2009; Enever 2015; Johnston 2009; Murphy 2014; Murphy and Evangelou 2016).

With these cautions in mind we will explore the following topics, considering what is needed in order to adopt LLTP effectively:

1   Teachers: teacher English language levels; teacher education.
2   Approach and methods: learner-centred education and context.

Teachers and LLTP

Although there lacks a consistent definition of teacher language skills in the literature, the Early Language Learning in Europe (ELLiE) summary concludes that CEFR (Common European Framework of Reference) C2 is needed, along with training in an age-appropriate methodology (Enever 2011, p. 5). Hayes (2014, p. 2) recommends at least CEFR B2, ideally C1. However, research shows that there are problematic gaps in the supply of adequately prepared teachers (Enever and Moon 2009; Emery 2012; Rixon 2013; Rixon 2015). Moreover, Alvarez et al. (2015, p. 259) report on a pilot of an English language and methodology project which showed that of the 97 generalist teachers in primary schools who took part, 41 (42%) scored A0-A1 in the British Council's Aptis test (CEFR equivalent).

In short, there seems to be a shortfall of teachers with either the training in appropriate TEYL methodology or adequate English language levels. This has implications for the delivery of LLTP, as it needs teachers who have both the linguistic skills and training in age-appropriate methodology in order to plan, prepare and deliver LLTP effectively.

Approach and methods

LLTP is based on LCE (Learner-Centred Education), which Schweisfurth (2011, p. 425) says is a 'culturally nuanced perspective (which) raises questions about how teaching and learning are understood in different contexts' and which, as a 'western approach' may be inappropriate for application in all societies and classrooms. Holliday (1994, pp. 175–177) also concurs, and goes on to say that LCE has been 'responsible for the failures in making the communicative approach work outside the BANA (British Australian North American) classroom' because 'it presupposes that we know a great deal about the learner' (ibid.), when the contrary is often true. Furthermore, Garton et al. (2011, pp. 5–6) reference multiple cases where there is evidence that CLT and at least one of its offshoot/derived methods, TBLT, have been adapted in certain contexts to align to the context-specific value and belief systems. In addition, there are multiple references to querying the application of CLT for TEYL because of issues such as 'over-crowded classrooms with few resources' and 'different educational traditions', as well as imperfect understanding of the method by teachers and the perceived inappropriate nature of the method (Garton et al 2011, p. 9). However, Holliday (1994, pp. 175–177) argues that by focusing on a 'learning-centred' approach together with 'culture-sensitive features', this could become appropriate classroom methodology.

Furthermore, Arnold and Rixon note that the speed with which TEYL has been introduced has 'outpaced the teacher education and creation of suitable materials'. Materials need to be both 'child-friendly' and 'teacher-friendly' so that they can support teachers who may be inexperienced in TEYL (2008, pp. 39–40). Arnold and Bradshaw (2012, p. 5) caution that a 'top down, aspirational, prescriptive' curriculum has a direct impact on the materials designed for young learners, which could result in materials that are too complex to either be delivered by the teacher or understood by the YL. They argue for a 'bottom up, pragmatic and experiential' (ibid.) curriculum that is relevant to the needs of the YL and the abilities of the teachers.

In short, due to the possible resistance to an LCE approach it is critical that teachers and learners are exposed to LLTP and are given time to understand the benefits. Teachers would need training as there is a role change for both learners and teachers in this approach.

Summary

Two critical concerns are therefore (a) the lack of readily available teachers with the appropriate linguistic competency and methodological training in order to deliver LLTP; and (b) appropriate materials to guide the teacher and their learners on using an approach which focuses on both content and language learning in parallel.

The teacher's role is critical, and without adequate levels of English language and knowledge of an age-appropriate methodology, no methodology will be successful. Murphy and Evangelou (2016, p. 300) agree, suggesting that the areas that need developing are: 'i) developing a skilled workforce through professional training, ii) developing quality environments in early years settings, and iii) the need for more research into children's development both within and across settings.'

Current contributions and research

In this section, we will present a review of recent and current research into the use of projects in different educational contexts, identifying relevant contributions to the TYL field. Unsurprisingly, given the wide-spread use reported in mainstream contexts, extensive reports on research into Project-Based Learning in schools and universities exist (Thomas 2000). There seem, however, to be fewer reports on the use of projects in ELT or, specifically, in TEYL, as Mukhurjee (2015) notes. Furthermore, as discussed previously, there is a wide variety in the interpretation, design and implementation of projects in classroom practice, and commonality of defining features of 'projects' among the reports on research is largely lacking.

Nonetheless, as we have noted, the aim in language education to young learners is not limited to the development of language skills, but is to address the development of the whole child, so as to include other skills, such as cognitive, social-emotional or twenty-first century skills. As such, it is useful to draw on the findings of research within this broad area, in order to contribute to a definition of good practice in LLTP and to further explore research findings related to some of the critical issues noted in the previous section. To this end, a review of around 30 reports on recent research and a number of reviews of current research in the field was undertaken. In addition, an online global survey of young learner English language teachers was conducted by the authors to find out what teachers of English knew about the use of projects in language learning.

Overall, findings of much of the research into the use of projects across contexts and ages are positive in terms of academic gains, cognitive, metacognitive and co-operative skills development and in student engagement, especially in Western mainstream educational contexts (Beckett and Slater 2005). Margaret Holm (2011, pp. 5–8) reviewed research conducted in mainstream state and private pre-school, primary and secondary education in Turkey, the USA, Hong Kong, Qatar and Israel, concurring with Beckett and Slater (2005). Some report overall benefits, at the primary level in ESL in Asia, such as Wong (2001) and Chua (2004; both cited in Liu et al. 2006), although this positivity is not entirely mirrored on a global level or in EFL contexts, where students do not always see the value in project work for language development (Beckett and Slater 2005).

Results from our online global survey indicated that 34% (of the 90 respondents) used 'learning through projects' at the end of a unit or topic, and 25% at the end of each term. Respondents felt that success in LLTP was mostly due to the learners: their critical thinking and application of knowledge (both 67%); choice in what they learn and how they present it (58%); and working independently, in pairs or groups (47%). No question was asked about challenges incurred.

Loosely based around Holm's (2011) review categories, the following thematic areas have been identified in the literature. These areas are intended to link into and build on the critical issues identified in the previous section.

1   Student factors: attitude, self-perception and autonomy; development, learning and skills.
2   Teacher factors: teacher beliefs; teacher role; professional development and training.
3   Project and contextual factors: design and authenticity; curriculum fit; learning context.

Student factors

Within this broad area, a number of points arose from the review. Firstly, studies in non-ELT mainstream education (e.g., Thomas 2011; Holm 2011) and tertiary ELT contexts

(Kaldi et al. 2011) found the impact of project work on student attitude, motivation and self-perception generally positive. Indeed several studies in TEYL contexts reported similarly positive findings in relation to student engagement, often attributed to the opportunity for student choice, such as in the decision-making processes (Pinter et al. 2016) or tasks (Riga 2011). Kogan (2003) also reported raised self-motivation, excitement, interest and willingness to work hard in her bilingual context.

The provision of choice seems to be supported by several studies, which undertook to investigate impact on learner autonomy and self-direction. Arnold (2006, p. 17), for example, notes that projects undertaken with young learners of English in Hong Kong where choice was permitted, 'encourage[d] learner autonomy by promoting responsibility in making choices'. In a study related to the hole-in-the-wall experiments in rural India (Mitra 2000), Mitra and Dangwal (2010) found that different children self-organised and assumed different roles. Other mainstream studies, however, suggest students need support in developing learning to learn skills or may be less willing to have such a shift of role. Fragoulis (2009), for example, reports that several Greek EFL primary-aged students would have preferred more teacher direction and less choice. As such, it seems that in order for learner autonomy to develop, learning to learn skills may also need specific attention in preparation for projects.

The need to prepare students for LLTP, by raising student awareness of the benefits and values of project work, was clear in several studies especially in language teaching. For example, Gibbes and Carson (2004), looking at the tertiary level, mention that a lack of preparedness may negatively impact students' acceptance. In TEYL, the children in Pinter et al.'s (2016) study were positive about the change from rote and book-based learning. Nonetheless, this would seem to be a potential issue, especially as children may have relatively fixed views due to their limited experience, even at a younger age. To this end, Beckett and Slater (2005) developed and tested their 'Project Framework', a tool which aims to raise such awareness in older learners before and during project work, finding that students' perceptions became more positive over time, as is echoed in other studies, including those in bilingual/ESL contexts, such as Kogan (2003) and Liu, et al (2006).

Several studies reviewed by Holm (2011) support the claim that project work can address diverse learning needs. This is also reflected in TEYL, such as Fragoulis's (2009) study, which reported raised intrinsic motivation among Greek primary-aged learners, even those with lower self-esteem or confidence in their language skills. Similarly, an improvement in levels of engagement, participation, motivation and children's sense of pride in their work was reported as being common among students at different stages of ESL development in India (Mukhurjee 2015). Cusen (2013) further found increased desire to develop perceived weaknesses in language skills in an ESL setting.

Many studies indicate the value of learning through projects in terms of skills development:

- Twenty-first century skills (Bell 2010, in mainstream primary).
- Transferable skills (Gibbes and Carson 2004, at the tertiary level).
- IT skills (such as Arnold 2003, as a particular benefit to boys in TEYL).
- Cognitive skills such as creativity, planning, decision making, problem solving and critical thinking in young learner contexts, such as Kogan (2003) and Chang and Chang (2003, cited in Liu et al. 2006).
- Collaborative and co-operative skills (especially in TEYL: Fragoulis 2009; Mukhurjee 2015; Pinter et al. 2016).

- Greater depth and richness of content knowledge was found in many studies, particularly in mainstream contexts (such as Holm 2002; Kaldi et al. 2014).
- Greater long-term retention and flexibility of learning were noted (cited in Thomas 2000), also in mainstream contexts.

Further investigations into learning through projects within content-based approaches in TEYL would be welcome.

Moving on to linguistic skills development, a number of issues were identified. Bicaki and Gursoy's (2010, cited in Holm 2011) study in a Turkish mainstream pre-school found improved mother tongue skills. In EFL and ESL environments, results were more mixed, however. Some reported language development as a result of real language use and an inter-relatedness with content (Beckett 1999, cited in Beckett and Slater 2005), or an increase in children's L2 risk-taking and experimentation (Fragoulis 2009). Others, meanwhile, voiced more negativity, for example in the development of lexis, syntax and grammar (Gibbes and Carson 2014).

Interestingly, a number of EFL and ESL studies noted students' high use of mother tongue during group interaction in project work, and a number of comments and recommendations for project work with young English language learners came through, such as the need for guidance and encouragement (Fragoulis 2009), language input (Gibbes and Carson 2014) and constant monitoring (Mukhurjee 2015). Nonetheless, others argued that the language input and output at other stages of the project more than suffice for acquisition, and that project work encouraged quieter or less confident students to begin to participate in English (Fragoulis 2009), or that the desire to ask questions pushed children to mix languages in order to convey meaning and form questions (Kogan 2003).

Teacher factors

Teacher beliefs are highly influential in the success of project approaches, making projects easier for some teachers to implement than others, depending on a range of factors such as teaching philosophy, current and previous teaching and learning experiences (Clark 2006). In several contexts around the world, both in language and mainstream education, such as in Hong Kong (Arnold 2003) and West Bengal (Mukhurjee 2015), project work has been introduced through educational reforms, but this does not always seem to imply a change in sometimes deep-seated beliefs held by teachers, who may be resistant to change (Clark 2006). Indeed, Cusen (2013) noted resistance and difficulty in implementation across Asia due to the prevalence of traditional and exam-oriented teaching practices. Nonetheless, it seems that even reluctant teachers who try using projects in their teaching develop an awareness of their value over time and continue to use – or at least want to use – projects after the research period (Mukhurjee 2015, in an Indian ESL context). Interestingly, Kogan (2003, n.p.), in a bilingual setting, reports change in attitude among colleagues of research participants, who were 'amazed' by the effects of project work on learners, reaffirming the need for awareness raising and reflective practice as teachers adopt LLTP.

Teachers' response to the shift in role away from controller and giver of knowledge was also an initial stumbling block in some studies (Clark 2006; Thomas 2001), as new teaching skills are needed in, for example, classroom management, planning, interaction with students and open-ended and student centred questioning (Tal, Krajcik, and Blumenfeld 2006, cited in Holm 2011, p. 7). Chard's (1999) pre-school study confirms teachers are initially challenged by ongoing responsive planning and negotiation with students, and at higher levels, skills in scaffolding learning can be lacking (Thomas 2001). While some teachers report negativity about this need for change, given time, most resolved this (Thomas 2001), and some come to view a project approach as an opportunity for professional development (Pinter et al. 2016), or as improving professionalism (Thomas 2001).

Project and contextual factors

A number of factors in project design come through in the review. Firstly, Fragoulis (2009) and Grant (2009) concluded with warnings against over-extending projects as students lose interest and motivation, while Cusen (2013) suggests that topics which induce an emotional response and inspire varied tasks can lengthen engagement. Difficulties related to curriculum fit, that is aligning project content or scenarios with curriculum guidelines, can also be identified (Thomas 2000), especially 'with increased competition among curricular objectives, the quantities of time dedicated to in-depth inquiries are difficult for teachers to reconcile' (Veermans et al. 2005, cited in Grant 2009, n.p.). This may equally be of concern in many TEYL contexts, depending perhaps on the type of institution, curriculum or syllabus. It was, indeed, cited as an issue by Mukhurjee (2015) in an Indian ESL environment.

Contextual or school factors have also been shown to be problematic in the implementation of projects, namely colleagues, head teachers, time and curriculum (Fragoulis 2009). Further obstacles include timetable, lack of support, school culture, time and space for learning in a different way (Leat et al. 2014); also resources, finance and facilities limited several studies (Leat et al. 2014; Mikulec and Chamnus-Miller 2011; Mukhurjee 2015). Nonetheless, Mitra and Dangwal's (2010) fascinating study in India, investigating self-directed learning in three different settings, a hole-in-the-wall (public computer facility) setting, a local state school setting and a high performing private city school, found that progress made by students in the hole-in-the-wall setting was considerable, and that they caught up with their peers in the local school when a mediator, a non-specialist adult who was known to the children and who supervised but did not teach them (Mitra and Dangwal 2010, p. 678), was present. This suggests that lack of, or inadequate, resources and facilities may be perceived as limiting, but are issues which can be overcome, even in situations where teachers may lack specific training.

Summary

Benefits to the development of a wealth of skills, including linguistic skills, are clearly evident in many reports, and with support and pre-project preparation in terms of learning-to-learn skills development as well as awareness-raising regarding these benefits, students largely seem to be brought on board with LLTP.

The teacher's change of role may be the biggest challenge to LLTP, especially in contexts such as Asia where there is a more traditional approach to learning. However, teachers who used LLTP found that over time the advantages outweighed the initial disadvantages such as longer time for planning and learning new skills.

Finally, the length of time of a project seems to be a challenge, and if it continues for too long, this can impact the motivation of the YL. Some TEYL contexts also had challenges with the school environment and fitting LLTP into the already crowded timetable, if it was supplementary to published materials.

Recommendations for Practice

This section will identify some recommendations for implementing LLTP in TEYL contexts derived from the discussions above. There are two main areas: (1) trainer training: training the teacher on their role, and (2) learner training: the need to prepare the students, allowing them to take a more active role in learning-to-learn and collaborating with others.

Teacher training

It is recommended that the design of LLTP should clearly define the role of the teacher, and that for successful adoption of these roles, training will generally be necessary. Two possible role scenarios are given, adoption of which depends on whether it is the teacher or the published materials that take the more active role in guiding the learners. The roles are outlined in Table 18.1.

Within Teacher Role 1 there may also be sub-scenarios, which include:

a   Teachers with adequate English language levels, e.g., CEFR C2+ but unused to developing LLTP materials.
b   Generalist primary teachers with inadequate English language levels, e.g., CEFR A0-A1 who are unconfident with language and methodology to teach language.

In order for these roles to be embraced, teacher training is needed. The nature and extent of this training may vary between different contexts, but some general recommendations include:

i   In-service, age-appropriate and extensive English language and LLTP methodology courses for generalist primary teachers who have been asked to teach English. Alvarez et al (2015) provide a model that could be modified to focus on LLTP concepts.
ii   Pre-service age-appropriate English language and LLTP methodology courses for generalist primary, subject primary and secondary teachers. There should be multiple opportunities for teaching practice to develop skills and understanding.
iii   If published materials are used, they need to be carefully checked to ensure that they are realistic in terms of the teacher's language and methodology abilities, and age appropriate for learners.

Table 18.1 Teacher roles

Teacher role 1 (design project to i) supplement, or (ii) complement published material or (iii) deliver the English syllabus and guiding the learning)	Teacher role 2 (using published materials which lead learning)
• Planning the project	• Leading the learners through the tasks/activities in the published materials using an enquiry (questions)
• Provider of the language arising from the communicative needs of the learners	• Providing additional resources and opportunities for the enquiry, e.g., reference books, a visit to the community, inviting a speaker
• Making the connections to cross-curricular subjects	• Implementing the assessment according to the design of the published materials.
• Sequencing the tasks/activities	
• Designing the structure of the authentic enquiry	
• Guiding the authentic enquiry, possibly using a problem, cause, effect and solution.	

iv   Such short, intensive teacher training courses require monitoring and evaluation in order to gauge short and long-term impact and sustainability (Ellis and Read 2015, p. 129).

v   Teachers themselves need to be pro-active and willing to develop both the linguistic and methodological skills needed.

Learner training

The second recommended area is the preparation of the students to understand the importance of their role in taking responsibility in learning-to-learn, as well as the benefits of collaboration and co-operation with peers. Beckett and Slater's (2005) Project Framework was developed to make LLTP more successful by supporting teachers in managing students' beliefs, goals and expectations, as we noted above. This framework is a tool composed of two elements, the 'planning graphic' and the 'project diary' (Beckett and Slater 2005, p. 110). These serve to show students the development of language content and skills from the project work, and hence, not only raise their awareness of their value but also raise meta-cognitive awareness of the learning process and strategies.

Wilhelm (1999, p. 16) also addresses the concern that 'students accustomed to more traditional, teacher-directed classrooms will generally respond with anxiety and confusion if expected to take responsibility for decision making too soon'. Arising from her studies into English language learners at the tertiary level, she identified five areas of student need to be analysed for planning collaborative project-based work:

1   Developing trust and interpersonal relationships.
2   Explaining and demonstrating student and teacher roles and responsibilities.
3   Modelling the collaborative learning approach.
4   Nurturing participant feedback, reflection and peer negotiation.
5   Utilizing well-balanced, appropriate grading systems.

These areas would clearly be relevant to YLs, developing various skills, and would help raise awareness and understanding of the value of LLTP. As such, it is strongly recommended that teachers take the time to prepare their students for LLTP, having identified the needs of their class, and continue by formalizing the process by using a tool similar to or derived from Beckett and Slater's (2005) Project Framework, designed with their specific learners, their context and their needs in mind.

Future directions

This chapter has discussed the emergence of LLTP as an approach at a time when education reforms have moved away from rote learning towards integrated learner-centred approaches. There is a need for more Ministries of Education to take the long-term view to education reform, such as Hong Kong, who started their reform in 2000. In the short-term development, one of the strategies to develop learning how to learn was project-based learning (Cheng 2009, p. 69).

In the future, research is needed into the impact of LLTP in various areas. Firstly, research is needed related to the transition to LLTP from more traditional approaches, which may be part of education reform at the policy level. Research into age-appropriate LLTP materials that are also at a suitable level for teachers would also be welcome. A number of issues relating to teacher and school management training have been highlighted in this chapter and would also warrant investigation. Lastly, the potential and actual impact that LLTP has on students and their language development would certainly be a valuable area to scrutinise through, for example, action research. Studies in any one of these areas would greatly contribute to the limited body of literature on LLTP.

Further reading

Alvarez, L. C., Arnold, W., Bradshaw, C., and Gregson, M. (2015). Capacity building and empowerment: A primary teacher-training project in Venezuela. In Giannikas, C. N., McLaughlin, L., Fannin, G., and Muller, N. D. (eds.) *Children learning English: From research to practice*. Reading: Garnet Education and IATEFL

A chapter in this publication outlines how a pilot project in a developing country, Venezuela, was implemented across 11 cities over a period of 10 months to generalist primary teachers. It consisted of 100-hour language development/basic primary methodology based on the British Council's English for Teachers (EfT) A0/A1 syllabus, with workshop materials written by British Council-trained local university lecturers. This could be modified to include LLTP and used as a model to train generalist primary teachers with low English language levels in age-appropriate language and methodology.

Phillips, D., Burwood, S., and Dunford, H. (1999). *Projects with young learners*. Oxford: Oxford University Press

This publication gives both experienced and less experienced teachers a simple, easily accessible, step-by-step format to setting up and delivering projects. There are visuals to make the meaning clear, as well as variations to extend the project. Level of learner, age group, timing, description, language, skills, materials, preparation and steps are all defined.

Related topics

CLIL, assessment, mobile learning, materials

References

Alan, B., and Stoller, F. L. (2005). Maximising the benefits of project work in foreign language classrooms. *English Teaching Forum*, 43(4).

Alvarez, L. C., Arnold, W., Bradshaw, C., and Gregson, M. (2015). Capacity building and empowerment: A primary teacher-training project in Venezuela. In Giannikas, C. N., McLaughlin, L., Fanning, G., and Muller, N. D. (eds.) *Children Learning English: From research to practice*. Reading: Garnet Publishing Ltd.

Arnold, W. (2003). Collaborative learning explored through the use of projects: Does freedom of choice promote collaboration? In Begley, J., and Hughes, A. (eds.) *Teaching English to Young Learners: Second international TEYL research seminar papers, 2003*. York: Department of Education, University of York.

Arnold, W. (2006). Promoting collaboration through project work: practical implications of ongoing longitudinal research. In Schuitevoerder, R. M., and Mourao, S. (eds.) *Teachers and Young Learners: Research in our classrooms*. Canterbury: IATEFL.

Arnold, W., and Bradshaw, C. (2012). A balancing trick between curriculum materials design and teacher ability. *MA in TEYL Module Materials*. York: University of York, Department of Education.

Arnold, W., and Rixon, S. (2008). Materials for young learners. In Tomlinson, B. (ed.) *English Language Learning Materials*. London: Continuum International Publishing Group.

Beckett, G. H. (1999). *Project-based Instruction in a Canadian Secondary School's ESL Classes: Goals and evaluations*. Unpublished PhD thesis, University of British Columbia.

Beckett, G. H. (2002). Teacher and student evaluations of project-based instruction. *TESL Canada Journal/Revenue TESL Du Canada*, 19(2).

Beckett, G. H., and Slater, T. (2005). The project framework: A tool for language, content, and skills integration. *ELT Journal*, 59(2).

Bell, S. (2010). Project-based learning for the 21st century: Skills for the future. *The Clearing House: A Journal of Educational Strategies, Issues and Ideas*, 83(2), 39–43.

Bradley-Levine, J., and Mosier, G. (2014). *Literature Review on Project-based Learning*. Center of Excellence in Leadership of Learning University of Indianapolis. http://cell.uindy.edu/wp-content/uploads/2014/07/PBL-Lit-Review_Jan14.2014.pdf [Accessed 13 October 2016].

Bruner, J. (1978). The role of dialogue in language acquisition. In Sinclair, A., Jarvelle, R. J., and Levelt, W. J. M. (eds.) *The Child's Concept of Language*. New York: Springer-Verlag.

Cambridge Global English, 2014 Grade 1 to 6. Cambridge: Cambridge University Press. http://education.cambridge.org/uk/subject/english/english-as-a-second-language/cambridge-global-english-(1-6) [Accessed 6 November 2016].

Cambridge Global English, 2014 Grade 7 to 9. Cambridge: Cambridge University Press. http://education.cambridge.org/uk/subject/english/english-as-a-second-language/cambridge-global-english-(7-9) [Accessed 6 November 2016].

Chard, S. C. (1999). From themes to projects. *Early Childhood Research & Practice*, 1 (1). http://ecrp.illinois.edu/v1n1/chard.html [Accessed 10 October 2016].

Cheng, Y. C. (2009). Hong Kong educational reforms in the last decade: Reform syndrome and new developments. *International Journal of Educational Management*, 23(1), 66–86. www.eduhk.hk/apclc/dowloadables/Publications/2009/Hong%20Kong%20educational%20reforms%20in%20the%20last%20decade.pdf [Accessed 11 November 2016].

Clark, A-M. (2006). Changing classroom practice to include the Project Approach. *Early Childhood Research & Practice*, 8(2). http://ecrp.uiuc.edu/v8n2/clark.html [Accessed 07 January 2016].

Cusen, O. M. (2013). The child soldiers project: Employing a project-based learning and teaching curriculum. *Language Education in Asia*, 4 (2).

Dewey, J. (1926). *Democracy and Education: An introduction to the philosophy of education*. New York: Palgrave Macmillan.

EdB Education Bureau Hong Kong. (2004). *English language curriculum guide primary 1 to 6*. Hong Kong: Curriculum Development Council. www.edb.gov.hk/attachment/en/curriculum- development/kla/eng-edu/primary%201_6.pdf [Accessed 25 October 2016].

Ellis, G, and Read, C. (2015). Course design and evaluation in primary teacher education. In Giannikas, C. N., McLaughlin, L., Fanning, G., and Muller, N. D. (eds.) *Children Learning English: From research to practice*. Reading: Garnet Publishing Ltd.

Emery, H. (2012). A global study of primary English teachers' qualifications, training and career development. In *ELT Research Papers*, 12(08). London: British Council.Enever, J. (2011). *Early Language Learning in Europe (ELLiE)*. London: British Council. www.teachingenglish.org.uk/sites/teacheng/files/B309%20ELLiE%20Book%202011%20FINAL.pdf [Accessed 28 October 2016].

Enever, J. (2015). The advantages and disadvantages of English as a foreign language with young learners. In Bland, J. (ed.) *Teaching English to Young Learners: Critical issues in language teaching with 3–12 year olds*. London: Bloomsbury.

Enever, J., and Moon, J. (2009). New global contexts for teaching primary ELT: Change and challenge. In Enever, J., and Moon, J. (eds.) *Young Learner English Language Policy and Implementation: International perspectives*. Reading: Garnet Education and IATEFL.

English for Palestine, 2011 to 2014, Grades 1 to 12. Oxford: Macmillan Education. www.englishforpalestine.com/wp-content/uploads/2016/01/English-for-Palestine-Curriculum-Document-19.01.2016.pdf [Accessed 6 November 2016].

Fragoulis, I. (2009). Project-based learning in the teaching of English as a foreign language in Greek primary schools: From theory to practice. In *CCSE*, 2(3), 113–119.Garton, S., Copland, F., and Burns, A. (2011). Investigating global practices in teaching English to young learners. *ELT Research Papers*, 11(01). London: British Council. http://englishagenda.britishcouncil.org/sites/ec/files/B094%20FINAL%20Aston%20University%20A4%20report_2column_V3.pdf [Accessed 26 October 2016].

Garvie, E. (1990). *Story as Vehicle*. Avon: Multilingual Matters Ltd.

Gibbes, M., and Carson, L. (2014). Project-based language learning: An activity theory analysis. *Innovation in Language Learning and Teaching*, 8(2), 171–189.

Grant, M. M. (2009). *Understanding Projects in Project-based Learning: A student's perspective*. San Diego: American Educational Research Association. April 16, 2009.

Hayes, D. (2014). *Factors Influencing Success in Teaching English in State Primary Schools*. London: British Council. www.teachingenglish.org.uk/sites/teacheng/files/E324_Factors_influencing_success_in_teaching_English_in_state_primary_schools_FINAL%20v3_WEB.pdf [Accessed 11 November 2016].

Hedge, T. (2004). Key concepts: Project work. In Ellis, G., and Morrow, K. (eds.) *ELTJ Year of the Young learner. Special Collection*, 47(3), 275–277.

Holliday, A. (1994). *Appropriate Methodology and Social Context*. Cambridge: Cambridge University Press.

Holm, M. (2011). Project-based Instruction: A review of the literature on effectiveness in Prekindergarten through 12th grade classroom. INSIGHT: *Rivier Academic Journal*, 7(2). www.rivier.edu/journal/ROAJ-Fall-2011/J575-Project-Based-Instruction-Holm.pdf [Accessed 10 October2016].

Jacobs, G. M., and Farrell, T. S. C. (2003). Understanding and implementing the communicative language teaching paradigm. *RELC Journal*, 34(1). http://people.exeter.ac.uk/msp203/MEd%20Formative%20Assignment/Understanding%20and%20Implementing%20the%20CLT%20Paradigm.pdf [Accessed 10 October 2016].

Johnstone, J. (2009). An early start: What are the key conditions for generalized success? In Enever, J., and Moon, J. (eds.) *Young Learner English Language Policy and Implementation: International perspectives*. Reading: Garnet Education and IATEFL.

Kaldi, S., Filippatou, D., and Anthopoulou, B. (2014). The effectiveness of structured co-operative teaching and learning in Greek primary school classrooms. *Education*, 3–13, (42), 6, 621–636.

Kaldi, S., Filiappatou, D., and Govaris, C. (2011). Project based learning in primary schools: Effects on pupils' learning and attitudes. *Education*, 3–13, (39), 1, 35–47.

Katz, L. (1994). The project approach. In *ERIC Digest*. Champaign: ERIC Clearinghouse on Elementary and Early Childhood Education.

Katz, L. G., and Chard, S. (1993). The project approach. In Roopnarine, Jaipaul L., and Johnson, J. E. (eds.) *Approaches to Early Childhood Education*, 2nd ed. New York: Merrill, 209–222.

Katz, L. G., and Chard, S. (2000). *Engaging Children's Minds: The project approach*, 2nd ed. Norwood: Ablex.

Kilpatrick, W. H. (1918). *The Project Method: The use of the purposeful act in educative process. Teachers college record*. New York: Columbia University Press.

Knoll, M. (1997). The project method: Its vocational education origin and international development. *Journal of Industrial Teacher Education*, 34(3).

Kogan, Y. (2003). A study of bones. *Early Childhood Research & Practice*, 5(1). http://ecrp.illinois.edu/v5n1/kogan.html [Accessed 10 October 2016].

Larmer, J., Mergendoller, J., and Boss, S. (2015). Setting the standard for project based learning: A proven approach to rigorous classroom instruction. www.bie.org/blog/gold_standard_pbl_essential_project_design_elements [Accessed 27 October 2016].

Leat, D., Thomas, U., and Lofthouse, R. (2014). Project based and enquiry based learning – The professional development challenge. *Professional Development Today*, 16(4), 12–18. http://library.teachingtimes.com/articles/pbl-and-enquiry-professional-development-challenge.htm [Accessed 10 November 2016].

Liu, W-C, Wong, A. F. L., Divaharan, S, Peer, J., Quek, C-L., and Williams, M. D. (2006). Students' intrinsic motivation in project-based learning using an asynchronous discussion platform. *Educational Research Journal*, 21(2).

Mikulec, E., and Chamnus-Miller, P. C. (2011). Using project-based instruction to meet foreign language standards. *The Clearing House*, (84), 81–86.

Mitra, S. (2000). Minimally invasive education for mass computer literacy. Paper presented at *CRIDALA 2000 Conference*, Hong Kong, 21–25 June, 2000. www.hole-in-the-wall.com/docs/Paper01.pdf [Accessed 4 November 2016].

Mitra, S., and Dangwal, R. (2010). Limits to self-organising systems of learning – Tehe Kalikuppam experiment. *British Journal of Educational Technology*, 41(5), 672–688.

Mukhurjee, K. (2015). Investigating impact of project-based learning in an Indian ESL classroom. In Giannikas, C. N., McLaughlin, L., Fanning, G., and Deutsch Muller, N. (eds.) *Children Learning English: From research to practice*. Reading: IATEFL, Garnet Education.

Murphy, V. A. (2014). *Second Language Learning in the Early School Years: Trends and contexts*. Oxford: Oxford University Press.

Murphy, V. A., and Evangelou, M. (2016). Foreword. In Murphy, V. A., and Evangelou, M. (eds.) *Early Childhood Education in English for Speakers of Other Languages*. London: British Council. www.teachingenglish.org.uk/sites/teacheng/files/F240%20Early%20Childhood%20Education%20inners%20FINAL%20web.pdf [Accessed 24 October 2016].

New Magic, 2008. Grades 4 to 6. Oxford: Oxford University Press.

Oxford Discover, Grade 1 to 6, 2013 to 2014. Oxford: Oxford University Press.Phillips, D. (2012). *Project Work with Young Learners*. Oxford: Oxford University Press. https://oupeltglobalblog.com/2012/10/31/project-work-with-young-learners/ [Accessed 10 June 2016].

Phillips, D., Burwood, S., and Dunford, H. (1999). *Projects with Young Learners*. Oxford: Oxford University Press.

Piaget, J. (1952). *The Origins of Intelligence in Children*. New York: Viking.

Pinter, A. (2006). *Teaching Young Language Learners*. Oxford: Oxford University Press.

Pinter, A., Mathew, R., and Smith, R. (2016). Children and teachers as co-researchers in Indian primary English classrooms. *ELT Research Papers*, 16(03).

Projects Fourth Edition, 2014. Level 1 to 5. Oxford: Oxford University Press. https://elt.oup.com/catalogue/items/global/teenagers/project/1/?cc=gb&selLanguage=en [Accessed 6 November 2016].

Rich, S. (2014). Taking stock: Where are we now with TEYL? In Rich, S. (ed.) *International Perspectives on Teaching English to Young Learners*. London: Palgrave Macmillan.

Riga, M. (2011). An investigation of the application of the Choice Theory and the effectiveness of the satisfaction of the four psychological needs in raising students' intrinsic motivation and improving the classroom atmosphere in a class of 11 year-old students. In Hughes, A., and Taylor, N. (eds.) *Teaching English to Young Learners Sixth International TEYL Research Seminar 2010 Papers*. York: University of York, Department of Education.

Rixon, S. (2013). *British Council Survey of Policy and Practice in Primary English Language Teaching Worldwide*. London: British Council. www.teachingenglish.org.uk/sites/teacheng/files/D120%20Survey%20of%20Teachers%20to%20YLs_FINAL_Med_res_online.pdf (Retrieved: 21 Oct 16).

Rixon, S. (2015). Primary English and critical issues: A worldwide perspective. In Bland, J. (ed.) *Teaching English to Young Learners: Critical issues in language teaching with 3–12 year olds*. London: Bloomsbury.

Schweisfurth, M. (2011). Learner-centred education in developing country contexts: From solution to problem? *International Journal of Educational Development*, 31(5), 425–432. www.deepdyve.com/lp/elsevier/learner-centred-education-in-developing-country-contexts-from-solution-r0pYPoY9SI [Accessed 27 October 2016].

Show and Tell, Level 1 to 3, 2014. Oxford: Oxford University Press.

Stoller, F. L. (1997). Project work: A means to promote language and content. *Forum*, 35(4). http://exchanges.state.gov/forum/vols/vol35/no4/p2.htm [Accessed 19 March 2002].

Taylor, C. C. W., Hare, R. M., and Barnes, J. (1998). *Greek Philosophers – Socrates, Plato, and Aristotle*. New York: Oxford University Press.

Thomas, J. (2000). *A Review of Research on Project Based Learning*. Report prepared for The Autodesk Foundation. www.bie.org/index.php/site/RE/pbl_research/29 [Accessed 27 October 2016].

Vygotsky, L. S. (1978). *Mind in Society: The development of higher psychological processes*. London: Harvard University Press.

Wilhelm, K. H. (1999). Collaborative do's and don't's. *TESOL Journal*, 8(2), 14–19.

PART 4

Technology and young learner curriculum

19

Gaming and young learners

Yuko Goto Butler

Introduction

Given the recent emphasis on active and autonomous learning as well as situated learning in education, digital games (games played through any digital device, including computers, videos, tablets and mobile phones) have gained growing attention as a learning tool among educators. Games contain features that are central to learning, such as setting clear goals, providing visible outcomes and instant feedback, having challenging tasks and fostering collaboration and interaction (e.g., Garris et al. 2002; Gee 2007; Prensky 2001). Because an increasing number of young learners are familiar with technology from an early age in their lives, digital games can place this new generation of learners 'at the heart of the learning and teaching processes' (Reinders 2012, p. 2). Although research on digital games has until relatively recently largely concentrated on science, engineering and math, second and foreign language (L2 and FL) educators have shown growing interest in digital games for their potential to provide students with authentic learning tasks and opportunities to use language for communication (García-Carbonell et al. 2001). The use of digital games for L2/FL education is sometimes referred to as *digital game-based language learning* (Cornillie et al. 2012).

The aim of this chapter is to provide L2/FL educators and researchers with an overview of how digital games can be and have been used as educational tools by examining major studies conducted in L2/FL learning as well as other educational settings. As I discuss below, major issues examined in general educational research are largely relevant to L2/FL learning, while there are L2/FL domain-specific issues as well. Studies also suggest that digital games may not always be effective for learning and motivation. Therefore, this chapter aims to identify conditions under which digital games can be effectively used for educational purposes. It also addresses potential challenges, especially when digital games are used with young language learners.

In this chapter, I define *young language learners* as children ages 5–15 who are learning an L2 or FL. The limited number of digital game-based studies in L2/FL research have mostly targeted learners in their early teens and older, although some studies report participants' grade level(s) but not their ages. In the following sections, I indicate participants' ages only when the authors reported them explicitly.

Historical perspectives

The use of digital games for L2/FL learning and instruction is relatively new, with origins in early computer-assisted language learning (CALL) during the 1980s (Cornillie et al. 2012). Although digital games are a relatively recent phenomenon, *games* themselves have been part of every culture as an important human activity since ancient times. In this section, I first define *games*. I then discuss how games, including digital games, have come to be used for educational purposes. I conclude this section with a description of the major learning theories underlying gaming.

Definitions of games

Games can be considered a type of play with goals and rules. Games have been used by people in all cultures to acquire various knowledge and skills (cognitive, social, emotional and physical skills) as well as to have fun. Despite the ubiquity of games, however, researchers have reached little consensus on a precise definition of them. One may recall the famous argument made by philosopher Ludwig Wittgenstein (1953) that there is no essential feature that characterises all games; instead, he argued, we can only see some complicated, overarching network of similarities across games. Other researchers have tried to identify essential features of games. Garris et al. (2002) reviewed game features that have been proposed in past research. They found that while there has been little consensus on the precise features, those features can be categorised into six dimensions: fantasy, rules/goals, sensory stimuli, challenge, mystery and control.

Engineers first developed basic digital games in late 1950s and early 1960s, but digital games did not reach wider audiences until the 1970s. With the development of home computing environments, home consoles and PC games drastically expanded the reach of digital games in 1980s and 1990s. Since the 2000s, gaming on smartphones, tablets and other mobile devices has been the fastest growing segment in the digital game industry (Williams 2017).

Digital games have been characterised in a number of different ways. For example, they have been classified by genre (e.g., action games, adventure games, role-playing games), player configuration (e.g., single-player game, multiplayer games, massively multiplayer games), type (e.g., casual game, social network games) and so forth (Sykes and Reinhardt 2013). Researchers have also categorised digital games according to their purposes. From an instructional point of view, games have been classified into *serious games* and *commercial games*. Serious games (also referred to as *instructional games*) are specifically designed for educational purposes and are often distinguished from commercial games designed primarily for entertainment purposes (also referred to as *entertainment games*, *commercial off-the-shelf games*, or *vernacular games*). As I discuss below, however, reflecting a paradigmatic shift in learning theories towards more focus on playing and active engagement in learning processes, some researchers (e.g., Thomas 2012) came to question the dichotomy between serious learning and entertainment. Indeed, in recent years, a growing number of researchers have examined not only serious games but also commercial games to see if they have an effect on students' learning and motivation.

Focusing on digital games in L2 education, Reinhardt and Skyes (2012) characterised L2 learning and pedagogical environments as *game-enhanced* and *game-based* environments.

Game-enhanced environment refers to general game-playing contexts (i.e., commercial games, including massively multiplayer online games and social network games), whereas *game-based environment* refers to cases in which learners work with serious games or in synthetic game-immersive environments specifically designed for L2 development and pedagogy. Research on game-enhanced environments concerns the general potential of digital games as learning and pedagogical tools, either as part of formal L2 curriculum or not. Research on game-based environments primarily examines the specific design of serious games for L2 learning and their effect on outcomes (learning, motivation, etc.).

The role of games in learning

Modern learning theories as well as major L2 learning and pedagogical approaches have supported the potential of digital games as a significant educational tool. As mentioned above, games are a form of play with goals and rules, and psychologists have long paid close attention to the role of play in children's social/emotional, cognitive and language development. Through play, children develop their sense of self (Mead 1934) and facilitate communication and metacommunication abilities (Bateson 1972). Piaget (1962) focused on the role of play in children's development of mental representation and abstract thinking. Most notably, Vygotsky (1978,p. 101) viewed children's play as 'a leading factor in development'. For Vygotsky, cognitive development is realised by transforming information from the external world and internalising it primarily through language. When children are at play, they make sense of the external world by engaging in dialogue with themselves or with others. They imagine and perform different roles and experience different language uses. Through play, children engage in social interaction. They observe others, imitate them and receive feedback. Vygotsky argued that since children at play always go beyond their everyday activities, play creates a *zone of proximal development (ZPD)*: a distance between a child's actual developmental level and the potentially achievable level with the help of capable others. Social interaction that happens within a child's ZPD is considered to be a basis for his or her learning. This concept of learning as being essentially a type of social interaction – as opposed to a mental change residing in individuals – is one of the strongest theoretical supports for using games, a form of play, for learning.

Games are also 'structured on the very notion of player-driven choice' (Sykes and Reinhardt 2013, p. 17). Games rest on a player's agency and active engagement in game tasks. Bruner's sociocognitive theory (1966) highlighted the importance of active observations and hands-on activities in learning for both children and adults. Children start encoding information through hands-on activities (enactive learning), and store such active-based information first iconically (e.g., visual images) and then symbolically (e.g., language). Bruner believed that humans are active problem solvers from birth and that learning can take place at any age as long as the instruction is organised in such a way that concepts are introduced with graduated levels of difficulty and in a spiral fashion through observing and engaging in problem-solving activities. Learners' self-directed engagement is critical in this pedagogical approach. Games in computer formats can be well suited to providing learners with opportunities to perform various activities organised around problems of concern to them. They can offer increasing levels of difficulty in rich, multimodal contexts that allow learners to interact with others.

Moreover, the goal-oriented and player-driven features of games align well with the notion of task-based language teaching (TBLT), a well-recognised approach to L2 learning and pedagogy. TBLT primarily focuses on meaning in communicative language use through performing tasks. A task is not a random activity but 'results in language use where learners treat the language as a "tool" for achieving a communicative outcome rather than as an "object" to be studied, analyzed and displayed' (Ellis and Shintani 2014, p. 136). According to Sykes and Reinhardt (2013), TBLT was developed with the intention of making language education more learner-centred. In practice, however, teachers usually pre-identify goals and design tasks for their students' learning; L2 learners have little agency in setting their own goals and selecting tasks for their learning. In this respect, tasks in classrooms have been largely implemented in a 'learning driven, rather than learner driven' (18) fashion. Sykes and Reinhardt suggested that the goal-oriented and player-driven features of digital games (i.e., players have to know the goal of the game and choose to engage in the game) can potentially provide learners and educators with opportunities for finding an optimal balance between learning-driven and learner-driven use of tasks in L2 learning. Moreover, new technology can give learners greater exposure to authentic uses of the target language and opportunities to negotiate meaning (Peterson 2010). Technology also makes it possible to develop more complicated and integrative tasks that better fit learners' needs (Thomas 2012).

In addition to the potential benefits of digital games for learning, it has been argued that certain characteristics of digital games create intrinsically motivating instructional environments. Malone (1981), for example, proposed three such characteristics: *challenge, fantasy* and *curiosity*. A challenging environment is realised by having personally meaningful and achievable goals with optimal difficulty levels. Mental images created by fantasy environments are perceived to be fun and interesting. Curiosity brings 'surprisingness with respect to the knowledge and expectation a learner has' (Malone 1981, pp. 337–338). According to self-determination theory, one's intrinsically motivated behaviours rest on satisfying one's own 'innate psychological needs': namely, *feeing of competence* (self-efficacy), *a sense of autonomy* and a sense of *relatedness* (a sense of belonging or connectedness to other people, group, community and culture) (Ryan and Deci 2000, p. 57). Social contexts that support such innate psychological needs allow a learner to be intrinsically motivated and to make extrinsically motivated behaviours more self-determined. Digital games can provide learners with such social contexts.

Critical issues and topics

As discussed in the previous section, theoretically speaking, digital games should be effective both in terms of learning and motivation. However, there is some skepticism among the general public when it comes to the actual use of digital games for educational purposes (Gee 2007). Thus, researchers have primarily focused on two topics. First, they are concerned with whether or not digital games are indeed effective in enhancing students' learning and motivation and, if so, under what conditions. Second, although somewhat less explored, researchers have been interested in understanding elements in digital games that would promote students' learning and motivation (issues related to game designs) as well as understanding how best to implement digital games in instruction (issues related to game implementation). For L2/FL researchers, especially those who are interested in young L2/FL learners, concerns include domain-specific effectiveness (i.e., effectiveness on language learning) as well as age-related effectiveness (i.e., effectiveness among young learners) of digital games.

Current contributions and research

In this section, I offer an overview of major findings concerning the two topics identified above. Research on digital games has been conducted largely in the fields of science, technology, engineering and health (Boyle et al. 2016), although studies on L2/FL learning are slowly on the rise. Therefore, I offer reviews of the current research, first in general educational contexts, followed by specific issues addressed in research in L2/FL learning contexts. Finally, while the number of studies on digital games among *young* L2/FL learners remains very limited, I examine these studies closely.

Digital games for learning and pedagogy – general educational contexts

A few recent meta-analyses reveal the state of understanding concerning the effectiveness of digital games in education. Wouters et al. (2013) focused on serious games and examined their effectiveness in relation to nongame-based conventional instructional methods such as lectures, practices/drills and reading. They found that serious games were more effective than the conventional methods not only in learning (i.e., gaining knowledge and skills) but also in the retention of learning (the effect lasts longer); however, no such benefit was found for motivation. Moreover, while serious games improved learning for children and young adults, the benefits did not extend to adult learners. The study further indicated that serious games worked better (a) when they were supplemented with other instruction such as explicit practice and follow-up discussions, (b) when multiple training sessions were offered, and (c) when learners played games in groups. A higher degree of realistic visualisation and the inclusion of narratives did not necessarily result in more effective learning, suggesting that serious game designers should pay attention to learning content rather than visual realism, and that they should avoid heavy cognitive processing of narrative information. In a finding that is especially relevant to this chapter, the effect size on learning was particularly large in language acquisition compared with other educational domains.

A more recent meta-analysis by Clark et al. (2016) and a literature review by Boyle et al. (2016) included entertainment games as well as serious games. Consistent with Wouters et al. (2013) on serious games discussed above, these studies also found advantages for digital games in learning (not only in the acquisition of knowledge and skills but also in interpersonal learning outcomes such as intellectual openness and conscientiousness) over nongaming conditions. No significant relation was found between the amount of time spent on game playing and the learning outcome (Clark et al. 2016).

Researchers have also attempted to identify game features that promote learning. According to Clark et al. (2016), simple games, as opposed to more sophisticated games, can have an effect on improving certain types of learning, such as lower order thinking skills. *Competition* did not necessarily contribute to learning (Boyle et al. 2016). However, the inclusion of *uncertainty* elements in games enhanced learners' motivation as well as their learning (Howard-Jones and Demetriou 2009; Ozcelik et al. 2013). While such information can be useful from an instructional design point of view, caution is necessary in order to avoid 'an overly positivistic view of discrete game elements and a corresponding lack of attention to the broader ecology and "alchemy" of professional game design and player experiences' (Cornillie et al. 2012, p. 249).

The motivational effects of digital games – and the consequences of those effects on learning – are not yet very clear. For example, Iten and Petko (2016) examined the relationship between enjoyment and learning among 74 primary school children (ages 10–13) in Switzerland. The researchers found that enjoying or having fun with games was not the primary reason the children used serious games; instead, the games' anticipated usefulness or simplicity motivated the children to use them. Greater enjoyment in playing games increased their interest in the subject matter but did not lead to greater learning (measured by self-reported cognitive gains). Iten and Petko suggested that there are 'complex inter-relations' between game enjoyment and learning (161). The lack of a clear understanding of the association between digital games and motivation and its relation to learning appears to be, in part, due to conceptual and methodological shortcomings. Key concepts such as *enjoyment*, *fun*, and *engagement* are inconsistently or unclearly conceptualised. Player *enjoyment* is often viewed as equivalent to the notion of *flow*, a mental state in which a player is involved in a task with complete concentration and engagement (Csikszentmihalyi 1991) and 'a key aspect of motivating game play experiences' (Sykes and Reinhardt 2013, p. 97). Based on this assumption, various measurements have been developed independently among researchers to capture game enjoyment and engagement. Such measurements include questionnaires, interviews, observations and other behavioural measurements (e.g., attention to time and the number of intermissions during games in Sharek and Wiebe 2014; time to complete tasks and eye movement in Jennett et al. 2008). However, the validity of such measures is often unknown.

Digital games for learning and pedagogy – L2/FL learning contexts

The major issues in general educational research on digital games discussed above largely apply to L2/FL learning contexts as well. However, L2/FL researchers also recognise that the multimodal interactions that occur within digital gaming spaces provide learners with rich target language resources and opportunities for language learning.

One of the fruitful areas of research on digital games in L2/FL learning is the examination of how language learning takes place when L2/FL learners engage in digital games and interact with other players. A number of studies have been conducted on commercial/ entertainment game environments, often by employing discourse analyses, observations and interviews. Such studies (e.g., Coleman 2002; Peterson 2012; Reinders and Wattana 2012; Thorne 2008), mostly conducted among college students, generally found that L2/FL learn-ers have extensive exposure to authentic use of the target language and intensive language practice with other players in natural and often playful ways. The goal-oriented nature of games pushes learners to produce the target language, and users have plentiful opportuni-ties to negotiate meaning and to employ a variety of pragmatic strategies (e.g., clarifica-tion requests) during the interactions. Frequent self- and other-corrections and repairs are observed. L2-speaking players also tend to actively interact with other players and exhibit positive perceptions of the interaction in L2/FL during game playing. In addition, game-enhanced environments can support learners' language socialisation by providing them with expert guidance on immersing themselves into the target culture and communities of prac-tice. Some researchers, such as Thorne et al. (2009), consider digital space as a ground for learners to experiment with and form identities. For example, by using avatars during game-play or having multilingual and hybrid uses of language in interaction, learners experiment with new identities, which can help reduce anxieties or develop sociocultural competencies related to language.

Caution is necessary when generalising from these findings. Many of the studies that examined players' interactions tended to have a small number of participants, and it is likely that players' interactions vary substantially depending on the nature of the digital games, the characteristics of players (e.g., age, gender, language proficiency and game-playing proficiency) and their motivation and reasons for playing games. Some games con-tain more narrative or verbal components than others. In Reinders and Wattana (2012), although their Thai college students showed higher degrees of willingness to communicate in English in digital game playing (a massive multiplayer online role-playing game, MMORPG) over time, no improvement in accuracy and complexity in their English language use was observed, leading the researchers to speculate that the participants were not able to pay attention to forms and meaning simultaneously during the gameplay. A similar point was made by deHaan, Reed, and Kuwada (2010), who did not see any advantage among players of FL music video games compared with game watchers (the students who were asked to watch the game on different monitors); the game players performed poorly in their incidental vocabulary learning (measured by both immediate recall and delayed recall of vocabulary). deHaan et al. ascribed the result to the excessive cognitive demands required for gameplay. It is important to remember that players of commercial/entertainment games usually focus on completing game tasks or missions rather than learning a language (or any other content knowledge and skills). In Reinders and Wattana (2012), participants expressed positive attitudes about their communication experience during gameplay, but when they were specifically asked about English learning, they expressed concerns about 'the use of abbreviations, emoticons, smileys, simple words and ungrammatical sentences to communicate, because they felt that over-use of these would not contribute to their accuracy and complexity in language production' (181). Therefore, if commercial/entertainment games are to be used for L2/FL learning/teaching purposes, we need to better understand how to maximise the games' potential benefits for learning and pedagogy in relation to learners' and educators' needs and goals.

Research on serious games/instructional game designs also concerns how best to make use of digital games as learning/pedagogical tools. According to Kao's (2014) small-scale meta-analysis on the effectiveness of serious games in Asia (based on 25 studies), serious games were more effective in English learning in general than traditional instruction that did not involve gaming (e.g., grammar-translation methods), and the effects were greater if (a) the games required meaningful engagement (as opposed to drill-based games), (b) learners were involved in a long-term gameplay engagement (defined as engagement that lasted more than a month), and (c) the target of language learning was procedural knowledge (as opposed to declarative knowledge). Whether or not the games were *networked* (connected to the Internet) did not matter. Although *feedback* was not included in Kao's moderator analysis, the existence of precise feedback functions seems to play a critical role in game-based language learning (Jackson et al. 2012).

Stakeholders' attitudes and behaviours towards digital games vary as well. Learners' varying attitudes and behaviours appeared to influence their learning outcomes. For example, Sykes (2010) observed her Spanish-learning students for 120 hours when they played *Croquelandia* (a synthetic immersive environment specifically designed for pragmatic learning) as part of their regular class activities. She identified four types of gameplay behaviours (which she named *explorer*, *student*, *presenter* and *non-player*) depending on the learners' approaches to the game (the extent to which the learners explore the game space beyond the course requirements), frequencies of entering the game and time spent playing. This study highlights the importance of paying attention to individual differences in players' behaviours during the gameplay when examining game effectiveness. Finally, teachers' computer literacy or virtual world literacy skills were closely related to their attitudes towards game-based learning, and their attitudes in turn are considered potentially influential over students' learning outcomes (e.g., Chik 2012; Franciosi 2015; Proctor and Marks 2013). The precise interrelations between teachers' attitudes and students' L2/FL learning outcomes, however, are not well understood.

Digital games for learning and pedagogy – Young learners' L2/FL learning

Although empirical research on digital games among young L2/FL learners is in its infancy, in the following sections I address our current understanding with respect to (a) the effectiveness of digital games in L2/FL learning; (b) how to design effective digital games; and (c) how to implement digital games in instruction.

Effectiveness among young L2/FL learners

Serious games appear to be effective among young L2/FL learners for vocabulary learning (e.g., Aghlara and Tamjid 2011), grammar learning (e.g., Sadeghi and Dousti 2013) and content subject learning in Content and Language Integrated Learning (CLIL) contexts (e.g., Dourda et al. 2014). Positive effects were reported even among children as young as kindergarteners, as in Segers and Verhoeven's (2002, 2003) research on L2-vocabulary learning among immigrant kindergarten children in the Netherlands. Longer duration of gameplay tends to bring better results. Segers and Verhoeven's data (2002) suggest that kindergarteners may need to have a certain minimum number of encounters during the game in order to learn a new word, perhaps due to their less-developed memory and information-processing capacities.

Positive results also have been reported for game-enhanced environments. For example, in Suh, Kim, and Kim (2010), South Korean fifth- and sixth-grade students who received English instruction through MMORPG (40 minutes of instruction twice a week for two months) performed better in listening, reading and writing (but, curiously, not in speaking) compared with students who received regular instruction. Similarly, Sylvén and Sundqvist (2012) showed a positive relationship between young Swedish students' (ages 11–12) engagement of a MMORPG during extramural activities and their L2-English proficiency (measured by tests in vocabulary, listening and reading comprehension). Boys benefitted more in vocabulary learning than girls, perhaps because they spent more time playing the digital game. According to Zheng et al. (2009), however, Chinese seventh-grade students who engaged in a game-like 3-D virtual world with native-English speaking players (60 minutes per week for 25 weeks) exhibited higher self-efficacy in their use of English than the students in the control group, but they did not have better English performance (measured by an achievement test).

Due to the limited number of studies, it is premature to conclude anything definitive. While published studies generally found positive effects of digital games, they vary in the learning and affective domains examined (e.g., vocabulary, reading, etc.), types of games implemented, the way that digital games were implemented, duration of the students' gameplay, measures used, ages of participants and social-educational contexts of implementation. Any of these factors can potentially influence outcomes.

Most critically, there is little information on how age-related factors uniquely interact with L2/FL learning through digital games. The benefits (or challenges) of using digital games in L2/FL learning among young learners remain largely unknown, especially in relation to age-related cognitive, social, affective and L1 language factors. Based on observations of Turkish children (ages 10–14) playing digital games in English at Internet Cafés, Turgut and Irgin (2009) identified some of the unique behaviours and attitudes among young learners who grew up with technology. Such characteristics included quickly adapting to new computer applications and functions, figuring out the meaning of unknown words by asking peers, having a strong desire to understand and participate in dialogues with other players and being aware of both pros and cons of game playing. Piirainen-Marsh and Tainio (2009) focused on lexical and prosodic repetition in interactions during videogame playing in English among Finnish boys (ages 10–14). It is thought that repetition plays a significant role in children's language acquisition (e.g., Cook 2000). Using Conversational Analysis, Piirainen-Marsh and Tainio showed how repetition can be a resource for 'engaging with the second language, analyzing it, and putting it to use in ways that enable players to display and develop their linguistic and interactional competence' (153). We need more studies such as those by Turgut and Irgin (2009) and Piirainen-Marsh and Tainio (2009), which shed light on young learners' specific characteristics in understanding their digital game language learning.

Game task designs for young L2/FL learners

There is very little research on digital game-task designs specifically targeting young L2/FL learners. Examining Japanese children's (ages 4–12) behaviours towards serious games that were part of an online learning kit for a standardised English proficiency test, Butler, Someya, and Fukuhara (2014) found that attractive games (measured by frequencies of game-playing) shared certain elements. These elements included (a) having optimal cognitive challenge; (b) evoking children's curiosity; (c) allowing players great control over the gameplay; and (d) having multiple players. Importantly, however, the attractive games did not necessarily contribute to the children's English learning, as measured by standardised test scores. Butler (2015, 2017) further explored this topic by asking Japanese sixth graders (ages 11–12) to work in groups to design English digital games for vocabulary learning. Treating children as experts in the new digital learning paradigm, Butler first asked them to examine some existing serious English games and to identify a series of motivational elements (elements that make the game attractive) and learning elements (elements that promote learning). The children then designed games based on their self-identified motivational and learning elements and conducted peer- and self-evaluations of their designs. Learning elements that the children highly valued included (a) having repetition/reviewing; (b) utilising multiple modalities; and (c) allowing autonomy over learning. Motivational elements valued highly included (a) challenging; (b) fantasies/stories; (c) granting a great deal of control; and (d) instant feedback. Importantly, the challenging elements were almost always combined with learner-controlled functions in their game designs, suggesting that children prefer to choose what to learn and the level of challenge. The children were also aware that unexpected elements that disrupt linear relationships between the result of learning and the game scores can be a great source of motivation, including for children with lower proficiency (i.e., giving them a chance to win). Finally, the children acknowledged that creating and maintaining an attractive avatar was a great motivational source for them. In a study conducted among college students, Yee and Bailenson (2007) found that players' interactive behaviours changed according to the attractiveness of their own avatars. We can thus expect that this phenomenon, what Yee and Bailenson called 'the Proteus Effect', can have significant implications for designing digital games for young learners as well.

Digital game implementation for young L2/FL learners

As noted above, research suggests that digital games are more effective for learning in general if they are combined with regular instruction. Although our understanding of how best to implement digital games for L2/FL instruction for young learners is far from sufficient, some studies provide insights. In Sandberg, Maris and de Geus (2011), a game-based mobile application was introduced to Dutch fifth-grade students. The participants were divided into three conditions: (a) a group that received regular English lessons only; (b) a group that used the mobile application as part of the formal instruction in addition to the regular lessons; and (c) another group that was allowed to access to the mobile application at home as well as in class. The third group learned the target vocabulary better than the other two groups. The researchers argued that for effective implementation of the mobile application, it was important to secure autonomous learning spaces for children in and outside of school and to have parents and teachers provide support for the children's game-based learning.

Teachers play a critical role in implementing game-based instruction in formal classrooms. Meyer (2009) reported interesting cases of two teachers from Danish primary schools in which serious games were implemented. In one fifth-grade class, the teacher allowed children to choose digital activities from the game platform. The children tended to choose play- or game-like activities that resembled the web-based games that they were accustomed to playing in their spare time rather than typical school-like activities. As a result, the teacher's role as 'a mediator between game activities and learning activities' (p. 717) became important. Despite the fact that the children were instructed that they would be learning English, they kept 'out of school identities as players and gamers' and brought 'unsolicited and unwanted entertainment into the classroom' (717). Under such a context, the teacher was required to reconceptualise the role of gaming in learning. In a fourth-grade classroom, the activities were more structured, pre-selected, and supervised by the teacher, and the children showed more concentration. The children were allowed to work on more playful tasks only as a reward after they finished their learning-focused tasks. These two cases highlight the critical role that teachers play in implementing digital games. The cases also illustrate challenges that teachers face in promoting autonomous and situated learning while dealing with changing expectations of teachers' and students' roles in the new paradigm of teaching and learning.

Recommendations for practice

Based on the preceding discussions, it is apparent that digital games have potential for young learners' L2/FL learning and motivation, but that to maximise their effectiveness certain considerations must be made. In this section, I discuss practical issues related to game design and implementation.

Game designing: making the best use of games' potential while meeting young learners' needs

In designing or choosing digital games for young L2/FL learners, it is important to make best use of a game's potential while paying close attention to learners' characteristics and needs. We can draw on research findings to help ensure that digital games provide learners with maximum opportunities for authentic communication. Instead of drill-based games, we should design games that require meaningful engagement and highlight the development of procedural knowledge. At the same time, we need to remember that young learners are in the midst of cognitive, linguistic and social-affective development. If nonlinguistic cognitive and interaction demands are too high to complete the game tasks, learners may not be able to invest sufficient mental resources in L2/FL language. Being too immersed in gaming or having excessive emotional engagement may hinder their learning (Butler et al. 2014; Meyer 2009). Young learners who grow up with technology may possess unique characteristics that differ from older generations. Prensky (2001) listed a number of changes of cognitive style that he observed among the generation growing up with computer games. Major characteristics included (a) processing information at a very high speed; (b) being good at parallel processing; (c) accessing graphics before texts; (d) showing preference for active learning over passive learning; and (g) considering play as work (52). While we need more empirical evidence to confirm Prensky's observation, we can expect that game designs that correspond well with young learners' preferred cognitive styles would be more likely to motivate them and facilitate their learning. Caution is necessary, however, not to overgeneralise these characteristics. More effort is necessary to observe children's behaviours during gameplay and to find out their own perspectives in order to better understand their needs and individual differences and incorporate such information into game designs.

Game implementation: teachers' deeper understanding of their changing roles is necessary

Game-enhanced and game-based instruction should not replace existing classroom instruction. Digital games appear to be most effective if they are used to supplement existing instruction, and, as Reinhardt and Skyes (2012) stated, 'even with the most comprehensive all-encompassing game-mediated L2 learning environment, a human instructor should play a key role' (pp. 34–35). Because learning in game-enhanced or game-based environment entails autonomous, situated and collaborative learning, teachers are asked to play different roles in these new learning spaces – whether they are in and outside of the classroom. While playing games, children may exhibit undesirable behaviours in light of the specific cultural and educational tradition of teaching. Meyer (2009) reported that even in Denmark, which has a long history of communicative language teaching and has been open to playful and innovative approaches to language learning/teaching in general, primary school teachers are somewhat skeptical about the use of digital games in instruction. Teachers seem to need assistance in developing (a) a deeper understanding of both the possibilities and limitations of digital games for young learners, (b) digital literacy skills, and (c) different and/or flexible conceptualisations of their role in instruction.

Future directions

Research on digital games for young L2/FL learners is largely unexplored, and there is no question that we need more empirical studies. In this section, I focus on the following three areas of research that are in particular need of investigation: (a) research on effectiveness in learning and motivation; (b) research on game task design and implementation; and (3) game-based assessment.

Research on effectiveness: unpacking the effective elements

Studies on the effectiveness of digital games have mostly examined a specific digital game implemented in a specific way in a specific context, often using holistic measurements. Such studies have relatively limited application beyond the particular case examined. It would be more informative if we could unpack the elements (e.g., cognitive and interactional demands, game procedures, learner characteristics, conditions for implementation, etc.) that contribute to specific language-learning outcomes. We also need to better understand the *process* of learning through digital games – for example, log functions can be used efficiently to capture the process of learning over time. Not only short-term effects but longer-term effects need to be investigated. We also need to better understand how learning through digital games is taking place outside of formal classroom L2/FL instruction and how such autonomous learning may influence learning in the classroom. Moreover, it is important to know how learning observed in a game-enhanced or game-based environment can be applied in wider contexts, going beyond the specific game context. As mentioned already, attention should be paid to the interaction between age-related factors and young learners' L2/FL learning. Individual differences in learners' learning styles and in their learning through digital games should be investigated as well, instead of simply assuming that young learners are all well-equipped to benefit from digital learning. Finally, the relationship between game engagement and learning should be better understood. As I have discussed, game engagement does not necessarily guarantee learning.

Research on game task design and implementation

Although it has been suggested that digital games should supplement existing language teaching, we're still in the early stages of this research. It would be useful to have more case studies that describe the detailed process of game implementation and the challenges that teachers and students face during the process. Such information would have substantial implications for curriculum designers and teachers. In addition, we do not know enough about teachers' attitudes and behaviours towards digital games, their digital literacy and game-playing experiences and how such factors may influence their implementation of digital games. Action research by teachers with different attitudes and knowledge about digital games would be very informative.

Game-based assessment

Assessment and instruction are tightly connected. Although hardly any research has been conducted on the use of digital games for assessment, this is a promising possibility. There are a number of potential merits of using digital games for young learners' L2/FL assessment – not just in an *assessment of learning* (a traditional measurement-oriented approach to assessment primarily aiming at capturing one's ability) capacity but also in an *assessment for learning* (a learning-oriented assessment approach primarily focusing on assisting learning) capacity (Butler 2016). First, typical characteristics of digital games, such as instant feedback and autonomy, can help learners to see their performance and progress, and assist them in setting a next step/goal for their own learning. Second, as mentioned already, log records, chats and other interactional and performance-related records can allow teachers and learners to access the process of learning during a single gameplay as well as during a series of gameplays over time. This could be a positive means of obtaining authentic assessment information without making learners feel self-conscious about being assessed. Third, digital games, as with other digital devices, are better equipped for use with individualised assessments. Finally, digital games, especially in a game-enhanced environment, can be used for capturing implicit learning because learners may not pay attention to the target language use. Considering these potential merits, it is a fruitful new area for future inquiry.

In conclusion, digital games have great potential for enhancing young learners' L2/FL learning and motivation. However, we need to better understand how best to design and implement digital games in and outside of classroom instruction in order to maximise their effects. We also need to be aware of potential limitations and challenges of using digital games for educational purposes. Teachers play a crucial role in the process of identifying the best practices when using digital games.

Further reading

1 Reinders, H. (Ed.). (2012). *Digital games in language learning and teaching*. New York: Palgrave Macmillan.

This is one of the first collections of papers focusing on the use of digital games in L2/FL learning and pedagogy. It includes papers concerning theoretical foundations for digital computer learning as well as a series of empirical studies. While most of the papers deal with older learners, the issues discussed in this volume are largely relevant to L2/FL learning and pedagogy for young learners as well.

2 Sykes, J. M., and Reinhardt, J. (2013). *Language at play: Digital games in second and foreign language teaching and learning*. New York: Pearson.

This book provides a comprehensive overview of the research on digital games in L2/FL education. Discussion is organised around five major concepts in second language acquisition research: goal, interaction, feedback, context and motivation. The book is written in a very accessible manner and is a good introduction to the topic.

Related topics

Motivation, language outside the classroom

References

Aghlara, L., and Tamjid, N. H. (2011). The effect of digital games on Iranian children's vocabulary retention in foreign language acquisition. *Procedia: Social and Behavioral Sciences*, 29, 552–560.

Bateson, G. (1972). A theory of play and fantasy. In Bateson, G. (ed.) *Steps to an Eology of Mind: Collected essays in anthropology, psychiatry, evolution, and epistemology*. Northvale, NJ: Jason Aronson, 183–198.

Boyle, E. et al. (2016). An update to the systematic literature review of empirical evidence of the impacts and outcome of computer games and serious games. *Computers & Education*, 94, 178–192.

Bruner, J. S. (1966). *Toward a Theory of Instruction*. Cambridge, MA: Belknap Press.

Butler, Y. G. (2015). The use of computer games as foreign language learning tasks for digital natives. *System*, 54, 91–102.

Butler, Y. G. (2016). Assessing young learners. In Tsagari, D. (ed.) *Handbook of Second Language Assessment*. Berlin: Mouton de Gruyter, 359–375.

Butler, Y. G. (2017). Motivational elements of digital instructional games: A study of young L2 learners' game designs. *Language Teaching Research*, 21, 735–750.

Butler, Y. G., Someya, Y., and Fukuhara, E. (2014). Online games for young learners' foreign language learning. *ELT Journal*, 68, 265–275.

Chik, A. (2012). Digital gameplay for autonomous foreign language learning: Gamers' and language teachers' perspectives. In Reinders, H. (ed.) *Digital Games in Language Learning and Teaching*. New York: Palgrave Macmillan, 95–114.

Clark, D. B., Tanner-Smith, E. E., and Killingworth, S. S. (2016). Digital games, design, and learning: A systematic review and meta-analysis. *Review of Educational Research*, 86(1), 79–122.

Coleman, D. W. (2002). On foot in SIM CITY: Using SIM COPTER as the basis for an ESL writing assignment. *Simulation & Gaming*, 33(2), 217–230.

Cook, G. (2000). *Language Play, Language Learning*. Oxford: Oxford University Press.

Cornillie, F., Thorne, S. L., and Desmet, P. (2012). Digital games for language learning: From hype to insight? *ReCALL*, 24(3), 243–256.

Csikszentmihalyi, M. (1991). *Flow: The psychology of optimal experience*. New York: Harper Perennial.

deHaan, J., Reed, W. M., and Kuwada, K. (2010). The effect of interactivity with a music video game on second language vocabulary recall. *Language Learning & Technology*, 14(2), 74–94.

Dourda, K., et al. (2014). Content and language integrated learning through an online game in primary school: A case study. *The Electronic Journal of e-Learning*, 12(3), 243–258.

Ellis, R. E., and Shintani, N. (2014). *Exploring Language Pedagogy through Second Language Acquisition Research*. London: Routledge.

Franciosi, S. J. (2015). Acceptability of RPG simulators for foreign language training in Japanese higher education. *Simulation & Gaming*, 47(1), 31–50.

García-Carbonell, A., et al. (2001). Simulation/gaming and the acquisition of communicative competence in another language. *Simulation & Gaming*, 32, 481–491.

Garris, R., Ahlers, R., and Driskell, J. E. (2002). Games, motivation, and learning: A research and practice model. *Simulation & Gaming*, 33, 441–467.

Gee, J. P. (2007). *What Video Games Have to Teach us about Learning and Literacy?* New York: Palgrave Macmillan.

Howard-Jones, P. A., and Demetriou, S. (2009). Uncertainty and engagement with learning games. *Instructional Science*, 37(6), 519–536.

Iten, N., and Petko, D. (2016). Learning with serious games: Is fun playing the game a predictor of learning success? *British Journal of Educational Technology*, 47(1), 151–163.

Jackson, G. T., Dempsey, K. B., and McNamara, D. S. (2012). Game-based practices in a reading strategy tutoring system: Showdown in iSTART-ME. In Reinders, H. (ed.) *Digital Games in Language Learning and Teaching*. New York: Palgrave Macmillan, 115–149.

Jennett, C., et al. (2008). Measuring and defining the experiences of immersion in games. *International Journal of Human-Computer Studies*, 66, 641–661.

Kao, C. (2014). The effects of digital game-based learning task in English as a foreign language contexts: A meta-analysis. *Educational Journal*, 42(2), 113–141.

Malone, T. W. (1981). Toward a theory of intrinsically motivating instruction. *Cognitive Science*, 5(4), 333–369.

Mead, G. H. (1934). *Mind, Self and Society*. Chicago: University of Chicago Press.

Meyer, B. (2009). Designing serious games for foreign language education in a global perspective. In Mendez-Vilas, A., Mesa Gonzalez, J., Mesa Gonzalez, J., and Solano, M. A. (eds.) *Research, Reflections and Innovations in Integrating ICT in Education: Vol. 2*. Badajoz, Spain: Formatex, 715–719.

Ozcelik, E., Cagiltay, N. E., and Ozcelik, N. S. (2013). The effect of uncertainty on learning in game-like environments. *Computers & Education*, 57(1), 1240–1254.

Peterson, M. (2010). Computerized games and simulations in computer-assisted language learning: A meta-analysis of research. *Simulation & Gaming*, 41(1), 72–93.

Peterson, M. (2012). Language learning interaction in a massively multiplayer online role-playing game. In Reinders, H. (ed.) *Digital Games in Language Learning and Teaching*. New York: Palgrave Macmillan, 70–92.

Piaget, J. (1962). *Play, Dreams and Imitation in Childhood*. New York: Norton.

Piirainen-Marsh, A., and Tainio, L. (2009). Other-repetition as a resource for participation in the activity of playing a video game. *Modern Language Journal*, 93(2), 153–169.

Prensky, M. (2001). *Digital Game-based Learning*. New York: McGraw-Hill.

Proctor, M. D., and Marks, Y. (2013). A survey of exemplar teachers' perceptions, use, and access of computer-based games and technology for classroom instruction. *Computers & Education*, 62, 171–180.

Reinders, H. (Ed.). (2012). *Digital Games in Language Learning and Teaching*. New York: Palgrave Macmillan.

Reinders, H., and Wattana, S. (2012). Talk to me! Games and students' willingness to communicate. In Reinders, H. (ed.) *Digital Games in Language Learning and Teaching*. New York: Palgrave Macmillan, 156–188.

Reinhardt, J., and Skyes, J. M. (2012). Conceptualizing digital game-mediated L2 learning and pedagogy: game-enhanced and game-based research and practice. In Reinders, H. (ed.) *Digital Games in Language Learning and Teaching*. New York: Palgrave Macmillan, 32–49.

Ryan, R. M., and Deci, E. (2000). Intrinsic and extrinsic motivations: Classic definitions and new directions. *Contemporary Educational Psychology*, 5, 54–67.

Sadeghi, K., and Dousti, M. (2013). The effect of length of exposure to CALL technology on young Iranian EFL learners' grammar gain. *English Language Teaching*, 6(2), 14–26.

Sandberg, J., Maris, M., and de Geus, K. (2011). Mobile English learning: An evidence-based study with fifth graders. *Computers & Education*, 57, 1334–1347.

Segers, E., and Verhoeven, L. (2002). Multimedia support in early literacy learning. *Computers & Education*, 39, 207–221.

Segers, E., and Verhoeven, L. (2003). Effects of vocabulary training by computer in kindergarten. *Journal of Computer Assisted Learning*, 19, 557–566.

Sharek, D., and Wiebe, E. (2014). Measuring video game engagement through the cognitive and affective dimensions. *Simulation & Gaming*, 45(4–5), 569–592.

Suh, S., Kim, S.-W., and Kim, N.-J. (2010). Effectiveness of MMORPG-based instruction in elementary English education in Korea. *Journal of Computer Assisted Learning*, 26, 370–378.

Sykes, J. (2010). Multi-user virtual environments: User-driven design and implementation for language learning. In Vicenti, G., and Braman, J. (eds.) *Teaching through Multi-user Virtual Environments: Applying dynamic elements to the modern classroom*. Hershey, PA: IGI Global, 283–305.

Sykes, J., and Reinhardt, J. (2013). *Language At Play: Digital games in second and foreign language teaching and learning*. New York: Pearson.

Sylvén, L. K., and Sundqvist, P. (2012). Gaming as extramural English L2 learning and L2 proficiency among young learners. *ReCALL*, 24, 302–321.

Thomas, M. (2012). Contextualizing digital game-based language learning: Transformational paradigm shift or business as usual? In Reinders, H. (ed.) *Digital Games in Language Learning and Teaching*. New York: Palgrave Macmillan, 11–31.

Thorne, S. L. (2008). Transcultural communication in open Internet environments and massively multiplayer online games. In Magnan, S. (ed.) *Mediating Discourse Online*. Amsterdam: Benjamins, 305–327.

Thorne, S. L., Black, R. W., and Sykes, J. M. (2009). Second language use, socialization, and learning in Internet interest communities and online gaming. *Modern Language Journal*, 93, 802–821.

Turgut, Y., and Irgin, P. (2009). Young learners' language learning via computer games. *Procedia Social and Behavioral Sciences*, 1, 760–764.

Vygotsky, L. S. (1978). *Mind and Society*. Cambridge, MA: Harvard University Press.

Williams, A. (2017). *History of Digital Games: Development in art, design and interaction*. Boca Raton, FL: Focal Press.

Wittgenstein, L. (1953). *Philosophical Investigations*. New York: Palgrave Macmillan.

Wouters, P., et al. (2013). A meta-analysis of the cognitive and motivational effects of serious games. *Journal of Educational Psychology*, 105(2), 249–265.

Yee, N., and Bailenson, J. (2007). The Proteus effect: The effect of transformed self-representation on behavior. *Human Communication Research*, 33, 271–290.

Zheng, D., et al. (2009). Attitudes and self-efficacy change: English language learning in virtual worlds. *CALICO Journal*, 27(1), 205–231.

20

Mobile learning for young English learners

Florià Belinchón Majoral

Introduction

It is well-known that we live in the age of technology, so much so that the use of Information and Communication Technology (ICT) has spread to all corners of the globe and has infiltrated every aspect of our lives. One of these places is our educational systems which, in recent years, have provided research, infrastructure and resources to integrate ICT into learning environments. In particular, this chapter looks at mobile devices in the hands of young English learners and the challenges and opportunities that these handheld portable devices and wireless technologies represent for supporting the process of teaching and learning to young learners, also identified as *mobile learning* or *mLearning*.

Towards a definition of mLearning

As the term denotes, mLearning is a compound of two different but powerful words: mobile and learning. The first one, *mobile*, immediately conjures up images of learning through smartphones, but it also refers to learning via a wide range of mobile technology, such as tablets, PDAs (or personal digital assistants), audio players, netbooks, laptops and digital readers. All of them share a series of characteristics that help define what is understood as mLearning.

Traditionally, the educational implications of mobile devices have been associated with the concept of *elearning* because most of the preceding electronic technologies were used to access the educational curriculum outside a physical classroom. That was the case when elearning platforms, such as WebCT (1997) or Moodle (2002), educational web platforms or other Virtual Learning Environments were web applications that integrated a set of tools for online teaching-learning, as an alternative to face-to-face teaching. However, the twenty-first century has seen an evolution and elearning now refers to the use of ICT in conjunction with traditional face-to-face methods, where Internet teaching is combined with experiences in the face-to-face classroom (Ramboll 2004, Jenkins et al. 2005).

Nowadays, due to the fast evolution of mobile devices and the ambiguity of the term 'mobile', there is no agreed upon definition. Does 'mobile' refer to the technology itself?

Or, does the concept have to do with the notion of learner mobility? Hashemia et al. (2011, p. 2478) propose: 'Mobility needs to be understood not only in terms of spatial movement but also the ways in which such movement may enable time-shifting and boundary-crossing'.

Providing a single definition of mLearning in this chapter is therefore challenging because of the growth and diversification of mobile devices (Sharples 2006). However, a reasonable definition of mLearning, and the one that will be used for this chapter, is that offered by Molenet (an initiative which supported 104 projects involving approximately 40,000 learners and over 7,000 staff from 2007 to 2010 to introduce and support mLearning): 'the exploitation of ubiquitous handheld technologies, together with wireless and mobile phone networks, to facilitate, support, enhance and extend the reach of teaching and learning'. mLearning therefore implies learning anything, anywhere, at any time, through mobile devices.

Historical perspectives

The emerging area of mLearning, a development from online learning, originates in the junction between technological development and learner-centred pedagogy (Crompton 2013). Briefly, the origin of mobile technologies began during the 60s and 70s with a series of experiments such as head-mounted devices (1968), the development of the first mobile phone (1973) and the conceptual articulation of the Dynabook, a hand-held electronic book (1972). In the next two decades, the functionality of these devices was improved and both size and cost were reduced, triggering a sharp rise in their use. With the arrival of Web 2.0 (O'Reilly 2005) and the access to computer technology and the Internet through small devices such as smartphones or tablets, powerful products such as iPhones (2007), Android operating systems (2008), iPad (2010), Google Glass (2013), Apple Watch (2014) and all their related applications, or apps, have become the face of innovation.

These advances in technology, underpinned by philosophical and conceptual pedagogies regarding learning, have generated the pre-requisites for new models of education such as mLearning (Crompton 2013). These pedagogies are principally based on learner-centredness. That is to say, educational approaches and methods that focus instruction on the student in order to develop learner autonomy, responsibility, problem solving and lifelong learning and to let the students construct meaning from new information and prior experience (Collins and O'Bien 2003). Particularly, these theories can be synthesised as follows: discovery learning (1970s) which considers that knowledge develops through active participation; constructivist learning (1980s) which takes into consideration interaction with the environment in the process of learning; constructionism (1980s) which contemplates knowledge achievement through the active creation of social objects; problem-based learning (1990s) which develops knowledge as the result of the work on authentic tasks and skills in a context in which they would be used; and socioconstructivist learning (1990s) which studies how knowledge is constructed interdependently between the social and the individual.

Although the evolution of learning and technologies has thus far been described dichotomously, it is important to understand that learning and technology have not occurred as disconnected theories; they have developed as interconnected theories in the digital age. In Crompton's words (2013, p. 10): 'the essence of m-learning is not in the learning or in the technology, but in the marriage of the two entities'. For this reason, current trends in mLearning should follow the theoretical assumptions of connectivism (Siemens 2004), which supports the connection of specialised information sources that can be improved by plugging them into an existing network, including those offered by mobile devices. The starting point of connectivism is the individual. Personal knowledge is comprised of a network or a database, which in turn feeds back into the network, and then continues to provide learning to individual. This cycle of knowledge development (Personal Learning Environments (PLEs) and Open Network Learning; Ozan and Kesim 2013) allows learners to remain updated in their field through the connections they have formed.

Succinctly and to conclude, drawing on a theory of mLearning means accounting for the mobility and the competences of learners; that is, learner autonomy, responsibility, problem solving and lifelong learning and letting students construct meaning from new information and prior experience (Collins and O'Brien 2003). It also means accounting for formal and informal learning, the constructivist and social processes of learning, which are implicit in the fact of being connected through mobile devices, and the analysis of learning as a personal activity mediated by technology (Sharples et al. 2010).

ICTs, and especially mLearning cannot be dissociated from the development of learning in early childhood education, since the attraction experienced by children in the face of technology and multimedia devices is undoubtedly a very important aspect. mLearning can be attractive, for instance, for the development of reading and writing in the foreign language; it can involve the first contact with letters, sounds, pronunciation of new words and chunks of language, as well as be a vehicle for learning how to produce language, initially by trial and error, and later by interacting with other children, always taking into account that mLearning tools can facilitate language learning and the development of cognitive skills.

Critical issues and topics

When mobile devices become teaching and learning tools, they come with their share of complications. In the following paragraphs, I look at some of the critical issues in the use of mlearning with young English learners. In particular, I explain the limitations of mLearning and some of the challenges teachers must deal with, together with feasible ways of overcoming these challenges. I also consider some of the ideal characteristics of mLearning content.

With the adoption of more and more smartphones and other mobile devices, the scope of mobile communication has clearly broadened, as young people engage in new practices and address new audiences (Bertel and Stald 2013; Ling and Bertel 2013). In the last decade, children and adolescents have learned to skillfully manage computers and all kinds of handheld devices; nevertheless, although they can be experienced users, most of them ignore the potential risks and issues of mobile communication and mobile devices.

One of the most widespread critiques of mobile devices is the belief that, far from supporting learning, they distract from schoolwork (Kuznekoff 2015). This is because young people use them assiduously in their social life, mainly for things that are unrelated to class. The solution to reduce this possible handicap is that, when using mobile devices for learning, teachers need to set the content to be addressed and make the learning objectives clear before starting any activity.

In this sense, it is important to point out many researchers support the idea that the implementation of mobile technology in the classroom requires careful planning and commitment from all those involved in the learning process, including teachers, the educational administration and parents (see, e.g., Wang et al. 2012). In the case of young learners, it is adults who are responsible for the use of mobile technology and must monitor in some way the work done in classrooms or at home. As has previously been said, mobile devices used in a school context give the opportunity to enrich learning, but also offer the possibility of being tools of distraction or leading to unethical behaviour (such as cheating and cyber-bullying). Moreover, there may be health concerns due to an excessive time in front of screens and privacy problems when children overshare personal information or when unsuitable sites are not limited by adults. One solution to these issues is to include digital literacy in the Primary curriculum, since websites and mobile applications can often track user behaviour and collect user data. Applications used for mobile learning should comply with national privacy laws and generally accepted mobile privacy principles. Measures should be in place to ensure that private and possibly sensitive data collected by educational institutions are kept safe and are only available to those with access rights (i.e., the learner and his or her teachers). As McQuiggan et al. (2013, p. 14) argue: 'Teaching digital literacy is certainly preferable to, as is often the case, letting the risk of liability lead to overly restrictive policies'.

A second important issue to consider is that we currently know very little about the efficacy of mLearning content (or apps) or about the experience needed to deliver on the software's educational promises. While a few studies show students improving in certain skill areas after using particular pieces of software (Ananiadou and Claro 2009), a set of generalizable rules, hallmarks and features that might guide early educators' choices is not yet available. Related to this second issue is the importance of how engaging content is, both in terms of language learning and from a cognitive or pedagogical point of view. The findings suggest, for example, that when hot spots (a place where a wireless Internet connection is available) support, reinforce or extend the e-story children are reading, the children are better able to retell the story (Stewart and Gachago 2016), whereas extraneous or incidental 'bells and whistles' from the app had the opposite effect.

The aim of a particular app is also an important concern for teachers. Some badly designed learning apps are simply a collection of buttons, and the role of the child is either to keep tapping on random images and switches to see them move or make noises or to listen to a narrator and then tap on a button to advance the game. The first type is an open-ended game with no meaningful learning experience behind it; the second type is essentially a multiple-choice quiz without useful feedback. Instead, an app should offer young learners a real and interactive experience, whether it is an open-ended experience or a structured one, toward a certain learning goal, or a language focus (i.e., naming the parts of the body, making pairs, etc.). The key aspect of apps lies in how they empower a child to try different things and experience the consequence of their actions in that virtual world, whether it is a 'correct' action or an 'incorrect' one. Knowing *why* a decision or an answer is incorrect (choosing a picture that matches a noun in a memory game, for instance) is much more important than just knowing it is not correct, since it has to do with cognitive processes and decision-making actions. To sum up, before the process of teaching-learning begins, the teacher has to take into consideration device usability, social technology and interaction technology (Koole 2009) and ensure that the learning experience truly brings advantages over other learning modalities.

Another important topic is how an app adapts to the learner's progress. This issue has to do with the term *adaptive learning*.

A learning environment is considered adaptive if it is capable of: monitoring the activities of its users; interpreting these on the basis of domain-specific models; inferring user requirements and preferences out of the interpreted activities, appropriately representing these in associated models; and, finally, acting upon the available knowledge on its users and the subject matter at hand, to dynamically facilitate the learning process.

> The preceding informal definition should differentiate the concept of adaptivity from those of tailorability/configurability, flexibility/extensibility, or the mere support for intelligently mapping between available media/formats and the characteristics of access devices.
>
> *(Paramythis and Loidl-Reisinger 2004 p. 182)*

When teaching language to young learners, this means that as the child masters one skill set, the app needs to recognise their progress and give them more complex problems to solve. If they require a little more time in one area, it should recognise that as well and give them the guidance they need on that subject.

Motivation and the will of the learner to explore the app is another important aspect. The best apps are the ones that children return to again and again with enthusiasm. It is relevant that teachers spend some time observing children as they play to familiarise themselves with the characteristics of apps that a particular group of children find engaging and thereby support appropriate selection of content. Maybe the music in the app is not appealing, or perhaps the learner cannot make sense of what is going on in the app and needs some additional guidance, both in terms of language or actions.

Together with motivation, another important aspect to take into account is what happens after the implementation of the mLearning activity. As with any learning activity, it is necessary to assess the activity and the learning that has taken place. Vavoula and Sharpes (2008) propose six challenges for evaluating mLearning through a framework of three levels (usability, learning experience and integration within the educational and organisational context): capturing and analysing learning in context and across context, measuring mLearning processes and outcomes, respecting learner/participant privacy, assessing mobile technology utility and usability, considering the wider organisational and sociocultural context of learning and assessing in/formality. Through all these actions, the teacher is assessing not only the mobile device used in the mLearning activity, but also the process of learning of his/her students. At the same time, learners are evaluating their progress, both in knowledge (content) and experience (process).

Other critical points to consider are the problems technology could have *per se*. For example, the fact that some software needed for an activity could be incompatible with the device used is an issue which must be solved before the implementation of the activity. The limited information that some devices can store may also be a challenge. Using mobile technology that is connected to the cloud helps ease concerns about the weight of the files and to work simultaneously in the classroom and at home, or anywhere else. There is also the question of the screen size and resolution. Some technologies can strain the eyes after long periods of reading or writing and, therefore, it would be counterproductive to write a 100-word text in a mobile phone instead of doing it on a tablet, for instance.

Some other limitations that do not depend on the control of those involved (teachers or students) in the learning process but which must be considered when teaching are the connectivity and the cost. Sometimes, poor or totally absent mobile network signals or overloading when users are uploading or downloading content could cause connectivity problems and, as a result, a stop in the learning process. In relation to the cost, some governments and/or schools purchase mobile devices but if children must bring their own devices, there would be issues of inequality of access due to economic differences between the most privileged and the least fortunate students.

Current research

As Liu et al. (2014) pointed out, the most well documented possibilities of mobile devices are their inherent portability (the small size allows mobility with the user) and their wireless connectivity (access to information on the network). In addition, the literature indicates that because of the ubiquity and the immediacy of mobile devices, students have access to knowledge from any place at any time and can continue learning beyond the classroom (Fallon 2008). Additionally, these technologies, compared to other tools such as laptops or desktop computers, have a lower cost, so their accessibility means they can be used in the classroom by most students (Liu et al. 2009). Other studies (Banister 2010) consider that app access and multifunction sensors (GPS, camera, etc.) incorporate intrinsic characteristics of mLearning that encourage students through their process of learning.

However, taking into account the technical characteristics of mobile devices must be accompanied by an understanding of what mLearning means pedagogically. Research has identified the educational advantages of technological tools as being motivation, activation, individualization, responsibility and interactivity.

To begin with, the level of motivation will influence what and how effectively students learn, so motivation could be contemplated as an essential precondition for student involvement in any type of learning activity. Thus if teachers use mobile devices for learning purposes, students' motivation plays a significant role in engaging and sustaining them in the process of mlearning (Vogel et al. 2009). Secondly and related to activation, using mobile technology as a cognitive tool enhances constructivist learning whereby learners become the centre of the didactic process and play a more active role (Herrington, Herrington, Mantei, Olney and Ferry 2009). Third, individualization has been mentioned as an educational characteristic derived from the use of mobile devices (Grant and Basye 2014) because their utilization gives students the chance to work at their own pace, taking extra time in the areas where they need it most or going in depth when they wish to. Therefore, working with these tools allows teachers to adapt the process of learning to the needs of each learner (Banister 2010). The fourth listed characteristic, responsibility, comes from the possibilities that mobile devices provide to educators to motivate, activate and individualise learning, giving a greater sense of ownership to learners (mobile devices belong to each user) and responsibility for their own learning (Ridenour, Blood et al. 2011). Last but not least, interactivity is believed to play a significant role in the use of mobile devices thanks to the fact that learners interact with the instructor and their peers and can access course materials and collaborate with each other.

Current research in mobile learning has illustrated learning across different educational contexts (universities, schools, both formal and informal learning contexts, professional development and workplace settings), with diverse target groups including children, adult learners, vocational schools and professionals (Kukulska et al. 2009) and there have been a number of recent reviews.

Petrova and Li (2009) analyzed more than 300 articles about mLearning, identifying three main research domains: technology, educational technology and pedagogy. Their analysis also indicated that there was a shift from focus on technology to focus on theory in 2006 and 2007, whereas reasearch on the pedagogical implications of mLearning still remains today in third place.

According to the review carried out by Rikala (2013), Cheung and Hew (2009) found four main research areas: usage profile, viability as an assessment tool, learning outcomes and attitudes.

Wu et al. (2012) also carried out a review of research in the area of mlearning between 2003 and 2010. They found that 58% of the 164 studies they reviewed took *evaluating the effectiveness of mobile learning* as the primary research purpose, and the second-most frequently cited research purpose was *mobile learning system design* (32%). Research into mobile learning has therefore focused most on user acceptance and attitudes, the effectiveness of mobile learning, personalization and the design principles and recommendations for educational purposes (Rikala 2013).

In spite of the number of recent reviews, it must be noted that research specifically related to young language learners and mobile learning is minimal. However, there are some relevant recent studies, for example, related to mobile assisted language learning (Chinnery 2006), the challenges of vocabulary teaching through mobile devices (Snow and Kim 2007) and mobile-device-supported peer-assisted learning systems for collaborative early EFL reading (Lang, Sung, and Chang 2007). From 2013 onwards, attention seems to have shifted mainly to tablet technologies, such as Apple iPads, and how these devices are used, for example, to promote L2 motivation through exploiting its affordances to enhance collaborative learning and social development (Alhinty 2015). Bannister and Wilden (2013) and Kukulska-Hulme et al. (2015) both elaborate on the numerous ways in which tablets can be used in foreign language classrooms as a research tool, a recording tool and a sharing tool. Details of these practices are discussed in the next section.

Recommendations for practice

How to make mLearning work

In the previous section, it was claimed that the use of mobile devices and the implementation of mLearning activities in a classroom requires careful planning. Thus, a 'pre-teaching' phase is required to integrate mobile technologies and it is necessary to develop a framework that exploits the possibilities of mLearning.

According to Lara (2012) some useful recommendations before starting are: defining the learning objective to be achieved; being aware of whether the technology available allows the creation of the task; considering the skills needed (for both teachers and learners); thinking about the cost of implementation (the mobile device itself and the access to some applications which may require paying extra fees); asking how to facilitate the motivation from the users towards the device, and how to measure the success of learning; and ensuring that all students have a mobile device, that they know how to use it and that there is a good connectivity.

While the mLearning activity is being implemented, it is essential to undertake continuous monitoring of the experience with a view to getting feedback from the learners and confirming that the objectives are still active and that the activity continues accomplishing the language learning aims the teacher had planned. It is also recommended that simple activities are designed, promoting the use of audiovisual language (photos, video, etc.), at least at the beginning of the experience. Another important aspect is the storage of the files created. Choosing the right cloud service in advance is essential, as it offers numerous benefits including lower costs, faster experimentation, user-friendly experience and no physical infrastructure to manage. Children are also likely to be more used to it, since most of the devices they use today are based on cloud services. Lastly, there is a need to consider the extremely dynamic mobile learning context and the different ways that mobile technologies can be used to support teaching and learning for young children, such as individual tasks, group work, data collection, recording reflections/diaries, skills practice, feedback/questions to teacher, peer-to-peer communication/support, reviewing knowledge and warm-up/cool-down exercises (Attewell et al. 2010).

Practical applications of mLearning for young learners can have a number of different foci and there are many tools for each. The following paragraphs explain the main types of practical applications, while some examples of specific tools are given in the appendix. Web 2.0 Tools can be used to teach curriculum content, store data, create/edit video, edit photos, collaborate and so much more. These programmes are often free and are used by teachers, students and sometimes parents, both in and out of the classroom, on a regular basis. However, when using Web 2.0 tools, teachers need to remember that it is not about the specific tools themselves, but why and when the tool is needed, taking into consideration the learning outcomes and the key competences the students already have, or will need, to use them as learning tools. Ideally there also needs to be a culture within the school that values technology use in the classroom, and teachers trained in both the use of mobile devices and good teaching skills. Finally, it is also important to mention that these tools were current at the time of writing the chapter, but because of the constant evolution of mobile technology, they are likely to be replaced by others very quicky.

Before reviewing the tools, it is worth reiterating concerns regarding possible risks for children. When using 2.0 tools, teachers need first of all make sure that these are intended for educational use, instruction, research and the facilitation of communication, collaboration and other educational-related purposes. When teaching children in an mLearning environment, careful consideration of the *privacy policy and terms of service*; that is, what is happening with children's personal data that they are providing, is of paramount importance. One key component of keeping young children safe from having their data misused is to teach them to be digital citizens who can assess the risk associated with putting information on the Internet and identify trustworthy software providers, apps and tools. It is imperative that children be taught the skills needed to guard secure information and evaluate threats. Consequently, teachers need to make sure that the terms of service and privacy policies of the tools we choose to use are appropriate. A straightforward way of doing so is to use websites and 2.0 services that do not need registration, since most 2.0 tools that require a registration are intended for users aged 13 or older. Of course, there are many other websites and 2.0 tools that can be used without age restrictions and that are fully intended for children and educational purposes (i.e., Edmodo, Edublogs, Glogster EDU, Google Apps accounts, Kahoot or story bird, among others).

Tools for expressing and creating

There are four main types of applications for expressing and creating content: image and multimedia processing, graphics and diagrams, movement and virtual books.

First, some tools offer an active place for image and multimedia processing. Highly technical skills are not required because they use very intuitive interfaces and any student can make their own creations. Tools such as Storybird or VoiceThread can help children create short, visual stories. Students can select artwork, drag and organise photos and add their own text. These creations can then be published on the web with adjustable privacy settings. In most cases, there is also the option to allow comments, which is perfect for teachers to encourage student collaboration

Secondly, elaborating graphics and diagrams is also a good activity for organizing knowledge and involving creative thinking. Students can create flowcharts, mind maps, concept maps and many types of helpful visual communication.

Thirdly, there are also multiple 2.0 options, both within the programme usually used by Windows and online options that allow children to play (see Tamis-LeMonda and Rodriguez 2009 for the role of play in early language learning). In general, these types of tools are also easy to use and useful, for example, for creating and editing audiovisual texts, fostering children's movement while learning or listening to music.

Lastly, with tools focused on virtual books, students can make creations combining text and images, fixed or mobile and in many different formats, from the traditional book to the magazine or the newspaper. These applications develop the digital competence not only of an individual, but also collaboratively, since most offer possibilities for collaborative writing.

Tools for publishing and sharing content

The concepts of publishing and spreading must be understood as active processes in which students interact with the contents and with other users, in the sense of sharing information. There are four applications in this section: photos, audio and podcasts, multimedia presentations and videos and television.

To publish photos and share them with other users, learners can use various applications. Photos are organised into albums, turning the space into an image catalogue. This is particularly useful to facilitate the learning of vocabulary and to work on oral and written expression by means of the insertion of photos into a blog, in a wiki (a website or database developed collaboratively by a community of users, allowing any user to add and edit content) or in a class web page.

Another group of tools are characterised by enabling the publication of and collaboration on audio files, generally in mp3 format. These files are downloaded through the podcast syndication. As Godwin-Jones (2005) comments, the use of podcasts develops oral communication, in the sense that it enables the practice of oral comprehension and expression through the recording and editing of oral productions. Other content, such as music, stories or oral presentations, can also be downloaded, which can support the teaching-learning process.

The applications called multimedia presentations are web services that host content. In them, teachers and pupils can create works, add to them and control the downloads and readings that a specific document has had. The teacher and the students are enriched by the collaboration and the search for diverse content to support the materials offered.

Videos and television are very useful tools for the teaching-learning process. These applications allow users to share stored videos and tag, download and comment on them and are particularly useful in promoting understanding of content. In addition, teachers and students can use them to publish videos to support learning and view activities, for example. Undoubtedly, the best-known video and television application is YouTube (www.youtube.com). However, its restrictions of use are limited to over thirteen years old, so its educational use must always be supervised by the teacher who needs to review the contents.

Tools for searching and accessing information

All applications with the ability to express and create, and/or publish and spread are stored on the Internet and, consequently, they become tools that allow access to information.

Therefore, a comic book or a video, for example, constitute published content to be located and used in the classroom. In this category of searching and accessing information, it is opportune to include those tools that contain search engines, aggregators, maps and music. As in the two previous sections, the following lines explain them and their applicability in the primary classroom.

Search engines are tools that allow for the location of information in various formats (documents, images, videos, etc). One of the main concerns of all educators is the large amount of information to which their students have access that is not appropriate to their age. To this end, there are adapted search engines that detect and eliminate the adult content of their search result. As an example, there is *Googlekids*.

An aggregator is an Internet programme or service. Its main function is to collect the latest news published on the Web 2.0. For this, the user has to predefine a favourite news list. In the classroom, it is beneficial if there is another application for expressing and creating or publishing and sharing, such as a virtual book or a multimedia presentation to build students' collaborative skills. The aggregator will keep users informed of the changes that are being made on the web.

At a first sight, it could seem that maps are educational resources for specific subjects, namely, geography and natural sciences, among others. Maps, however, make it easy to locate content, find different geographical locations, view images from satellites and explore landscapes from different places, often inaccessible to many students.

Tools for sharing and thinking

The applications based on social networks put people in contact according to some kind of common interest. Social networks can be of two types: vertical or horizontal. The former are created by users, whereas the latter already exist and users are incorporated into them. Many authors have addressed the potential benefits of social networks in the educational process. De Haro (2010), for instance, considers that they allow centralisation in a single site of all teaching activities; there is an improvement of the work environment by allowing students to create their own objects of interest; they increase the fluency and the simplicity of communication between teachers and students; they increase the effectiveness of the practical use of ICT, by acting as a means of agglutinating people, resources and activities; and, they facilitate the coordination and work of diverse learning groups by creating them.

Currently, the most widespread social network among the population in terms of its use is *Facebook* (www.facebook.com), but its restrictions mean it cannot be used with young learners. However, there are some networks focused on the educational field that can be used in the primary classroom.

There are also a number of useful tools which cannot be classified within the above-mentioned categories because they contain several of the features listed; these include storage, calendars, social bookmarks, online office, microblogging, Virtual Learning Environments, wikis, blogs and generators, and are described below.

Storage

Storage applications store information in web services. This allows people to have the information available at any time and from any site through the network. At the same time, these tools facilitate not only the download of files, but also their distribution between the teacher and the student.

Calendars

As its name implies, calendars are online calendars. The educational applicability allows the creation of shared calendars through which students can know the temporary organization of contents of the subject and the notification of events, for example, the delivery of a task.

Social bookmarking

Social bookmarks are Web 2.0 applications that serve to store, classify and share Internet links. They are virtual libraries that allow the realization of customised and/or collective webography and the organization of information according to the user's interests. They can be very useful for teachers and students. For example, the teacher can create a database to structure the contents of the subject while the student can have a list of all those web pages integrated in his/her process of learning.

Online office

These Web 2.0 tools create and share the work online. Consequently, teamwork, collaboration in projects and content editing are promoted simultaneously by several students and/or the teacher. For example, in the elaboration of a group multimedia presentation, the students can upload the document in the *Prezentit*, and each one can participate from wherever they want.

Microblogging

The microblogging or nanoblogging is a short messaging service, usually text, but to which you can add photos or audio. The program authorises the creation of messages, and the user publishes them to be read and/or commented on by the other members or followers. Lomicka and Lord (2009) recognise that the microblogging makes easier and maximises the interactions between the students and the teacher with a fluent communication. In addition, through this tool, students can work as a team in a collaborative task.

Virtual Learning Environments (VLE)

A VLE, also called a virtual classroom or platform, is an environment through which the computer simulates a classroom with teaching and learning activities, such as documents, exercises, work, etc. Thus, a VLE gives the possibility of presenting to the participants of the learning process a new space on the Internet to develop the teaching and learning act. Boenu (2007) proposes four essential characteristics for any virtual classroom: interactivity (learner as the protagonist), flexibility (with the institution, the curriculum and the content and pedagogical styles), scalability (ability to work with any number of users) and standardization (possibility to import and export courses). Belloch (2003) is more specific and proposes a series of technical and pedagogical characteristics. In reference to the technical aspects, the author emphasises if the VLE is free or not, if there is the possibility of changing the language, if the system is operative with the organization that implements it, if there are manuals or documentation of support for the users and if there is a community of users to consult problems and/or doubts about the dynamics of the virtual platform. In terms of pedagogical aspects, the author lists six characteristics: management, personalization, communication, interaction, collaboration and evaluation. The knowledge of these characteristics of EVA and its possibilities in the teaching-learning processes will be the elements that have to determine its use in an mLearning context and the pedagogical methodology according to the tools that it offers.

Wikis

A wiki is a website where users can create, modify and/or delete information they share. Their educational applications are multiple: to plan and to carry out works promoting constructivist and collaborative work; to create web content banks, glossaries, dictionaries, manuals, etc., with photographs, videos, files and/or links to expend the curricular content; and to interact with students.

Blogs

A blog is a website that collects information chronologically in entries (or post), composed of texts, images, audios, videos, etc. There are several educational applications, mainly: creating, publishing and spreading knowledge, opinions, questions, etc. The most popular blogs in the educational field are:

Blogger → www.blogger.com
Blogspot → www.blogspot.es

Future Directions

As stated in the Current Research section, if teachers use mobile devices for learning purposes, aspects such as students' motivation, learning in a constructivist way, working on their own pace, responsibility and interactivity are believed to play a significant role. However, research in these areas is still lacking.

Cheung and Hew (2009) also identified four main research areas that need to be addressed in the future: (1) usage profile, (2) viability as an assessment tool, (3) learning outcomes and (4) attitudes.

Research in the field of mobile learning should offer explicit proof of educational outcomes and impacts: how the the use of mobile technology helps young learners learn better, develop digital competences and make learning a positive experience while they develop their learning-how-to-learn competence. These educational outcomes and impacts cannot be assessed before the use of mobile devices in education has been fully integrated into the day to day operations of the classroom. Consequently, one major challenge is that mobile learning practises have not become endemic to educational contexts or to classroom practices. There should be a cohesive theoretical mobile learning framework and a set of best practices addressed to young learners for educational purposes. As Jenni Rikala (2013) suggests, without these it simply takes too much of teachers' time and energy to interweave all crucial aspects together. Teachers alone will unlikely be able to bring the breadth of implementation needed.

Also, as has been shown in the previous section, mLearing tools are especially relevant to the young learner English classroom, as they enable access to all kinds of information and educational materials, as well as offer a communicative channel. They offer teachers and learners a new educational paradigm without spacial or time barriers for information and communication.

Furthermore, according to McQuiggan et al. (2015), the future adoption of mobile learning and the success of such efforts require continuous awareness and integration of new technologies and functions, especially in regard to teaching. Thus, teachers must stay informed of the latest updates to these devices. The landscape of mobile learning has shifted dramatically in just the past five to seven years, with the advent of new and cheaper tablets, and the proliferation and evolution of other types of handheld devices and wearable technologies. The capabilities of today's smartphones and tablets have revolutionised the concept of mobile learning, and according to edtech experts, the majority of the hardware and software can be moved to 'the cloud' and the product itself will mainly be the input and the display (Huiyu 2015). Similarly, although the theoretical foundations behind mobile learning remain relevant (i.e, constructivism, motivation, collaborative learning), research in the field is very much in its infancy.

It can be concluded that as current or future teachers of young learners we must not forget that the main focus in education today is learning, not technology, despite the rapid growth of technological changes. All the information and the tools mentioned in this chapter are means to help create exciting, engaging and effective activities for young learners, which can be achieved by learning about, implementing and redesigning mLearning to enrich the curriculum in the areas of creativity and innovation, collaboration, critical thinking, problem solving and communication.

Further reading

Berge, Z. L., and Muilenburg, L. (June 19, 2013). *Handbook of Mobile Education*. Hoboken: Taylor and Francis.

The chapter begins by explicating the philosophical, pedagogical and conceptual underpinnings regarding learning, particularly towards learner-centred pedagogies. This is followed by a discussion of the technology, covering the evolution of the hardware and software, its adoption in society and how these technological advancements have led to today's new affordances for learning.

Gawelek, M. A., Spataro, M., and Komarny, P. (March 01, 2011). Mobile perspectives: On iPads – Why mobile? *Educause Review*, 46(2), 28.

This article was written by a group studying an iPad pilot program and focuses on technical infrastructure, administrator and leadership buy-in and redesigning instruction with iPads in mind. This article asks some of the same questions as this chapter: are the devices a distraction? Does the time setting up and using the devices take away from reflection? Ultimately, this article supports the notion of integrating instruction into learning devices that today's students are familiar with and continually planning for the technology changes of the future.

Troutner, J. (2010). Mobile learning. *Teacher Librarian*, 38, 1

This article focuses on practical applications for mobile learning and information to find apps and other resources. The article links to blogs of teachers who use mobile devices in their classrooms. This article reinforces some of the resources already mentioned but provides a peer-reviewed source of quality information for beginning teachers and instructors to use when piloting a mobile device program.

Related topics

Motivation, projects, CLIL, English outside the classroom, classroom management

APPENDIX

1 Tools for expressing and creating

A Image processing

Picnik → www.picnik.com
Pixton → www.pixton.com
Glogster → www.glogster.com
Canva → www.canva.com

B Elaborating graphics and diagrams

Text2mindmap → www.tex2mindmap.com
Sketchboard → https://sketchboard.io/

C For the management of movement

Jango → http://es.jango.com/music/Tool
Kidjo → www.kidjo.tv/

D Virtual books

Storybird → http://storybird.com/

2 For publishing and spreading

A To publish photos

Flickr → www.flickr.com/
Picasa → http://picasa.google.com/

B For the publication and collaboration of audio files

Evoca → www.evoca.com/
Odeo → www.odeoenterprise.com/

C Multimedia presentations

Prezi → www.prezi.com
Slideshare → www.slideshare.net/

D Videos and television

Teachertube → www.teachertube.com
- *Livestream* → www.livestream.com/
- *Blip* → http://blip.tv/

For searching and accessing information

All applications with the ability to express, create, publish and spread are online tools that facilitate finding information. Therefore, a comic book or a video, for example, is published content that can be located and used in the classroom. Nevertheless, in this section on searching and accessing information, it is useful to include the following tools: search engines, aggregators, maps and music. As in the two previous sections, explanations of the tools and their applicability in the classroom, especially the primary one, are provided below.

Search engines are tools that allow you to locate information in various formats, namely, documents, images, videos, etc. The most popular search engines are:

Google → www.google.com
Yahoo → www.yahoo.com

One of educators' main concerns is the large amount of information to which their students have access that is not age appropriate. To alleviate this concern, there are adapted search engines that can detect and eliminate explicit content, e.g., *Googlekids*.

An **aggregator** is an Internet program or service that collects the latest news published on the Web 2.0, based on the user's predefined list of favourites. In the classroom it is helpful to use one in tandem with another application for expressing, creating, publishing and spreading, such as a virtual book or multimedia presentation. The aggregator will keep users informed about the updates to the web. The most famous one is:

Feedly → http://feedly.com/i/welcome

At a first impression, it could seem that maps are educational resources for very specific areas and their geography, natural sciences and so forth. However, maps make it easy to locate content, find different geographical locations, view images from satellites and explore landscapes from different places which are often inaccessible to students. Two applications for maps are:

Community walk → www.communitywalk.com/
Google maps → http://maps.google.com/maps?hl=en&tab=wl

The Web 2.0 contains applications for listening to **music**, creating and sharing distribution lists. Therefore, the Web 2.0 facilitates the search for music and its digital reproduction, thanks to software such as:

Lastfm → www.lastfm.es/
Yes → www.yes.fm/
The radio → www.theradio.com/

3 For sharing and thinking

Neo LMS → www.neolms.com/
Edmodo → www.edmodo.com/

4 Storage

Dropbox → www.dropbox.com/
Box → http://box.net/
Live drive → www.livedrive.com/

5 Calendars

Google calendar → www.google.com/intl/es/googlecalendar/tour.html

6 Social bookmarking

Delicious → www.delicious.com/
Mister-wrong → www.mister-wong.es/
Diigo → www.diigo.com/

7 Online office

Stilus → http://stilus.daedalus.es/stilus.php
ArtPad → http://artpad.art.com/artpad/painter/
Prezentit → www.prezentit.com
Zoho → www.zoho.com/
Schoolrack → www.schoolrack.com/.

8 Microblogging

Twitter → http://twitter.com/ (as with Youtube and Facebook, Twitter is restricted to users over age 13)
Tumblr → www.tumblr.com/
You are → http://youare.com/

9 Wikis

Wikispaces → www.wikispaces.com
Escolar → www.escolar.net7wiki
Nirewiki → http://nirewiki.com/en

10 Blogs

Blogger → www.blogger.com
Blogspot → www.blogspot.es

References

Adell, J. (2010a). Web 2.0 y Escuela 2.0. *DIM-UAB, 16*. http://dim.pangea.org/revistaDIM16/revistanew.htm [Aaccessed 3 August 2017].

Adell, J. y Castañeda, L. (2012). Tecnologías emergentes, ¿pedagogías emergentes? En Hernández, J., Pennesi, M., Sobrino, D., y Vázquez, A. (coord.). *Tendencias emergentes en educación con TIC*. Barcelona: Asociación Espiral, Educación y Tecnología, 13–32.

Ala-Mutka, K., and Koskinen, T. (2014). Digital Literacies and eCompetence. *eLearning Papers*, (38).

Anderson, T., and Dron, J. (2010). Three generations of distance education pedagogy . . . . Review of research in open and distance learning. Retrieved from www.irrodl.org/index.php/ irrodl/article/ view/890.

Aston, M. (2002). The development and use of indicators to measure the impact of ICT use in education in the United Kingdom and other European countries. In *Developing Performance Indicators for ICT in Education*. UNESCO Institute for Information Technology (IITE), 62–73. www.unescobkk.org/education/ict/ict-in-education-projects/monitoring-and-measuring-change/performance-indicators-on-ict-use-in-education-project/consultative-workshop/experiences/uk-and-other-european-countries/?type=98.

Aubusson, P., Schuck, S., and Burden, K. (2009). Mobile learning for teacher professional learning: Benefits, obstacles, and issues. ALT-J. *Research in Learning Technology*, 17(3), 233–247.

Castañeda, L., y Adell, J. (Eds.). (2013). Entornos personales de aprendizaje: claves para el ecosistema educativo en red. Linda Johanna Castañeda Quintero (ed. lit.), Jordi Adell Segura (ed. lit.). Editorial Marfil.

Cheung, W., and Hew, K. (2009). A review of research methodologies used in studios on mobile handheld devices in K-12 and higher education settings. *Australasian Journal of Educational Technology*, 25(2), 153–183.

Dede, B. C. (2005). Planning for Neomillennial Learning Styles. *Educause*, (1), 7–12.

Delgado, E. (2013). 5 key areas of a highly successful K-12 tech integration plan/PME: Beyond technology education. www.youtube.com/watch?v=UZePBZ-edfE

Delialioglu, Ö. (2012). Student engagement in blended learning environments with lecture-based and problem-based instructional approaches. *Educational Technology & Society*, 15, 310–322. http://ifets.info/journals/15_3/24.pdf.

Ding, G. (2010). New theoretical approach to integrated education and technology. *Frontiers of Education in China*, 5(1), 26–36.

Domingo, M. Y Marques. (2011). Aulas 2.0 y uso de las TIC en la práctica docente. *Comunicar*, 37(XIX), 169–175.

Educause Learning Initiative (ELI). (2010). 7 things you should know about . . . Mobile apps for learning. http://net.educause.edu/ir/library/pdf/ELI7060.pdf [Accessed 2 October 2014].

ELearning Guild. (2013). 158 Tips on mLearning: From Planning to Implementation. www.elearning guild.com/publications/index.cfm?id=35&from=home [Accessed 2 October 2014].

European Commission. (2007). *Safer Internet for Children: Qualitative study in 29 European countries*. Summary Report. Versailles: European Commission [online]. http://ec.europa.eu/commfrontoffice/ publicopinion/archives/quali/ql_safer_internet_summary.pdf [Accessed 25 November 2017].

Gawelek, M. A., Spataro, M., and Komarny, P. (March 01, 2011). Mobile perspectives: On iPads why mobile? *Educause Review*, 46(2), 28.

Goh, T., and Kinshuk, D. (2006). Getting ready for mobile learning-adaptation perspective. *Journal of Educational Multimedia and Hypermedia*, 15(2), 175–198.

Hernández, J. (2012). Móviles y apps. Realmente aportan algo a la Educación. *Comunicación y Pedagogía*, 259–260, 41–46.

Herrington, J., Herrington, A., Mantei, J., Olney, I., and Ferry, B. (Eds.). (2009). *New Technologies, New Pedagogies: Mobile learning in higher education*. Wollongong: Faculty of Education, University of Wollongong.

Holzinger, A., Nischelwitzer, A., and Meisenberger, M. (2005). Mobile phones as a challenge for mlearning. *Proc. IEEE International Conference on Pervasive Computing and Communications, IEEE Press*, 307–311.

Johnson, L., Adams Becker, S., Estrada, V., Freeman, A., Kampylis, P., Vuorikari, R., and Punie, Y. (2014). *Horizon Report Europe: 2014 schools edition*. Luxembourg: Publications Office of the European Union, and Austin, Texas: The New Media Consortium.

Keegan, D. (2005). The incorporation of mobile learning into mainstream education and training. *Proceedings of mLearn2005–4th World Conference on mLearning*, Cape Town, South Africa, 25–28 October 2005. www.mlearn.org.za/CD/papers/keegan1.pdf [Accessed 2 October 2014].

Koole, M. L. (2009). A model for framing mobile learning. In Ally, M. (ed.) *Mobile Learning: Transforming the delivery of education and training, Edmonton*. Edmonton, Canada: Athabasca University Press, 38.

Karsenti, T., and Fievez, A. (2013). *The iPad in Education: Uses, beneits, and challenges – A survey of 6,057 students and 302 teachers in Quebec (Canada)*. Montreal, QC: CRIFPE.

Kucirkova N (2013) Response to By-passing the debate: Beyond the 'technology question' in the early years by Associate Professor Suzy Edwards, Tactyc 2013. http://tactyc.org.uk/pdfs/Response-Kucirkova.pdf [Accessed 2 August 2017].

Kukulska-Hulme, Agnes, Sharples, Mike, Milrad, Marcelo, Arnedillo-Sánchez, Inmaculada, and Vavoula, Giasemi. (2009). Innovation in mobile learning: A European perspective. *International Journal of Mobile and Blended Learning*, 1(1), 13–35.

Madrid, D., Mayorga, M. J., and Núñez, F. (2013). Aplicación del m-learning en el aula de primaria: Experiencia práctica y propuesta de formación para docentes. EDUTEC, Revista Electrónica de Tecnología Educativa, 45. Recuperado el dd/mm/aa de. http://edutec.rediris.es/Revelec2/Revelec45/aplicacion_mlearning_primaria_experiencia_formacion_docentes.html.

MoLeNET. (2007) The mobile learning network (MoLeNET). http:// www.molenet.org.uk/ [Accessed 2 October 2014].

Padrós, J. (2011): El Projecte EduCAT1x1. Què en pensen els implicats. Documento en llínea. Espiral, educació i tecnologia. http://ciberespiral.org/informe_espiral1x1.pdf.

Petrova, K., and Li, C. (2009). Focus and setting in mobile learning research: A review of the literature. *Communications of the IBIMA*, 10, 219, 226.

Pollara, P., and Kee Broussard, K. (2011). Student perceptions of mobile learning: A review of current research. *Proceedings of Society for Information Technology & Teacher Education International Conference 2011*. Chesapeake, VA: AACE, 1643–1650.

Sharples M., Taylor J., Vavoula G. (2010) A Theory of Learning for the Mobile Age. In: Bachmair B. (eds) Medienbildung in neuen Kulturräumen. VS Verlag für Sozialwissenschaften

Sharples, M., Milrad, M., Arnedillo Sánchez, I., and Vavoula, G. (2009). Mobile learning: ‹Small devices, big Issues.› In Balacheff, Nicolas, Ludvigsen, Sten, Ard Lazonder, Ton de Jong, and Barnes, Sally (eds.) *Technology Enhanced Learning: Principles and products*. Heidelberg: Springer, 233–249. www.lsri.nottingham.ac.uk/msh/Papers/KAL_Legacy_Mobile_Learning.pdf [Accessed 10 December 2017].

Siemens, G. (2004). Connectivism: A learning theory for the digital age. Retrieved from http://www.elearnspace.org/Articles/connectivism.htm.

United Nations Educational, Scientific and Cultural Organization (UNESCO) and Commonwealth of Learning (COL). (2011). *Guidelines for Open Educational Resources (OER) in Higher Education*. Paris/Vancouver, BC, Authors. http://unesdoc.unesco.org/images/0021/002136/213605e.pdf.

United Nations Educational, Scientific and Cultural Organization (UNESCO) and Commonwealth of Learning (COL). (2012). *Mobile Learning and Policies: Key issues to consider*. Paris, BC, Authors. http://unesdoc.unesco.org/images/0021/002176/217638E.pdf.

Veletsianos, G. (2011). Designing opportunities for transformation with emerging technologies. *Educational Technology*, 51(2), 6.

21

Classroom technology for young learners

Shona Whyte and Euline Cutrim Schmid

Introduction

Nowadays it is probably as rare to find an English classroom without a single computer or smartphone as it is to find distance learners of English who are isolated from any authentic exchange with others. Although early work in computer-assisted language learning (CALL) compared teaching and learning with and without technology – often contrasting traditional, face-to-face teaching with learning via computer – this boundary is now blurred due to developments both in teaching and learning practices and in technologies themselves. Face-to-face teaching with perhaps only traditional blackboards and textbooks, for instance, may be supplemented with homework requiring technology use outside class time, in what is popularly termed the 'flipped classroom'. Here technology is not used directly in the class-room, but class teaching depends on it all the same. Should our definition include this use of technology? Conversely, a virtual class for a distance course taught exclusively online may employ the same tools with the same affordances as in the physical classroom, and may permit teacher-learner interaction which is very similar. Shouldn't our definition therefore also include this kind of virtual classroom?

For this reason, it is difficult to define the term 'classroom technology', and to determine which technologies and uses fit this appellation. In their recent review of 'technology use in the classroom', Mama and Hennessy (2013) list Powerpoint, educational software, web-based video and display of images on the interactive whiteboard (IWB) as examples of somewhat conservative use of classroom technology. In his handbook on technology for foreign language teachers, however, Blake (2013) uses the umbrella term 'digital classroom' to include a much wider range of tools and resources, including use of web pages, CALL programmes and applications, computer-mediated communication (CMC), distance learning, social networks and games, thus encompassing technology use both in and outside the traditional physical classroom. We shall follow this broad definition in the present chapter to focus on teachers' and learners' use of technology in traditional classrooms, including both equipment and devices employed in physical classroom settings, as well as CMC reaching beyond the classroom walls.

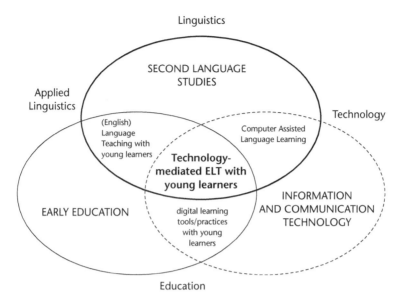

Figure 21.1 Dimensions of technology-mediated ELT with young learners

The use of classroom technology with young learners of English, like many areas of applied linguistics, and indeed education studies, stands at the intersection of several academic disciplines. Figure 21.1 provides a schematic representation of the overlapping interests of three main domains. Second language (L2) studies focus on second language acquisition (SLA) and informs both English language teaching (ELT) and CALL. Information and communication technology (ICT) also intersects with education studies as the field of educational technology.

In many ways the findings of research in each area have not been communicated and applied effectively in others, leaving the field of technology-mediated language education with young learners somewhat bereft of both theoretical underpinning and empirical findings. We begin with a brief historical overview of work in classroom technology for young English language learners (YELLs), and then focus on critical issues related to the affordances of digital tools, the distinction between language interaction and technology, the pedagogical advantages of technology-mediated task-based language teaching (TBLT), and the challenges of orchestrating complex CMC interactions with YELLs. The chapter continues with a review of current CALL research with young learners, before considering recommendations for practice and future directions.

Historical perspectives

CALL research can be summarised in a succession of overlapping phases, beginning with *structural CALL* in the 1970s and 1980s (Gruba 2004; Warschauer 2004; Chun 2016). In this approach to technology-mediated language teaching and learning, computers were used to drill and practice the target language from grammar-translation or audiolingual perspectives, with a view to improving L2 accuracy. By the end of the twentieth century, cognitive views of acquisition and learning led to new uses of personal computers to develop fluency through communicative exercises in what has been termed *communicative CALL*.

The sociocultural turn of the early 2000s coincided with the arrival of multimedia and wide-spread use of the internet, leading to greater attention to authentic resources for both content and language learning, and to social interaction, in the form of *integrative CALL*. Finally, Chun (2016) has proposed the term *ecological CALL* to cover a very recent phase of global and ubiquitous learning via mobile devices, involving the broader educational goals of inter-cultural competence and digital literacies.

This account of historical developments in the field gives the somewhat misleading impression of linear progress, suggesting that new technologies and new pedagogical approaches advance hand in hand. While it is true that early CALL programmes were largely based on structural linguistic analysis and behaviourist pedagogical assumptions, the same criticism applies to many recent applications designed for modern smartphones and tablets. Language apps for beginners, for example, often rely on decontextualised practice of single lexical items, or discrete-item multiple-choice grammar exercises, rather than on communicative or sociocultural approaches to language learning. Just as many individual teachers experience a form of pedagogical backsliding when integrating new technologies into their regular teaching repertoire, in the form of Fullan's (2001) 'implementation dip', it appears that publishers and developers, too, often show signs of pedagogical regression when adapting teaching and learning resources for new platforms and devices. For Gimeno Sanz (2016, p. 1104),

> the maturity we had acquired in the 1990s both in making the most of what technology had to offer at the time and how to apply that technology to the full benefit of peda-gogically sound multimedia materials has not yet been paralleled even with the recent incorporation of social network applications or sophisticated virtual world software.

Researchers in other educational sectors have also adopted a critical stance with respect to technology integration. Early research on interactive software (Plowman 1996; Aldrich et al. 1998) decried the predominance of drill-and-practice activities, offering learners only what they termed *reactive interactivity* or indeed *gratuitous interactivity*, lacking any clear pedagogi-cal purpose. Technological progress and a better understanding of technology integration have led to the development of different frameworks to describe the different types of interactivity afforded by different technologies, a crucial dimension which is examined in the next section.

Finally, the historical focus of CALL on adult learners should not be forgotten. Many find-ings have not filtered through to early language educators, where technology is viewed as a means of increasing L2 exposure, given what many consider insufficient time allotted to language instruction and the opportunities to access English-language media outside the class-room (Copland and Garton 2014). YELL researchers are aware of the emergence of 'a wealth of small-scale classroom studies' such as those reported in Pim (2013), but feel that 'substan-tially more research is now needed throughout the primary sector' (Enever 2016, p. 359).

Critical issues and topics

Some recent studies have examined the use of a broad range of tools and applications under the heading classroom technology, from language learning software and interactive white-boards and mobile technologies to both asynchronous and live CMC, and of course web-based materials. In Table 21.1, we list examples of technology use together with some of the main affordances and challenges of each.

Among the difficulties teachers and researchers have identified with the use of these technologies in the YELL classroom is the question of **interactivity**: in work with IWBs,

Table 21.1 Tools and activities for technology-mediated ELT with young learners

Tools /Activities	Uses	Affordances	Challenges	Examples from the literature
Language learning software	Digital storytelling Digital games Interactive exercises Extensive listening	Interactivity Multimedia dimension Rich input Individual, autonomous practice	Predominance of drill-and-practice and grammar activities Multimedia dimension is often underexploited	Elsner (2014)
IWBs	Multisensory presentations Interactive tools (e.g., drag and drop, hide and reveal) to encourage learner participation Anonymous quizzes using learner response systems	Enhanced interaction Authentic, rich input Facilitating understanding of grammar concepts and rules (e.g., reordering categorizing)	Teacher centredness and learner passivity Predominance of drill-and-practice activities Insufficient ready-made material Superficial or gratuitous interactivity Cognitive overload	Kegenhof (2014) Yáñez and Coyle (2011)
Tablets/mobile phones	Creating own digital products (e.g., videos, digital stories) Sharing and revisiting work by listening to audio and video recordings	Ubiquitous and user-friendly technology Seamless access to recording and playback functions allowing focus on meaning and form	Some apps provide little room for spontaneous and creative language output	Alhinty (2015) Pellerin (2014)
Asynchronous CMC	Collaborative writing on wikis Sharing content via blogs and podcasts Use of online platforms (e.g., Moodle) to support telecollaboration between remote classes	Authentic audience for learners' L2 production Opportunities for meaningful interaction and collaboration	Younger learners have limited competence with written language Exchanging pre-recorded audio or video messages beyond 'here and now' context can be frustrating	Dooly and Sadler (2016)

(Continued)

Table 21.1 (Continued)

Tools /Activities	Uses	Affordances	Challenges	Examples from the literature
Live CMC	Interviews with native speakers Online debates or discussions between remote classes Collaborative projects	Access to peer or expert interlocutors who do not share learners' L1 Authentic tasks based on genuine communicative intent and real gaps in knowledge or opinion	Learners may lack communication strategies for dealing with interactional breakdowns Teachers may limit spontaneous interaction by controlling exchanges too tightly	Whyte (2011), Cutrim Schmid and Whyte (2015)
Web-based materials	Internet material for presentation of new content (e.g., YouTube videos, film sequences, digital images) Internet search, reference tools (dictionaries, encyclopedias) Online games and learning activities	Access to authentic, rich and motivating input Facilitating comprehension of language input (e.g., images, video.) Supporting autonomous learning	Cognitive overload and disorientation Lack of skills for finding and evaluating online material	Sailer et al. (2014)

tablets and phones, or web-based activities, for example, studies found examples of superficial interactivity without adequate pedagogical underpinning which failed to allow space for creative language use, or which led to cognitive overload and disorientation (Pellerin 2014; Kegenhof 2014; Sailer et al. 2014; Yañez and Coyle 2011). Language learning software has also attracted criticism, this time concerning the design of **learning tasks** which frequently involve drill-and-practice exercises rather than more cognitively demanding communicative activities (Elsner 2014). Other limitations on children's opportunities to interact in English in ostensibly more challenging CMC environments were found to be imposed by teachers in both design and implementation of tasks (Whyte 2011). A third challenge emerging from this body of research is therefore the exploitation of opportunities for **rich CMC exchanges** in ways which provide sufficient support for YELLs (Cutrim Schmid and Whyte 2015; Dooly and Sadler 2016).

This section focuses on these three critical issues in technology integration, namely, (a) classroom interaction and digital interactivity, (b) the design and implementation of teaching and learning tasks and (c) the challenges of orchestrating complex technology-mediated interaction with young beginners.

Classroom interaction and digital interactivity

A key affordance of the technologies listed in Table 21.1 is the opportunity to enhance interactivity in a constructivist environment where learning constitutes an active process of knowledge creation. However, there have also been debates in the literature about the nature and quality of technology-supported interaction. For instance, several studies on the use of IWBs (e.g., Whyte, Cutrim Schmid and Beauchamp 2014) and videoconferencing (Whyte 2011) in the EFL primary classroom reveal no clear-cut positive effects on classroom interaction associated with these technologies, which were mostly used to maintain teacher control of learning processes and manage pupil behaviour.

Based on findings of classroom-based research, some authors propose multidimensional models to analyse technology-enhanced classroom interaction, including technical, physical and conceptual interactivity (Jewitt et al. 2007) or didactic, interactive and enhanced interactivity (Glover et al. 2007). These frameworks provide ways of analysing classroom practice not only in terms of the technical competence of teachers and/or learners, but also with respect to the pedagogical goals pursued. One influential approach to teaching with technologies involves a four-stage developmental model, moving from the *authoritative* class, where the teacher controls technological interactivity, through the *dialectic* class, where space is allowed for learners to respond, and the more flexible *dialogic* class, to a *synergistic* stage where all participants have the power to shape learning events (Beauchamp and Kennewell 2010). Increased interactivity is thought to meet diverse learning needs (Wall et al. 2005), enhance motivation (Gitsaki and Robby 2014) and contribute to the development of digital literacies (Warschauer 2012).

In the language classroom, too, the nature and quality of technology-supported interaction have attracted interest (Favaro 2011; Cutrim Schmid and Whyte 2015; Dooly and Sadler 2016). CALL frameworks suggest that technology supports interaction by

- Making key linguistic features salient.
- Offering modified input and supporting modified interaction.
- Allowing learners to participate actively in tasks.
- Facilitating the noticing of errors and incorporation of feedback (Chapelle 2001).

These principles inform instructional design conforming to L2 research recommendations for learners of all ages and are particularly well served by task-based pedagogical approaches discussed next.

Design and implementation of teaching and learning tasks

Many researchers have linked the enhanced interactivity made possible with technology to TBLT, an approach which 'seeks to facilitate language learning by engaging learners in the interactionally authentic language use that results from performing a series of tasks' (Ellis 2013, p. 1). The main tenets of this approach are summarised from Ziegler (2016):

1. The **primary focus is on meaning**: learners are focused on the content, including semantic and pragmatic meaning, rather than the form.
2. The task must provide **communicative purpose**, stimulated by learners' need to impart information, solve a problem or express an opinion. The learners' use of language is necessary to achieve the desired outcome and is not necessarily the goal in and of itself.
3. The task should be **learner-centred**, requiring learners to draw mainly on their own linguistic and nonlinguistic resources.
4. Tasks are **authentic** and representative of the real world, drawing on real-world processes of language use and integrating form and function.
5. Opportunities for **reflective learning** are also provided. This offers learners the chance to consider the process as well as the outcome, encouraging cyclical and reflective learning.

Over the past twenty years an important body of CALL research has followed the TBLT approach (Chapelle 1998a; 1998b; Doughty and Long 2003; Gonzalez-Lloret and Ortega 2014). For Ziegler (2016), 'technology-mediated TBLT provides an ideal framework in which technology and tasks provide great potential for a mutually beneficial relationship'. With its focus on non-linguistic outcomes, TBLT also allows teachers to develop more general digital literacies. In the recommendations for practice section, we will discuss research related to three criteria for technology-mediated TBLT most relevant to YELLs: learner-centredness, authentic language use, and reflective learning.

Orchestrating complex technology-mediated interactions with young beginners

A paradox of technology-mediated language learning with young beginners is that real-time L2 interaction requires the competence to orchestrate very limited resources in sophisticated ways, yet this competence can only be acquired through active participation in such complex interactions. Discussing CMC with YELLs, Milton and Garbi (2000, p. 287) note the particular challenges of controlling L2 interaction to limit cognitive load and build confidence:

> An application for use by young beginners must somehow contrive a situation where young learners can use what language they have in a realistic, meaningful and communicative way. Equally, the application must contrive that learners are not frequently exposed to language they cannot understand.

Dooly and Sadler (2016, p. 55) identify similar challenges for telecollaboration, including the need for sophisticated oral language, with limitations on interests and topics, technological skills and use of written input. A further problem concerns teaching and learning materials. As Milton and Garbi (2000, p. 287) point out, 'the content of beginners' textbooks can be highly idiosyncratic'. This causes problems especially when young learners have to interact with interlocutors from a different educational context, who do not always share the same knowledge of linguistic structures and vocabulary. The challenge for technology-mediated language teaching is thus to accommodate the restricted linguistic resources and capabilities of YELLs, while still providing opportunities for authentic target language use.

Some responses to the challenges presented by CMC interaction, technology-mediated TBLT and technical versus pedagogical interactivity are reviewed in the next section.

Current research

As noted earlier, the three disciplines informing technology-mediated YELL teaching share blind spots: both SLA and CALL research tend to neglect young learners, while early language educators often adopt an uncritical stance with respect to technology. Concerning CALL research, the increasing use of technology for second language learning and teaching has led to a large volume of work, as evidenced by a number of recent meta-studies and overviews (Grgurovic et al. 2013; Golonka et al. 2014; Lin 2015; Plonsky and Ziegler 2016). There is some disagreement about findings. While Golonka et al. (2014, 92) claim that 'for most technologies, actual increases in learning or proficiency have yet to be demonstrated', the bulk of CALL research to date is tentatively positive with respect to SLA effects, suggesting that technology-mediated learning is at least as effective as traditional face-to-face teaching. However, young learners are largely absent from this picture. Lin (2015), for example, noted that only 5 of the 59 studies she examined focused on younger learners (aged 9–15); none involved very young learners. Similarly, in their systematic review of 47 CALL studies conducted in ESL 'concerned with the acquisition of linguistic knowledge or skills' in compulsory education, Macaro et al. (2012) identified only nineteen concerning young learners (primary school level). The study found much to criticise in terms of scientific rigour and concluded that the link between technology use and language learning has not been clearly established, arguing that 'future research needs to provide a tighter link between technological applications, Second Language Acquisition (SLA) theory, and learning outcomes' (Macaro et al. 2012, p. 30).

One recent small-scale study involving twenty-eight 10–11-year-old EFL learners in Barcelona appears to answer this call. Tragant et al. (2016) compared an intervention class based on individual reading-while-listening with audiobooks, with a control class receiving teacher-generated input. They found 'that the students in the intervention group progressed at least as much as the students in the comparison group, despite their having had much less teacher-led instruction time'. The authors consider these findings encouraging 'in particular for difficult learning contexts where teachers are in short supply and input may be accessed multi-modally' (Tragant et al. 2016, 252).

As noted, however, technology specialists and language educators do not necessarily communicate or collaborate effectively, and YELL teacher educators are not well represented or well served by mainstream CALL research. Indeed, Pazio (2015) notes 'a move away from the term CALL in the primary MFL context' in favour of the term 'ICT for MFL'. This focus on tools rather than learning is echoed in a study of digital technology use in USA schools, where the authors found that 'although many teachers both advocate and use digital tools in instruction', they generally 'use technology more for preparation and administration than for instruction' (Underwood et al. 2013, 480). In our own work we have found a similar preference for non-pedagogical use of technology among both novice and more experienced language teachers in primary and secondary foreign language classrooms across Europe. Other caveats against undiscriminating technophilia apply. In their review of global YELL practices, Garton, Copland and Burns (2011) remind readers that 'in many schools computers remain a luxury and internet access is limited', while Golonka and colleagues warn that 'using technology in delivering a lesson or instructional unit will not make bad pedagogy good. Nor does a lack of technological tools or applications prevent effective teaching' (2013, p. 93). The mere presence of technology does not ensure automatic learning gains, as we will show in this section.

Over the past ten to fifteen years, both national and European funding has been specifically targeted at foreign languages and digital education. Projects which have been the focus of published research are listed in Table 21.2.

All of the telecollaborative projects in Table 21.2 involved young learners communicating with remote interlocutors, both teachers and learners, including native speakers and other L2 learners. Many involved live oral interaction via video communication or virtual worlds, and some also included a teacher education dimension. All reported a strong motivational effect for all participants in the projects, but few documented learning effects. All gave special attention to both the design of teaching and learning tasks, and to support for learner L2 interaction.

Some projects investigated technology-supported YELL interaction (Favaro 2011; Cutrim Schmid and Whyte 2015; Dooly and Sadler 2016). Studies of IWB use and videoconferencing (VC) in the primary EFL classroom, for instance, found that concerns about maintaining teacher control of learning processes and managing pupil behaviour often outweighed goals related to L2 interaction and learning (Gruson 2011; Whyte 2011; Cutrim Schmid and Whyte 2015). IWB research conducted in primary schools in the UK, France, Germany and Spain suggest that interactivity is often limited to physical interactivity, where a single learner manipulates elements on the IWB in front the class (Yañez and Coyle 2011; Whyte, Cutrim Schmid and Beauchamp 2014). Research from the iTILT project (Whyte, Cutrim Schmid, van Hazebrouck Thompson & Oberhofer 2014), which analysed 81 lessons by 44 language teachers at four educational levels in six European countries, also revealed a general preference for activities involving lower levels of interactivity. The majority of IWB-based drill-and-practice activities conducted by project teachers were observed in primary EFL classes, where there was very little focus on using the technology to support communicative-oriented activities. Instead, the IWB was mainly used to support stepwise knowledge building by drilling. Research on learners' and teachers' perceptions of IWB-mediated activities also reveals dissatisfaction with levels of interaction during lessons. Sailer et al. (2014) note the risk of using technology to increase lesson pace rather than improve interactivity and interaction, and suggest that a major challenge is the lack of CALL materials designed for YELLs. In general, teachers tend to design CALL materials with only superficial interactivity, where learners use the IWB to move pictures or textboxes across the screen, or to reveal answers embedded in the electronic files (Coyle et al. 2010; Gray 2010; Yáñez and Coyle 2011).

A number of projects have involved VC with young learners and these typically report motivational effects (Gruson 2011; Macrory et al. 2012; Phillips 2010; Pritchard et al. 2010). Phillips (2010) used VC to allow young learners of French to communicate with native speakers and found increased motivation for L2 learning in participants. However, although the objective was authentic communication, learners' L2 output was highly controlled, limited to recalling previously learned chunks or performing minor substitutions.

Table 21.2 Funded digital language research projects involving young learners

Projects	Name	Languages	Learner age/level	Technology	Publications
VIRLAN (2000)	Virtual Languages	DE, EN, FI, GR	6–12 years	virtual world	Milton and Garbi (2000)
1000 visios (France, 2008)	1000 videoconferences	EN	6–11 years	VC, IWB	Gruson (2011) Whyte (2011)
PADS (Spain, 2010)	Plurilingual, Audiovisual and Digital Competences	EN	7–8 years	virtual world	Dooly and Sadler (2016)
MustLearnIT (2010)	Must Learn IT	EN, FI, GR, PL	7–11 years	VC	Pritchard et al. (2010)
TELLP (2010)	Technology Enhanced Language Learning in Primary schools	EN, ES, FR	7–11 years	VC	Macrory et al. (2012)
MuVit (2011)	Multilingual Virtual Talking Books	EN, GR, RS, ES, TK,	7–11 years	Software, CMC	Elsner (2014)
iTILT (2011)	Interactive Technology In Language Teaching	CY, DE, EN, ES, FR, NL, TK	all sectors	IWB	Whyte, Cutrim Schmid, van Hazebrouck Thompson & Oberhofer (2014)
TILA (2013)	Telecollaboration for Intercultural Language Acquisition	DE, EN, ES, FR, NL	primary, secondary	CMC	van der Kroon et al. (2015)
ITILT2 (2014)	Interactive Teaching in Languages with Technology	CY, DE, EN, FR, NL, TK	all sectors	smartphones, tablets, CMC	Whyte and Cutrim Schmid (2017); Cutrim Schmid and Cvetkovic (2016)

Other studies report similar findings. A number of small-scale projects have attempted to address these concerns: Cardoso (2011) used learner response systems to increase interactivity, while Kegenhof (2014) used Web 2.0 tools in IWB storytelling activities to enhance participation and engagement.

Perhaps one of the most promising avenues for improving both techno-pedagogical interactivity and L2 interaction, however, is live oral communication. Recent work in synchronous CMC with YELLs has sought to combine VC with other technologies to provide additional support for L2 interaction. Our own study of VC interaction between primary EFL learners in France and Germany using live audio/video and screen-sharing in a TBLT framework found higher levels of learner-learner interaction and spontaneous L2 production than in previous projects (Whyte and Cutrim Schmid 2014; Cutrim Schmid and Whyte 2015). Another project involved VC and machinima (short video clips featuring virtual world avatars) in a CLIL initiative in Spain (Dooly and Sadler 2016). Tackling health education with 7–8 year-old YELLs, this project achieved a high level of conceptual interactivity by providing opportunities for learners to explore complex concepts through authentic interaction with both real and virtual remote interlocutors.

These studies raise a number of issues in CMC with young L2 learners. As noted earlier, Dooly and Sadler (2016, p. 55) highlight 'the need for somewhat sophisticated oral language use if the pedagogical design aims for telecollaboration with other speakers'. Because of young learners' restricted linguistic resources, the majority of project tasks in the French-German exchange imposed a tight framework that often prevented spontaneous language interaction. Teachers and learners expressed a desire for greater learner-centredness to allow more creative and experimental language use, and develop appropriate communication strategies for dealing with interactional breakdowns on their own. Both studies stressed the importance of providing adequate support for the complex interactional demands of VC tasks.

Other efforts to improve interactivity and interaction with YELLs involve tablets and smartphones. Our previous distinctions between technical versus pedagogical or conceptual interactivity, and limited drill-and-practice versus communicative interaction also apply to these technologies. **Closed apps**, with a predetermined language bank, allow memorisation and practice in reading, writing, listening and sometimes also speaking (e.g., Duolingo, MyWordbook). L2 use is limited to repetition of the language provided by the app, with little room for spontaneous and creative language output. **Open apps**, on the other hand, offer much more freedom (e.g., Book Creator, Puppet Pals, iMovie). Here, a choice of templates seems more likely to inspire and invite language production in ways both familiar and stimulating for learners growing up surrounded by technology. Little research into use of these apps with YELLs has been conducted to date. Alhinty (2015) investigated the open apps Puppet Pals and Show Me in L2 interactions in and outside the classroom. Learners worked in groups to create multimodal e-books by combining these apps with the tablets' built-in camera and voice recognition functions. She reported motivational effects, and particularly a preference for synchronous mobile interactions, which created an impression of 'relatedness'.

The studies reviewed in this section indicate that technology has the potential to enhance the levels of interaction and interactivity in the YELL classroom. However, our discussion also highlights the importance of designing didactically meaningful language learning tasks to fully exploit the potential of technology-mediated environments for authentic L2 interaction.

With respect to our focus on technology-mediated ELT with young learners in this chapter, a number of conclusions can be drawn. First, there are persistent calls for more focused CALL research, in particular, research driven by theory rather than policy, and which addresses learning rather than motivational effects. Second, technology-mediated L2 teaching with young learners involves unique difficulties related to a mismatch between learner competence and task demands: solutions proposed to date have involved videocommunication and virtual worlds. Finally, both SLA and CALL have neglected young learners; this population has specific characteristics and needs with clear consequences for teaching, learning and research. In our recommendations for practice in the next section we focus on three dimensions of technology-mediated TBLT of particular importance for YELLs.

Recommendations for practice

We have suggested elsewhere that 'technology can help teachers to implement task-based approaches that are likely to foster interlanguage development by providing access to rich language input and supporting opportunities for output, interaction and reflection, which are necessary for effective language learning' (Whyte 2014, p. 13). As proposed earlier, we now return to three key dimensions of technology-mediated TBLT to draw research-based lessons for the language classroom.

Learner-centredness

A main requirement in TBLT is for learners to rely on their own resources, rather than repeat memorised words, expressions or dialogues. In the French VC project discussed earlier, primary school learners met with native speakers in a videoconference to exchange information and play a game (Phillips 2010). The teacher used songs and rhymes to help learners memorise formulaic questions, and linked gestures to meanings to help them retrieve words and expressions during live CMC. Phillips concluded that 'the use of associative codes appeared to aid pupils' procedural learning by mediating both their initial apprehension of the language and also their rapid language retrieval, seemingly without threatening their sense of independence' (p. 232). However, the project did not seem to encourage learners to use their own linguistic resources, since the interactions mostly involved 'prescribed' questions (*Comment t'appelles-tu ?*) inviting 'slot-and-frame' responses (*Hier j'ai mangé ____*).

In the telecollaborative project cited earlier (Whyte and Cutrim Schmid 2014; Cutrim Schmid and Whyte 2015) primary pupils aged seven to nine Germany and France used English as lingua franca to interact with the remote class in three collaborative tasks: making ID cards, a supermarket exchange and a breakfast invitation. Participants saw the tasks as authentic and relevant in design, but in early stages of the project, the actual implementation of these tasks did not sufficiently encourage learners to use their own resources. Transcriptions of the first CMC interactions showed high levels of teacher mediation in learner-learner exchanges. In later phases, the teachers made efforts to help learners develop communication strategies to negotiate meaning and repair communication breakdowns on their own. Similarly, both teachers and pupils felt the planned tasks imposed a tight framework which prevented spontaneous use of language, and so later phases of the project aimed to allow more open activities. Thus, in preparation for one of the supermarket sessions, 15 German learners showed and described the content of their lunch boxes without preparation, using any linguistic resources at their disposal. Since the learners had not prepared or practiced in advance for the activity, they could not rely on memorised chunks, but had to adapt language online during interaction. An important challenge with YELLs is thus the balance between adequate linguistic and emotional support, on one hand, and space to create on the other.

Authentic real-world tasks

Another important TBLT criterion is the real-world relevance of tasks and the opportunity to integrate form and function in authentic contexts. Dooly and Sadler (2016) achieved this in their CMC project where primary school children took on the role of scientists investigating the consequences of good and bad habits related to personal hygiene, physical exercise and diet. Learners interacted with virtual world avatars to learn new information, which they then communicated online with telecollaborative partners. The authors report that a majority of learners assimilated the core curricular objectives, and several were able to produce target language structures far beyond the output expected for their age and L2 proficiency. They attribute this success to the nesting of telecollaborative tasks in a range of pre- and post-tasks designed to introduce and recycle the target L2 items in different modes throughout the project. The authors claim: 'through the carefully scaffolded, meticulously planned task sequencing, the learners gradually developed more sociopragmatic competences in their use of formulaic chunks in contextualized "everyday" talk' (Dooly and Sadler 2016, 73).

Reflective learning

The third TBLT dimension addressed in this section is the provision of opportunities for reflecting on learning, with respect to both the process and outcome of tasks. Pellerin (2014), for instance, investigated the contribution of mobile technologies (iPods and tablets) to the interpretation of tasks by young language learners. She notes that these technologies can allow young learners to create their own learning environment and meaningful language tasks, as well as help them self-regulate their language learning process. She describes how learners in a French immersion class were allowed to select the iPad tools they would use to demonstrate their learning about a specific science topic in an assessment task, and encouraged to consider their own needs and preferences as well as the task requirements. This is the same approach used by Alhinty (2015), where learners were encouraged to create their own digital content, which could then be transformed into language learning tasks for other students.

This type of technology-mediated task can also facilitate L2 learning by allowing 'focus on form' (explicit focus on grammar during a communicative language activity). Individual or small-group tasks using mobile technologies may promote the noticing of forms, and, in particular, gaps between learners' interlanguage and the target language. Pellerin (2014) provides an example where 6–7 year-old anglophone learners of French became aware they lacked the vocabulary necessary to describe an object while recording their description of a picture. As she points out, technologies such as tablets allow seamless access to recording and playback functions, meaning learners can record their spoken language in various activities and then revisit their work by listening to the audio and video recordings. This revision process allows students to become consciously aware of their strengths, as well as notice gaps in their oral competencies in the target language.

Future directions

A crucial factor determining the future of technology use in the EFL young learner classroom is institutional policy. Considering the fact that ICTs are usually promoted as symbols of progress and economic prowess, it is reasonable to expect continuing investment in ICT in education. Therefore, one can speculate that new technologies will continue to find their way into the young learner classroom in the years to come. The question is whether these new developments will make a positive impact on language learning and teaching. The research reviewed in this chapter points to several factors that need to be addressed in order to achieve this aim.

First, as in CALL research more generally, there is a dearth of rigorous studies of language learning outcomes in relation to technology-mediated YELL instruction. More longitudinal work is needed to investigate sustained effects over time, and to compare use of technology in and/or outside class (Lin 2015), with and without direct teacher mediation (Tragant et al. 2016). Then, while TBLT offers an attractive framework for technology-mediated teaching and learning activities, attention to task design is essential to further our understanding of how emergent technologies such as videoconferencing and mobile technologies can support the language learning process of YELLs, as well as address digital literacies. This chapter has shown how TBLT principles can inform the conception and implementation of technology-mediated tasks in order to balance young learners' needs for support in sophisticated real-time interactions with their propensity for playful, spontaneous use of language. Careful planning is required to sequence activities which allow learners to understand and gradually acquire new language in meaningful contexts while also leaving room for individual initiative and choice (Cutrim Schmid and Whyte 2015, Whyte and Cutrim Schmid 2014; Dooly and Sadler 2016).

A third concern involves materials design and, more broadly, teacher education. Communicative technology-based materials are not readily available commercially, placing additional demands on teachers as materials designers. Clear principles for materials design and examples of good practice are needed to help teachers develop an increased awareness of the different types and levels of interactivity and language interaction supported by technology, and empower them to exploit new technologies in ways that are consistent with SLA theory. Many challenges faced by CALL practitioners derive from a lack of adequate pedagogical training for the integration of new technologies in ways that enhance language learning and teaching. There should be a special focus on the education of pre- and in-service language teachers, who are pivotal players in the mediation of digital technologies in the language classroom and in wider processes of technology adoption in schools. In spite of widespread technological investment in many parts of the world, teachers can and do resist educational and pedagogical hegemonies in ways that affect learning (Cutrim Schmid and Whyte 2012; Gray 2010). For this reason, the quality of professional development available to teachers will be critical in shaping the uptake of new technologies in the young learner classroom in years to come.

A number of models of CALL teacher education have been proposed, from situated practice and experiential modelling to novice-expert tandems and the development of open educational resources and practices. Key principles underlying these models are (a) CALL pedagogy rather than technical aspects (Hubbard and Levy 2006), (b) authentic language teaching scenarios (Egbert 2006; Cutrim Schmid and Hegelheimer 2014), (c) peer collaboration that supports the development of communities of practice (Whyte 2011, 2015), and (d) reflective practice and engagement (Guichon 2009). The findings reported in this chapter can contribute to CALL teacher education of L2 teachers of young learners to assist them in developing the necessary competencies for transformative practice in the challenging context of the young learner CALL classroom.

Further reading

1 Cutrim Schmid, E., and Whyte, S. (Eds.) (2014) *Teaching languages with technology: Communicative approaches to interactive whiteboard use: A resource book for teacher development.* London: Bloomsbury.

This book presents seven case studies which focus on the use of interactive whiteboards for the teaching of languages, covering special educational needs, teacher training, materials design, gamification and CLIL. Four chapters focus on the young learner classroom.

2 Whyte, S. (2015). *Implementing and researching technological innovation in language teaching: The case of interactive whiteboards for EFL in French schools.* London: Palgrave Macmillan.

This case study investigates the integration of IWBs into the teaching of EFL in French schools, and includes four primary teachers. It provides an analytical framework for documenting the development of their IWB-mediated teaching practice, and highlights the challenges and opportunities inherent in the process of technological innovation involving IWB use.

Related topics

Materials, motivation, classroom management

References

Aldrich, F., Rogers, Y., and Scaife, M. (1998). Getting to grips with "interactivity": helping teachers assess the educational value of CD-ROMs. *British Journal of Educational Technology*, 29(4), 321–332.

Alhinty, M. (2015). Young language learners' collaborative learning and social interaction as a motivational aspect of the iPad. *International Journal of Emerging Technologies in Learning*, 10(2), 24–29.

Beauchamp, G., and Kennewell, S. (2010). Interactivity in the classroom and its impact on learning. *Computers & Education*, 54(3), 759–766.

Blake, R. J. (2013). *Brave New Digital Classroom: Technology and foreign language learning*. Washington, DC: Georgetown University Press.

Cardoso, W. (2011). Learning a foreign language with a learner response system: The students' perspective. *Computer Assisted Language Learning*, 24(5), 393–417.

Chapelle, C. (1998a). Multimedia CALL: Lessons to be learned from research on instructed SLA. *Language Learning and Technology*, 2(1), 22–34.

Chapelle, C. (1998b). Research on the use of technology in TESOL: Analysis of interaction sequences in CALL. *TESOL Quarterly*, 32(4), 753–757.

Chapelle, C. (2001). *Computer Applications in Second Language Acquisition*. Cambridge: Cambridge University Press.

Chun, D. M. (2016). The role of technology in SLA research. *Language Learning & Technology*, 2(2), 98–115.

Copland, F., and Garton, S. (2014). Key themes and future directions in teaching English to young learners: Introduction to the Special Issue. *ELT Journal*, 68(3), 223–230.

Coyle, Y., Yañez, L., and Verdúa, M. (2010). The impact of the interactive whiteboard on the teacher and children's language use in an ESL immersion classroom. *System*, 38(4), 614–625.

Cutrim Schmid, E., and Cvetkovic, A. (2016). Digitale Medien im Englischunterricht der Grundschule. In Peschel, M., and Irion, T. (eds.) *Neue Medien in der Grundschule 2.0*. Frankfurt: Grundschulverband, 178–188.

Cutrim Schmid, E., and Hegelheimer, V. (2014). Collaborative research projects in the technology-enhanced language classroom: Pre-service and in-service teachers exchange knowledge about technology. *ReCALL*, 26(3), 315–332

Cutrim Schmid, E., and Whyte, S. (2012). Interactive whiteboards in school settings: Teacher responses to socio-constructivist hegemonies. *Language Learning and Technology*, 16(2), 65–86.

Cutrim Schmid, E., and Whyte, S. (2015). Teaching young learners with technology. In Bland, J. (ed.) *Teaching English to Young Learners: Critical issues in language teaching with 3–12 year plds*. London: Bloomsbury, 239–259

Dooly, M., and Sadler, R. (2016). Becoming little scientists: Technologically-enhanced project-based language learning. *Language Learning & Technology*, 20(1), 54–78.

Doughty, C. J., and Long, M. H. (2003). Optimal psycholinguistic environments for distance foreign language learning. *Language Learning & Technology*, 7, 50–80.

Egbert, J. (2006). Learning in context: Situating language teacher learning in CALL. In Hubbard, P., and Levy, M. (eds.) *Teacher Education in CALL*. Amsterdam: John Benjamins, 167–182.

Ellis, R. (2013). Task-based language teaching: responding to the critics. *University of Sydney Papers in TESOL*, 8, 1–27.

Elsner, D. (2014). Multilingual Virtual Talking Books (MuViT) – A project to foster multilingualism, language awareness, and media competency. In AbendrothTimmer, D., and Hennig, E.-M. (eds.) *Plurilingualism and Multiliteracies: International research on identity construction in language education*. Frankfurt/M.: Peter Lang, 175–190

Enever, J. (2016). Primary ELT. In *The Routledge Handbook of English Language Teaching*, 353.

Favaro, L. (2011). Videoconferencing as a tool to provide an authentic foreign language environment for primary school children: Are we ready for It? In Rata, Georgeta (ed.) *Academic Days in Timisoara: Language education today*. Newcastle Upon Tyne: Cambridge Scholars Publishing, 331–339

Fullan, M. (2001). *Leading in a Culture of Change*. San Francisco, CA: Jossey-Bass.

Garton, S., Copland, F., and Burns, A. (2011). *Investigating Global Practices in Teaching English to Young Learners*. London: British Council.

Gimeno-Sanz, A. (2016). Moving a step further from "integrative CALL": What's to come?. *Computer Assisted Language Learning*, 29(6), 1102–1115.

Gitsaki, C., and Robby, M. (2014). Using the iPads for teaching English: Teachers' perspectives. In Dodigovic, Marina (ed.) *Attitudes to Technology in ESL/EFL Pedagogy*. Dubai, UAE: TESOL Arabia, 277–291.

Glover, D., Miller, D., Averis, D., and Door, V. (2007). The evolution of an effective pedagogy for teachers using the interactive whiteboard in mathematics and modern languages: An empirical analysis from the secondary sector. *Learning, Media and Technology*, 32(1), 5–20.

Golonka, E. M., Bowles, A. R., Frank, V. M., Richardson, D. L., and Freynik, S. (2014). Technologies for foreign language learning: A review of technology types and their effectiveness. *Computer Assisted Language Learning*, 27(1), 70–105.

González-Lloret, M., and Ortega, L. (Eds.). (2014). *Technology-mediated TBLT: Researching technology and tasks*. Amsterdam: John Benjamins.

Gray, C. (2010). Meeting teachers' real needs: New tools in the secondary modern foreign languages classroom. In Thomas and Schmid, Cutrim (eds.) *Interactive Whiteboards for Education: Theory, research and practice*. Hershey, NY: Information Science Reference, 69–85.

Grgurovic, M., Chapelle, C., and Shelley, M. (2013). A meta-analysis of effectiveness studies on computer technology-supported language learning. *ReCALL Journal*, 25(2), 165–198.

Gruba, P. (2004). Computer Assisted Language Learning (CALL). In Davies, A., and Elder, C. (eds.) *The Handbook of Applied Linguistics*. Oxford: Oxford University Press, 623–648.

Gruson, B. (2011). Analyse comparative d'une situation de communication orale en classe ordinaire et lors d'une séance en visioconférence, *Distances et Savoirs*, 8(3), 395–423.

Guichon, N. (2009). Training future language teachers to develop online tutors' competence through reflective analysis. *ReCALL*, 21(2), 166–185.

Hubbard, P., and Levy, M. (2006). *Teacher Education in CALL*. Amsterdam: John Benjamins.

Jewitt, C., Moss, G., and Cardini, A. (2007). Pace, interactivity and multimodality in teachers' design of texts for interactive whiteboards in the secondary school classroom. *Learning, Media and Technology*, 32(3), 303–317.

Kegenhof, A. (2014). Digital storytelling in the primary EFL classroom. In Cutrim Schmid, E., and Whyte, S. (eds.) *Teaching Languages with Technology: Communicative approaches to interactive whiteboard use: A resource book for teacher development*. London: Bloomsbury, 80–116.

Lin, H. (2015). A meta-synthesis of empirical research on the effectiveness of computer-mediated communication (CMC) in SLA. *Language Learning & Technology*, 19(2), 85–117.

Macaro, E., Handley, Z., and Walter, C. (2012). A systematic review of CALL in English as a second language: Focus on primary and secondary education. *Language Teaching*, 45(1), 1–43.

Macrory, G., Chrétien, L., and Ortega-Martín, J. L. (2012). Technologically enhanced language learning in primary schools in England, France and Spain: Developing linguistic competence in a technologically enhanced classroom environment. *Education 3–13: International Journal of Primary, Elementary and Early Years Education*, 40(4), 433–444.

Mama, M., and Hennessy, S. (2013). Developing a typology of teacher beliefs and practices concerning classroom use of ICT. *Computers & Education*, 68, 380–387.

Milton, J., and Garbi, A. (2000). VIRLAN: Collaborative foreign language learning on the Internet for primary age children: Problems and a solution. *Educational Technology & Society*, 3(3), 286–292.

Pazio, M. (2015). Normalising computer assisted language learning in the context of primary education in England. Unpublished PhD thesis, University of Bedfordshire.

Pellerin, M. (2014). Language tasks using touch screen and mobile technologies: Reconceptualizing task-based CALL for young language learners. *Canadian Journal of Learning and Technology*, 40(1), 1–23.

Phillips, M. (2010). The perceived value of videoconferencing with primary pupils learning to speak a modern language. *Language Learning Journal*, 38(2), 221–238.

Pim, C. (2013). Emerging technologies, emerging minds: Digital innovations within the primary sector. In *Innovations in Learning Technologies for English Language Teaching*. London: British Council, 20–42.

Plonsky, L., and Ziegler, N. (2016). The CALL – SLA interface: Insights from a second-order synthesis. *Language Learning & Technology*, 20(2), 17–37.

Plowman, L. (1996). Designing interactive media for schools: A review based on contextual observation. *Information Design Journal*, 8(3), 258–266.

Pritchard, A., Hunt, M., and Barnes, A. (2010). Case study investigation of a videoconferencing experiment in primary schools, teaching modern foreign languages. *Language Learning Journal*, 209–220.

Sailer, H., Cutrim Schmid, E., and Koenraad, T. (2014). The IWB in the CLIL classroom: Using visuals to foster active learning with young beginners. In Cutrim Schmid, E., and Whyte, S. (eds.) *Teaching Languages with Technology: Communicative approaches to interactive whiteboard use: A resource book for teacher development*. London: Bloomsbury, 129–158.

Tragant, E., Muñoz, C., and Spada, N. (2016). Maximizing young learners' input: An intervention program. *Canadian Modern Language Review*, 72(2), 234–257

Underwood, C., Parker, L., and Stone, L. (2013). Getting it together: Relational habitus in the emergence of digital literacies. *Learning, Media and Technology*, 38(4), 478–494.

van der Kroon, L., Jauregi, K., and Jan, D. (2015). Telecollaboration in foreign language curricula: A case study on intercultural understanding in video communication exchanges. *International Journal of Computer-Assisted Language Learning and Teaching (IJCALLT)*, 5(3), 20–41.

Wall, K., Higgins, S., and Smith, H. (2005). 'The visual helps me understand the complicated things': Pupil views of teaching and learning with interactive whiteboards. *British Journal of Educational Technology*, 36(5), 851–867.

Warschauer, M. (2004). Technological change and the future of CALL. In Fotos, S., and Brown, C. (eds.) *New Perspectives on CALL for Second Language Classrooms*. Mahwah, NJ: Lawrence Erlbaum, 15–25.

Warschauer, M. (2012). *Learning in the Cloud: How (and why) to transform schools with digital media*. New York: Teachers College Press.

Whyte, S. (2011). Learning to teach with videoconferencing in primary foreign language classrooms. *ReCALL*, 23(3), 271–293.

Whyte, S. (2014). Theory and practice in second language teaching with interactive technologies. In Cutrim Schmid, E., and Whyte, S. (eds.) *Teaching Languages with Technology: Communicative approaches to interactive whiteboard use: A resource book for teacher development.* London: Bloomsbury.

Whyte, S. (2015). *Implementing and researching technological innovation in language teaching: The case of interactive whiteboards for EFL in French schools.* London: Palgrave Macmillan.

Whyte, S., and Cutrim Schmid, E. (2014). A task-based approach to video communication with the IWB: a French – German primary EFL class exchange. *Teaching Languages with Technology: Communicative Approaches to Interactive Whiteboard Use,* 50–79

Whyte, S., and Cutrim Schmid, E. (2017). Synchronous video communication with young EFL learners: A multimodal analysis of task negotiation. Paper presented at AILA, Rio de Janeiro, 23–28 July.

Whyte, S., Cutrim Schmid, E., and Beauchamp, G. (2014). Second language interaction with interactive technologies: The IWB in state school foreign language classrooms, Paper presented at AILA conference, Brisbane, Australia, 10–15 August 2014.

Whyte, S., Cutrim Schmid, E., van Hazebrouck Thompson, S., and Oberhofer, M. (2014). Open educational resources for CALL teacher education: The iTILT interactive whiteboard project. *Computer Assisted Language Learning,* 27(2), 122–148.

Yáñez, L., and Coyle, Y. (2011). Children's perceptions of learning with an interactive whiteboard. *ELT Journal,* 65(4), 446–457.

Ziegler, N. (2016). Taking technology to task: Technology-mediated TBLT, performance, and production. *Annual Review of Applied Linguistics,* 36, 136–163.

22

Syllabus development in early English language teaching

Virginia Parker and David Valente

Introduction

Early English language teaching (EELT) can be considered the most important development in English language teaching in the past few decades (Rich 2014; Rixon 2013). As English has become the dominant global language for economics and politics, governments have seen it necessary to ensure their competitiveness on the world stage through the encouragement of an English-speaking workforce (Garton et al. 2013; Rich 2014). This has led to the introduction of ELT programmes at ever earlier ages, generally under the questionable assumption that *earlier is better* for eventual English proficiency. We do not seek to join the ongoing debate over the decision to teach English to younger children (see Singleton and Pfenninger, this volume), but instead to simply recognise that it is happening. The issue in EELT is not necessarily the age of introduction, but rather the question of syllabus fit and related methodology, materials, assessment targets and standards which are too often based on adult ELT programmes and criteria, such as CEFR indicators (Hasselgreen 2013; Hayes 2014; Rich 2014; Rixon 2013). Throughout the chapter, we will be applying Bourke's (2006) definition of 'syllabus' in an EELT context: encompassing course contents, reflecting a particular pedagogical approach and views of SLA as well as explicitly stated goals and related learning aims and objectives. While 'syllabus' and 'curriculum' are often used interchangeably in ELT literature, in order to unpack key issues and principles involved in what Pantaleoni (1991) calls 'syllabusing at the primary level', it is crucial for us to differentiate. A 'curriculum' operates at the macro (often national and Ministerial) level while a 'syllabus' is 'a more day-to-day, localised guide for the teacher . . . a statement of approach . . . a rationale for how that content should be selected and ordered' (Pantaleoni 1991, p. 302).

Other terms which warrant clarification include the numerous ways children learning English are referred to globally including Young Learners (YL), Very Young Learners (VYL), Early Years (EY) and Primary Learners (Ellis 2004; Garton et al. 2013; Rich 2014; Rixon 2013). We will be focusing on the life stage of between ages 6–10, or Grades 1–5 (while recognizing that grades do not always correspond with years of age), which we will refer to as Early English language teaching. We are also cognizant that English instruction for children, including at the primary and pre-primary levels, does not only occur within the context of state schools, and that private education providers (i.e., language schools) are also significant influencers.

Young learner English language proficiency examinations, benchmarked on the Common European Framework of Reference (CEFR), have also dictated EELT syllabus content in recent years. These high-stakes examinations which can determine not only progress or achievement of learning outcomes, but also admission to further education, migration rights or the awarding of certification (Hayes 2014; Rixon 2013), also reflect the growing influence of washback on EELT syllabuses. The trend towards starting English language instruction in the lower primary years or even earlier, without due consideration of children's readiness, whether teachers are appropriately qualified as well as institutional and other sociocultural factors, have resulted in considerable mismatch when it comes to the age relevance of syllabus content worldwide.

Historical perspectives

Historically, English Language Teaching developed to meet the needs of adult learners, and as such, syllabuses for primary-aged children were initially based on linguistic items more appropriate for older learners (Littlejohn 2016a; Read 2016; Pantaleoni 1991). Adults tend to have specific reasons for learning an additional language, such as migration, employment or further academic study (White 1988), which differ greatly from children, who may not actually understand why they need to study English or French or Japanese, beyond its inclusion in their school timetables (Cameron 2001; Enever 2011; Jin et al. 2014; Moon 2005).

A major twentieth-century trend in language learning for adults – which inevitably influenced children's English language syllabuses – were the oral-structural-situational syllabuses, popular until the 1970s (Littlejohn 2016a; Richards and Rodgers 2001; White 1988). Structural syllabuses are still in use with primary learners, both overtly and woven into the contexts of child-friendly stories, songs and activities (Littlejohn 2016a; Stec 2013).

A structurally determined, linear syllabus is relatively easy to apply and assess, and demands less English language proficiency from the teacher (Pantaleoni 1991; Bowman et al. 1989; White 1988). It is very practical for publishers, policy makers and assessors, as language targets are arranged in a nominally logical sequence (Anderson 2016; Richards and Rodgers 2001). It is also familiar to EELT teachers, who may be tempted to teach as they were taught, despite the introduction of newer, more age-appropriate approaches to syllabus design such as activity-based, topic-based, content-based and story-based syllabuses which may however present a cultural mismatch (Anderson 2016; Bowman et al. 1989; Clifford and Htut 2015; Enever 2014; Schweisfurth 2013). Although supporters extol its virtues with lower level learners, including primary-aged children (Anderson 2016), a structural syllabus is ill-suited to teach children as 'the ability to see, focus on and manipulate conscious rules of grammar, or follow controlled patterns based on form . . . [is] beyond the developmental stage of all but the oldest learners in the primary school age' (Littlejohn 2016a, p. 31).

Communicative Language Teaching (CLT) saw a shift away from its grammatically structured syllabuses towards a more functional approach. For learners and teachers, the focus was now on meaningful communication in the classroom rather than forms, with the overall objective of communicative competence (Guerrero 2014; Thornbury 2006). As CLT gained in popularity, ELT syllabuses, including those for children, began to integrate functional language and related exponents such as asking for directions or ordering a meal (Richards and Rodgers 2001; Thornbury 2006; White 1988). Assessment also came to be influenced by this new approach to syllabus design, which moved English towards a communications-based standard (Read 2016; Thornbury 2006), including the decision by Cambridge Assessment English to omit translation and literature-focused questions in favour of more authentic skills-based listening and reading papers in the mid-1970s (Weir 2013). However, with the global boom in international language examinations EELT syllabuses came to be heavily modelled on task types typically found in these high-stakes skills-based exams, even at younger stages of learning (Read 2016).

While arguably more appropriate for children than rote memorization, translation or explicit grammar instruction, many classroom tasks specified in CLT syllabuses for children remain largely 'a rehearsal for future possible experiences' (Littlejohn 2016a, p. 32), existing outside the sphere of children's immediate authentic communication needs (Moon 2005). Bourke (2006, p. 208) further argues that we need to, 're-discover and inhabit the world of the child. Children live in a world of fantasy and make-believe, a world of dragons and monsters, talking animals, and alien beings. In their world there are no tenses, nouns or adjectives; there are no schemas labeled "grammar", "lexis", "phonology" or "discourse"'.

Young Learner-specific ELT pedagogy was not explicitly researched until the late 1990s (Rich 2014). And while EELT has tended to be divergent from research in mainstream Early Childhood Education, influenced more broadly by existing adult-focused language programmes, child-centred approaches have also become influential in EELT syllabus design, including Vygotsky's concept of learning as a social construct within a zone of proximal development (ZPD), and Bruner's focus on scaffolding and routines to support (L1) learning (Cameron 2001). In learning either their first or additional languages, children remain meaning bound, focusing on 'what language says, not how it works' (Littlejohn 2016a, p. 31), thereby further reinforcing Bourke's (2006) assertion that children respond to age-accessible content rather than language in the abstract, which has significant implications for EELT syllabus design.

The CEFR has become another major influencer in English language syllabus design for adults, teenagers and children. This Council of Europe project sought to clarify and codify needs of the *adult* language learners of its member states, considered by some to be a bureaucratic standardisation exercise that may have ignored the specifics of individual learners, including young learners (Howatt and Widdowson 2004; White 1988). The CEFR grew out of this project, not just for English, but for all the official languages of Europe (Cambridge English 2011), with a research-based focus on functional language rather than knowledge of grammar, and a view towards European plurilingualism (Thornbury 2006).

The CEFR has become a widely accepted benchmark for developing English language syllabuses throughout the world, which was never its intended purpose (Cambridge Assessment English 2011; Howatt and Widdowson 2004), particularly not with children (Enever 2011; Rixon 2013). Conversely, such influence could be regarded as positive, leading to more genuinely communicative teaching globally. By focusing on everyday linguistic competencies and outcomes, the CEFR has facilitated the creation of communicative language targets embodied by both national and local syllabus documents within and outside its intended domain of Europe (Enever 2011; Hayes 2014; Rixon 2013). However, by describing and codifying the criteria necessary for a learner to be deemed proficient in a language, the CEFR inadvertently created a top-down interpretation of successful language proficiency. As mentioned, this has influenced syllabus and related coursebook content, and in turn assessment via high-stakes ELT examinations for children, often as future proficiency targets.

To assume however that adult ELT approaches are no longer prevalent in EELT syllabuses would be misleading (Read 2016). Structural syllabus design continues to influence the learning of English by young children reflected in the use of particular classroom techniques (such as explicit highlighting of grammatical forms), and the favouring of examination-preparation tasks over authentic age relevant communication, as well as the inclusion of certain themes in coursebooks. The movement towards starting English instruction earlier means that these adult-focused approaches are being found in syllabuses for younger and younger children, potentially to the detriment of their wellbeing and motivation. Expected thresholds of achievement via overly rigorous application of the CEFR are also a key issue in EELT, which will be explored in the next section.

Critical issues and topics

Primary educational practice and syllabus mistmatch

It is generally accepted that children acquire languages in vastly different ways than older age groups, tending to need less overt instruction (Cameron 2001; Moon 2005; Rich 2014). Bourke (2006, p. 282) asserts, 'The language has to be packaged in a way that makes sense to children . . . Children need exposure to "whole instances of language use" and not a series of disjointed bits of language'. Furthermore, best practice at this level should also take into consideration that:

- Materials must 'respond to the specific needs' of children and be 'founded on an understanding of how young children learn languages' (Hayes 2014, p. 2).
- Children's motivation to learn a language differs greatly from an adult's or adolescent's motivation, but is key to the success of in-school foreign language programmes (Enever 2011).
- While linguistic outcomes can be assessed, other factors such as intercultural awareness and social development cannot, making them easier to omit in practice (Rixon 2015).
- Overt in-class test preparation is often more stressful for children, who tend to be more emotionally vulnerable than older learners when faced with assessments (Otomo 2016).
- Explicit grammar and lexical instruction is counter-intuitive to children's natural language learning (Littlejohn 2016a).
- Every child has a different English literacy 'entry point', which may be influenced by how their L1 writing system differs from English (Cameron 2001).

A successful EELT practitioner, and by extension successful EELT syllabus, must therefore carefully consider both the linguistic and unique age-related needs of the learners. Pedagogical weaknesses which stem from faulty syllabus design can cause primary children's motivation to learn English to decline as they progress through school (Enever 2011; Jin et al. 2014; Littlejohn 2016a). Shortcomings arising from syllabus documents which do not sufficiently take into account the life stage of the learners include inappropriate procedures, techniques and materials, further exacerbated by a perennial lack of support and training for teachers of this age group in how to implement the syllabus in classroom practice (Enever and Moon 2009; Garton et al. 2013; Hayes 2014; Rich 2014), alongside an unfortunate reliance on syllabuses that are heavily influenced by secondary-level ELT (Robinson et al. 2015; Stec 2013). This means that 'despite the enormous expenditure and effort put into primary school language teaching, the promised gains frequently fail to materialise' (Littlejohn 2016a, p. 31).

CEFR dominance in syllabus design

Syllabuses aligned with the CEFR are 'wholly inappropriate' for primary learners of English (Enever 2011, p. 5). Although developed specifically for European adult learners, the CEFR is now widely used in syllabuses to quantify English proficiency throughout the world, for even the youngest learners (Enever 2011; Hasselgreen 2013; Rixon 2013), though it may be little more than an easy, but inappropriate, way to validate language goals within a syllabus document (Rixon 2015). Furthermore, taken out of their intended context, the CEFR outcomes are overly used in syllabuses to determine what learners *should* achieve at the end of a term or year, rather than as a proficiency check on what they are able to do. As the CEFR was developed with adult and young adult (but not younger than adolescent) learners in mind, many of the topics are ill suited to the reality of a child's immediate world. Take, for example, that travel, employment and shopping are all repeatedly mentioned in the CEFR A1-A2 level (CEFR 2001), yet primary-aged children are not expected to shop alone, attend job interviews, nor make travel arrangements. Therein lies the mismatch between 'global generalizations and local circumstances, between specifications and specificity' (Howatt and Widdowson 2004, p. 268) whereby a syllabus may be developed with learning outcomes based on the CEFR, but without a fully informed notion of the implications of adopting such a framework in a particular localised learning and teaching context (Cambridge Assessment English 2011; Little 2014; Rixon 2015).

This has not prevented a wide range of countries from adopting the CEFR A1-A2 descriptors as a de facto EELT syllabus (Enever 2011). The longitudinal ELLiE study of EELT in practice in Europe used the CEFR as targets (Enever 2011), even while acknowledging that these were 'not developed for use with young learners' (Hayes 2014, p. 12), while Rixon's 2013 survey of global EELT found approximately a third of the surveyed countries included explicit language learning aims linked to the CEFR in syllabus documents (p. 35). Cyprus, for example, has fully aligned its EELT outcomes to the CEFR A1-A2 descriptors, stating, 'It is expected that all children will have sufficiently covered the A1 level whereas stronger children will be able to move into the A2 scale during the 5th or 6th year' (p. 10). The Cypriot EELT syllabus also provides teachers with explicit structural language foci related directly to the CEFR A1-A2 descriptors over a period of six years (Cyprus Ministry of Education, n.d.).

Proficiency exams based on the CEFR (i.e., those moderated by external examinations boards such as Cambridge Assessment English, Pearson Education and Trinity College London) and internationally marketed coursebooks have a mutually influential relationship (Weir 2013). Although these examinations were initially based on what learners were taught, i.e., the syllabus, the inverse is now more common, with international English language coursebook content for children based directly on the target exam task types underpinned by the syllabus (Read 2016), and all with a CEFR level prominently displayed on the cover. In EELT contexts where these publications are Ministry approved, they are often treated as an official syllabus document by the teachers in practice (Garton et al. 2013; Read 2016). Where coursebooks are versioned for a specific market, such as Italy, the UAE, Greece or South Korea, both the overt and covert applications of CEFR-type indicators or themes influenced syllabuses are frequently evident. The government-approved South Korean coursebook for Grade 3 includes the following chapter titles: *Hello, I'm Minsu, Wash your hands., I Can Swim,* and *It's Snowing* (Yuasa 2010, p. 149), again a reflection of a list published in the CEFR suggesting appropriate 'communication themes', including personal identification, daily routines, leisure activities and the weather (2001, p. 52).

Teachers will often opt to follow the coursebook as a safe way to ensure that lessons satisfy the prescribed syllabus, while preparing learners for an assessment situation that may be in the distant future (Bowman et al. 1989; Enever and Moon 2009; Garton et al. 2013). Where a structural syllabus, a particularly popular choice in internationally marketed coursebooks (Anderson 2016), is married to future CEFR-indexed examinations, as in China, the result may be an explicit form and structure practice with little interaction with children as young as six to seven years old (Chen and Wang 2014). Similar form-focused practice with EELT learners has also been reported in Poland (Stec 2013), Sweden (Rich 2014) and Malaysia (Garton et al. 2013).

The role and impact of high-stakes examinations in EELT syllabuses

As highlighted previously, high-stakes examinations remain a key influencer and therefore warrant further exploration here. The influence of internal and external high-stakes examinations on syllabus design cannot be understated. The influence of assessment – both positive and negative – on syllabus is commonly known as *washback*, defined by Taylor (2005) as the way examinations affect the design of teaching and learning content for classroom use.

While many countries do not have Ministry-mandated examinations at the primary level (Rich 2014), teachers do still need to assess their learners for administrative purposes (Moon 2005). Examinations that may be used in upper primary or secondary may also exert an influence over primary teachers' syllabus choices, in an extreme case of washback (Hayes 2014). For primary-level language learning, any alignment to outcomes based on *future* assessment criteria ignores accepted best practice in English language instruction with this age group.

External and national or local assessments may be used by policy makers in different ways, including as quality control at different levels (i.e., between schools, regions or even nations), to determine teacher promotion, or to influence classroom practice through washback (Hayes 2014). This can put enormous pressure on teachers to focus on specific items in their syllabuses that may be tested in later years, especially where teaching skills are evaluated in relation to students' performance and results in examinations. Where there are no examination specifications, teachers are still expected to assess and report on their students' progress (Rixon 2013). Existing external examinations may be seen as an objective scale by which to measure the effectiveness of both EELT teachers and the syllabus, or attempts may be made to link standardised proficiency examinations (such as the Cambridge Assessment English YLE tests) to the EELT syllabus. In Taiwan for example, as the age of introduction of English was recently lowered from Grade 7 to Grade 1, there was a need to determine whether the EELT syllabus was effective. Researchers compared Ministry guidelines and teachers' syllabuses with the Cambridge YLE tests, finding a positive correlation, with the exception of songs and stories (neither of which is assessed in the YLE Starters, Movers or Flyers). By comparing syllabus documents to an existing, reputable and valid examination suite, governments and teachers may also be validating their syllabus decisions, policies on EELT and related classroom practices (Wu and Lo 2011).

Age-appropriate teaching skills and syllabus

The nearly universal decision to lower the age of introducing English in schools has led to a major increase in the demand for English language teachers. Whereas the ideal EELT practitioner might be a proficient English user with specific teaching qualifications in primary pedagogy (Hayes 2014), the reality is that many who teach English to primary learners do not fit this narrow definition (Bowman et al. 1989; Garton et al. 2013; Hasselgreen 2013; Rixon 2013). In her 2013 survey of EELT teachers in practice, Rixon found the profile of EELT teachers to be inconsistent and often ambiguous, ranging from EELT specialists to 'a qualified teacher who has no formal qualifications in English [to] Someone who is not qualified as a teacher but who knows English' (p. 21). Other studies have also found that many primary practitioners are expected to teach English, but without the support, training or resources necessary to make this a successful endeavour (Littlejohn 2016a; Moon 2005). Where teachers are lacking in either specific primary pedagogical training or English proficiency, this inevitably results in significant discrepancies between syllabuses and classroom practice (Garton et al. 2103), with the former designed around communicative competence, and setting primary-level language outcomes that are inaccessible to teachers (Hayes 2014; Rich 2014; Schweisfurth 2013). The application of more communicative or age-appropriate methodologies in syllabus design may be misunderstood by untrained or unsupported teachers (Garton et al. 2013), while teachers who are less confident in their English proficiency, or who feel pressure to teach towards an examination, will tend to opt for more traditional instruction, even if this is not mandated by the syllabus itself (Bowman et al. 1989; Garton et al. 2013; Schweisfurth 2013). This was the case in Hong Kong, when a task-based EELT syllabus was introduced. In practice, teachers were resistant, citing a lack of appropriate resources, difficulty understanding the theory behind the reforms, increased noise in the classroom and concern over student success in the high-stakes Grade 6 examination (Adamson and Davison 2003, p. 35). Rather than embracing the task-based syllabus, the teachers tended to default to traditional activities and techniques such as dictations and focus on decontextualised grammar (ibid.). This situation is found in EELT classrooms worldwide where 'teachers still use what are seen as more traditional formal grammar-focused approaches despite the fact that official curricula are promoting more communicative, activity-oriented approaches suitable for [children]' (Enever and Moon 2009, p. 10).

In their 2013 study of global EELT classroom practice, Garton, Copland and Burns found that the most common EELT classroom activities included repeating after the teacher (75% in every class), reading out loud (70%) and doing gap-fills or grammar exercises (56–65%) (p. 48). While it was encouraging to see child-friendly activities such as songs and games (70%) and role plays (61%) also in use (ibid.), details were not given on how these were used: for enjoyment and communication, or as structural memorization? Were the songs used only as a veneer to hide a grammar-driven syllabus (Littlejohn 2016a)? Or were they written into the syllabus in a way that categorically removes all the enjoyment, replacing it with an assessable outcome as with the United Arab Emirates' Grade 2 indicator: 'Recite songs, poems and rhymes with clear diction, pitch, tempo and tone; retell a story with appropriate facts and relevant details, speaking clearly and at an appropriate pace' (United Arab Emirates 2014).

The issues in EELT are thus multifaceted, but also interrelated. Structural syllabuses with form-focused lessons are still in use globally, based around topics that are listed in the limited A1-A2 descriptors of the CEFR. Where the CEFR is not explicitly used in syllabus documents to determine success criteria or language targets, there may be a 'closed loop' of teaching towards an examination, using coursebooks that are CEFR-based, regardless of cultural relevance or age-appropriacy. Meanwhile, the teachers, who may not be proficient enough in English to access the terminology used in the syllabus documents, find themselves pressured by outside forces to ensure success in future examinations, often in situations where class sizes are unmanageably large, with few resources and little outside support or training. Where teachers do make pedagogical decisions in relation to their syllabuses, this often occurs in order to maintain the status quo of outdated and inappropriate teaching methods.

Current contributions and research

Redefining linguistic outcomes in primary syllabuses

In an attempt to address the issues identified here, CEFR-based syllabuses have been adapted to better suit children's life stages (Hasselgreen 2013; Rixon 2013). The European Language Portfolio (ELP) sought to facilitate the use of the CEFR in primary to tertiary schools, including more learner-driven self-reflection, while also favouring intercultural awareness and learner autonomy (Little et al. 2011; Little 2014). Unfortunately, it has 'failed to secure significant purchase in any [European] member states' (Little 2014, p. 33), and is virtually unheard of outside of Europe. Another proficiency-based syllabus tool which has gained traction recently is the Global Scale of English (GSE). The GSE is unique in that it is made up of different scales according to the target learner and was developed over a number of years in collaboration with teachers, ELT authors and language specialists. The GSE for YLs includes such objectives as 'Can follow short, basic classroom instructions, if supported by pictures or gestures' or 'Can recognise familiar words and basic phrases in short illustrated stories, if read out slowly and clearly' (Pearson 2017, p. 12), both of which better reflect a child's reality in the communicative language classroom than a more generic adult-focused scale like the CEFR. However, the GSE for YLs syllabus document was developed by a publishing company. This can be problematic whereby a for-profit company sets the assessment scales, researches impact and sells books and materials explicitly designed to improve proficiency. Clearly then, there is a conflict of interest in terms of a coursebook provider also setting the assessment agenda, where the influence of corporations on syllabuses, policies, assessments and materials in syllabus design risks potential bias (Mansell 2012).

Topic, cross-curricular and content-based syllabuses

The dearth of research in EELT syllabus design and implementation underscores how neglected the area is. Our review of the indexes of 60 'top landmark primary ELT methodology books and articles' (as compiled by Rixon 2016) revealed that a mere 16 titles included any reference whatsoever to 'syllabus'. Despite the predominance of proficiency descriptors and examinations-influenced coursebooks as the basis of EELT syllabuses outlined so far, this remains a partial picture. It is important to also consider other types of syllabus currently in use with primary learners to provide a sufficiently balanced view of global syllabus practice. Pinter (2017, pp. 127–128) demonstrates how recent syllabus outlines found in international coursebooks also adopt topic, cross-curricular and content-based approaches. Authentic child-friendly 'Big Questions' facilitate the integration of other school subjects such as social studies, art and science. She further highlights the influence of a child-relevant genre-based approach to syllabus design where both fiction and non-fiction act as springboards for each unit of work. In addition, twenty-first century skills are woven throughout syllabuses found in up-to-date coursebooks including the development of collaboration, critical and creative thinking skills, clearly reflective of inquiry-based and learner-centred approaches.

Lourenço and Mourão (2018) also refer to a number of innovative Content Language Integrated Learning (CLIL) projects in Portugal over the past decade where history and science syllabuses are taught via English. The use of CLIL as an approach for primary syllabus design has gained significant traction in a number of teaching and learning contexts in recent years; however, as Lourenço and Mourão (ibid.) caution, 'despite the positive effects of these innovative approaches, they remain locally and narrowly circumscribed, lacking adequate government support and teacher preparation' (p. 55), further highlighting the need for more favourable conditions for successful syllabus implementation. When unpacking such conditions, it is also necessary to clearly differentiate between state and private EELT sectors, whereby the latter tends to have greater freedom in terms of syllabus choice and, in turn, ability to successfully implement. Bourke (2006, pp. 280–281) argues that any syllabus for primary children needs to be planned in an 'experientially appropriate' manner and should include the following aspects:

- Topics of interest to children
- Stories
- Games
- Doing and making activities
- Songs, chants and rhymes
- Pairwork and groupwork tasks
- Web-based materials
- Children's literature.

The above can all be readily attended to by a topic- and content-based syllabus such as Read's (2010) project-based materials *Amazing World of Animals* and *Amazing World of Food* underpinned by a topic and content syllabus with outcomes such as 'children create a food chain' and 'children design a poster to draw attention to world hunger', with each lesson teaching real content in an age-accessible manner and language support embedded throughout. Innovative materials such as these demonstrate how topic, content and cross-curricular approaches to syllabus design can also be used to richly supplement and inject creativity into an existing structurally orientated syllabus for children.

Recommendations for practice

Age-based syllabuses and teacher education

The shortcomings of EELT syllabus design which we have highlighted so far in this chapter reflect what Sahlberg refers to as the adverse impact of the *Global Education Reform Movement* or 'GERM' (2012). This captures the 'spread and infection' of overly scripted pedagogy including an oppressive classroom culture of 'right answerism' (Grinder 1989; Holt 1969), a narrowly linguistic syllabus accompanied by heavy testing of outcomes and all within the increasingly corporate management of educational institutions. To prevent the spread of GERM in EELT syllabuses worldwide, there is a particular need to provide ongoing support to EELT practitioners and better enable them to implement alternative syllabus types and thereby teach in more age-appropriate ways.

The widespread use of the term 'young learner' when referring to children in EELT programmes, particularly in the private sector, is vague and causes confusion and lack of clarity for teachers. It has created a tendency to refer to learners with a varying range of characteristics as if they form a homogenous group. While they may share commonly accepted needs and rights as children, learners in EELT around the world differ greatly in terms of their physical, psychological, social, emotional, conceptual, cognitive and literacy development. The first key recommendation for practice therefore is the development of genuinely, age-relevant English language syllabuses for primary children in line with the best practice principles outlined in the chapter (Copland and Garton 2014; Ellis 2014, Enever and Moon 2009).

Ministries of education and private language education providers have a responsibility to equip EELT practitioners with appropriate skills to work with the age groups they are teaching. Initial training as well as CPD needs to be both based around and driven by syllabus design fully congruent with learners' life stages. In recognition of the urgent need for greater age appropriacy in syllabus design, the Council of Europe (2018) recently developed new CEFR-related descriptors specifically for primary learners aged seven to 10. Clearly, elements of content and topic-based approaches have been incorporated in an attempt to situate the can-do statements in the child's world, such as 'I can read and understand a simple illustrated text about means of transport and transportation, e.g. how fruit travels from the farmer to my home' (ibid., p. 68). For these new descriptors to be adopted with any real success, ELLT practitioners will require ongoing planned and systematic support with ways to implement them at the lesson planning, teaching and assessment levels, thereby enabling them to better bridge the often stark gap between syllabus-related policy documents and actual classroom practice.

Furthermore, EELT needs to move beyond teacher education and training only focused on teaching *language* to a model which balances the roles of being a *teacher of language* with those of a *teacher of children*, including practical ways to develop learning to learn and life skills as a core part of any syllabus for primary-aged learners of English (Brewster et al. 2002; Ellis and Ibrahim 2015; Pinter 2017). With regard to language specifically, we advocate for the development of a corpus of child language to move further toward what Read (2016, p. 33) refers to as an 'evidence-based approach to primary ELT syllabus content'.

Integrating mainstream education approaches

To counter the influence of limiting and inadequate linear structural syllabuses, Littlejohn argues the need for practitioners to break free from 'the traditional confines of language teaching' (2016b, p. 50) by integrating mainstream education approaches into syllabus design, thereby aligning classroom content with children's ages and better reflecting developments in how they learn. Such approaches include application of the revised Bloom's taxonomy for developing children's critical and creative thinking skills in tandem with providing them appropriate language support (Littlejohn 2016b; Westbrook 2014). For example, Littlejohn suggests syllabus content should enable children to develop higher order thinking skills including 'creating', e.g., via designing a poster with ideas for a recycling scheme and 'evaluating', e.g., by giving opinions on story characters (2016b).

This *language support* approach to syllabus design is content- rather than language-driven and is clearly anchored in the child's world which in turn contributes towards practitioners' wider educator remit. Using the revised version of Bloom's taxonomy develops twenty-first century skills in age-appropriate ways (Pinter 2017, Reis 2015). Therefore, as with a CLIL approach to syllabus design, language is no longer the driver and instead becomes a vehicle for meaningful child-friendly content (Lourenço and Mourão 2018).

Embedding learning to learn

Learning to learn is based on a philosophy of constructivism and social interactionism and clearly has its roots in Bruner's theories of instruction (Pinter 2017; Ellis and Ibrahim 2015; Fisher 2005). Underpinning all learning are its links with learner autonomy, which is one of the most important aspects of a child's overall educational development. It values diversity and takes into account that children develop and learn in different ways and at different rates and have different learning preferences. Implementing learning to learn in EELT syllabuses involves embedding both *metacognitive strategies*, i.e., thinking about learning: planning, monitoring, evaluating along with *cognitive strategies* which are task specific and involve children doing things with the language and their learning materials related to key skills areas.

According to Ellis and Ibrahim (2015), learning to learn in EELT provides teachers insight into what children think and helps plan next steps in learning, thereby encouraging learners and teachers to become more reflective throughout the course. This *flexible framework* approach to syllabus design helps teachers become more aware of the importance of routines and time management when planning their lessons. A key principle in EELT classrooms which adopt learning to learn in the syllabus is the need for regular and systematic reflective reviewing, as exemplified in the Plan-Do-Review model (Ellis and Ibrahim 2015).

Curricula and schemes of work

Given the issues highlighted in this chapter, we question whether the entire notion of 'syllabus' is relevant or even appropriate when working with children in the EELT classroom. Littlejohn (2016b) maintains a *curriculum approach* with its related schemes of work would be a better suited to determining and defining how English language teaching and learning is organised at the primary level. The challenge for adopting such a novel approach in EELT is to identify engaging, child-friendly 'points of entry' on which to base curriculum plans and schemes of work. One example which has gained popularity in multiple EELT contexts is the use of picturebooks as 'springboards' for course design. Children's picturebooks enable children to access and deal with what Ghosn (2013, p. 40) refers to as 'universal aspects of the human condition' including equality, diversity and inclusion themes such as gender, ethnicity, religion and disability in age-appropriate and meaningful ways.

Ellis and Brewster (2014) demonstrate how between five to six picturebooks can comprise the annual EELT curriculum:

> This would mean spending about five to six weeks on each story and about ten to twelve lessons per story, if the class has approximately one and a half to two hours of English per week. In this way, a storybook provides the starting point for a wide range of related language-learning activities.
>
> *(ibid., p.11)*

This *story-based* approach strongly favours an acquisition-oriented methodology and additionally helps address the numerous issues with structural syllabuses alluded to earlier. It can be adapted for challenging learning contexts where access to picturebooks is lacking by using contextually relevant stories and enabling children to create their own modern retellings, which further develops higher order thinking skills. If such an approach is to be implemented with any degree of success, it needs to be an integral component of teacher education programmes such as the BEd course at the University of Zagreb developed for Croatian primary ELT undergraduates (Narancic Kovač 2016), which emphasises how teachers need to be trained to use picturebooks specifically for ELT purposes, and this is where medium to longer-term curriculum planning and schemes of work play a key role.

Assessment for learning

To alleviate the effects of washback in EELT curricula, Rixon (2012) advocates implementation for *assessment for learning*, whereby:

1   Lesson objectives are systematically shared with children in accessible language and/or the mother tongue.
2   Peer and self-assessment are commonplace.
3   Children are provided with immediate feedback.

Such feedback on children's tasks and activities therefore progresses beyond task achievement and gives them concrete support about what to do next. Accessible language can be provided by EELT practitioners by using the following acronyms, again inspired by primary mainstream education:

WALTs – we are learning to . . .
WILFs – what I'm looking for . . .

Such a *framing approach* enables primary children to perceive their learning as purposeful and coherent which in turn enhances their metacognitive awareness. Rixon (2012) adds

WAGOLL – what a good one looks like

Thus, this underlines the crucial importance of providing models and robust scaffolding when enabling children to achieve lesson outcomes. Use of varied formative assessment tools in EELT fosters a far greater age-appropriate and child-friendly approach to assessment when compared to daunting high-stakes English language examinations. Practitioners should also recognise the particular value of embedding systematic use of learning portfolios which involve primary learners in decision making regarding which work is to be included as well as providing the children with a tangible sense of progress (Ellis and Ibrahim 2015, Ioannou-Georgiou and Pavlou 2003). As to how extensively these 'new' types of assessment are ultimately adopted in EELT curricula will depend on the particular learning context, as with all the innovations we are proposing in this chapter.

Future directions

Values education in EELT

It is increasingly common in international EELT coursebooks to see a 'values related' lesson in each unit with fostering empathy, resolution of conflict and empowering children to be responsible citizens as frequent examples (Hird 2016). As we highlighted previously, coursebooks often are interpreted by schools, teachers and parents/caregivers as the actual syllabus. Therefore, such a 'values' focused trend is worthy of serious attention, particularly given the numerous contexts worldwide where teachers are currently not provided with adequate support or CPD, including how to incorporate values education in their schemes of work. Given the level of global conflict coupled with the increasing rhetoric of hate in many contexts, incorporating a robust values education focus in EELT is laudable; however, it may result in a somewhat limited and tokenistic values syllabus grafted on almost as an afterthought, which would be counterproductive to developing children's intercultural competence (Kramsch 1993). Furthermore, incorporating values education in EELT is not without controversy, with many questions surrounding the issue, such as: what values should be taught? Whose values are they? Do 'global values' exist? Best EELT practice also maintains that children should be given age-relevant *choices* to accept or reject particular values. This respects their rights as learners, and pedagogical approaches should influence them to make informed choices (Bilsborough 2016).

Based on insights from research conducted on mainstream education in the UK and Australia where a *whole school approach* to modelling values in primary level curricula and schemes of work has been successfully adopted, Read (2018) has developed a flexible 'pedagogy of values' according to the following principles:

- Encourage children to notice values.
- Help them to understand reasons for particular values.
- Encourage them to reflect on their own and others' values.

She emphasizes the need for this to remain fully age appropriate as focusing on values with a five-year-old is very different from doing so with a 10-year-old. Read goes on to highlight the usefulness of discovery learning and advises EELT practitioners to avoid being overly quick to explain values. Such *discovery approaches* in schemes of work act as springboards into values education, and practitioners can make use of picturebooks and storytelling as well as discussion and personalization via drama and role play (but never in a vacuum) to open up thinking around values in the safe environment of the classroom.

Integrating the United Nations Sustainable Development Goals

Closely related to children's rights is the need to enable them to consider their futures by tackling poverty, caring for the environment and ensuring prosperity, as reflected in the United Nations Sustainable Development Goals (SDGs). These 'global goals' can be used in age-accessible ways in EELT to raise children's awareness of key issues while drawing on the *language support* approach to simultaneously develop their creativity, critical thinking and language skills. Real, meaningful and up-to-date content is once again clearly the driver for course design by using the SDGs as 'entry points' into lessons. Read (2017) has developed materials aimed at upper primary children which provide EELT practitioners inspiration and a flexible framework for developing their own contextually relevant schemes of work around the SDGs. She makes use of freely downloadable Getty Images to raise children's awareness of world problems and convey meaning of related lexis. Circle time can also be used to enable children to predict the goals while fostering respect for diverse opinions, turn-taking and active-listening sub-skills. Read's (ibid., p. 18) 'global goals spider gram' provides an opportunity for children to create their own goals, which develops higher order thinking skills and enables them to further personalise content and language in a contextually relevant manner. While EELT practitioners may feel raising children's awareness of the SDGs is complex and daunting, the creative approaches outlined above demonstrate the far-reaching potential achievable in EELT classrooms. It is also an important reminder of the need to avoid underestimating what children are capable of and to provide them with plenty of opportunities for creative exploration in curricula and related schemes of work.

Children's voices in EELT

Throughout this chapter, we have been focusing on the need for a critical analysis of the way teaching and learning in EELT are organised, and while teacher support and optimising learning are both crucial, all too often children's voices are absent from the discussion. Article 12 of the UN Convention on the Rights of the Child (2010) affirms that, 'You have the right to give your opinion and for adults to listen and take it seriously'. The idea of 'mainstreaming' in EELT means developing curricula and schemes of work with related classroom routines and procedures where children's voices are included as a norm. This further underlines the importance of providing choice and reflective reviewing in age-relevant ways and makes the notion of 'needs analysis' and 'the negotiated syllabus' (both commonplace in adult and secondary ELT) an age-accessible reality for children in EELT. This enables them to become active and questioning participants in and contributors to their own learning process. By becoming involved in curricula-related decision making, children's motivation for learning English increases as well as develops their collaborative learning and communication skills (Bilsborough 2016; Ellis and Ibrahim 2015). There is an increasing body of innovative EELT research which foregrounds children's voices (Pinter et al. 2013; Pinter et al. 2016). Classroom practitioners, academic managers, private education providers and ministries of education need to listen to their voices and make them the starting point for decision making around EELT curricula and schemes of work, for this is the very essence of genuine child-centredness.

Further reading

1 Pinter, A. (2017). *Teaching young language learners*, 2nd ed. Oxford: Oxford University Press.
   The chapter on materials evaluation and design includes the integration of a topic and content-based syllabus both with published coursebooks and authentic, age-appropriate texts. It also includes an explicit focus on integrating twenty-first century skills in syllabus design.

2 Ellis, G., and Ibrahim, N. (2015). *Teaching children how to learn*. Surrey: Delta Publishing.
   This book unpacks the pedagogical principles underpinning the integration of learning to learn in primary ELT syllabus design. It also includes a range of pedagogical routines and practical strategies to scaffold the implementation of learning to learn in everyday primary ELT classroom practice.

3 Read, C. (2017). Developing children's understanding of the Global Goals. In Maley, A., and Peachy, N. (eds.) *Integrating global issues in the creative English language classroom: With reference to the United Nations Sustainable Development Goals*. London: British Council. www.teachingenglish.org.uk/sites/teacheng/files/PUB_29200_Creativity_UN_SDG_v4S_WEB.pdf.
   The tasks and activity cycles included in this chapter demonstrate to teachers of upper primary ways to integrate a focus on the United Nations Sustainable Development Goals into the ELT syllabus in age-accessible ways.

4 *Onestopenglish* – Amazing World of Animals
   This subscription site with a project on wild animals for young learners provides a blueprint for teachers of primary ELT aiming to use topic-, project- and content-based learning in their syllabuses and schemes of work. www.onestopenglish.com/clil/young-learners/animals/project-amazing-world-of-animals/

5 *Onestopenglish* – Amazing World of Food

This subscription site with a project on food for young learners provides a blueprint for teachers of primary ELT aiming to use topic-, project- and content-based learning in their syllabuses and schemes of work. www.onestopenglish.com/clil/young-learners/science/food/project-amazing-world-of-food/

6   *TeachingEnglish* – Promoting Diversity Through Children's Literature

This site provides primary ELT practitioners freely downloadable materials based on a story-based syllabus. The teachers' notes demonstrate how to use picturebooks as the basis of an ELT syllabus as well as to develop children's awareness of values education issues such as equality, inclusion, racism, recycling, climate and responsible consumption. http://tinyurl.com/z9pzj7n

Related topics

Assessment, materials, grammar, vocabulary, speaking and listening, reading and writing

References

Adamson, B., and Davison, C. (2003). Innovation in English language teaching in Hong Kong primary schools: One step forward, two steps sideways? *Prospect*, 18(1), 27–41.

Anderson, J. (2016). Why practice makes perfect sense: The past, present and potential future of the PPP paradigm in language teacher education. *ELTED*, 19, 16–22.

Bilsborough, K. (2016). The neglected 'C' – Implementing choice in the YLT English language classroom. *TEYLT Worldwide: The Newsletter of the IATEFL Young Learners and Teenagers Special Interest Group*, 70–75.

Bourke, J. M. (2006). Designing a topic-based syllabus for young learners. *ELT Journal*, 60(3).

Bowman, B., Burkart, G., and Robson, B. (1989). *TEFL/TESL, Teaching English as a Foreign or Second Language*. Peace Corps (U.S.) Information Collection and Exchange.

Cambridge English (2011). *Critique of the CEFR (Video 1 of 2)*. Video recording, YouTube: www.youtube.com/watch?v=rhCYc7rGOUo.

Cameron, L. (2001). *Teaching Languages to Young Learners*. Cambridge: Cambridge University Press.

Chen, Z., and Wang, Q. (2014). Examining classroom interactional practices to promote learning in the young learner EFL classroom in China. In Rich, S. (ed.) *International Perspectives on Teaching English to Young Learners*. New York: Palgrave MacMillan, 45–65.

Clifford, I., and Htut, K. P. (2015). A transformative pedagogy for Myanmar? *Paper Presented to 13th International Conference on Education and Development*, UKFIET, Oxford, 15–17 September 2015.

Copland, F., and Garton, S. (2014). Key themes and future directions in teaching English to young learners: Introduction to the Special Issue. *ELT Journal*, 68(3), 223–230.

Council of Europe (2001). *Common European Framework of Reference for Languages: Learning, teaching, assessment*. Cambridge: Cambridge University Press.

Council of Europe (2018). *Collated Representative Samples of Descriptors of Language Competences Developed for Young Learners Aged 7–10 Years*. Council of Europe: Language Policy Unit. https://rm.coe.int/1680697fca.

Cyprus (no date). *Pilot curriculum English as a foreign language in Cyprus Primary Schools (Years 1–6)*. www.moec.gov.cy/dde/programs/eniaio_oloimero/pdf/analytika_programmata/curriculum_english.pdf.

Edwards, V., and Li, D. (2011). Confucius, constructivism and the impact of continuing professional development on teachers of English in China. *ELT Research Papers* 11–02. British Council.

Ellis, G. (2004). Young learners: Clarifying our terms. *ELT Journal*, 68(1), 75–78.

Ellis, G., and Brewster, J. (2014). *Tell it Again! The storytelling handbook for primary English language teachers*. London: British Council.

Ellis, G., Brewster, J., and Girard, D. (2002). *The Primary English Teacher's Guide*, 2nd ed. London: Penguin English.

Ellis, G., and Ibrahim, N. (2015). *Teaching children how to learn*. Surrey: Delta Publishing.

Enever, J. (ed.) (2011). *ELLiE: English language learning in Europe*. London: British Council.

Enever, J. (2014). Primary English teacher education in Europe. *ELT Journal*, 68(3), 231–242.

Enever, J., and Moon, J. (2009). New global contexts for teaching Primary ELT: Change and challenge. In Enever, J., Moon, J., and Raman, U. (eds.) *Young Learner English Language Policy and Implementation: International perspectives*. Reading: Garnet Publishing, 5–17.

Fisher, R. (2005). *Teaching Children to Think*. 2nd edition. Oxford: Oxford University Press.

Garton, S., Copland, F., and Burns, A. (2013). Investigating global practices in teaching English to Young Learners. In Sheehan, S. (ed.) *British Council ELT research papers volume 1*, 35–56.

Ghosn, I. (2013). Humanizing teaching English to young learners with children's literature. *Clele Journal*, 1(1), Article 1.

Guerrero, S. (Ed.). (2014). *Primary Methodology Handbook: Practical ideas for ELT*. Oxford: Richmond.

Hargreaves, A. (2002). Sustainability of educational change: The role of social geographies. *Journal of Educational Change*, 3 (3–4), 189–214.

Hasselgreen, A. (2013). Adapting the CEFR for the classroom assessment of young learners' writing. *The Canadian Modern Language Review/La revue canadienne des langues vivantes*, 69(4), (November), 415–435.

Hayes, D. (2014). *Factors Influencing Success in Teaching English in State Primary Schools*. London: British Council.

Hird, E. (2016). *Teaching Social Values in the Primary Language Classroom*. https://emilyhirdblog. wordpress.com/2016/12/14/teaching-social-values-in-the-language-classroom/.

Holt, J. (1969). *How Children Fail*. Harmondsworth: Penguin.

Howatt, A. P. R., and Widdowson, H. G. (2004). *A History of ELT, Second edition*. Oxford: Oxford University Press.

Ioannou-Georgiou, S., and Pavlou, P. (2003). *Assessing Young Learners*. Oxford: Oxford University Press.

Jin, L., Jiang, C., Zhang, J., Yuan, Y., Liang, X., and Xie, Q. (2014). Motivations and expectations of English language learning among primary school children and parents in China. *ELT Research Papers*, 14(1).

Kramsch, C. (1993). *Context and Culture in Language Teaching*. Oxford: Oxford University Press.

Little, D. (2014). Learning, teaching, assessment: An exploration of their interdependence in the CEFR. *Presentation to the 11th EALTA Conference*, University of Warwick, 29 May–1 June 2014.

Little, D., Goullier, F., and Hughes, G. (2011). *The European Language Portfolio: The story so far (1991–2011)*. [Executive Summary]. www.coe.int/en/web/portfolio/the-european-language-portfolio-the-story-so-far-1991-2011-executive-summary.

Littlejohn, A. (2016a). How young learners learn language. *IATEFL Young Learners & Teenagers SIG Newsletter: C&TS Digital Special Pearl Anniversary Edition*, 31–32.

Littlejohn, A. (2016b). Task types and cognitive engagement. *TEYLT Worldwide: The Newsletter of the IATEFL Young Learners and Teenagers Special Interest Group*, 50–53.

Lourenco, M., and Mourão, S. (2018). Learning English (and other languages) in Portugal. *Language Issues*, 28(2), 53–55.

Mansell, W. (2012). Should Pearson, a giant multinational, be influencing our education policy? *The Guardian*. www.theguardian.com/education/2012/jul/16/pearson-.

Moon, J. (2005). Teaching English to young learners: the challenges and the benefits. *In English!*, 30–34.

Narancic Kovač, S. (2016). Picturebooks in educating teachers of English to young learners. *Clele Journal*, 4(2), Article 1.

Pantaleoni, L. (1991). Syllabusing at primary level: The Italian perspective. In Brumfit, C., Moon, J., and Tongue, R. (eds.) *Teaching English to Children*. London: Harper Collins.

Patrinos, H. A., Osorio, F. B., and Guáqueta, J. (2009). *The Role and Impact of Public-private Partnerships in Education*. Washington, DC: The World Bank.

Pearson Education Ltd. (2017). *GSE Learning Objectives for Young Learners Photocopiables*. Harlow: Pearson.

Pinter, A. (2017). *Teaching Young Language Learners*, 2nd ed. Oxford: Oxford University Press.

Pinter, A., Kuchah, H., and Smith, R. (2013). Researching with children. *ELT Journal*, 67(4), 1 October 2013, 484–487.

Pinter, A., Mathew, R., and Smith, R. (2016). Children and teachers as co-researchers in Indian primary English classrooms. ELT Research Papers 16.03. British Council.

Read, C. (2010). *Amazing World of Animals*. Onestopclil: Macmillan Education. www.onestopenglish.com/clil/young-learners/animals/project-amazing-world-of-animals.

Read, C. (2010). *Amazing World of Food*. Onestopclil: Macmillan Education. www.onestopenglish.com/clil/young-learners/science/food/project-amazing-world-of-food/.

Read, C. (2016). An ABC of changes in primary English language teaching and learning over the last 30 years. *IATEFL Young Learners & Teenagers SIG Newsletter: C&TS Digital Special Pearl Anniversary Edition*, 33–37. www.carolread.com/wpcontent/uploads/2015/01/ABC-of-changes-in-PELT-over-the-last-30-years.pdf.

Read, C. (2017). Developing children's understanding of the global goals. In Maley, A., and Peachy, N. (eds.) *Integrating Global Issues in the Creative English Language Classroom: With reference to the United Nations sustainable development goals*. London: British Council, 11–20.

Read, C. (2018). *Values Education for Children: Issues, challenges and solutions*. TEYLT Worldwide: The newsletter of the IATEFL Young Learners and Teenagers Special Interest Group, Issue 1, 2018.

Reis, V. (2015). 21st Century learning for 21st century young learners. *Modern English Teacher*, 24(1), 14–16.

Rich, S. (2014). Taking stock: Where are we now in TEYL? In Rich, S. (ed.) *International Perspectives on Teaching English to Young Learners*. New York: Palgrave MacMillan, 1–22.

Richards, J., and Rodgers, T. (2001). *Approaches and Methods in Language Teaching*. Cambridge: Cambridge University Press.

Rixon, S. (2012). *How young learners learn languages and how to test them*. ALTE. www.alte.org/attachments/pdfs/files/alte_plenary_final_shelagh_rixon_ta2w1.pdf.

Rixon, S. (2013). *British Council Survey of Policy and Practice in Primary English Language Teaching Worldwide*. London: British Council.

Rixon, S. (2015). Primary English and critical issues: A worldwide perspective. In Bland, J. (ed.) *Teaching English to Young Learners: Critical issues in language teaching with 3–12 year olds*. London: Bloomsbury, 31–50.

Rixon, S. (2016). 30 years of top young learner reads. *IATEFL Young Learners & Teenagers SIG Newsletter: C&TS Digital Special Pearl Anniversary Edition*, 23–25.

Robinson, P., Mourão, S., and Kang, N. J. (2015). English learning areas in pre-primary classrooms: An investigation of their effectiveness. *ELT Research Papers*, 15.02. British Council.

Sahlberg, P. (2012). *Global education reform movement is here*. https://pasisahlberg.com/global-educational-reform-movement-is-here/.

Schweisfurth, M. (2013). *Learner-centred Education in International Perspective: Whose pedagogy for whose development?* London: Routledge.

Shamim, F., Negash, N., Chuku, C., and Demewoz, N. (2007). Maximizing learning in large classes: Issues and options. *Milestones in ELT*. ELT 16. British Council.

Stec, M. (2013). English course books and language awareness of young learners. *Literacy Information and Computer Education Journal* (LICEJ), 4(3), 1171–1177.

Taylor, L. (2005). Washback and impact. *ELT Journal*, 59(2), 154–155.

Thornbury, S. (2006). *An A-Z of ELT*. London: Macmillan Books for Teachers.

UNICEF (2010). *A Summary of the UN Convention of the Rights of the Child*. UK: UNICEF. https://downloads.unicef.org.uk/wp-content/uploads/2010/05/UNCRC_summary-1.pdf?_ga=2.249554503.1162392707.1509926263-249914037.1501700505.

The United Arab Emirates (2014). *English as an International Language: National unified K-12 learning standards framework 2014*. www.moe.gov.ae/Arabic/Docs/Curriculum/Learning%20Standard/UAE%20English%20Framework.pdf

Weir, C. J. (2013). Measured constructs: A history of Cambridge English language examinations 1913–2012. *Cambridge English Research Notes*, (51), 2–10.

Westbrook, C. (2014). *Teaching critical thinking using Bloom's taxonomy*. www.cambridge.org/elt/blog/2014/04/18/teaching-critical-thinking-using-blooms-taxonomy/

White, R. V. (1988). *The ELT Curriculum: Design, innovation and management*. Oxford: Blackwell.

Wu, J., and Lo, H-Y. (2011). The YLE tests and teaching in the Taiwanese context. *Cambridge English Research Notes*, (46), 2–6.

23

Materials for early language learning

Irma-Kaarina Ghosn

Introduction

Since English language teaching (ELT) was introduced into grade school curricula, the onset of instruction has usually been around age eleven or above. However, the early 1990s saw a push in Europe to lower the onset of foreign language (FL) instruction, and the same trend has since been observed in many countries outside Europe. In the early twenty-first century, ELT found its way also into pre-school and even into nursery classes. Following the European framework, Teaching English to Very Young Learners (TEVYL) refers to three- to six-year-olds and Teaching English to Young Learners (TEYL) refers to seven- to 12-year-olds. The practice of introducing ELT to ever younger age groups raises concerns not only about pedagogy but also instructional materials, which include the coursebook and any other materials used in the classroom. Often the internationally marketed 'global' coursebooks for upper primary school have been modelled after materials for older learners, and are increasingly often geared towards standardised language tests. Yet, a coursebook-based approach is not necessarily developmentally appropriate in the pre-school and lower primary school classes, in particular.

TEYL programs range from enrichment programs, where children receive English instruction for perhaps one hour a week, to immersion programs, where some academic content is also taught in English. English as a foreign language (EFL) here refers to programs where children learn English as a subject, whether for one or more weekly hours. English as a second language (ESL) refers to partial or total immersion programs, whether children live in an English-speaking country or not. Needless to say, with such a wide range of aims, a wide range of instructional materials should be available. TEVYL must also take into account the fact that the youngest learners have not yet developed literacy in their first language (L1), and that children's linguistic development, even in their L1, varies widely from child to child depending on the richness of their linguistic environment. In addition to the above variables, materials should also consider the level of teacher qualifications and experience in teaching young and very young learners.

'Materials' here includes coursebooks and any supplementary materials such as workbooks, flashcards, posters, cassettes, CD-ROMs, videos, dictionaries, worksheets and supplementary readers, etc. Needless to say, teachers around the world often also prepare their own instructional materials, either because there are no funds for coursebooks or to supplement commercial materials. There is such a vast array of teacher-made materials from flashcards to worksheets and bulletin-board posters that they are beyond the scope of this article.

Historical perspectives

Birth of TEYL materials

Although TEFL has a long history in secondary schools, TEYL is relatively new. In the early 1900s, the US policy was to assimilate immigrants as soon as possible, and immigrant children were immersed in English-only classrooms (with few exceptions) until the mid-1960s. However, since the 1950s, large population shifts have resulted in considerable numbers of linguistic minorities in North America and Britain (Howatt 1984), and 1966 witnessed the establishment of TESOL (Teachers of English to Speakers of Other Languages) followed by IATEFL (International Association of Teaching English as a Foreign Language) in 1967.

In the UK, Schools Council *Scope* project was developed to teach English to immigrant children, with *Scope 1* published in 1969, followed by two more levels in 1972. Howatt (1997, p. 275) describes how

> *Scope* broke new ground in English language teaching by bringing together the EFL tradition of the linguistically organized syllabus (structured patterns, controlled vocabulary, etc.) and the primary school tradition of activity methods which required the children to use the new language co-operatively to make puppets, charts, models of various kinds.

Examination of TEYL materials published after *Scope* reveals that the approach has had a long-lasting impact that can still be seen in some EFL courses published in the UK, such as *Stepping Stones* (Ashworth and Clark 1990), *English Together* (Webster and Worrall 1992), *New Stepping Stones* (Ashworth and Clark 1997) and *Tops* (Hanlon and Kimball 2008). *Let's Learn English* (Dallas and Iggulden 1990), *Way Ahead* (Ellis and Bowen 1998) and *Blue Skies* (Holt 1999) represented a more traditional structured approach but with communicative flavor, possibly easier for a teacher teaching large classes.

Increasing numbers of immigrant children in American schools in the 1970s brought about innovations in teaching English to children in the country. In 1971, Hap Palmer published *Songbook: Learning Basic Skills through Music*, aimed at children learning ESL. Carolyn Graham's (1978) *Jazz Chants for Children* was based on the notion that chants provide exposure to natural intonation patterns and promote listening and speaking skills. Other innovations followed. Story Experience activity was developed for Jefferson County Public Schools in Colorado in 1979 and involved rhymes, physical action, acting out story scripts and other activities (Richard-Amato 1988). *Random House book of poetry for children* (1983) aimed to teach children English through poetry, *Games for language learning* (Wright, Beteridge and Buckley 1984) presented a variety of games and *Storytelling for children* (Wright 1984) (in its 9th impression in 2004) promoted storytelling. Some of these popular approaches eventually found their way to ESL coursebooks published in the USA, albeit with minor modifications.

American primary level ESL courses have followed a communicatively oriented, yet structured approach, with a variety of songs, rhymes, TPR and short-story scripts in *Kids*

(Walker 1989c) and *ESL* (Addison Wesley 1989b). *Parade* (Herrera and Zanatta 1996) and *New Parade* (Herrera and Zanatta 2000) added content connections and hands-on projects, while *Amazing English* (Walker 1989a) incorporated multicultural content reflecting the multicultural characteristics of American society. These courses remained popular throughout the 1990s. *Backpack* (Herrera and Pinkley 2005) integrates vocabulary, grammar and the four skills and has also Little Books for levels 1–3 and Magazines for levels 4–6. *Hip Hip Hooray!* (Eisele et al. 2004) is structured around updated and abbreviated classic stories that develop in the course of the lesson units. At the time of this writing, both *Backpack* and *Hip Hip Hooray!* were in second edition. The earlier courses were often accompanied by pictures cards, posters and audiocassettes, while the more recent courses come with VHS/DVD, CD-ROMs and companion websites.

Story-based materials

One of the early studies on young learner materials was Michael West's study of his *New Method Series*, which he piloted in 1923–1925 with Bengali children in India (Howatt 1997). The focus of his approach was reading of simplified stories, which West believed would eventually enable children to use the language themselves (West 1937). In one of his experimental classes, pupils made two-year gains in reading and one-year gains in vocabulary in only 141 class hours (Tickoo 1988, p. 297). The readers became a commercial success and were used for a number of years in India, then-Ceylon, Palestine, Persia, Nigeria, Kenya and Uganda (Smith, n.d.).

Reading and storybooks were also central in 'book flood' studies conducted by Warwick Elley and others based on an approach developed in New Zealand in the 1970s. The approach entailed shared reading of numerous storybooks and related follow-up activities. Significant gains were noted in reading and listening comprehension, with positive effects having carried over to other subject matter areas (e.g., Elley and Mangubhai 1983; Elley 2000).

In the 1990s, story-based instruction gradually found its way into TEYL and has gained popularity steadily as attested by the many research projects and programs carried out in different parts of the world. In 1997, Opal Dunn founded the *RealBook News* (www.realboos.co.uk), in 1998 Ghosn's (1999) story-based, thematically structured *Caring Kids: Social Responsibility through Literature* was awarded the Mary Finocchiaro Award for Excellence in the Development of [unpublished] Pedagogical Materials from TESOL, and in 2013 *CLELE (Children's Literature in English Language Education) Journal* was launched. The motivating power and low cost are some advantages of story-based instruction. Children's literature can work even in contexts with limited resources, especially if one Big Book version is used. These are large, illustrated books that can be placed on an easel and seen by a group of children as the teacher reads the story while pointing at the words.

Diversity of TEYL and TEVYL materials

In the early twenty-first century a push for TEVYL began, with increasing number of countries introducing English in the lower primary school as well as in pre-school (see Enever 2011; Rixon 2013). Publishers quickly followed with courses for the very young learners. *Pockets* (Herrera and Hojel 2009a) is aimed at children between the ages of three and five, while *Little Pockets* by the same authors is promoted for two-year-olds.

Since the 1980s, there has been a significant increase in TEYL materials and since mid-2000 TEVYL materials. Arnold and Rixon (2008) mention 36 titles aimed at TEYL, while a brief examination of three well-known international publishers' online catalogs of 2016–2017 showed 44 titles designated for pre-primary and 75 for primary school. In addition to commercial print materials, there are numerous web-based resources for TEYL, such as https://learnenglishkids.britishcouncil.org, www.learninggamesforkids.com and www.eslgamesplus.com, as well as language learning apps for children offered by https://elearningindustry.com and others.

YL materials selection varies, with some countries prescribing one textbook for each grade level, while in others a wide array of textbooks is available for schools to choose from, either freely from the market or from a government-approved list (Arnold and Rixon 2008). The global TEYL books published in the UK and the USA have been adopted by many countries, while others have begun to produce their own materials specially commissioned and written to the specifications of a ministry of education or other educational authority. International materials – often called 'global coursebooks' – have also been adapted to local needs with some modifications (Arnold and Rixon 2008). In many cases, teachers make their own materials, as there is no budget for books, while others make materials to supplement the coursebook. As Rixon (2013, p. 32) notes, 'there is a very wide range of solutions to the provision of class materials and this reflects the resources and often the political conditions in each context'.

The well-designed coursebook has many advantages in the classroom: it provides a clear syllabus, a comprehensive teacher's guide and motivating content (Harmer 2001), as well as appropriately sequenced and structured lessons that save teacher's time regarding lesson planning (Halliwell 2006). Nearly 30 years ago, Sheldon (1988) argued that that assessment of coursebooks is not well researched, although the ELT publishing business is a multimillion pound industry. It seems things have not changed much, especially in regards to TEYL and TEVYL coursebooks.

Enever (2011, p. 29) argues that publishers have been 'slow to respond' to the needs of the YLs and their teachers. She suggests that this is likely due to 'high costs, the uncertainty of the market and the well-established tradition of coursebooks for older learners'. It might also be due to 'a closed and possibly vicious circle', as Rixon (2009, p. 4) argues, with international examination syllabuses being based on coursebooks, which in turn are based on examination syllabuses. With the demands of accountability, standardised tests for young learners are increasingly popular. For example, approximately 150,000 children sat for the UCLES Test for Young Learners in 2000 (Cameron 2003).

Critical issues and topics

What are 'Good' materials for TEYL and TEVYL?

Numerous suggestions regarding successful ELT materials are available and the key points can be summarised as follows. Good materials should reflect topics relevant, interesting and meaningful to learners, language that is contextual and natural, and focus ought to be on meaning rather than form of language, with skills integrated and concepts recycled (Richard-Amato 1988). Materials should provide repetition of input and opportunities for learner output, be culturally appropriate (Watt and Foscolos 1998) and in the case of TEYL and TEVYL be also age appropriate in terms of content, approach and expectations (Ghosn 2013a).

In the wake of the push for ever earlier TEVYL, publishers are turning out coursebooks even for nursery and kindergarten children. Yet, teaching children as young as five and six (let alone two or three) using a coursebook is not necessarily appropriate. First, children at this age are not yet literate in their first language, although they might have acquired a sizeable vocabulary and know how the language works. Second, children at this age do not respond well to formal, teacher-fronted and coursebook-based instruction implied by the materials available at the time of writing (Ghosn 2017).

For young children, who may have little intrinsic motivation to learn a new language, especially in EFL contexts, materials must also be interesting enough for children to be motivated to engage in the lessons. Jalongo (2007) argues that motivation and interest have a profound influence on learning, and Artelt (2005) considers interest as a key form of intrinsic motivation. There are two types of interest; individual interest and situational interest (Jalongo op cit.), the latter playing a particularly important role in TEYL and TEVYL.

Situational interest has been studied for over twenty years, and according to Hidi and Harackiewizc (2000, p 152) certain features in texts can trigger situational interest: texts that are easy to understand, present unusual, novel or surprising content and feature characters and topics with which learners can identify, and/or involve high levels of activity. In a classroom, it is more difficult to meet the personal interests of all learners, which can vary widely from dinosaurs and comic books to puzzles, Pokémons and Barbie dolls. However, Hidi and Harackiewizc (ibid.) also found situational interest can evoke personal interest, meaning that content of lessons can trigger students' personal interests.

Instructional approaches

Cameron (2003, p. 105) argues that the spread of TEVYL 'is not a minor change that can be left to YL experts, but a shift that will have knock-off effects for the rest of ELT'. She further cautions against 'over-reliance at primary level on literacy skills in English' (2003, p. 106) at the expense of listening and speaking because 'some children will always begin to fall behind or fail – not because they cannot learn to speak English, but because they need more time to master the complications of reading and writing' (ibid.). Her cautions are well placed, as the majority of internationally available TEYL courses feature little or no explicit instruction in word study or reading skills.

'New TEYL curricula have generally emphasized communicative competence' (Garton et al. 2011, p. 5), leading to 'some form of Communicative Language Teaching (CLT) or task-based Learning and Teaching (TBLT)'. However, the CLT syllabus originated in Western countries and was aimed at adult learners. Thus, while it may work well in contexts with small classes and ample resources, it might not be realistic in countries with large classes, limited resources and possibly a shortage of teachers experienced in teaching young learners. CLT might also not work in countries where different classroom cultures prevail. For example, in highly hierarchical cultures, where the teacher is perceived as the source of knowledge with students respectfully listening, it might be difficult for both teachers and students to adapt to CLT. The following quotes from two teachers who were trying to use a communicatively oriented coursebook illustrate this point. The first quote is from Japan and the second from Lebanon:

> If I do group work or open-ended communicative activities, the students and other colleagues will feel that I'm not really teaching them. They will feel that I didn't have anything really planned for the lesson and that I'm just filling time.
>
> *(Richards and Lockhart 1994, 108)*

> When I first started teaching at [the school], I tried to follow the teacher's book and I think students liked it . . . but anyway, the coordinator told me stop doing it because

some parents were complaining. They said my class was out of control and that I wasn't teaching children anything, and that they were just talking to each other and playing games. So, now I don't do that anymore.

(Ghosn 2004, 114)

One must wonder how the typical coursebook activities involving pair- and small-group work can be realised in such situations. The following dialogue shows what happened in one Lebanese fifth-grade class. Children are expected to talk about their favourite seasons and seasonal activities. The text provides options of swimming, sailing, bike riding, playing in the autumn leaves and planting flowers.

T: OK. Rami and Boutors. Please do the conversation.
S3:   [Reading] What is your favorite season?
S4:   [Reading] My favorite season is spring.
S3:   Why?
S4:   [Reading] I like warm, rainy days.
S9:   [Reading] What is your favorite season?
T: OK. Now Rania, you answer him.
S10:   [Reading] My favorite season is winter.
T: Why do you like winter?
S10:   Because it's cold.
T: Because it's cold or because you like to play in the snow?
S10:   I like to play in the snow.
T: Now Hani and Zeina, you do the conversation.
S11:   [Reading] What is your favorite season?
T: [to S12] And don't say winter!
S12:   [no response]

(Ghosn 2003, pp. 295–296)

The intended pair-dialogue became just another drill with the teacher correcting form errors.

The above episode brings to attention another potentially problematic issue in the global coursebooks: culture-specific content. Some content in the TEYL coursebooks reflects a pre-supposed shared reality, which might not exist. For example, in the above case, the only activity options that were relevant and familiar to the children were swimming and bike riding.

ELT materials developed in the USA reflect the multicultural characteristics of the country, while UK-developed materials reflect the British culture. Although one might argue that these books are 'local', they are, in fact, marketed globally. Incorporating aspects of Anglo culture, although undoubtedly a key aspect of any ELT program, may not be appropriate at the very early stages of TEVYL outside the target language culture. If lesson content features topics very unfamiliar in the learners' home culture, young children may not be able to relate to the concepts and may even find them confusing. Unfamiliar cultural content may also result in awkward classroom interactions even at the upper primary classroom, as the above episode illustrates and as shown by Ghosn (2003, 2004, 2013a, 2017).

During the author's teacher development sessions in the Middle East over two decades, TEYL teachers, especially in rural areas, have voiced their concerns about cultural content in their coursebooks, with which they themselves are not familiar. When children act out coursebook dialogues that feature unfamiliar concepts, the interaction is unauthentic and drill-like, and perhaps not very meaningful for them. Locally developed materials can better be tailored to the local context and needs.

When developing materials for children, one must consider children's cognitive development and also their psycho-social needs. For example, maintaining focused attention is a demanding skill, which children develop gradually during the pre-school and elementary school years. The more salient the lesson content, the greater the likelihood that children will maintain attention (Kail 2010), while unfamiliar or too-abstract content makes it more difficult for children to maintain attention. Memory is another important factor for learning, and only around age seven do children begin to utilise memory strategies that improve remembering, such as rehearsal and repetitive naming of the information to be learned (ibid.). This has implications on what young children can be expected to remember from one lesson to another, especially if the lessons are a week apart.

Developmentally appropriate practice (DAP) (Copple and Bredekamp 2009) calls for a learning environment reflecting the predictable sequences of growth observed in children, and this applies also to language and literacy development, whether in L1 or L2. Children must be exposed to experiential, interactive and appropriately challenging learning experiences, which should allow plenty of opportunities for play, especially dramatic play, which contributes to children's cognitive (Golinkoff et al. 2006), psycho-social (Berk et al. 2006) and language and literacy development (Christie and Roskos 2006). Play also develops children's communication skills, vocabulary and storytelling skills, and promotes development of attention and concentration. Thus play would have an important place also in the TEVYL classroom and should be considered in materials development for this age group.

In DAP classrooms, children interact physically with people and their environment and engage in hands-on activities, materials and interactions, constructing their new knowledge, which builds on their prior knowledge (Beaty 2009). Needless to say, this goes contrary to the coursebook-driven instructional practice promoted by publishers of TEVYL and some early TEYL materials.

Current contributions and research

Evaluation of materials

Bearing in mind the central role a textbook plays in the classroom, it is surprising that research on the quality of TEYL materials and how they are actually used in the classroom is rather limited. Some research has emerged that reviews and evaluates available TEYL textbooks and other materials. Ellis (2017, p. 216) aptly notes that young learners are not very 'adept at treating language as an object that needs to be studied, analyzed, understood and memorized' and calls for 'plentiful input, interactive input-based tasks and text-creation materials' (ibid.). Citing an internationally marketed course for young learners as an example, he argues that published TEYL materials 'sadly' (ibid.) do not meet the criteria, pointing out that 'text-manipulation work' dominates.

Arnold and Rixon (2008) mention 35 TEYL courses published between 1992 and 2007, and review 16 of them in detail. International textbooks produced by three large international publishers accounted for 19 of the 21 titles intended for international distribution, and of locally targeted books five were also produced by these international publishers. In other words, the pedagogical philosophies of a few major publishers determine the content and approach of the global coursebooks.

Although Arnold and Rixon (op cit., p. 48) note that the coursebook authors' stated rationales for their materials were 'all in line with current YL thinking', they also point out that the materials fell into two main categories: those which promoted 'structural/grammatical' preparation for specific examinations, and those which were more activity based with less focus on 'linguistic content'. They also found the cultural content of the materials to be Western-specific and suggest that 'many teachers' guides rely too much on the written word alone' (ibid., p. 51) rather than guide teachers in the use of available technologies.

Dickinson (2010) examined a primary school course from an international publisher intended for use in Japan. The series adopts a method similar to the traditional present-practise-produce approach and adheres to a controlled grammatical syllabus. Dickinson notes this restricts what students can actually say during the question-and-answer dialogues, which have been a staple in TEYL courses, and as the earlier cited dialogue illustrates. Dickinson (2010, p. 12) also found some of the content 'irrelevant' to learners in his context, a lack of 'diversity of registers', as well as some 'socially inappropriate content' (such as calling someone fat).

At the time of writing, the field of TEVYL is still new, so it is not very surprising that there is little research evaluating materials. Hughes (2014) reviewed courses aimed at children between the ages of three and seven; two for three- to five-year-olds; one for four- to five-year-olds; and first levels of two other primary school courses. She points out that comparing TEVYL courses is complicated because of differences in style, methodology, target market and the clarity of type of approach advocated. She found considerable variety regarding the 'density and complexity of the pages' (ibid., p. 336) in the student books. Yet, her review is positive overall, although she questions the value-based approach in one course aimed at three- to five-year-olds.

Ghosn (2014) reviewed the first level of two series aimed at children ages three to five, one global course and one aimed at the Middle Eastern market. Although themes and topics were fairly age appropriate with some exceptions, some of the activity pages in the regional coursebook were inappropriate in terms of image sizes. For example, some images that children were expected to count were so small that it would be very difficult for a child who still needs to point to the objects to count them. The focus of both courses was on form rather than meaning, and children were expected to produce complete sentences in the very early stages. She found a clear lack of alignment with DAP.

Arnold and Rixon (2008, p. 45) surveyed 76 teachers in 28 countries worldwide for their views on materials they use. The authors note that 'EYL provision is so varied across sectors and cultures that it does not make sense to seek a "typical" use of materials'. According to their questionnaire, the great majority of the teachers responding were happy with their materials, and the authors speculate that this was because they had participated themselves in the selection. The characteristics valued by teachers the most were materials being based on fun and enjoyment, with emphasis on aural/oral language, and promoting interaction. Least-valued characteristics were a heavy emphasis on grammar or vocabulary.

Materials in the classroom

The central role of the textbook in the classroom is well demonstrated in research. Barton (1994, p. 181) has argued that 'much of schooling can be characterized as talk around texts', in a process referred to as 'instructional conversations' by Tharp and Gallimore (1988, p. 11). These comments refer to classroom interactions in general, rather than just language classroom interactions. Typically, the teacher initiates the interaction (often with a question), the student responds and then the teacher evaluates or gives feedback, a sequence that puts 'the teacher in the position of mediator between student and text' (Martin 1999, p. 40).

Although extensive research over the years has examined interactions in the language classroom, much of this research has focused on upper primary levels and above. Less research is found from TEYL classrooms and what teachers and learners do with the available materials, and the research tends to be comparative in nature. Chen-Ying Li and Seedhouse (2010, p. 288) compared interactions around story-based lessons and traditional lessons in Taiwanese primary schools. They found 'more variations of interaction patterns' and 'a lot more pupil initiations, expressing a wide range of language functions' during story lessons than the standard choral drills and task-based activities. During story lessons children talked about the story content and made predictions and engaged in storytelling. Their study resonates with Ghosn's (2001) study in six fifth-grade English classes, where she found more interactive discourse around stories and content area topics than around traditional language practice. In other words, the coursebook activities do play a key role in classroom interactions, and the textbook is in an authority position. Teachers reported they were expected to cover everything in the book, and teachers frequently referred to 'they' (presumably meaning the authors) when initiating an activity in the textbook. Expressions similar to the following were recorded in all six classrooms:

Teacher 6:　They want us to practice conversation here.
Teacher 1:　Let's see what they want us to do here.
Teacher 3:　They always give us problems to solve.
Teacher 2:　They want us to circle the answers here.
(Ghosn 2001, p. 220)

Clearly, the textbook is in control, at least in the case of these four teachers. However, Ghosn (ibid.) found also differences in how interactions around distinctly different lesson activities were realised. While question-answer dialogues produced limited student output, story- and content-based lessons generated richer student output and more negotiated interactions between teachers and students. In the following episode, the teacher is inviting the pupils to discuss Tom Sawyer's fence-painting event using the illustrations as a guide:

Teacher:　Let us listen to Batul's suggestion about the first picture.
Sa:　Tom Sawyer said for her 'oh, you are you are painting'
Teacher:　Painting
Sa:　Painting and I'm and I eating and playing
Teacher:　Yes, I am free, you are busy. I am eating I'm not working free to go whatever where ever I like and you are here to whitewash. We'll see.
Teacher:　Sabine
Sb:　I think I think so that that Tom saw the apple, so he said for his Ben
Teacher:　To his friend, yes
Sb:　Friend Ben that (unintelligible) can you give me the apple and I will let you to to to wash the [several students calling out] Wash wash!
Teacher:　Wait, wait, listen, yes. She is saying something important and the others, shh.
Sb:　and I will let you
Teacher:　Have a turn
Sb:　Have a turn to paint.
Teacher:　To paint. Maybe, maybe. Very good.
(Ghosn 2001, p. 174)

Although children are struggling with the language, they are eagerly participating, and the discourse is more interactive in quality that in the earlier seasonal activity, which had a very drill-like quality.

Little research exists at the time of this writing on how materials are actually used by teachers in the TEVYL classroom with children between the ages of three and six, and what kind of interactions can be observed around the texts. One report from Poland (Szulac-Kurpeska 2007) describes pre-service teachers' attempts to engage five- and six-year-old kindergarten children in English. The teachers found the most successful activities to be those involving a lot of movement, as well as chanting, role play and music, which kept children actively engaged in the lesson. The most difficult aspect according to participants was maintaining children's attention.

Materials and language learning outcomes

The longitudinal Early Language Learning in Europe (ELLiE) study assessed seven- to eight-year-old language learners' achievement over a three-year period (Enever 2011). The ELLiE study did not compare different materials but examined teacher characteristics and out-of-school factors and learner achievement. Perhaps because primary school ELT is a relatively recent practice, little research has been conducted on the relationship between different language teaching materials and learning outcomes. One strand of research has been focusing on storybook reading and language learning.

Reading comprehension

Several experimental studies point to the benefits of storybook reading on development of second language skills, particularly reading, writing and vocabulary. Replication of the 'book floods' cited earlier have produced significant gains in both reading and listening comprehension in Sri Lanka (Kuruppu 2001), Singapore (Ng and Sullivan 2001), South Africa (Schollar 2001; Elley et al. 1996) and Poland (Sadowska-Martyka 2006). All these studies involved hundreds of children and numerous storybooks. Several smaller studies have also produced similar results (e.g., Aranha 1985; Ghosn 2003b). Studies with kindergarten or pre-school aged children have produced similarly positive outcomes (e.g., Eade 1997; Tunnell and Jacobs 1989). Some retrospective studies also support the use of storybooks in TEYL, including Ng (1994), de'Ath (2001), Singh (2001) and Ghosn (2001; 2006; 2010). These studies point to the importance of reading for young language learners, yet very few TEYL coursebooks focus on reading.

Vocabulary acquisition

Vocabulary learning presents a challenge to young second language learners and for their reading development in particular. Word knowledge means many things, as Nation (1990), Cameron (2001) and others have pointed out. Knowing a word implies conceptual knowledge, whether receptive or productive; morphological knowledge which helps determine meanings of inflections and derivational affixes (Nagy and Scott 2000); grammatical knowledge; semantic knowledge because words are interrelated (Nagy and Scott 2000); pragmatic knowledge which helps to know how to use a word correctly in a real world-situation; and phonological knowledge to be able to pronounce a word or to recognise it in spoken and written language. Developing such complex word knowledge is a gradual process happening over time, as children hear, see and use a given word. The more often the target word is encountered, the more likely it is learned (Beck and McKeown 1991; Laufer 2005), and Nation and Wang (1997) suggest that a minimum ten encounters are necessary for likely acquisition. Elley (1997, p. 6) argues that 'much of our vocabulary development is a result of incidental learning from silent reading'. His argument is supported by research of Verhallen and Bus (2010), Ghosn (2010; 2013a) and others.

Writing

Writing is a skill given very little attention in TEYL coursebooks, with tasks consisting mainly of filling in the blanks, compiling lists and composing short messages and letters, and serving merely as an exercise function. Samway (1987, p. 3) argued in the 1980s that even 'the most advanced levels of most ESL texts for elementary grade children present writing in an artificial way'. When Ghosn (2013b) examined four TEYL courses produced between 2000 and 2010 by the largest international publishers, she found writing tasks still very limited. For example, in the highest level of a five-level course, there were a total of 72 lessons but only 20 writing tasks in all, of which ten were letters or poems. Teachers' guides revealed no explicit writing instruction, as if children just somehow pick up the skill on their own. As Graves (1983, p. 43) argues, children need modelling in order to develop as writers so that they would not perceive writing as magic, as if 'we only need to hold the pen and a mysterious force dictates stories, poems, and letters'. This is of particular concern in ESL contexts, where children must develop academic literacy and take written tests. Research suggests that when young language learners write, their writing resembles their instructional texts (e.g., Hudelson 1989; Huie and Yahya 2003; Ghosn 2007, 2012).

Recommendations for practice

In the early 1980s, Tongue (1984, p. 113) proposed alternatives to the then-traditional, tightly controlled language practice typical in primary ELT. He proposed 'content-based extracts', content drawn from local social studies curriculum and 'concentration on games, puzzles, verses, stories, competitions, quizzes and simple dramatisations, together with songs and music, drawing, colouring' as 'particularly suitable perhaps for the first years of primary'. Since then some of his suggestions have found their way to newer TEYL courses.

In the TEVYL classroom, learners should engage with content that is interesting, meaningful and motivating for them, as motivation and interest have a profound influence on learning (Jalongo 2007; Artelt 2005). Meaningful material is learned faster and remembered better than material less meaningful (Anderson 1995; Mayer 1996). Similarly, novel, emotionally relevant or personally significant information gets the learners' attention and gets it processed to the working memory better (Barkley 1996). Ullman (2001) found that when learning L2 syntax, young children employ their procedural memory, which implies they learn grammar by repeated exposure and practice *in context*, not by explicit instruction in rules. This poses a challenge because young foreign language learners are typically exposed to the target language only for short lesson periods, possibly only once or twice a week (Enever 2011). The instructional materials and pedagogical approaches must therefore provide sufficient repeated exposure to target language vocabulary and structures for learning to happen. According to Laufer (2005), several exposures to a word are required for it to be remembered, and according to Nation and Wang (1997) a minimum of ten are required. In the early TEVYL classes, nursery rhymes, songs, physical activities, games, illustrated picture books and big easel books will provide enjoyable repetition of both vocabulary and structures and would also be more developmentally appropriate choices as children are naturally drawn to them. With the rich range of high quality illustrated children's books in English, it will be possible to structure a TEVYL syllabus solely around such books – especially in Big Book format – and nursery rhymes and songs with physical movement (such as *Teddy bear, teddy bear, turn around*, *This is the way we wash our hands*, and *Hokey pokey*). This approach, described in Ghosn (2013b) has proven successful in UNRWA[1] schools catering to Palestinian refugee children in Lebanon since 2011. In brief, developmentally appropriate TEYL and TEVYL materials will provide plenty of opportunities for meaningful, contextualised activities and experiential learning through rhymes, songs, chants and games, as well as interesting content (Cameron 2001; Ghosn 2017; Hughes 2010).

Primary school TEYL materials, although focusing initially on aural/oral language, should gradually incorporate basic reading comprehension strategies, word study and spelling instruction, and modelling of the writing process. The language presented ought to reflect more how people actually use language in daily discourse. One particularly troubling aspect of TEYL courses has been the delay of past tense verbs in the lower levels, which does not reflect language in use. For example, a brief search of the British National Corpus (www.natcorp.ox.ac.uk) yielded 195,306 instances of *said* but only 67,135 of *say*. The absence of the past verb tense also denies children the opportunity to talk about things meaningful to them, such as interesting experiences they had or stories they have heard, which would enable them to 'create their own personal history' in the new language (Escott 1995, p. 20). Although we know that children's L2 development occurs in a sequence, with past-tense forms *emerging* after present, it does not follow that we should not *expose* them to past-tense verb forms early on. A good example is the verb *ate* in Eric Carle's classic *The Very Hungry Caterpillar*, where it appears seven times, while *eat* does not appear at all. Many teachers of young second language learners have observed children effortlessly pick up the word even when they are not familiar with its present tense form. As regards culturally unfamiliar content, it is better introduced gradually, once children have acquired language that allows them to talk about familiar concepts around them. Difficulties may arise when young language learners and their instructional texts inhabit different worlds, as Gregory (1998) and others have shown.

Future directions

Research needs to examine teachers' and learners' perceptions about the materials and how teachers actually use the materials in the classroom, and what kind of discourse the materials generate. There is also a need for longitudinal studies on learning outcomes as regards learners' ability to use the language beyond passing a test. With the apparent rapid spread of TEVYL, it will be very important to assess the longitudinal benefits of the practice, and to ensure, through DAP, that all children can succeed and nobody is left behind because of TEVYL.

Authors of TEVYL materials should break away from the coursebook model and take into consideration the developmental needs of very young language learners. In TEVYL teacher handbooks with rhymes, songs and games, possibly with accompanying Big Books, would be more aligned with DAP than a traditional coursebook.

Further reading

1 Cameron, L. (2001). *Teaching languages to young learners*. Cambridge: Cambridge University Press.

This book provides a theoretical framework for how children learn languages in the classroom and practical suggestions on how to structure lessons.

2 Ghosn, I.-K. (2013). *Storybridge to second language literacy. The theory, research and practice of teaching English with children's literature*. Charlotte, NC: Information Age Publishing.

This volume outlines the theoretical benefits of children's literature for L2 language learning, presents an overview of research studies from around the world to support the theory, and provides classroom vignettes of actual classrooms.

3 Tomlinson, B. (Ed.). (2016). *SLA research and materials development for language teaching*. New York: Routledge.

An important book that focuses on the interaction between second language acquisition (SLA) and materials development. Chapters comprise position statements, SLA theory driven materials, materials evaluation and recommendations for action.

Related topics

Motivation, technology in the classroom, mobile learning, syllabus, differentiation

Note

1 The United Nations Relief and Works Agency for Palestine Refugees in the Near East.

References

Arnold, W., and Rixon, S. (2008). Materials for teaching English to young learners. In Tomlinson, B. (ed.) *English Language Teaching Materials: A critical review*. London: Bloomsbury, 38–58.

Artelt, C. (2005). Cross-cultural approaches to measuring motivation. *Educational Assessment*, 10(3), 231–255.

Barton, D. (1994). *Literacy: An introduction to the ecology of written language*. Oxford: Blackwell.

Beaty, J. (2009). *Preschool Appropriate Practices*. New York: Cengage Learning.

Berk, L., Mann, T. D., and Ogan, A. T. (2006). Make-believe play: Wellspring for development of self-regulation. In Golinkoff, R. M., and Hirsch-Pasek, K. (eds.) *Play=Learning: How play motivates and enhances children's cognitive and social-emotional growth*. New York: Oxford University Press, 74–100.

Cameron, L. (2003). Challenge for ELT from the expansion in teaching children. *ELT Journal*, 57(2), 105–112.

Cameron, L. (2001). *Teaching Language to Young Learners*. Cambridge: Cambridge University Press.

Chen-Ying Li, and Seedhouse, P. (2010). Classroom interaction in story-based lessons with young learners. *The Asian EFL Journal*, 12(2), 288–312.

Christie, J., and Roskos, K. (2006). Standards, science, and the role of play in in early literacy education. In Singer, D., Golinkoff, R., and Hirsch-Pasek, K. (eds.) *Play=learning: How play motivates and enhances children's cognitive and social-emotional growth*. New York: Oxford University Press, 57–73.

Copple, C., and Bredekamp, S. (2009). *Developmentally Appropriate Practice in Early Childhood Programs: Serving children from birth through age 8*. 3rd ed. Washington, DC: NAEYC.

Dickinson, P. (2010). *Evaluating and Adapting Materials For Young Learners*. Thesis (MA). University of Birmingham.

Elley, W. (2000). The potential of book floods for raising literacy levels. *International Review of Education*, 46(3/4), 233–255.

Elley, W., and Mangubhai, F. (1983). The impact of reading on second language learning. *Reading Research Quarterly*, 14(1), 53–67.

Ellis, R. (2008). Principles of instructed second language acquisition. *CAL Digest*. www.cal.org/resources/digest/instructed2ndlang.html [Accessed 25 April 2016].

Ellis, R. (2017). Language teaching materials as work plans. In Tomlinson, B. (ed.) *SLA Research and Materials Development for Language Learning*. New York: Routledge, 203–218.

Enever, J. (2011). Policy. In Enever, J. (ed.) *ELLiE: Early language learning in Europe*. London: The British Council, 23–41.

Escott, C. (1995). Bridging the gap: Making links between children's reading and writing. In Bearne, E. (ed.) *Greater Expectations: Children reading writing*. London: Cassell, 18–24.

Garton, S., Copeland, E., and Burns, A. (2011). Investigating global practices in teaching English to young learners. *ELT Research Papers* 11–01, London: The British Council.

Ghosn, I.-K. (2001). *Teachers and Children Interacting Around the Textbook: An exploratory study of children developing academic second language literacy in primary school English language classes in Lebanon*. Thesis (PhD). University of Leicester (UMI No. 3049590).

Ghosn, I.-K. (2004). Story as culturally appropriate content and social context for young English language learners: A look at Lebanese primary schools. *Language, Culture and Curriculum*, 17(2), 109–126.

Ghosn, I.-K. (2014). Teaching the very young learners: An alternative to kindergarten textbooks. In Enever, J., Lindgren, E. and Ivanov, S. (eds.) *Early Language Learning: Theory and practice, 2014*. Sweden: Umeå University, 57–63.

Ghosn, I.-K. (2013a) *Storybridge to Second Language and Literacy: The theory, research and practice of teaching English with children's literature*. Charlotte, NC: Information Age Publishing.

Ghosn, I.-K. (2013b) Developing motivating materials for refugee children: From theory to practice. In Tomlinson, B. (ed.) *Developing Materials for Language Teaching* (2nd. revised edn.), London: Bloomsbury, 247–265.

Ghosn, I.-K. (2017). No place for a coursebooks in the very young learner classroom. In Tomlinson, B. (ed.) *SLA Research and Materials Development for Language Acquisition*. New York: Routledge, 50–66.

Golinkoff, R. M., Hirsch-Pasek, K., and Singer, D. G. (2006). Why play = learning: A challenge for parents and educators. In Golinkoff, R. M., and Hirsch-Patek, K. (eds.) *Play=Learning: How play motivates and enhances children's cognitive and social-emotional Growth*, New York: Oxford University Press, 3–12.

Graham, C. (1978). *Jazz Chants for Children*. New York: Oxford University.

Graves, D. (1983). *Writing: Teachers and children at work*. Portsmouth, NH.: Heinemann.

Halliwell, S. (2006). *Teaching English in a Primary Classroom*. Harlow: Pearson Education.

Harmer, J. (2001). *The Practice of English Language Teaching*. Harlow: Pearson Education.

Howatt, A. P. R. (1984). Teaching languages to young learners: Patterns of history. In Brumfit, C., Moon, J., and Tongue, R. (eds.) *Teaching English to Children: From practice to principle*. Harlow: Addison Wesley Longman, 289–301.

Howatt, A. P. R. (1997). *A History of English Language Teaching*. London: Oxford University Press.

Hughes, A. (2010). Why should we make activities for young language learners meaningful and purposeful? In Mishan, F., and Chambers, A. (eds.) *Perspectives on Language Learning Materials Development*. Bern: Peter Lang, 175–200.

Hughes, A. (2014). Five courses for 3–6/7-year-old learners of British English as a foreign language. *ELT Journal*, 68(3), 330–344.

Jalongo, M. (2007). Beyon benchmarks and scores: Reasserting the role of motivation and interest in children's academic achievement: An ACEI position paper. *Childhood Education, International Focus Issue* 395–407.

Kail, R. (2010). *Children and their Development*, 5th ed. Upper Saddle River, NJ: Pearson Prentice Hall.

Laufer, B. (2005). Instructed second language vocabulary learning: The fault in the "Default Hypothesis". In Hausen, A., and Pierrard, M. (eds.) *Investigations in Instructed Second Language Acquisition*. New York: Mouton de Gruyter, 311–332.

Nation, P., and Wang, R. (1997). Vocabulary size, text coverage, and word lists. In Schmitt, N., and McCarthy, M. (eds.) *Vocabulary: Description, acquisition, and pedagogy*. Cambridge: Cambridge University Press, 6–19.

Palmer, H. (1971). *Songbook: Learning basic skills through music*. Freeport, NY: Educational Activities.

Random House Book of Poetry for Children (1983). New York: Random House.

Richard-Amato, P. (1988). *Making It Happen*. New York: Longman.

Rixon, S. (2013). *British Council Survey of Policy and Practice in Primary English Language Teaching Worldwide*. London: The British Council.

Rixon, S. (2009). Supporting innovation and best practice in EYL: The role of publishing. In Enever, J., Moon, J., and Raman, U. (eds.) *Young Learner English Language Policy and Implementation: International perspectives*. Reading: Garnet Education, 211–214.

Sheldon, L. (1988). ELT textbook and materials evaluation: goals, obstacles and solutions. *ELT Journal*, 42(2/3), 237–246.

Smith, R. C. (n/d) *Michael West's life and career*. www.2warwick.ac.uk/fac/ soc/al/ research/collections/ elt_archive/halloffame/west/life [Accessed 1 August 2017]

Szulac-Kurpeska, M. (2007). Teaching and reaching very young learners: "They are unpredictable". In Nikolov, M., Mihaljevic, J., Mattheoudakis, M., Lundberg, G. and Flanaga, T. (eds.) *The TeMoLaYoLe Book: Teaching modern languages to young learners: Teachers, curricula and materials*. Graz, Austria: European Center for Modern Languages/Council of Europe, 35–46.

Tharp, R., and Gallimore, R. (1988). *Rousing Minds to Life: Teaching, learning, and schooling in social context*. Cambridge: Cambridge University Press.

Tickoo, M. L. (1988). Michael West in India: A centenary salute. *ELT Journal*, 42(4), 294–300.

Watt, D., and Foscolos, D. (1998). Evaluating ESL software for the inclusive classroom. *International Electronic Journal for Leadership in Learning*, 2 (6). www.ucal.ca/~ieljj/volume2/Watt_6.html [Accessed 10 March 2012]

Wright, A. (1995). *Storytelling with Children*. Oxford: Oxford University Press.

Wright, A., Beteridge, D., and Buckley, M. (1984). *Games for Language Learning*. Cambridge: Cambridge University Press.

Coursebooks mentioned

Ashworth, J., and Clark, J. (1990). *Stepping Stones*. Addison Wesley Longman.

Ashworth, J., and Clark, J. (1997). *New Stepping Stones*. Addison Wesley Longman.

Dallas, D., and Iggulden, M. (1990). *Let's Learn English*. Longman.

Eisele, B., Yang Eisele, C., York Hanlon, R., Hanlon, S., and Hojel, B. (2004). *Hip Hip Hooray!* White Pearson Education.

Ellis, P., and Bowen, M. (1998). *Way Ahead*. MacMillan.

Hanlon, R., and Kimball, J. (2008). *Tops*. Pearson Education.

Herrera, M., and Hojel, B. (2009). *Pockets*. Pearson Education.

Herrera, M., and Hojel, B. (2009). *Little Pockets*. Pearson Education.

Herrera, M., and Pinkley, D. (2005). *Backpack*. Pearson Education.

Herrera, M., and Zanatta, T. (1996). *Scott Foresman*.

Herrera, M., and Zanatta, T. (2000). *New Parade*. Addison Wesley Longman.

Holt, R. (1999). *Blue Skies*. Addison Wesley Longman

Walker, M. (1989). *Amazing English*. Addison Wesley.

Walker, M. (1989). *ESL*. Addison Wesley.

Walker, M. (1989). *Kids*. Addison Wesley.

Webster, D., and Worrall, A. (1992). *English Together*. Addison Wesley Longman.

24

Assessment of young English language learners

Szilvia Papp

Introduction and definitions

Assessment of young learners' English as a second or foreign language has 'come of age' and matured into a field of enquiry with its own identity and integrity (Rixon 2016). It has its own questions, concerns and methodologies relevant to a wide range of highly involved stakeholders: ministries of education, assessment providers, publishers, school leaders, teacher trainers, teachers, parents and students.

The field has moved on from an assessment of general language proficiency to include the assessment of the language of schooling (academic English) and the integrated assessment of content and language learning (Bailey and Huang 2011; Inbar-Lourie and Shohamy 2009; Nikolov 2016). Several approaches and methods populate the field, reflecting variation in constructs and their measurement. What type of assessment is most effective and beneficial for young learners depends on their age, context of instruction, amount and type of exposure to English, purpose of assessment and use of results.

This chapter reviews some of the current research on instruments used in classroom assessment and large-scale national and international tests of English developed for young learners. Knowledge about alternative approaches to assessing young learners' English language competence may help stakeholders (parents, teachers, policy makers) make informed decisions on what assessment is appropriate in their context for the young people in their charge and how to use results generated by such assessments to make sound decisions.

Who are young learners of English?

The label 'young English language learners' has been used mainly for primary/elementary school age children who learn English as a second or foreign language. However, it sometimes encompasses adolescents in lower secondary/middle school contexts, as well as very young learners in early years or kindergarten settings. As a result, the age range designated by the label of 'young learners' may vary between three and 16. Within this wide age range, there are milestones in cognitive, linguistic, social and emotional development, which stages of schooling tend to recognise and build on. However, large variations in educational systems exist in terms of start of compulsory schooling and start and nature of English language instruction. Even wider differences exist among stakeholders' views on whether and how young learners' English language development should be assessed. In this chapter, we take the widest definition of 'younger learners' (within the range of 3–16 years of age) and will bring examples of assessment from pre-school, primary and lower secondary school contexts.

What is assessment?

Educational assessment is used to identify levels of ability within a target population in a particular learning domain such as English language competence in order to distinguish between strong and weak performance. Masters (2014) argues that there is only one purpose of assessment: to find out individual learners' current standing in a learning domain. However, the results may be put to various use, such as readiness checking, diagnosis, screening, placement, selection or certification. The ultimate aim in generating assessment information is to answer important and well-articulated questions about young learners' English language learning in order to make sound educational decisions. Assessment thus involves gathering and analysing evidence to make valid inferences about learning and teaching. Importantly, the evidence collected is always a sample of all the information that could be collected, and decision making will need to take this into account. Typical questions for which assessment data is used include:

- Which learner is ready to proceed, which needs help/support and which needs additional challenge?
- What are the levels of progression on the learning ladder?
- What are achievable targets for young learners in various contexts?
- What is the minimum standard for a particular purpose, such as learning content (maths, science, history, geography) through the medium of English?
- What are the skills profiles of young learners?
- Where are the achievement gaps?
- What does each learner/class/school/region/country need in terms of appropriate next steps?
- How does this assessment predict future achievement (e.g., performance in further assessments or in future study)?
- Which school needs improvement? Which one needs additional challenge to excel further?
- What are the conditions of success as demonstrated by best practice in learning and teaching?

Assessment data at the individual level is used to find out about readiness to learn or proceed, current achievement, rate of progress or potential future performance of individual children. At group level, assessment data is sometimes used for establishing a baseline to develop a new strategy or for benchmarking against an external (national or international) standard. Historical assessment data is used for information on learning gains, growth and trends over time.

A traditional dichotomy is usually made between internal versus external assessment in terms of purposes and use of results. It is usually assumed that classroom assessment is carried out by teachers to make sound pedagogical decisions, while large-scale tests are usually used for policy decisions such as accountability or gatekeeping purposes. Whether internal or external, the differences in the intended use of assessment results will have implications for reporting: whether diagnostic feedback on strengths and weaknesses at the task/skill level is reported or information on overall proficiency is provided. Assessment results can be used to monitor progress, plan future action or predict future performance of individuals and groups (usually referred to as formative use of assessment data) or evaluate the effectiveness of teaching and learning in programmes by individual learners, teachers, classes, schools, regions or nations (usually termed summative use of assessment data).

It follows that assessment design and reporting will vary according to whether the intended use has more formative and developmental aspects that require a domain, skill or task-centred interpretation with domain-, skill- or task-specific criteria (achievement) or whether the intended use is a construct-centred summative interpretation in terms of generic criteria and standards (communicative competence or proficiency). Reporting should match the purpose of the use of assessment results (e.g., readiness checking, diagnosis, screening, placement, monitoring progress, selection, certification) (Moss 2015).

In interpreting the results, the frame of reference can be the performance of other students of the same age, in the same class or other classes, schools, regions or nations (norm referencing). Alternatively, the frame of reference can be external standards, benchmarking frameworks or curriculum expectations specifying certain learning outcomes in terms of target knowledge, skills and abilities (criterion referencing) or the student themselves in their earlier performance (ipsative referencing). Whether the purpose of using the results is instructional, evaluative or predictive, the overarching aim of all assessment should be to improve learning outcomes by increasing student motivation and to ensure positive impact. It follows that the stakes of all assessment with young people are always very high.

Teachers use a variety of information (e.g., observation of learner classroom performance, periodic teacher-made or textbook tests at the end of unit of learning, term or year, portfolio of classwork, homework) to monitor students' progress in English language learning. Once recorded, these informal assessments can be used to check if a set of learning outcomes have been achieved and to provide feedback to inform subsequent teaching and learning. Teacher-based assessment is also used in some national curriculum testing regimes for summative purposes, such as in the UK. In large-scale international tests, trained examiners assess the performance of candidates against specific criteria and standards. Learning aims and assessment criteria can also be used for self- and peer-assessment for formative purposes.

Historical perspectives

In the last 60 years or so, a wide variation in instructional contexts and educational purposes have emerged in response to different English language learner needs that require a range of approaches to teaching and assessment. Learning objectives and assessment outcomes depend on the role English language plays in instruction: whether English is used as a vehicle for learning other subjects, as in full immersion, in various types of bilingual/trilingual schooling or in content and language integrated learning (CLIL); or whether English is a subject to be learnt as in traditional modern foreign language classes (Bailey and Huang 2011, Bailey et al. 2014, Inbar-Lourie and Shohamy 2009, Murphy 2014). In the following we discuss assessment instruments used in contexts where students learn English as a foreign language and also contexts where learners receive all or part of their education in English.

Assessment in English as foreign language (EFL) contexts

While national tests of general English language proficiency have existed for a long time as secondary school leaving exams, large-scale international assessments for younger English language learners have appeared only in the last 35 years.

Pearson's Test of English Young Learners formerly known as London Test of English for Children has been in existence since 1982. The Cambridge English Young Learners tests were launched in 1997, the for Schools version of Cambridge Key and Preliminary was introduced in 2009 and Cambridge First for Schools followed in 2011. The Pearson and Cambridge tests measure general English language competence. Both Pearson and Cambridge tests have explicit exam syllabuses specifying what vocabulary and grammatical structures learners need to have mastered for successful achievement.

In the USA, Educational Testing Service (ETS) developed TOEFL Junior in 2011 and TOEFL Primary in 2012 to expand their family of assessments. With no clearly specified exam syllabus, TOEFL Primary provides 'information about the English proficiency of young English learners in countries where English is not typically used in daily life' (ETS 2015a, 2015b). On the other hand, TOEFL Junior measures English language proficiency needed in English language instructional contexts (So et al. 2015), which is reflected in the construct and content of the tests. Existing international tests for under six-year-olds are Trinity Stars and Anglia's First Step.

In these assessments, children's oral skills are assessed face-to-face (individually, in pairs of groups) with an examiner (or two) and using traditional paper-and-pencil tests for listening, reading and writing. Alternatively, there are computer-based versions, such as those for all Cambridge English exams for children and teenagers, the Oxford Young Learners Placement Test or British Council's Aptis for Teens. The mode of delivery will define the construct and inevitably have a backwash effect on teaching. In these tests, the stakes vary at different levels, with the pedagogical motivational purpose at the lower levels overtaken by arguably higher stakes of certification at higher levels.

Tests for young learners tend to measure the four skills of listening, speaking, reading and writing and contain items and task types (closed/selected and open/constructed response items) similar to tests developed for adults. Well-designed restricted response items (multiple choice questions, short answer questions, matching) can measure knowledge at word and phrase levels but also some higher order skills at sentence, text and discourse levels. Their use in assessments is not out of line with modern theories of learning, as there is a place for logical reasoning, use of analogy and elimination and even informed guessing from context in current cognitive psychological theories. Single best answer questions used in medical education are an example of how well-constructed MCQs can measure higher order thinking skills such as problem solving and application of knowledge. However, authentic direct tests of performance have the highest fidelity to the real world and therefore greater relevance to learners' lives. The respective weighting of restricted and constructed response items in a test for young learners should be dictated by the purposes for which test results are used.

Assessment in English as a second language/ content-based instruction

In English as a second language (ESL) contexts (e.g., USA, Australia, Canada), assessment of English language competence is part of the national standards-based educational system. In these contexts, minimum standards are specified in English language development/

proficiency frameworks of competences (e.g., WIDA 2012, McKay et al. 2007). In the USA, assessment of both content knowledge and language development is carried out in substantive ways. Schools are held accountable for reaching the minimum standards; therefore assessments are subjected to close scrutiny (Bailey and Carroll 2015). Typically, in these frameworks, the learning domain is mapped and progression is charted using a learning ladder. The WIDA framework integrates age/level of schooling with language and academic content in core subject areas (maths, science, social studies and language arts). These standards help teachers understand and assess the required academic language skills for each core subject at each level of the curriculum. If such a map is based on empirically validated developmental sequences and learning trajectories, it can chart out critical paths for high achievers. In the UK, the document linked to the previous National Curriculum entitled 'National Curriculum 2000 A Language in Common: Assessing English as an Additional Language' (QCA 2000) dealt with the four skills but not the academic language requirements in primary and secondary schools. A national framework to be used with EAL learners in the UK has recently been developed (Evans, Jones et al. 2016a) to more accurately assess the needs of English language learners and guide their teaching in both language and content areas (Arnot et al. 2014, Evans et al. 2016b).

Assessment in content and language integrated learning (CLIL)

Content and language integrated instruction (CLIL) is an increasingly popular methodology within Europe and beyond, typically at primary and secondary levels, where the L2, usually English, apart from being a target language to be learnt as a school subject, is also used as a vehicle to deliver content knowledge and target domain-specific skills. CLIL describes any learning activity where an additional second or foreign language is used as a tool to develop new learning in a subject area or theme. CLIL can range from total immersion to a single subject or topic taught in the L2. It may help maintain motivation of children who start learning English as foreign language at a young age (Nikolov 2016). CLIL theory has clear links with general education theory and modern cognitive and assessment theories (e.g., reference to lower/higher order thinking skills, balancing of cognitive challenge with linguistic support, differentiation in assessment and continuous assessment as integral part of instruction providing feedback to inform subsequent teaching and learning). However, true integration of language and content is still rare and remains a major issue in both instruction and assessment (Massler et al. 2014). It is recognised that assessment is fundamental to the success of CLIL. However, how teachers assess progress and attainment in CLIL is still something of a 'blind spot' (Massler et al. 2014, p. 137). This is due to lack of clear policy decisions on assessment in CLIL and the scarcity of assessment tools. Successful CLIL implementation calls for continuity across school levels; thus coherent assessment principles and procedures are needed that bridge educational stages (Stotz and Megías 2010). Llinares et al. (2012, p. 280) point out that to be useful and beneficial, assessment has to be an integral and indispensable part of instruction that should be planned before any teaching takes place.

In CLIL, especially at the beginning stages and at lower levels of language and academic proficiency, short-term learning goals should be set and assessed to build student confidence. It is necessary to design a variety of cognitively appropriate instructional tasks with clear assessment criteria for their achievement: challenging but not too frustrating for the learners, graded in terms of difficulty. Individual feedback needs to be provided on whether the student has achieved the outcomes or not.

Also, in CLIL, a range and variety of assessment tools is recommended. This should give the students greater confidence and provide more reliable data, because it can measure individual progress and check a wider range of competences and desirable learning outcomes. A range of assessment tools can consist, among others, of graded mini-assessments of each building block for each learning outcome, visual representations of students' understanding of content (tables, graphs, visual organisers), self- and peer-correction, self- and peer-assessment and portfolios. If feedback is provided on all these, assessment can usefully guide learning of both content and language. It is very important that the scores on each of these assessments are not averaged to derive a final score, as that would break all the principles of formative developmental assessment. A student's final assessment could be based on their progression in tackling similar content and tasks aimed at one learning goal or closely related set of leaning goals, and their ability to take feedback on board, reflecting their final achievement of the learning objectives.

Surveys

With this wide array of instructional contexts and purposes, a number of questionnaires and empirical surveys have been initiated to find out the state of play in young learners' language assessment worldwide. Early on, Rea-Dickins and Rixon (1999) found that primary teachers used internal assessment by way of paper-and-pencil tests in spite of the universal declaration that speaking and listening were teaching priorities. The focus on written assessment in primary schools mirrored the tradition in secondary schools where instruction and assessment has traditionally emphasised formal language study and reading and writing skills. Performance assessment of communicative language ability has been a recent addition in a lot of assessment regimes (Rixon 2013).

Since the advent of standards-based assessment, many countries have set explicit target attainment levels for the end of primary and secondary schooling. Selecting or developing instruments to assess whether targets have been reached has been the focus of intense effort in many countries with widely differing assessment cultures ranging from a largely egalitarian view (e.g., Norway, Carlssen 2008) to much more competitive examination-focused cultures (e.g., Butler and Lee 2010; Carless and Lam 2014). Some South American and European countries have developed their own national EFL examinations for young learners (e.g., in Uruguay, Fleurquin 2003; Norway, Hasselgreen 2005b; Germany, Rupp et al. 2008; Slovenia, Pizorn 2009; Switzerland, Haenni Hoti et al. 2009; Hungary, Nikolov and Szabo 2012; Poland, Szpotowicz and Campfield 2016).

Recently, two large scale empirical surveys have been carried out on attainment levels at the end of primary and secondary schooling in Europe (Enever 2011, European Commission 2012). These studies combine assessment results with questionnaire data in order to identify variables that contribute to high attainment in foreign language learning.

Critical issues and topics

Ethics

As the review above indicates, young English language learners have become the focus of intense attention, and the stakes in assessing them have become higher. Therefore, ethical considerations should be at the forefront of all assessment activity involving young learners. Ethics of assessment is a branch of philosophy dealing with issues of right and wrong decisions and actions; it is a synonym for morality. Codes of conduct offer ethical guidelines about professional responsibilities and accountabilities (e.g., BERA 2011). Assessment should only be carried out to do good and for the benefit of learners, not for surveillance or the exercise of power that may harm young learners either directly or indirectly through their effect on teachers, schools, curriculum, educational systems or society. When conducting research with or assessment on children, children's rights must be observed (United Nations 1989). Criteria to evaluate the ethics of assessments for young learners include (a) whether assessment is in the children's best interests, (b) whether it is universal in that it allows equal opportunities to learning and access to assessment, (c) whether it attends to matters of diversity and individual difference and (d) whether it allows children's voices to be heard (Elwood 2013, Pinter 2011, 2014).

Desirable test qualities

One of the major responsibilities of assessment providers is to make sure tests for young learners have desirable test qualities, validity, positive impact, reliability.

Validity

Based on a review of the literature on validity, including the work of scholars (e.g., Messick 1989, Frederiksen and Collins 1989, Kane 2013), the *Standards for Psychological and Educational Testing* (AERA et al. 2014) and documents developed by assessment providers (e.g., Cambridge English 2013, SQA 2015), an assessment can be said to be valid when it fits the following criteria:

- Is appropriate for its purpose.
- Is a catalyst for curricular, instructional change and improves learning.
- Allows candidates to show that they have the required knowledge, understanding and skills to demonstrate the assessment outcomes, assessment standards or performance criteria.
- Allows all assessors to make reliable assessment decisions.
- Allows the interpretation and inferences which can be drawn from the scores/grades to be meaningful, useful, appropriate and justifiable.

A valid use of an assessment or its outcomes is when decisions made are sound and follow-up actions are justified, closely linked to the original intended purpose and supported by the results.

Impact

Impact of an assessment on learners can be gauged by investigating fitness for purpose, e.g., how well it motivates learners to learn English and/or how well it prepares them for the next level of study. Motivation is a central critical issue in the reporting of results in young learners' assessment, as children and adolescents tend to suffer from test anxiety and may get demotivated by assessment results. Tests can have devastatingly negative impact on learning and young learners' future prospects (Carreira 2012, Kim and Seo 2012). It is very important that assessments do not alienate them from taking tests in the future and ultimately from learning English.

In addition, assessments, when misused or abused, can have negative effects on teachers, educational systems and society. Two recent large-scale global surveys carried out by Cambridge English (Papp et al. 2011, Papp and McElwee 2015) found that there is uncertainty, concern, fear or even distrust of tests developed for young learners among some stakeholders. Those who oppose testing young learners warn of the danger of over-testing children. Some are concerned that increasing standards of achievement may be demanded of young learners, which will entail more pressure in terms of competition that might generate a fear of failure, especially among the weaker learners. There is a distrust of large-scale testing as, if used for accountability purposes, it may foster test-orientedness (teaching to the test) among teachers, which might be linked with a loss of enjoyment and interest in teaching and learning. Some test users fear that results may not reflect the true ability of learners. Some see a risk that standards might ultimately be lowered as a result of a focus on accountability. Diagnostic testing is felt to be more appropriate in order to cater to young learners' individual needs and for the provision of feedback to improve learning and teaching among them. Assessment providers should be committed to carrying out ongoing research on the consequences of using assessments in young learners' education.

Reliability

Reliability relates to how much confidence users of tests can have in the results, in terms of the accuracy of test scores or consistency of classification.

It is commonly believed that with the fundamental requirement to be motivational, young learners' tests may not be psychometrically optimal (Jones 2002). Lower reliability may be due to the high facility of these tests, which means that they are designed so that most candidates can answer most items correctly, resulting in a skewed distribution. In addition, data generated by young learners may not be reliable as children are easily distracted and affected by physical and mental variations. It is very easy to get children to fail items by using the wrong assessment type or method in research or assessment. For instance, young learners may not be familiar with the content of the test, choose responses for idiosyncratic reasons or may be confused by test instructions. This is another reason why it is good practice to collect data from young learners at several different occasions and in several different ways from several sources. It is imperative that assessment of young learners' performance does not punish unexpected but clearly ingenious responses because that will stifle children's creativity (Cameron and McKay 2010). This principle should be reflected in scoring and assessment criteria.

Studies containing technical qualities or measurement properties of tests developed for young learners are rare. The same applies for many national tests designed for primary and secondary school aged learners. Even less information is available on teacher-made and textbook tests.

Current contributions and research

Alignment with external frameworks, benchmarks and standards

International standards such as the Common European Framework of Reference (CEFR, Council of Europe 2001) offer a way to set attainment targets and establish and compare standards among various assessment instruments. The CEFR's positive 'can do' approach is well suited to the principles of assessment of young learners. International tests aligned with external frameworks such as the CEFR can be used as an aid to increase standardisation of learning and teaching, which may lead to improved teaching and higher levels of proficiency.

Major international large-scale tests of English for young learners, such as Cambridge English Young Learners and for Schools exams, Pearson Test of English Young Learners, TOEFL Primary and Junior, Oxford Young Learners Placement Test and British Council APTIS for Teens, all claim alignment to the CEFR levels, with some reporting formal alignment procedures (Papp and Salamoura 2009, Baron and Papageorgiou 2014). However, until the CEFR is adapted with young learners' needs and development in mind, all such linkage is tentative (Hasselgreen 2005a, McKay 2006, Papp and Salamoura 2009, Enever 2011). Nevertheless, in most countries, CEFR A1 and A2 levels have been set as a target of primary schooling (Rixon 2013). One of the authors of the CEFR, John Trim, has stated that in EFL settings in Europe:

'As a very rough guide,

- A1 (Breakthrough) is appropriate to progress in the first foreign language at the 10 or 11 year primary/secondary interface,
- A2 (Waystage) to around 14,
- B1 (Threshold) to 16+, the lower secondary goal,
- B2 (Vantage) to 18+, the completion of upper secondary education, and
- C1 and C2 to specialist university level'. (Trim 2005, p. 4)

In the face of the diversity inherent in international language learning, Jones and Saville (2009, p. 37) have argued, 'our default expectation must be that different countries' interpretations will be culturally determined (in a broad sense) and therefore may differ'. Indeed, Trim (2001/2009, p. 6) recalls how, when working on the Breakthrough/CEFR A1 specifications with groups of educators from a range of European countries, 'it became clear from different specimen descriptions that very different interpretations of words like "simple", "basic", "familiar", etc. were possible'.

How far young learners can progress in L2 proficiency due to linguistic, cognitive, emotional, social and literacy development was investigated by Hasselgreen and Caudwell (2016) for the British Council. In their analysis, the highest potential levels attainable by different age groups are as shown in Table 24.1. These represent much more ambitious targets than Trim's estimates above.

It is important to note that both of these sets of targets were not based on empirical research on young learners' language development in specific contexts. As Trim argued, '*I say a rough guide since the speed of learning depends greatly on such factors as the learner's age and aptitude, the curricular time available, extra-curricular contact, the relation of*

Table 24.1 Target CEFR attainment levels for different age groups (Hasselgreen and Caudwell 2016, p. 34)

Age groups	Typical limits of CEFR levels potentially attainable
Young children (roughly between 5/6 years and 8/9 years)	A2
Older children (roughly between 8/9 years and 12/13 years)	B1
Teenagers (roughly between 13 and 17 years)	B2
Exceptional older teenagers	C1

Table 24.2 Cambridge English guidance on learning hours

CEFR Level	Cambridge English Exam	Number of Hours (approximate)
C2	*Cambridge English: Proficiency (CPE)*	1,000–1,200
C1	*Cambridge English: Advanced (CAE)*	700–800
B2	*Cambridge English: First (FCE)*	500–600
B1	*Cambridge English: Preliminary (PET)*	350–400
A2	*Cambridge English: Key (KET)*	180–200

L1 to L2, etc.' Trim (2005, p. 4). How long it takes to go from one level to the next depends on the factors pointed out by Trim as well as the intensity and quality of instruction, learner motivation, etc. However, a very general rule of thumb is that 180 hours are required to move within the A levels, 200 hours at B levels and 220+ at C levels (see Table 24.2).

Little (2007) pointed out that above the B-levels the CEFR attainment levels are probably not achievable for learners below the age of 16, as they require high levels of educational experience with the associated tasks that most young learners have not had exposure to. There is consensus that learners below 16 lack cognitive and social maturity that the tasks in the C-levels require (Hasselgreen and Caudwell 2016, Goodier and Szabo 2017).

The Finnish National Certificates of Language Proficiency (2011) uses the CEFR to identify targets for English and Finnish and Swedish as L2. The proficiency scale in the Finnish framework uses the levels of the CEFR and targets are set for both English and national languages. For instance, the University of Helsinki website states

> the foreign language requirement for a lower university degree is B2 in English/B1 in other languages. The minimum requirement for Finnish/Swedish as a second national language is B1.

Härmälä et al. (2015) found:

- Students at the age of 12/13 are required to have a minimum level of language competence mirroring B1 in all skills in order to succeed in history/mathematics.
- 15/16-year-old students need a B2 competence in the same skills/subjects.

These ambitious but realistic targets are corroborated by assessments created for L2 learners who live and learn in an environment where English is spoken. Cambridge Lower Secondary English as L2 by Cambridge International Examinations (CIE) specifies high B1/low B2 targets for 11–14 year-olds. Shaw and Imam (2013) also suggest that CEFR B2 represents a critical level for 16-year-old learners who are assessed through the medium of English in subjects such as history. They found that linguistic range and accuracy at B2 level are essential, but some C1-level skills provide added advantage. Especially influential are the written cognitive-academic skills (e.g., Thematic Development, Propositional Precision, Coherence and Cohesion, Overall Written Production, Text Processing). However, Goodier and Szabo (2017, p. 16) point out that written skills in a foreign language environment need specific support:

> The treatment of descriptors relating to written reception, production and integrated skills therefore should take a 'bias for best' approach, assuming what is reasonable/possible for the age range given optimum literacy support.

Various sets of level descriptors have been collected by assessment boards, either reflecting typical or likely performance of candidates at a target level (Papp 2009), from teachers (Pearson Education 2015, Benigno and de Jong 2016) or based on specific exam content (So et al. 2015). Each of these sets of can-do statements are context specific in the way they were developed and validated. With the extended set of descriptors for young learners (aged 7–10 and 11–15) collated by the Council of Europe (Goodier and Szabo 2017), it is now easier and more meaningful to align young learners assessments with the CEFR and set attainment targets more directly relevant for each age group.

Accountability

Assessment of young learners is increasingly used as a policy instrument for accountability purposes or to evaluate educational reform. One such use of assessment is to establish a baseline against which achievable targets can be set, growth can be measured and evaluated and standards maintained. For plans on introducing such a baseline assessment in the UK among four- and five-year-old children, see Bradbury and Roberts-Holmes (2016). It is clear from the reaction to these plans, that to be useful and beneficial, young learners' assessments must be very well conceived and should not be used as surveillance, judgement or to exert power. Their use should be with the express aim to bring about improvement in learning. It should be ensured through reporting, use of results, decision making and follow-up action that the effect of assessment is transformational, productive and empowering (Earl 1999, Klenowski and Wyatt-Smith 2014). Assessment providers have a moral obligation to work toward this aim.

Examination boards are responding to calls for transparency and accountability. For instance, Cambridge English is about to publish an account of the Cambridge approach to assessing young learners aged between six and 16 within the school contexts (Papp, and Rixon Field forthcoming). The volume, within the Studies in Language Testing series, will set out the theoretical foundations, language competence model, development and validation framework within Weir's (2005) sociocognitive model, and test specifications to provide evidence for the validity of Cambridge English's range of assessments for children and teenagers. Cambridge English also works with ministries and governments on various education reform projects across the school sectors (see Cambridge English Case Studies 2015).

In the USA, there is a similar response to a need to show accountability. ETS has set out an extensive research programme on the development of the TOEFL Primary and Junior tests, providing systematic evidence for their validity within Kane's (2013) interpretive/assessment use argument. On the other hand, Pearson has been developing the Global Scale of English Learning Objectives for Young Learners (Pearson 2015). These developments prove that the field of young learners English language assessment has truly come of age.

Recommendations for practise

What is good assessment for young learners?

Good assessment measures 'critically explored and clearly defined constructs' (Daugherty 2012). Test developers for young learners must justify what knowledge, skills and abilities are assessed and clearly state the intended purpose of test use. Test score interpretations should be made very clear so that test users can make the right inferences from the results. There should be recommendation for legitimate uses of test results and some examples of illegitimate interpretations of score data and use of test results. Test developers should encourage informed and responsible use of results among stakeholders.

Since learning is central for children, teaching and assessment should foster meaning making through language, both in their L1 and L2 English. Therefore, the centrality of concept formation, critical thinking and problem solving through language should take priority in young learners' assessment (Butler 2016). This is a fundamental principle in CLIL and has also been emphasised in current thinking on the future of assessment. However, focus on form should not fall prey and traditional standards of accuracy and fluency should also be promoted.

Good assessments for young learners manage to balance two seemingly opposing requirements: cognitive challenge with the right amount of support. Tests that take into account young learners' cognitive, social and emotional development are learner friendly and offer a positive experience to candidates. Useful assessments help learners prepare for the 'real world', either in terms of promoting real-life abilities or general learning to learn skills or soft interpersonal or intrapersonal skills.

When it comes to the ethics of assessing young learners, best practice strives for fairness, equity and equal access. Quality large-scale tests should be equally accessible to all candidates – geographically, financially and in terms of special needs.

Assessment literacy

Teachers play a crucial role as decision makers, users of results and developers of various types of assessment. This makes assessment literacy one of the most important aspects of teacher training and professional development. Increasing assessment literacy among teachers of primary and lower secondary school learners is a capacity-building exercise. The aim is to build confidence among teachers in designing and/or selecting assessments that are valid, reliable, fit for purpose and have positive consequences for young English language learners, so that teachers can make sound decisions based on test results.

In addition, to help teachers make valid and reliable judgements of language use, it would be useful to ask them to act as examiners for large-scale tests in order to familiarise themselves with assessment criteria and standards, and in order for them not to be biased and underestimate some groups' achievement (SEN, disabilities, some ethnic minorities) (Harlen 2004, Campbell 2013). This would also enhance their 'diagnostic competence' (Edelenbos and Kubanek-German 2004).

According to Swaffield and Dudley (2003/2014), Popham (2009) and Taylor (2009, 2013) increasing assessment literacy may help tackle negative emotions, views and attitudes towards assessment among language teachers and the general public. Taylor (2013) proposes that language teachers need an understanding of the purposes and social role of assessment in education; an awareness of test consequences (impact and washback), accountability, ethics and of the responsibilities of stakeholders. Teachers need to have an understanding of the link between various assessment purposes, tools or instruments, methods and the curriculum. They need to be equipped with knowledge of the principles of sound assessment: an ability to identify and evaluate, develop and analyse a quality test. They should ideally have an in-depth knowledge of language competence: the trait to be measured, the link between learners' cognitive, social, emotional development and language learning for social and academic purposes. They should also have some understanding of how to use statistical information from classroom and large-scale test data: a basic grasp of numbers and measurement and an ability to extract data and interpret results for various purposes. And finally, they need to have the wisdom to apply assessment information to inform decision making. This is an ability to make sensible decisions and critical choices, the know-how required to use effective assessment to maximise learning and minimise negative consequences and the wisdom to integrate assessment into the overall teaching and decision-making process.

Coherent educational framework

The challenge for policy makers and assessment providers is to create a coherent assessment framework with achievable targets and appropriate reporting at each transition point (between pre-school and primary, between primary and junior secondary and between junior and senior secondary education). There should be tight coherence in curriculum, assessment and teacher professional development. Without a clearly articulated progression in all three areas, support for teachers and provision of resources, there is a risk of overestimating feasible attainment levels within a given timeframe. If assessment information on children's attainment is not used in an informed and responsible way at various transition points in the education process, there is a 'continued danger that the achievements at primary school will be undervalued and underexploited at secondary school. This has serious consequences for ultimate attainment' (Rixon 2013, p. 40).

Future directions

The importance accorded to English language learning by parents, teachers and education authorities is likely to lead to a growing demand for English language instruction and an expansion of assessment among children and teenagers. Tasks ahead include the dissemination of the CEFR's extended set of descriptors for young learners in school contexts, to cater for communicative situations that fit better with young learners lives and experiences (BICS). In addition to this, there is a growing need to develop assessments to address and measure children's language learning needs related to academic achievement, both general language of schooling/academic English (CALP) and subject literacy in CLIL and other English as a medium of instruction contexts.

Future research is still due on the following:

- Attainable targets/standards of achievement by age groups in various contexts.
- Young learners' progression in social and instructional target language use domains.
- Technical qualities of young learners' tests.
- In-depth impact studies in specific contexts to investigate issues relating to:

    - Learner and teacher motivation.
    - The link between educational aims, curricula, teaching and assessment.

Technology

Technology has already produced computer-based and computer adaptive tests (e.g., Papp and Walczak 2016). Current developments point towards a revolution in assessment. Item-level data from large-item banks can be put to best use in adaptive assessments. Adaptive tests can be taken when ready, offer the right level of challenge and support and provide instant diagnostic feedback to inform learning and teaching. This is the promise of next-generation instructional design and learning-oriented assessment. Automated assessment of open constructed response items is already firmly on the research and development agenda of major assessment boards (e.g., Evanini et al. 2015). Technology can also be exploited for the marking of speaking performances and writing scripts by human raters. Markers can be asked to make paired comparisons/comparative judgements (Jones 2016, McMahon and Jones 2015). This would lead to the creation of a reliable scale of quality by making holistic judgements about pairs of performances or scripts, making marking criteria redundant.

Assessing valued outcomes

The view on what desirable outcomes should be measured in educational assessments for young learners is constantly changing. 'Understanding of what makes up effective performance in [. . .] languages [. . .] is constantly changing; as are the content of educational programmes, societal expectations, and requirements in the economy' (Cambridge Assessment 2009, p. 8). Apart from communicative competence, a wider range of competences have been identified for assessment in the future. Some are relevant for the use of English as an international language: e.g., collaborative problem solving, creativity, concept formation, learning to learn skills and computer literacy (Masters 2013, The Gordon Commission 2013, Hill and Barber 2014, AQA 2015). Assessment of these broad desirable dispositions and competences can build on existing knowledge in the field of second language assessment among young learners.

Further reading

Bailey, A. L., and Carroll, P. (2015). Assessment of English language learners in the era of new academic content standards. *Review of Research in Education*, 39, 253–294.

A discussion of academic English, and the validity of assessments of English language learners who are learning content through the medium of English in the USA.

Butler, Y. G. (2016). Assessing young learners. In Tsagari, D., and Banerjee, J. (eds.) *Handbook of second language assessment*. Berlin: Mouton de Gruyter, 359–376.

A recent overview of the characteristics of young learners, issues related to construct, i.e., communicative language ability and academic English, age-appropriate tasks and assessment formats and impact of assessment.

Nikolov, M. (Ed.). (2016). *Assessing young learners of English: Global and local perspectives*. Dordrecht: Springer.

A collection of recent research on assessing young learners by major international examination boards, and national examination providers as well as academic research on individual differences contributing to success, self and peer assessment.

Swaffield, S., and Dudley, P. (2003/2014). *Assessment for wise decisions*, 4th ed. Association of Teachers and Lecturers. London. https://www.atl.org.uk/Images/Assessment_and_literacy_for_wise_decisions_May_2015.pdf

A useful publication originally published in 2003 now in its fourth edition, used as part of teacher training for assessment literacy in the UK.

Related topics

Differentiation, syllabus, grammar, vocabulary, speaking and listening, reading and writing.

References

AERA, APA, NCME. (2014). *Standards for Educational and Psychological Testing*. Washington, DC: American Educational Research Association, American Psychological Association, and National Council on Measurement in Education.

AQA. (2015). *The Future of Assessment, 2025 and Beyond*. AQA.

Arnot, M., Schneider, C., Evans, M., Liu, Y., Welpy, O., and Davis-Tutt, D. (2014). *School Approaches to the Education of EAL Students: Language development, social integration and achievement*. Cambridge: The Bell Foundation.

Bailey, A. L. Heritage, M., and Butler, F. A. (2014). Developmental considerations and curricular contexts in the assessment of young language learners. In Kunnan, A. J. (ed.). *The Companion to Language Assessment*. Hoboken, NJ: Wiley-Blackwell.

Bailey, A. L., and Huang, B. H. (2011). Do current English language development/proficiency standards reflect the English needed for success in school? *Language Testing*, 28, 343–365.

Baron, P. A., and Papageorgiou, S. (2014). *Mapping the TOEFL® Primary™ Test onto the Common European Framework of Reference (TOEFL Research Memorandum ETS RM 14–05)*. Princeton, NJ: Educational Testing Service.

Baron, P. A., and Tannenbaum, R. (2011). *Mapping the TOEFL® Junior™ Test onto the Common European Framework of Reference (TOEFL Research Memorandum ETS RM-11–07)*. Princeton, NJ: Educational Testing Service.

Beacco, J.-C. (2010). *Items for a Description of Linguistic Competence in the Language of Schooling Necessary for Teaching/Learning History (End of Compulsory Education)*. Strasbourg: Council of Europe.

Beacco, J.-C., Byram, M., Cavalli, M., Coste, D., Egli Cuenat, M., Goullier, F., and Panthier, J. (2016). *Guide for the Development and Implementation of Curricula for Plurilingual and Intercultural Education*. Strasbourg: Council of Europe.

Beacco, J.-C., Coste, D., van de Ven, P.-H., and Vollmer, H. (2010). *Language and School Subjects – Linguistic dimension of knowledge building in school children*. Strasbourg: Council of Europe.

Benigno, V., and de Jong, J. (2016). A CEFR-based inventory of YL descriptors: Principles and challenges. In Nikolov, M. (ed.). *Assessing Young Learners of English: Global and local perspectives, educational linguistics volume 25*. New York: Springer, 43–64.

Bradbury, A., and Roberts-Holmes, G. (2016). The introduction of reception baseline assessment. "They are children . . . not robots, not machines" ATL, NUT, UCL: London. http://www.teachers.org.uk/files/baseline-assessment--final-10404.pdf

British Educational Research Association (BERA) (2011) *Ethical guidelines for educational research*. London. http://www.bera.ac.uk/wp-content/uploads/2014/02/BERA-Ethical-Guidelines-2011.pdf

Butler, Y. G. (2009). Issues in the assessment and evaluation of English language education at the Elementary school level: Implications for policies in South Korea, Taiwan, and Japan. *The Journal of Asia TEFL*, 6(2), 1–31.

Butler, Y. G., and Lee, J. (2010). The effects of self-assessment among young learners of English. *Language Testing*, 27(1), 5–31.

Cambridge Assessment. (2009). *The Cambridge Approach: Principles for designing, administering and evaluating assessment*. Cambridge: Cambridge Assessment Available online.

Cambridge English Language Assessment. (2013). *Principles of Good Practice: Quality management and validation in language assessment*. Cambridge. http://www.cambridgeenglish.org/images/22695-principles-of-good-practice.pdf

Cameron, L., and McKay, P. (2010). *Bringing Creative Teaching into the Young Learner Classroom*. Oxford: Oxford University Press.

Campbell, T. (2013). *Stereotyped at Seven? Biases in teacher judgements of pupils' ability and attainment* (CLS Working Paper 2013/8). London: University of London, Institute of Education, Centre for Longitudinal Studies.

Carless, D., and Lam, R. (2014). The examined life: Perspectives of lower primary school students in Hong Kong. *Education 3–13*, 42(3), 313–329.

Carlssen, C. (2008). The role of testing in an egalitarian society. *Research Notes*, 34, 2–6.

Carreira, J. M. (2012). Motivational orientations and psychological needs in EFL learning among elementary school students in Japan. *System*, 40, 191–202.

Cho, Y., Ginsburgh, M., Morgan, R., Moulder, B., Xi, X., and Hauck, M. C. (2016). *Designing the TOEFL® PrimaryTM tests (Research Memorandum No. RM-16–02)*. Princeton, NJ: Educational Testing Service.

Council of Europe. (2001). *Common European Framework of Reference for Languages: Learning, teaching, assessment*. Cambridge: Cambridge University Press.

Daugherty, R. (2012). Alternative perspectives on learning outcomes: Challenges for assessment. In Gardner, J. (ed.). *Assessment and Learning*. London: Sage, 76–78.

Earl, L. M. (1999). Assessment and accountability in education: Improvement or surveillance? *Education Canada*, 39 (3), 4–47.

Edelenbos, P., and Kubanek-German, A. (2004). Teacher assessment: The concept of "diagnostic competence". *Language Testing*, 21(3), 259–283.

Elwood, J. (2013). Educational assessment policy and practice: A matter of ethics. *Assessment in Education: Principles, Policy & Practice*, 20(2), 205–220.

Enever, J. (ed.) (2011). *ELLiE: Early language learning in Europe*. London: British Council.

ETS. (2015a). *Understanding TOEFL primary reading and listening score reports* (PDF). Educational Testing Service. https://www.ets.org/s/toefl_primary/pdf/understand_reading_listening_score_reports.pdf

ETS. (2015b). *Understanding TOEFL primary speaking score reports* (PDF). Educational Testing Service. https://www.ets.org/s/toefl_primary/pdf/understand_speaking_score_reports.pdf

European Commission. (2012). *First European survey on language competences*. Final Report, Technical Report, Executive Summary.

Evanini, K., Heilman, M., Wang, X., and Blanchard, D. (2015). *Automated scoring for the TOEFL Junior® Comprehensive Writing and Speaking Test (ETS Research Report No. RR-15–09)*. Princeton, NJ: Educational Testing Service.

Evans, M., Jones, N., Leung, C., and Liu, Y. (2016a). *EAL Assessment Framework for Schools*. Cambridge: The Bell Foundation.

Evans, M., Schneider, C., Arnot, M., Fisher, L., Forbes, K., Hu, M., and Liu, Y. (2016b). *Language Development and School Achievement: Opportunities and challenges in the education of EAL students*. Cambridge: The Bell Foundation.

Fleurquin, F. (2003). *Development of a Standardized Test for Young EFL Learners: Spaan Fellow Working Papers in Second or Foreign Language Assessment, Volume 1*. English Language Institute, University of Michigan.

Fredericksen, J., and Collins, A. (1989). A systems approach to educational testing. *Educational Researcher*, 18(9), 27–32.

Goodier, T., and Szabo, T. (2017). The CEFR, ELP and lifelong learning – relating a collated sample of ELP descriptors for Young Learners to the updated CEFR illustrative scales. *4th Meeting of the EALTA CEFR Special Interest Group*, London, 11 February 2017. Eurocentres.

Haenni Hoti, A., Heinzmann, S., and Müller, M. (2009). "I can you help?": Assessing speaking skills and interaction strategies of young learners. In Nikolov, M. (ed.) *The Age Factor and Early Language Learning*. Berlin and New York: Mouton de Gruyter.

Harlen, W. (2004). *A Systematic Review of the Evidence of Reliability and Validity of Assessment by Teachers Used for Summative Purposes*. Research Evidence in Education Library. London: EPPI-Centre, Social Science Research Unit, Institute of Education, University of London.

Harlen, W. (2005). Trusting teachers' judgement: Research evidence of the reliability and validity of teachers' assessment used for summative purposes. *Research Papers in Education*, 20(3), 245–270.

Härmälä, M., Lee Kristmanson, P., Moe, E., Pascoal, J., and Ramonienė, M. (2015). Language skills for successful subject learning. CEFR-linked descriptors for mathematics and history/civics (Language

Descriptors). https://www.ecml.at/Portals/1/Language%20Descriptors/Moe%20&%20Härmälä% 20-%20EALTA%20-%20Language%20descriptors%20for%20history%20and%20maths.pdf

Hasselgreen, A. (2005)a. Assessing the language of young learners. *Language Testing*, 22(3), 337–354.

Hasselgreen, A. (2005)b. *Testing the Spoken English of Young Norwegians: A study of testing validity and the role of 'smallwords' in contributing to pupils' fluency.* Cambridge: Cambridge University Press.

Hasselgreen, A., and Caudwell, G. (2016). *Assessing the Language of Young Learners*. Equinox: British Council.

Hill, P., and Barber, M. (2014). *Preparing for a Renaissance in Assessment.* London: Pearson.

Hönig, I. (2010). *Assessment in CLIL: Theoretical and empirical research.* Saarbrücken: VDM Verlag.

Inbar-Lourie, O., and Shohamy, E. (2009). Assessing young language learners: What is the construct? In Nikolov, M. (ed.), *The Age Factor and Early Language Learning.* Berlin and Germany: Mouton de Gruyter, 83–96.

Jones, N. (2002). Linking YLE levels into a single framework. *Research Notes*, 10, 14–15.

Jones, N. (2016). "No more marking": An online tool for comparative judgment. *Research Notes*, 63, 12–

Jones, N., and Saville, N. (2009). European language policy: assessment, learning and the CEFR. *Annual Review of Applied Linguistics*, 29, 51–63.

Kane, M. T. (2013). Validating the interpretations and uses of test scores. *Journal of Educational Measurement*, 50(1), 1–73.

Kim, T.-Y., and Seo, H.-S. (2012). Elementary school students' foreign language learning demotivation: A mixed methods study of Korean EFL context. *The Asia Pacific Education Researcher*, 21(1).

Klenowski, V., and Wyatt-Smith, C. (2014). *Assessment for Education.* California: Sage, 101–103.

Little, D. (2007). The Common European Framework of Reference for Languages: Perspectives on the making of supranational language education policy. *The Modern Language Journal*, 91, 645–655.

Little, D. (2011). The Common European Framework of Reference for Languages: A research agenda. *Language Teaching*, 44, 381–393.

Llinares, A., Morton, T., and Whittaker, R. (2012). *The Roles of Language in CLIL.* Cambridge: Cambridge University Press.

Massler, U. (2010). Assessment in CLIL learning. In Ioannou-Georgiou, S. and Pavlou, P. (eds.) *Guidelines for CLIL Implementation in Primary and Pre-primary Education.* Cyprus Pedagogical Institute, pp. 115–137. http://arbeitsplattform.bildung.hessen.de/fach/bilingual/Magazin/mat_aufsaetze/ clilimplementation.pdf

Massler, U., Stotz, D., and Queisser, C. (2014). Assessment instruments for primary CLIL: The conceptualisation and evaluation of test tasks. *The Language Learning Journal*, 42(2), 137–150.

Masters, G. N. (2013). *Reforming Educational Assessment Imperative, Principles and Challenges.* Camberwell, Victoria: Australian Council for Educational Research.

Masters, G. N. (2014). Assessment: Getting to the essence. In *Designing the Future*, Issue 1, Centre for Assessment Reform and Innovation. www.acer.edu.au/files/uploads/Assessment_Getting_to_the_ essence.pdf

McKay, P. (2006). *Assessing Young Language Learners.* Cambridge: Cambridge University Press.

McKay, P., Hudson, C., Newton, M., and Guse, J. (2007). The NLLIA ESL bandscales Version 2. In McKay, P. (ed.) *Assessing, Monitoring and Understanding English as a Second Language in Schools.* Brisbane: Queensland University of Technology and Independent Schools Queensland.

McMahon, S., and Jones, I. (2015). A comparative judgement approach to teacher assessment. *Assessment in Education: Principles, Policy and Practice*, 22(3), 368–389.

Messick, S. (1989). Meaning and values in test validation: The science and ethics of assessment. *Educational Researcher*, 18(2), 5–11.

Murphy, V. A. (2014). *Second Language Learning in the Early School Years: Trends and contexts.* Oxford: Oxford University Press.

Nikolov, M., and Szabó, G. (2012). Developing diagnostic tests for young learners of EFL in grades 1 to 6. In Galaczi, E. D., and Weir, C. J. (eds.). *Voices in Language Assessment: Exploring the impact of language frameworks on learning, teaching and assessment – Policies, procedures and challenges.* Cambridge: UCLES/Cambridge University Press, 347–363.

Papp, S. (2009). Development of can do statements for KET and PET for schools. *Research Notes*, 36, 8–12.

Papp, S., Chambers, L., Galaczi, E., and Howden, D. (2011). *Results of Cambridge ESOL 2010 Survey on Young Learners Assessment.* Research and Validation Report Number: VR1310. Cambridge: Cambridge ESOL internal report.

Papp, S., and McElwee, S. (2015). *Development and Trialling of a New Test for Very Young Learners aged 4–6. Research and Validation Report Number: VR1550.* Cambridge: Cambridge English Language Assessment internal report.

Papp, S., Rixon, S. with Field, J. (forthcoming). *Examining Young Language Learners: The Cambridge English approach to assessing children and teenagers in schools.* Cambridge: Cambridge University Press.

Papp, S., and Salamoura, A. (2009). An exploratory study into linking young learners' examinations to the CEFR. *Research Notes*, 37, 15–22. Cambridge: Cambridge ESOL.

Papp, S., and Walczak, A. (2016). The development and validation of a computer-based test of English for children: the computer-based Cambridge English: Young Learners tests. In Nikolov, M. (ed.). *Assessing Young Learners of English: Global and local perspectives.* New York: Springer, 139–190.

Pearson Education. (2015). *GSE learning objectives for young learners.* https://dbxmrk3ash14o.cloudfront.net/englishfiles/GSE_LO_YoungLearners_beta_Dec15.pdf

Pinter, A. (2011). *Children Learning Second Languages.* Basingstoke: Palgrave Macmillan.

Pinter, A. (2014). Child participant roles in applied linguistics. *Research Applied Linguistics*, 35 (2), 168–183.

Pizorn, K. (2009). Designing proficiency levels for English for primary and secondary school students and the impact of the CEFR. In Figueras, N., and Noijons, J. (eds.) *Linking to the CEFR Levels: Research perspectives.* Arnhem: Cito/EALTA, pp 87–100.

Popham, W. J. (2009). Assessment literacy for teachers: Faddish or fundamental? *Theory Into Practice*, 48, 4–11.

QCA (2000). *National curriculum 2000 a language in common: Assessing English as an additional language.* Qualifications and Curriculum Authority. www.naldic.org.uk/Resources/NALDIC/Teaching%20and%20Learning/1847210732.pdf

Rea-Dickins, P., and Rixon, S. (1999). Assessment of young learners' English: Reasons and means. In Rixon, S. (ed.) *Young Learners of English: Some research perspectives.* Harlow: Addison Wesley Longman/The British Council, 89–101.

Rixon, S. (2013). *Survey of Policy and Practice in Primary English Language Teaching Worldwide.* London: British Council.

Rixon, S. (2016). Do developments in assessment represent the "coming of age" of young learners English language teaching initiatives? The international picture. In Nikolov, M. (ed.) *Assessing Young Learners of English: Global and local perspectives.* New York: Springer, 19–41.

Rupp, A., Vock, M., Harsch, C., and Köller, O. (2008). *Developing Standards-based Assessment Tasks for English as a Foreign Language: Context, processes, and outcomes in Germany.* Münster: Waxmann.

Shaw, S., and Imam, H. (2013). Assessment of international students through the medium of English: Ensuring validity and fairness in content-based examinations. *Language Assessment Quarterly*, 10(4), 452–475.

Short, D. J. (1993). Assessing integrated language and content instruction. *TESOL Quarterly*, 27(4), 627–656.

So, Y., Wolf, M. K., Hauck, M. C., Mollaun, P., Tumposky, D., and Wang, L. (2015). *TOEFL Junior design framework (TOEFL Young Students Research Report No. TOEFL Jr-02).* Princeton, NJ: Educational Testing Service.

SQA. (2015). *Guide to Assessment. Scottish Qualification Agency.* www.sqa.org.uk/files_ccc/25GuideToAssessment.pdf

Stotz, D., and Megías, R. M. (2010). Moving on, broadening out. A European perspective on the transition between primary and secondary foreign language learning. *Babylonia*, 1, 30–34.

Szpotowicz, M., and Campfield, D. (2016). Developing and piloting proficiency tests for Polish young learners. In Nikolov, M. (ed.). *Assessing Young Learners of English: Global and local perspectives*, pp. 109–137.

Taylor, L. (2009). Developing assessment literacy. *Annual Review of Applied Linguistics*, 29, 21–36.

Taylor, L. (2013). Communicating the theory, practice and principles of language testing to test stakeholders: Some reflections. *Language Testing*, 30(3), 403–412.

The Gordon Commission. (2013). The Gordon Commission Final Report: To Assess, To Teach, To Learn: A Vision for the Future of Assessment, Technical report.

United Nations. (1989). *Convention on the Rights of Child*. www.unicef.org/rightsite/files/uncrcchilld friendlylanguage.pdf

Vollmer, H. (2010). *Items for a Description of Linguistic Competence in the Language of Schooling Necessary for Teaching/learning Sciences (End of Compulsory Education)*. Strasbourg: Council of Europe.

Weir, C. (2005). Limitations of the Common European Framework for developing comparable examinations and tests. *Language Testing*, 22(3), 281–300.

WIDA. (2012). *English Language Proficiency Standards for English Language Learners in Kindergarten through Grade 12.* Board of Regents of the University of Wisconsin System, on behalf of the WIDA Consortium. www.wida.us

PART 5
Researching young learners

25

Research issues with young learners

Annamaria Pinter

Introduction

Given the spread of English into primary and pre-primary contexts all over the world in the last decades, research with young learners in EFL/ESL is on the increase (e.g., Rich 2014, Mourão and Lourenço 2015, Bland 2015, Copland and Garton 2014, Enever 2011). In the last decade more research has been done than ever before and this trend is likely to continue. Thus questions about how research with children might be different or similar to research with adults will continue to dominate discussions among those interested in working with children. The community of researchers interested in child second/foreign language learning will also continue to be interested in tools and techniques that 'work particularly well' with children in research.

Children's special status in research is generally ignored or left implicit. Most books covering research methods in applied linguistics have been written with adult learners in mind, for example, Dörnyei 2007, Paltridge and Phatiki 2015, Nunan 1992, Mackey and Gass 2005 and Richards 2003, just to list a few. These books offer comprehensive guidelines about the research process in general; however they devote very little space, if at all, to children. For example, Paltridge and Phatiki (2015) devote only one chapter to child research participants, while Dörnyei (2007) makes only occasional mentions of children where data collection in schools is discussed. Mackey and Gass (2005) refer to children only on a handful of occasions (see pp. 32–33 and 209–213). Recently Murphy and Macaro (2017) have reported about the challenges and common obstacles of working with children as research participants in school contexts, but this review is also mostly focused on the practicalities of collecting data in schools.

Some would argue that this apparent lack of interest in children as research participants in second language education is explained by the assumption that there is nothing special about undertaking research with child participants because research with all subjects (adult or child) has to meet rigorous methodological or ethical criteria, and research tools and approaches need to be appropriate to the participants' needs no matter who they are. On the other hand it could be argued that there are indeed specific challenges that emerge in research with child participants, and undertaking research with children is therefore qualitatively different from that with adults. For example, children do not always take an interest in adult research and may resist taking part by showing reluctance in answering questions or even staying silent altogether (e.g., Spyrou 2016). If unaware or uninterested, children find concentrating on research activities tiring or meaningless, and as seemingly reluctant contributors they are quickly dismissed as 'difficult' research participants (Bucknall 2014).

In this chapter I will first of all explore trends in research involving children from a historical perspective. I will address some critical issues in more traditional approaches to researching children and then move on to current contributions. In this part the discussion will focus on the variety of ways children can be involved in research as active contributors.

Current approaches also present considerable challenges which will be discussed next. Finally, ethical issues, practical considerations and future directions in researching with children will be offered.

Definitions of research

Any research is enquiry that leads to new insights and understandings. Academic research undertaken by university researchers has the highest status because the researchers are highly skilled and experienced; however, such research is not routinely accessible or available to others, such as teachers. In fact to address the gap between academic research and teaching or classroom practice, and to encourage teachers to engage with research that is more meaningful to them, Burns (2011) and others have long promoted the idea of different types of practitioner research such as Action Research or Exploratory Practice (Hanks 2017).

Research involving child participants can be undertaken by both academic researchers or teachers, and these two types of perspectives have their own advantages and drawbacks. Typically, academic researchers who come into schools to work with children do not have any prior relationships with the children, and they often do not understand the context of the school and find the children's life worlds difficult to understand. Such researchers are outsiders with an 'etic' perspective. They might find it challenging to get the children to open up in conversations and thus may not get rich data. On the other hand, they can notice aspects of the context that insiders might not be immediately conscious of or might take for granted. In contrast, teacher researchers are almost always insiders with an 'emic' perspective, and they establish strong relationships with the children before embarking on any study. This existing relationship allows teachers to base their research work on strong foundations of trust and mutual understanding. However, emic perspectives also have disadvantages such as the difficulty of differentiating between the roles of being a teacher and researcher at the same time.

Whether adults work with children as outsiders or insiders, from etic or emic perspectives, in the majority of cases they are still in charge of all aspects of the research process. Traditionally adults conduct research *on* children and children remain passive objects of interest throughout the research process.

In this chapter, however, I argue that research does not have to be an exclusively adult territory and children are able to contribute actively.

Definitions of child research participants

Since both children and adults can undertake research, it is useful here to conceptualise the different roles and status positions children can take. Following Kellett (2010a) we can identify four distinct ways in which children can participate in research. Accordingly, any research can be conducted '*on*' them, '*about*' them, '*with*' them or '*by*' them. When adults alone are in charge, research is either 'on' or 'about' children. In both these roles children are rather passive and have no input on the shape of the research. When we talk about research 'with' children or 'by' children, the difference is that the children themselves can influence the research process in an active way. They can offer unique insights and perspectives, and some can go as far as becoming co-researchers or researchers themselves.

On the whole, applied linguistics has been dominated by research '*on*' and '*about*' children. The second two options '*with*' and '*by*' are less familiar and more contentious (see Pinter 2014; Pinter and Zandian 2012, 2014; Pinter et al. 2016) even though it is clear from studies that have taken alternative perspectives that children benefit in various ways (Kellett et al. 2004). Nonetheless, due to this current lack of focus on children in more active roles in research, very little is actually known about children's perspectives and views about English language learning.

Historical perspectives

A great deal of research has been undertaken with children as language learners in the broad field of applied linguistics over the last few decades, as every chapter in this book illustrates, but almost all of it is adult focused and adult motivated.

The most popular and traditional approach across different disciplines has been research '*on*' children. In these types of studies children are objects of systematic adult enquiry which encourages objectivity, a dispassionate predisposition, often adopting a tightly controlled experimental design. This approach is associated with the 'developmental psychology' paradigm which has its roots in the work of Darwin and dates back to the time of the industrial revolution. Developmental psychology is interested in the universal processes and stages of development in childhood with an emphasis on the general rather than the individual child. In order to understand children such research is interested in plotting the path of development from birth to adulthood and either explicitly or implicitly; children are viewed as immature, incompetent and irrational. Since they are being compared and contrasted to adults, their abilities and performances are routinely described in negative terms, i.e., emphasising what they are still lacking.

In this paradigm children appear as 'depersonalised' objects of study' (Woodhead and Faulkner 2008, p. 14). As Alderson (1995, p. 40) comments, such research is undertaken so that adults can ultimately influence school curricula, mass education and health provision for large populations. Children are usually left in the dark about the purposes of the research, and the data gained from children are interpreted according to 'adult discourses' (Woodhead and Faulkner 2008, p. 13) and evaluated with adult priorities in mind.

Within this paradigm, one of the most well-known and comprehensive developmental theories of childhood was proposed by Piaget (1963) and his colleagues in the early part of the twentieth century. Most children, according to Piaget, progress through the same stages, becoming more skilled at handling questions of formal logic. Universal processes apply in learning to think about problem solving, to consider others' views and positions and to learning about extending one's thinking from immediate problems in the here-and-now to abstract ideas and hypotheses. Even though Piaget's claims have been criticised heavily, this is still the most well-known framework describing age-related abilities in a universal framework, thus illustrating the essence of this tradition. In addition, the methodology used in Piaget's experiments also fits with research '*on*' children in the sense that children were typically questioned and tested in somewhat decontextualised situations where their under-standing of adult concepts was carefully measured.

In addition to the numerous large-scale studies that have focused on children's progress towards adulthood (studies on children), research '*about*' children has also emerged. Within this approach, more qualitative studies focussing on fewer children as unique individuals have been undertaken. In such studies adult researchers have been making efforts to under-stand children as individuals with their unique views and perspectives. Accordingly, chil-dren might be studied individually or in small groups and the research design may be more longitudinal and may draw on various different data sets in order to get a comprehensive dynamic view of the participants. In a quest to understand individual children a holistic approach to data collection is applied: e.g., observation of the children in and out of school may be combined with interviewing them or collecting and analysing their written work or drawings or photos. However, the majority of these studies still sit within the developmental psychology paradigm, because despite the efforts to get to know the children as individu-als, all decisions and responsibilities in the research process remain adult initiated and adult focused, and the needs-benefits scale is still heavily tipped in favour of the adult.

For example, In Hawkins (2005), the adult researchers were interested in understanding the L2 development of kindergarten children in the USA. The teacher and the academic researcher worked collaboratively and used a wide range of appropriate tools to track the children's L2 development. They conducted regular observations both in the classroom and the playground, interviewed the parents and the focal children on several occasions and also analysed the children's friendships networks and interactions by constructing 'sociograms'. Nonetheless, as Hawkins remarks, despite the fact that they were able to follow these chil-dren around using a variety of appropriate research tools, they (the adults) were still the ones who designed all the tools and interpreted the children's voices from an exclusively adult perspective (ibid. 2005, p. 79).

Overall, in research *about* children, even though the more qualitative methods are more conducive to showcasing individual differences and special learning trajectories than tradi-tional experiments, for example, children's voices are still reported from an adult perspec-tive. In this sense both studies *on* and *about* children ultimately rely on adult perspectives and adult interpretations.

Critical issues and topics

What we know today about children as language learners originates from contributions of the traditional paradigm, i.e., research *on* children and research *about* children. How-ever, criticism has been mounting regarding the dominance of such adult perspectives. Hogan (2005, p. 26) comments that approaches where children are studied as objects appear context-free, because it is the universal that is being studied by detached and neutral observ-ers, and children's individual unique trajectories together with their contextual affordances and their perspectives are often ignored. The object position also implicitly assumes that children have less to offer even about themselves than adults do. This leads to a conclusion that children are passive and dependent, and they are unreliable informants. Some go as far as saying that research '*on*' children is therefore unethical (Fraser et al. 2014) because of the adult-biased view.

Research about children has offered an alternative approach and has helped us broaden our understanding about children's individual trajectories as well as promoted the emergence of a range of so-called 'child-friendly' methods and approaches. For example, researchers have attempted to embed interview questions into more meaningful events such as circle time conversations (Eder and Fingerson 2002) and have suggested using drama, stories and drawings to elicit better quality data from children.

In the ELLiE study (Enever 2011), for example, the researchers incorporated a child-friendly tool to explore young learners' perspectives on classroom layouts (from more traditional contexts with rows of desks to classrooms where children were sitting in groups working together). The children in different contexts were asked to select one classroom they would most like to join and then explain why they selected this classroom. It is clear that the adult researchers' aim was to use an appropriate, child-friendly tool which contained visual clues and allowed the children to link the visuals to their own personal experiences. Nevertheless, it is important to acknowledge that the prompts were designed by adults based on their judgments as to what was appropriate. Interesting questions therefore arise, such as: how do adults know what is 'child-friendly' for a particular group of children? Where do accommodations come from that help adult researchers ask age-appropriate questions and/or use language that is deemed meaningful to the children? Adults' ideas about child-friendly approaches come from knowledge, experience and assumptions all rooted in the traditional developmental psychology paradigm.

Current contributions

Research *'with'* and *'by'* children reflects a major perspective change whereby adult researchers acknowledge that in order to understand children *in their own right* (rather than as developing 'would-be' adults) they need to seek children's own interpretations and involve them in research as *partners* and *collaborators*. 'Childhood Studies' has played an important role in this paradigm shift. Originated by scholars in sociology and anthropology (James and Prout 2015) it is now gaining strength in second language education. Childhood Studies is a movement that devotes itself to understanding children from their own point of view by acknowledging them as experts in their own lives.

Childhood Studies emerged as a radical approach to studying children following the impact of the United Nation Declaration on the Rights of the Child (UNRC 1989), in particular in relation to Articles 12 and 13 that focus on children's rights as decision makers when it comes to important aspects of their lives. The change of perspective from conceptualising children as passive objects of the adult gaze to children as 'active social agents' means that children's rights are to be taken much more seriously and their input should be sought systematically. The Childhood Studies approach is based on the idea that children are competent social actors and, as Scott (2000, p. 88) argues, 'the best people to provide information on the child's perspective, actions and attitudes are children themselves'. Children provide reliable responses if questioned about events that are meaningful to their lives'.

Even though the UNRC articles do not directly mention children's rights to research, the wording 'all important aspects of their lives' (Articles 12) has been interpreted rather broadly and scholars working in Childhood Studies have been designing and undertaking studies with children as research collaborators, exploring both school and out-of-school issues. Some children have been promoted to important roles in research such as advisors or even fully fledged researchers. Publications promoting research training for children have also become popular (e.g., Kellett 2005).

For adult researchers the explicit shift from thinking about children as objects to children as social actors can lead to unexpected opportunities of gaining new insights and understandings. For example, in my own work I have seen how some children who participate as active subjects can suddenly become interested in contributing more and/or take a genuine interest in adults' research. In Pinter and Zandian's (2012) study, the participating children were originally invited to respond to a questionnaire about intercultural issues such as welcoming newcomers in their school. This initial phase was followed up by group interviews which were organised in a way that a range of participatory activities were included. Participatory activities (O'Kane 2008) are recommended in the literature because they allow flexible participation through drama, role play or drawings rather than just responding verbally. The children enjoyed the participatory activities and contributed fully. When the research study was written up in an MA dissertation, we decided to go back to the children to talk about the research they participated in some months earlier. We also wanted to get the children's reflections on the whole process. During these discussions, the children took an unexpected interest in the actual MA dissertation that was on the table and wanted to look through it. When they discovered their own transcribed utterances on the pages in the data analysis section, they asked spontaneous questions about transcribing conventions, pseudonyms and representation. They were genuinely surprised that their own words were so frequently quoted word by word in the final text, and they wanted to understand why their exact words (even if fragmented and with hesitation) were used rather than adult reformulations. In fact they expected that adults would 'correct' what they had said. They also wanted to know why pseudonyms were necessary. The follow-up session with the children therefore turned into a 'research training session', where the adult researchers were explaining to the children the conventions of writing up research and the way data were represented in an academic text. These children were keen to understand more about research and academic conventions, but a space for such spontaneous discussions would not have opened up had we not made a conscious effort to listen to the children's agenda rather than just following our own. This study started off as research about children but as we progressed, the discussions with the children opened our eyes to the possibility of researching 'with' children. Adult researchers and facilitators should be encouraged to approach children's input with a genuine willingness to take the research in directions that the children suggest, and resist the urge to brush to the side their suggestions, comments and questions as irrelevant, unimportant or vague.

In another study by Kuchah and Pinter (2012), children's views were sought about good English teaching. The study's primary interest was the exploration of inspirational teachers' practice in primary schools in Cameroon. The children's English teacher had already been identified as an inspirational teacher using a careful bottom-up approach, but in order to complement the findings gained from adults, it was decided that children would also be interviewed about their views regarding inspirational/good teachers. When the children were invited to talk about the characteristics of good English language teachers, they insisted that their regular teacher (the one who was identified earlier) was not their best English teacher. They suggested that another teacher in the school (who was a less established teacher) was much better at teaching English. They explained their viewpoints and persuaded the researcher to observe and interview this other English teacher. The adult researcher could have simply ignored the children's suggestion and could have persevered with their own agenda, but that would have been a missed opportunity. Listening to the children, taking their views seriously and observing the new teacher they recommended led to a better understanding of the differences between children's and adults' views on good teaching and has led to an alternative research focus compared to the original adult focus.

Children as co-researchers and researchers

Children can take various roles when working with adults as interested, active subjects. They can help with data collection by interviewing each other (i.e., act as interviewers and interviewees). For example, in a study by Coppock (2011) 10-year-old children interviewed their peers in pairs, one of them asking the questions and the other one acting as a scribe. Children may also comment on, design and evaluate tools initially designed by adults (e.g., Zandian 2015; Horgan 2017; Pinter and Zandian 2014) and thus can contribute to producing tools that are more authentic and more in tune with children's life experiences in a given context. Children can also suggest new research questions and angles of enquiry or new topics to explore. They can also analyse data and disseminate findings, but these are less frequently reported in the literature (but see Kellett et al. 2004 or Kirova and Emme 2008).

Children may first take on limited roles as co-researchers first, but over time they may take on more roles and different roles in new projects. Hart (1992) discussed issues about levels of involvement and introduced the concept of a 'participation ladder', i.e., a continuum from pretence or tokenistic involvement all the way to shared work and projects fully initiated and directed by children. Many would argue that tokenistic participation is of little benefit and significance, but the debate is ongoing about the practicalities of achieving full participation.

Taking more and more responsibility means being involved in increasing numbers of roles such as identifying research questions, undertaking data collection and analysis or writing up and disseminating results. Kellett, in this respect, (2010a:49) explains that:

> the co-researcher role is a partnership where the research process is shared between adults and children. A distinguishing element is that co-researchers can be involved in any number of the research phases from design to dissemination. If we were to think of a sandwich as a metaphor: participant researchers always form part of the filling, co-researchers also form part of the bread.

In order for the child to develop independent skills, the relationship between children as co-researchers and the facilitating adults needs to be open and honest and requires a great deal of rapport building and reflexivity. Christensen (2004, p. 174) suggests that rapport building can be achieved through a reflective dialogical approach whereby ongoing communication between adult researchers and the children becomes the basis for meaningful engagement. Reflexivity, the conscious attempt to switch back and forth between the researcher's own ideas and understandings and the children's perspectives, requires the adult researcher to work out 'when to step back both figuratively and physically from the discussion, allowing the children's voices to become more dominant and their deliberations more independent at each stage' (Coppock 2011, p. 442).

Some children are enabled to work as researchers in their own rights. When children undertake research for themselves, they initiate and direct research and take responsibility for all the stages. Alderson (2008, p. 287) argues that this is qualitatively different from children undertaking research in their everyday lives at school, or being involved in adult-initiated research.

Kellett (2010a, p. 105) promotes child research for a number of reasons. She argues that children ask different questions compared to adults. She also (ibid, p. 8) proposes that 'accepting children as researchers in their own right promotes their democratic involvement in all phases of decision-making'. Some go as far as to suggest that children themselves are best suited to researching children's experiences (Alderson 2008) as they are successful at, for example, getting responses from their age group. Research is an important vehicle for children's voices, and participation is an empowering process. Parents also often comment on their children's increased self-esteem (Kellett et al. 2004).

Mann et al. (2014, p. 299) also emphasise a range of benefits that affect the self-development of young researchers; these include raised self-esteem, increased confidence, development of transferable skills, sharpening of critical thinking, heightened ethical awareness, enhanced problem solving abilities, more effective communication, development of independent learning, increased participation in other aspects affecting their childhoods and contribution to knowledge being valued.

Overall, the benefits are holistic and long lasting:

> When children realise their research is valued and listened to by adults, they have an increased sense of personal worth, of childhood as an important stage in life and of their ability to influence the quality of that childhood.
>
> *(Kellett 2010b, p. 201–202)*

Pinter et al. (2016) also quote specific benefits, not just for the children but also for the adult facilitators/teachers. Children who acted alongside their teachers as co-researchers in an Indian project developed both their proficiency and confidence in using English and autonomous learning skills such as critical thinking and working collaboratively. They also enjoyed engaging with authentic texts such as interview data which they had collected themselves, which they contrasted with passive learning from books. The children also commented that the projects they chose were important to them, that they carried on working on these even when the teacher was absent and they felt proud and empowered to be able to share their work with wider audiences. Additionally, benefits were also significant for teacher-researchers working with these children (Pinter et al. 2016). Teachers reported that they grew and changed as professionals in their acceptance that everyone in their classrooms was learning all the time, including themselves. They also commented on the fact that they had changed their conceptions about children and learning in general, and many became firm believers that children should take a central role in decision making, choosing activities and evaluating their learning. For example, one teacher said (quoted in Pinter et al. 2016, p. 22):

> Today I believe learners can be good researchers, I strongly believe that. What next? [Research] will be an ongoing activity in my classroom. It will continue as long as I am in the profession. I hope it will become a part of the curriculum someday. And it will go on because the children are not letting me stop.

Current critical issues

How children are viewed and how adults decide to work with them will depend on the adults' system of beliefs regarding children and childhood. Whether adults will invite children as objects or subjects in the research project will vary according to their aims and their research questions but more importantly according to what they believe about what children can or cannot do or be trusted to do. In fact many academic researchers or practitioner researchers do not believe that children can do their own research (e.g., Ellis and Ibrahim, forthcoming).

At the same time, Gallacher and Gallagher (2008, p. 511) rightly comment that 'children should be approached as experts in their own lives', but they are of course not the *only* experts. It would not be sensible just to focus on what children tell us about their experiences; we need to continue listening to adults who also know them well. Komulainen (2007) warns us that we must not replace one essentialism 'children are incompetent' with another, 'children are competent'. Children's voices are always multilayered and messy and they are the product of relevant institutional, interactional and discourse contexts (Spyrou 2011, 2016), and therefore the interpretations of these voices are never straightforward.

Many scholars also suggest that there are certain roles that children cannot take over. Mayall (1994) argues, for example, that no matter how much we try to involve children in all stages of research, the interpretation and analysis of the final representation (at least for some purposes) requires knowledge that children simply do not have.

In addition to methodological challenges, there are also critical voices questioning the value of children's research. Kim (2017), for example, suggests that quality issues can be raised about children's research. Is children's research really 'research'? Is it scholarly? Kim (ibid.) comments that much research that children undertake is not aimed directly to promote genuine participation or the core purpose of knowledge production but is undertaken simply for educational benefits. In fact she argues that research undertaken for pedagogical purposes at schools allows teachers to *'achieve their own pedagogical goals'* (Kim 2017, p. 12) and this goes back to traditional perspectives *on* children because research for educational purposes focuses on adults' agendas. Kim further argues that, 'as children's research is vulnerable to being subsumed under the pedagogical intentions of adults, and given the ethical questions that arise when that happens, it seems necessary not to fuse conceptually children's research as a tool for their participation and pedagogy. If so, tensions arising from balancing these objectives seem inevitable, as are those concerning children's status as 'beings' and 'becomings'.

Overall, perhaps research undertaken with a pedagogic purpose is a stepping stone for research that is for true participation if we conceptualise different types of research on a continuum.

Ethics

The role of ethical guidelines in any research is to protect the research participants by offering anonymity, confidentiality and an opportunity to withdraw from the research without negative consequences of any kind. Working with children, whether in the role of objects or subjects or social agents, will mean that adults may have to consider complex ethical dilemmas of all kinds. Academic institutions and other organisations will have their own ethical guidelines about working with children but it is the duty of the adult researcher to monitor and navigate ethical dilemmas as they arise in any one study. For example, one issue that causes concern is the increasing over-bureaucratization of ethical procedures which leads to a situation where children are sometimes excluded from research (Darian-Smith and Henningham 2014) even though they themselves would very much like to participate. The more active roles children take, the more there is a tension between how far they can make decisions and when and how their parents and guardians can potentially override these decisions. Children are considered 'vulnerable' research participants because of their social status, and in all research their parents' or guardians' permissions (often interpreted as written consent) will be needed in order to for them to participate. However, when children are active contributors or even initiators of their own research, their own consent is most important and the requirement for adult permission can be brought into question (e.g., Coyne 2010).

Good quality research rests on a trusting relationship between the adult researcher and the children, and confidentiality is a cornerstone of this relationship. However, should any issues about child abuse or any other harm or danger to the child come to the attention of the adult researcher, they cannot continue with confidentiality.

There are important cultural dimensions to consider as well. In some contexts it is not the norm to approach parents with letters from the school about research because it is believed that whatever activity that goes on at school is authorised by the teachers and the head teacher/principal. In some contexts, parents might also find signing official letters threatening as they might not fully understand the content and/or fear potential negative consequences, based on past negative experiences.

Ethical guidelines have been inherited from the field of medicine, and much of the scrutiny about harm, for example, does not really apply in the kind of social sciences research that children will be involved in (see Copland and Creese 2016). In the majority of cases, especially the kind where children are encouraged to become researchers themselves, participating in the research is in fact beneficial and enjoyable for children.

Recommendations for practice

In our rapidly changing societies there is now a growing realisation that new approaches are needed to meet the ever-changing educational needs of school children. Many scholars recommend that schools should embrace the development of twenty-first century skills (P21 2009) focussing on cultivating skills such as creativity, critical thinking, communication and collaboration. These 4 skills (4Cs) have been widely accepted to be core for primary school children (Trilling and Fadal 2009). In view of the importance of these skills, the goal of developing competent and confident young researchers equipped with rudimentary research skills does not seem such a far-fetched idea. To become a child researcher presupposes certain autonomous skills, and those children who can undertake research in collaboration with adults or by themselves with minimal adult facilitation are by definition autonomous, motivated learners who can communicate well, collaborate with their friends and think critically and creatively.

It is therefore important for future research and practice to identify opportunities where children are encouraged and enabled to take control of their own learning and to undertake projects, enquiries or research into their own learning.

Future directions

To date, very little research within second language education has been undertaken with children in active roles, participating in research as active social agents. Whilst all research with children is valuable (whether children are subjects, objects or active participants), there is a need to open up new possibilities which would allow more research to be undertaken *with* or *by* children as part of larger projects.

Researchers interested in children as language learners need a broader framework that embraces all types of research with children in a more balanced way. This would mean undertaking research of all kinds including on, about, with and by children. This would further stimulate future work that would cover a wider range of options in terms of children's status, roles and general involvement in research.

Teacher education programmes of all kinds will need to incorporate awareness raising about teachers' own conceptions of childhood and children (Ellis and Ibrahim, forthcoming) and familiarise teachers with various roles children can take on (Pinter and Mathew 2017). Depending on specific contexts, different ways in which children can contribute to more meaningful classroom research could be explored and critically evaluated.

Academic research could also benefit from exploring the opportunities around involving children as social agents. Longitudinal studies that explore the trajectories of children and groups of children working jointly on classroom research projects alongside their teachers will also present interesting opportunities to understand how children develop and move forward to become researchers, acquiring new skills and learning to do more and more sophisticated research.

How and why (under what circumstances and with what kind of support) children actually take interest in being involved in research and how and why they may want to develop their skills to learn to function as co-researchers and in some cases as fully fledged researchers is an interesting empirical question. As Tisdall (2012, p. 188) comments, 'There is too little research, and particularly too few large-scale and sustainable models of research that involve children as researchers or other deep levels of involvement'. Children should have opportunities to engage in different roles as developing researchers to gain long-term benefits.

The principles that suggest that children's views and opinions need to be taken seriously should of course permeate all aspects of the teaching-learning process, including materials, activities, ways of working and assessment as well. All these areas may be good entry points for teachers and learners to begin joint enquiry in their own classrooms.

Conclusions

Traditionally, applied linguistics research involving child participants has been very much focused on children as objects of research. While this focus has resulted in a useful pool of knowledge and understanding about how adults make sense of children's language learning, there is further scope to include children's own views, perspectives and experiences. Such alternative opportunities would complement the findings of studies where children are objects of adult investigation.

If children are engaged in research alongside adults on an ongoing basis, an additional benefit is that the adult researcher is also on a path of professional development, learning about how to facilitate children's research and helping them to move forward and progress from less formal to more formal types of research. I have worked with teachers who have supported children's research and who have been inspired to undertake their own academic research as graduate students, moving forward on their own paths of professional development.

Finally, it is important to acknowledge most child-initiated research is ultimately represented by adults, and not all contexts will be conducive to working with children as co-researchers or researchers, and indeed not all children will be interested. Nevertheless, we should not give up on pushing the boundaries that provide space for children to make their voices heard within the field of second language learning.

Further reading

1 Christensen, P., and James, A. (Eds.). (2008). *Research with children: Perspectives and practices*. London: Routledge.

This is a collection of chapters illustrating how children can be engaged as active collaborators or co-researchers in different contexts. Many of the chapters discuss participatory tools and approaches that can be directly implemented in language classrooms as well.

2 Sargeant, J., and Harcourt, D. (2012). *Doing ethical research with children.* Maidenhead: Open University Press.

This is a hands-on handbook that takes the reader through many of the common ethical dilemmas that occur in working with children. Illustrative case studies focus on problems and possible solutions to ethical dilemmas in various contexts.

3 Kellett, M. (2005). *How to develop children as researchers* London: Sage.

This book starts with an excellent introductory chapter about why it is important to teach children research skills. The rest of the chapters are devoted to a step-by-step guide to teaching children research concepts; introducing them to research questions, methodological solutions, data collection techniques and analysis; and finally reporting and presenting research. There are real examples from children to illustrate a variety of different topics and interests, and there are activities with guided commentary as well as additional reading, games and key reflection questions in each chapter. The content is suitable for children aged 10–14.

Related topics

Researching very young learners, research on learners outside the classroom, the age debate

References

Alderson, P. (1995). *Listening to Children: Ethics and social Research*. Barkingside: Barnardo's.

Alderson, P. (2008). Children as researchers: Participation rights and research methods. In Christensen, P., and James, A. (eds.) *Research with Children*. Abingdon: Routledge, 276–290.

Bland, J. (ed.) (2015). *Teaching English to Young Learners: Critical issues in language teaching with 3–12 year olds*. London: Bloomsbury.

Bucknall, S. (2014). Doing qualitative research with children and young people. In Clark et al. (eds.), *Understanding Research with Children and Young People*. London: Sage, 69–84.

Burns, A. (2011). Action research in the field of second language teaching and learning. In Hinkel, E. (ed.), *Handbook of Research in Second Language Teaching and Learning*. Vol. II. New York: Routledge, 237–253.

Christensen, P. (2004). Children's participation in ethnographic research: Issues of power and representation. *Children and Society*, 18(2), 165–176.

Copland, F., and Creese, A. (2016). Ethical issues in linguistic ethnography: Balancing the micro and the macro. In De Costa, P. I. (ed.) *Ethics in Applied Linguistics Research: Language researcher narratives*. Second Language Acquisition Research Series, New York: Routledge, 161–178.

Copland, F., and Garton, S. (2014). Key themes and future directions in teaching English to young learners: Introduction to the Special Issue. *ELT Journal*, 68(3), 223–230.

Coppock, V. (2011). Children as peer researchers: Reflections on a journey of mutual discovery. *Children and Society*, 25(6), 435–466.

Coyne, I. (2010). Research with children and young people: the issue of parental proxy consent *Children and Society*, 24, 227–237.

Darian-Smith, K., and Henningham, N. (2014). Social research and the privacy and participation of children: Reflections on researching Australian children's playlore. *Children and Society*, 28(4), 327–338.

Dörnyei, Z. (2007). *Research Methods in Applied Linguistics*. Oxford: Oxford University Press.

Eder, D., and Fingerson, L. (2002) Interviewing children and adolescents. In Gubrium, J. F., and Holstein, J. A. (eds.) *Handbook of Interview Research*. London: Sage, 181–202.

Ellis, G., and Ibrahim, N. (forthcoming). Teachers' image of the child in ELT. In Pinter, A., and Kuchah Kuchah, H. (eds.) *Ethical and Methodological Issues in Researching Young Learners in School Contexts*. Bristol: Multilingual Matters.

Enever, J. (ed.) (2011). *ELLiE, early language learning in Europe*. London: the British Council.

Fraser, S., Flewitt, R., and Hammersely, M. (2014). What is research with children and young people. In Clark, A. et al. (eds.) *Understanding Research with Children and Young People*. London: Sage, 34–50.

Gallacher, L., and Gallagher, M. (2008). Methodological immaturity in childhood research? *Childhood*, 15(4), 499–516.

Hanks, J. (2017). *Exploratory Practice in Language Teaching*. Basingstoke: Palgrave Macmillan.

Hart, R. (1992). *Children's Participation: From tokenism to citizenship*. UNICEF International Child Development Centre, Florence, Italy.

Hogan, D. (2005). Researching the child in developmental psychology. In Greene, S., and Hogan, D. (eds.), *Researching Children's Experiences*. London: Sage, 22–42.

Horgan, D. (2017). Child participatory research methods: Attempts to go deeper. *Childhood*, 24(2), 245–259.

James, A., and Prout, A. (2015). *Constructing and Reconstructing Childhood*. London: Routledge.

Kellett, M. (2005). *How to Develop Children as Researchers: A step-by-step guide to teaching the research process*. London: Sage.

Kellett, M. (2010a). *Rethinking Children and Research: Attitudes in contemporary society*. London: Continuum.

Kellett, M. (2010b). Small shoes, big steps! Empowering children as active researchers. *American Journal of Community Psychology*, 46, 195–203.

Kellett, M., Forrest, R., Dent, N., and Ward, S. (2004). Just teach us the skills, please, we'll do the rest! Empowering ten-year-olds as active researchers. *Children and Society*, 18,329–343.

Kim, C-Y. (2017). Participation and pedagogy: Ambiguities and tensions surrounding the facilitation of children as researchers. *Childhood*, 24(1), 84–98.

Kirova, A., and Emme, M. (2008). Fotonovela as a research tool in image-based paarticpatory research with immigrant children. *International Journal of Qualitative Methods*, 7(2), 35–57.

Komulainen, S. (2007). The ambiguity of the child's "voice" in social research. *Childhood*, 14(1),11–28.

Kuchah Kuchah, H., and Pinter, A. (2012). Was this an interview? Breaking the power barrier in adult-child interviews in an African context. *Issues in Educational Research*, 22(3), 283–297.

Mackey, A., and Gass, S. (2005). *Second Language Research Methodology and Design*. London: Routledge.

Mann, A., Liley, J., and Kellett, M (2014). Engaging children and young people in research. In Clark, A. et al. (eds.), *Understanding Research with Children and Young People*. London: Sage, 286–304.

Mayall, B. (ed.) (1994). *Children's Childhoods*. London: Falmer Press.

Mourăo, S., and Lourenço, M. (Eds.). (2015). *Early Years Second Language Education*. London: Routledge.

Murphy, V., and Macaro, E. (2017). It isn't child's play: Conducting research with children as participants. In McKinley, J., and Rose, H. (eds.) *Doing Research in Applied Linguistics: Realities, dilemmas, and solutions*. London: Routledge, 103–113.

Nunan, D. (1992). *Research Methods in Language Learning*. Cambridge: Cambridge University Press.

O'Kane, C. (2008). The development of participatory techniques: Facilitating children's views about decisions which affect them. In Christensen, P. and James, A. (eds.), *Research with Children: Perspectives and practices*. London: Routledge, 125–155.

P21. (2009). Learning environments: A 21st century skills implementation guide. www.p21.org/storage/documents/p21-stateimp_learning_enviroenments.pdf.

Paltridge, B., and Phakiti, A. (2005). *Research Methods in Applied Linguistics: A practical resource*. London: Bloomsbury.

Piaget, J. (1963). *The Language and the Thought of the Child*. London: Routledge and Kegan Paul.

Pinter, A. (2014). Child participant roles in applied linguistics research. *Applied Linguistics*, 35(2), 168–183.

Pinter, A., and Mathew, R. (2017). Links between teacher development and working with children as co-researchers. In Wilden, E., and Porsch, R. (eds.), *The Professional Development of In-service and Pre-service Primary EFL Teachers: National and international research*. Münster: Waxmann, 141–152.

Pinter, A., Mathew, R., and Smith, R. (2016). *Children and Teachers as Co-researchers in Indian Primary English Classrooms: ELT research papers 16.03*. London: British Council.

Pinter, A., and Zandian, S. (2012). 'I thought it would be tiny little one phrase that we said, in a huge big pile of papers': Children's reflections on their involvement in participatory research. *Qualitative Research*, 15(2), 235–250.

Pinter, A., and Zandian, S. (2014). I don't ever want to leave this room: Benefits of researching with children. *ELT Journal*, 68(1), 64–74.

Rich, S. (ed.) (2014). *International Perspectives on Teaching English to Young Learners*. London: Palgrave Macmillan.

Richards, K. (2003). *Qualitative Inquiry in TESOL*. Basingstoke: Palgrave.

Scott, J. (2000). Children as respondents: The challenge for quantitative methods. In Christensen, P., and James, A.(eds.) *Research with Children: Perspectives and practices*. London: Falmer Press, 98–119.

Spyrou, S. (2011). The limits of children's voices: From authenticity to critical reflexive representation. *Childhood*, 18(2), 151–165.

Spyrou, S. (2016). Researching children's silences: Exploring the fullness of voice in childhood research. *Childhood*, 23(1), 7–21.

Tisdall, E. K. M. (2012). The challenge and challenging of Childhood Studies: Learning from disability studies and research with disabled children. *Children and Society*, 26,181–191.

Trilling, B., and Fadal, C (2009). *21 Century Skills: Learning for life in our time*. San Francisco, CA, Jossey-Bass Publishers.

United Nations (1989). *United Nations Conventions on the Rights of the Child*. New York: United Nations.

Woodhead, M., and Faulkner, D. (2008). Subjects, objects or participants: Dilemmas of psychological research with children. In James, A., and Christensen, P. (eds.) *Research with Children: Perspectives and practices*. London: Routledge, 10–39.

Zandian, S. (2015). *Children's Perceptions of Intercultural Issues: An exploration into an Iranian context*. Unpublished PhD dissertation, University of Warwick.

26

Research into the teaching of English as a Foreign language in early childhood education and care

Sandie Mourão

Introduction and definitions

Early childhood education and care (ECEC) – care and education services before entry into formal schooling – has a variety of labels around the world: for example, nursery, day care, pre-kindergarten, kindergarten and pre-school. The referent for early childhood education and care used by the United Nations is 'Early Childhood Education' (UNESCO-UIS 2012), which covers 'early childhood educational development' – children from birth to two years old (infants and toddlers), and 'pre-primary education' – children from three years to the start of primary education, which varies between five and seven years old. I will be using these latter terms in this chapter, which focuses on foreign language (FL) learning in pre-primary education.

Foreign language education, also referred to as 'language exposure programmes', is said to 'prepare and help children to learn a new language' (European Commission 2011, p. 15). Children receive a restricted amount of exposure to the FL in a classroom setting – often as little as 30 minutes, once a week; there may be little or no access to this language outside the classroom, and there are no opportunities for interacting with peers who speak the FL, for children share a common classroom language. English in these circumstances has been referred to as a drip-feed language programme (Baker 2011), turning English into a subject, which is hardly comparable to bilingual or immersion education, where children learn through the medium of another language and experience a higher degree of exposure to this language.

Historical perspectives

The development of early childhood education and care

Early childhood education and care has secured increased policy attention since the 1960s, mainly due to the recognition that care and education is a child's right. According to Papatheodorou (2012, p. 4) research has shown that:

- Early exposure to rich and diverse educational experiences through quality provision improves development and learning.

- Provision in ECEC increases children's educational opportunities and counters social and economic disadvantage.
- Provision of ECEC contributes to reducing poverty and increases household income as a result of enabling parental employment or by being a source of employment.
- With a relatively small investment, the above results in reduced dependency on state welfare and later criminal activity costs.

In all, Papatheodorou highlights that provision of ECEC is 'a service to children, their families and communities and to society in general' (p. 4). Commitment to children's rights and educational requirements are reflected in five of the eight Millennium Developmental Goals (United Nations 2000), and as a result enrolments in pre-primary education worldwide have increased by 64% since 1999 (UNESCO 2015).

Compulsory education in most countries begins with primary education, with just one-fifth of the world's nations with statutory pre-primary education laws (UNESCO 2015, pp. 63–64). Israel (since 1949), Peru (since 2003) and Hungary (since 2015) are the only countries to mandate pre-primary education from the age of three, at the moment of writing. Despite the low number of countries assuring free statutory pre-primary education, recent figures from OECD reports show that as many as 71% of all three-year-olds are enroled in some form of early childhood education programme (OECD 2016, p. 298) – with public provision also on the increase, resulting in 68% of children enroled in pre-primary education attending public institutions (OECD 2016, p. 299).

Pioneers in early childhood education, such as Friedrich Froebel in Germany, Maria Montessori in Italy and Rudolf Steiner in Austria, were all influential educational thinkers who left their mark on the different approaches to early childhood education around the world. These approaches also integrate the ideas of twentieth-century cognitive psychologists like Lev Vygotsky, Jean Piaget and Jerome Bruner. However, practices in each country will vary according to the different perspectives that distinct societies and their specific cultures have towards the child and childhood in general (Cambell-Barr and Georgeson 2015).

Pre-primary education is recognised, in Europe at least, as being qualitatively different to primary education (European Commission 2011), and according to de Botton (2010, p. 7) the different philosophical traditions sit at opposite ends of a continuum: a teacher-led, education-focused approach related to school-readiness skills such as numeracy and literacy (for example, in the USA and China); and a child-directed, social, pedagogic approach, where attention is given to educational goals, play and interactivity with both teachers and peers (for example, in Nordic countries and Germany). In reality, most early-years programmes fall somewhere between the two extremes; however, UNESCO recommends that pre-primary education focus on children's language and social skills, logical and reasoning skills and alphabetical and mathematical concepts, and should aim to develop a child's understanding of the world (UNESCO-UIS 2012, p. 27).

Foreign language education in early childhood education and care

Foreign language education in ECEC has no clear tradition or history in relation to implementation. However, Edelenbos et al. (2006) note that early language learning (mostly English) existed at the beginning of the twenty-first century, especially in the private sector. The latest British Council report on policy and practice suggests English is 'cascading into Early Years teaching' (Rixon 2013, p. 13). With a growing recognition of the importance of ECEC, it is not surprising that English, in particular, is rapidly being introduced into this sector, where parents are also highly influential (Edelenbos et al. 2006; Enever 2015; Rokita-Jaśkow 2013).

The last fifteen years in Europe have also been influenced by language education policy stressing the importance of 'teaching at least two foreign languages from a very early age' (Barcelona European Council 2002, p. 19). The most recent Eurydice report (2017) showed that just over a third of the European community officially implements second or foreign language teaching to children of six years and under. These countries include Cyprus and Poland, where English was introduced as a compulsory part of their pre-primary programme from the age of five in September 2015. At the time, both countries began their statutory pre-primary education law for five-year-olds; however, under the new government in Poland plans were revoked and compulsory education, including English, returned to the last year of pre-primary education at age six.

In Spain, bilingual Spanish and English projects in pre-primary began as pilots in 1996, with English becoming part of the pre-primary programme in 2006 (Andúgar et al. forthcoming; Fleta 2016). English is now compulsory in ten of the seventeen Autonomous Regions, with 2015 figures showing that 79% of all pre-primary children learned English starting at age three in Spain. Since 2008, a select number of bilingual Spanish-English schools in the Madrid community have included two 45-minute sessions of English per week in the final year of pre-primary education. However, the Madrid Community recently announced that these programmes would be expanded in September 2017, to begin at age three, with at least three sessions of 45 minutes a week, increasing to five sessions a week at age five, if these schools have the appropriate staff – pre-primary trained with at least C1 level of English (Comunidad de Madrid 2017).

The lack of national regulations does not deter early English initiatives – for they are well established in many European countries where pre-primary education is not mandatory, bringing about a variety of learning experiences and varied quality (Mourão and Lourenço 2015). English is reportedly taught as a FL in around 50% of the pre-primary institutions in the Czech Republic (Černá 2015), Portugal (Mourão and Ferreirinha 2016), Romania (Dolean 2015), Slovakia (Portiková 2015) and Slovenia (Brumen 2010), and in many cases starting at age three. In Italy a report by Langé et al, (2014) showed that English was taught in 84% of the ECEC centres.

In Eastern Asia, Zhou and Ng (2016) describe English being introduced at ever earlier ages due to parents wanting to give their children 'the best start in life' and accordingly they state that 'the majority of very young (aged three to six) [. . .] are therefore learning English as a foreign language' (p. 137). Ng and Rao (2013), writing about Hong Kong, confirm that 97% of local pre-primary institutions teaching through the medium of Chinese offered English to children from age three by 2008. The emphasis, as in most East Asian countries, is on developing academic skills with the support of a textbook, resulting in a focus on developing early literacy skills over oral skills.

The more cosmopolitan cities of China introduced English into pre-primary education at the beginning of the twenty-first century, and gradually this has escalated to parents sending their pre-primary children to after-school and private English lessons despite Chinese educational authorities advising institutions not to run extra-curricular English activities 'in order to reduce "study pressure" on children' (Jin et al. 2016, p. 3). Similar accounts have been given in relation to Taiwan, where enthusiastic parents are also sending their pre-primary children to English classes as an after-school activity (Tseng 2008) or English only pre-primary institutions, despite government restrictions on their creation (Butler 2009). Furthermore, in South Korea, there are a growing number of fee-paying pre-primary establishments claiming to be 'English kindergartens' (Song 2012, p. 40). Reports that learning English starts in the womb have also been associated with South Korea, where mothers are including English in pre-natal routines to ensure their children survive in a 'hypercompetitive educational environment' (Park 2015).

The trend for languages, mostly English, entering the Latin American educational agenda emerged towards the end of the twentieth century (Banfi 2017). In Mexico, English has been mandatory from the final year of compulsory pre-primary education since 2009; however actual implementation averages at 25% for the primary school population (Sayer et al. 2017) with no data regarding pre-primary. Argentina begins English in Grade 1; however, it has had private, fee-paying bilingual education since the early 1800s, which usually includes pre-primary. The majority of these bilingual schools teach through English and Spanish, though vary dramatically with regards to their socioeconomic student population and curricular content and approach (Banfi and Day 2004). Finally, in Peru where 80 percent of the pre-primary provision is public, a recent baseline study (Mourão 2018a) confirmed that 85 percent of private pre-primary institutions included an early English initiative, compared with 15 percent in the public sector.

The lack of clear research directions beyond surveying national situations is a consequence of the fragility of ECEC due to the insufficiency of formal policy around statutory provision and attendance. In Europe, a European Commission Policy Handbook (European Commission 2011) containing a set of guidelines for early language learning was published with the intention of supporting the already growing initiatives. Since 2015 more robust academic volumes are also becoming available, discussing, to some extent, the issues related to FL learning. However, it is clear that early language learning in ECEC still needs to formulate effective language policies and (re)consider appropriate programmes of implementation (Mourão and Lourenço 2015; Murphy and Evangelou 2016).

Critical issues and topics

The emerging evidence that English is being introduced at an ever earlier age on a worldwide scale could, in itself, be called critical, for guaranteeing that any language policy is effectively and sustainably implemented is complex when a system often lacks an educational policy of its own (Mourão 2016). The different issues can be teased apart, however they are interrelated.

Beliefs

The impact of global processes on policy and practice is responsible for forging English into a 'generic skill' (Enever and Moon 2009, p. 6) to be included in compulsory education as early as possible. Within ECEC, governments and policy makers may not be interested in taking official action towards ensuring a FL is included in pre-primary education due to the absence of statutory early years provision; however, parents continue to be hugely influential, as they foresee the social and economic benefits of their child learning English in a pre-primary education they may already be paying for (Černá 2015; Jin et al. 2015; Portiková 2015; Rokita-Jaśkow 2013). Decisions to enrol a child in English are often supported by the 'the earlier the better' belief, despite the inexistence of research to support this notion (Jaekel et al. 2017; Murphy 2014; Munõz 2006; Singleton and Pfenniger, this volume). Research has also shown that parents are keen to ensure their child is successful in compulsory education by getting a head start in pre-primary education (Jin et al. 2015; Rokita-Jaśkow 2013).

Equal access

Despite an increase in the number of children attending pre-primary education around the world, there is 'considerable difference between urban and rural areas, rich and poor families and communities, and thriving and deprived regions within countries' (UNESCO 2015, p. 59). Butler (2015) laments the scarcity of research into socioeconomic status (SES) and FL education and highlights a concern regarding the gaps in opportunities 'based on region, student SES and ethnic/linguistic status in many parts of the world' (p. 413). Rokita-Jaśkow (2013) has indicated that a child's SES is the major factor contributing to inequality in her study into parental aspirations in Poland.

The staff and teacher education

The ideal teacher profile for English in pre-primary is unclear – a pre-primary professional who speaks English well enough, or an English teacher who has training in early years pedagogies. European Commission guidelines highlight the relevance of staff qualifications as a critical factor in the quality of pre-primary settings and the children's learning experiences. This holds for staff supporting early language learning activities (European Commission 2011, p. 17). Teachers working with such young children require an understanding of the principles of ECEC pedagogy and child development, age-appropriate foreign language methodologies as well as a competence in English that gives them confidence to speak fluently and spontaneously to children in the L2. Hanušová and Najvar (2006, in Černá 2015, p. 173), suggest that 'the younger the child starting to learn an L2, the higher the importance of teacher qualifications'; proficiency in English alone is not sufficient, for English should not be seen as a discrete subject within an ECEC curriculum that generally takes a holistic approach to educating children.

Age-appropriate practices

The European Commission Policy Handbook highlights what they call 'proven orientations' (2011, p. 8) for pedagogical processes and states:

> Language-learning activities should be adapted to the age of the learners and to the pre-primary context. Children should be exposed to the target language in meaningful and, if possible, authentic settings, in such a way that the language is spontaneously acquired rather than consciously learnt.
>
> *(European Commission 2011, p. 17)*

These orientations show, above all, that we should be ensuring the FL takes into consideration the educational attributes of pre-primary education; these focus on educating the whole child – learning and developing through a language, not learning a language for the sake of the language. Unfortunately, a review of practices undertaken by European member states implementing language-learning projects shows that there is 'little evidence of agreed processes, uniformity of approach or established indicators of achievement in early language learning' (ibid.). Edelenbos et al. (2006) describe a variety of language-learning models that have been observed in pre-primary education. These range along a continuum from low to high exposure:

- *A language awareness model*, which provides access to a number of languages and cultures in order to develop a plurilingual curriculum.
- *A language exposure model* to a FL, which sees the language learning experience as an end in itself.
- *Content and language integrated learning model* (CLIL), which associates the language with individual subjects, such as music.
- *Bilingual or partial/full immersion models*, where children are taught in an official or minority/regional language other than the child's home, community or heritage language.

The very nature of pre-primary education, following a curriculum supporting the holistic development of the child, would suggest that the language exposure model, viewing language as a specific subject and not as a 'communication tool to be used in other activities' (European Commission 2011, p. 14), is inappropriate for pre-primary education. In addition, where CLIL is subject-based it might also challenge the relevance of its suitability with such young children. As such, an *integrated model* (Brumen, Fras Berro and Cagran 2017; Moja Guijarro 2003; Mourão 2015b; Robinson et al. 2015) has been described which proposes emulating the way children learn in their ECEC context and would appear more suitable for low-exposure initiatives. An integrated model also suggests that the FL is planned to accompany what the children are doing in their daily ECEC activities so connections can be made between learning through the languages (Dolean 2015). Such a model also implies a collaborative approach between the pre-primary professional and FL teacher, if they are indeed two different staff members (Mourão and Robinson 2016).

Current contributions and research

Parental motivations

Parental involvement in a young child's education is recognised as being highly relevant and this naturally holds true with FL learning. Rokita-Jaśkow (2013) describes the educational aspirations of Poland's emerging middle class as one of their defining features, and as a result, she suggests that Polish parents' visions of their children's future linguistic competence contribute to arousing their child's own educational aspiration, therefore developing intergenerational success. Rokita-Jaśkow concludes that 'an investment into child FL education does require some financial resources' (p. 221) and appeals to policy makers to provide quality pre-primary FL education for all children, not just those whose parents can afford it.

Jin et al. (2015) have also researched attitudes and experiences of Chinese parents with pre-primary children learning English. They describe parents (and grandparents) in China putting 'all their hopes and resources on the single child of each family' (p. 3) in the belief that English will 'help ensure a child's future' (ibid.). The study involved 243 parents of children attending pre-primary institutions in urban and rural areas in three different locations in China. Their data suggests that parents with undergraduate or graduate qualifications were more likely to support their child's FL experience, either due to higher expectations, or because they were able to spend more time with their child. Just over half of the parents in the study paid extra for their child's English education and though SES, regional and urban and rural divides were significant in relation to parental attitude, the authors highlight how difficult it is to interpret their data as it is sometimes contradictory. Nevertheless, it is clear that parental views have an impact on the children's perceptions of English, which were generally positive.

Parental motivation can result in a variety of different approaches to ensuring a child is taught English. As such, research into home-schooling in English (and other languages), which usually involves families of a higher SES, is also emerging (Pirchio et al. 2015; Prosic-Santovac 2016; Sokol and Lasevich 2015).

Policy

Coherent, clear policy regarding the official implementation of FLs in pre-primary education is rare, and research into these policies and their implementation is negligible. Andúgar et al. (forthcoming) share an exhaustive analysis of how the eighteen Autonomous Regions in Spain approach the national regulations of 2006, which suggests that it is the responsibility of the local education authorities to include a FL from three to six years old. The variety of interpretations includes a difference in guidelines around who is responsible for the English teaching (the pre-primary professional, an English teacher or both); the teachers' language competence; whether language assistants are involved; the number of hours devoted to English; and the different approaches, which may or may not be labelled bilingual language education or CLIL. Andúgar et al.'s study concludes that only three Autonomous Regions – Andalucía, Cantabria and Navarra – successfully implement pre-primary language education according to the criteria established by the European Commission (2011). Fewer than half of the regions have elaborated a comprehensive plan for English in pre-primary education and many regions are limited for economic reasons. The relationship between English and the regional languages, such as Catalan or Basque, has also affected implementation. Andúgar et al. consider the heterogeneity of the regions to be the major stumbling block in a successful nationwide implementation, which is likely to be the reason in most countries where there are larger differences between urban and rural areas, e.g., Mexico or China.

Staff profiles

In primary education, C1 level is considered more desirable 'as it enables teachers to be fully functional in the informal and incidental language regularly required in primary classrooms' (Enever 2011, p. 26). The opportunities for informal and incidental language use in ECEC contexts would appear to warrant this higher proficiency, so C1 may well be the level of competence required for pre-primary professionals teaching English. In Cyprus, where English is generally spoken to a fairly high proficiency, due to its history as a British colony, pre-primary professionals are said to be of C1 level (Ioannou-Georgio 2015). Here, a structured in-service training programme has ensured that pre-primary professionals are given training in FL teaching methodologies to teach English in the last year of statutory pre-primary provision (ibid.). Those professionals who were trained initially showed concern about their ability to implement the project, mostly due to lack of confidence in their own language proficiency. However, after two years of the programme their self-assurance increased as they began to 'identify emerging results in their children's learning' (p. 101), which included a high level of listening comprehension, development in language production and communication strategies, a positive attitude towards English, languages and cultures generally and a positive response from children with learning difficulties.

In Italy, the pre-primary professionals are generally responsible for early language learning with a required language proficiency of B2 (Langé et al. 2014). Ng and Rao (2013) have reported that in Hong Kong there is a relative balance between native English speakers and pre-primary professionals teaching English; however, just 15% of these professionals have training in ECEC and English teaching, and around 30% of the pre-primary professionals have received no training in English. Andúgar et al. (forthcoming) reveal that in Spain nine of the autonomous regions recommend that English be taught by pre-primary professionals with a level of English at B2, with one autonomous region recommending a C1 level, and four autonomous regions recommending that specialist English teachers teach English. Fleta (2016) surveyed the Madrid Community in particular, where she found that just over 50% were trained primary teachers who had re-qualified as English teachers and around 40% were pre-primary professionals. Seventy percent claimed to be B2 or C1 level English. The present law (Comunidad de Madrid 2017) requires that all Madrid Community English teachers be C1 level.

Other studies have reported that staff trained to teach English to older children and adults are brought into pre-primary as peripatetic English teachers as well as individuals who may not have any formal qualifications in English or ECEC (see Cortina-Pérez and Andúgar 2017; Černá 2015; Lugossy 2018; Mourão and Ferreirinha 2016; Ng 2013; and Portiková 2015). The section below shares research that looks at the extent to which these different models are successful or not; however, it is clear that due to the lack of legislation generally, national standards or quality control visits to regulate practices are non-existent. Where policies exist, they are often implemented without consideration of who would eventually be responsible for teaching English.

Classroom practices

Classroom practices will be affected by any number of specific contextual concerns, which include national or localised approaches to ECEC, existence of national FL policy, stakeholder interest, funding, staff profiles and training as well as access to resources. The following section looks at research into learning outcomes and specific approaches to teaching and learning in a FL.

Peripatetic staff and collaborative practices

When English teachers are peripatetic, and do not belong to a school's permanent staff, making connections between the children's learning and English is challenging. Ng (2013) shares research undertaken in Hong Kong, where the pre-primary professional teaches English with the support of a visiting English teacher. The English teachers in the study came from different educational backgrounds: a local pre-primary professional with no training in English, a native speaker English teacher with no training in ECEC and a native speaker with neither ECEC or English training. Ng suggests that the low-exposure setting resulted in a 'product-oriented approach' by all visiting English teachers, which was characterised by the use of 'teacher-dominated strategies, with fewer chances for teacher-child or child-child free interaction but a major focus on the form-focused activities like drilling of language items, in particular the vocabulary learning' (p. 18). Limited professional knowledge together with an inappropriate textbook was also considered a reason for form-focused activities, which were even observed in the English teacher who had ECEC training. Another result emerging from the study was the lack of sensitivity shown by the native speaker with no teaching qualifications. In another report of this study Ng (2015) highlights the absence of three enabling factors in these contexts:

- The pedagogical factor, where neither staff has the knowledge or training to develop a professional relationship which was beneficial for all involved.
- The logistical factor, focusing on the peripatetic staff's part-time status which hindered joint planning and the necessary creation of a professional relationship.
- The interpersonal factor exasperated by the lack of time for collaboration.

On a more positive note, research by Mourão and Robinson (2016) has shown that when peripatetic and permanent staff collaborate and both take responsibility for the children's English experience, English was integrated and meaningful. In a project which investigated the set-up of an English learning area to foster opportunities for child-led play in English, English was seen as part of the children's everyday activities and not restricted to the teacher-led English sessions which made sure 'children were exposed to English in a systematic way' (p. 262). During the rest of the time, the pre-primary professional was a key motivator, 'ensuring children saw English as part of their everyday lives' (ibid.). She was also 'responsible for organising the space and planning time for English to be part of the classroom' (ibid.), and was essential in guaranteeing parental involvement by helping them understand what was happening to support and motivate their children at home.

Pre-primary children's attitudes and motivation

Jin et al. (2016) used elicited metaphor analysis to gain insights into pre-primary children's 'conceptual thoughts' towards English (p. 11) in China. In a study involving 243 children from urban and rural settings, the authors ascertained that just over 50% of the children's metaphors were positive and 36% were neutral, suggesting that children's attitudes towards English were positive. The same study also provided evidence that these children's attitudes, and consequently their motivation, towards English were dependent upon peers' attitudes and parents' views towards English and learning in general (p. 22), as well as the kinds of activities they engaged in during English sessions. Jin et al.'s study did not include detailed analysis of the learning environment.

Regarding intrinsic motivation and its relationship with environmental variables, Wu (2003) reported on a quantitative study with 72 pre-primary children (four to six years old) learning English in Hong Kong. Using an experimental and control group, a setting was created which furnished a predictive learning environment for meaningful and genuine communication; included challenging and open-ended activities that encourage creativity and initiative; provided opportunities for variety in learner organisation (e.g., whole group, pair work, small group work); and allowed for formative assessment activities and strategy training to facilitate self-improvement. Results show clear evidence that the teaching method was a significant predictor of intrinsic motivation. In addition, perceived competence and perceived autonomy exhibited direct relationships with intrinsic motivation. Brumen (2010) has also described Slovenian pre-primary children's motivation towards English in a study where 120 children ages four to six years old were involved in semi-structured interviews after participating in English and German lessons. Intrinsic motivation was noted as being very positive in a context where 'children learnt the foreign language on the basis of concrete experiences and active participation in activities' (2010, p. 723). Taking a more qualitative approach, Brumen concluded that children showed intrinsic motivation through an

evident desire to learn the FL for its own sake. This was also demonstrated in their awareness of, and pride shown in, their ability to use the FL in a variety of different ways. Elvin
et al. (2007) report on a qualitative study which makes similar assertions around the visits
of a dynamic English teacher to two pre-primary institutions in Norway.

Developmentally appropriate practices

The studies described above demonstrate that by creating a learning environment that
is developmentally appropriate in terms of learning content, as well as child-centred in
approach, children's motivations and attitudes are positive. Developmentally appropriate
practices include the use of songs, chants and nursery rhymes, stories and picturebooks,
games and game-like activities, movement and hands-on interactive pursuits and an integrated approach to learning experiences which develop the whole child (Brumen 2010;
Elvin et al. 2007; Fleta 2006; Ghosn 2016; Ordóñes 2016; Robinson et al. 2015; Wu 2003).
For research into quantitative studies around using song, see Coyle and Garcia (2014) and
Davis and Fan (2016). For a more qualitative example of research into using picturebooks,
see Mourão (2015a).

A report on a recent comparative study in the Madrid Community (Ramirez and Kuhl
2017) provides an excellent description of optimal conditions for an early language learning
initiative, albeit with infants from seven to 33 months old. The study involved 126 infants in
intervention groups and 124 matched infants attending the bilingual Spanish English initiatives mentioned earlier. The intervention grouped 12 infants, in homogeneous age groups,
who spent one hour a day with four different native English speakers who had been trained
in a method which involved:

- High quantities of English input, organised around weekly topics.
- Use of parentese (higher pitch, slower tempo and exaggerated intonation contours).
- Highly social interactions, meaningful and engaging activities (routines, game-like
  activities and picturebook reading), all supported with prompt and contingent responses
  by adults.
- Children being encouraged to talk and interact.
- Access to multiple native speakers (groups of 12 children with four adults).
- Play-based activities.

After 18 weeks, the intervention group showed rapid gains in English word comprehension
and English speech production. SES levels were not considered a significant factor in their
learning. Though difficult to replicate such conditions, mainly due to the high child-adult
ratio of 3 to 1, this study reinforces the importance of quality interaction and the relevance
of more time dedicated to developmentally appropriate activities in and with the target
language.

In countries where a more academic perspective is associated with pre-primary education, English activities may involve the use of a textbook and focus on acquiring early literacy skills, though this is an approach which has been attested (Ghosn 2016; Ng 2013; Ng
and Rao 2013). Research into these specific activities in FL settings remains scarce.

Including free play in English is considered highly relevant in pre-primary English as it
emulates good practice in ECEC. Mourão (2014) elaborates on the importance of providing
for a balance of child-initiated and adult-led activities in FL learning, and in order for this
to be possible, English is made available to children in an English learning area (ELA). An

ELA is one of any number of learning areas in an open plan classroom set up to promote child-initiated play. Research by Robinson et al. (2015) in Portugal and South Korea has shown that children learning English in low exposure settings enjoy playing in ELAs and interacting in English with the resources they find there. Child-initiated play in the ELA extends the amount of time children are exposed to English, as this play occurs outside the formal English sessions with the English teacher. Robinson et al. suggest that the resources stimulate memories of teacher-led English sessions, as children re-enacted teacher-led activities, took on the role of teacher and student and replicated familiar sequences of English associated with teacher-led activities (p. 28). Nevertheless, play in the ELAs also prompted experimental use of English, which implies children are creative with English during play. Mourão (2018c) has shown that children scaffold each other in novice/expert interactions during child-initiated play in the FL as well as make the most of their linguistic repertoires by using both Portuguese and English, thus assuring peer interaction takes place successfully.

Classroom language

Llinares Garcia (2007) has investigated pre-primary learners' functional use of language in low exposure FL sessions. Using Halliday and Painter's six main language functions – heuristic, informative, personal, regulatory, informational and interactional – she analysed transcriptions of lessons where a teacher used 'activities and role-plays that promoted the pupils' discourse initiations in the L2 and the use of this language to perform the same communicative functions as in the L1' (p. 41). Her results show that children were able to initiate interaction very successfully in the FL and used less L1 after the treatment. Llinares Garcia suggests this was due to the teacher's controlled activities which were adapted to the learners and the move from using display questions to providing children with real reasons for using and interacting in English. The most common function used by both experimental and control groups in the classroom language was the personal function, but in the experimental group this function was greater in English. Llinares Garcia concludes that appropriate use of activities to encourage the personal function can succeed in more use of the target language.

Mourão (2018b) has reported on similar interactive language use in teacher-led activities during English sessions, which later support child-initiated activities in ELAs. She highlights the relevance of routines which provide what Bruner (1983, p. 45) describes as occasions for 'systematic use of language with an adult', and refers to them as 'closely circumscribed format(s)' (1983, p. 46). 'Formats' contain a structure, clearly marked turn-taking roles and a script-like quality, which combines action and communication. The repetitive nature of circle time, where routines are paramount accompanied by teacher-led, often game-like activities which naturally contain multiple closely circumscribed formats, provide children with opportunities for prediction to support their understanding as well as favour language development.

Recommendations for practice

First and foremost, we have seen that policy is rarely existent, so the implementation of sound policies, which take national contexts into consideration, are essential to support the implementation of English in a pre-primary education system. This policy should take into account the staff available to teach English, the time required to train them, together with the opportunities for continuation into primary education. Parents should also be better informed of the limitations of a low-exposure learning model, which is nothing like immersion or bilingual education, and as their voice appears to contribute to policy making, they should be encouraged to insist on quality language education by trained staff. Teacher education is of essence, for as yet institutions that train pre-primary professionals to teach English or English teachers to teach in pre-primary are rare.

Classroom approaches require an understanding of how children learn in ECEC, so recommendations should clearly emulate local ECEC approaches, which are likely to include providing a balance of child-initiated and adult-led activity. English should also be integrated into the children's everyday learning and not seen as a separate subject, isolated from their daily realities. In addition, expectations of what children can do in English require care and attention, and opportunities should be created for language to be used in meaningful situations which are relevant to children. Finally, all staff involved in the children's education need to work together to ensure that the children's English experience is a positive and joyous one.

Future directions

Precious little research involves pre-primary FL learners, so research in any direction would be welcome. But of extreme importance is research that looks at the learning journey a child follows when beginning English at age three – data from longitudinal studies in a variety of low-exposure FL contexts would be very useful. Comparative studies where learners begin in pre-primary versus those that begin later would also be of relevance. Research into different staff profiles and the resulting learning approaches and outcomes including the systematic collection of examples of good practices seen in relation to different settings would contribute to a greater understanding of the relevance of these factors to successful learning outcomes.

Investigating different practices using both quantitative and qualitative research approaches would contribute to a more robust collection of data to support policy making. Areas that desperately require evidence from research to inform practice include literacy development in the FL, FL education in settings where children come from minority language backgrounds, peer interaction in the FL, classroom interactional language and collecting evidence of progression in a FL.

Further readings

1 European Commission (2011). *Language learning at pre-primary school Level: Making it efficient and sustainable. A policy handbook*. Brussels: European Commission. http://ec.europa.eu/dgs/education_culture/repository/languages/policy/language-policy/documents/early-language-learning-handbook_en.pdf.

   A European document, available online, which provides useful guidelines for implementing early language learning, with a collection of good practices from different countries.

2 Mourão, S. (2014). Taking play seriously in pre-primary English classes. *ELT Journal*, 63(3), 254–264.

   A useful article which discusses the importance of incorporating play into FL education and provides a suggestion of how this can be organised.

3 Mourão, S., and Lourenço, M. (Eds.). (2015). *Early years second language education: International perspectives on theories and practice*. Abingdon: Routledge.

   This is a collection of chapters that draws on a synthesis of theory, research and practice to explore language learning in a range of geographical contexts and includes second language learning, foreign language learning, bilingual education, plurilingualism and home-schooling.

4 Murphy, V., and Evangelou, M. (Eds.). (2016). *Early childhood education in English for speakers of other languages*. London: British Council. www.teachingenglish.org.uk/article/early-childhood-education-english-speakers-other-language

This is a collection of chapters that provides a more focused look at the issues involved in teaching English in the early years (up to age seven) including English as a second language, English as a foreign language and English immersion. It is also available online.

Related topics

Materials, research methods for investigating TEYL, projects, listening and speaking

References

Andúgar, A., Cortina-Pérez, B., and Tornel, M. (forthcoming). Tratamiento de la lengua extranjera en Educación Infantil en las distintas comunidades autónomas españolas. *Revista de Profesorado*.

Baker, C. (2011). *Foundations of Bilingual Education and Bilingualism*, 5th ed. Bristol: Multilingual Matters.

Banfi, C. (2017). English language teaching expansion in South America: Challenges and opportunities. In Kamhi-Stein, L. D., Diaz Maggioli, G., and de Oliveira, L. C. (eds.) *English Language Teaching in South America: Policy, preparation, and practices*. Clevedon: Multilingual Matters, 13–30.

Banfi, C., and Day, R. (2004). The evolution of bilingual schools in Argentina. *International Journal of Bilingual Education and Bilingualism*, 7(5), 398–411.

Barcelona European Council (15–16 March 2002). Presidency conclusions. http://ec.europa.eu/invest-in research/pdf/download_en/barcelona_european_council.pdf [Accessed 17 June 2017].

Brumen, M. (2010). The perception of and motivation for foreign language learning in preschool. *Early Child Development and Care*, 181(6), 717–732.

Brumen, M., Fras Berro, F., and Cagran, B. (2018). Preschool Foreign Language Teaching and Learning – a Network Innovation Project in Slovenia. *European Early Childhood Education Research Journal*, 25 (6), 904-917.

Bruner, J. (1983). *Child's Talk: Learning to use language*. New York: Norton.

Butler, Y. G. (2009). Teaching English to young learners: The influence of global and local factors. In Enever, J., Moon, J., and Raman, U. (eds.) *Young Learner English Language Policy and Implementation: International practices*. Reading: Garnet Education, 23–29.

Butler, Y. G. (2015). English language education among young learners in East Asia: A review of current research (2004–2014). *Language Teaching*, 48(3), 303–342.

Cambell-Barr, V., and Georgeson, J. (2015). *International Perspectives on Early Years Workforce Development*. Northwich: Critical Publishing.

Černá, M. (2015). Pre-primary English language learning and teacher education in the Czech Republic. In Mourão, S., and Lourenço, M. (eds.) *Early Years Second Language Education: International perspectives on theories and practice*. Abingdon: Routledge, 165–176.

Comunidad de Madrid (2017). *Extensión del Programa Bilingüe español-inglés al segundo ciclo de Educación Infantil en los colegios públicos bilingües de Educación Infantil y Primaria de la Comunidad de Madrid*. ORDEN 2126/2017. Madrid, Consejería de Educación, Juventud y Deporte.

Cortina-Pérez, B., and Andúgar, A. (2017). An exploratory study on English teachers' opinions in multicultural preschools. *Procedia Social and Behavioural Science*, 237, 334–340.

Coyle, Y., and Gómez Gracia, G. (2014). Using songs to enhance L2 vocabulary acquisition in preschool children. *ELT Journal*, 68(3), 276–285.

Davis, G. M., and Fan, W. (2016). English vocabulary acquisition through songs in Chinese kindergarten students. *Chinese Journal of Applied Linguistics*, 39(1), 59–71.

Dolean, D. D. (2015). How early can we efficiently start teaching a foreign language?. *European Early Childhood Education Research Journal*, 23(5), 706–719.

Edelenbos, P., Johnstone, R., and Kubanek, A. (2006). *The Main Pedagogical Principles Underlying the Teaching of Languages to Very Young Learners: Languages for the children of Europe*. Final Report of the EAC 89/04, Lot 1 study. Brussels: European Commission.

Elvin, P., Maagerø, E., and Simonsen, B. (2007). How do the dinosaurs speak in England? English in kindergarten. *European Early Childhood Education Research Journal*, 15(1), 71–86.

Enever, J. (2015). Advantages and disadvantages of EFL with young learners. In Bland, J. (ed.) *Teaching English to Young Learners: Critical issues in language teaching with 3–12 year olds*. London: Bloomsbury, 13–29.

Enever, J., and Moon, J. (2009). New global contexts for teaching primary ELT: Change and challenge. In Enever, J., Moon, J., and Raman, U. (eds.) *Young Learner English Language Policy and Implementation: International practices*. Reading: Garnet Education, 5–21.

European Commission (2011). *Language Learning at Pre-primary School Level: Making it efficient and sustainable. A policy handbook*. Brussels: European Commission.

Eurydice (2017). *Key Data on Teaching Languages at School in Europe*. Brussels: Education, Audiovisual and Culture Executive Agency.

Fleta, T. (2006). Stepping stones for teaching English L2 in the early years. In Mitchell-Schuitevoerder, R., and Mourão, S. (eds.) *Teachers and Young Learners: Research in our classrooms*. Kent: International Association of Teachers of English as a Foreign Language, 43–51.

Fleta, T. (2016). El aprendizaje temprano de lenguas extranjeras en la Comunidad de Madrid: Implicaciones del perfil y metodologías de los docentes. *Didáctica. Lengua y Literatura, 28*, 87–111.

Ghosn, I.-K. (2016). No place for coursebooks in the very young learner classroom. In Tomlinson, B. (ed.) *SLA Research and Materials Development for Language Learning*. Abingdon: Routledge, 50–66.

Ioannou-Georgiou, S. (2015). Early language learning in Cyprus: Voices from the classroom. In Mourão, S., and Lourenço, M. (eds.) *Early Years Second Language Education: International perspectives on theories and practice*. Abingdon: Routledge, 95–108.

Jaekel, N., Schurig, M., Florian, M., and Ritter, M. (2017). From early starters to late finishers? A longitudinal study of early foreign language learning in school. *Language Learning*, 67(3), 631–664.

Jin, L., Zhou, J., Hu, X., Yang, X., Sun, K., and Zhao, M. (2016). *Researching the Attitudes and Perceived Experiences of Kindergarten Learners of English and their Parents in China*. London: British Council.

Langé, G., Marrocchi, D., Lopriore, L., Benvenuto, G., Cinganotto, L., and Vacca, M. (2014). Esperienze di insegnamento in lingua straniera nella Scuola dell'Infanzia. Report presented at 'Early Childhood Education and Care and Early Language Learning', Reggio Children – Loris Malaguzzi Centre Foundation, 16–18 December 2014, Reggio Emilia, Italy. www.istruzione.it/allegati/2015/INFANZIA_Lingue_Straniere_Rapporto_Monitoraggio_Dicembre%202014.pdf [Accessed 17 June 2017].

Llinares Garcia, A. (2007). Young learners' functional use of the L2 in a low immersion EFL context. *ELT Journal*, 61(1), 39–45.

Lugossy, R. (2018). Whose challenge is it? Learners and teachers of English in Hungarian preschool contexts. In Schwartz, M. (ed.) Preschool Bilingual Education: Agency in Interactions between Children, Teachers, and Parents. Dordrecht, Netherlands: Springer.

Moja Guijarro, A. J. (2003). La adquisición/aprendizaje de la pronunciación, del vocabulario y de las estructuras interrogativas en lengua inglesa. Un estudio por edades. *Didáctica, Lengua y Literatura*, 15, 161–177. https://revistas.ucm.es/index.php/DIDA/article/view/DIDA0303110161A [Accessed 17 June 2017].

Mourão, S. (2014). Taking play seriously in pre-primary English classes. *ELT Journal*, 63(3), 254–264.

Mourão, S. (2015a). Response to picturebooks: A case for valuing children's linguistic repertoires during repeated read alouds. In Mourão, S., and Lourenço, M. (eds.) *Early Years Second Language Education: International perspectives on theories and practice*. Abingdon: Routledge, 62–79.

Mourão, S. (2015b). English at pre-primary: the challenges of getting it right. In Bland, J. (ed.) *Teaching English to Young Learners: Critical issues in language teaching with 3–12 year olds*. London: Bloomsbury, 51–70.

Mourão, S. (2016). ELT in early childhood education: From a trickling stream to a cascading river. *Children and Teenagers* (1), 15–19.

Mourão, S. (2018a). *English Teaching in the Early Years: Research in Peru*. Lima: British Council. http://docplayer.net/74534175-English-teaching-in-the-early-years-research-in-peru-report.html [Accessed 19 May 2018].

Mourão, S. (2018b). Playing in English: The emerging voices of pre-primary children in a foreign language context. In Copland, F., and Garton, S. (eds.) *Voices from the TESOL Classroom: Participant inquiries in young learner classes*. Alexandria, VIC: TESOL, 67-76.

Mourão, S. (2018c). The social and linguistic benefits of peer interaction in a foreign language-learning programme. In Schwartz, M. (ed.) *Preschool Bilingual Education: Agency in Interactions between Children, Teachers, and Parents*. Dordrecht, Netherlands: Springer

Mourão, S., and Ferreirinha, S. (2016). Early language learning in pre-primary education in Portugal. Unpublished report. www.appi.pt/activeapp/wp-content/uploads/2016/07/Pre-primary-survey-report-July-FINAL-rev.pdf [Accessed 17 June 2017].

Mourão, S., and Lourenço, M. (Eds.). (2015). *Early Years Second Language Education: International perspectives on theories and practice*. Abingdon: Routledge

Mourão, S., and Robinson, P. (2016). Facilitating the learning of English through collaborative practice. In Murphy, V., and Evangelou, M. (eds.) *Early Childhood Education in English for Speakers of Other Languages*. London: British Council, 253–264.

Munõz, C. (2006). *Age and the Rate of Foreign Language Learning: Second language acquisition*. Clevedon: Multilingual Matters.

Murphy, V. A. (2014). *Second Language Learning in the Early School Years: Trends and contexts*. Oxford: Oxford University Press.

Murphy, V., and Evangelou, M. (Eds.). (2016). *Early Childhood Education in English for Speakers of Other Languages*. London: British Council.

Ng, M. L. (2013). Pedagogical conditions for the teaching and learning of English as a foreign language in Hong Kong kindergartens. *English Teaching and Learning*, 37(3), 1–35.

Ng, M. L. (2015). Difficulties with team teaching in Hong Kong kindergartens. *ELT Journal*, 62(2), 188–197.

Ng, M. L., and Rao, N. (2013). Teaching English in Hong Kong kindergartens: A survey of practices. *The International Journal of Literacies*, 19 (3), 25–47.

OECD (2016). *Education At a Glance: 2016 indicators*. OECD Publishing. http://download.ei-ie.org/Docs/WebDepot/EaG2016_EN.pdf [Accessed 17 June 2017].

Ordóñes, C. L. (2016). Just singing, role playing and reading: A case study in education for bilingualism. In Murphy, V., and Evangelou, M. (eds.) *Early Childhood Education in English for Speakers of Other Languages*. London: British Council, 241–253.

Pirchio, S., Taeschner, T., Colibaba, A. C., Gheorghiu, E., and Jursová Zacharová, Z. (2015). Family involvement in second language learning: The Bilfam project. In Mourão, S., and Lourenço, M. (eds.) *Early Years Second Language Education: International perspectives on theories and practice*. Abingdon: Routledge, 204–217.

Portiková, Z. (2015). Pre-primary second language education in Slovakia and the role of teacher training programmes. In Mourão, S., and Lourenço, S. (eds.) *Early Years Second Language Education: International perspectives on theories and practice*. Abingdon: Routledge, 177–188.

Rokita-Jaśkow, J. (2013). *Foreign Language Learning at Pre-primary Level: Parental aspirations and educational practice*. Kraków: Wydawnictwo Naukowe Uniwerytetu Pedagogicznego.

Papatheodorou, T. (2012). *Debates on Early Childhood Policies and Practices: Global snapshots of pedagogical thinking and encounters*. Abingdon: Routledge.

Park, S. (2015). Tae-gyo: Prenatal intensive mothering in South Korea. https://thesocietypages.org/socimages/2015/09/09/tae-gyo-prenatal-intensive-mothering-in-south-korea/ [Accessed 17 June 2017].

Prosic-Santovac, D. (2016). Popular video cartoons and associated branded toys in teaching English to very young learners: A case study. *Language Teaching Research*. doi:10.1177/1362168816639758.

Rixon, S. (2013). *British Council Survey of Policy and Practice in Primary English Language Teaching Worldwide*. London: British Council.

Robinson, P., Mourão, S., and Kang, N. J. (2015). *English Learning Areas in Preschool Classrooms: An investigation of their effectiveness in supporting EFL development*. London: British Council. https://www.teachingenglish.org.uk/article/english-learning-areas-pre-primary-classrooms-investigation-their-effectiveness [Accessed 19 May 2018].

Sayer, P., Ban, R., and López de Anda, M. (2017). Evaluating the educational outcomes of an early foreign language programme: The design of an impact study for the primary English programme in Mexico. In Enever, J., and Lindgren, E. (eds.) *Early Language Learning: Complexity and mixed methods*. Bristol: Multilingual Matters.

Sokol, A., and Lasevich, E. (2015). Supporting parents in building learning activities in another language. In Mourão, S., and Lourenço, M. (eds.) *Early Years Second Language Education: International perspectives on theories and practice*. Abingdon: Routledge, 218–235.

Song, J. J. (2012). South Korea: language policy and planning in the making. *Current Issues in Language Planning*, 13(1), 1–68.

Tseng, C-L. (2008). Understanding the desirability of English language education in Taiwan. *Contemporary Issues in Early Childhood*, 9(1), 83–86.

UNESCO (2015). *Education for all 2000–2015: Achievements and challenges*. Paris: UNESCO.

UNESCO-UIS (2012). *International Standard Classification of Education ISCED 2011*. Montreal: UNESCO Institute for Statistics.

United Nations (2000, September 18). General Assembly resolution 55/2. United Nations Millennium Declaration A/RES/55/2. www.un.org/millennium/declaration/ares552e.pdf [Accessed 17 June 2017].

Wu, X. (2003). Intrinsic motivation and young language learners: The impact of the classroom environment. *System*, 31(4), 501–517.

Zhou, Y., and Ng, M. L. (2016). English as a foreign language (EFL) and English medium instruction (EMI) for three- to seven-year old children in East Asian contexts. In Murphy, V., and Evangelou, M. (eds.) *Early Childhood Education in English for Speakers of Other Languages*. London: British Council, 137–158.

27

Research on learning English outside the classroom

Peter Sayer and Ruth Ban

Introduction

The relative advantages of learning a second language in a formal classroom setting versus 'picking it up' in a natural or informal context have long been debated. An early second language acquisition (SLA) theory proposed by Krashen (1981) held that there was a fundamental distinction between L2 *acquisition* and *learning*. He argued that true language acquisition came not from consciously studying language rules and grammatical structures, but rather unconsciously through receiving significant amounts of input in the target language. Although most contemporary SLA researchers reject the strong version of the learning versus acquisition distinction (called a 'non-interface position', cf. MacWhinney's (2008) 'Competition Model'), many note that successful L2 learners often have many opportunities for informal learning. In L2 teaching, immersion and study abroad programmes are modelled after input-intensive approaches (Christian 2006). However, most younger students in the world still learn English predominantly through traditional face-to-face classroom instruction. This reality prompts the questions: what is the current state of research on children's informal L2 English learning? What is the potential for out-of-school L2 English learning for younger learners?

Disconnects between early L2 learning outside the classroom and SLA research

Mainstream SLA research dating back to the 1960s has tended to focus on adult or late adolescent learners (Myles 2010). Central concepts such as *interlanguage, native/non-native speakers,* and *target language* were developed within a cognitivist framework that assumed these were relatively fixed and unproblematic. Within the past decade applied linguists approaching SLA from a sociocultural orientation (Atkinson 2011; Block 2003) have argued that SLA theory needs to account far better for the social aspects of L2 learning, such as the social context and learner's identity. Likewise, Ortega (2013) has argued that SLA should take a 'bi/multilingual turn', which would include attention to heretofore neglected areas such as child early second language acquisition and bilingual first language acquisition. It is our opinion that when considering young L2 learners' use of English we need to expand our view of what counts as engagements with the target language. New language policies have been instrumental in creating programmes to teach English in the primary grades; the introduction of these programmes has lowered the age at which many students begin to study the language, and have – some significantly – expanded the amount of instruction they receive (Cha and Ham 2008; Enever 2012). The expansion of formal English instruction mirrors another trend: the expansion of opportunities children have for informal language learning outside of school (Edelenbos et al. 2006). While the research to date on early L2 English programmes has grown, focusing mostly on policies, pedagogy and acquisition, the role of children's exposure and use of English outside the classroom remains largely unexplored (cf. Nikolov and Mihaljevic Djigunovic 2011). Murphy (2014) explains that young learners' opportunities to use English are shaped by the social context beyond the classroom. However, typically, and especially in countries in the expanding circle or English as a foreign language (EFL varieties) settings as defined by Kachru (1990), the assumption is that the amount of exposure children have to English outside of class time is quite restricted because the language is not widely used in the social context (Sayer and Ban 2014).

We would argue that, on the contrary, using English in informal settings outside class now forms part of many children's everyday lives, even in so-called EFL settings. There is a growing recognition amongst researchers that as English has become established as the global lingua franca, children are increasingly being exposed to and engaging with English in diverse social activities. English continues to gain prominence in global popular culture (McKay and Bokhorst-Heng 2008), mainly through television, movies, music, videogames and online social networks. As they live more of their lives online, accessibility to English through digital venues is becoming ever more relevant to children in many countries. The Internet and other emerging platforms, such as smartphone applications (apps), often lead to incidental exposure and learning of English. Whereas there used to be a strong 'digital divide' across countries and socioeconomic status, more people from more diverse backgrounds are now connected and possibilities to use and learn English informally have thus expanded (Thorne et al. 2009).

Therefore, an examination of early learning of L2 English outside the classroom considers aspects of L2 learning that are not necessarily aligned with research done in mainstream SLA. As Ortega (2013) has pointed out, the bi/multilingual turn will broaden the scope of SLA work, and it will also challenge applied linguists to confront the gaps where existing (and previously agreed upon) theories and concepts need to be stretched or re-thought. We can think of these as 'disconnects' between the traditional focus of SLA research and the areas into which we need to extend current research in order to contemplate young learners' out-of-school L2 experiences. These disconnects include:

- Research on SLA and research on bilingualism.
- Research on adults and younger L2 learners.
- Research on L2 learning inside (instructed) and outside (informal/naturalistic) the classroom.
- The distinction between incidental and informal L2 learning.
- The learning of L2s in digital or virtual spaces versus other 'real' social environments.

In this chapter, we will refer to these disconnects as we review and synthesise work on children's informal learning of English beyond school settings.

Historical perspectives

Most of our learning in daily life occurs without receiving explicit instruction. Cross (2007) argues that learning happens as we figure out how to participate in our social and work spaces, and that this 'informal learning is the unofficial, unscheduled, impromptu ways people learn to do their jobs' (Cross 2007, p. 19). Learning is, then, very much a quotidian and 'situated' activity that is part-and-parcel of living and working (Lave and Wenger 1991). Aligned with this approach, Toffoli and Sockett (2010) hold that informal language learning is best understood within socioconstructivist models, where learning is seen as a co-constructed activity – carrying out meaningful tasks with others – in a social environment. However, in the history of the development of research on second language acquisition, young children's informal L2 learning has been largely overlooked.

Research on informal L2 learning

There are two related ways of approaching out-of-school language learning, as *informal* or *incidental* L2 learning. The distinction is not always clear. 'Incidental' refers to language learning that happens when the L2 user is trying to accomplish something else through the language, without the intention or focus on improving her or his language. Gass (1999, p. 319) defines it as 'a by-product of other cognitive exercises involving comprehension'. In this sense, incidental learning is contrasted with intentional learning, either in a classroom or self-instructed setting, and has long been studied in SLA, even if researchers did not frame it as such. Hulstijn (2003) points out that the term *incidental learning* in SLA research has usually been applied to work on vocabulary, but almost not at all on work in areas of phonology or grammar. However, he points out that well-known studies such as Doughty's (1991) study of adult L2 learners' acquisition of relative clauses clearly examine incidental learning, since although the learners were in a classroom setting, the main focus of instruction was not on relative clauses.[1] 'Informal' on the other hand refers to language learning that happens outside a traditional classroom setting. Informal may well be intentional, for example, purposively changing the audio track on the television to English or studying song lyrics in order to practise. Informal learning may also be incidental, such as when a child is playing a video game in English. For our purposes here, we will equate L2 learning outside the classroom as informal learning, since 'informal' usually refers to both the context (a 'naturalistic' setting, not in-school instruction) whereas 'incidental' refers to the intentionality of the learning (whether in a classroom setting or not).

Some early work in SLA did examine learners in informal settings, although it was not explicitly framed as informal L2 learning. Krashen's (1981) formulation of his monitor model included a whole chapter on 'formal and informal linguistic environments in language acquisition and language learning'. An important insight he and other researchers had at the time was that L2 *exposure* is necessary but by itself does not guarantee L2 *intake*. However, the studies from the 60s and 70s that Krashen reviews are with L2 adult learners, which he contrasts with L1 child acquisition. Two other early seminal studies in SLA are case studies of informal language learning. Schumann's (1978) study of Albert, an L2 learner from Costa Rica, noted that despite extended time living in the United States, Albert's English was still marked by many ungrammatical or 'pidgin' forms. Schumann posited that the problem with Albert's L2 progression was not linguistic, but rather that he felt he was not a part of and therefore rejected the culture he connected with English, a theory Schumann called the *acculturation model*. Likewise, Schmidt's (1983) study of Wes, an adult Japanese learner of English living in Hawaii, traced how he developed aspects of his L2. Schmidt used the notion of *communicative competence* (Hymes 1972; Canale and Swain 1980) as a framework. By carefully describing how Wes, a talented artist who interacted frequently with English speakers, used his 'broken' English successfully in his everyday dealing with people, Schmidt showed that Wes was an effective communicator despite deficiencies in his L2 grammatical system. That is, whereas by traditional SLA measures Wes would be considered a poor L2 learner, the data demonstrated that in many settings he was clearly a successful language learner, in spite of his lack of grammatical accuracy.

These early case studies were of adult L2 learners. Researchers looking at children in similar contexts usually did not frame their work as 'SLA research', but rather research on bilingualism. They typically focused on questions relevant to bilingual development, such as the relation of the two languages in the brain (what is the nature of a unitary or underlying linguistic system?) and the phenomenon of language mixing or codeswitching (Genesee 2002). Some research in SLA did include work with children, such as the morpheme acquisition studies by Dulay and Burt in the 1970s and 80s (see Goldschneider and DeKeyser 2005). Like the adults in the studies by Schumann and Schmidt, participants included in these studies were learning English in an English-speaking environment, in this case, California. They were therefore probably learning English in both instructed and out-of-school settings. However, the researchers were not looking at differences in explicit/formal and implicit/informal learning, but rather were mapping the progression of the learning structures in the L2, regardless of the participants' age or mode of learning the target language.

Later researchers, while not framing their work as studying informal learning per se, were seeking to understand the role of the social context, and hence everyday informal language use, in shaping L2 learning. Norton's (2000) seminal ethnographic study of immigrant women in Canada showed that despite the commonly held notion that English as a second language (ESL) settings are contexts where learners are fully immersed in the L2, many of her participants had only limited occasions for meaningful interactions with 'native speakers'[2] of English. One participant who worked at a restaurant related that she was treated by her English-speaking co-workers 'as a broom', and denied opportunities to move into positions in the restaurant where she would be able to interact with customers. Because they were marginalised members of society, many of the women's chances for interaction and negotiation of meaning that foster second language acquisition were quite restricted. This work shows that social structures often constrain the ways that less powerful members of society, immigrant women and minorities in particular, are able to access opportunities for informal L2 learning (Norton 2013).

In the mid 1990s, inspired by the work on language socialization by linguistic anthropologists such as Schieffelin and Ochs (1986), applied and sociolinguists started to look at how emergent bilingual children acquired their languages through social interaction. Zentella's (1997) seminal study of bilingual children in New York City illustrates children's development of a keen contextual awareness of when and how to use their various languages for different social functions. In the same vein, Willett (1995) employed a language socialization approach to document the English learning of three recently arrived first-grade immigrant girls in the United States. Although she did the study in the girls' school, her interest was in how they acquired the language through interactions during the school day. She attached an audio recorder to the girls, and recorded their interactions throughout the day. She found that for small children, significant amounts of L2 learning happened as they negotiated their relationships with peers and their place within the group. A similar approach was employed by Day (2002) in her study of Hari, a kindergarten-aged immigrant boy in Canada from

Pakistan. Like other language socialization studies, she used audio recordings and careful observation of peer interactions to follow Hari's language learning as part of his trajectory to becoming a competent member of the English-speaking group, such as the following interaction between Hari and a classmate (Day 2002, p. 83):

Casey: Know what I did, watch, good, I'm almost away from him, and you said, 'Get him, bud' and I went like this, and he said 'Ah psh::: pshhhh::: pshhhh::: rrrr rrr[rr

Hari: [Don't you know, I was (smashing over) to him and the (roller) too and um don't you know (. . . [.)

Casey: [And pretend you said: Bu:::d look

Hari: Rrrrrrrr[rr

Casey: [Pretend you said, 'Hy Hari says: "Bu:d, look out::.." '

Hari: Bu:d, look out (*same intonation as Casey*)

Casey: And I fell in the water.

Hari: Don't you know, rrrr rrrr vrr[rr

Casey: [eeeah pyew

Day (2002, p. 84) explains that 'the interchange shows how in their play the boys pass the role of conversational initiator and director back and forth'. The data illustrate that Hari is not just learning vocabulary and linguistic structures, but an ability to use his L2 to navigate the norms and conventions of the group, as in his use of the discourse marker 'Don't you know' to take the floor by claiming the right to speak and get others to pay attention to what he is saying. Conversely, Valdes's (2001) study of adolescent Latina girls in California found that because they were linguistically and socially isolated they missed out on many of the types of interactions that Willett's and Day's younger participants had had, and that had provided plentiful informal language learning opportunities within school. These studies emphasise that even within school settings, L2 learners benefit greatly beyond classroom instruction from informal opportunities for social interaction with peers.

With the exception of these studies, mainstream SLA research has rarely examined younger learners' informal L2 learning. However, as cognitive and psycholinguistic approaches to SLA have been complimented by 'socio-' approaches (sociocultural, socio-constructivist, sociolinguistic, language socialization), more attention is now being paid to how the learner's identity and the social context influence learning. Researchers themselves may not explicitly frame their work as 'research on informal L2 learning', but they are examining how aspects of L2 learning are shaped by everyday social encounters outside of formal classroom instruction. Wagner (2016) terms research on informal language use 'L2 learning in the wild'. Using a conversation analytic (CA) approach, he argues that real-world talk is chaotic and unpredictable, and cannot therefore be modelled through neat or linear models (cf. the collaboration efforts of Scandinavian scholars: http://languagelearn inginthewild.com/). He concludes that, like Albert, Wes or the women in Norton's study, and the children in Willett's, Day's and Valdes's studies, L2 learning is as much about becoming a member in a new community as it is about mastery of linguistic forms. In this sense, these scholars approach L2 learning as a form of sociocultural engagement, and hence they prioritise studying informal learning through everyday interactions. Another important similarity Wagner (2016) makes between these early studies on informal L2 learning is that they employ related research methodologies. They are qualitative studies (case studies, ethnography, language socialization and conversation analysis) that use naturalistic data (audio recordings of naturally occurring interactions, field notes of observations and interviews with participants), and tend to find evidence for language learning by documenting changes in L2 use by following participants longitudinally, for months or even years.

Critical issues and topics

There are several reasons why few researchers have looked at younger L2 learners in informal settings. First, as mentioned previously, SLA research has predominantly focused on instructed contexts or been carried out in controlled or clinical settings. The psycholinguistic tradition of SLA research, upon which the field was built, still approaches questions of L2 learning from a (post)positivist perspective and therefore tends to prefer quantitative, and in particular experimental, research where variables can be accounted for and controlled. For example, a study might look at how a group of learners who share certain characteristics perform on a given L2 task. Evidence of L2 learning can be garnered by comparing the learners' performance before and after a particular intervention (called 'pre-post design') or by comparing them to a similar group of learners who did not receive the intervention (comparing a control and experimental group). The evidence being measured is usually some type of linguistic element or structure, such as grammar, phonology or vocabulary. In informal settings, it is difficult to distinguish in research terms what constitutes actually learning the language versus merely using the language, without being able to show whether any learning – change in the L2 learner's interlanguage system – has taken place. Gass (1999), studying incidental vocabulary learning, notes a related problem of how a researcher can know whether a particular word was really learned through incidental exposure.

A second issue is the difficulty of collecting data in natural settings. While anthropologists, conversation analysts and sociolinguists have long done fieldwork in communities, workplaces, churches and so forth, applied and educational linguists are less accustomed to working in settings outside of schools. Traditionally, this may have been partially due to the difficulty in collecting data 'in the wild'. Recording devices were expensive, cumbersome and obtrusive, and written field notes of linguistic data can be construed as less reliable. However, nowadays audio and video recorders are small and readily available, and though transcribing audio recordings is still time consuming it can now be aided by voice recognition programmes, and analysis is greatly facilitated by qualitative analysis software such as NVivo or ATLAS.ti. Mitchell et al. (2013) note that much of the SLA research from a functionalist perspective, in particular Perdue's (2002) study of adult immigrants in the large-scale European Science Foundation study, documents naturalistic language learning. Likewise, the DYLAN project (Berthoud et al. 2013), a large-scale study of multilingualism across workplaces and government institutions in Europe, is a good example of a conversation analysis approach to studying everyday language use, although it focused exclusively on adults and its purpose was not to document informal language learning.

Another critical issue that has emerged is the changing scope of young children's informal learning of L2 English. As public primary programmes expand rapidly in many countries, more children are being exposed to English from a younger age (Kaplan et al. 2011). What is not as clear is to what extent and how the nature of English exposure and use for young children across the globe is changing. Consider the diagram of L2 learning contexts in figure 27.1.

Here, instructed English as a foreign language (+classroom/-community) is the opposite of naturalistic language learning (-classroom/+community). Intuitively, this makes sense, but according to the diagram then, there are no opportunities for naturalistic learning in EFL

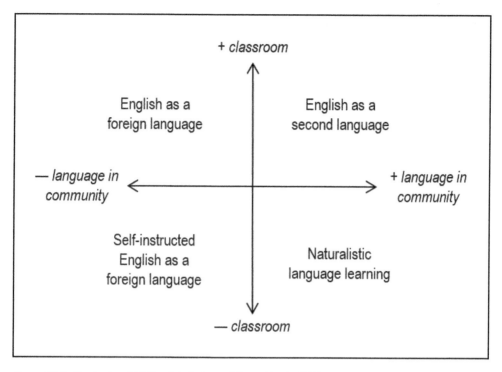

Figure 27.1 Contexts of L2 English (adapted from Block 2003)

settings. However, Sayer and Ban (2014) researching young EFL students' out-of-school use of English in Mexico noted that the children reported using English fairly often in their daily lives. They documented 14 different out-of-school activities that 12–13-year-olds did in English, including listening to pop music, watching movies and TV shows, playing video games, watching videos on YouTube and interacting with family members in the United States through Facebook. They also found that there was a mismatch between what the children's teachers thought they did with English outside of school, which was very little, and what the children themselves reported. Likewise, Idris's (2016) study of adolescent English learners in Indonesia found that, although the goal of their EFL program was to allow them to access academic information through English, most of the participants reported not using English for emails or for consulting reference materials, but that they did use it for movies, songs, browsing web pages related to personal interests and sending text messages. Sockett (2014) and Sayer and Ban (2014) suggest that the growing accessibility to and preponderance of English in everyday activities mediated through digital means is breaking down the established distinction between ESL and EFL contexts, and making Figure 27.1 above somewhat obsolete.

Current contributions and research

Clearly, both the areas of informal language learning and children's second language learning are expanding and starting to converge. We focus on three areas related to SLA research and online learning.

Young learners' informal learning and language acquisition research

Current SLA research continues to expand our understanding of the differences between instructed and informal language learning. There is a general consensus that informal L2 learning has advantages over formal instruction at least in terms of retention or memory. Pavlenko (2015, n.p.) summarises the results to date:

> Psycholinguistic findings suggest that the key differences between second language learning in the classroom and 'in the wild' lie in the memory systems involved and in the depth and nature of language processing. Memory is a set of dynamic integrated systems, commonly divided into *implicit* memory that requires little to no conscious awareness and *explicit* memory that encodes our knowledge about the world and is subject to conscious recall. Foreign language learning in the classroom engages explicit memory, both for memorization of new words and rules and for their conscious recall during classroom activities, quizzes, and tests.

The implicit/unconscious versus explicit/conscious memory systems recalls the earlier discussion of acquisition and learning. However, as with this distinction, this theory is mostly developed based on adult learners, and it is not clear whether the memory-involved L2 acquisition processes are similar or different in younger learners.

Recently, SLA scholars have begun to examine specifically the question of informal learning and younger learners, particularly as it relates to the development of particular L2 skills. The results so far have been mixed. For example, in Europe, Unsworth et al. (2015) concluded that 'incidental exposure' to English outside the classroom for four- to five-year-olds did not seem to affect vocabulary or grammar development. At the same time, Lindgren and Muñoz (2013) found that for somewhat older children it had a positive impact on reading and listening. They identified the parents' education and socioeconomic levels as being related to the amount and type of exposure that children had to English, and pointed especially to movie watching as a main source of input in the home. An early study by Y'dewalle and Van de Poel (1999) of 8–12-year-olds' incidental L2 learning through watching cartoons had two interesting findings. First, that the children's level of formal study in the language did not predict the amount of incidental learning and, second, that compared to adults children benefited more from having the L2 in the soundtrack rather than in the subtitles. Likewise Sylvén and Sundqvist's (2012) study of 11–12-year-old children in Sweden found a positive correlation between their English proficiency level and the hours per week they spent playing online video games.

Narrative and retrospective research

As researchers became more interested in the social aspects of L2 learning, they began considering other types of data. Researchers adopting a sociocultural lens inspired by the theories of Vygotsky were particularly interested in narrative and retrospective accounts of language learning (Pavlenko and Lantolf 2000). Retrospective narratives often entail the participant, now as an adult, autobiographically recalling learning experiences she had as a child. They can be in the form of a written introspective diary or memoir or as a life-history interview (Benson 2004). Swain et al. (2015) used language learners' narratives from various sources, stories elicited through email, as part of class assignments, and interviews, and theorised them through key concepts of Vygotskyan sociocultural theory such as the zone of proximal development and activity theory. One woman, Mona, recalled her early experiences with English:

> I began learning English at age twelve in junior high school in China. At that time [in 1971], because it was during the Cultural Revolution [1966–76], we didn't learn much English actually. After high school [. . .] I settled down in the countryside and worked on a farm, and the village school needed an English teacher and I happened to know ABC. So that is how I became an English teacher, even though I didn't know much English! I listened radio broadcasts designed to teach the English language. The opportunities to learn English were so limited.
>
> *(Swain et al. 2015, pp. 3–4)*

Mona's story exemplified the concept of *mediation*, the way that learning happens in conjunction with the use of other material, cultural or symbolic means. This concept of mediation is more fully discussed by Lantolf et al. (2015). Based on Vygotsky's theory of higher mental functioning, mediation is the process through which humans use higher-level symbolic artefacts – language being the most important – to socially control the biological aspects of learning.

There is a growing body of narrative studies of L2 learning which include retrospective accounts of how participants learned languages informally when they were younger (cf. the edited volume by Ogulnick 2000); a review of the literature reveals researchers have not framed them as studies of younger learner per se. Nevertheless, there seems to be a strong potential for using retrospective narrative studies to understand the experiences of younger learners. Barkhuizen et al. (2014) provide an excellent overview of carrying out narrative research including methods for analysing these data.

Technology, online affinity spaces and informal L2 learning

Clearly, digital platforms provide multiple ways for English learners to learn informally by engaging in activities they enjoy through English. Newgarden and Zheng (2016) discuss the many ways that the massive multiplayer online game (MMOG) *World of Warcraft* provides affordances for L2 English users to acquire the language. Bytheway (2015) provides a taxonomy of 15 vocabulary learning strategies of L2 MMOG players from noticing the frequency of words to recognizing knowledge gaps. Two other studies, in Japan (Butler et al. 2014) and Sweden (Sundqvist and Sylvén 2014), also point to the positive connection between children's videogame playing and English learning. They document several advantages for younger learners who engage in activities involving 'extramural English', including increased levels of confidence in using English and the development of strategies for negotiating meaning and conversation repair, and discuss the implications for designing pedagogical activities based on gaming features (see 'recommendations for practice' below). Sayer and Ban (2014) document the multiple ways that children in Mexico engage with English, including through music and social media. In their study, 12-year-olds describe how they are adept at combining various resources to figure out what something they encounter in English in a song or video means. Most of the children did not think of this as learning or even practising English, as this extract reveals:

Damien: I have this video game it's like a little cube and all the instructions are in English [. . .] It's called Super Mario Sunshine.

Interviewer: So to beat the level you have to figure out what they're saying in English . . .?
Teresa: They talk . . . and I have to open two tabs [windows on the computer]. One is the Google translator, and so I write it [what they say in the video game], and I see what it means. And then I go back to the game and back and forth like that until I get it.

(Sayer and Ban 2014, p. 324)

Others explained how they used YouTube tutorials to get through levels in a video game. Google Translator was also used to understand song lyrics: the lyrics could in turn be referenced in comments posted on friends' Facebook walls.

Researchers studying children's informal use of English are increasingly going where their participants are: online. One of the most promising recent areas of research in informal language learning is the work on how young L2 learners engage in online affinity spaces (Gee 2004). An affinity space is characterised by Gee as an online space organised around the endeavour or interest around which the space is organised. An early important study was Lam's (2000) examination of Almon, a Chinese high school student whose family had immigrated to the USA. In school, Almon struggled with English and was placed in remedial classes. He was acutely aware that this cast him as a low-achieving, ineffective English user, and would have consequences for his career beyond school. However, Almon was an effective user of English amongst an online community of J-pop (Japanese pop music) fans. In this virtual setting, he was able to participate as an equal member and gained significant confidence and language skills, since the online spaces provided a safer context for self-expression and feedback, where he was familiar with the communicative norms of the community and could position himself as a content expert.

In a later study, Lam (2004) found that bilingual chat rooms provided a powerful forum for young second language learners to explore and validate their identities, by using code-switching to talk to peers about issues of relevance to them. Black (2009) documented how adolescents with diverse backgrounds – both so-called 'native speakers' and L2 learners of English – come together in online fan-fiction communities. These are sites organised around a common interest, such as *Harry Potter*, where members write their own stories within the same world, and read and comment on each other's stories. Black (2009) found that within these communities, participation was evaluated less on language skills per se, and more on a writer's creativity, originality of ideas and knowledge of the milieu. Li (2012) traces the progress of a fourth-grade Chinese English language learner who, as she discovers her passion for manga stories, transforms from a struggling ESL student to an avid reader, illustrator and writer. Thorne et al. (2009, p. 807) maintain that 'the support feedback and positive language experiences that ELL [English language learners] youth gain though voluntary literacy activities can provide a 'counterbalance' (Yi 2007, p. 35) for the frustrations they experience when using English in the classrooms'. They explain that these spaces are often 'hybridised', meaning that users take existing cultural and linguistic elements and combine them into new communicative practices. Traditional written and spoken forms are combined with emojis, memes and short embedded video clips to create new multimodal communications.

Recommendations for practice

The studies reviewed here speak to the richness and potential of informal, out-of-school L2 learning for younger learners. However, does research in this area hold any promise for language educators? Can informal learning be brought into the classroom? Out-of-school language learning is difficult to bottle and bring into the classroom. Eskildsen and Theodórsdóttir (2015, p. 18) observe that the challenge facing L2 users, and therefore researchers as well, is that 'what L2 users need to learn [is] the ability to navigate competently in locally contextualised settings, socially and linguistically' and that these 'in the wild' social interactions are very difficult to replicate in the classroom.

Many of the activities children do when they are informally learning English, especially watching movies, cartoons and playing video games, would not be appropriate in most classroom settings. They may be highly motivating, but they are also time-consuming. At home, learning two or three new words randomly or incidentally while playing games or watching television for three hours may be acceptable, but not at school. School learning is packaged to be efficient and designed to meet certain objectives which can be measured in terms of outcomes. For the same reasons informal learning is difficult to research, it is also difficult to assess since the outcomes are often less tangible. For these reasons, informal learning belies direct translation into classroom practice. One notable exception is a study by Reinders and Wattana (2014), who modified the game *Ragnarok Online* for EFL students in Thailand to consist of six 90-minute lessons. The game's missions were designed to include special instructions and quests requiring students to use English. They measured the students' willingness to communicate (WTC) and found students felt less anxious and more confident in their ability to use English while playing the game.

In reviewing the research on young learners' L2 use in non-school settings, we can see that there are at least five characteristics which tend to make it more successful.

1   It is 'student-centred' in the sense that the learner is completely autonomous and has maximum control over the selection of content and pace.
2   Learning English is often secondary to doing some kind of social activity.
3   The learner willingly chooses to engage in social activity because it is of interest to her.
4   The social activity is usually 'authentic' in the sense that the linguistic content was not prepared with an L2 learner in mind.
5   The learners develop strategies while doing the activity which serve to scaffold their L2 use, such as the use of tutorials, lyrics or translators.

Note that these characteristics have been recognised, in different ways and at different times, as principles of good second or foreign language teaching. Brown (2015), for example, includes meaningful learning, intrinsic motivation and autonomy as key principles of communicative language teaching. Task-based (Beglar and Hunt 2002), project-based (Stoller 2002) and content-language integrated learning (CLIL) approaches aim to engage learners with some kind of activity through which L2 learning will happen.

Again, technology may be the area where the lines between formal and informal L2 learning are being blurred. Whereas independent but semi-guided learning used to take place in self-access centres and language labs equipped with VCRs and audio cassette players, they are being replaced by iPad and smartphone apps. In many ways, the apps are better suited for younger children than traditional language labs. Duolingo (www.duolingo.com) is an example that is well designed; besides having an excellent layout, interface and graphics, the app tracks the learner's progress and rewards the user with prizes as one 'levels up'. It is designed to be used as a stand-alone language learning program, or as a tool for teachers to supplement classroom instruction. Interestingly, the 20+ language courses include minority and heritage languages such as Welsh and Irish, the 'universal' language Esperanto, and an 'incubator' function for user-based content to be contributed to build new courses. One of the main features that seems to make the Duolingo programmes successful, and one which it shares with many informal L2 activities, is that it incorporates game and play dynamics, referred to as *gamification* (Kapp 2012). Reinhardt and Sykes (2012) argue that the use of technology to include gaming dynamics in language learning in educational settings is a huge potential area for future work. Butler et al. (2014) argue that good design features of video games can inform pedagogical principles, and list nine features: fantasy (or reality), rules and goals, sensory stimuli, optimal level of challenge/difficulty, mystery/curiosity, control and choice, assessment, speed and action and multiple players.

Future directions

Moving forward, research on young learners' L2 learning outside the classroom calls on scholars to connect areas of SLA work that have traditionally been disconnected. We suggested that this includes bridging research on SLA and bilingualism (Ortega 2013), research on adult and younger L2 learners, research on learning in instructed classroom settings and informal, naturalistic settings and work on digital and real-world social environments.

Clearly, technology in its various forms will continue to permeate young children's lives and play an ever bigger role in informal language learning (Thorne and Black 2007). Social media and social networks like Facebook and Snapchat incorporate multimodal forms of communication which provide opportunities for young English learners to do many of the things that have been shown to promote L2 acquisition: authentic interactions with negotiation for meaning, taking risks with language, integrating practice of various skills and so forth. As Lam (2004) shows, chat rooms and affinity sites can provide 'safe' spaces for learners to explore their L2 identities. When incorporating social networking sites (SNS) like Facebook into the classroom-based language learning, Lantz-Andersson et al. (2013, p. 293), in a study of children aged 13–16 from four different countries, argue that it must be 'deliberately, collaboratively and dynamically negotiated by educators and students to form a new language-learning space with its own potentials and constraints'.

Another promising area that has received almost no attention in the research on younger learners is the role that siblings play in supporting L2 learning. Kibler, Palacios, and Simpson Baird (2016) report that pre-school aged children in Spanish-speaking families in the USA who had older siblings were more likely to use English and acquired the language more quickly than children without older siblings. Amongst immigrant families, sibling interaction aids English learning, but at the same time it may lead to language shift away from the family's language. Orellana (2009) describes how children in immigrant families act as 'language brokers', and are often called upon to mediate adult situations, like disagreements with landlords, and use their languages in ways that most children do not. In English foreign language settings, it stands to reason that siblings and peers will promote informal language learning through shared interests in social activities in English such as video gaming, music and cartoons, although currently there is no research that supports our understanding of how these activities support L2 learning.

Finally, as Benson and Reinders (2011, p. 2) in the introduction to the volume *Beyond the language classroom* note:

> It is common knowledge among teachers that the progress made by students who learn languages only in the classroom tends to be limited, especially in their ability to use the language for spoken or written communication as contrasted with receptive skills.

Well-rounded communicative proficiency, it seems, depends to a large extent on the learner's efforts to use and learn the language beyond the walls of the classroom. For this reason alone, settings for language learning beyond the classroom deserve much more attention in research than they have received hitherto.

Therefore, not only should researchers better understand what types of informal L2 practices younger learners engage in and how these affect their acquisition, but the research to date also suggests that there are some important potential implications for developing pedagogical approaches that connect in-school and out-of-school learning.

Further reading

1 Benson, P., and Reinders, H. (Eds.). (2011). *Beyond the Language Classroom*. Basingstoke: Palgrave Macmillan.

An edited volume, mostly focused on L2 English, that addresses various aspects of learning in out-of-school contexts. It includes several chapters on adolescent learners.

2 Gee, J. P. (2004). *Situated Language and Learning: A critique of traditional schooling*. London: Routledge.

Gee approaches the topic of language in learning through a critical literacy lens. While it does not focus on L2 learning, it does illuminate the differences many young people find between how they use language to learn in their daily lives, including gaming and affinity spaces and how language is treated and taught in school.

3 Sockett, G. (2014). *The Online Informal Learning of English*. Basingstoke: Palgrave Macmillan.

The book addresses how younger learners navigate online spaces through English. He specifically casts this as 'online informal learning of English' (OILE), discusses its processes through various types of online activities and also considers pedagogical implications.

4 Thorne, S. L., Black, R. W., and Sykes, J. M. (2009). Second language use, socialization, and learning in internet interest communities and online gaming. *The Modern Language Journal*, 93, 802–821.

The article looks at L2 learning in two Web 2.0 environments through a language socialization lens, examining how adolescent learners acquire English through participation in fan-fiction and gaming sites.

Related topics

Gaming, motivation, materials, contexts of learning, multilingualism

Notes

1 Likewise, of the six studies Gass (1999) discusses in the special issue of *Studies in Second Language Acquisition* on incidental learning, none includes younger learners.

2 Although Norton's participants referred to native speakers of English, the term 'native speaker' here is in quotes to recognise that it is a problematic concept (Faez 2011). Indeed, part of Norton's critique of SLA is that the field has addressed relations of power and negotiations of identity as 'non-native' speakers try to gain recognition with 'native speakers' as legitimate speakers of English.

References

Atkinson, P. (ed.) (2011). *Alternative Approaches to Second Language Acquisition*. New York and London: Routledge.

Barkhuizen, G., Benson, P., and Chik, A. (2014). *Narrative Inquiry in Language Teaching and Learning Research*. New York and London: Routledge.

Beglar, D., and Hunt, A. (2002). Implementing task-based language teaching. In Richards, J. C., and Renandya, W. (eds.), *Methodology in Language Teaching: An anthology of current practice*. Cambridge: Cambridge University Press, 96–106.

Benson, P. (2004). (Auto)biography and learner diversity. In Benson, P., and Nunan, D. (eds.) *Learners' Stories: Difference and diversity in language learning*. Cambridge: Cambridge University Press, 4–21.

Benson, P., and Reinders, H. (eds.). (2011). *Beyond the Language Classroom*. Basingstoke: Palgrave Macmillan.

Berthoud, A. C., Grin, F., and Lüdi, G. (eds.). (2013). *Exploring the Dynamics of Multilingualism: The DYLAN project*. Amsterdam and Philadelphia: John Benjamins.

Black, R. W. (2009). Online fan fiction, global identities, and imagination. *Research in the Teaching of English*, 43(4), 397–425.

Block, D. (2003). *The Social Turn in Second Language Acquisition*. Edinburgh: Edinburgh University Press.

Brown, H. D. (2015). *Teaching by Principles: An interactive approach to language pedagogy* (4th ed.). White Plains, NY: Pearson Longman.

Butler, Y. G., Someya, Y., and Fukuhara, E. (2014). Online games for young learners' foreign language learning. *ELT Journal*, 68(3), 265–275.

Bytheway, J. (2015). A taxonomy of vocabulary learning strategies used in massively multiplayer online role-playing games. *CALICO Journal*, 32(3), 508–527.

Canale, M., and Swain, M. (1980). Theoretical bases of communicative approaches to second language teaching and testing. *Applied Linguistics*, 1(1), 1–47.

Cha, Y.-K., and Ham, S.-H. (2008). The impact of English on the school curriculum. In Spolsky, B., and Hult, F. M. (eds.) *The Handbook of Educational Linguistics*. Malden, MA: Wiley-Blackwell, 313–327.

Christian, D. (2006). Introduction. In Genesee, F., Lindholm-Leary, K., Saunders, W. M., and Christian, D. (eds.) *Educating English Language Learners: A synthesis of research evidence*. New York: Cambridge University Press, 1–13.

Cross, J. (2007). *Informal Learning: Rediscovering the natural pathways that inspire innovation and performance*. San Francisco: Pfeiffer.

Day, E. M. (2002). *Identity and the Young English Language Learner*. Clevedon: Multilingual Matters.

Doughty, C. (1991). Second language instruction does make a difference: Evidence from an empirical study of SL relativization. *Studies in Second Language Acquisition*, 13(4), 431–469.

Edelenbos, P., Johnstone, R., and Kubanek, A. (2006). *The Main Pedagogical Principles Underlying the Teaching of Languages to Very Young Learners Languages for the Children of Europe*. Brussels: European Commission.

Enever, J. (2012). Current policy issues in early foreign language learning. *CEPS Journal*, 2(3), 9–26.

Eskildsen, S. W., and Theodórsdóttir, G. (2015). Constructing L2 learning spaces: Ways to achieve learning inside and outside the classroom. *Applied Linguistics*, 1–23.

Faez, F. (2011). Are you a native speaker of English? Moving beyond a simplistic dichotomy. *Critical Inquiry in Language Studies*, 8(4), 378–399.

Gass, S. (1999). Incidental vocabulary learning. *Studies in Second Language Acquisition*, 21(2), 319–333.

Gee, J. P. (2004). *Situated Language and Learning: A critique of traditional schooling*. London: Routledge.

Genesee, F. (2002). Portrait of the bilingual child. In Cook, V. (ed.), *Portraits of the L2 User*. Clevendon: Multilingual Matters, 167–198.

Goldschneider, J. M., and DeKeyser, R. M. (2005). Explaining the "natural order of L2 morpheme acquisition" in English: A meta-analysis of multiple determinants. *Language Learning*, 55(S1), 27–77.

Hulstijn, J. H. (2003). Incidental and intentional learning. In Doughty, C. J., and Long, M. H. (eds.) *The Handbook of Second Language Acquisition*. Malden, MA: Wiley-Blackwell, 349–381.

Hymes, D. (1972). Communicative competence. In Pride, J. B., and Holmes, J. (eds.), *Sociolinguistics*. Harmondsworth: Penguin Books, 269–293.

Idris, S. (2016). *The Impact of Globalization, Language Policy, and Language Learning on Identity Construction: An ethnographic case study of high school students in Bima, Indonesia.* Unpublished PhD dissertation. San Antonio, TX: The University of Texas at San Antonio.

Kachru, B. B. (1990). World Englishes and applied linguistics. *World Englishes,* 9(1), 3–20.

Kaplan, R., Baldauf, R. B., and Kamwangamalu, N. (2011). Why educational language plan sometimes fail. *Current Issues in Language Planning,* 12(2), 105–124.

Kapp, K. (2012). *The Gamification of Learning and Instruction: Game-based methods and strategies for training and education.* San Francisco, CA: Pfeiffer.

Kibler, A. K., Palacios, N., and Simpson Baird, A. (2016). The influence of older siblings on language use among second generation Latino preschoolers. *TESOL Quarterly,* 50(1), 164–175.

Krashen, S. (1981). *Second Language Acquisition and Second Language Learning.* Oxford: Pergamon Press.

Lam, W. S. E. (2000). L2 literacy and the design of the self: A case study of a teenager writing on the internet. *TESOL Quarterly,* 34(3), 457–482.

Lam, W. S. E. (2004). Second language socialization in a bilingual chat room: Global and local considerations. *Language Learning and Technology,* 8(3), 44–65.

Lantolf, J., Thorne, S. L., and Poehner, M. (2015). Sociocultural theory and second language development. In B. van Patten & J. Williams (eds.), *Theories in Second Language Acquisition* (pp. 207–226). New York Routledge.

Lantz-Andersson, A., Vigmo, S., and Bowen, R. 2013. Crossing boundaries in Facebook: Students' framing of language learning activities as extended spaces. *Computer-Supported Collaborative Learning,* 8, 293–312.

Lave, J., and Wenger, E. (1991). *Situated Learning: Legitimate peripheral participation.* Cambridge: Cambridge University Press.

Li, G. (2012). Literacy engagement through online and offline communities outside school: English language learners' development as readers and writers. *Theory into Practice,* 51(4), 312–318.

Lindgren, E., and C. Muñoz. 2013. The influence of exposure, parents and linguistic distance on young European learners' foreign language comprehension. *International Journal of Multilingualism,* 10(1), 105–129.

MacWhinney, B. (2008). A unified model. In Robinson, P., and Ellis, N. C. (eds.), *Handbook of Cognitive Linguistics and Second Language Acquisition.* New York: Routledge, 341–371.

McKay, S. L., and Bokhorst-Heng, W. D. (2008). *International English in its Sociolinguistic Contexst: Towards a socially sensitive EIL pedagogy.* London: Routledge.

Mitchell, R., Myles, F., and Marsden, E. (2013). *Second Language Learning Theories* (3rd ed.). London and New York: Routledge.

Myles, F. (2010). The development of theories of second language acquisition. *Language Teaching,* 43(3), 320-332.

Murphy, V. A. (2014). *Second Language Learning in the Early School Years: Trends and contexts.* Oxford: Oxford University Press.

Newgarden, K., and Zheng, D. (2016). Recurrent languaging activities in World of Warcraft: Skilled linguistic action meets the Common European Framework of Reference. *ReCALL,* 28(3), 274–304.

Nikolov, M., and Mihaljevic Djigunovic, J. (2011). All shades of every color: An overview of early teaching and learning of foreign languages. *Annual Review of Applied Linguistics,* 31, 95–119.

Norton, B. (2000). *Identity and Language Learning: Gender, ethnicity and educational change.* Harlow: Longman.

Norton, B. (2013). *Identity and Language Learning: Extending the conversation.* Clevedon: Multilingual Matters.

Ogulnick, K. (ed.). (2000). *Language Crossings: Negotiating the self in a multicultural world.* New York: Teachers College Press.

Orellana, M. F. (2009). *Translating Childhoods: Immigrant youth, language, and culture.* Piscataway, NJ: Rutgers Press.

Ortega, L. (2013). SLA for the 21st century: Disciplinary progress, transdisciplinary relevance, and the bi/multilingual turn. *Language Learning*, 62(S1), 1–24.

Pavlenko, A. (2015). Learning language in the classroom and "in the wild". *Psychology Today*. www.psychologytoday.com/blog/life-bilingual/201501/learning-languages-in-the-classroom-and-in-the-wild [Accessed 1 September 2016].

Pavlenko, A., and Lantolf, J. (2000). Second language learning as participation and the (re)construction of selves. In Lantolf, J. (ed.), *Sociocultural Theory and Second Language Learning*. Oxford: Oxford University Press, 155–178.

Perdue, C. (2002). Development of L2 functional use. In V. Cook (ed.), *Portraits of the L2 user* (pp. 121–144). Clevedon, UK: Multilingual Matters.

Reinders, H., and Wattana, S. (2014). Can I say something? The effects of digital game play on willingness to communicate. *Language Learning and Technology*, 18(2), 101–123.

Reinhardt, J., and Sykes, J. (2012). Conceptualizing digital game -mediated L2 learning and pedagogy: Game-enhanced and game-based research and practice. In Reinders, H.(ed.) *Digital Games in Language Learning and Teaching*. New York: Palgrave Macmillan, 32–49.

Sayer, P., and Ban, R. (2014). Young EFL students' engagements with English outside the classroom. *ELT Journal*, 68(3), 321–329.

Schieffelin, B., and Ochs, E. (1986). Language socialization. *Annual Review of Anthropology*, 15, 163–191.

Schmidt, R. (1983). Interaction, acculturation, and the acquisition of communicative competence: The case study of an adult. In Wolfson, N., and Judd, E. (eds.) *Sociolinguistics and Language Acquisition*. Rowley, MA: Newbury House, 137–174.

Schumann, J. (1978). The acculturation model for second language acquisition. In Gingras, R. C. (ed.), *Second Language Acquisition and Foreign Language Learning*. Washington, DC: Center for Applied Linguistics, 27–50.

Sockett, G. (2014). *The Online Informal Learning of English*. Basingstoke: Palgrave MacMillan.

Stoller, F. L. (2002). Project work: A means to promote language and content. In Richards, J. C., and Renandya, W. (eds.) *Methodology in Language Teaching: An anthology of current practice*. Cambridge: Cambridge University Press, 107–120.

Sundqvist, P., and Sylvén, L., K. (2014). Language-related computer use: Focus on young L2 English learners in Sweden. *ReCALL*, 26(1), 3–20.

Swain, M., Kinnear, P., and Steinman, L. (2015). *Sociocultural Theory in Second Language Acquisition*. Bristol: Multilingual Matters.

Sylvén, L., K., and Sundqvist, P. (2012). Gaming as extramural English: L2 learning and L2 proficiency among young learners. *ReCALL*, 24(3), 302–321.

Thorne, S. L., and Black, R. (2007). Language and literacy development in computer-mediated contexts and communities. *Annual Review of Applied Linguistics*, 27, 133–160.

Thorne, S. L., Black, R. W., and Sykes, J. M. (2009). Second language use, socialization, and learning in internet interest communities and online gaming. *The Modern Language Journal*, 93, 802–821.

Toffoli, D., and Sockett, G. (2010). How non-specialist students of English practice informal learning using web 2.0 tools. *ASp*, 58, 125–144.

Unsworth, S., Persson, L., Prins, T., and De Bot, K. (2015). An investigation of factors affecting language learning in the Netherlands. *Applied Linguistics*, 36(5), 527–548.

Valdés, G. (2001). *Learning and Not Learning English: Latino students in American schools*. New York: Teacher's College Press.

Wagner, J. (2016). Designing for language learning in the wild: Creating social infrastructures for second language learning. In Cadierno, T. and Eskildsen, S. W. (eds.) *Usage-based Perspectives on Second Language Learning*. Berlin: Mouton de Gruyter.

Willett, J. (1995). Becoming first graders in an L2: An ethnographic study of L2 socialization. *TESOL Quarterly*, 29(3), 473–503.

Y'dewalle, G., and Van de Poel, M. (1999). Incidental foreign-language acquisition by children watching subtitles television programs. *Journal of Psycholinguistic Research*, 28(3), 227–244.

Yi, Y. (2007). Engaging literacy: A biliterate student's composing practices beyond school. *Journal of Second Language Writing*, 16(1), 23–39.

Zentella, A. C. (1997). *Growing Up Bilingual: Puerto Rican children in New York*. Malden, MA: Blackwell.

PART 6

Teaching English to young learners

Regional perspectives

28

Early English language learning in Africa

Challenges and opportunities

Medadi E. Ssentanda and Jacob Marriote Ngwaru

Introduction

Africa is comprised of 54 independent countries, each with their own Indigenous peoples and languages. Of the 7,099 languages spoken in the world, about 2,144 languages are spoken on the African continent (Simons and Fennig 2017). The most populous country is Nigeria (186 million people) with approximately 527 languages; the smallest is Rwanda with 11,883,000 people (Simons and Fennig 2017). There are four languages said to be spoken in Rwanda: Kinyarwanda, English, French and Swahili (National Institute of Statistics of Rwanda 2012), and only one of these is Indigenous, i.e., Kinyarwanda. Although other African countries may not have Nigeria's size, a complexity of Indigenous peoples and languages, which range from one or more million speakers to those which are on the verge of extinction, is typical of most. Multilingualism, whereby in any community more than one language or dialect may be spoken and any one person may be able to use two or three languages, is also typical.

Among the features that have significant bearing on the teaching of English to young learners in Africa is the impact of European colonialism in the nineteenth and first half of the twentieth century. This includes the work of missionaries alongside the colonial powers to create written forms of a few Indigenous languages, mainly for Bible translation. At the same time, African cultures and religions were being stigmatised. After the First World War, Britain, France and Portugal were able to divide Africa among themselves. When countries won their Independence, mostly in the early 1960s, they found themselves retaining the ex-colonial language as the official language for several reasons, not least neo-colonialism. This meant that ex-colonial languages became the languages of government and administration, higher education and law courts, as well as almost all the formal qualifications necessary to attain salaried employment. However, this did not mean that a large majority of the population either spoke or understood the ex-colonial languages. Sadly, this situation continues today, and it is in school that most children learn the official language for the first time, especially in rural areas where 80% of the population typically lives (Nakayiza 2013).

Finally, countries in Africa tend to be classified by degrees of poverty (Beegle, Christiaensen, Dabalen, and Gaddis 2016). On the one hand, this marks the wealth of human skills and creativity, and of natural resources that exist – a huge potential. On the other hand it is also true that the prestigious schools are few, maintaining an elite, while many government schools are inadequate for basic needs of teaching and learning (Ssentanda 2013) – these last factors are behind some of the significant challenges addressed in this chapter.

While these features form a general background across the continent, we also need to note some important distinctions. First, North Africa is part of classical Mediterranean civilisations, and now Arabic is a significant language of wider communication. In sub-Saharan Africa, some countries were French and Portuguese colonies and therefore have a history of speaking French and Portuguese, while Ethiopia and Liberia maintained their own independence. What is clear, though, is that English has functions in countries that were British colonies, especially as the main official language. It is remarkable how far a conference presentation from Zimbabwe in South Central Africa, Ghana in West Africa or Uganda in East Africa, will reveal the same challenges and opportunities for learning English in education – and for the same reasons. Even post-apartheid South Africa faces issues in common. For the sake of economy, this chapter will draw mainly from examples from East Africa, especially Uganda, Kenya and Tanzania.

The chapter examines language-in-education policies (LiEP) in Africa and the reasons for them. These policies are highly contested, often ambiguous and do not match realities in the classroom (Nankindu 2015; Ssentanda 2016; Ssentanda, Huddlestone, and Southwood 2016) – with consequences for the quality of learning and teaching, including early English language learning. The main questions we ask include the following: how far are poor results in literacy and numeracy at the national level due to the focus on English? Is it the LiEP or are other factors also involved? We use three case studies to show how the focus on English has created challenges for the acquisition of literacy skills and how teachers are creatively supporting learners by use of scaffolding mechanisms to acquire literacy skills.

We show how the focus on English in LiEPs not only hinders child learning directly, but also creates a negative cycle of disregard for Indigenous languages, failure to write and publish appropriate materials, failure to train teachers effectively in teaching through two languages and lack of connection between home and school (Stroud 2002). Ngugi wa Thiong'o famously wrote that there is need for 'de-colonisation of the mind' (wa Thiong 1986). Our first case study illustrates what can happen in an English lesson when teachers do not have adequate training.

African countries tend to have very weak infrastructure in education. The lack of educational facilities impacts learning in schools and teacher training alike – illustrated in our second case study. In such contexts Mother tongue-based multilingual education (MTBMLE) may not be an immediate panacea. However, in our Current Contributions and Research section we discuss ongoing programmes to introduce MTBMLE and support it with materials. We also discuss research evidence that the learning of English may improve along with literacy and numeracy; research into how teachers may use English and mother tongues in African classrooms through languaging methods; and research into the value of community libraries and digital technology for support.

In *Recommended Practices* we provide examples of how, even in a congested classroom (Altinyelken 2010) with few resources, teachers find creative means to enable pupils to participate in meaningful language learning. In *Future Directions*, we present the features of a contextually appropriate LiEP and ask for further research on how the learning of English can build on African children's linguistic repertoires (additive bilingual development) rather than 'destroy' it (subtractive language development).

Historical perspectives: an overview of language and education

Before we move on to discussing historical perspectives on the learning of English in Africa, we need to state that the examples we draw here are mostly from East Africa, Uganda, Kenya and Tanzania – all three countries that were British colonies. However, given the multilingual nature of African countries, the issues discussed here are similar in many ways across the continent.

Until the 1900s, the colonialists had not engaged in education, leaving it almost entirely in the hands of missionaries and offering only financial assistance. As alluded to earlier, when missionaries established schools in Africa, they taught in the mother tongues of the communities in which the schools were established. In most cases, they chose dominant languages in the communities (Nakayiza 2013). As time went on, education reviews were conducted to determine the quality and management of education and how to proceed with it. Several commissions were sent to Africa to review education. Although it is pertinent to point out that these were not to promote the interests of the African people, and therefore did not seek to prioritise the African languages. The Phelps-Stokes Commission (1924–1925), the de La Warr Commission (1937) and the Binns Study Group (1951) (Ssekamwa 2000) are good examples. Of all the commissions, the Phelps-Stokes Commission's recommendations had the most significant impact in various parts of Africa (East, Central and Southern Africa) (Berman 1971; Schomburg Center for Research in Black Culture, n.d.; Ssekamwa 2000).

With the advice of the Phelps-Stokes Commission in Africa, colonial governments began to take a direct interest in education and, as such, established Education Ordinances (Ssekamwa 2000) or laws to govern education. The Schomburg Center for Research in Black Culture (n.d.) and Berman (1971) state that the Phelps-Stokes Commission recommended vocational education, with an empahsis on agriculture and religion. Before the arrival of the Phelps-Stokes Commission in Africa, local languages were the medium of instruction (MoI) in the early years (primary 1 to primary 3) of education and English was the MoI in upper classes (primary 4 to primary 7) and then later in colleges. Even though it is not explicitly stated in the literature, it is inferable that the language-in-education policies which colonial governments supported, encouraged and funded were deliberately aimed at promoting English; leaving African langauges at the lower level of education and English (or French, German or Portuguese) in upper primary classes, secondary schools and in colleges. This form of language use in colonial education had a hidden agenda, as Shohamy (2006) was later to observe, as the beginning of a creation of an English-speaking administrative class to carry out colonial tasks. As a result of this form of language planning, African langauges were portrayed as inferior and only fit for lower-level education. Negative attitudes towards African langauges were created, and it is no wonder that even the current language-in-education policies, curricula and pedagogy continue to limit African languages to lower education levels.

According to Abdulaziz (2003), Bamgbose (1999) and Stroud (2002), the nature of mother tongue (MT) education in Africa relates to the inherited colonial education policies and practices: in countries where African languages had been used in education, they remained in such use after independence; and where they had been excluded from use in education or where their use had been limited to the initial three or four school years, this situation also often remained unchanged (also see Chimbutane 2009, 2011; Ouane and Glanz 2010). For example, in the case of Uganda, before independence, MTs were the languages of learning and teaching (LoLT) in lower primary school, the transition to English as LoLT took place only in the fourth or fifth grade (see Lasebikan, Ismagilova, and Hurel 1964). This was the practice up until the 60s. However, gradually, since Independence, English has replaced MT education and in most cases, it is simultaneously introduced with MTs (Ssentanda 2014a, 2014c). As is well documented in the literature, this is counterintuitive – one would expect African governments to be promoting MTBE and teach English from an additive perspective. The persistence of promoting English at the expense of African languages is largely an inherited colonial practice which portrayed English as the language of affluence – colonial administrators and all white-collar jobs demanded proper knowledge of English. Such colonial structures are present up to today (see Ssentanda 2013 for the causes of failure of implementation of mother-tongue education in postcolonial Uganda).

From the foregoing, we learn that the increasing use of English as LoLT and exclusion of MTs has been informed by politics, economics and ideology rather than by educational considerations (Ball 2011; Ferguson 2013; Tollefson 1991a). This practice has generally resulted in very low literacy levels, high dropout rates and low throughput rates (Glanz 2013) as children are required to learn through unfamiliar languages and live in various forms of social inequality in various countries and communities (Ssentanda 2013; Tollefson 2006).

The introduction of English as LoLT as part of the drive to master ex-colonial languages has had negative effects on all people's lives: in education, political participation, etc. For example, Stroud (2002) explains how the focus on Portuguese and neglect of local languages in Mozambique after independence contributed to the people's poverty and powerlessness. Over time, educational achievements have declined, and the challenge appears to be at its peak within the last 10 years. Educational review reports, for example, Uwezo (Uwezo 2010, 2011, 2012, 2013), with a focus on East Africa have continuously asked *Are our children learning?* In addition, studies in Kenya (e.g., Nyaga 2013) and Uganda (e.g., Ssentanda 2014) have revealed that the challenges children experience in learning both content and English language are that English is introduced at a very early age, teaching and learning is conducted in English without prior exposure and so children are experiencing a dual-challenge: acquiring the language as well as learning through a language which they are in the process of learning.

Given this bleak situation, there have been modifications to language-in-education policies and curricula in many countries of Africa with an aim of improving education quality: literacy acquisition and better acquisition of English and children's MTs. These declining levels of education have triggered calls for, recourse to and advocacy for MT education across Africa. The questions we ask are about how much the low educational outcomes or, for that matter, pedagogical challenges in Africa south of the Sahara are attributable to language policy – with the impact this has on the teaching and learning of English – and how far are they attributable to the generally weak human resources and infrastructure – schools, classrooms, teaching and learning materials, teacher training and so on. This now brings us to discussing some critical issues and topics around the teaching and learning of English in the African multilingual context.

Critical issues and topics

Attitudes to Indigenous African languages

In the last two to three decades, issues related to linguistic hegemony have become more contentious because of the inescapable reality of their implications (e.g., see Bourdieu 1991;

Tollefson 1991b, 2002). For example, Kwaa Prah (2009) maintains that if Africa were to have a realistic chance of development, African languages needed to become central in all levels of education and all areas of social life across the continent. Kwaa Prah (2009) dismisses the arguments that (a) Africa has too many languages to be able to settle for a few as languages of learning and teaching; (b) the quality of African languages is too poor to carry modern notions of science and technology; (c) the languages hardly have any literature; (d) English and other ex-colonial languages are already in place performing the MoI role; and (e) that Africans do not want to work in their own languages. He points out and demonstrates that implicit in the arguments against the use of African languages is a cultural inferiority complex compared to western languages since no language is incapable of being developed: 'No language, as is now well understood, by all serious linguists and other social scientists, is incapable of development as a language of science and technology' (ibid., p. 10).

Above all, the rise of Afrikaans in South Africa as a language of literacy and education following the Anglo-Boer War (1881); the use of Mali to teach physics and chemistry at tertiary level in Banama (Ouane and Glanz 2010); and a recently produced PhD thesis in Xhosa are illustrative examples of struggles to assert the usage of different languages in the face of English hegemony. To make the point about possibilities of developing minority languages into official languages, it is important to observe that after South Africa's independence in 1994 Afrikaans has remained a language of domination, a language of education up to university level, and many discoveries and innovations in science and technology have been generated in this language.

Attitudes towards English

The historical attitudes towards both English and MTs can still be seen today in the day-to-day school practices and in the linguistic landscape of the school. For example, schools put up posters to 'encourage' learners to learn to speak English as fast as they can and parents to admire that their children acquire English as early and as fast as possible. Both teachers and parents believe that when children become proficient in English at an early age, their educational journey becomes lighter and brighter. For example, one school in Uganda had a poster proclaiming 'Speak English for smart brains' (Ssentanda and Nakayiza 2017).

This poster is representative of the many others in school compounds which 'encourage' learners to speak English all the time. The message on this poster paints a bad picture of African languages for the learners; they regard their MTs as inferior and of little help in their quest for knowledge.

Current language-in-education policies: arguments and misconceptions

A critical look at the current language-in-education policies in Africa reveals that there are misconceptions and practices towards the teaching and learning of English and African languages which have clouded the proper employment of African languages in education. These misconceptions have played in favour of English. Firstly, countries limit MT education to only the early school years, citing the seemingly overwhelming linguistic diversity in African communities. Policy makers argue that it is difficult and expensive to train and deploy teachers who can teach all MTs in various communities.

Another common misconception held by people in multilingual contexts is that if a language is not used as an MoI and if it is not taught as early as possible (including kindergarten), it cannot be acquired successfully (Benson 2008; Dutcher 1997; McLaughlin 1992).

This belief has affected many African children, who are experiencing a dual challenge as they struggle to acquire the language of the school (English, French or Portuguese) and at the same time acquire the concepts and academic content of the curriculum in the language in which they have no knowledge. In this regard, Benson (2002, p. 308) argues that there is 'failure to apply established principles of bilingual education to local practices'. Research shows that that it is vital that children who are attempting to acquire oral and written proficiency in English need first to have a solid foundation in their MT both orally and in writing (see examples below).

There are cases of very successful MT projects which have demonstrated that learning is very possible in MTs. For example, the Ife Project in Nigeria (Fafunwa et al. 1989); the Rivers Readers Project in Nigeria (Fyle 2003); the Kom Project in Cameroon (Walter and Chuo 2012); the use of Somali language for up to 12 years in formal schooling (Abdulaziz 2003; Ouane and Glanz 2010); and the use of Ethiopian languages in primary schools for up to eight years (Heugh et al. 2007). These projects have demonstrated that subject matter learning not only improves with learning through MTs but that learners who are in the MT projects learn English better than those in the English-only medium.

Consequences of the LiEP: classroom practices

In the classrooms where the LiEP does not match with the linguistic repertoires of learners and teachers, teachers try to negotiate the interactions. In most cases, such classrooms are full of translanguaging as a strategy to meet learners' communicative needs (e.g., see Chick 1996; Chimbutane 2011; Hornberger and Chick 2001). In many contexts translanguaging is a powerful learning device and a scaffolding mechanism that is usually employed to support the transition from MT education to English medium and/or in contexts where children are not conversant in English (e.g., see Garcia 2009; Velasco and Garcia 2014). However, in some cases, such classrooms are constrained because of fear of non-compliance with the LiEP (Ssentanda 2016).

Herewith we present cases of classroom vignettes to show how teachers strive to negotiate learning amidst lack of joined up approaches to teaching and learning of English and MTs.

Case study I

One of the problems is that teachers in Uganda have little understanding of phonics and children are taught to recite the spellings of words from the board by letter name either in English or in the MT. Furthermore, teachers are not always comfortable with literacy in MTs. However, there cannot be any training in how to use both languages productively as the Uganda Ministry of education and Sports guidelines do not allow teachers to do so in the same lesson. But teachers certainly 'stealthily' do it through their creative means in order to enhance learning (see Ssentanda 2014b).

In what follows below, we reproduce a classroom interaction in which Ssentanda (2014b, p. 9–10) reports on the challenge that exists in a classroom where the teaching of sound letter names is not joined up in Luganda (MT) and English, yet this would be possible.

Traditionally, letters and sounds have been taught differently in Luganda and English. Luganda shares an alphabet with English except for two letters, /ŋ, ɲ/, which Luganda employs in its orthography. In English, sounds/letters have names e.g., [bi] for /b/, [em] for /m/, [kei] for /k/, etc. In Luganda similar sounds are assigned different names e.g., [ba] for /b/, [ma] for /m/, [ka] for /k/, etc. In sum, all letter names in Luganda have /a/ added on to every consonant. Therefore, as teachers teach Luganda and English, they need children to remember that the letters in each language have different names, even though the letter looks the same in the orthography.

The extract below comes from an English lesson in P1 in a government school (School A). There were 34 learners in this class. As the teacher was teaching English, she expected learners to respond to questions 'in English' not 'in Luganda'. In this lesson the teacher asked the learners to spell the words that they had been learning about that day. There were learners who pronounced the letter names 'in Luganda' rather than 'in English'. The teacher's response to this is revealed in the following extract. The teacher turns are indicated with T and the learners' turns with L. A singular L shows a turn taken by one pupil and the plural form (Ls) shows a turn taken by several pupils. K stands for the learner, *Kaweesi* (pseudonym). The Luganda text is in bold, the translation is in italics and the English text is in normal typeface.

Extract (1)

1 T: Ok, sit on your desk. Can you spell, let us spell this word. We are going to spell the word bananas. Let us spell it. Letterˆ . . .

2 Ls: 'bi' [Some learners say 'ba']

3 T: Letter . . .

4 Ls: 'bi' [Some learners say 'ba']

5 T: This is letterˆ . . .?

6 Ls: 'bi' [Some learners say 'ba']

7 T: **Bannange Kaweesi,** [*Friends, Kaweesi*] is this letter 'ba'? We are in English. We are not in Luganda **Kaweesi. Owulidde Kaweesi**? [*Kaweesi. Have you heard, Kaweesi?*] This is letter 'bi'

8 Ls: 'bi' [there is one child who still says 'ba'].

9 T: Kaweesi come. Kaweesi come. Letter ba yo gy'oyogerako, olwo Luganda, **owulidde?** [Your letter ba is in Luganda but we are now in English. Have *you heard*] But now we are inˆ . . .? English. We are inˆ . . . ?

10 K: English.

11 T: We call it letter 'bi'. Letterˆ . . .?

12 K: bi

13 T: Can you write it for me there? Write letter 'bi' for me. Get this piece of chalk. Kaweesi is going to write letter bi. Uhm, get a piece of chalk, write it there. Write letter 'bi'. Letter 'bi'. **Bannange Kaweesi** [*Oh Kaweesi*] is that letter 'bi'? **Nedda nedda, bannange Kaweesi** [*No, no Kaweesi*] this is not letter 'bi' Who can write for us letter 'bi'? Kaweesi cannot. Uhm, Kimera get . . . That's why we call it letter 'bi' when we are in English. **Wamma** Kimera [*Please Kimera*] help us. Eeeh, bannange labayo akatwe kano, **naye nki? Ntuufu.** [Look at this long stick, but is it what . . . it is right] Let us give him soda.

14 Ls: **Saanukula, saanukula omuwe.** [*Open, open, give him*]

This extract clearly illustrates how learners can be confused about the two 'names' given to the same letter in the two different languages which they are in process of learning to read. The case study shows that teachers are not prepared for using English and the MT for children to learn to read in either language. Teachers want to keep English and the MT separate and this can be confusing to the learners. If teachers could use phonics (as in the RTI SHRP[1] project) the problem would be reduced, as the letter < b > represents the same /b/ in both English and Luganda. Moreover, the case study shows how the English-only policy is transgressed for the sake of communication (Nankindu 2015).

Consequences of the LiEP: teacher training

Another challenge that constrains the learning of English relates to teacher training. Pryor, Akyeampong, Westbrook and Lussier (2013) have studied teacher preparation and professional development in Ghana, Kenya, Mali, Senegal, Tanzania and Uganda and found that there are many discrepancies between teacher training and what their actual demands in practice are. For example, the training of teachers did not match the demands of the curriculum to be taught. Similarly, in a study conducted to explore how teachers understand and manage the process of transitioning from MT education to English-medium education, Ssentanda (2013) found that out of the 36 languages listed as LoLT at the primary level, only six were examinable at senior four. In Uganda, Primary Teachers' Colleges (PTCs) admit senior four leavers to be trained as primary school teachers. So many candidates for and graduates from PTCs have no background in the MTs that they later encounter in their practice. Moreover, there is no training for teaching in the MTs in PTCs in Uganda. At the policy level, when teachers are being transferred, no attention is given to which teacher will be teaching which language where, so teachers may be in a context where they do not share a MT with their learners. Accordingly, the implementation of MT education is negatively affected with poor teacher transfers.

Consequences of the LiEP: writing and publishing

One of the biggest challenges facing MT education in Africa is the inadequacy of teaching and learning materials (e.g., Bamgbose 2004; Dutcher 2004; Stroud 2002). While the materials for teaching and learning English may not be entirely adequate, the situation for the MTs is dire in many contexts with, for example, very limited publishing in the MTs, and hence reading materials for pupils and teachers are not readily available.

Moreover, as reported by Ssentanda et al. (2016), the provision of these materials involves influence peddling: teachers do not receive the materials they request from the publishers they consider as producers of quality materials; they instead receive those from other publishers which teachers consider to be poor quality, and the materials do not arrive on time.

It is however, encouraging that there are initiatives on the African continent to provide reading materials. For example, there is the African Storybook Project (www.africanstorybook.org) which provides reading materials under a Creative Commons licence – these materials are being translated into many languages including English. This will further be elaborated in the Current contribution and research section.

Poor school conditions?

Another potential challenge that complicates the teaching and learning of English is the nature and availability of conducive learning environments. We refer to two cases of schools, one government and one private school in Kenya and Uganda, to illustrate how the school and classroom environment can negatively affect the learning process.

First, climate is a factor affecting classroom conditions. For example, Tanzania is a hot country year round, which means that classrooms need to be kept cool and well aerated. This explains why many of the classrooms have open doors and windows with no latches or locks. Consequently, the room is open to the elements and is very dirty and dusty. In some extreme cases teaching goes on in partially collapsed buildings, exposing both teachers and students to great danger. In other contexts, the school structures are semi-permanent. Of course, conditions vary greatly; in some countries, private schools have admirable permanent buildings and government schools have relatively poorer structures (for example, South Africa), while in other countries the opposite is true.

Such conditions are not suitable for reading and writing activities, since teachers cannot use the chalkboards or store any teaching and learning materials in these classroom structures. Moreover, classrooms lack furniture. In some classrooms, half the pupils sit on desks while the other half sits on the floor. In other contexts, all pupils are forced to share the fewer desks in the classroom, something that compromises the effective development of writing skills. In other contexts, the learner numbers are very large (Altinyelken 2010) with few resources, so teachers have to be very creative in getting learners to learn.

A comparative study carried out in Uganda (Ssentanda 2014) found that challenging conditions similar to those described above, together with the shortage of literacy texts (charts), storybooks or any reading materials, severely limited literacy development opportunities for children in these contexts.

Although the situation regarding infrastructure facilities appears extremely challenging, teachers work out ways to ensure that children learn even amidst such constraints. Teachers are commended for being creative and for getting learners to begin to learn to write and read amidst such challenges. We are hopeful that the conditions will eventually improve.

Current contributions and research

An overview of research work in the 1970s and 1980s reveals that languages were kept separate – developing first proficiency in the MT; then later English in the fourth year of schooling was initiated and continued to the tertiary level. A number of studies were conducted, and children were assessed as doing better than those who were immersed in English right from the start. For example, see the Ife Project in Nigeria (Akinnaso 1993; Fafunwa et al. 1989), the Rivers Readers Project of 1970 (Fyle 2003) in Nigeria and the Mozambique bilingual education study in Mozambique (Benson 2000, 2002). Unfortunately, these studies do not appear to have been replicated elsewhere in Africa.

That aside, numerous research projects by individuals and NGOs have inquired how best children can learn English without having to lose proficiency in their MTs (e.g., see Walter and Chuo 2012 in Cameroon). In addition, governments in East Africa (and others elsewhere) have put in place language-in-education policies that support the teaching and use of MTs as MoI owing to the advantages which come with this practice. Below is some of the current research in various parts of Africa to show efforts that scholars are making to understand how best MTs and English can be taught.

This section is premised on the fact that in multilingual contexts (the whole of Africa), it is common to attribute academic failure to poor proficiency in the language of instruction, which is often the learner's second or even foreign language (Chimbutane 2011). We want, therefore, to reiterate the bilingual education theory and international practice that initial literacy and academic development can only be better achieved when the child's first language is used as a medium of instruction. This is why we highlight that research around

Africa recognises the fact that African children grow up to be multilingual rather than monolingual (Banda 2009, 2010; Brock-Utne 2004; Glanz 2013; Makalela 2016). For that reason, we reiterate that the manner through which they learn English should be different from that of children in the global north. Most communities in the global north are monolingual, so children in fact begin to learn and continue learning through their MTs. Makalela (2016) has argued that it is wrong to consider African communities as though they are similar to those of the Western world, while Makalela (2016) and Nkadimeng and Makalela (2015) have also argued that classroom interactions should be reflective of the linguistic repertoires of learners rather than assuming that learners are purely monolingual (cf. Banda 2010). Nkadimeng and Makalela's (2015) study revealed that children in the Soweto town in South Africa speak about six languages by the time they are six years of age, and by age 13 they can freely and easily converse with these languages in a single sentence, and that they carry this practice with them into the classroom environment. Makalela (2016) is of the view that the notion of mother tongue, first language or third language have little meaning in a context where one grows up speaking many languages and all can be equated to 'mother tongue'. It is therefore wrong, as Banda (2010) observed, to keep the languages in class separate (Garcia 2009), as this practice is not reflective of the learners' identity (Makalela 2016).

As underlined by UNESCO as early as in 1953 and later in 1990 and echoed in research by Bamgbose (2000), Cummins (2000b, 1991) and Hornberger (1988), the second or foreign language should never be the medium used for children in learning. Therefore, all possible innovations towards promoting effective ESL are welcome. One recent such innovation has been the African Storybook Project (www.africanstorybook.org; see Tembe and Reed 2016). This project involves producing reading materials through a Creative Commons licence. The project is currently running in South Africa, Uganda, Kenya and Lesotho. These stories are freely accessible online, they can be downloaded or printed out for use and individuals are free to translate and/or translate them in any African language and English. What is more, most of the stories available at the website in African languages have been translated into English. If children and teachers are well prepared to make use of the materials at this website, the transition from MTs to English medium will be supported.

There are also studies into reading methodologies that are meant to improve learners' levels of reading fluency. As indicated in section 3.4, the practice of teaching reading has been problematic and this has been observed as a challenge to the mastery of reading. The School Health and Reading Program in Uganda is out to study and address this challenge. The practice of phonics is yet to be embraced by all teachers across the country (NORC at the University of Chicago 2015). It is hoped that these efforts will greatly enhance the acquisition of reading fluency in both the MTs and English and eventually improve literacy acquisition.

Recommendations for practice

The issues discussed above point to useful action points which can be handled both nationally and locally to make teaching and learning meaningful. In addition, the learning of English in the context of multilingual education will greatly be enhanced when such challenges are considered. At this point in time we want to recommend a shift from the general sweeping narrative in African governments' language policy that MT should be used in the first three years followed by the introduction of L2 from Grade 4 onwards. We specifically want to recommend that different countries come up with more specific policies based on specific case studies about bilingual English teaching and learning in their own contexts. This will ensure that language policies become more ecological by being framed by linguistic ethnography (see, e.g., Chimbutane 2011). The relationships that people establish between language and social and economic mobility should become a part of the basis of policy decisions that can ensure effective language pedagogies.

We say this believing that if the learning of English is to make sense and remain relevant to school learning, children in the African context ought to be taught English in a manner that builds on their specific linguistic repertoires but does not promote English only. For example, Banda's (2010) and Makalela's (2016) studies speak about language realities in African communities and schools. Classifying learners and teachers as monolingual speakers of particular languages prior to school entry is misleading and denies children and teachers of their identities. The learning of English should be approached from an additive point of view (learning a language to add to those already known by the learner and to further develop those they already known prior to school entry; see Cummins 2000a, 2000b). With this approach, the learning of English will become more beneficial and exciting to learners.

Banda's study feeds in well to that of Makalela (2016) in advocating for a learning of languages that is reflective of learners' linguistic repertoires. The practice of translanguaging (some scholars refer to it as codeswitching) is widespread across Africa (see, e.g., Merritt, Cleghorn, Abagi, and Bunyi 1992; Ncoko, Osman, and Cockcroft 2000; Nkadimeng and Makalela 2015; Nyaga and Anthonissen 2012; Yevudey 2015). Learners who join school are proficient in many languages ranging from two to six. So, the teaching of these languages, including English, should be handled in a complementary or unified manner to reflect the linguistic practices of the learners – this is how learning will be meaningful and beneficial to the learners. In sum, translanguaging should be developed further to support language learning and mastery of classroom content. Moreover, translanguaging as a practice on the part of teachers has revealed that the classroom interactions become lively, interactional and participatory (Chimbutane 2011; Ssentanda 2016; Yevudey 2015) when teachers attempt to employ the realities of learners' linguistic repertoires in the teaching and learning process.

Furthermore, research has revealed that teachers are 'policy makers' (Johnson 2009) themselves. In situations where the language-in-education policies are far removed from the school and/or classroom realities, teachers create environments in which learning is negotiated through languaging means (Garcia 2009) familiar to learners. This then means that meaningful and beneficial language policies should involve studies involving classroom interactions.

As the world is intensely moving into mobile technology, there is need to invest in and conduct studies on how technology can be tapped to enhance language learning not only in schools but also at home. For example, many homes have mobile technology and therefore investment into digital educational resources is a welcome idea as many children are technologically literate even before they join school. One thing remains sure, however – that 'reading, writing, and use of print and screen texts are now crucial means of getting things done in the world of work and education, as well as in local life worlds' (Martin-Jones 2011, p. 249).

Finally, studies into language and work are mostly lacking in East Africa and Africa at large. The languages of the school do not match the languages required for work outside of the school. Children become proficient in English and graduate as engineers, doctors and lawyers who can only practice their professions in English and yet the community in fact demands that they communicate in their mother tongue. Therefore, graduates from school must struggle to 'reconceive' the knowledge they have and find ways to practically render it into their mother tongue. This means that the learning of English in the African context has to be tailored to the needs of children and look beyond life after school. Consequently, the learning of English has to be rethought and replanned.

Future directions

As we reflect on the future directions of teaching and learning and research into the use of English in Africa, we would like to draw on Heugh's (Heugh 2006, pp. 57–58) observations.
    There is consensus in the recommendations about

- A need for further development and use of African languages in education systems across the continent.
- The better provision and teaching of an ILWC (international language of wider communication) in each case.

Here is where there is not yet consensus:

- The point at which the medium should change from MT to ILWC; whether a change in medium is necessary if the ILWC is taught efficiently as a subject.
- Whether it is possible to use both MT and ILWC as complementary mediums of instruction through the school system.

Given these observations, a joint effort for the development of all African languages at all educational levels would be beneficial for the future. All stakeholders ranging from parents, teachers, politicians and all educators to publishers need a greater understanding of child learning and language learning. Furthermore, as there should be a motivation for learners to learn their MTs, today MTs are not examined at the end of primary school in many African countries, which has been a big excuse for dropping MTs from the school system. There is a need to manage these examinations because they are a source of negative attitudes towards the learning of MTs, especially in the early years of schooling.
    In addition, there is a need to collect information about pertinent language-related issues on the distribution, dialects and level of development of languages as well as individual linguistic repertoires in schools and communities. This information is imperative in the formulation of local school language policies. In addition, this information can be useful in national teacher allocation and deployment. Useful and beneficial language-in-education policies emanate from ethnographic research, as observed by Johnson (2009) and Hornberger and Johnson (2011).
    Last but not least, there is a need to conduct more research and respond to calls of classroom-based linguistic research that aim to understand how teachers negotiate learning.

Further reading

Ssentanda, M. E. (2016). Tensions between English medium and mother tongue education in rural Ugandan primary schools: An ethnographic investigation. In Christiane, Meierkor, Bebwa, I., and Namyalo, S. (eds.) *Ugandan English: Its sociolinguistcs, structue and uses in a globalising post-protectorate*. Amsterdam and Philadelphia: John Benjamins, 95–117. https://doi.org/10.1075/veaw.g59.05sse.
    This chapter discusses how teachers understand and manage the process of transition from MT education to English-medium education in uganda. It illustrates how teachers grapple with language policy stipulations of MT use and english to negotiate learning in the classroom environment, though at different levels of compliance with policy in government and private schools.

Nankindu, P. (2015). Contesting language choices in Uganda: English as a high value language. In Michieka, M., and Elhindi, Y. (eds.) *The changing roles of English in Eastern Africa*. Illinois, IL: Common Ground Publishing, 58–77.

> In this chapter, Nankindu discusses the status of english in Uganda and how such official status holds the langauge in high regard compared to the local languages in the country. In addition, she shows how the status of English dictates its use throught out the education system in uganda.

Nyaga, S., and Anthonissen, C. (2012). Teaching in linguistically diverse classrooms: Difficulties in the implementation of the language-in-education policy in mulitingual Kenyan primary school classrooms. *Compare: A Journal of Comparative and International Education*, 42(6), 863–879.

> In this article, Nyaga and Anthonissen describe how teachers struggle to handle teaching and learning in linguistically diverse classrooms. The authors discuss how English is given prominence in the language-in-education policy in Kenya, in classrooms and how teachers give it emphasis because it is the language of examination. The article shows that English is in fact a second language to the majority of learners in schools.

Related topics

Policy, difficult circumstances, contexts of learning, critical pedagogy

Note

1 Research Triangle International runs a project in Uganda called the School Health and Reading Project whose primary aim is to enhance reading fluency through a phonics approach.

References

Abdulaziz, M. H. (2003). The history of language policy in Africa with reference to language choice in education. In Ouane, A. (ed.), *Towards a Multilingual Culture of Education*. Hamburg, Germany: UNESCO Institute for Education, 103–112.

Akinnaso, F. N. (1993). Policy and experiment in mother-tongue literacy in Nigeria. *International Review of Education*, 39(4), 255–285.

Altinyelken, H. K. (2010). Curriculum change in Uganda: Teacher perspectives on the new thematic curriculum. *International Journal of Educational Development*, 30(2), 151–161. http://doi.org/10.1016/j.ijedudev.2009.03.004

Ball, J. (2011). *Enhancing Learning of Children from Diverse Language Backgrounds: Mother tongue-based bilingual or multilingual education in the early years. Analytical review commissioned by the Unesco Education Sector*. France: United Nations Educational, Scientific and Cultural Organization.

Bamgbose, A. (1999). African language development and language planning. *Social Dynamics*, 25(1), 13–30. http://doi.org/10.1080/02533959908458659

Bamgbose, A. (2004). *Language of Instruction Policy and Practice in Africa*. Office for Education in Africa, UNESCO.

Banda, F. (2009). Critical perspectives on language planning and policy in Africa: Accounting for the notion of multilingualism. *Stellenbosch Papers in Linguistics PLUS*, 38, 1–11.

Banda, F. (2010). Defying monolingual education: alternative bilingual discourse practices in selected coloured schools in Cape Town. *Journal of Multilingual and Multicultural Development*, 31(3), 221–235.

Beegle, K., Christiaensen, L., Dabalen, A., and Gaddis, I. (2016). *Poverty in a Rising Africa: Africa Poverty Report*. The World Bank: Washington.

Benson, C. (2000). The primary bilingual education experiment in Mozambique, 1993 to 1997. *International Journal of Bilingual Education and Bilingualism*, 3(3), 149–166.

Benson, C. (2008). Common themes and areas for further work: Questions, answers and remaining issues. In Haddad, C. (ed.), *Improving the Quality of Mother Tongue-based Literacy and Learning:*

Case Studies from Asia, Africa and South America. Bangkok, Thailand: Unesco Asia and Pacific Regional Bureau for Education, 182–183.

Benson, C. J. (2002). Real and potential benefits of bilingual programmes in developing countries. *International Journal of Bilingual Education and Bilingualism*, 5(6), 303–317.

Berman, E. H. (1971). American influence on African education: The role of the Phelps-Stokes fund's education commissions. *Comparative Education Review*, 15(2), 132–145. Comparative Education Review. Retrieved from www.jstor.org/stable/1186725.

Bourdieu, P. (1991). *Language and Symbolic Power*. Ed. J. B. Thompson. Cambridge: Polity Press.

Brock-Utne, B. (2004). "But English is the language of science and technology" – The language of instruction in Africa – with special look at Tanzania. *CIES Conference in Salt Lake City*, 2004.

Chick, J. K. (1996). Safe-talk: Collusion in apartheid education. In Coleman, H. (ed.), *Society and the Classroom*. Cambridge: Cambridge University Press, 21–39. http://ematusov.soe.udel.edu/CH-SIG/Document Library/Chick, Safetalk in SA apartheid classroom, 1996.pdf

Chimbutane, F. (2011). *Rethinking Bilingual Education in Postcolonial Contexts*. Bristol, Buffalo, Toronto: Multilingual Matters.

Chimbutane, F. S. (2009). *The Purpose and Value of Bilingual Education: A critical, linguistic ethnographic study of two rural primary schools in Mozambique*. School of Education, The University of Birmingham.

Cummins, J. (1991). Interdependence of first- and second-language proficiency in bilingual children. In Bialystock, E. (ed.), *Language Processing in Bilingual Children*. Cambridge: Cambridge University Press, 70–89.

Cummins, J. (2000a). *BICS and CALP*. Available online: http://iteachilearn.org/cummins/bicscalp.html. [Accessed May 22, 2012].

Cummins, J. (2000b). *Language, Power and Pedagogy: Bilingual children in the crossfire*. Clevedon: Multilingual Matters.

Dutcher, N. (1997). *The use of the first and second languages in education: A review of international experience*. Pacific Islands Discussion paper series, No 1. East Asia and Pacific region.

Dutcher, N. (2004). *Language Policy and Education in Multilingual Societies: Lessons from three positive models*. Barcelona, Spain: Linguapax Congress.

Fafunwa, A. B., Macauley, J. L., and Sokoya, J. A. F. (1989). *Education in Mother Tongue: The Ife primary education research project (170–1978)*. Ibadan, Nigeria: University Press Limited.

Ferguson, G. (2013). The language of instruction issue: Reality, aspiration and the wider context. In McIlwraith, H. (ed.) *Multilingual Education in Africa: Lessons from the Juba language-in-education conference*. London: British Council, 17–22.

Fyle, C. N. (2003). Language policy and planning for basic education in Africa. In Ouane, A. (ed.) *Towards a Multilingual Culture of Education*. Hamburg, Germany: UNESCO, 113–120.

Garcia, O. (2009). *Bilingual Education in the 21st Century: A global perspective*. Oxford: Wiley-Blackwell.

Glanz, C. (2013). Why and how to invest in African languages, multilingual and multicultural education in Africa. In McIlwraith, H. (ed.), *Multilingual Education in Africa: Lessons from the Juba language-in-education conference*. London: British Council, 57–67.

Heugh, K. (2006). Theory and practice – Language education models in Africa: Research, design, decisionmaking, and outcomes. In Alidou, H., Boly, A., Brock-Utne, B., Diallo, S. Y., Heugh, K., and Wolff, H. E. (eds.) *Optimizing Learning and Education in Africa – The language factor: A stocktaking research on mother tongue and bilingual education in Sub-Saharan Africa*. Association for the Development of Education in Africa (ADEA) UNESCO Institute for Education, 56–84.

Hornberger, N. H., and Chick, J. K. (2001). Co-constructing school safetime: Safetalk practices in Peruvian and South African classrooms. In Heller, M., and Martin-Jones, M. (eds.), *Voices of Authority: Education and linguistic difference*. Stanford: Ablex, 33–55.

Hornberger, N. H., and Johnson, D. C. (2011). The ethnography of language policy. In McCarty, T. L. (ed.), *Ethnography and Language Policy*. New York and London: Routledge, 274–289.

Johnson, D. C. (2009). Ethnography of language policy. *Language Policy*, 8(2), 139–159. http://dx.doi.org/10.1007/s10993-009-9136-9.

Lasebikan, E. L., Ismagilova, R., and Hurel, R. (1964). *Report of the Study on the Use of the Mother Tongue and the Preparation of Alphabets for Literacy*. Ibadan: Unesco.

Makalela, L. (2016). Ubuntu translanguaging: An alternative framework for complex multilingual encounters. *Southern African Linguistics and Applied Language Studies*, 34(3), 187–196. http://doi.org/10.2989/16073614.2016.1250350

Martin-Jones, M. (2011). Languages, texts, and literacy practices: An ethnographic lens on bilingual vocational education in Wales. In MacCarty, T. L. (ed.), *Ethnography and Language Policy*. New York and London: Routledge, 232–253.

McLaughlin, B. (1992). *Myths and misconceptions about second language learning: What every teacher needs to unlearn*. University of California, Santa Cruz. Available online: http://people.ucsc.edu/~ktellez/epr5.htm. [Accessed November 16, 2013].

Merritt, M., Cleghorn, A., Abagi, J. O., and Bunyi, G. (1992). Socialising multilingualism: Determinants of codeswitching in Kenyan primary classrooms. *Journal of Multilingual and Multicultural Development*, 13(1–2), 103–121. http://doi.org/10.1080/01434632.1992.9994486

Nakayiza, J. (2013). *The Sociolinguistics of Multilingualism in Uganda: A case study of the official and non-official language policy, planning and management of Luruuri-Lunyara and Luganda*. London: University of London.

Nankindu, P. (2015). Contesting language choices in Uganda: English as a high value language. In Michieka, M., and Elhindi, Y. (eds.) *The Changing Roles of English in Eastern Africa* (pp. 58–77). Champaign, IL: Common Ground Publishing.

National Institute of Statistics of Rwanda. (2012). General Population and Housing Census – 2012.

Ncoko, S. O. S., Osman, R., and Cockcroft, K. (2000). Codeswitching among multilingual learners in primary schools in South Africa: An exploratory study. *International Journal of Bilingual Education and Bilingualism*, 3(4), 225–241. http://doi.org/10.1080/13670050008667709

Nkadimeng, S., and Makalela, L. (2015). Identity negotiation in a super-diverse community: The fuzzy languaging logic of high school students in Soweto. *International Journal of the Sociology of Language*, 2015(234), 7–26. http://doi.org/10.1515/ijsl-2015-0002

NORC at the University of Chicago. (2015). *Perfomance and impact evaluation (P&IE) of the USAID/Uganda School Health and Reading program: Result I interventions*. Chicago.

Nyaga, S., and Anthonissen, C. (2012). Teaching in linguistically diverse classrooms: Difficulties in the implementation of the language-in-education policy in mulitingual Kenyan primary school classrooms. *Compare: A Journal of Comparative and International Education*, 42(6), 863–879. http://doi.org/10.1080/03057925.2012.707457

Nyaga, S. K. (2013). *Managing Linguistic Diversity in Literacy and Language Development: An analysis of teachers' attitudes, skills and strategies in multilingual classrooms in Kenyana primary schools*. Stellenbosch: Stellenbosch University. http://scholar.sun.ac.za/handle/10019.1/79899

Ouane, A., and Glanz, C. (2010). *Why and How Africa Should Invest in African Languages and Multilingual Education: An evidence- and practice-based policy advocacy brief*. Hamburg, Germany: UNESCO Institute for Lifelong Learning All rights reserved, Association for the Development of Education in Africa (ADEA).

Pryor, J., Akyeampong, K., Westbrook, J., and Lussier, K. (2013). Rethinking teacher preparation and professional development in Africa: An analysis of the curriculum of teacher education in the teaching of early reading and mathematics. *The Curriculum Journal*, 23(4), 409–502.

Schomburg Center for Research in Black Culture. (n.d.). *Phelps-Stokes Fund Records*. New York: New York Public Library.

Shohamy, E. (2006). *Language Policy: Hidden agendas and new approaches*. New York: Routledge.

Simons, G. F., and Fennig, C. D. (2017). *Ethnologue: Languages of the world, Twentieth edition*. Dallas, Texas: SIL International. www.ethnologue.com.

Ssekamwa, J. C. (2000). *History and Development of Education in Uganda* (2nd ed.). Kampala, Uganda: Fountain Publishers Ltd.

Ssentanda, M. E. (2013). Exploring connections: Reflections on mother-tongue education in postcolonial Uganda. *Stellenbosch Papers in Linguistics Plus*, 42, 281–296.

Ssentanda, M. E. (2014a). "Have policy makers erred?" Implications of mother tongue education for pre-primary schooling in Uganda. *Per Linguam*, 30(33), 53–68. http://doi.org/http://dx.doi.org/10.5785/30-3-547

Ssentanda, M. E. (2014b). *Mother Tongue Education and Transition to English Medium Education in Uganda: Teachers' perspectives and practices versus language policy and curriculum.* Stellenbosch: Stellenbosch University.

Ssentanda, M. E. (2014c). The Challenges of Teaching Reading in Uganda: Curriculum guidelines and language policy viewed from the classroom. *Apples – Journal of Applied Language Studies*, 8(2), 1–22.

Ssentanda, M. E. (2016). Tensions between English medium and mother tongue education in rural Ugandan primary schools: An ethnographic investigation. In Meierkor Christiane, I. Bebwa and Namyalo, S. (eds.) *Ugandan English: Its sociolinguistcs, structue and uses in a globalising post-protectorate.* Amsterdam: John Benjamins, 95–117. http://doi.org/10.1075/veaw.g59.05sse

Ssentanda, M. E., Huddlestone, K., and Southwood, F. (2016). The politics of mother tongue education: the case of Uganda. *Per Linguam*, 32(3), 60–78.

Ssentanda, M. E., and Nakayiza, J. (2017). "Without English There Is No Future": The case of language attitudes and ideologies in Uganda. In Ebongue, A. E. and Hurst, E. (eds.) *Sociolinguistics in African Contexts: Perspectives and challenges.* Switzerland: Springer International Publishing, 107–126.

Stroud, C. (2002). *Towards a Policy for Bilingual Education in Developing Countries.* Stockholm: Swedish International Development Cooperation Agency.

Tembe, J., and Reed, Y. (2016). Languaging in and about Lunyole: African Storybook materials as a catalyst for re-imagining literacy teaching and learning in two Ugandan primary schools. *Reading & Writing*, 7(2), 2308–1422. http://doi.org/http:// dx.doi.org/10.4102/rw. v7i2.115

Tollefson, J. W. (1991a). *Planning Language, Planning Inequality: Language policy in the community.* London and New York: Longman.

Tollefson, J. W. (1991b). *Planning Language, Planning Inequality: Language policy in the community.* London and New York: Longman Inc.

Tollefson, J. W. (2002). *Language Policies in Education: Critical issues.* London: Lawrence Erlbaum Associates, Publishers.

Tollefson, J. W. (2006). Critical theory in language policy. In Ricento, T. (ed.), *An Introduction to Language Policy: Theory and method.* London: Blackwell Publishing Ltd, 42–59.

Uwezo. (2010). *Are Our Children Learning? Annual learning assessment report 2010.* Uganda, Kampala: Uwezo Uganda.

Uwezo. (2011). *Are Our Children Learning? Annual learning assessment report 2011.* Uganda, Kampala: Uwezo Uganda.

Uwezo. (2012). *Are Our Children Learning? Literacy and numeracy across East Africa.* Nairobi, Kenya: Uwezo Uganda.

Uwezo. (2013). *Are Our Children Learning?: Literacy and Numeracy across East Africa.* Nairobi, Kenya: Uwezo Uganda.

Velasco, P., and Garcia, O. (2014). Translanguaging and the writing of bilingual learners. *Bilingual Research Journal: The Journal of the National Association for Bilingual Education*, 37(1), 6–23.

wa Thiong, N. (1986). *Decolonising the Mind: The politics of language in African literature.* Kenya: East African Educational Publishers.

Walter, S. L., and Chuo, K. G. (2012). *The Kom Experimental Mother Tongue Education Pilot Project Report for 2012.* Cameroon: MTB-MLE Network.

Yevudey, E. (2015). Translanguaging as a language contact phenomenon in the classroom in Ghana: Pedagogic relevance and perceptions. In Angouri, J., Harrison, T., Schnurr, S., and Wharton, S. (eds.), *Learning, Working and Communicating in a Global Context: Proceedings of the 47th annual meeting of the British Association for applied linguistics.* British Association for Applied Linguistics, 258–270.

29

Early English language learning in East Asia

Lixian Jin and Martin Cortazzi

Introduction

In East Asia, education currently combines widespread features of innovation, development and social change alongside stable pedagogic practices, including the maintenance of long-standing features of heritage and traditional cultures of learning. This combination, with productive and uneasy tensions, can be seen in the enthusiasm for English language learning (ELL), including English for young learners (EYL). The East Asia region in this study includes China, Japan, South Korea, Mongolia, Hong Kong and Taiwan. For most children in the region, English is a foreign language since most young learners will have few opportunities to use English for out-of-class communication, but forms of bilingual education are emerging in places where English is a medium of instruction. The popular urge to learn English has elements of fashion – often labelled 'a craze', 'frenzy', 'fever' or 'obsession' – particularly in China and Korea (Hu 2009; Butler 2015). It includes strong perceptions that English is useful, especially for younger learners, and it reflects the popular belief that it is better to start early (see Singleton and Pfenniger, this volume).

Somewhat polarised features are visible in the rapidly expanding sector of EYL (which here refers to kindergarten and primary age learners, aged 3–12). One development is the move away from practices of memorizing vocabulary and grammar towards learning in more communicative approaches: children learn English for fun and through play, but they are also encouraged to use the language to discuss and solve problems and thus develop foundations of critical and creative thinking. Interactive and learner-centred learning have been much promoted: Hong Kong, Korea and Japan have a record of emphasising task-based approaches (see, e.g., Carless 2003, 2004) and more recently this has become current in China, and this often melds with communicative and activity-based orientations, including in Taiwan and Mongolia. However, to outsiders, many observed teaching and learning methods seem stable but static, often as largely teacher-centred or directed whole-class activities. These may reflect more traditional cultures of learning, in what are often – sometimes misleadingly – labelled as 'Confucian heritage cultures' but which do reflect sociocultural beliefs about learning (Li 2012; Chan and Rao 2009; Jin and Cortazzi 1998, 2004, 2006; Cortazzi and Jin 2013). Such beliefs, together with institutional constraints, mediate such policy innovations as task-based learning in Chinese primary schools and may weaken them (Zhang and Adamson 2007).

This chapter concerns East Asian contexts, but we give particular attention to China because the Chinese education system has by far the greatest number of participants involved in English learning and includes the world's largest group of young learners (Pan 2015; Morgan et al. 2017). It seems likely that through Chinese economic and social influence, developments in Chinese EYL will be influential throughout this region. We sketch features of the general education context and indicate common EYL pedagogic practices through a discussion of critical issues. We highlight influences of parents and likely roles of digital technology, and briefly discuss English as a medium of instruction and needs for research.

Historical perspectives and the educational context

Each country within this region has different historical perspectives. China and Mongolia both had a post-1950s educational and linguistic tradition which emphasised Russian. In Mongolia, since the turn of the century, there has been a swing towards English, whereas a swing was evident more than 20 years earlier in China. In Mongolia, introducing English has recently moved from secondary to primary education, and the expansion of EYL, even more than elsewhere, has been constrained by teachers' limited knowledge and training, school resources and the demography of a scattered population with traditional nomadic lifestyle, often living in remote areas (Cohen 2004). Arguably, Japan and Korea have had traditions of over fifty years of widespread ELL in schools but only extended this to EYL in the 2000s.

In Chinese education, English has had an ambiguous role in a chequered history: since 1949 the language found or lost favour periodically within social movements (Adamson 2004). Even in Hong Kong with its own long-time external contact with and internal use of English, there have been attitudinal swings towards English, which have limited the provision of English-medium primary schools. Putonghua (Mandarin) has rapidly expanded alongside the native Cantonese language in a system of 'one country, two systems and three languages'. In China, the current popularity for learning English continues apace with China's increasing international role; the expansion of Chinese business, commerce and tourism; students aiming for international study; and popular perceptions of the utility of English.

In East Asia institutionalised exams have long dominated the focus of school learning (Carless 2011; Butler 2015). The gatekeeping effect of university entrance exams affects perceptions of English at school levels; a washback affects tests to enter the best secondary schools and, successively, tests to enter prestigious primary schools. This exam-orientation affects EYL as a feature of East Asian education, and although China, Japan and South Korea are modifying such exams and broadening school curricula, an exam-oriented mindset remains a significant influence for EYL (Zhang and Wang 2011). Other traditional regional influences include large classes, more teacher-centred approaches and caution towards more interactive teaching, but more learner-centred pedagogies which many teachers desire are constrained by institutional and parental influences (Cortazzi and Jin 2001; Li 2012).

Historically, EYL remains an innovation in much of East Asia. Official starting ages in schools are around the age of eight or nine. In China children should start learning English at Grade 1 or 3 of primary schools (age 7 or 9). However, with the widespread and ever-increasing parental demand for English, some kindergartens start classes before that, particularly in urban areas. A common belief holds that an earlier start is beneficieal. In Korea, children start at Grade 3 (age 9); in Japan, children start in Grades 5 or 6 (ages 11–12), but again many start earlier. In Hong Kong, with a stronger ELL legacy from the colonial era up to 1997, English is introduced in kindergarten (age 3) and is established from primary Grade 1. In many East Asian cities, the age of beginning EYL is cascading downwards. In an accelerating urban trend, English is introduced not only in the lower primary grades but also at pre-school stages in kindergartens (ages 3–6). However, this waterfall effect has been slow to reach more outlying or rural areas, most notably in Mongolia, yet a similar pattern is observable in Japan and Korea.

A historical issue unique to China was the 'one child' policy from 1979, which was modified in 2016 to allow parents to have a second child. A surge in birth rates showed couples wanted a sibling for their only child. Predictably, this will affect the availability of places in child-care centres, kindergartens and primary schools, and underline current shortages of trained teachers, including EYL teachers. The previous policy affected child-rearing and educational attitudes as parents and grandparents strove to put maximum investment into the envisaged future for a single child in the family; for many this included EYL.

Significant challenges for EYL can be highlighted within the wider ELL background in China (Cortazzi and Jin 1996a, 1996b; Jin and Cortazzi 2004) and research which focuses on Chinese learners (Jin and Cortazzi 2006, 2011, 2012), but challenges also need to be seen in the context of early childhood education and positive EYL practices. ELL has been influenced by successful reforms and continuing progress of the Chinese economy and society. Kindergarten and primary stages are widely recognised as fundamental to further learning, and therefore curricula and pedagogic models are changing, including philosophies and pedagogic programmes adapted from the West, such as Maria Montessori and Reggio Emilia programmes, perspectives derived from John Dewey or project- and task-based learning (Lau 2012).

Situational features affecting EYL in China include continuing education reform to consolidate the start of English teaching, coupled with the ever-increasing public demand for English, allied with the belief held by many teachers, but particularly parents: the 'earlier the better' (Hu 2007, 2009). ELL implementation at primary stages, however, has been variable; this is unsurprising considering the vast Chinese geography, the huge number of children, the difficulties of providing educational resources in some areas and the availability of teachers. Some of these features apply widely in Japan and Korea, too (Hu and McKay 2012). The social and parental drive towards ELL is pushing down the starting ages in many places to beginning primary stages, then down to many kindergartens and even in nurseries and child-care centres when teachers are available. English is not, in fact, an official kindergarten curriculum subject in China, Japan or Korea, though 'first rank' kindergartens have initiated ELL.

Critical issues

Identifiable critical issues include early childhood demographic features; private sector ELL provision and business issues; educational values and parental attitudes; and teacher training and development. Other issues, such as resources, materials and methods or sustaining long-term learning and evaluating progress towards more proficient levels and broader educational and cultural development, are implicated within these.

Demographic issues

In China, significant demographic features of the early childhood education context impact ELL. The nearly 1.4 billion population and the geographic size of China has led to the world's largest centralised school system but with some regional and local diversity. The number of young learners who had entered Chinese kindergartens by 2016 reached over 44 million, which is an increase of 2.4% from 2015. Over 90 million children entered primary schools in 2016 (Ministry of Education 2016). These figures exclude children in the private sector of kindergartens and primary schools. Some estimates state that 67.2% of Chinese children before the age of five have started learning English (NA 2016). This is surely an overestimate nationally, but evidence of the early start can clearly be seen in metropolitan and larger cities.

Large-scale rapid educational development in cities has left a challenge of developing some aspects of EYL teaching and learning (Zhao and Hu 2008). This issue is also evident in Japan, Korea and Taiwan, but is highlighted in China by the sheer numbers and the social issue of some children's differing backgrounds, with large-scale migration from countryside to metropolitan areas. Millions of migrant children from countryside areas now residing in cities have different educational backgrounds and linguistic experiences from their urban-born peers, which affects early schooling, home-school links and EYL. Conversely there is a 'left behind' generation of young children cared for by grandparents who remain in rural or outlying areas while the children's parents work in cities, often so far away that visits to children can be rare.

The private sector

In increasingly competitive East Asian societies, the private sector for EYL is expanding as newly prosperous families strongly support their child's education and see the value of ELL. In addition to normal school classes for English, with their limited curriculum hours, many children also go to private 'training schools' for English (sometimes known as 'after-class' or 'cram' classes). Around 20,000 such schools are registered in China (Ministry of Education 2016). The common use of the term 'training' is indicative: this is language training often with little emphasis on education, whereas early years' specialists stress links of language development and EYL with overall child development and broader educational values. In some training schools, carers and parents are often nearby during classes and some observe from the back of the class. This helps parents to support children's learning at home or to learn English themselves. Commonly, young urban learners have private home tutors and attend summer school programmes, perhaps in target language countries. These features are also common in Japan, Korea and Taiwan.

Often in this region the provision of early EYL classes has become a marketing feature for an institution for both educational and commercial values: within the private business sector, EYL is seen as a lucrative investment opportunity. Children's attendance is a source of perceived social status for families whose child is learning English. This is particularly the case if teachers are 'native speakers' or 'westerners'. The underlying pressures are influenced by parental perceptions that education is an investment in children's futures: it is widely understood that learning English early is helpful to gain children's entry into good secondary schools, and thence into good universities. EYL is seen to have a long-term value for personal advancement, future employment, socioeconomic achievement and internationalised futures. Apparently, fewer parents and learners understand how EYL is valuable for cognitive, social and cultural reasons that go beyond such utilitarian outcomes.

Cultural values

The high value put on East Asian children's education has been a major factor in increasing numbers of private and pre-school education, including ELL. It accrues social status to declare that one's child is learning English before the nationally specified age. Early East Asian education in general has three strands: traditional culture (recently made more explicit in the case of 'Confucian kindergartens'); modern local culture expressing some traditional values; and Western culture (Zhu and Zhang 2008).

Significantly, the expansion of EYL is predicted to increase further but is mediated by parental and social values. China has put more investment into basic education so that kindergartens and primary schools are better resourced. Also, Chinese parents are increasingly willing to invest heavily in the early years' education of their children. This reflects a traditional East Asian value for education, for which parents sacrifice, but it is combined with a keen sense of competitiveness. Given such values, providing high quality schools and qualified teachers will remain a demanding issue for society, in state or private institutions. Local diversity can affect the implementation of the national policy of the EYL starting age. Variation in provision is due to a number of factors: geographical location, school size, available funding and resources, and especially the availability of appropriate teachers (Cohen 2004; Hu 2007). Within such expansion with huge numbers of learners involved in sometimes quite diverse contexts there is inevitably an issue of quality control regarding pedagogic practices, appropriate teaching staff, resources and materials (see 'culture in classroom practices' below).

Teachers, teacher training and development

A challenge throughout East Asia is the inadequacy of English skills, specific pedagogic training and development of EYL teachers (see Garton, et.al. 2011). In Korea and Hong Kong, teacher tests of English proficiency skills have been used to try to ensure teachers have appropriate skill levels: the effect of this as a policy depends on the precise nature of such tests, teachers' attitudes towards them (often these are negative), and provision of appropriate programmes to enable teachers to meet relevant standards.

Kindergarten and primary teachers are often trained as generalist teachers and in Korea and Japan may teach multiple subjects besides English (Butler 2015); this is less likely in China, Taiwan and Hong Kong. While many are graduates – some with master's degrees – many still have relatively little training to teach English. In China, in 2007 there were not enough primary teachers of English to cover needed classes; many had no more than a two-year college training course (Liu 2007); even now, some barely have basic language proficiency. Many EYL teachers in Korea, Japan and Taiwan are aware that their own current levels of English do not meet minimum levels despite in-service courses and this impacts their confidence and pedagogic skills and affects learners' motivation (Butler 2004; Hayes 2014). Employing 'native' English speakers is widespread in East Asia, but some are unqualified or without previous EYL experience. Their effectiveness depends partly upon how policies specify their expected roles and how they should help EYL and the education system (Butler 2015).

The Japanese practice of employing English-speaking teaching assistants to co-teach alongside primary teachers clearly has benefits of bringing different role models and cultural experiences to classrooms, but in itself this is unlikely to resolve the issue of enhancing local teacher training and skills, particularly if assistants are unqualified (Zhou and Ng 2016). Learners may rely on the Japanese teacher to translate major elements of lessons into Japanese; arguably, this weakens the effectiveness of language classes. In Korea, Taiwan and China, some teachers employed for their English language skills (including local graduates, some international graduates or undergraduate students of English) are not professionally trained. The present regional shortage of English teachers for younger learners partly stems from relatively small numbers of specifically qualified teachers emerging from national training colleges and universities. Within the Chinese training curriculum for English teachers, courses tend to be general, with an emphasis on language knowledge and theory. They may not specifically equip students for competent English language teaching, and when courses do so, they rarely specifically train teachers for the EYL age group. Thus, in many East Asian contexts, EYL teachers may be trained to teach younger learners, but not specifically trained to teach English; others with good English language qualifications may lack specific training related to younger learners. An underlying public perception which adds to this problem is the popular myth that EYL involves simple language and therefore does not need special skills or advanced knowledge of pedagogy.

Fortunately, some teachers obtain recognised teaching qualifications through studying abroad, but for most this is not feasible. While the Chinese education system has strengths in ELL teacher development activities and training courses, including online programmes, these remain less developed for EYL. Many current EYL teachers want to earn specific qualifications, yet they cannot easily find good programmes to get appropriate comprehensive skills training. In addition, state universities in China have yet to establish advanced TEYL courses at the master's level. This is a general issue in the East Asian region. Some local training is available via modelling, in which experienced English teachers give carefully planned demonstration lessons, watched by groups of teachers (Cortazzi and Jin 2001). This performance can be inspiring, insightful and suggestive for an audience but would not be considered training as such in 'Western' contexts. Overall, training EYL teachers seems likely to remain a problem in East Asia (Hayes 2014; Butler 2015). The lack of English teacher trainers who specialise in EYL constrains the establishment of high quality programs.

Current contributions

Digital technologies

It is clear that primary education and ELL in East Asia have developed and changed dramatically in some ways (Tobin et al. 2009). This is evident in the use of interactive whiteboards, digital media resources for stories, visuals, games and language activities. For individual learners – possibly at home with parents – there are burgeoning uses of ELL applications on handheld devices, besides online lessons with a remote English 'tutor', who is as likely an unqualified student as an experienced teacher.

In China, Japan and Korea (but much less in Mongolia because of resource availability), teachers are encouraged to use ICT for ELL in primary classes; this appears to be especially helpful for teachers to prepare resources for classes, especially for reading and vocabulary activities (Samad et al. 2013), but increasingly teachers use interactive whiteboards in class and access websites for stories and thematic vocabulary materials. In the rapidly developing private sector which drives China's digital economy, new developments in online education, mobile phone and tablet applications (apps) are becoming popular for learning English. For EYL this includes the expanding area of one-on-one online tutoring (Li 2018). Frequently this focuses on reading and vocabulary, but sometimes on speaking in which one teacher works online with a single student (Liang and Yan 2014; Zhang 2017). Some apps have been specifically designed for young learners aged 3–8 in China, for use alongside their parents; these may use brief animated episodes and feature teachers and children engaging in contextualised oral practice activities to teach words and phrases (de Groat 2015). Other apps intended for nine- to 12-year-olds may involve reading, pronunciation and vocabulary activities. Given the widely recognised Chinese digital innovations associated with mobile phones, the current government support for artificial intelligence developments and the considerable commercial and educational opportunities in such a huge educational system, ICT will develop rapidly in Chinese schools. This can be expected to affect EYL. Thus, ELL classes in some Chinese middle schools now use handheld electronic devices (e.g., tablets) for internet access for all students and for homework activities. EYL Internet resources will spread rapidly to primary schools and kindergartens for teachers, learners and parents (Zhou et al. 2010). For teachers, language and content information with lesson planning resources may be shared within and across institutions to give professional support for lesson planning and enhance socializing within a teaching community. For learners, resources may be organised thematically to accompany classroom learning, carefully related to a current national curriculum, and designed to encourage independent learning and to follow-up classwork at home. For parents, access to relevant websites can enable tracking children's progress and obtaining additional guidance about ELL issues. Ideally, digital resources would be multisensory with colours, music and animation to aid memory and should be related to national or local contexts (Zhou et al. 2010).

Culture and classroom practices

While technology increasingly influences EYL in East Asia, there is evident continuity in cultural beliefs about how children learn and how teachers should teach. Such 'cultures of learning' (Cortazzi and Jin 1996b; Jin and Cortazzi 2006) mediate classroom pedagogies and may determine whether and precisely how innovations are enacted. Cultures of learning are not simply traditional practices but are contextualised by current social values and the local contexts of teachers' experience in schools in large classes, often of 30–40 or more learners in primary school (Jin and Cortazzi 1998; Cortazzi and Jin 2001). Features of cultures associated with English-speaking countries or other cultures around the world are introduced orally or in textbooks at primary stages (e.g., introducing food or festivals; see Reilly and Ward 1997). In China this is within the now expected practice that appropriate aspects of Chinese cultures are also featured so that learners can talk about them in English to visitors. This is reflected in primary English textbooks but is underdeveloped towards intercultural understanding (see Driscoll and Simpson 2015) or intercultural communication. Hence, the English curriculum practices may be seen to maintain Chinese identity for learners, developing some knowledge of other cultures, but it does not yet seek to establish an intercultural identity.

In China, there are noticeable features of Chinese cultures of learning related to EYL classroom practices. These include a predominance of organised whole class activities. Activities are introduced, demonstrated, modelled and conducted by the teacher (or two teachers in kindergartens). Typically, activities include songs, verbal games and action routines (see Reilly and Ward 1997). Teachers make use of pictures and stories for labelling, simple retelling and perhaps for developing tasks (see Cameron 2001; Pinter 2015b). Some use role plays with greetings, simple enquiries and requests, shopping activities with simple realia or language routines with puppets. For learners aged 9–11 this can include textbook-based reading and writing activities such as reading aloud, copying words, matching and grouping flashcards and pictures, vocabulary games with objects, pictures or flashcards, use of picture books (see Mourão 2015) or brief presentations by learners after preparation and practice. Such presentations may include descriptions of people, clothing, everyday activities or classroom objects. Wall posters may be actively used for short games and lexical sets, such as number and counting activities, days and months, and 'word families'. Some classes use internet resources and electronic media, say, for animated stories or phonic activities with letters and short words (see Schmid and Whyte 2015, and this volume). Nevertheless, these are mainly organised as whole class events in a planned lesson structure which includes teacher-directed routines combining known and previously practised elements with new words or structures. This can be effective 'learner-trained learning' in disciplined, highly attentive and responsive classes (Jin and Cortazzi 1998). Some ELL teachers use pair activities to practice short dialogues, mainly carried out according to a textbook. Learners may read aloud and memorise a brief text.

Clearly, such activities can be effective. However, challenges remain: there are few voluntary individual or group activities and few creative extensions of activities or more spontaneous uses of English. While 'learner-centred' ideas are fairly current throughout East Asia there are still few developments towards more independent learning or ideas about meeting individual children's needs for English (see Djigunovic and Lopriore 2011). There is, so far, little development towards 'learning to learn' (see Moon 2000; Cameron 2001; Pinter 2006). There is relatively little public knowledge or educational awareness of EYL special needs (except in specialist schools where progress is noticeable).

In Korea, a policy to 'teach English in English' may not help younger learners to understand. It seems to deny children's L1 abilities and some difficulties might be overcome with some L1 use (Hayes 2014) or a translanguaging approach. While Chinese and Japanese EYL teachers are generally aware of communicative approaches and the need to emphasise the target language use, many are more flexible about L1 explanations or brief translations in classrooms.

Literacy and oral skills

Another contribution relates to reading, writing and spelling English. East Asian languages do not employ the Roman script used for English (though children will be exposed to English in the visual environment, e.g., in shops, advertisements and t-shirts). Therefore, the introduction of writing needs to be careful and gradual in relation to a first language script. In the case of ELL in China, kindergartens introduce the well-established *pinyin* system to children: this means that early literacy in Chinese is mediated by this Roman alphabet system as a transitional measure to assist learning Chinese characters. *Pinyin* is used throughout primary and later educational stages as a reference system for pronouncing Chinese characters, since the written characters themselves generally contain few clues for pronunciation. However, the relationship between *pinyin* and the far more complex system of phonics for English reading, writing and spelling is not straightforward. Understandably, some EYL teachers in China use 'Western' produced L1 materials to practice phonics. This has the advantage of providing systematic introduction and practice activities such as rhymes, songs and games, perhaps supported by interactive whiteboard and internet resources, but often the extensive vocabulary range and cultural examples in these is not suitable for East Asian contexts. Homework with reading and some writing may be given for ELL primary age groups, but this is likely more routine literacy practice and vocabulary learning; this is often supported at home by parents, who expect homework to be given.

English as a medium of instruction and bilingual schooling

In East Asia, with the current demand for English it is no surprise that there is strong interest in primary schools which use English as a medium of instruction (EMI) or in those international schools which develop content-based language learning and various forms of bilingual or immersion schooling. The shortage of appropriate teachers and relevant resources for EYL limits this. However, Hong Kong, with its own education system, has a tradition of bilingual kindergartens usually with trained EYL teachers and often highly proficient speakers. Yet local language policy shifts have reduced the number of EMI primary schools to a relatively few private institutions. In China, Taiwan and Korea English-only or bilingual kindergartens are popular among those parents who can afford them (Butler 2015). 'English villages' in Korea reportedly experienced financial difficulties (Jeon 2012); others seem viable in China. A 2001 Chinese law states that oral and written Chinese must be the medium of education except for recognised minority groups; apparently, early EMI can be seen as a threat to national identity (Feng and Adamson 2015). This apparently limits bilingual and EMI programmes to experimental contexts (e.g., in Xi'an, Shanghai, Wuhan and Beijing) or to international schools (for which many parents are willing to pay considerable fees). An EYL Content and Language Integrated Learning (CLIL) programme in China, using English-medium instruction, is held as 'Chinese-English bilingual education' (Wei and Feng 2015).

A Taiwan study showed how learners in CLIL participated more in classroom interaction (Huang 2011). A Canada-USA-China collaboration programme developed partial-immersion principles in over 50 experimental schools in China, including at kindergarten and primary levels (Qiang et al. 2011). Teachers use multimedia-supported resources to emphasise listening; then speaking and engagement in classroom activities within curriculum themes. Success is reported not only for English but also for more interactive learning, without impeding the learning of Chinese or maths (Cheng et al. 2010). Similarly, a whole-school EMI approach studied in China (Liang *et al*. 2013) shows not only possibilities of greatly raising children's English proficiency but demonstrates modifications of classroom interaction. In this case, 11-year-olds were observed to engage in peer assistance for English by giving each other repetitions, translations, explanations, clarifications, challenges and task-organization and emotional support (fostered over time by teachers). This is dramatically different from teacher-centred error correction in which teachers usually correct individuals directly or occasionally ask another learner to locate and repair an error. Thus, particular approaches or specific EYL contexts can modify cultures of learning. However, bilingual and other EYL programmes are problematic to compare: the former attracts learners from better educated and wealthier backgrounds, and quality learning is mediated by teachers' English proficiency and professional development (Qiang et al. 2011).

Research: parental roles and children's attitudes and motivation

Many East Asian parents consider their child's academic performance a top priority. Increasingly, this includes ELL: proficiency in English is considered a mark of academic and social prestige. Such parents often believe in the motto 'younger and higher': children should start English early and can thus be expected to achieve higher proficiency (Zou and Zhang 2011). Related beliefs are that their children learn best under pressure and that the more time given to learning, the better. Hence many East Asian parents send their children in the evenings or on weekends to private chains of schools for individual English tuition or small group classes to supplement full-time schooling. A Shanghai study (Zhou et al. 2014) found 28% of children started ELL in kindergarten and another 31% started in after-kindergarten classes. Other young learners attend full-time private or international schools in which English plays a prominent role. Increasingly, brief visits to English speaking countries are part of this enthusiastic push towards ELL. Such parents are largely those of higher socioeconomic status (SES) in the rapidly expanding prosperity. Thus, SES seems to be a contextual factor in children's access to ELL in both early stages before the official ELL starting point of primary Grade 3 and in later stages. However, this is complex: parents with high education background themselves help children learn better with social support (Zou and Zhang 2011). However, a survey of Chinese parents of learners in Grades 4, 6 and 8 (Butler 2013) examined the socioeconomic status (SES) of parents in a medium-sized city and found that SES was not related to any differences in parents' beliefs about English or the perceived value of ELL. Nevertheless, this study found large differences by Grade 4 regarding how parents helped their children to learn English, which affected the learners' speaking performance.

An extensive online survey of Chinese parents (China Daily 2013) found apparently contradictory attitudes. Although 86% of the children had had English classes starting in kindergarten or lower primary grades (47% between ages 3 and 6, and 16% from the age of three), only 10% of their children were 'really interested' in English and a majority of the parents knew their children did not like learning the language. Parents nevertheless wanted their children to learn English in the strong belief that this would increase their children's chances to enter a better middle school and thence university for a better future. Other research (cited in Li 2018, p. 38) claims that 87% of Chinese parents are in favour of children studying English before the age of five and that 63% would send their children to English classes at training institutions.

In contrast, a kindergarten study in China using both quantitative and qualitative methods (Jin et al. 2016) reported how nearly 50% of this age group spent up to 30 minutes a day learning English, largely through songs and watching cartoons. Most children said they liked learning English: it was 'good', 'fun' and many 'loved it' and were happy and engaged, though some found it 'hard' and anticipated it would get harder in later stages. A few expressed negative attitudes of 'unhappiness' or 'loathing': apparently, they disliked 'reciting and memorizing English words'. Significantly, many children were influenced by parental attitudes and whether their parents were themselves involved with English and supported children by obtaining materials. Graduated parents were more likely to show explicit support, while those few who were against an early start wanted their children to learn Chinese well before starting English.

Studies in Japan show how learners' willingness to communicate in English declines in later primary stages (Nishida 2012), which aligns with the general finding of loss of interest in later primary grades (Carreira 2011; Butler 2015), but this is complex and is affected by attitudes towards learning (Adachi 2011, 2012) and learners' perceptions of 'classroom atmosphere' (Nishida and Yashima 2009). In China, a study of primary Grade 1 and 3 children (Jin et al. 2014b) found children agreed that learning English is 'interesting', 'useful' and 'helpful for the future'; they considered it 'important in the world' and thought that it made them 'knowledgeable'. Through eliciting metaphors for learning, the study revealed that 56% of these learners had positive attitudes while only 8% had negative attitudes about English; others were neutral or ambivalent. For Grade 3 children, motivation to learn was more dynamic: they were more willing to talk to 'foreigners', had a stronger desire to gain competence and were more aware of the role of English in the curriculum. While many parents had modest or limited attainments in English themselves, their great financial and time investment for their children in EYL is striking evidence of their support. Parents' and children's expectations, attitudes and practices towards English seem intertwined and mutually influential on learners' progress.

Recommendations for practice

East Asian practices for EYL can be greatly enhanced by teacher development for experienced staff and training for those with little or no specialist training. This key recommendation could focus on both broad issues of language, child development and education, and on extending, developing and innovating within classroom practices, yet to consolidate identifiable progress which has clearly been made. This should include developing and validating uses of digital technologies, developing both literacy and oral communication skills and developing the roles of parents and their understanding of language learning and use. Given how EYL is a foundation for later learning, for English but also for children's general educational, personal, social and cultural development, more resources should be allocated to this area, especially for materials and methods which engage learners in active participation, develop critical and creative thinking, and sustain their interest and motivation. Further recommendations relate to digital technologies and research.

Researching EYL

EYL in East Asia, despite huge interest and the millions of learners involved at ever younger ages, remains one of the least researched areas in ELT. Of course, research methods with children need careful consideration for feasibility, appropriateness, ethics and validity (see Pinter, this volume). Using established questionnaire surveys may be appropriate for investigations with teachers, and such methods fit an East Asian perception that in research measurements are expected. Current topics which need research include EYL teachers' and learners' beliefs, values and practices and those of children's parents and carers; home-school links regarding EYL; teachers' training, pedagogic and professional career development; the roles and effectiveness of training centres, summer programmes and extracurricular activities; the range, uses and value of different classroom activities, textbooks and digital materials; and the functions and effects of English through drama, stories, art, sciences, singing and music, and how these relate to developments towards holistic learning (development of 'the whole child'). Longitudinal studies to evaluate the effectiveness of EYL on later language learning (Liu 2007), communication and attitudes towards peoples and cultures, and on subsequent educational achievement, are needed. Research to investigate parental beliefs about how English relates to school achievement and 'dreams' for their children's futures would have educational and social significance. Research into the effectiveness of digital affordances will be useful, not only to track how devices and digital resources are used but also on how they affect classroom interaction and progress in learning and to ascertain the value they add to ELL.

Further research methods exploring children's self-evaluations and informed classroom observations (either systematically using checklists quantitatively or more qualitative field studies and ethnographies) are needed (Pinter 2006, 2011, 2015a). Innovative methods using narrative and metaphor analysis are worth exploring right through this age group because they engage children's interest and creativity and are shown to yield fascinating insights (Jin et al. 2014a, 2014b, 2016). Such methods use pictures, coloured cards, toys and objects to help elicit stories and metaphors in a play context. These methods, alongside interviews, show young learners' dynamic thinking about their English learning experiences. They bring insights into children's experiences, attitudes and feelings, even with primary learners with special needs, such as Singaporean children with dyslexia (Jin et al. 2011). These methods potentially give an insider perspective through children's eyes and minds, complementing quantitative research. Such perspectives should include how children and teachers see multilingual skills and their identity development (Lo Bianco et al. 2009)

Future directions

Even with extensive developments and innovations in East Asia, traditional practices and pedagogies remain influential within cultures of learning. This may be expected, given the diversity of contexts (geographically, economically, linguistically and culturally). Parents are important stakeholders in EYL: their views and attitudes need to be known by teachers to support parental roles and foster home-school links for English. Key challenges include specific EYL teacher training and pedagogic development, the improvement of methods and availability of better resources, and perhaps the wider education of parents about English and foreign or second language learning. These factors limit – or can enhance – EYL. Increased use of digital technologies for ELL in this region seem inevitable; this might assist teachers to meet some identified challenges but this would depend on the quality of software provision and the actual value of use both in and outside classrooms. The social valuation given to early years' education in this region now often includes the element of EYL and this will be enhanced with progressive internationalization. If challenges can be met competently, with research-based developments, imagination and enthusiasm, the EYL future in the region is bright.

Further reading

1 Uchiyama, Takumi. (2011). Reading versus telling of stories in the development of English vocabulary and comprehension in young second language learners. *Reading Improvement*, 48, 168–178.

     This study focused on the use of two storytelling methods, Character Imagery (CI) and Simple Reading (SR), to 10–12-year-old Japanese primary school learners of English. It was found that the CI method had achieved a greater effect on the vocabulary and comprehension of English.

2 Lee, Ho-Young, and Hwanga, Hyosung. (2016). Gradient of learnability in teaching English pronunciation to Korean learners. *Journal of Acoustical Society of America*, 1859–1872.

     This is an experimental study of the learnability of Korean young learners receiving the teaching of English pronunciation through a high variability phonetic training (HVPT) program. This study indicates a greater benefit of using HVPT to these young learners, particularly if they are highly motivated.

Related topics

Motivation, listening and speaking, assessment, research issues with young learners

References

Adachi, R. (2011). The effect of increased English activities on sociocultural attitudes and intercultural communicative attitudes of young Japanese learners. *JACET Journal*, 52, 1–18.

Adachi, R. (2012). A motivational model in Japanese elementary students' foreign language activities. *Language Education and Technology*, 49, 47–64.

Adamson, B. (2004). *China's English: A history of English in Chinese education*. Hong Kong: Hong Kong University Press.

Butler, Y. G. (2004). What level of English proficiency do elementary school teachers need to attain to teach EFL? Case studies from Korea, Taiwan and Japan. *TESOL Quarterly*, 38(2), 245–278.

Butler, G. B. (2013). Parental factors and early English education in English as a foreign language: A case study in Mainland China. *Asia Pacific Education, Language Minorities and Migration (ELMM) Network Working Paper Series*, 8.

Butler, G. B. (2015). English language education among young learners in East Asia: A review of current research (2004–2014). *Language Teaching*, 48(3), 303–342.

Cameron, L. (2001). *Teaching Languages to Young Learners*. Cambridge: Cambridge University Press.

Carless, D. R. (2003). Factors in the implementation of task-based teaching in primary schools. *System*, 31, 485–500.

Carless, D. R. (2004). Issues in teachers' reinterpretations of task-based innovations in primary schools. *TESOL Quarterly*, 38(4), 639–661.

Carless, D. (2011). *From testing to Productive Students Learning: Implementing formative assessment in confucian heritage countries*. New York: Routledge.

Carreira, J. M. (2011). Relationship between motivation for learning EFL and intrinsic motivation for learning in general among Japanese elementary school students. *System*, 39, 90–102.

Chan, C. K. K., and Rao, N. (Eds.). (2009). *Revisiting the Chinese Learner: Changing contexts, hanging education*. Hong Kong: Springer.

Cheng, L. Y., Li, M., Kirby, J. R., Qiang, H. Y., and Wade-Wooley, L. (2010). English language immersion and students' academic achievement in English, Chinese and mathematics. *Evaluation and Research in Education*, 23(3), 151–169.

China Daily (no author) (2013). Most Chinese kids learn English just for entrance exams. *China Daily*, 14 November 2013. www.chinadaily.com.cn/beijing/2013-11/14/content_17112871.html.

Cohen, R. (2004). The current status of English in Mongolia. *Asian EFL Journal*, 6(4).

Cortazzi, M., and Jin, L. (1996a). English language teaching and learning in China (State of the Art article). *Language Teaching*, 29(2), 61–80.

Cortazzi, M., and Jin, L. (1996b). Cultures of learning: Language classrooms in China. In Coleman, H. (ed.) *Society and the Language Classroom*. Cambridge: CUP, 169–206.

Cortazzi, M., and Jin, L. (2001). Large classes in China: "good" teachers and interaction. In Watkins, D., and Biggs, J. (eds.) *Teaching the Chinese Learner: Psychological and pedagogical perspectives*. Hong Kong: CERC/ACER, 115–134.

De Groat, B. (2015). Mobile app helps Chinese kids learn English. *Michigan News*, 23 June 2015. http://ns.umich.edu/new/releases/22968-mobile-app-helps-chinese-kids-learn-english

Djigunovic, J. M., and Lopriore, L. (2011). The learner . . . do individual differences matter? In Enever, J. (ed.) *ELLiE: Early language learning in Europe*. London: The British Council, 43–60.

Driscoll, P., and Simpson, H. (2015). Developing intercultural understanding in primary schools. In Bland, J. (ed.) *Teaching English to Young Learners, Critical Issues in Language Teaching with 3–12 Year Olds*. London: Bloomsbury, 167–182.

Feng, A., and Adamson, B. (2015). Contested notions of bilingualism and trilingualism in the People's Republic of China. In Wright, W. E., Boun, S., and Garcia, O. (eds.) *The Handbook of Bilingual and Multicultural Education*. Chichester: Wiley-Blackwell.

Garton, Sue, Copland, Fiona and Burns, Anne (2011). Investigating global practices in teaching English to young learners. *ELT Research Papers* 11–01

Hayes, D. (2014). *Factors Influencing Success in Teaching English in State Primary Schools*. London: British Council.

Hu, G. (2009). The craze for English medium education in China: Driving forces and looming consequences, *English Today*, 25(4), 47.

Hu, G., and McKay, S. (2012). English language education in East Asia: Some recent developments. *Journal of Multilingual and Multicultural Development*, 33(4), 345–362.

Hu, Yuanyuan (2007). *China's Foreign Language Policy on Primary English Education: From policy rhetoric to implementation reality*, PhD thesis, Purdue University, Indiana, USA.

Huang, K.-M. (2011). Motivating lessons: a classroom-oriented investigation of the effects of content-based instruction on EFL learners' motivated behaviours and classroom interaction. *System,* 39,186–201.

Jeon, M. (2012). English immersion and educational inequality in South Korea. *Journal of Multilingual and Multicultural Development,* 33(4), 395–408.

Jin, L., and Cortazzi, M. (1998). Dimensions of dialogue: Large classes in China. *International Journal of Educational Research*, 29(8), 739–761.

Jin, L., and Cortazzi, M. (2004). English language teaching in China: A bridge to the future. In Ho, W. K., and Wong, R. Y. L. (eds.) *English Language Teaching in East Asia Today, Changing Policies and Practices*, 2nd ed. Singapore: Eastern Universities Press, 119–134.

Jin, L., and Cortazzi, M. (2006). Changing practices in Chinese cultures of learning. *Language, Culture and Curriculum*, 19(1), 5–20.

Jin, L., and Cortazzi, M. (Eds.). (2011). *Researching Chinese Learners: Skills, perceptions, intercultural adaptations*. Basingstoke: Palgrave Macmillan.

Jin, L., and Cortazzi, M. (Eds.). (2012). *Researching Chinese Learners: Skills, perceptions, intercultural adaptations*. A Chinese and English bilingual edition, Beijing: FLTRP; Palgrave Macmillan.

Jin, L., Liang, X. H., Jiang, C. S., Zhang, J., Yuan, Y., and Xie, Q. (2014a) Studying motivation of Chinese young EFL learners by metaphor analysis. *ELT Journal,* 68(3), 286–298.

Jin, L., Jiang, C. S., Zhang, J., Yuan, Y., Liang, X. H., and Xie, Q. (2014b) *Motivations and Expectations of English Language Learning among Primary School Children and Parents in China*. London: British Council.

Jin, L., Smith, K., Yahya, A., Chan, M., Choong, M., Lee. A., Ng, V., Poh-Wong, P., and Young, D. (2011). *Perceptions and Strategies of Learning in English by Singapore Primary School children with dyslexia – A metaphor analysis*. London: British Council.

Jin, L., Zhou, J., Hu, X. Y., Yang, X. L., Sun, K. Zhao, Md., and Yang, F. (2016). *Researching the Attitudes and Perceived Experiences of Kindergarten Learners of English and their Parents in China*. London: British Council.

Lau, Grace (2012). From China to Hong Kong: A reflection of the impact of educational reform in the Deweyan perspective on early childhood education in the Land of the Dragon. *International Journal of Educational Reform*, 21(1), 2–23.

Li, M. (2018). After-class war. *China Report*, English edition, 56, January, 36–38

Li, J. (2012). *Cultural Foundations of Learning: East and West*. Cambridge: Cambridge University Press.

Liang, Jun and Yan, Meng (2014). Chinese parents passionate for kids early English learning. *English People*, 21 May 2014.

Liang, Xiaohua, Jin, L., and Cortazzi, M. (2013). Peer assistance in an English immersion context in China. In Jin, L., and Cortazzi, M. (eds.) *Researching Intercultural Learning: Investigations in language and education*. Basingstoke: Palgrave Macmillan, 99–116.

Liu, J. (2007). Critical period hyspothesis retested: The effects of earlier English education in China. In Liu, J. (ed.) *English Language Teaching in China: New approaches, perspectives and standards*. London: Continuum,170–191.

Lo Bianco, J., Orton, J., and Gao, Y. (Eds.). (2009). *China and English, Globalization and the Dilemmas of Identity*. Bristol: Multilingual Matters.

Ministry of Education (2016). *Educational Statistics*. Beijing: Chinese Ministry of Education. www.moe. edu.cn/jyb_sjzl/sjzl_fztjgb/201707/t20170710_309042.html.

Moon, J. (2000). *Children Learning English, A Guidebook for English Language Teachers*. London: Macmillan Education.

Morgan, W. T., Gu, Q., and Li, F. (Eds.). (2017). *Handbook of Chinese Education*. Cheltenham: Edward Elgar.

Mourão, S. (2015). English in pre-primary: The challenges of getting it right. In Bland, J. (ed.) *Teaching English to Young Learners, Critical Issues in Language Teaching with 3–12 Year Olds*. London: Bloomsbury, 51–70.

NA: No author (2016). *The white paper on English learning by Chinese children.* http://education. news.cn/2016-05/13/c_128980586.htm. http://wreport.iresearch.cn/uploadfiles/reports/636161223 706866082.pdf.

Nishida, R. (2012). A longitudinal study of motivation, interest, can-do and willingness to communicate in foreign language activities among Japanese fifth-grade students. *Language Education & Technology*, 49, 23–45.

Nishida, R., and Yashima, T. (2009). An investigation of factors affecting willingness to communicate and interest in foreign countries among young learners. *Language Education & Technology*, 46, 151–117.

Pan, L. (2015). *English as a Global Language in China: Deconstructing the ideological discourses of English in language education.* London: Springer.

Pinter, A. (2006). *Teaching Young Language Learners.* Oxford: Oxford University Press.

Pinter, A. (2011). *Children Learning Second Languages: Research and practice in applied linguistics.* Basingstoke: Palgrave Macmillan.

Pinter, A. (2015a). Researching young learners. In Paltridge, B., and Phakiti, A. (eds.) *Research Methods in Applied Linguistics.* London: Bloomsbury, 339–455.

Pinter, A. (2015b). Task-based learning with children. In Bland, J. (ed.) *Teaching English to Young Learners, Critical Issues in Language Teaching with 3–12 Year Olds.* London: Bloomsbury, 113–128.

Qiang, H., Huang, X. Siegel, L., and Trube, B. (2011). English immersion in mainland China. In Feng, A. (ed.) *English Language Education across Greater China.* Bristol: Multilingual Matters, 169–188.

Reilly, V., and Ward, S. M. (1997). *Very Young Learners.* Oxford: Oxford University Press.

Samad, R. S. A., Houque, K. E., Yu, M., Othman, A. J., Sukur, M. I. R., and Daud, M. A. K. M. (2013). Uses of ICT in English teaching in primary schools in Wei Nan city, China. *International Journal of Language and Development*, 3(4) 78–86.

Schmid, E. C., and Whyte, S. (2015). Teaching young learners with technology. In Bland, J. (ed.) *Teaching English to Young Learners, Critical Issues in Language Teaching with 3–12 Year Olds.* London: Bloomsbury, 239–260.

Tobin, Joseph, Hsieh, Yeh and Karasawa, Mayumi (2009). *Preschool in Three Cultures Revisited: China, Japan, and the United States.* Chicago: University of Chicago Press.

Wei, Rining and Feng, Jieyun (2015). Implementing CLIL for young learners in an EFL context beyond Europe: Grassroots support and language policy in China. *English Today,* 31(1), 55–60.

Zhang, E. Y., and Adamson, B. (2007). Implementing language policy: Lessons from primary school English. In Feng, A. (ed.) *Bilingual Education in China: Practices, policies and concepts.* Clevedon: Multilingual Matters, 166–181.

Zhang, Y., and Wang, J. (2011). Primary school English language teaching in South China: Past, present and future. In Feng, A. (ed.) *English Language Education across Greater China.* Bristol: Multilingual Matters, 151–168.

Zhang, Zefeng (2017). English learning goes online. *China Daily*, 17 May 2017. www.chinadaily.com. cn/life/2017-05/17/content_29377631_2.htm

Zhao, Lin and Hi, Xinyun (2008). The development of early childhood education in rural areas in China. *Early Years: An International Journal of Research and Development*, 28(2), 197–209.

Zhou, J., Chen, S., and Jin, L. (2010). Using digital resources for the ECE curriculum in China: Current needs and future development. *International Journal of Knowledge Management & E-Learning*, 1(4), 285–294.

Zhou, J., Han, C. H., Tang, J. Y., Huang, J. Z., Chen, S. Zhang, L. Li, C. J., and Xia, S. S. (2014). *Are We Immersed in the Multicultural and Multilingual Context? A survey on parents and teachers of young children in Shanghai*, Keynote conference presentation, Zhongnan University of Economics and Law, China, 1–2 March 2014.

Zhou Y., and Ng, M. L. (2016). English as a Foreign Language (EFL) and English medium instruction (EMI) for three-to seven-year old children in East Asian contexts. In Murphy, V. A., and Evangelou, M. (eds.) *Early Childhood Education in English for Speakers of Other Languages.* London: British Council, 137–156.

Zhu, Jiaxiong and Zhang, Jie (2008). Contemporary trends and developments in early childhood education in China. *Early Years: An International Journal of Research and Development*, 28(2), 173–182.

Zou, W., and Zhang, S. (2011). Family background and English learning of compulsory stage in Shanghai. In Feng, A. (ed.) *English Language Education across Greater China*. Bristol: Multilingual Matters, 189–211.

30

Teaching English to young learners in Europe

Shelagh Rixon

Introduction

This chapter discusses the history and development of Early English Language Learning in Europe.

The historical period in focus is the four decades from the 1980s to the time of writing, although the context for this period is provided in discussion of developments in the earlier part of the twentieth century. Research and development dating from the decade of 2006 to 2016 is highlighted in Section 4: Current Contributions and Research.

The term *Early Language Learning* in this chapter covers children of any age up to about 11, which in many countries is the upper limit for what is variously termed 'primary' or 'elementary' education. It therefore also takes in pre-primary school language learning, which has become increasingly important in Europe in recent years. According to the definition used by Doyé and Hurrell (1997), writing of The Council of Europe Modern Languages Programme, the years of primary level education in Europe fall between the ages of 5–6 and 10–11, although in some countries children remain in the same institution until the age of 12–13. The focus of this chapter is on English teaching and learning in the state school sector, although in some countries interaction with a vigorous system of private provision is also relevant.

The term *Europe* has both geographical and political connotations. For the purposes of this chapter, Europe is considered to be those countries which currently fall within the European Economic Area (EEA). This includes members of the European Union (EU), plus three countries which are part of the European Union's single market although they are not EU members. Switzerland is not part of either the EU or the EEA but is clearly within the geographical territory commonly accepted as Europe and is also part of the single market, which means that its nationals have the same rights of movement and residence as EU members. Over the historical period discussed, the EU has gained a considerable number of members so that statistics may not always allow for a comparison of like with like at different points in time. However, the very useful documentation dealing with school level education published since 1980 under the name of Eurydice, now part of the Education, Audio-visual and Culture Executive Agency (EACEA) in the EEA region, has made provision for information on EEA countries and on other countries prior to their accession to the EU. This means that when using this source comparisons may be made safely between one period and another.

At the time of writing in 2016, the EU countries were: Austria, Belgium, Bulgaria, Croatia, Republic of Cyprus, Czech Republic, Denmark, Estonia, Finland, France, Germany, Greece, Hungary, Ireland, Italy, Latvia, Lithuania, Luxembourg, Malta, Netherlands, Poland, Portugal, Romania, Slovakia, Slovenia, Spain, Sweden and the UK.

The EEA but not EU member countries were Iceland, Liechtenstein and Norway. Switzerland, neither an EEA nor an EU country, is also included in this account.

Historical perspectives

For the period discussed, developments in the teaching of English need to be considered alongside the teaching of other languages. This is firstly because in a region of such cultural and linguistic diversity the choices to be made have always been amongst many candidates. Secondly, it is only in the years since the Second World War that English has been moving into its present position of very high priority within most school curricula, largely owing to growing US influence on industry, world politics and the media (Graddol 2000, p. 7). Thirdly, despite the growth of the appeal of English, the predominant philosophy within European institutions with a social or educational remit is one of plurlingualism.

From 1900 to the end of the Second World War

Although English had been present in many curricula since the late nineteenth century, when industrialisation and increases in international trade made command of 'living/modern' rather than 'dead/classical' languages a priority for most, it had not, during the first 40 years of the twentieth century, assumed the important role in public and government attention within Europe that it has today. Additionally, the norm at that time was for foreign language learning to be reserved for secondary level education, which was not available to all.

From 1950–1979

After the Second World War, in Europe many states underwent massive reorganisation, which included educational systems and the role of foreign language learning within them. In territories in Eastern Europe with new or existing affiliations to the Soviet Union, Russian became the dominant foreign language taught and from 1949 was also taught at the primary school level in most of these countries (Eurydice 2001, p. 49). In Western Europe, foreign languages tended still to be reserved for secondary school learning until a movement for change in the 1960s. The main impetus seems to have been widespread dissatisfaction with the attainments of learners who were taught languages at secondary school. Rationales for lowering the starting age for foreign language centred around, firstly, a view that devoting more school years to the process would raise standards and, secondly, a belief, stimulated by first- and second-language acquisition research of the time (e.g., Penfield 1953) that younger children would have superior capacities for learning languages in instructional situations. In 1961, the Second Conference of European Ministers of Education in held in Hamburg included the following statement (Council of Europe 1961) as part of its *Resolution No. 6 on the Expansion and Improvement of Modern Language Teaching:*

> Experience in certain European countries has shown that a great extension of the teaching of modern languages is practicable. This seems to hold good also for relatively

young pupils. The Ministers recommend that periodical surveys be made in each country in order to ascertain the proportion of children following modern language courses. The results should be published in order to show the progress made.

Stern and Weinrib (1977, p. 6) record two international meetings in 1962 and 1966 organised by UNESCO at their Institute for Education in Hamburg at which similar emphasis was given to the need to gather empirical evidence for the optimum starting age as well as survey evidence on the actual state of language teaching in territories worldwide. However, in much of Europe, evaluation of primary school language teaching during this period was often frustrated either by the lack of contexts in which substantial and systematic teaching for a significant amount of time had taken place or by lack of systematic data collection (ibid., p. 6).

A contrast, in terms of planned evaluation and systematic research methodology, was provided by an experiment in England and Wales during that time. The 'French from Eight' project, whose piloting began in 1963, is still one of the best-known and most influential sets of research into primary level foreign language teaching. However, the interpretation put on the data in the final report (Burstall et al. 1974) was, and remains, controversial. The key finding, that by the age of 16 participants in the project differed in no significant way in attainment from children who had started French only at secondary school, resulted in the abandonment of the project after loss of government support. This research and its outcome were widely debated, and the findings were by no means accepted by all (Bennett 1975; Buckby 1976). They seem not to have had a dampening effect on piloting and research concerning early language learning in other regions.

A European symposium held in Copenhagen in September 1976 (Council of Europe 1977) involving representatives from 22 Western European countries was evidence of continued interest. As a lead-in to the symposium, P.H. Hoy, an Inspector of Schools from the UK and early member of the committee of the International Association of Teachers as a Foreign Language (IATEFL), conducted a questionnaire-based survey whose results suggested 'that the European picture is one of a general trend towards lowering the starting age for modern languages' (Hoy 1975). The debate remained alive, however. As Stern and Weinrib (1977, p. 15) expressed it, findings so far:

> all point in the same direction: the provision of languages in the education of younger children has not come to be considered the *sine qua non* of effective language learning over the last 25 years.

The period 1980–2016

Despite the caution from Stern and other authorities, interest in implementing primary school foreign language teaching at nationwide levels gained new vigour during the 1980s, with greater interest and intervention by national politicians and administrations. This was often accompanied by a focus on the teaching of English. As has been documented by Graddol (2006, p. 88), this may partly be accounted for by the rise in the influence of English as a global language.

The narrative of the development of English for Young Learners in Europe from this point onwards is extremely complex, with the many internal changes in political and economic alignment in the region and an increasing number of states joining what was to become the European Union. That is even without considering the different ways in which school systems are structured within individual countries and the different phases of piloting and experimentation that may precede official ratification of the introduction of primary foreign languages. The passing of a law or decree to give foreign language teaching a place in primary school has not always coincided with its actual active presence, and there has often been language teaching activity before full official recognition was obtained. Detailed chronology and statistics are obtainable from two very useful sets of documents from the Council of Europe, available online. These are the Eurydice 2001 document *Foreign Language Teaching in Schools in Europe* and the Eurydice *Key Data on Teaching Languages in Europe* series, with volumes published about every four years. The most recent at the time of writing was that for 2012.

In the 1980s and 1990s, countries such as Austria, Italy and France were amongst the first to lower the starting age for foreign language learning. This was after extended periods of pilot or experimental teaching. The change of starting age was radical, with children starting English or another language several years younger than the previous norm of 11 or 12.

In the Scandinavian countries, the lowering of the starting age was normally gradual with changes only of a year or so made at any one time. For example, in Denmark with the 1994 *folkeskole* reform, the starting age was reduced by one year and English became compulsory from the fourth to the ninth year.

The breakup of the Soviet Union in the late 1980s and the fall of the Berlin Wall in 1989 led to wide-ranging political and administrative changes in countries which had, after the Second World War, been under Soviet rule or direct influence. One manifestation of this change in many cases was a rejection of the teaching of Russian in schools and a massive retraining of teachers of Russian to teach other languages, usually English. Since Russian was already being taught in primary schools, this left an opening for the teaching of other languages at this level and in countries such as Hungary and Poland, and major changes in pre-service and in-service training took place (see Pugsley and Kershaw 1996 for a summary). During this period, financial and advisory support for countries in this region became abundantly available from the outside world with, for example, funding from the British Foreign Office and the British Council ELTECs (English Language Teaching Contacts Scheme) fostering travel and professional support for teachers, together with similar aid from the USA and loans from the World Bank for the creation and publication of new teaching materials. Much of this funding had an impact that also affected primary English language education.

Within the European Union, the Lingua programme was adopted in July 1989 and came into force on January 1, 1990, with the aim of improving the amount and quality of language teaching in the area. The programme was later (1995) integrated within the broader Socrates programme. Through these schemes, provision was made for co-operation amongst EU countries to promote the teaching and learning of languages. In addition to the actions in Lingua, other actions of the Socrates programme such as Comenius (cooperation in school education) also had a language teaching dimension.

It should be noted that the major movement in the period between the late 1990s and the present has been towards plurilingualism. In most countries pupils have the chance to study several languages during their school career. Currently, in almost all countries except the UK, learning a first foreign language is compulsory at the primary school level, with a second language in place certainly in the early years of secondary school and in several cases starting in primary school. (Within the UK, Scotland is alone in promoting two languages at the primary level from 2017 onwards.) In the year 1998–1999 (Eurydice 2001, p. 96) eight countries (Denmark, Greece, the Netherlands, Sweden, Liechtenstein, Norway, Cyprus and Latvia) had already made English the first compulsory foreign language at primary school, and in other countries where there was a choice of first foreign language English was by far the most chosen.

In 2004, the following countries joined the European Union: Cyprus, the Czech Republic, Estonia, Hungary, Latvia, Lithuania, Malta, Poland, Slovakia and Slovenia. Accession to the EU seems to have coincided in many cases with a rise in their take up of English at primary school level (Eurydice 2012, p. 61). The two most dramatic rises over this period were in Slovenia (from 11.1% to 49%) and in Poland (50.7% to 88%). Steep rises, of 20–30 percentage points, were also recorded for Bulgaria, the Czech Republic and Slovakia. The position in Cyprus and Malta where, owing to previous colonial contacts with the UK, English was already an important curricular subject, was little changed. During the same period, Iceland and Croatia also experienced steep rises in take up of English. Overall, in the five years between 2004–2005 and 2009–2010 there was an increase from about 60.7% of primary pupils over the whole European area learning English to about 73% in 2009–2010 (Eurydice 2012, pp. 60–61). These figures are rendered more striking if it is considered that they are calculated based on the total numbers of pupils at that time in primary education, not all of whom would have started a language yet, and that increases were generally the result of lowering the age at which English was started. By 2010, English was already the most widely taught foreign language in primary education in almost all education systems. Exceptions were the Flemish Community of Belgium and in Luxembourg, in both of which French and German were compulsory.

Developments in the teaching of English in pre-primary education

The 1998 publication (Blondin et al. 2008) *Foreign Languages in Primary and Pre-School Education: Contexts and Outcomes*, intended for policy makers and administrators, evidenced a growing interest in teaching very young children. However, the Eurydice document of 2001 reported little foreign language teaching at the pre-primary level. This was soon to change. By the time of the data collection in 2011–2012 leading to the report in a British Council survey (Rixon 2013), the signs of activity were evident enough for the researcher to include specific questions about this area. The results worldwide showed significant interest in English teaching at the pre-school level, and this was particularly the case in the European countries covered, with responses from some countries, such as Croatia, suggesting very considerable coverage at an official level, while in others, such as the Czech Republic, although English was not yet a compulsory part of the state Early Years curriculum, it was very frequently taught.

Where pre-primary education was not part of the state-supported system, there were also reports of English being offered at pre-school levels in private institutions, for example in Greece. In 2014, after the publication of the survey, British Council Teaching Centres in the EU began offering courses for children as young as two years old.

Critical issues and topics

English in a Europe which values multilingualism

It should always be remembered that developments within Europe take place among a set of highly diverse countries with extremely different historical backgrounds, economic fortunes and cultural assumptions. The teaching of English in Europe is part of a wider spectrum of language learning, conditioned by the policy in almost all countries, since the

Resolution of the Council of Europe of 1995, to ensure that all pupils study at least two foreign languages during their school years. An additional factor in some countries is the existence of more than one local language or language variety to which proper attention must be also paid. This commitment to multilingualism could be seen to be endangered if one language gains too great a dominance over others in school-based learning. For example, in some of the countries where Russian once dominated the primary and secondary languages syllabus, it has been noted that the aspiration for all EU children to learn two languages in addition to the mother tongue has become attenuated, and in practical terms English is the single language of choice. See Bruen and Sheridan (2016), for example, for a discussion of the situation in the ex-German Democratic Republic region and Hungary. In the Foreword to the document 'Foreign Language Teaching in Schools in Europe' (Eurydice 2001, p. 3) Viviane Reding, then European Commissioner for Education and Culture, acknowledges the issue as follows:

> what is required to ensure that the consistently strong preference among pupils for learning English, or even the status of English as the first compulsory foreign language, do not compromise preservation of the linguistic and cultural diversity of Europe?

Optimum age or optimum conditions?

One issue has remained constant for at least the past 50 years: that is the assumption, at least in non-expert circles, that beginning to learn another language at a young age is a powerful guarantee of success. More extreme forms of this view hold that success will be limited unless the learner starts young (the so-called 'younger the better' view). Most experts, both linguists and educationists, have long ago moved on from and refined such age-dominated/ biological development concepts as that of a Critical Period (Lenneberg 1967) or even a Sensitive Period (Oyama, 1976). See Singleton and Lengyel (1995) and Johnstone (2002), for example, for further discussion. Such views have nonetheless frequently been used by politicians and administrators to support an early start in foreign or second language learning in schools. Specialists today are careful to factor in with the age of the learners the peculiar conditions and multiple variables offered by instructed school-based learning. Optimum conditions include adequate exposure to the language within the curriculum, activities which are engaging and lead to interaction and, above all, language use that is meaningful to the learners (see Rixon (2000) for a summary of these issues).

However, while politicians, parents and members of the public still press for an ever-earlier start to foreign language learning, even when favourable conditions are difficult to set up, the comment by Stern and Weinrib (1977, pp. 19–20) is worth reflecting on:

> An understanding of the role of a second language in a community, and an appreciation of its educational and cultural value are perhaps more important than the search for a psychologically or biologically optimal age.

Purposes for teaching foreign languages at primary school level

The pro-forma used by 'Foreign Language Teaching in Schools in Europe' (Eurydice 2001) for gathering information concerning objectives for primary school language learning unsurprisingly asks for responses concerning linguistic/grammatical objectives, but other objectives are also included as key:

- Reflecting on language.
- Sociocultural aspects (knowledge of other cultures, understanding people from other cultures).
- Cognitive and affective aspects (fostering independent learning, fostering personality development).

This may be considered good evidence of what is agreed to be of value in an 'ideal' delivery of a foreign language programme. However, it is notable that not all countries have responded concerning the aspects listed above.

Teacher supply and education needs

A much-debated issue in Europe is who is the most appropriate figure to teach primary school children a language. Eurydice (2001, p. 114) sets up a typology of eligible teachers:

- Generalist teacher: a teacher qualified to teach all subjects in the curriculum, including foreign language(s).
- Semi-specialist teacher: a teacher qualified to teach a group of subjects including foreign language(s); s/he may be in charge of foreign language(s) exclusively or several other subjects as well.
- Specialist subject teacher: a teacher qualified to teach one or several foreign languages.

A frequent debate concerning teachers of English is about the benefits of ensuring that a generalist primary school teacher, in the form of the children's own 'home room' teacher, has a subject repertoire that includes English, compared with the value of bringing in a specialist English teacher whose experience may not have previously included teaching younger children. The British Council survey (Rixon 2013, pp. 20–23) revealed different responses to this issue. Frequently all three of the possible solutions above were in place.

Whatever the preference regarding the ideal figure as teacher, one of the greatest obstacles to smooth implementation of a programme of English for younger children is the shortage of sufficiently qualified and competent teachers of any sort, especially when the demand is suddenly increased by a hurried lowering of the starting age. We may take as an example the case of Italy where in 1992 one foreign language was made compulsory in primary school, from the age of seven onward (Eurydice 2001, p. 56). However, several years later, in 1998/1999 when the data for the 2001 report was collected, a shortage of adequately qualified teachers meant that only 65% of schools were able to implement the policy.

In the 1990s, in countries such as Hungary and Poland, in response to the decision to teach other languages than Russian in schools, measures were taken to increase the numbers of appropriately trained primary school language teachers through setting up new initial teacher training courses and institutions as well as in-service courses, but this wholesale approach has not applied across the whole European region. As Enever (2014) notes, in spite of the creation of the European Profile for Language Teacher Education (Kelly and Grenfell 2004), which might be thought to encourage greater consistency, the teacher education picture varies, and in some countries pre-service teacher training courses for primary level may contain little or no specific preparation for the role of language teacher. Additionally, in-service courses may contain very diverse subject matter and often present problems of access or of timing from the point of view of would-be trainees (Enever 2014).

Attempted solutions to difficulties with supply of suitable teachers include officially or unofficially allowing people without required qualifications or skills to teach a language. Even in more recent years, experts from some of the European countries covered by the British Council survey (Rixon 2013, p. 27) reported such compromises:

> Although the required qualifications to that effect are stated by the Ministry of Educa-
> tion, the shortage of qualified teachers has led it to taking applicants on the basis of their
> 'relevant curricula' which have been judged continuously. Such practice has proved
> that some applicants lack both academic and pedagogical qualifications and have been
> taken as teachers at this level.
>
> *(Portugal)*

Transition between levels of schooling as a major factor in ultimate success

As early as the report by Burstall et al. (1974) the importance was emphasised of giving a positive reception at the next level of schooling to children's primary school linguistic attainments and of the need to build on them rather than ignore them. The problem has been referred to many times and in many other contexts since then. In the British Council survey (Rixon 2013, pp. 39–40) the same issues seemed apparent, with only a few reports (Rixon 2013, p. 220) of positive measures in place, such as teachers from both levels meeting in order to ensure continuity and appreciation of children's attainments so far.

Social equity in access to English – public and private provision

The social and social-symbolic value of a knowledge of English as a badge conveying a good standard of education and a key to success has been a widely experienced phenom-enon for some time (Rogers 1982). In some societies, however, truly effective English lan-guage teaching is a scarce resource. This can lead to serious ethical considerations and social discontent when what is considered good quality English teaching is available only to the economically affluent who can pay for private tuition but is also desired by those less privileged.

Such perceptions of English as a necessity for success in life often result in parents making financial sacrifices to support their offspring that are out of proportion to what an informed valuation of the power of an early start can logically support. The dynamics between public and private provision in some countries thus are vivid and the source of much discussion.

A factor for the history of EYL in Europe has been the existence in some countries, at least since the end of the Second World War, of a vigorous tradition of teaching English as a foreign language in the private sector. Children whose parents could afford it were often learners of English at these institutions even in the years before English became part of the primary school curriculum. In the British Council Survey (Rixon 2013, p. 44), there were reports of high attendance at private language institutes from five of the European contexts responding. It was claimed that in Croatia and Spain between 40% and 59% primary-aged children attended private language institutes. The claim for Cyprus, Greece and Serbia was that over 60% attended private language institutes. From Greece in 2012 the comment was 'English is considered to be an unimportant subject at school as it is seriously offered at private language institutions'. By contrast, in other contexts such as Finland (Rixon 2013, p. 105) there is confidence in the quality of public provision which means that almost no children study English at private language institutes. Similarly, the comment from Sweden (Rixon 2013, p. 218) was 'There is no market for private language institutions in Sweden'.

Suitable methodological choices

According to Eurydice (2001, p. 158), in most contexts in Europe a version of Communicative Language Teaching (CLT) is explicitly or implicitly recommended for primary school language teaching. It is doubtful, however, whether this is actually in place, considering the difficulties of defining the approach and above all the generally low levels of training in language teaching methodology of many of the teachers concerned. We also need to consider that CLT was developed with adults in mind and would need considerable modifications to become 'child-friendly'.

It might be more accurate to say that where teaching languages to children has been successful, methodological principles have been developed from experience and have often involved putting good general primary school educational practice to the service of language learning. In these 'child-friendly' approaches, communication and meaningful language use have been dominant without the methodology necessarily aligning itself with mainstream CLT. As an example, since the 1970s, language teaching to children in Croatia with the work of the late professor Mirjana Vilke and colleagues in English, French, German and Italian has become emblematic of an integrated playful approach which is yet systematic in its underlying planning. It has also been carefully researched as to its results (VIlke 1998).

In other cases, adaptations of mainstream primary teaching practices have been made for the teaching of English. Topic-based teaching, once the main framework for mainstream primary school teaching in the UK, was promoted in the early 1990s through teaching materials (e.g., Stepping Stones, Collins 1991). What this and other approaches such as story-based teaching and CLIL (discussed below) have in common is that the activities involved are intended to engage attention and rouse interest and the language is used in a way that is meaningful to the child rather than presented as a set of exponents of a linguistic system.

Teaching based on storytelling, such as is advocated by Garvie (1989), has been highly effective in EAL contexts in the UK, but this approach needs to be distinguished from teaching using picture-story books as a starting point and stimulus. This latter approach has been more widely discussed in the European context and in some places is highly developed. In 1991, Ellis and Brewster published a highly influential handbook on storybook use, with a revised version a decade later (Ellis and Brewster 2002). Since this time, numerous publications with a European focus (e.g., Enever and Schmid-Schönbeim 2006) have reported on research and classroom experiences with both storybook use and storytelling.

Content Language Integrated Learning (CLIL) traces its origins to innovations in Finland in the early 1990s (Coyle et al. 2010) and has since been promoted worldwide. The 2012 Key Data report (Eurydice 2012) claims that in all EEA countries, except Denmark, Greece and Iceland, some schools give students the opportunity to have CLIL-type provision. However, it seems to take place in limited areas, and outside these focal zones numbers are very small and the provision patchy. Examples where the willingness of authorities to devote resources has contributed to success have been projects with the Ministry of Education and British Council in Spain, starting in 1996, in the Basque country and Slovakia. It is only in Belgium (German-speaking community), Luxembourg and Malta that all schools operate on a 'CLIL' basis, in which English is involved as well as other languages. Trentino, in Northern Italy, and Switzerland are notable for the literature that has been based on CLIL activity and research in their schools (see Lucietto 2008). More recently (Rixon 2013, p. 9) a CLIL approach in primary schools has received official support in Cyprus. For a collection of case studies and accounts of experiences from European contexts, see Ioannou-Georgiou and Pavlou (2011) and Bentley (2015).

It is probably true to say that although the approaches above have been influential and are much discussed in the literature, outside high-profile projects they may not be greatly in evidence at the level of day-to-day teaching. This is possibly because of the high levels of language competence required on the part of the teacher in order to sustain the flexible exchanges with pupils essential to such approaches. Enever (2014), using the findings from the ELLiE study of seven European countries (see Current Contributions and Research below), comments:

> classroom observations throughout the ELLiE study indicated that not all teachers had the necessary FL [Foreign Language] skills for the types of classroom interaction needed with this primary age group.

Language level goals and age-appropriate assessment

Although collections of research papers on assessment have been published since the early twenty-first century (e.g., Rea-Dickins 2000) with an increase in interest in the second decade of the century (e.g., Nikolov 2015), the issues of appropriate approaches to the assessment of language learning in young children are far from settled.

Since its publication, the Common European Framework of Reference (CEFR) for Languages (Council of Europe 2001) has been used in most European countries as a way of expressing goals for language attainment at the end of primary schooling. Most have chosen the A1 or A2 level (Rixon 2013, p. 35). However, it should be remembered, as discussed by, e.g., Hasselgren (2005), McKay (2006) and Enever (2011, p. 34), that as yet there is no version of CEFR adapted for the capacities and centres of interest of children. The current use of CEFR levels to define goals for English at primary school should therefore be taken as only a rough guide to aspirations. In most countries, assessment to determine if the level is reached takes place within the school.

Approaches to classroom assessment thought to be suited to primary school aged children have been described (Rea-Dickins and Rixon 1997) but tend to be time-consuming and are often based on one-on-one interactions. There is thus a tension, even for highly motivated and skilled professionals, between what is optimal and what is practically feasible in the allocated time. A phenomenon noted in the late twentieth century (Rea-Dickins and Rixon 1999), but continuing into the twenty-first (Brumen et al. 2009), is the mismatch between stated aims of primary language teaching and the assessment methods and instruments used by teachers. The most common mismatch (found in all the studies mentioned above) has been the use for assessment of classroom 'pencil and paper' tests which were heavily dependent on reading and writing, despite the teachers' stated interest in developing oral and aural skills. On the other hand, in assessment used for research and project evaluation purposes, where more resources of time and expertise are usually available, some highly innovative and child-friendly instruments have been created, particularly in Norway (Hasselgren 2000) and as part of the ELLie project (Szpotowicz and Lindgren 2011).

At the time of writing, modern mainstream educational developments of formative assessment such as assessment for learning (Black and Wiliam 1998), which puts emphasis on supporting children in reflection, self-assessment and deciding their own next learning steps, have reached the young learners literature (e.g., Rixon 2015) but are not yet widely established in classrooms. On the other hand, portfolio work which also encourages reflection and self-assessment by the children is more widespread and is supported by the various locally adapted versions of the Junior Version of the European Languages Passport (ELP), which is calibrated with the CEFR. For an example from Norway, see: http://elp.ecml.at/Portals/1/documents/Norway-100-2009-Model-for-young-learners-aged-6-12.pdf. It should be pointed out that the ELP, in keeping with the plurilingual ambitions in Europe, is a useful tool for building a profile of a child's capacities in several languages and is not intended as an instrument for assessment of English or any other language alone.

Current contributions and research

From the late 1980s until the end of the twentieth century there were numerous surveys and state of the art articles concerning early language learning (e.g., Rixon 1992, Kubanek-German 1998, Rixon 2000; Moon and Nikolov 2000). More recently, there have been volumes giving detailed accounts of experiments or projects in specific countries. Rich (2014) contains chapters covering experiences in Poland and Germany, while Bland (2015) covers issues and research with a particularly European focus. Examples of volumes reporting research on specific topics are Nikolov 2015 on approaches to assessment and Wilden and Porsch (2017) on teacher education for primary school English teaching. Most of the discussions in these two volumes are focused on European case studies or examples.

What is feasible for children to achieve in normal instructional conditions?

One of the most significant contributions in recent years concerning the teaching of English in Europe has been the longitudinal comparative study of language teaching and learning in seven European countries (Croatia, England, Italy, Netherlands, Poland, Spain and Sweden) led by Enever under the auspices of the Council of Europe (Enever 2011). This study has provided data on the conditions and results of ordinary classroom learning of English in continental Europe that have already engendered numerous articles and will furnish material for discussion for many years.

With the increase of interest in pre-school learning of English in the twenty-first century has come an increase of research into this age group as language learners, much of it focused on work in Europe (see Mourão and Lourenço 2015).

Recommendations for practice

The following recommendations are derived from the discussions above.

Governments and administrations should consider the resource implications of any change in the stage of schooling at which English is introduced. Experience and research have shown that short-term hurried changes are unlikely to be implemented as intended or to have the desired impact.

More successful learning outcomes are regularly associated with approaches and methods in which activities are intrinsically engaging, have meaning for the learners and foster interactions in the target language. However, successful teaching of this sort requires fluency and confidence in target language use on the part of the teacher.

Assessment practices and instruments should fit with the style and the goals of primary school English teaching and be based more on observation and sampling of work than on pencil-and-paper tests.

It is particularly important to confront the problems of transition from pre-school to primary levels of education, already a lingering problem with the move from primary to secondary level.

Future directions

The post-Brexit fortunes of English as a foreign language in European schools

It is an obvious irony that in June 2016 the result of a referendum held in the UK was that the then UK government expressed its intention to leave the EU – so-called Brexit. Thus, a major English-speaking country and major reference point for many teachers of English in Europe elected to part company with Europe in the political and economic sense. It seems unlikely, since English remains a global lingua franca, that this will affect the take-up of English as the main foreign language learning option for primary school children in Europe, but the nature of continuing co-operation between the European Union and the UK in the field of English language learning is an area that will merit attention. It may be less likely that major research projects such as the ELLie project, discussed above, funded by the European Commission and initiated from the UK, will be part of the future.

Increased pre-school teaching of English

It is highly likely that the push for starting English teaching at ever-younger ages will continue. More research is needed not only into appropriate approaches for children as young as two or three but into what aspects of English language learning are feasible to address in instructional situations with very young children and how their achievements can be validly and reliably measured for research purposes. The drive to provide commercially available tests of English for younger and younger children has so far stopped short of this age group, but increased teaching may result in attempts by testing bodies to capitalise on this level.

More appropriate specification of goals for young learners of English

Work that has started on adapting the CEFR to reflect the interests and capacities of children under 12 will, once completed, provide a framework for more realistic goal-setting and support those attempting to devise more appropriate instruments for assessing their English attainments and supporting its progress.

Online and blended learning routes to teacher education

Different, accessible and affordable, ways need to be sought of supporting teachers both at pre-service and in-service levels in language and methodological preparation. Online and blended learning courses in areas such as Early Childhood Language Learning (e.g., The Norwich Institute for Language Education 2016) are starting to cater to Teacher Subject

Knowledge and have been shown to be effective. These along with free online MOOCs (Massive Online Open Courses; e.g., futurelearn and the British Council 2017) seem to offer viable and affordable sources of continuous professional development for primary school teachers of English in Europe.

Further reading

Bland, J. (Ed.). (2015). *Teaching English to young learners: Critical issues in language teaching with 3–12 year olds*. London: Bloomsbury.
  Fifteen chapters by different authors, covering topics related to the teaching of English to pre-school and primary school aged children, many with a focus on classroom activities such as the use of drama, storybooks, CLIL, task-based learning and portfolio-based assessment.

Eurydice Key Data on Teaching Languages at School in Europe 2012.
  Key Data reports are published every three to four years. This most recent one at the time of writing provides a useful snapshot of the situation regarding the teaching of all languages in the then 27 member countries of the European Union, plus Croatia, Iceland, Liechtenstein, Norway and Turkey.

Mourão, S., and Lourenço. M. (2015). *Early years second language education: International perspectives on theory and practice*. Abingdon: Routledge.
  One of the first works to focus specifically on the teaching of English to children under six years old. The contexts covered are mainly European.

Related topics

The age debate, contexts of learning, CLIL, assessment, language policy, learning through literature, teacher education

References

Ashworth, J., and Clarke, J. (1991). *Stepping Stones*. London: Collins.

Bennett, S. N. (1975). Weighing the evidence: A review of Primary French in the balance. *British Journal of Educational Psychology*, 45(3), 337–340.

Black, P., and Wiliam, D. (1998). Inside the black box: Raising standards through classroom assessment. *Phi Delta Kappa*, 80(2), 139–148.

Bland, J. (Ed.). (2015). *Teaching English to Young Learners: Critical issues in language teaching with 3–12 year olds*. London: Bloomsbury.

Blondin, C. et al. (2008). *Foreign Languages in Primary and Pre-school Education: Context and outcomes: A review of recent research within the European Union*. London: CILT.

British Council/futurelearn. (2017). MOOC English in early childhood: Language learning and development. www.futurelearn.com/partners/british-council

Bruen, J., and Sheridan, V. (2016). The impact of the collapse of communism and EU accession on language education policy and practice in Central and Eastern Europe: Two case-studies focussing on English and Russian as foreign languages in Hungary and Eastern Germany. *Current Issues in Language Planning*, 17(2).

Brumen, M., Cagran, B., and Rixon, S. (2009). Comparative assessment of young learners' foreign language competence in three Eastern European countries. *Educational Studies*, 35(3), 269–295.

Buckby, M. (1976). Is primary French really in the Balance?. *The Modern Language Journal*, 60(7), 340–346.

Burstall, C., Jamieson, M., Cohen, S., and Hargreaves, M. (1974). *Primary French in the Balance*. Slough: National Foundation for Educational Research.

Council of Europe (1961). *Standing Conference of European Ministers of Education 2nd Session*. Hamburg, Germany, 10–15 April 1961. Strasbourg: Council of Europe.

Council of Europe (1974). *Symposium on the Early Teaching of a Modern Language*. Wiesbaden, 11–17 November 1973, Strasbourg:: The Council of Europe.

Council of Europe (1977). *Symposium on Modern Languages in Primary Education*. Copenhagen, 20–25 September 1976, Strasbourg: The Council of Europe.

Council of Europe (2001). *Common European Framework of Reference for Languages: Learning, teaching, assessment (CEFR)*. Cambridge: Cambridge University Press.

Council of Europe (2009). *European Language Passport 6–12, Norway*. http://elp.ecml.at/Portals/1/documents/Norway-100-2009-Model-for-young-learners-aged-6-12.pdf

Coyle, D., Hood, P., and Marsh, D. (2010). *CLIL: Content and language integrated learning*. Cambridge: Cambridge University Press.

Doyé, P., and Hurrell, A. (1997). *Foreign Language Learning in Primary Schools (age 5/6 to 10/11)*. Strasbourg: Council of Europe.

Ellis, G., and Brewster, J. (1991). *The Storytelling Handbook: A guide for primary teachers of English*. Harmondsworth: Penguin Books.

Ellis, G., and Brewster, J. (2002). *Tell it Again! The new storytelling handbook for primary teachers*. Harmondsworth: Penguin Books.

Enever, J. (ed.) (2011). *ELLiE: Early language learning in Europe*. London: British Council.

Enever, J. (2014). Primary English teacher education in Europe. *ELT Journal*, 68(3), 231–242.

Enever, J., and Schmid-Schönbeim, G. (Eds.). (2006). *Picture Books and Young Learners of English. MAFF Band 14*. Munich: Langenscheit ELT.

Eurostat (2016). *Foreign language learning statistics*. http://ec.europa.eu/eurostat/statistics-explained/index.php/File:Proportion_of_pupils_in_primary_education_learning_foreign_languages,_by_language,_2014_(%C2%B9)_(%25)_YB16-II.png.

Eurydice (2001). *Foreign Language Teaching in Schools in Europe*. Brussels: Directorate-General for Education and Culture, European Commission.

Eurydice (2012). *Key data on Teaching Languages at School in Europe*. Brussels: Directorate-General for Education and Culture, European Commission.

Garvie, E. (1989). *Story as Vehicle: Teaching English to young children*. Clevedon: Multilingual Matters.

Graddol, D. (2006). *English Next: Why global English may mean the end of "English as a Foreign Language"*. London: The British Council.

Hasselgren, A. (2000). The assessment of the English ability of young learners in Norwegian Schools: An innovative approach. In Rea-Dickins, P. M. (ed.) *Language Testing, Special Issue: Assessing young language learners. vol. 17,2*. London: Edward Arnold, 261–277.

Hasselgren, A. (2005). Assessing the language of young learners. *Language Testing*, 22(3), 337–354.

Hoy, P. H. (1975). *The Early Teaching of Modern Languages: A summary of reports from fifteen countries*. Strasbourg: Council of Europe.

Ioannou-Georgiou, S., and Pavlou, P. (Eds.). (2011). *Guidelines for CLIL Implementation in Primary and Pre-primary Education*. Strasbourg: Socrates (Comenius) European Commission.

Johnstone, R. (2002). *Addressing 'the age factor': Some implications for languages policy*. Strasbourg: Council of Europe.

Kelly, M., and Grenfell, M. (2004). *European Profile of Language Teacher Education*. Southampton: University of Southampton.

Kubanek-German, A. (1998). Primary foreign language teaching in Europe – trends and issues. *Language Teaching*, 31(4), 193–205.

Kubanek-German, A. (2000). Early language programmes in Germany. In Nikolov, M., and Curtain, H. (eds.) *An Early Start: Young learners and modern languages in Europe and beyond*. Graz: European Centre for Modern Languages/Strasbourg: Council of Europe Publishing, 59–69.

Lenneberg, E. H. (1967). *Biological foundations of language*. New York: Wiley.

Lucietto, S. (2008). A model for quality CLIL provision. *International CLIL Research Journal*, 1(1), p. article 7.

Moon, J., and Nikolov, M. (2000). *Research into Teaching English to Young Learners*. Pecs, Hungary: University of Pecs Press.

Mourão, S., and Lourenço, M. (Eds.). (2015). *Early Years Second Language Education: International perspectives on theory and practice*. Abingdon: Routledge.

Nikolov, M. (Ed.). (2015). *Assessing Young Learners: Global and local perspectives*. New York: Springer.

Nikolov, M., and Curtain, H. (Eds.). (2000). *An Early Start: Young learners and modern languages in Europe and beyond*. Strasbourg: Council of Europe Publishing.

NILE, Norwich Institute for Language Education. (2016). Online course Early Childhood Language Learning. www.nile-elt.com

Oyama, S. (1976). A sensitive period for the acquisition of a nonnative phonological system. *Journal of Psycholinguistic Research*, 5, 261–285.

Penfield, W. (1953). A consideration of the neurophysiological mechanisms of speech and some educational consequences. *Proceedings of the American Academy of Arts and Sciences*, 82, 201–214.

Pugsley, J., and Kershaw, G. (1996). *Voices from the New Democracies: The impact of British E LT in Central and Eastern Europe*. London: The British Council.

Rea-Dickins, P. M. (2000). Language testing. *Special issue: Assessing young language learners*. 17(2). London: Edward Arnold.

Rea-Dickins, P. M., and Rixon, S. (1999). Assessment of young learners' English: Reasons and means. In Rixon, S. (ed.) *Young Learners of English: Some research perspectives*. Harlow: Pearson Education, 89–101.

Rea-Dickins, P., and Rixon, S. (1997). The asssessment of young learners of English as a foreign language. In Clapham, C., and Corson, D. (eds.) *Encyclopedia of Language and Education: Language testing and assessment*. Dordrecht: Kluwer, 151–161.

Rixon, S. (1992). English and other languages for younger children: practice and theory in a rapidly changing world. *Language Teaching*, 5(2), 73–93.

Rixon, S. (2000). *Optimum Age or Optimum Conditions?* London: The British Council.

Rixon, S. (2013). *British Council Survey of Policy and Practice in Primary English Language Teaching Worldwide*. London: British Council.

Rixon, S. (2015). Do developments in assessment represent the "Coming of Age" of young learners English language teaching initiatives? The international picture. In Nikolov, M. (ed.) *Assessing Young Learners of English*. New York: Springer, 19–42.

Rogers, J. (1982). The world for sick proper. *ELT Journal*, 36(3), 144–151.

Singleton, D., and Lengyel, Z. (Eds.). (1995). *The Age Factor in Second Language Acquisition*. Clevedon: Multilingual Matters.

Stern, H., and Weinrib, A. (1977). Foreign languages for younger children: Trends and assessment. *Language Teaching and Linguistics Abstracts*, 10(1), 5–5.

Szpotowicz, M., and Lindgren, E. (2011). Language achievement: A longitudinal perspective. In Enever, J. (ed.) *ELLie: Early language learning in Europe*. London: British Council, pp. 125–142.

Vilke, M. (1998). Introducing English into Croatian primary schools. In de Beaugrande, R., Grosman, M., and Seidlelhofer, B. (eds.) *Language Policy and Language Education in Emerging Nations*. Stamford, CT: Ablex Publishing Corporation, 87–92.

Wilden, E., and Porsch, R. (Eds.). (2017). *The Professional Development of Primary EFL Teachers: National and international research*. Münster: Waxmann.

31

Teaching English to young learners

Some reflective voices from Latin America

Inés K. Miller, Maria Isabel A. Cunha, Isabel Cristina R. Moraes Bezerra, Adriana N. Nóbrega, Clarissa X. Ewald and Walewska G. Braga

Introduction

Countries where English as a Foreign or Additional Language (EFL/EAL) is taught have undergone the pressure of a worldwide trend by which English is being included in school curricula from the early years of education (Banfi 2015). Such is the situation of Teaching English to Young Learners (TEYL) within the last decade in most countries in Latin America, and, in this chapter, we will focus on Argentina, Brazil, Chile, Colombia and Uruguay.

As indicated in our title, we bring into discussion some voices from Latin American contexts from which we could draw sources to substantiate our research, while not claiming to represent the vast region in a conventional sense. We take this stand because we do not believe in reified views of EFL or EAL, of teaching and learning, of Young Language Learners (YLLs) or of bilingualism – a related notion that underlies the discourse generated by the TEYL enterprise.

Despite the complex sociopolitical backdrop in which TEYL is expanding in Latin America (Ramírez-Romero and Sayer 2016), reports on the national programs launched in these countries usually focus on the urge to educate bilingual learners for the international globalised scenario in which proficient command of English is required for communication and for the workplace. Nonetheless, there are researchers (Guevara and Ordoñez 2012) who problematise this linguistic imposition across diverse sociolinguistic teaching-learning contexts, especially when children under the age of five are taught English before becoming literate in their own mother tongue. Other concerns raised are the dearth of specialised teacher preparation and of teaching resources that take into account the social, cognitive and affective development of young learners as well as the lack of consideration for social and historical local issues.

Some central concepts need to be defined. First, the notion of language, here understood as social practice (Fairclough 1989). Taking a political and critical view of language use, we are inspired by César and Cavalcanti's (2007) metaphor of language as a kaleidoscope, thus breaking away from reductionist dichotomies such as oral/written, literate/illiterate, standard/

nonstandard, among others. Furthermore, we align ourselves with a post-structuralist perspective of language, which includes psychological and affective dimensions, and does not conceive language as a mere 'instrument of communication' (Revuz 1998, p. 217).

The second idea regards the teaching and learning of EFL/EAL by taking a critical stance towards a tradition of English teaching as transmission of linguistic rules. This might be the case when it is taken for granted that once learners learn linguistic rules, as well as cultural conventions that underpin language use, they will get their message across. Following Kincheloe (2004) and Ramanathan (2002), Polo and Guerrero (2010) also point out that English teachers tend not to problematise the sociopolitical aspects embedded in English Language Teaching (ELT), nor the asymmetry among different curricular components.

A third notion regards the age range covered within TEYL. In reaction to the acknowledged attempt to establish a specific age range for the area, Pinter (2006, p. 2) argues that 'all children are unique, and two children at the same chronological age can exhibit markedly different characteristics'. Araos (2015) asserts that TEYL is understood as teaching English to children from five to 11 years old. Yet, despite the developmental individualities identified among YLLs and the little empirical support available, a major trend worldwide is to introduce TEYL at earlier and earlier ages (Cameron 2001, 2003), under the justification that it encourages motivation, expands intercultural experiences and prepares children for the future. This issue will be critically appraised later in this chapter.

The fourth key issue to be addressed is the systematic association being made between TEYL and the alleged social advantages of bilingualism. Given the scope of this chapter, our intention is to briefly acknowledge some of the implications for the settings in which immersion or bilingual programs have been implemented. The international drive for multilingual education, which can be traced back to the UNESCO 1999 conference (Banfi 2015), is based on an unproblematised definition of bilingualism as 'the ability to use two languages in everyday life' (Byers-Heinlein and Lew-Williams 2013, p. 97).

The fifth key idea that needs to be critically reflected upon is the centrality of technology in TEYL classrooms. When discussing innovation in YLLs' classrooms, Banfi (2015) describes some TEYL programs in Latin America and stresses the expanding role that publishers and technology development companies have played in this scenario. In alignment with Banfi, Figueiredo (2014, p. 159) raises the danger involved in an excessively 'festive' view of digital literacies, which leads schools to embrace technology in order to attract and entertain YLLs.

Historical perspectives

This section will offer a panoramic overview of the historical perspectives of TEYL in Argentina, Brazil, Chile, Colombia and Uruguay. While in most of these countries EFL has been compulsorily incorporated into primary schools, mainly by national programs, in Brazil there is no official national program aimed at TEYL.

In Argentina, the teaching of a foreign language is mandatory in primary and secondary schools under the 2006 National Education Law (Ley de Educación Nacional 26.206) and most provinces have tended to select English, starting at the age of six. In 2013, the local project Jornada Ampliada was implemented, integrating English and art in the later years of primary school.

In Chile, the inclusion of EFL in primary education was part of a reform implemented in 1998 by the Ministry of Education (MINEDUC), as an explicit attempt to advance quality and equity in Chilean education (MINEDUC 2012; 2013). The justification was that English would be needed increasingly to participate in the global economy and information network. The English Opens Doors Programme (EODP) was created by MINEDUC in 2003 in agreement with the United Nations Development Programme, proposing actions that foster the improvement of national economic competitiveness and provide opportunities to enable all students in public schools to learn English (Araos 2015).

Concerned with the quality of English teaching/learning and the students' future competitiveness in the workplace, the National Bilingual Program (NBP) started in Colombia in 2004 as an initiative of the Ministry of Education (MEN). It provides all students with opportunities to become bilingual in English and Spanish and was originally designed to last from 2004 to 2019, with the cooperation of the British and North American governments regarding in-service teacher development (Mejía 2009). The MEN also implemented the 'Basic Standards of Foreign Language Competences: English', a document created in 2006, based on the Common European Framework of Reference for Languages (CEFRL) (Byram and Parmenter 2012). Mejía (2009, p. 104) claims that 'the National Bilingual Programme's aims are quite ambitious'.

In Uruguayan programs, English has also been considered essential for the country to integrate the global market. However, as Brovetto et al. (2007) state, the focus has been on teaching English through a succession of programs that have not necessarily fulfiled these requirements. Differently from Argentina, Chile and Colombia, Uruguay had the initiative to socially include students through the use of technological resources and, in 2007, proposed the Ceibal Plan. First developed in public schools, the program was based on the One Laptop per Child Program and was adapted to Uruguayan educational settings.

According to Oliveira (2015), the Ceibal Plan in English was implemented as a way of beginning TEYL and of improving teachers' proficiency. In 2014, students from four to seven years old were finally given a tablet with ludic activities. By 2015, the program had already reached 570 schools, 3,300 groups and 80,000 YLLs in fourth, fifth and sixth grades.

Brazilian policies prescribe the teaching of at least one foreign language starting at the sixth grade of Basic Education – National Education Base and Guidelines (Lei de Diretrizes e Bases da Educação, Brasil 1996) and Foreign Language National Curricular Guidelines (Parâmetros Curriculares Nacionais-Língua Estrangeira, PCN-LE, Brasil 1998). Even though it is possible to choose among English, Spanish, French or any other language according to local decision, English has been, by far, the first choice.

The PCN-LE, prepared by a group of university professors, defined the basic guidelines for the teaching of foreign languages in schools from grades six to nine but not for the previous ones. Despite this lack of orientation, for decades, EFL has been taught from prekindergarten to fifth grade in several schools of the private sector and language courses. Gimenez (2013) indicates that TEYL programs have been implemented in the public sector, primarily in São Paulo, Rio de Janeiro, Minas Gerais, Paraná and Rio Grande do Sul, to improve the quality of education and to follow the new demands of globalisation.

Critical issues and topics

Taking a critical perspective towards TEYL in Latin America, and echoing research on this theme (Ramírez-Romero and Sayer 2016; Moraes Bezerra and Aceti 2015), four issues will be addressed in the following subsections.

The very age of young language learners

It is important to understand the worldwide trend by which TEYL is being introduced at earlier and earlier ages (Garton et al. 2011), a trend also found in the case of the countries surveyed in this chapter. However, there seems to be little empirical research support in the literature for the notion that younger second language learners learn more efficiently or successfully than older learners (Singleton 1989, p. 37, cited in Nunan 2013, p. 234; Cameron 2003).

Based on Pinter (2011; 2012) and Zandian (2012), Araos (2015, p. 20) notes that YLLs need to be considered a particular group of learners, 'especially because their learning experiences and motivations are different from adults and teenagers'. Some contemporary sociologists (Corsaro 2011) urge practitioners to consider children's specific characteristics, respecting their cognitive, affective and social growth. Linse (2005, cited in Nunan 2013, p. 235), in the United States, and Valenzuela (2016), in Chile, have argued for a 'whole-learner' approach, by taking a holistic, anthropological and educational view on classroom management, classroom organization and teaching techniques. In Brazil, Rocha (2007) asserts that YLLs need to feel comfortable and self-confident when involved in learning situations.

The imperialistic attitude and the imposition of English bilingualism

Some importantly interrelated aspects are central to a critical discussion of language policies and TEYL educational practices in Latin America. As reported in evaluations of the national programs which have incorporated the teaching of English as a compulsory subject in the Primary Education curricula of Argentina, Chile and Colombia, authors from these countries (Corradi 2014; Araos 2015; Guevara and Ordoñez 2012, respectively) question the imposition of English at early ages and the policy of bilingualism. The notion of Spanish-English bilingualism has been problematised, especially in countries with long traditions of bilingualism and multilingualism in indigenous languages. Mejía (2009, p. 105) highlights the plurilingual composition of Colombian society, which presents 'around 65 separate indigenous languages in existence, as well as two native Creoles, Colombian Sign Language and Romani'. Relevant bilingualism has always been present in Uruguay, with Spanish being the general language but, as linguistic diversity is considered positive, in certain border regions Italian and Portuguese are taught in primary schools. Although Brazil has no official Portuguese-English bilingual policy, Maher (2013, cited in Liberali and Megale 2016, p. 97), points out that besides Portuguese, 'two hundred and twenty two languages are spoken in Brazil'.

Parra et al. (2012) voice a similarly critical position on TEYL programs as ideological processes of control. We can relate this standpoint to Phillipson's ideas about linguistic imperialism, which the author defines as being 'asserted and maintained by the establishment and continuous reconstitution of structural and cultural inequalities between a dominant language and other languages' (Phillipson 1992, p. 47).

The production and/or use of specific materials

Our understanding of the Latin America situation is that public and private institutions tend to adopt or adapt imported models because pedagogic coordinators and teachers perceive a lack of materials that meet their 'sense of plausibility' (Prabhu 1987) in their diverse class-room realities.

Research carried out in Chile by Araos (2015) shows that in order to minimise teachers' reliance on internationally published materials and resources, the Ministry of Education has adapted coursebooks to the Chilean National Syllabus, which is consistent with the inter-national standards of the CEFRL. Pedagogic materials produced in Brazil by some private schools engaged in TEYL have shown strong allegiance to what is published by foreign publishing houses (Soares 2007; Tílio and Rocha 2009). It is noticeable that these decisions are highly dependent on imported models.

The Brazilian National Textbook Program (PNLD), a federal project created to provide public sector teachers and students with textbooks for every subject, has not yet included materials for TEYL. In some Brazilian states, however, isolated initiatives have tried to address the issue of materials production for young learners in public schools.

Initial and continuing teacher education for TEYL

The prevailing orientation towards increasing efficiency in technique-oriented teacher train-ing practices must be questioned. As Miller (2013) points out, it is necessary to implement a move from efficiency to criticality and ethics in initial and continuing teacher education. This movement is especially relevant, as ethically oriented EYL teachers can contribute to the critical and ethical education of YLLs.

Abrahams and Farias's (2010, p. 46) critical interpretation of English language teacher education programs in the Chilean context is that they have 'a technical training compo-nent that disregards both the role of language as social practice [. . .] and the importance of (action) research'.

The delicate situation concerning teacher education in Colombia is that the NBP favours market-based teacher development and does not consider particular aspects of different cul-tures living in the country (Vargas et al. 2008).

In Brazil, most undergraduate Modern Languages (Letras) programs are not yet pre-pared to meet the needs of TEYL teachers (Tonelli and Cristóvão 2010). On the other hand, some actions are geared towards promoting discussion of theoretically supported practices in TEYL at the pre-service level (Moraes Bezerra 2011) and in-service teacher education (Santos 2010).

Current contributions and research

As compared to the widespread interest in implementing TEYL around the world, and more specifically in Latin America, it is surprising to see that 'systematic reflection on these issues often lags behind the implementation of policies that are driven by political imperatives' (Banfi 2015, p. 15). Despite the scarcity of systematic academic investigation in TEYL in Latin America perceived by Ramírez-Romero and Sayer (2016), this section presents a sample of studies to illustrate the body of research work conducted in the Latin American countries examined in this chapter.

In the context of bilingual education in Argentina, Renart (2005) focuses her case study on the development of communicative competence of seven-year-old children who are in two bilingual-biliterate programmes. Based on a detailed analysis of the children's dis-course, the observed teaching practices and teachers' language input, the author reinforces that, in order to understand communicative competence development, there is a need to reconsider the role of the learner, the input offered by the teaching context and the relation between the two (Renart 2005, p. 1942).

Compulsory TEYL in Chilean primary education was problematised by Araos (2015). Through a survey study and an intervention project, the investigator critically examined the challenges faced by Chilean early primary school teachers and the contextual factors that can facilitate or hinder the teaching-learning process. The findings of this research reveal that contextual features, 'such as limited time for planning, lack of parental involvement and a mismatch between policy and school reality, affected the teaching-learning process' (Araos 2015, p. ii).

Although many official programmes concerning the teaching of English in public primary schools have been proposed in Colombia, Mejía (2009) observes that not many studies about the results of these proposals have been carried out. Among these studies, Valencia Giraldo (2007) investigates how teachers in Bogotá positioned themselves regarding the language policies, such as the NBP (MEN 2004). The study suggests that 'the top-down model applied in language and education planning in Colombia leaves many voices silenced and does not allow for participation in these processes' (Mejía 2009, p. 110).

Cobo et al. (2016) describe an innovative large-scale action research involving Uruguay's participation in a global network of schools in six other countries (Australia, Canada, Finland, the Netherlands, New Zealand and the United States). The aim of this project was to implement a pedagogical approach called 'deep learning' where students are expected to develop their creativity, their ability to solve problems and to work collaboratively in an interdependent world.

In Brazil, Tonelli and Ramos (2007) as well as Rocha, Tonelli and Silva (2010) have been systematically compiling most of the research carried out in this area. With a focus on the advantages and disadvantages of teaching a foreign language to young learners, Rocha (2006, 2008) shows that the age factor does not operate alone, but is influenced by many other factors, such as teachers' lack of preparation to teach young children, the quality of both the teaching programs (immersion, situated teaching, critical learning/ teaching) and the teaching materials (Carvalho 2007). Research dealing with the personal characteristics needed by a professional in the area of Language Education for Children (Raquel Carvalho 2005) can be complemented by a study on the importance of teachers' and young learners' mutual construction of beliefs on learning a foreign language (Scheifer 2009).

Working with Exploratory Practice (Allwright and Hanks 2009), Leoni (2016) monitored groups of young learners at an NGO project in a low-income community in Rio de Janeiro, Brazil. She understood that she could propose 'constant inquiry about the reality in the classroom' (ibid., p. 28) and also could conduct reflexive practices about the groups' social affective conflicts. Similarly, Griffo (2017) reports her work with YLLs in a Brazilian bilingual school, where she proposed a written activity and a discussion about noise in the classroom. This led to deeper understandings of learners' social roles at school and their relationship with teachers and coordinators. Inspired by Vygotsky (1987), Peixoto (2007, p. 25) and her colleagues, working on their students' puzzles or questions, understood that 'in groups, students can accomplish more – and better – than any individual alone'.

As mentioned earlier, research in Latin American TEYL is not abundant and needs to be encouraged, so that sounder research-based suggestions for practice can be made.

Recommendations for practise

Based on a social view of childhood (Benjamin 1984), a sociocultural perspective of the classroom (Wells and Claxton 2002) and an ethical-professional view of teachers and learners as key developing practitioners of learning (Allwright and Hanks 2009), we believe that teaching, as any social practice, is intrinsically local and situated. Following a critical perspective (Freire 2001), we consider it unwise to make one-size-fits-all recommendations. In order to avoid or resist acritical implementation of TEYL programs, these need to be negotiated with (future) teachers, learners, teacher educators and parents in each of the countries of Latin America, so as to reflect their local wishes and needs in terms of TEYL.

Drawing on the sample of academic and practitioner research reported in this chapter, it is possible to hope for resistance to large-scale or country-wide policies to come from classrooms, where teachers and their (young) learners, based on their sense of plausibility (Prabhu 1987) and on local possibilities, know what they need and can do. Our overall proposal for implementation is that more voices from YLLs' classrooms be heard and shared systematically through publications or events.

Classroom language teaching and learning of the local vernacular(s) and English as an additional or foreign language – understood as social practice and not as a set of grammar rules – can become, even with young learners, the potential *locus* for negotiating situated meanings as well as personal opinions, beliefs and arguments (Pinter and Zandian 2015). These could be about issues of local interest, such as the usefulness of learning languages, the quality of classroom life and, whenever feasible, life outside the classroom. In our view, it is also desirable to replace structuralist conceptions of language by post-structuralist views (Fairclough 1996), as a way of transforming behaviouristic automatization of grammatical structures into teacher-learner or learner-learner meaningful interaction (Pontecorvo et al. 2005). Such contemporary notions need to inform teacher education curricula and teacher development programmes so as to disseminate these less-known perspectives among pre-service and in-service first and foreign language teachers. Familiarised with such views, it is hoped that language professionals can feel better equipped to co-construct meaningful language interaction with students of any age, especially YLLs.

The centrality of positive and negative affect in the social co-construction of foreign language classrooms has emerged more and more in contemporary research on teachers' and learners' lived emotions and identities (Zembylas 2005; Lewis and Tierney 2013; Barcelos 2013, among others). This aspect is, also, highly relevant for TEYL, if the area wishes to contribute to the development of (language) learners as practitioners of learning for life (Allwright 2006). As they implement their pedagogic practice, teachers of YLLs can find inspiration in ethical principles – they need to understand and respect their YLLs' capabilities, by creating opportunities for meaningful collaborative work and for mutual development (Nóbrega Kuschnir 2003).

A recommendation for practice, based on our own work as teacher educators, comes from the perceived need to integrate language learning and practitioners' (learners' and teachers') local reflexivity. Such integration has been developed within the framework of Exploratory Practice, characterised as an investigative and inclusive way of teaching (Allwright and Hanks 2009; Hanks 2017). Along these lines, some TEYL practitioners have been systematically involved in teaching while they work for understanding. Over the past twenty years, English classes have been inspired by the Exploratory Practice framework and have inspired pre-service and in-service teachers alike (Miller and Barreto 2015; Miller et al. 2015). Following the Exploratory Practice principles, pre-service teachers have been planning their classes in order to build local understandings instead of working to solve problems (Moraes Bezerra et al. 2016).

As we understand it, the shared experiences show that teachers and their learners can become involved in constructing knowledge about their locally intriguing issues in and around their YLLs' English language classrooms.

Future directions

This section echoes local realities voiced by the authors whose texts helped us construct this chapter. We share the view that further research has to be conducted, involving learners, teachers, teacher educators, supervisors and policy makers. Thus, deeper understandings of the practices may emerge, helping these agents to be more participative in TEYL choices and decisions. The following sections detail some areas that deserve careful attention for the future development of the field.

Teacher education in TEYL

When English is compulsorily introduced as part of a foreign language or bilingual policy into the curriculum of YLLs, the education of primary school teachers needs to become a central matter. Should future teachers engage in practical language and/or pedagogic courses or should they be encouraged to get a university degree? Do Latin American colleges and universities offer adequate programs that cater to pre-service and in-service teacher needs regarding knowledge of English, as well as theoretical and methodological aspects related to TEYL? These and many other questions have been asked by researchers in the area, such as Tonelli and Cristóvão (2010) and Santos (2010), but further research is needed. Teacher education curricula should be mapped, analyzed and discussed in view of the professional profile expected by educational institutions. Another focus of interest for teacher educators could be to motivate future teachers to reflect on the complexity of TEYL classroom life, working to understand its inextricable connections with first and second language literacy development.

Still in the realm of teacher education, the importance of the level of English required of EFL teachers, and of TEYL teachers in particular, needs to be problematised. Teachers' low proficiency language level, generally leading to a lack of confidence in the use of English in oral classroom interaction, has been highlighted as a global issue by Copland et al. (2014). It is our belief that TEYL teacher educators could encourage collaborative reflection about the specific needs and difficulties of pre-service and/or in-service teachers so as to work towards fluency development, for their professional use as well as for their personal aims.

YLLs' teachers as practitioner researchers

It is important to map specific initiatives for pre-service and in-service teacher education programs, so as to investigate whether they offer adequate language instruction, a theoretical basis for the development of professional practice and a space for teacher reflection. Pre-service and in-service teachers can thus be encouraged to join the practitioner researcher movement and contribute to the field (Pimenta and Ghedin 2002; Zeichner 2003; Allwright and Hanks 2009; Burns et al. 2017). Allwright and Hanks (2009) state that language learners are practitioners of learning, and, as such, they must be involved in the work to understand the puzzles related to the 'quality of their language classroom life' (Gieve and Miller 2006).

Likewise, as mentioned earlier, we make a plea for the introduction of 'children's perspectives' by doing research 'with' young learners through participatory activities (Pinter and Zandian 2015). In agreement with these ideas, we understand that pre-service and in-service teachers should consider involving YLLs in their research practices, not as mere participants but especially as research collaborators.

Pedagogies for YLLs

A genre-based TEYL seems promising, since the use of language happens within social practices and the use of a variety of genres can enhance the cooperative building of multiliteracies, which is 'needed to live a critical and protagonist citizenship' (Rocha 2009, p. 263, our translation). TEYL practices can be aligned with the rationale of critical literacy, as advocated by Lankshear and McLaren (1993) and Janks (2010, 2012). Adopting a critical stance can lead us to rethink the role of sociohistorical aspects in discursive classroom practices (Almeida 2016; Copland, Garton, and Burns 2014).

It is relevant to consider social and affective aspects as they permeate the teaching/learning process and are central to the motivational attitude that learners have about their learning practices. Obviously, the very age and social status of YLLs should also be a pedagogic concern. Rather than picturing those students who suffer from poverty, family violence, parent unemployment or unwanted pregnancy (Correa and González 2016) as lazy or demotivated, teachers and researchers could adopt approaches that aim to encourage YLLs to construct a more positive view of themselves.

By the same token, teachers and researchers can work to promote critical (multi)literacies by adopting and researching materials (books, resources, software) produced in alignment with a sociocultural-historical perspective of learning and with the tenets of genre and critical literacy. Hence, the mere transposition of materials produced for global use by YLLs and their teachers in Latin America is not advisable and their implementation should be reviewed.

TEYL policies in Latin America

In addition to research on the themes above, foreign language policies for TEYL in Latin America must be reviewed if real accomplishments in the proficiency levels of teachers and students are to be made. First and foremost, funding is essential to nurture and sustain teacher development programs and to provide physical, didactic and technological resources for urban and rural schools. Policy makers should also be sensitive to the need of allotting more time for English language classes per week and should abandon top-down measures, which do not acknowledge the views of teachers, coordinators and teacher educators, that is, those in charge of implementing these policies. Instead of being called to validate and implement political decisions, these local stakeholders should have a different role and ought to voice their beliefs. Moreover, following Levinson et al. (2009), Correa and González (2016) claim that a more critical sociocultural view of policy making should be undertaken.

Drawing on Coleman's (2011) and Rajagopalan's (2009) thoughts, we stress our belief in the need to: understand how to manage the complexity of language planning and development, develop research in specific contexts, acknowledge that educational change takes time and effort, critically engage students with the English language in their environment, teach English without underestimating students' mother tongues and respect YLLs' potential do develop as practitioners of learning (Allwright and Hanks 2009).

A more specific language-oriented direction for the future of TEYL in Latin American countries could be to adopt a post-structuralist view of language (Revuz 1998), so as to inspire a more ethical and formative take on the worldwide initiative of TEYL. Hence, the field could move from an instrumental justification for the experience to a more holistic perspective. Language would no longer be taught to and learnt by YLLs as a code for social communication but as a centrally constitutive element of human life. At this point, we now return to Coleman (2011, p. 22), with whom we learn that 'we need to venture out from our cosy and comfortable world of English language teaching and continue to ask ourselves challenging questions about the value of what we are doing'.

Further reading

1 Banfi, C. (2015). English language teaching expansion in South America: Challenges and opportunities. In Kamhi-Stein, L., Maggioli, G., and Oliveira, L. (eds.) *English language teaching in South America: Policy, preparation, and practices*. Clevedon: Multilingual Matters.

   Focusing on changes in educational policy, the author problematises the offer of foreign languages, particularly English, in Latin America. She critically appraises (English as) foreign language programs launched by education authorities that aim for the expansion and coverage from kindergarten through secondary education.

2 Enever, J., Moon, J., and Raman, U. (Eds.). (2009). *Young learner English language policy and implementation: International perspectives*. Reading: IATEFL, British Council, Garnet Publishing.

   This issue provides significant photographs of TEYL in various countries around the world. In this publication, Chapter 6, written by Gimenez, and Chapter 19, written by Corradi, are of special interest since these authors offer a variety of insights on TEYL in Brazil and in Argentina, respectively.

3 Rajagopalan, K. (2009). Exposing young children to English as a foreign language: The emerging role of world English. *Trabalhos em Linguística Aplicada*. 48(2), July/December, pp. 185–196.

   Rajagopalan's article brings a relevant discussion on children's language learning in multilingual contexts and the lessons that can be learned for language learning, in general. The article sets the background for the other articles in the same issue.

4 Ramírez-Romero, J. L., and Sayer, P. (Eds.) (2016). Introduction to the special issue on English language teaching in public primary schools in Latin America. *Education Policy Analysis Archives*, 24(79). EPAA/AAPE's Special Issue.

   The authors present an overview of articles about TEYL in Argentina, Brazil, Chile and Colombia, as well as in Mexico and Puerto Rico. The experiences, programs and policy processes related to the implantation of ELT in the region are discussed.

Related topics

Policy, teacher education, critical pedagogy

References

Abrahams, M. and Farias, M. (2010). Innovation and Change in the Chilean Initial Teacher T Curriculum for Teachers of English. In T. Gimenez and M. C. G. Monteiro, eds., *Formação de Professores de Línguas na América Latina e Transformação Social*. 1st ed. Campinas: Pontes, 45–67.

Allwright, D. (2006). Six promising directions for applied linguistics. In Gieve, S., and Miller, I. (eds.) *Understanding the Language Classroom*, 1st ed. Basingstoke: Palgrave Macmillan, 11–17.

Allwright, D., and Hanks, J. (2009). *The Developing Learner: An introduction to exploratory practice*. Basingstoke: Palgrave Macmillan.

Almeida, R. L. T. (2016). ELT in Brazilian Public Schools: History, challenges, new experiences and perspectives. *Education Policy Analysis Archives*, Special issue on *English Language Teaching in*

Public Primary Schools in Latin America, Guest Edited by José Luis Ramirez-Romero and Peter Sayer, 24(81), 1–17. http://epaa.asu.edu/ojs/article/view/2473 [Accessed 3 June 2017].

Araos, M. (2015). *Examining Challenges and Complexities in the Chilean Young Learners Classroom: A case of teaching English as a foreign language*. PhD. The University of Sheffield.

Banfi, C. (2015). *English Language Teaching Expansion in South America: Challenges and opportunities*. https://www2.warwick.ac.uk/fac/soc/al/research/groups/llta/activities/events/recorded_talks/banfi/english_language_teaching_expansion_cb_4.pdf [Accessed 27 November 2016].

Barcelos, A. M. F. (2013). Desvelando a Relação entre Crenças sobre Ensino e Aprendizagem de Línguas, Emoções e Identidades. In Gerhardt, A. F. M., Amorim, M. A., and Carvalho, A. M. (eds.) *Linguística Aplicada e Ensino: Língua e Literatura*. Campinas: Pontes Editores, 153–186.

Benjamin, W. (1984). *Reflexões: a Criança, o Brinquedo, a Educação*. São Paulo: Summus.

Brasil. ([1996]2005). Lei de Diretrizes e Bases da Educação Nacional. https://www2.senado.leg.br/bdsf/bitstream/handle/id/70320/65.pd [Accessed 26 June 2017].

Brasil. (1998). *Secretaria de Educação Fundamental. Parâmetros Curriculares Nacionais: Terceiro e Quarto Ciclos do Ensino Fundamental: Língua Estrangeira*. Brasília. http://portal.mec.gov.br/seb/arquivos/pdf/pcn_estrangeira.pdf [Accessed 26 June 2017].

Brasil. (2012). *Programa Nacional do Livro Didático (PNLD)*. www.fnde.gov.br/programas/livro-didatico [Accessed 27 November 2016].

Brovetto, C., Geymonat, J., and Brian, N. (2007). Una Experiencia de Educación Bilingüe Español – Portugués en Escuelas de la Zona Fronteriza. In Brovetto, C., Geymonat, J., and Brian, N. (eds.) *Portugués del Uruguay y Educación Bilingüe*, 1st ed. Montevideo: Anep, 9–47.

Burns, A., Dikilitaş, K., Smith, R., and Wyatt, M. (Eds.). (2017). *Teacher-researchers in Action* 1st ed. [ebook] Faversham: IATEFL. http://resig.weebly.com/uploads/2/6/3/6/26368747/burns_dikilitas_smith___wyatt_eds._2017.pdf [Accessed 25 May 2017].

Byers-Heinlein, K., and Lew-Williams, C. (2013). Bilingualism in the early years: What the science says. *LEARNing Landscapes*, 7(1), 95–112. www.researchgate.net/publication/259822414_Bilingualism_in_the_Early_Years_What_the_Science_Says [Accessed 13 February 2016].

Byram, M., and Parmenter, L. (Eds.). (2012). *The Common European Framework of Reference: The globalisation of language education policy (Languages for intercultural communication and education)*. 1st ed. Kindle Multilingual Matters. www.amazon.com/Common-European-Framework-Reference-Globalisation-ebook/dp/B01MZFOMVW/ref=tmm_kin_swatch_0?_encoding=UTF8&qid=&sr=/ [Accessed 20 June 2017].

Cameron, L. (2001). *Teaching Languages to Young Learners*. Cambridge: Cambridge University Press.

Cameron, L. (2003). Challenges for ELT from the expansion in teaching children. *ELT Journal*, 57(2), 105–112.

Carvalho, R. C. M. (2005). *A Teacher's Discourse in EFL Classes for Very Young Learners: Investigating mood choices and register*. M.A. Universidade Federal de Santa Catarina, Brasil.

Carvalho, T. (2007). Artes Visuais na Educação Infantil Bilíngue. In Tonelli, J. R. A., and Ramos, S. G. M. (eds.) *O Ensino de LE para Crianças: Reflexões e Contribuições*. Londrina: Moriá, 35–59.

César, A., and Cavalcanti, M. (2007). Do Singular para o Multifacetado: o Conceito de Língua como Caleidoscópio. In Cavalcanti, M., and Bortoni-Ricardo, S. (eds.) *Transculturalidade, Linguagem e Educação*, 1st ed. Campinas: Pontes Editores, 145–166.

Cobo, C., Brovetto, C., and Gago, F. (2016). A global network for deep learning: The case of Uruguay. www.cristobalcobo.net/2016/ . . . /an-innovative-large-scale-action-research-in-education . . . [Accessed 18 July 2016].

Coleman, H. (2011). Developing countries and the English language: Rhetoric, risks, roles and recommendations. In Coleman, H. (ed.) *Dreams and Realities: Developing countries and the English language*, 1st ed. London: British Council, 11–23.

Copland, F., Garton, S., and Burns, A. (2014). Challenges in teaching English to young learners: Global perspectives and local realities. *Tesol Quarterly*, 48(4), 738–762. http://onlinelibrary.wiley.com/doi/10.1002/tesq.148/abstract [Accessed 27 Mar. 2017].

Corradi, L. (2014). *Foreign language teaching policy in Argentina*. [pdf]. http://piap.cl/seminarios/archivos/2do-seminario/leonor-corradi/Leonor-Corradi-Foreign-Language-Teaching-Policy-In-Argentina.pdf [Accessed 9 May 2017].

Correa, D., and González, A. (2016). English in Public primary schools in Colombia: Achievements and challenges brought about by national language education policies. *Education Policy Analysis Archives*, 24(81), pp. 1–25. Special issue on *English Language Teaching in Public Primary Schools in Latin America*, Guest Edited by José Luis Ramirez-Romero and Peter Sayer. http://epaa.asu.edu/ojs/article/view/2459 [Accessed 1 November 2016].

Corsaro, W. (2011). *Sociologia da Infância*. 2nd ed. Porto Alegre: Artmed.

Fairclough, N. (1989). *Language and Power*. London: Longman.

Fairclough, N. (1996). Introduction. In Fairclough, N. (ed.), *Critical Language Awareness*. 1st ed. London: Longman, 1–29.

Figueiredo, D. (2014). Leitura e Escrita na Era Digital: Considerações Críticas para Professor@s de Línguas. In Mateus, E., and Oliveira, N. (eds.) *Estudos Críticos da Linguagem e Formação de Professores/as de Línguas*, 1st ed. Campinas: Mercado de Letras, 145–165.

Freire, A. M. A (2001). *Pedagogia dos Sonhos Possíveis*. São Paulo: Editora UNESP.

Garton, S., Copland, F. and Burns, A. (2011). Investigating global practices in teaching English to young learners. *ELT Research Papers*, British Council. www.stir.ac.uk/research/hub/publication/18928 [Accessed 8 May 2017].

Gieve, S., and Miller, I. K. (2006). What do we mean by "Quality of Classroom Life"? In Gieve, S., and Miller, I. K. (eds.) *Understanding the Language Classroom*. 1st ed. Basingstoke: Palgrave Macmillan, 18–46.

Gimenez, T. (2013). A Ausência de Políticas para o Ensino da Língua Inglesa nos Anos Iniciais de Escolarização no Brasil. In Nicolaides, C., Silva, K. A., Tílio, R., and Rocha, C. H. (eds.) *Política e Políticas Linguísticas*. Campinas: Pontes Editores, 199–218.

Griffo, M. (2017). *Mindfulness and Exploratory Practice*. Post-Graduation Monograph. Pontifical Catholic University of Rio de Janeiro (PUC-Rio). https://doi.org/10.17771/PUCRio.acad.29372

Guevara, D., and Ordoñez, C. (2012). Teaching English to very young learners through authentic communicative performances. *Colombian Applied Linguistics Journal*, 14(2), 9–23. www.scielo.org.co/scielo.php?script=sci_arttext&pid=S0123-46412012000200002&lng=pt&nrm=iso [Accessed 26 November 2016].

Hanks, J. (2017). *Exploratory Practice in Language Teaching*. London: Palgrave MacMillan.

Janks, H. (2010). *Language and Power*. London: Routledge.

Janks, H. (2012). The importance of critical literacy. *English Teaching: Practice and Critique*, 11(1), 150–163.

Kincheloe, J. (2004). *Critical Pedagogy*. New York: Peter Lang Publishing Inc.

Lankshear, C., and McLaren, P. (1993). *Critical Literacy: Politics, praxis, and the postmodern*. Albany: State University of New York.

Leoni, A. (2016). *Why Do My Students Believe they Cannot Learn English at School? – Exploratory practice promoting understanding in the classroom*. Post-Graduation Monograph. Pontifical Catholic University of Rio de Janeiro (PUC-Rio). https://doi.org/10.17771/PUCRio.acad.29138 [Accessed 26 June 2017].

Levinson, B., Sutton, M., and Winstead, T. (2009). Education policy as a practice of power: Theoretical tools, ethnographic methods, democratic options. *Educational Policy*, 23(6), 767–795. http://journals.sagepub.com/doi/pdf/10.1177/0895904808320676 [Accessed 23 June 2017].

Lewis, C., and Tierney, J. D. (2013). Mobilizing emotion in an urban classroom: Producing identities and transforming signs in a race-related discussion. *Linguistics and Education*, 24(3), 298–304.

Liberali, F. C., and Megale, A. (2016). Elite bilingual education in Brazil: An applied linguist's perspective. *Colombia Applied Linguistics Journal*, 18(2), 95–108.

Linse, C. (2005). *Practical English Language Teaching: Young learners*. New York: McGraw Hill.

Maher, T. M. (2013). Ecos de Resistência: Políticas Linguísticas e Línguas Minoritárias no Brasil. In Nicolaides, C., Silva, K. A., Tílio, R., and Rocha, C. H. (eds.) *Política e Políticas Linguísticas.* Campinas: Pontes Editores, 117–134.

Mejía, A-M. (2009). Teaching English to young learners in Colombia: Policy, practice and challenges. *MEXTESOL Journal,* 33(1), 103–114.

MEN. (2004). *Estándares Básicos de Competencias en Lenguas Extranjeras: Inglés.* Bogotá: Ministerio de Educación Nacional.

Miller, I. K. (2013). Formação Inicial e Continuada de Professores de Línguas: da Eficiência à Reflexão Crítica e Ética. In Moita-Lopes, L. P. (ed.) *Linguística Aplicada na Modernidade Recente: Festschrift para Antonieta Celani,* 1st ed. São Paulo: Parábola Editorial, 99–121.

Miller, I. K., and Barreto, B. (2015). A Formação de Professores de Línguas nas Licenciaturas em Letras da PUC-Rio: Horizonte Teórico e Decisões Curriculares. In Meyer, R. M., and Albuquerque, A. (eds.) *Português: Uma Língua Internacional,* 1st ed. Rio de Janeiro: Editora PUC-Rio, 77–94.

Miller, I. K., Côrtes, T. C. R., Oliveira, A. F. A., and Braga, W. G. (2015). Exploratory practice in initial teacher education: Working collaboratively for understandings. In: Bullock, D., and Smith, R. (eds.) *Teachers Research!* Faversham: IATEFL, 65–71. http://resig.weebly.com/teachers-research.html [Accessed 19 June 2017].

MINEDUC. (2003). *English Opens Doors Programme.* www.centrodevoluntarios.cl/the-english-opens-doors-program/ [Accessed 27 November 2016].

MINEDUC. (2012). *Bases Curriculares 2012: Idioma Extranjero Inglés Educación Básica.* Santiago. www.curriculumenlineamineduc.cl/605/w3-contents.html [Accessed 27 November 2016].

MINEDUC. (2013). *Bases Curriculares 2013: Idioma Extranjero Inglés 7mo a 2do medio.* Santiago. www.curriculumenlineamineduc.cl/605/w3-contents.html [Accessed 27 November 2016].

Moraes Bezerra, I. (2011). Ensino de Inglês para Crianças: Formando Professores Reflexivos. Initial Teacher Education Project. CETREINA, State University of Rio de Janeiro (UERJ), Brazil.

Moraes Bezerra, I., and Aceti, B. (2015). "Nossa que Menina Independente": Construção Identitária e Negociação de Enquadres em Sala de Aula de LEC. *Veredas: Revista de Estudos Linguísticos,* 19(1), 128–146. https://veredas.ufjf.emnuvens.com.br/veredas/article/view/44 [Accessed 26 November 2016].

Moraes Bezerra, I., Ferreira, A., Avelino, A., Souza, E., Ramon, K., Bernachi, L., and Santos, M. (2016). Refletindo sobre Representatividade de uma 'Family' no Ensino de LEC: Puzzles, Discussões, Surpresas, Escuta, Processo, Aprendizagem.

National Education Law. (2006). Ley de Educación Nacional 26.206. www.me.gov.ar/doc_pdf/ley_de_educ_nac.pdf. [Accessed 26 November 2016].

Nóbrega Kuschnir, A. (2003). *"Teacher", Posso te Contar uma Coisa? A Conversa Periférica e a Sócio-construção do Conhecimento na Sala de Aula de Língua Estrangeira.* M. A. Pontifical Catholic University of Rio de Janeiro (PUC-Rio), Brazil. http://www2.dbd.puc-rio.br/pergamum/tesesabertas/0115409_03_pretexto.pdf [Accessed 26 June 2017].

Nunan, D. (2013). Innovation in the young learner classroom. In Hyland, K., and ong, Wong, L. (eds.) *Innovation and Change in English Language Education,* 1st ed. New York: Routledge, 233–247.

Oliveira, V. (2015). *Uruguay Dá Computadores a Alunos para Combater a Desigualdade.* http://porvir.org/uruguai-da-computador-alunos-para-combater-desigualdade/ [Accessed 28 November 2016].

Parra, Y., Jiménez, J., and Vásquez, V. (2012). Retos del Programa Nacional de Bilingüismo. *Colombia Bilingüe. Educaton Education,* 15(3), 363–381. www.researchgate.net/publication/262639637_Retos_del_programa_nacional_debilinguismo_Colombia_bilingue [Accessed 28 November 2016].

Peixoto, M. (2007). The possibility of young children to work collaboratively. In Adour, T. (ed.) *Pesquisa, Ação e Colaboração: A Busca de um Entendimento sobre a Aula de Língua Estrangeira,* 1st ed. Rio de Janeiro: Publit Soluções Editoriais, 24–38.

Phillipson, R. (1992). *Linguistic Imperialism.* Oxford: Oxford University Press.

Pimenta, S. G., and Ghedin, E. (2002). *Professor Reflexivo no Brasil: Crítica de um Conceito.* São Paulo: Cortez.

Pinter, A. (2006). *Teaching English to Young Language Learners*. Oxford: Oxford University Press.

Pinter, A. (2011). *Children Learning Second Languages*. Basingstoke: Palgrave Macmillan.

Pinter, A. (2012). Is research relevant for teachers of English working with young learners? In *English for Young Learners – Forum 2012*. Upsala: Upsala Universitet, 11–27.

Pinter, A., and Zandian, S. (2015). "I Thought it Would Be Tiny Little One Phrase that we Said, in a Huge Big Pile of Papers": Children's reflections on their involvement in participatory research. *Qualitative Research*, 15 (2), 235–250.

Polo, A., and Guerrero, H. (2010). Dimensión Social de la Educación de Docentes de Inglés: Intersección entre Innovación Pedagógica e Investigación Formativa. In Gimenez, T., and Monteiro, M. C. G. (eds.) *Formação de Professores de Línguas na América Latina e Transformação Social*, 1st ed. Campinas: Pontes Editores, 167–186.

Pontecorvo, C., Ajello, A. M., and Zucchermaglio, C. (2005). *Discutindo se Aprende: Interação Social, Conhecimento e Escola*. Porto Alegre: Artmed.

Prabhu, N. (1987). *Second Language Pedagogy*. Oxford: Oxford University Press.

Rajagopalan, K. (2009). Exposing young children to English as a foreign language: The emerging role of world English. *Trabalhos em Linguística Aplicada*, 48(2), 185–196. www.scielo.br/scielo.php?script=sci_issuetoc&pid=0103-181320090002&lng=en&nrm=i [Accessed 8 June 2017].

Ramanathan, V. (2002). *The Politics of TESOL Education: Writing, knowledge, critical pedagogy*. London/New York: Psychology Press.

Ramírez-Romero, J. L., and Sayer, P. Eds. (2016). Introduction to the special issue on English language teaching in public primary schools in Latin America. *English Language Teaching in Public Primary Schools in Latin America*, 24(79), 1–7. http://dx.doi.org/10.14507/epaa.24.2635 [Accessed 8 May 2017].

Renart, L. (2005). Communicative competence in Children: Spanish-English bilinguality. In *4th International Symposium on Bilingualism*. Somerville, MA: Cascadilla Press, 1934–1944.

Revuz, C. (1998). A Língua Estrangeira entre o Desejo de um Outro Lugar e o Risco do Exílio. In Signorini, I. (ed.) *Linguagem e Identidade: Elementos para uma Discussão no Campo Aplicado*, 1st ed. Campinas: Mercado de Letras, 213–230.

Rio de Janeiro. (2012). Orientações Curriculares Revisitadas. Prefeitura da Cidade do Rio de Janeiro. Secretaria Municipal de Educação. Subsecretaria de Ensino. www.rio.rj.gov.br/dlstatic/10112/4246634/4104951/OCs_Ingles_versaofinal_jan_2.0.1.2.pdf [Accessed 26 June 2017].

Rocha, C. H. (2006). O Ensino de LE (Inglês) para Crianças por Meio de Gêneros: um Caminho a Seguir. *Contexturas*, 10, 65–93.

Rocha, C. H. (2007). O Ensino de Línguas para Crianças no Contexto Educacional Brasileiro: Breves Reflexões e Possíveis Provisões. *D.E.L.T.A.*, 23(2), 273–319. https://doi.org/10.1590/S0102-44502007000200005 [Accessed 26 June 2017].

Rocha, C. H. (2008). O Ensino de Línguas para Crianças: Refletindo sobre Princípios e Práticas. In Rocha, C. H., and Basso, E. A. (eds.) *Ensinar e Aprender Língua Estrangeira nas Diferentes Idades: Reflexões para Professores e Formadores*, 1st ed. São Carlos: Claraluz, 15–34.

Rocha, C. H. (2009). A Língua Inglesa no Ensino Fundamental I: Diálogos com Bakhtin por uma Formação Plurilíngue. *Trabalhos em Linguística Aplicada*, 48(2), pp. 247–274. www.scielo.br/scielo.php?pid=S0103-18132009000200006&script=sci_abstract&tlng=pt [Accessed 26 June 2017].

Rocha, C. H., Tonelli, J. R. A., and Silva, K. A. (Eds.). (2010). *Língua Estrangeira para Crianças: Ensino-aprendizagem e Formação Docente*. Campinas: Pontes Editores.

Santos, L. (2010). Presença de LE na Sociedade e em Contexto de Ensino Regular Público. In Rocha, C. H., Tonelli, J. R. A., and Silva, K. A. (eds.) *Língua Estrangeira para Crianças: Ensino-Aprendizagem e Formação Docente*, 1st ed. Campinas: Pontes Editores, 149–184.

Scheifer, C. L. (2009). Ensino de Língua Estrangeira para Crianças – Entre o Todo e a Parte – uma Análise da Dinâmica das Crenças de uma Professora e de seus Alunos. *Trabalhos em Linguística Aplicada*, 48(2), 197–216.

Singleton, D. (1989). *Language Acquisition: The age factor*. Clevedon: Multilingual Matters.

Soares, M. L. F. (2007). *The Role of the Author of Course Books for English Language Teaching: A study of authorial identity.* M. A. Pontifical Catholic University of Rio de Janeiro (PUC-Rio), Brazil. www.maxwell.vrac.puc-rio.br/10704/10704_1.PDF [Accessed 26 June 2017].

Tílio, R., and Rocha, C. (2009). As Dimensões da Linguagem em Livros Didáticos de Inglês para o Ensino Fundamental I. *Trabalhos em Linguística Aplicada,* 48(2), 295–315.

Tonelli, J. R.A and Cristovão, V. (2010). O Papel dos Cursos de Letras na Formação de Professores de Inglês para Crianças. *Calidoscópio,* 8(1), 65–76.

Tonelli, J. R. A., and Ramos, S. G. M. (Eds.). (2007). *O Ensino de LE para Crianças: Reflexões e Contribuições.* Londrina: Moriá.

Valencia Giraldo, S. (2007). *Empowerment and English language teaching (ELT) in public education in Colombia.* Presentation in Language, Education and Diversity Conference, University of Waikato, Hamilton, New Zealand, November.

Valenzuela, D. (2016). Teaching English to young learners in Chile: Towards a holistic approach. [Blog] hhtps://diegovalenzuelasec1.wordpress.com/author/diegovalenzuelasec1/ [Accessed 28 November 2016]

Vargas, A., Tejada, H., and Colmenares, S. (2008). Estándares Básicos de Competencias en Lenguas Extranjeras (Inglés): una Lectura Crítica. *Lenguaje: Revista de la Escuela de Ciencias del Lenguaje de la Universidad del Valle,* 36(1), 241–275.

Vygotsky, L. S. (1987) [2008]. *Pensamento e Linguagem.* 4th ed. São Paulo: Martins Fontes.

Wells, G., and Claxton, G. (Eds.). (2002). *Learning for Life in the 21st Century.* Oxford: Blackwell Publishers.

Zandian, S. (2012). Participatory activities, research and language classroom practice. In *English for Young Learners – Forum* 2012. Upsala: Upsala Universitet, 133–142.

Zeichner, K. (2003). Educating reflective teachers for learner centered-education: Possibilities and contradictions. In Gimenez, T. (ed.) *Ensinando e Aprendendo Inglês na Universidade: Formação de Professores em Tempos de Mudança.* Londrina: ABRAPUI, 3–19.

Zembylas, M. (2005). Beyond teacher cognition and teacher beliefs: The value of the ethnography of emotions in teaching. *International Journal of Qualitative Studies in Education,* 18(4), 465–487.

32

Teaching English to young learners across the Pacific

Fiona Willans

Introduction and definitions

This chapter surveys the teaching of English to young learners in the island countries of the Pacific. It focuses on those states that have either sovereign or self-governing status, listed in Table 32.1, but excludes those that remain dependent territories of countries. The island region is typically considered to be divided into three areas: Melanesia, Micronesia and Polynesia. The countries in Melanesia are by far the largest, most geographically spread out and most linguistically diverse, while those of Micronesia and Polynesia tend to be smaller and more linguistically homogeneous.

English shares either *de facto* or *de jure* status as a national/official language with one or more other languages in all countries. These other languages are referred to as the vernaculars. English is a compulsory subject in primary school and secondary school in all countries, beginning from Year 1 in all cases except Tonga, and it is a medium of instruction for a significant part of the formal education system. English is thus being taught to young learners in the Pacific through formal education, starting in early primary school.

Table 32.1 provides an overview of the countries surveyed, including population estimates (Secretariat of the Pacific Community 2015), the number of indigenous languages (Lynch 1998) and the policy regarding medium of instruction and which languages are taught as compulsory subjects (based on national curriculum documents and personal correspondence with ministries of Education).

English has two main roles in the Pacific today. Its first role is a language of official written purposes in many institutions, due to the colonial establishment of these institutions. English has been retained in this role to varying extents out of familiarity with the status quo and the perceived difficulties of change (Lynch and Mugler 1999). The second role of English is a means to participate in contemporary transactions that have far-reaching socioeconomic, environmental and political consequences: English is the language through which logging rights and land leases are negotiated with foreigners, small island states plead their case about climate change with the UN, the tourist industry thrives as the major source of income and ties with former colonial powers are maintained in their new roles as major aid donors (along with new donors such as China). In short, English is the language through

Table 32.1 An overview of the region

Country	Population estimates	Number of indigenous languages	Medium of instruction	Languages taught as compulsory subjects
Melanesia				
Fiji	867,000	3 plus Fiji Hindi	Year 1–2: Fijian/Hindi in homogeneous groups (or English in mixed groups) Year 3–13: English	Year 1–8: Fijian or Hindi Year 1–13: English
Papua New Guinea	8,083,700	More than 750 plus Tok Pisin and Hiri Motu	Year 1–13: English	Year 1–13: English
Solomon Islands	642,000	63 plus Pijin	Year 1–13: English[i]	Year 1–13: English
Vanuatu	277,500	105[ii] plus Bislama	Year 1–3: Vernacular or Bislama Year 4–13: English or French	Year 1–3: Vernacular Year 1–13: English (or French) Year 4–13: French (or English)
Micronesia				
Federated States of Micronesia	102,800	11	Transitional bilingual programme from the vernacular to English	
Kiribati	113,400	1	Year 1–2: Te taetae ni Kiribati Year 3–4: Transition from Te taetae ni Kiribati to English Year 5–13: English	Year 1–13: Te taetae ni Kiribati Year 1–13: English
Marshall Islands	54,880	1	Year 1–6: Marshallese Year 7–12: Marshallese (social science, health, PE, art); English (maths, science)	Year 1–12: Marshallese Year 1–12: English
Nauru	10,840	1	Year 1–13: English	Year 1–13: English
Palau	17,950	1	Bilingual programme in Palauan and English	Palauan
Polynesia				
Cook Islands	14,730	3	Year 1–3: Cook Islands Māori Year 4–6: Cook Islands Māori and English Year 7–13: English	Year 1–10: Cook Islands Māori Year 1–13: English
Niue	1,470	1	Year 1–3: Niuean Year 4: Transition from Niuean to English Year 5–13: English	Year 1–13: Niuean Year 1–13: English

(Continued)

Table 32.1 (Continued)

Country	Population estimates	Number of indigenous languages	Medium of instruction	Languages taught as compulsory subjects
Sāmoa	187,300	1	Year 1–6: Gradual shift from Sāmoan only to equal amounts of Sāmoan and English Year 7–13: Sāmoan and English	Year 1–13: Sāmoan Year 1–13: English
Tonga	103,300	2	Year 1–6: Tongan Year 7–13: English	Year 1–13: Tongan Year 4–13: English
Tuvalu	11,010	1	Year 1–2: Tuvaluan Year 3–13: English	Year 1–13: Tuvaluan Year 1–13: English

i A new policy for vernacular medium education was approved in 2010, but remains at the pilot stage at the time of writing.

ii The most recent estimate (François et al. 2015) is 138 plus Bislama. Discrepancies are predominantly due to differences of opinion in where to draw the lines between 'languages' and 'dialects', rather than to the discovery of previously undocumented languages.

which Pacific island countries manage what Crocombe (2008, p. 593) refers to as 'being small in a big world'.

My contribution to this volume is written based on my experience training English teachers at the University of the South Pacific, a regional institution co-owned by eleven of the countries surveyed, in addition to the dependent state of Tokelau. I currently teach at the University's main campus in Fiji, from which I make occasional visits to other campuses throughout the region, and I have previously taught English at secondary schools in the Solomon Islands and Vanuatu. In writing this chapter, I have accessed official policy texts, syllabus documents and teaching materials from ministry of education websites, contacted employees of ministries of education and their curriculum units, discussed a range of issues with my own students and conducted a literature review of research carried out in the region.

Historical Perspectives

English has had a presence in the region since the late eighteenth century when the first English-speaking explorers made landfall, although other Europeans had preceded their arrival. Missionaries, sandalwood traders, labour recruiters and plantation owners followed during the nineteenth century, and the increase in European activity resulted in a range of colonial arrangements initiated around the end of the century. The countries discussed in this chapter experienced some form of colonial relationship with one or more of Britain, Australia, New Zealand and the United States, with some also experiencing periods of German or Japanese rule. Vanuatu was administered jointly by Britain and France as the New Hebrides. The New Zealand territories of (then Western) Sāmoa and the Cook Islands were the first to gain independence, in 1962 and 1965 respectively, followed by all British and Australian colonies between 1968 and 1980, and finally the American territories of the Micronesian region between 1986 and 1994 (Crocombe 2008, p. 405).

By the time of independence, English was well established. Although early missionaries had tended to conduct initial education through the vernacular, the colonial governments had usually replaced this practice with an English-only model of formal education. The English syllabi of several countries were based on the South Pacific Commission (SPC) programme, which combined an oral component referred to as Oral Tate, and a reading supplement of workbooks and storybooks. Even Tonga, which had never been colonised, opted to follow this programme on the grounds that it was designed specifically for Pacific islanders learning English as a second language (Taufe'ulungaki 1979). The programme was based on a behaviourist view of language learning, consisting of scripted lessons for teachers to follow, using chorus drilling and repetition of decontextualised sentences (Vakaruru 1984). By the 1980s, concerns began to be raised about poor educational outcomes, and particularly literacy levels. The challenge was partly due to the rapid expansion of education after independence. While it had been possible to deliver education relatively successfully through English in a well-resourced, expatriate-staffed system that catered only to a tiny proportion of the population, new governments now found themselves responsible for educating the masses while localising their teaching forces. Their aim was to maintain high educational outcomes, while teaching through a medium of instruction that was now the second language of teachers and pupils alike.

However, literacy specialists attributed the problem to the SPC model of language teaching (Benson 1993; Lumelume and Todd 1996), and there followed a shift towards a whole-language approach. A number of reading programmes were trialled, including a shared reading approach in Niue with locally developed materials (De'Ath 1980), the Book Flood Project in Fiji (Elley and Mangubhai 1981), a story listening project in Fiji (Ricketts 1982) and the Ready to Read Project in Fiji, Kiribati, Tonga, Vanuatu, Marshall Islands, Sāmoa and Tuvalu (Lumelume and Todd 1996). The idea was to promote a range of literacy approaches, including phonics, but the emphasis on the acquisition of literacy appears to have masked the concern over whether children were learning to read in their first or second language. An unpublished study by Moore (1987) suggested that there was an enormous gap between the number of words that second language learners of English would obtain through the SPC readers and the number of words known by first language speakers of English. However, this and similar findings appear to have been used to support a shift to a pedagogical approach used in first language English contexts, rather than one designed to support the acquisition of English as a second or foreign language. According to Burnett (2013), relatively little has changed since the 1980s, and this view appears to be confirmed by syllabus documents from across the region that advocate a 'holistic' or 'integrated' approach to language teaching.

However, the region has seen a shift towards bilingual education, with an attempt to enable children to at least begin their formal education through the languages they speak at home. Almost all countries surveyed in this chapter now have policies in place to begin instruction through the vernacular, before a transition to English as the medium of instruction in at least some subjects. The result is that English is now theoretically taught as a subject prior to its use as a medium of instruction, and its syllabus should aim to prepare young learners to access content subjects across the curriculum through this language.

Critical issues and topics

English as a first, second or foreign language

The first critical issue is the ambiguity over whether English serves as a first, second or for-eign language for children in primary school. The attempt to designate the exact sequence in which languages are acquired is of course problematic, particularly in multilingual contexts in which children simply grow up with two or more languages simultaneously (Brock-Utne 2009; Dewey 2012). However, it remains useful to distinguish between an *English as a first language* situation in which children are exposed to English from a very young age at home and are completely comfortable interacting in this language by the time they start school; an *English as a second language* situation in which children hear and see the language used all around them in their daily lives, but do not speak it much at home; and an *English as a for-eign language* situation, in which children's exposure to the language is primarily restricted to the classroom. The syllabus and methodology used to teach English need to take account of the extent to which children actually use the language outside the English classroom.

Within each Pacific country there is considerable variation. Children who grow up in urban areas are generally exposed to more English than those in rural areas and the outer islands. This is due to the presence of tourism, internationally owned businesses, access to media and new media and, in some cases, the mixing of different ethnic groups for whom English is the only lingua franca. In such urban areas, some children do indeed grow up with English as their dominant first language, with exposure to their parents' or grandparents' languages restricted to sporadic visits to the village or island of origin. Many of today's par-ents and elders were banned from speaking their own languages in school, during the colo-nial period or its immediate aftermath, and this experience has impacted the way they have raised their own children, often promoting the use of English even at home. In countries such as the Cook Islands that are in free association with New Zealand, it is also common for families to relocate frequently between the two countries, with children therefore raised with greater exposure to English.

However, national curricula typically refer to English as the second language. For exam-ple, the first sentence of Sāmoa's primary English curriculum states, 'Sāmoa has two offi-cial languages: Sāmoan, the majority language, and English, the second language', (Sāmoa Ministry of Education, Sports and Culture 2013, p. 7) and the Kiribati and Cook Islands curriculum texts provide very similar statements. These statements cover up the variation in the extent to which children are actually exposed to English in their daily lives, and they appear to be using an idealised chronological definition of the way English should be intro-duced as a 'second language' for all. The language policy of the Solomon Islands is the only text obtained that refers specifically to English as a 'foreign language', explaining that the majority of students 'do not have ready access to spoken or written English in their out-of-school lives' (Solomon Islands Ministry of Education and Human Resources Development 2010, p. 26). Finally, Vanuatu makes use of the terms 'second' and 'foreign' language in a slightly different way, designating either English or French as the 'second language' (i.e., the medium of instruction) and the other as the 'foreign language' (i.e., taught as a subject), depending on whether children are enroled in Anglophone or Francophone schools.

Children who speak English as their first language are generally treated as an exception within these policy texts. For example, the Cook Islands curriculum framework advises that 'provisions will be made for students whose first language is not Cook Islands Māori'

(Cook Islands Ministry of Education 2002, p. 11); a Tongan media announcement about the change to Tongan-only instruction in the first three years of primary school stated that 'an exception will be for children whose mother tongue is not Tongan' (Tonga Ministry of Education 2012); and the Sāmoan primary English curriculum sets out a range of options for dealing with English-dominant children. Even in the very small countries, such as Niue with its single primary school, teachers struggle to deal with both first and second language speakers of English: 'There is not a strict expectation to only use Niuean in the early years, as we are faced with the challenge of English-speaking children that come to school. Teachers have adapted their methods to try and teach them Niuean' (Personal communication with curriculum officer, May 2017).

This issue is of critical importance. The syllabus and methodology used to teach English must take into account whether children speak it fluently already, are exposed to it outside school or are learning it entirely through formal classroom instruction. If this issue continues to be ignored, the region will become trapped between two deficit models: in some classrooms, children who arrive without prior exposure to English are considered to need some form of remedial attention in this language. In other classrooms, children who arrive with English only are considered to need remedial attention in the vernacular.

A multipurpose English syllabus

Following on from this complexity, the second critical issue is the set of competing demands placed on the English syllabus. A single syllabus in early primary school is typically expected to cover initial literacy development, explicit instruction in a second/foreign language and academic support for an English-medium content curriculum. This has ramifications in a number of areas.

Firstly, initial literacy is taught through what is a second or foreign language for many, despite rhetoric promoted regionally that 'children become literate far more readily, and better able to become competent in other languages, when they start school using their mother tongue' (UNESCO 2015, p. 67). The 2012 Pacific Islands Literacy and Numeracy Assessment results showed 'an alarming situation' with only 30% of children reading and writing at the expected level after four years, and 29% after six years (Secretariat of the Pacific Community 2014, p. 2). Other measures, such as the Early Grade Reading Assessment, have shown similar outcomes (Toumu'a 2016). Benson (1993), in advocating for a change from the SPC programme to a whole-language programme, had lamented an earlier literacy rate of 85%, and although the data from these periods cannot be compared in absolute terms, it is clear that the whole-language approach has not provided the panacea that was hoped for 25 years ago.

Among others, Fiji has enlisted the help of Australian-funded literacy specialists to tackle the problem. New guidelines and activity booklets for Years 1 to 4 have been produced and piloted, accompanied by informative videos showing teachers demonstrating the activities. However, in a section of 'notes on struggling readers', the guidelines state that 'oral language proficiency comes before reading and writing', and asks teachers whether they are 'speaking English every day, all day [so that they are] consistently and frequently providing each child with opportunities to use English'. The paragraph advises teachers to 'ask parents to speak in English for 20–30 minutes each day – perhaps at breakfast or when getting ready for school' (Fiji Ministry of Education, Heritage and Arts 2017, p. 40). Although the new activities appear engaging and user-friendly for teachers with limited training, they frame the children who do not speak English at home as in need of remedial attention.

Since this position is taken, there is insufficient discussion about how to teach English to young learners for whom it is a second or foreign language. There is a widespread belief that the earlier the language is learnt the better proficiency will be reached, but there has been very little critique of the approach used to actually teach the language. The shift to what is still referred to as a whole-language or integrated approach (Burnett 2013) has meant that there is very little attention paid to the learning of English as a second or foreign language, and school leavers reach secondary school and university with neither explicit knowledge about grammar nor the ability to use English to communicate their intended meaning (Deverell 1989; Griffen 1997). Instead, they have been trained to reproduce exam answers about short stories and the language of sports commentary, relying on rote memorisation of notes that are shared between teachers and schools. Moreover, there is a disconnect between what is learnt in the English classroom, and the purposes for which English is used across the rest of the curriculum.

Teacher training

The third critical issue is teacher training. Teachers responsible for teaching English to young learners in the Pacific may have a degree in primary education from one of the region's universities, or a diploma from a national teacher training college, but some have no qualifications at all. The Solomon Islands has one of the highest rates of untrained teachers, with only 54% of primary teachers holding any teaching qualification (UNESCO 2015). Secondary teachers are more likely to hold university degrees than primary teachers, and it can sometimes be seen as a promotion to be asked to teach at secondary level. As a result, many diploma-holding primary teachers enrol in degree programmes in order to become secondary teachers, which leads to something of a brain drain from the primary system. Worse still, a number of teachers who complete postgraduate degrees end up leaving the teaching profession and taking up positions in ministries of education. Even within the primary system, there is a tendency for teachers with higher qualifications or greater experience to be given responsibility for the older children, particularly where there is a national exam to pass in order to reach secondary school, leaving less experienced teachers responsible for the early years. In Vanuatu, for example, a survey of all primary schools in 2010 (Early 2015) revealed that only 10% of Year 1 teachers held any form of teaching qualification, while 40% were Year 12 leavers with no further education, 32% had completed either Year 10 or Year 11, and 14% had completed fewer than 10 years of formal education. The first exposure to English may therefore be from a teacher with limited teacher training or experience, and potentially limited English proficiency.

English proficiency requirements for teacher training programmes are low, or non-existent. A recent pilot of a new English proficiency test at the University of the South Pacific (conducted by the author) revealed that approximately a third of new trainee primary and secondary teachers scored in the lowest three bands out of seven for one or more language skills. The implication is that teachers with relatively low proficiency in English are entering teacher training institutions, possibly unable to cope with the demands of the training, and definitely without formal opportunities to improve their proficiency during the course of their programmes. The graduates of these programmes are then entering the region's classrooms and struggling to teach effectively. It is often assumed that teachers will improve their English proficiency by taking a teacher training course, as evidenced by views frequently expressed during both internal and external meetings regarding the University of the South Pacific's programmes, and by commentary in the media about tertiary providers of teacher training (e.g., Bola-Bari 2015). However, with such limited space in the teacher training curriculum to cover so many different elements, there is no opportunity for additional courses that focus solely on teachers' own English proficiency.

Current contributions and research

Research can very crudely be divided into three phases: a problem-solving phase in the 1980s and 1990s focused specifically on the teaching of English, and two separate but concurrent phases since the turn of the century that have tackled matters of either education or language, but with limited interface between the two areas.

The earliest, problem-solving phase saw a range of studies conducted into practical ways to enhance the educational use of English (see, e.g., Elley et al. 1996; Goetzfridt 1985; Institute of Education 1981). As noted earlier, the political changes across the region during the 1960s and 1970s had led to significant expansion of formal education, and the continued use of English as the medium of instruction began to be seen as an issue. The University of the South Pacific was founded in 1968, and concerns were raised by the end of its first decade that students were arriving with weak levels of English (Elley and Thompson 1978; Fitzcharles 1983; Deverell 1989). Studies and interventions focused particularly on the use of English as the language through which children learnt to read and write, such as the Pacific Islands Literacy Levels study (Withers 1991). Although a detailed evaluation was conducted of what might be wrong with the SPC programme and its drill-focused Oral Tate component (Vakaruru 1984), no empirical research appeared to be carried out into alternative approaches designed specifically for the teaching of English as a second or foreign language. Instead, Burnett (2009, p. 23) argues that the shifts to whole-language approaches during the 1980s and 1990s were supported only by research conducted in New Zealand, with children learning to read in their first language.

From around the end of the 1990s, the second and third phases of research have tended to tackle education and language rather separately. The education-focused of these phases has been one of rethinking ('Otunuku et al. 2014). Concerns were raised at the 1999 meeting of the Pacific Islands Forum that the region's education systems were failing to meet its human resource needs, due to poor curricula that were insufficiently focused on life skills. At the same time, Pacific academics Konai Thaman, 'Ana Taufe'ulungaki and Kabini Sanga were weaving together what would become known as the Rethinking Pacific Education Initiative, which helped to see the realisation of The Forum Basic Education Action Plan of 2001, the Rethinking Education Colloquium in Suva in 2001, the publication of Tree of Opportunity: Rethinking Pacific Education (Pene et al. 2002), a regional conference in 2003 on Rethinking Educational Aid in the Pacific and regional and national follow-up conferences, including the Rethinking Education in Micronesia conference in 2004 and the Rethinking Vanuatu Education conference in 2002, and the launching of a new five-year Pacific Regional Initiatives for the Delivery of Basic Education (PRIDE) project.

Puamau (2005, p. 1) opens her paper on 'Rethinking Education: A Pacific Perspective' with the following:

A groundswell of opinion on the critical importance of rethinking education in the Pacific is rising from Pacific nations and their educators. They recognise that their education systems are still caught up in a colonised time warp despite the fact that most Pacific nations have been politically independent for some decades.

She later states (2005, p. 4):

> It is not hard to understand why colonial practices, processes, structures and ways of knowing and doing continued in hegemonic ways after decolonisation . . . . An example of this is the continuing practice of valuing and elevating English in school, and in the home, above the mother tongue.

English has never been rejected by this rethinking movement. Burnett (2013, p. 351) explains that '[t]he importance of English is difficult to dismiss regardless of a wider Pacific culturalist discourse in education that links an at times over-emphasis in formal school curriculum on English literacy with neo-colonialism, Pacific Vernacular decline and cultural anxiety and loss'. However, the space for treating this language as a subject of research was perhaps narrowed by the drive to ground education in indigenous values. Although a number of articles and workshops focusing on language issues emerged as part of this general movement (e.g., Mugler 2005; Taufe'ulungaki 2003, 2005), they tended to focus on the role of the vernacular languages in early education, and the culturally embedded patterns of interaction that might be more conducive to learning, rather than tackling any questions about the role of English and what outcomes were intended to be met by an appropriate English syllabus.

The third phase of research, which has run concurrently with the second, has focused on language issues (including within classroom contexts), but with a descriptive, rather than critical, slant. For example, in an interesting descriptive study from Fiji, Shameem (2002) shows that primary teachers frequently underreported the amount of English they were using in their classrooms, while Franken and August (2011) report on another study, this time from Papua New Guinea, in which primary teachers underreported the multilingual strategies they used to help children learn English and transition to its use as the medium of instruction. A range of studies on classroom codeswitching have described the way the vernacular and English are used in tandem (e.g., Tamata 1996; Tanangada 2013; Willans 2011) while, outside the classroom, scholars have described the emergence of new Pacific varieties of English (e.g., Biewer 2015; Green 2012; Wigglesworth 1996). Such studies bring context to our understanding of language-in-education issues, but they remain separate from attempts to change or enhance the way languages are used or taught.

At the present time, it appears that transformation within the domain of language teaching is limited to short-term projects coordinated by donor partners, leading to relatively surface-level changes including reorganisation of curriculum contents into new strands, or their light repackaging according to new trends such as outcomes-based learning. There is very little new research being carried out into the way English is being taught to young learners, or how literacy acquisition occurs in a language that may not be spoken at home, or how an English syllabus can be brought to life with the help of other languages. In short, there is a lack of critical evaluation, and rethinking, of this aspect of education in the Pacific.

Recommendations for practice

Given the range of curriculum contexts across the Pacific, it is hard to give specific recommendations for the teaching of English that will apply in all countries. However, this section will present broad recommendations that apply across the region.

The first recommendation is that English be taught as a subject by designated teachers who have been trained specifically to teach English. The more typical arrangement currently is that one primary teacher is responsible for teaching all subjects across the curriculum to one class (often in multigrade classrooms). The result is that literacy acquisition and language teaching are often meshed together, along with socialisation into the practices of formal education. Where policies stipulate that literacy is taught through the vernacular, as is the case in most countries now, it would make sense to keep English as a separate subject. Moreover, by changing the division of labour slightly, it would be possible to deploy one teacher at each primary school to teach English across all grade levels, while the remaining teachers covered the content teaching of the same classes, without changing the total number of teachers required.

The second recommendation is that English is taught orally only during Years 1–3. While there is no clear evidence that children will gain any advantage from starting formal instruction in a second language right from the start of school, at the age of five rather than, say, the age of eight (Ortega 2009, p. 17), there is societal and political pressure in most Pacific countries to provide this. A principled syllabus of oral English for a few hours a week will provide a base for more formal study of the language from about the fourth year onwards, once children have mastered reading and writing in their own language. The specific syllabus and approach used to teach English must then be tied in with questions of medium of instruction across the content curriculum. If English will become a medium of instruction from the later stages of primary education or early secondary education, then an early English syllabus must adequately prepare children to learn through this language. In an ideal situation, English will be used alongside the vernacular in a plurilingual model of teaching and assessment, so the English syllabus should support readiness for such a scenario. The longer that children can learn English as a separate subject first, the better chance they will have of using it to engage critically with the content curriculum.

The third recommendation is that the selection, training and support of primary teachers is made a priority. If teachers are to teach English, or teach through English, it is important that they already have good proficiency in this language before entering a training programme. An incentive scheme may be needed to encourage proficient speakers to consider primary teaching an appealing career option. The curriculum for the training of primary teachers then needs to take into account the roles that they are expected to carry out. If one teacher is expected to be responsible for all subjects, including initial literacy and the teaching of English as a second or foreign language, then the curriculum will need to ensure that these elements are given sufficient attention. If specialised primary English teachers are to be trained, then a separate curriculum will be needed.

However, perhaps the most important recommendation that can be made for the region is that a far greater body of research is needed that is situated in the Pacific context, for which serious capacity building is needed. As Liyanage (2009, p. 737) notes with reference to Kiribati, 'before instigating major changes such as restructuring curriculum and mass teacher training, a comprehensive body of research is required regarding socially situated and preferred practices of learning and teaching'. National ministries of education therefore need local advisors who are well versed in research in fields of English teaching, language acquisition, literacy and multilingual education, and who can lead new research driven by questions that make sense in Pacific classrooms. We need contextually relevant data, both qualitative and quantitative, and we need the directions for such research to follow national and regional priorities.

Driving such a research agenda must be a series of questions that ask what English is doing in the Pacific in the first place, why it is so important to learn and how the language fits into the multilingual landscape of the region. More critical discussion of the place and power of English is needed within the wider Rethinking Education Initiative, so that practices that value indigenous languages and cultures are not pitted against those that promote proficiency in English.

Future directions

Recent developments suggest that some positive change is in progress. Firstly, most countries have now shifted, or are in the process of shifting, towards a bilingual or multilingual model of education through which English is recognised as an additional language. The positive impact this has on the perceptions held towards Pacific languages also helps shift the perceptions held towards English. Students at the University of the South Pacific who study either linguistics or a Pacific language as part of their teacher training discover that English is no different to any other language from a linguistic point of view, but has simply become dominant in the Pacific and worldwide due to colonialism and globalisation. Understanding that English is bound up in some of the darkest periods of Pacific history, but that it is still an important language in the present, helps to demystify the language and remove some of the fear surrounding it as a compulsory school subject. Teachers become more confident in talking about the language, and taking ownership of it as second language speakers. Similarly, as many children now learn to read and write through their own languages first, they are introduced to English as an additional language that is useful to add to their repertoires, rather than the only language through which life beyond the village is supposed to operate.

Secondly, the University of the South Pacific, responsible for training a large proportion of the region's teachers, has made good progress recently in restructuring the teacher training curriculum for secondary English teachers as well as introducing a new postgraduate diploma for English teachers of all levels. With these developments now underway, it is hoped that the primary teacher training curriculum can also be given some attention to ensure that teachers are trained to deal with the complexity of their roles – whether as specialist English teachers or as cross-curriculum teachers. Again, there is work to be done but, if carried out with good cooperation between the different groups responsible for teacher training and curriculum development, this work is not so complex.

A major barrier to positive change is political instability. With constant changes in government across the region, it can be hard to implement and support effective change. Moreover, given that many of today's leaders and senior civil servants are the success stories of colonial education that was delivered entirely through English, it can be hard to raise the issues of medium of instruction and the teaching of English as problems that even need to be addressed. It is too easy to blame falling standards of English on poor teachers or inadequately resourced schools, rather than ask difficult questions about the systemic issues that have been inherited from the colonial period and that are only beginning to make themselves fully known 40 or so years later.

A second barrier is the continued reliance on external assistance in the education sectors of most countries, which is not matched by the amount of empirical research within the region. When national education policy is shaped to such an extent by aid donors, international consultants and supranational targets, it can be hard to ensure that the right priorities are met, and that innovations are sustainable. A focused human resources plan is needed in all countries, through which an effectively trained workforce of researchers, analysts and policy advisors in the relevant areas can be produced.

Further reading

1 Burnett, G. (2009). Critically theorising the teaching of literacy and language in Pacific schooling: Just another Western metanarrative? *Critical Literacy: Theories and Practices*, 3(2), 17–32.
   This paper examines the apparent reluctance in the Pacific region to engage with critical approaches to the teaching of language and literacy.

2 'Otunuku, M., Nabobo-Baba, U., and Johansson Fua, S. (Eds.). (2014). *Of waves, winds, and wonderful things: A decade of rethinking Pacific education*. Suva, Fiji: University of the South Pacific.
   This edited collection summarises a decade of research and theorising within the Rethinking Pacific Education Initiative.

3 Taufe'ulungaki, A. (2005). Language and culture in the Pacific region: Issues, practices, and alternatives. *Directions: Journal of Educational Studies*, 27(1), 12–42.
   This paper examines a range of issues relating to language choice in education policy in the Pacific.

Related topics

Contexts of learning, multilingualism, policy, assessment, difficult circumstances

References

Benson, C. (1993). *Publishing Project for Educational Materials for the Pacific States*. www.accu.or.jp/appreb/report/aprb/aprb9301.html

Biewer, C. (2015). *A Sociolinguistic and Morphosyntactic Profile of Fiji English, Sāmoan English and Cook Islands English*. Amsterdam: John Benjamins.

Bola-Bari, V. (2015). Reddy points out flaws. *Fiji Times*, 8 September.

Brock-Utne, B. (2009). The adoption of the Western paradigm of bilingual teaching: Why does it not fit the African situation? In Prah, K., and Brock-Utne, B. (eds.) *Multilingualism: An African advantage*. Cape Town: CASAS, 18–51.

Burnett, G. (2009). Critically theorising the teaching of literacy and language in Pacific schooling: Just another Western meta-narrative? *Critical Literacy: Theories and Practices*, 3(2), 17–32.

Burnett, G. (2013). Approaches to English literacy teaching in the Central Pacific Republic of Kiribati: quality teaching, educational aid and curriculum reform. *Asia Pacific Journal of Education*, 33(3), 350–363.

Cook Islands Ministry of Education (2002). *The Cook Islands Curriculum Framework*. Rarotonga, Cook Islands: Ministry of Education.

Crocombe, R. (2008). *The South Pacific*, 7th ed. Suva, Fiji: Institute of Pacific Studies, University of the South Pacific.

De'ath, P. (1980). The shared book experience and ESL. *Directions: Journal of Educational Studies*, 4, 13–22.

Deverell, G. (1989). The relationship between English proficiency and academic success at the University of the South Pacific. *Directions: Journal of Educational Studies*, 11(1), 10–18.

Dewey, M. (2012). Beyond labels and categories in English language teaching: Critical reflections on popular conceptualization. In Leung, C., and Street, B. (eds.) *English: A changing medium for education*. Bristol: Multilingual Matters, 129–149.

Early, R. (2015). Language policy across Pacific polities. Paper presented at the Language, Education & Diversity conference, University of Auckland, 23–26 November.

Elley, W., Cutting, B., Mangubhai, F., and Hugo, C. (1996). *Lifting Literacy Levels with Story Books: Evidence from the South Pacific, Singapore, Sri Lanka, and South Africa*. Paper presented at the World Conference on Literacy, Philadelphia, March 12–15.

Elley, W., and Mangubhai, F. (1981). The impact of a Book Flood in Fiji primary schools, New Zealand Council of Educational Research and the Institute of Education, University of the South Pacific.

Elley, W., and Mangubhai, F. (1983). The impact of reading on second language learning. *Reading Research Quarterly*, 19, 53–57.

Elley, W., and Thompson, J. (1978). *The English Language Skills of USP Foundation Students*. Suva, Fiji: The University of the South Pacific.

Fiji Ministry of Education, Heritage and Arts. (2017). *Literacy Guide for Lower Primary: Years 1 & 2*. Suva, Fiji: Ministry of Education, Heritage and Arts.

Fitzcharles, K. (1983). *Report on Research into the Relationship between English Proficiency and Academic Success at USP*. Suva, Fiji: The University of the South Pacific.

François, A., Franjieh, M., Lacrampe, S., and Schnell, S. (2015). The exceptional linguistic density of Vanuatu. In François, A., Lacrampe, S., Franjieh, M., and Schnell, S. (eds.) *The Languages of Vanuatu: Unity and diversity*. Open Access Studies in the Languages of Island Melanesia: College of Asia and the Pacific, The Australian National University. 1–22

Franken, M., and August, M. (2011). Language use and the instructional strategies of Grade 3 teachers to support "bridging" in Papua New Guinea. *Language and Education*, 25(3), 221–239.

Goetzfridt, N. (1985). *An Annotated Bibliography for Teaching English as a Second Language in the South Pacific*. Suva, Fiji: University of the South Pacific.

Green, B. (2012). Pacific English: what is it, why is it and its implications. Unpublished PhD Thesis. The University of the South Pacific.

Griffen, P. (1997). *An Investigation of the Place of the English Language Competence in the Determination of A and D Grades at the University of the South Pacific*. Suva: Department of Literature and Language, The University of the South Pacific.

Institute of Education Report (1981). *Conference on English Language Teaching in the South Pacific in the 80s*. Suva, Fiji: The University of the South Pacific.

Liyanage, I. (2009). Global donors and English language teaching in Kiribati. *TESOL Quarterly*, 43(4), 733–738.

Lumelume, S., and Todd, E. (1996). Ready to read: A long-term literacy project in the South Pacific. *Compare: A Journal of Comparative and International Education*, 26(3), 347–363.

Lynch, J. (1998). *Pacific Languages: An introduction*. Honolulu: University of Hawai'i Press.

Lynch, J., and Mugler, F. (1999). English in the South Pacific. http://vanuatu.usp.ac.fj/paclangunit/English_South_Pacific.htm.

Moore, B. (1987). A comparison of the SPC basic word list with Standard word list. Unpublished manuscript.

Mugler, F. (2005). Introduction: Language policies and education in the Pacific. *Directions: Journal of Educational Studies*, 27(1), 1–11.

Ortega, L. (2009). *Understanding language acquisition*. London: Routledge.

'Otunuku, M., Nabobo-Baba, U., and Johansson Fua, S. (Eds.). (2014). *Of Waves, Winds, and Wonderful Things: A decade of rethinking Pacific education*. Suva, Fiji: University of the South Pacific.

Pene, F., Taufe'ulungaki, A., and Benson, C. (Eds.). (2002). *Tree of Opportunity: Re-thinking Pacific education*. Suva, Fiji: University of the South Pacific.

Puamau, P. (2005). *Rethinking Educational Reform: A Pacific perspective*. A paper presented at Redesigning Pedagogy: Research, Policy, Practice, National Institute of Education, Nanyang Technological University, Singapore, 30 May–1 June.

Ricketts, J. (1982). The effect of listening to stories on comprehension and reading achievement. *Directions: Journal of Educational Studies*, 8, 29–36.

Sāmoa Ministry of Education, Sports and Culture (2013). *English Years 1–8 Primary School Curriculum*. Apia, Sāmoa: Ministry of Education, Sports and Culture.

Secretariat of the Pacific Community (2014). Pacific Islands literacy and numeracy assessment (PILNA). www.forumsec.org/resources/uploads/attachments/documents/2014FEdMM.03_Attachment_PILNA_Rpt.pdf.

Secretariat of the Pacific Community (2015). 2015 Pocket statistical summary. www.spc.int/prism/images/downloads/2015_Pocket-Statistical-Summary.pdf.

Shameem, N. (2002). Classroom language use in a multilingual community – the Indo-Fijians in Fiji. *Journal of Intercultural Studies*, 23(3), 267–284.

Solomon Islands Ministry of Education and Human Resources Development. (2010). *Policy Statement and Guidelines for the Use of Vernacular Languages and English in Education in Solomon Islands*. Honiara, Solomon Islands: Ministry of Education and Human Resources Development.

Tamata, A. (1996). Code-switching in Fiji schools. In Mugler, F., and Lynch, J. (eds.) *Pacific Languages in Education*. Suva, Fiji: University of the South Pacific, 92–101.

Tanangada, L. (2013). A study of language use in secondary school classrooms in the Solomon Islands: Conceptions, practices and proficiencies. Unpublished MEd thesis, University of Waikato.

Taufe'ulungaki, A. (1979). Curriculum development in Tonga: Then and now. *Directions: Journal of Educational Studies*, 3, 25–35.

Taufe'ulungaki, A. (2003). Vernacular languages and classroom interactions in the Pacific. In Thaman, K. (ed.), *Educational Ideas from the Oceania*. Suva, Fiji: Institute of Education, University of the South Pacific.

Taufe'ulungaki, A. (2005). Language and culture in the Pacific region: Issues, practices, and alternatives. *Directions: Journal of Educational Studies*, 27(1),12–42.

Tonga Ministry of Education (2012). Media announcement, 30 January: The Ministry of Education will launch its new language policy for all Tongan schools at the beginning of the 2012 school year in February. www.mic.gov.to/ministrydepartment/14-govt-ministries/moet/3339-minister-of-education-introduces-new-language-policy-for-tongan-schools.

Toumu'a, R. (2016). Culturally and linguistically relevant resource development for literacy in the Pacific. In *Weaving Education Theory and Practice in Oceania: Selected papers from the second Vaka Pasifiki Education Conference*. Suva, Fiji: Institute of Education, University of the South Pacific, 118–122.

UNESCO. (2015). *Pacific Education for all 2015 Review*. Paris/Apia: UNESCO.

Vakaruru, N. (1984). Improving the teaching of English in primary schools in Fiji. *Directions: Journal of Educational Studies*, 12, 15–27.

Wigglesworth, A. (1996). *Cook Islands Maori English: A unique language variety from the South Pacific* MA thesis, American University

Willans, F. (2011). Classroom code-switching in a Vanuatu secondary school: Conflict between policy and practice. *International Journal of Bilingual Education and Bilingualism*, 14(1), 23–38.

Withers, G. (1991). The Pacific islands literacy levels: Some implications for learning and teaching. *Directions: Journal of Educational Studies*, 13, 3–17.

Index

Note: Page numbers in *italic* indicate a figure and page numbers in **bold** indicate a table on the corresponding page.